Environmental and Natural Resource Economics

Third Edition

Thomas H.

Tom Tietenberg
Colby College

HarperCollins*Publishers*

To Florence M. and Harry H. Tietenberg,
who provided me with a healthy environment conducive to development.

Sponsoring Editor: Bruce Kaplan
Project Editor: Thomas R. Farrell
Cover Design: Jaye Zimet
Cover Photo: Jack Elness/Comstock
Compositor: Publishing Synthesis, Ltd.
Printer and Binder: R. R. Donnelley & Sons Company
Cover Printer: The Lehigh Press, Inc.

Environmental and Natural Resource Economics, Third Edition

♻ PRINTED ON RECYCLED PAPER

Library of Congress Cataloging-in-Publication Data

Tietenberg, Thomas H.
    Environmental and natural resource economics / Tom Tietenberg. —
3rd ed.
        p.   cm.
    Includes bibliographical references and indexes.
    ISBN 0-673-46328-1
    1. Environmental policy.   2. Natural resources—Government policy.
3. Raw materials—Government policy. I. Title.
HC79.E5T525   1992
333.7—dc20   91-22564
                                                                  CIP

93   94   9 8 7 6 5

CONTENTS

9 *REPLENISHABLE BUT DEPLETABLE RESOURCES: WATER* 222

PREFACE

Saving the planet is very much in vogue.
It's also in Harper's Bazaar, Elle, *and* Mademoiselle.

THE NEW YORK TIMES (March 25, 1990)

When I began writing the first edition of this book in 1981, environmental and natural resource economics was a well-developed but underutilized field. Its impact on environmental policy could most generously be described as "emerging." That is no longer the case. Economics has become an indispensable part of the education of anyone dealing with environmental policy. As *Our Common Future* put it in 1987, "Economics and ecology bind us in ever-tightening networks ... economics and ecology must be completely integrated in decision-making and lawmaking processes ...."[1]

Signs of maturation abound. A number of journals are now devoted either exclusively or mostly to the topics covered in this book. One, *Ecological Economics*, is a new journal dedicated to bringing economists and ecologists closer together in a common search for appropriate solutions for environmental challenges. Interested readers can also find advanced work in the field in *Land Economics, Journal of Environmental Economics and Management, Environmental and Resource Economics,* and *Natural Resources Journal*, among others.

New resources for student research projects have been made available in response to the growing popularity of the field. Original research on topics

---

1 The World Commission on Environment and Development, *Our Common Future* (New York: Oxford University Press, 1987): 27, 37.

related to international environmental and natural resource issues was formerly very difficult for students because of the paucity of data. A number of good sources now exist including *World Resources: 1990–91* (Washington, DC: Oxford University Press, 1989), which has an extensive data appendix, and *OECD Environmental Data* (Paris: Organization for Economic Co-operation and Development, 1989).

Environmental and Natural Resource Economics attempts to bring those who are beginning the study of environmental and natural resource economics close to the frontiers of knowledge. Although it is designed to be accessible to students who have completed only a two-semester introductory course in economics or a one-semester introductory microeconomics course, it has been successfully used in several institutions in lower-level and upper-level undergraduate courses as well as lower-level graduate courses. Intertemporal optimization is handled within a discrete-time, mathematical programming framework, and all mathematics other than simple algebra is relegated to appendixes. Graphs and numerical examples are used to provide an intuitive understanding of the principles suggested by the math and the reasons for their validity. In this edition I have tried to retain the strengths that seem particularly valued by users, while expanding the number of applications of economic principles, clarifying some of the more difficult arguments, and updating the material to include the very latest developments around the world.

The structure and topical coverage of this book facilitate its use in a variety of contexts. For a survey course in environmental and natural resource economics, all chapters are appropriate, though many of us have found that the book contains somewhat more material than can be covered adequately in a quarter or even a semester. This surplus of material provides some flexibility for the instructor to choose those topics that best fit his or her course design. A one-term course in natural resource economics could be based on Chapters One to Thirteen and Twenty-one to Twenty-three. A brief introduction to environmental economics could be added by including Chapter Fourteen. A single-term course in environmental economics could be structured around Chapters One to Four and Fourteen to Twenty. Chapter Six could be added if a brief introduction to natural economics seemed desirable.

New to This Edition

This edition has a much more international focus. Additional attention has been paid to environmental problems and policies in Eastern and Western Europe, Japan, and the developing nations than was the case in previous editions.

Two new chapters have been added—"Growth, Poverty, and the Environment" and "The Quest for Sustainable Development"—reflecting the demonstrated, current global interest in sustainable development as a guide for the future. These new chapters include the latest research on the appropriateness of the traditional model of development for low-income countries, the relationships among trade policies, debt, poverty, and environmental degradation, and the role for economic incentives policies in achieving sustainable development. These chapters replace two chapters in the previous edition entitled "Growth in a Finite Environment" and "Further Economic Growth?" This edition also contains a completely new mathematical appendix entitled "The Simple Mathematics of Cost-Effective Pollution Control."

Ten new boxed examples highlight special topics, including (1) The Economics of Recycling: The Japanese Experience; (2) New Markets for Trash: Tires; (3) Using Economic Principles to Conserve Water in California; (4) Protecting Instream Uses of Water through Economics; (5) Success Stories in Conserving Tropical Forests; (6) Restricting Access to Common Property Resources: Harbor Gangs of Maine; (7) Geochemically Scarce Minerals: How Would the Economy React to Impending Scarcity?; (8) Innovative Mobile Pollution Control Strategies: Singapore and Hong Kong; (9) Anatomy of An Oil Spill: *Amoco Cadiz*; (10) Sustainable Development: Three Success Stories.

Several previously included topics have received considerably more attention in this edition, including the economics of recycling; the causes, consequences, and potential solutions for global deforestation; and economic incentive policies. The new material on economic incentive policies includes the actual experience with their use in France, Sweden, the Netherlands, and Japan; new applications in the United States (acid rain and ozone depletion) and potential applications to global warming and declining biodiversity.

New topics covered in this edition include oil spills and ocean dumping; the economics of limited liability for oil spills; the Gaia hypothesis; ethics of present value calculations for the allocation of depletable resources, including a new numerical example; informal arrangements for restricting access to common property resources; nuclear power around the world; new approaches by electric utilities to internalize environmental costs; the economics of renewable energy sources; the magnitude of subsidies for irrigation water; emerging water markets in the western United States; sustainable agriculture in the United States and Europe; economics of organic farming; debt-nature swaps; extractive reserves; policies for stemming decline of elephant populations; indoor air pollution; results from the National Acid Rain Precipitation Assessment Program; the London agreement on ozone depletion; citizen suits and the private enforcement of environmental laws; cost-benefit analysis of global warming; the cost effectiveness of alternative automobile fuels; joint and several liability doctrine for hazardous wastes; deficiencies of national income accounting from the point of view of sustainable development; examples of industrial waste reduction; strategies for preserving biodiversity; and the World Heritage Fund.

All data and references to governing legislation in the previous edition have been updated. Some completely new data have been included: global oil reserves, types of pricing systems used by U.S. public and private water utilities, global air quality comparisons, international comparison of gasoline taxes, noteworthy oil spills, and opportunities for enhanced energy efficiency.

This edition retains a strong policy orientation. Though a great deal of theory and empirical evidence are discussed, both are motivated by the desire to increase understanding of intriguing policy problems and are discussed in the context of those problems. This explicit integration of research and policy within each chapter avoids the problem frequently encountered in applied economics textbooks in which the theory developed in earlier chapters is only loosely connected to the rest of the book.

This is an economics book, but it goes beyond economics. Insights from the natural and physical sciences, literature and political science, as well as other disciplines, are scattered liberally through the text. In some cases these references raise unresolved issues that economic analysis can help resolve, while in others they affect the structure of the economic analysis or provide a contrasting point of view. They have an important role to play in overcoming the tendency to accept the material uncritically at a superficial level by highlighting those characteristics that make the economics approach unique.

Acknowledgments

Perhaps the most rewarding part of writing this book has been that it has put me in touch with so many thoughtful people I had not previously met. I very much appreciate the faculty and students who pointed out areas of particular strength or areas where coverage could be expanded in this edition. The support that my approach has received from faculty and students has been gratifying and energizing. One can begin to understand the magnitude of my debt to my colleagues by glancing at the several hundred names in the lists of references contained in the name index. Because their research contributions make this an exciting field, full of insights worthy of being shared, my task was easier and a lot more fun than it might otherwise have been.

Valuable assistance was received during various stages of the writing from the following:

Maurice Ballabon	Baruch College
Fikret Berkes	Brock University
Sidney M. Blumner	California State Polytechnic University, Pamona
Richard V. Butler	Trinity University
Duane Chapman	Cornell University
Charles J. Chicchetti	University of Wisconsin, Madison
Jon Conrad	Cornell University
William Corcoran	University of Nebraska at Omaha
Gregory B. Christiansen	California State University, Hayward
Maureen L. Cropper	University of Maryland
John H. Cumberland	University of Maryland
Herman E. Daly	World Bank
Diane P. Dupont	University of Guelph

Randall K. Filer	Brandeis University
Anthony C. Fisher	University of California, Berkeley
Marvin Frankel	University of Illinois, Urbana-Champaign
A. Myrick Freeman, III	Bowdoin College
James Gale	Michigan Technological University
Doug Greer	San Jose State University
A. R. Gutowsky	California State University, Sacramento
W. Eric Gustafson	University of California, Davis
Jon D. Harford	Cleveland State University
Gloria E. Helfand	University of California, Davis
John J. Hovis	University of Maryland
Craig Infanger	University of Kentucky
James R. Kahn	State University of New York, Binghamton
Dwight Lee	University of Georgia
Joseph N. Lekakis	University of Crete
Randolph M. Lyon	University of Texas, Austin
Giadomenico Majone	Harvard University
David Martin	North Carolina State University
Nicholas Mercuro	University of New Orleans
David E. Merrifield	Western Washington University
Frederic C. Menz	Clark University
Michael J. Mueller	Clarkson University
Thomas C. Noser	University of Alabama
Lloyd Orr	Indiana University
Raymond Prince	University of Colorado-Boulder
J. Barkley Rosser, Jr.	James Madison University
Milton Russell	University of Tennessee
Frederic O. Sargent	University of Vermont
Salah El Serafy	World Bank
W. Douglas Shaw	Vassar College
James S. Shortle	Pennsylvania State University
Leah J. Smith	Swarthmore College
V. Kerry Smith	North Carolina State University
Joe B. Stevens	Oregon State University
Kenneth N. Townsend	Hampden-Sydney College
Wallace E. Tyner	Purdue University
Myles Wallace	Clemson University
Patrick Welle	Bemidji State University
Anthony Yezer	The George Washington University

In preparing this edition I am especially indebted to David Martin, Davidson College; Lloyd Orr, Indiana University; and Gloria Helfand, University of California, Davis, for their detailed, helpful suggestions. Their support and their willingness to share ideas on how the manuscript could be improved are much appreciated.

I have been fortunate to have been aided by many extremely capable student research assistants over the years. Judi Greene, Alison Jones, Susan French, Fidel Fajardo, Elaine Johnson, Diane Peterec, Susan Charrette, Vicki Howe, Marc Gordon, Faith Delaney, Thom Menzies, Margaret Wimmer, Jill Stasz Harris, and Melissa Raffoni have all helped to shape previous editions. The current edition has been shaped primarily by David Edelstein, with substantial contributions made by Wendy Naysnerski, Elaine Jorgensen, and Rabia Mirza. Working with such fine young men and women has made it all the more obvious to me that teaching is the world's most satisfying profession.

Finally, I should like to say a deeply felt word of thanks to my family for putting up with a father and husband who spent time in writing that they deserved. I couldn't have done it without their support.

TOM TIETENBERG

CHAPTER ONE

Visions of the Future

From the arch of the bridge to which his guide has carried him, Dante now sees the Diviners . . . coming slowly along the bottom of the fourth Chasm. By help of their incantations and evil agents, they had endeavored to pry into the future which belongs to the almighty alone, and now their faces are painfully twisted the contrary way; and being unable to look before them, they are forced to walk backwards.

DANTE ALIGHIERI, *Divine Comedy: The Inferno,*
TRANSLATED BY CARLYLE (1867)

INTRODUCTION

The Self-Extinction Premise

About the time the American colonies became independent, Edward Gibbon completed his monumental The History of the Decline and Fall of the Roman Empire. In a particularly poignant passage which opens the last chapter of his opus, he recreates a scene in which the learned Poggius, a friend, and two servants ascend the Capitoline Hill after the fall of Rome. They are awed by the contrast between what Rome once was and what Rome had become:

> In the time of the poet it was crowned with the golden roofs of a temple; the temple is overthrown, the gold has been pillaged, the wheel of fortune has accomplished her revolution, and the sacred ground is again disfigured with thorns and brambles. . . .
> The forum of the Roman people, where they assembled to enact their laws and elect their magistrates is now enclosed for the cultivation of potherbs, or thrown open for the reception of swine and buffaloes. The public and private edifices, that were founded for eternity lie prostrate, naked, and broken, like the limbs of a mighty giant;

1

and the ruin is the more visible, from the stupendous relics that have survived the injuries of time and fortune [Vol. 6, pp. 650–651].

What could cause the demise of such a grand and powerful society? Gibbon weaves a complex thesis to answer this question, suggesting ultimately that the seeds for Rome's destruction were sown by the Empire itself.[1] Though Rome finally succumbed to such external forces as fires and invasions, its vulnerability was based upon internal weakness.

The premise that societies germinate the seeds of their own destruction has long fascinated scholars. In one historically significant study in the early nineteenth century, Thomas Malthus foresaw a time when the urge to reproduce would create a situation in which population growth would outstrip the growth of food supply, resulting in starvation and death.

The 1970s and 1980s have ushered in a revival of interest in Malthus's premise, mainly because of the growing number of writers who believe that modern society has embarked on a path that leads to self-destruction. Modern ecologists, for example, have suggested that the environment possesses a unique "carrying capacity" to support humans, and once that capacity is exceeded widespread ecological disruption occurs with disastrous consequences for humanity. The focus is no longer on individual societies but on the survival of the planet.

Sources of concern are not difficult to find. Since mid-century the world has lost nearly one-fifth of the topsoil from its cropland, a fifth of its tropical rain forests, and tens of thousands of plant and animal species. Human activity has increased carbon dioxide levels to the point where the global climate is being affected. The protective ozone shield is been depleted. Dead forests and lakes are common in parts of Europe.[2]

Writers have begun to suggest that we have reached a turning point. Bill McKibben put it this way:

> We can no longer imagine that we are part of something larger than ourselves . . . . now we make the world, affect every operation . . . . This is, I suppose, the victory we have been pointing to at least since the eviction from Eden—the domination some have always dreamed of. But it is the story of King Midas writ large—the power looks nothing like we thought it would. It is a brutish, cloddish power, not a creative one.[3]

---

1 Rome does not provide the only historical example of a powerful society which followed a path to self extinction. It has been suggested, for example, that the classic Maya civilization succumbed when its concentrated population proved too large to be supported by the soils around it. See Jeremy A. Sabloff, "The Collapse of Classic Maya Civilization," in *Patient Earth*, John Harte and Robert H. Socolow, eds. (New York: Holt, Rinehart and Winston, 1971): 16–27; Lester R. Brown, "World Population Growth, Soil Erosion, and Food Security," *Science* 214 (November 27, 1981): 995–1002.

2 For an up-to-date examination of the earth's vital signs see the first chapter of the current edition of *State of the World* (New York: W. W. Norton), an annual published by the staff of the Worldwatch Institute in Washington, DC.

3 Bill McKibben, *The End of Nature* (New York: Random House, 1989): 83–84.

Humans have negotiated the transition from "adapting to" nature to "managing" nature.[4] The scale of activity has become so large that we affect the life processes of the planet. Where will it all lead?

For several decades economists have been concerned with topics such as exhaustible resources and pollution, but during the last decade the frequency of related books and articles has accelerated rapidly.[5] Consequently, we've come to better understand the relationship between humanity and the environment and how that relationship affects, and is affected by, economic and political institutions.

The Use of Models

In this book you will study the rapidly growing field of environmental and natural resource economics. All of the topics covered will be examined as a part of the general focus on economic growth in the presence of limited environmental and natural resources. Because this subject is so complex, it is better understood when broken into manageable portions. Once we have mastered the components, we can then reassemble them to form a complete picture.

In economics, as in most other disciplines, we use models to illustrate complex subjects, such as relationships between the economy and the environment. In using these models, however, we should also be sensitive to their limitations.

Models are simplified characterizations of reality. For example, although a roadmap, by design, leaves a lot out, it is a useful guide to reality. The map shows how various locations relate to each other and gives an overall perspective. It cannot, however, capture the unique details which characterize any particular location. The map highlights only those characteristics crucial for the purpose at hand.

The models in this text are like that. Through simplification, less is held in view so that more can be understood of what is retained. Models allow us to rigorously study issues which are interrelated and global in scale, but, through their selectivity, models may yield conclusions that are dead wrong. What is omitted may turn out, in retrospect, to be crucial in understanding a particular dimension. Models are therefore useful abstractions that should always be viewed with some skepticism.

Most people's views of the world are based on models, though frequently those models are implicit rather than explicit. The assumptions and relationships involved may be hidden, perhaps even subconscious. In economics the models

---

4 Symptomatic of this transition was the title of the September 1989 issue of *Scientific American*. This special issue on the environment was entitled "Managing Planet Earth."

5 One article which is generally credited with sparking a renewed interest in natural resource problems is John Krutilla, "Conservation Reconsidered," *The American Economic Review* 57 (September 1968): 777–786.

are explicit; objectives, relationships, and assumptions are clearly specified so that the reader understands exactly how the conclusions were derived.

In this chapter we will use two models for thinking systematically about the future. While models can be used successfully to forecast future problems, this has not always been the case. Long-range forecasts may heighten our sensitivity to possible outcomes, but they must never be treated as fact (Example 1.1).

The two visions presented in this chapter (the basic pessimist model and the basic optimist model) demonstrate areas of concern that will be given closer scrutiny later in this text. They also highlight the key relationships that motivate the conclusions drawn by authors of those visions, so that we can assess the adequacy of these relationships as guides to reality.

The pessimist and optimist visions were chosen from the literally hundreds that exist because they define, in some sense, the end points of a spectrum. We shall, of course, want to explore not only these end points but the vast intervening territory as we proceed through the book.

THE BASIC PESSIMIST MODEL

One end of the spectrum is defined by an ambitious study published in 1972 under the title *The Limits to Growth.*[6] Based on a technique known as *systems dynamics,* developed by Professor Jay Forrester at MIT, a large-scale computer model was constructed to simulate likely future outcomes of the world economy. The most prominent feature of systems dynamics is the use of feedback loops to explain behavior. The *feedback loop* is a closed path that connects an action to its effect on the surrounding conditions which, in turn, can influence further action. As the examples presented subsequently in this chapter demonstrate, depending on how the relationships are described, a wide variety of complex behavior can be described by this technique.

Conclusions of Pessimist Model

Three main conclusions were reached by this study. The first suggests that within a time span of less than 100 years with no major change in the physical, economic, or social relationships that have traditionally governed world development, society will run out of the nonrenewable resources on which the industrial base depends. When the resources have been depleted, a precipitous collapse of the economic system will result, manifested in massive unemployment, decreased food production, and a decline in population as the death rate soars. There is no smooth transition, no gradual slowing down of activity; rather, the economic sys-

---

6 The popular version of this study appears as Donella H. Meadows et al., *The Limits to Growth* (New York: Universe Books, 1972).

EXAMPLE 1.1

The Dangers of Prognostication

One's view of the future can be limited by his or her understanding of the past and present, as well as of the technological possibilities which lie around the corner. Often that understanding is not what it should be and the forecasts based on it, in retrospect, can seem rather absurd.

In 1486, for example, a committee headed by Fray Hernando de Talavera was established by King Ferdinand and Queen Isabella to advise them on the merits of funding Christopher Columbus's plan to sail to the West Indies. Following four years of work, the committee reported its conclusion that a voyage of the type contemplated was impossible because (1) the western ocean was infinite and probably not navigable; (2) even if the antipodes (the expected landfall) were reached, the return journey would be impossible; and (3) there probably were no antipodes to be reached because most of the world was presumably covered by water; St. Augustine said so.

In 1835, Thomas Tredgold, a British railroad designer, declared, "Any general system of conveying passengers—at a velocity exceeding 10 miles an hour, or thereabouts—is extremely improbable."

The chief geologist of the U.S. Geological Survey reported in 1920 that only 7 billion barrels of petroleum remained to be recovered with existing techniques. He predicted that, at the contemporary annual rate of consumption of a half-billion barrels, American oil resources would be exhausted in 14 years—by 1934. However, when that fateful year arrived, 12, not 7, billion barrels had been produced, and there was an additional 12 billion barrels of proved reserves.

Economists are certainly not immune from the dangers of prognostication. In *The Coal Question: An Inquiry Concerning the Progress of the Nation and the Probable Exhaustion of our Coal Mines*, published in 1865, Stanley Jevons concluded that the rapid increase in coal consumption coupled with the finite nature of the supply of coal would cause progress to stop in the near future. In John Maynard Keynes's discussion of Jevon's work, he notes that Jevons had a similar fear of an increasing scarcity of paper. Jevons apparently acted on those fears for, some 50 years after his death, his children had not used up the stock of paper he had accumulated.

Sources: Glenn Hueckel, "A Historical Approach to Future Economic Growth," *Science* 191 (March 14, 1975): 925–31; Harry U. Spiegel, ed., *The Development of Economic Thought* (New York: John Wiley, 1952): 490–525; Edward Cornish et al., *The Study of the Future* (Washington, DC: World Future Society, 1977): 106–08.

FIGURE 1.1 The limits-to-growth standard run.

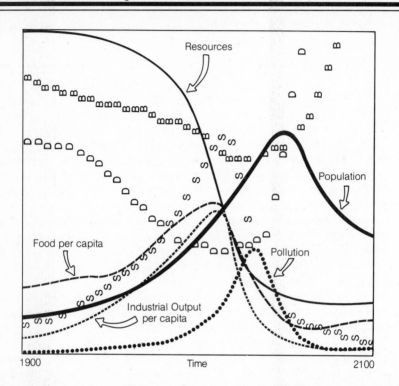

The "standard" world model run assumes no major change in the physical, economic, or social relationships that have historically governed the development of the world system. All variables plotted here follow historical values from 1900 to 1970. Food, industrial output, and population grow exponentially until the rapidly diminishing resource base forces a slowdown in industrial growth. Because of natural delays in the system, both population and pollution continue to increase for some time after the peak of industrialization. Population growth is finally halted by a rise in the death rate due to decreased food and medical services.

Source: From *The Limits to Growth: A Report for The Club of Rome's Project on the Predicament of Mankind,* by Donella H. Meadows, Dennis L. Meadows, Jorgen Randers, William H. Behrens, III. A Potomac Associates book published by Universe Books, N.Y., 1972. Graphics by Potomac Associates. Reprinted by permission.

---

tem consumes successively larger amounts of the depletable resources until they are gone. The characteristic behavior of the system is overshoot and collapse (see Figure 1.1).

The second conclusion of the study is that piecemeal approaches to solving the individual problems will not be successful. To demonstrate this point, the authors arbitrarily double their estimates of the resource base and allow the model to trace out an alternative vision based on this new higher level of resources. In this alternative vision the collapse still occurs, but this time it is caused by excessive pollution generated by the increased pace of industrialization permitted by the greater availability of resources. The authors then suggest that if the depletable resource and pollution problems were somehow jointly solved, population would grow unabated and the availability of food would become the binding constraint. In this model the removal of one limit merely causes the system to bump subsequently into another one, usually with more dire consequences.

As its third and final conclusion, the study suggests that overshoot and collapse can be avoided only by an immediate limit on population and pollution, as well as a cessation of economic growth. The portrait painted shows only two possible outcomes: the termination of growth by self-restraint and conscious policy—an approach that avoids the collapse—or the termination of growth by a collision with the natural limits, resulting in societal collapse. Thus, according to this study, one way or the other, growth will cease. The only issue is whether the conditions under which it will cease will be congenial or hostile.

The Nature of the Model

Why were these conclusions reached? Clearly they depend on the structure of the model. By identifying the characteristics that yield these conclusions, we can examine the realism of those characteristics.

The dominant characteristic of the model is exponential growth coupled with fixed limits. Exponential growth in any variable (for example, 3% per year) implies that the absolute increases in that variable will be greater and greater each year.[7] Furthermore, the higher the rate of growth in resource consumption, the faster a fixed stock of it will be exhausted. Suppose, for example, current reserves of a resource are 100 times current use and the supply of reserves cannot be expanded. If consumption were not growing, this stock would last 100 years. However, if consumption were to grow at 2% per year, the reserves would be exhausted in 55 years; and at 10%, exhaustion would occur after only 24 years.

Several resources are held in fixed supply by the model. These include the amount of available land and the stock of depletable resources. In addition, the supply of food is fixed relative to the supply of land. The combination of exponential growth in demand, coupled with fixed sources of supply, necessarily implies that, at some point, resource supplies must be exhausted. The extent to which those resources are essential thus creates the conditions for collapse.

---

7 Suppose, for example, that in some initial year there are 100 units of a specific variable. If that variable is growing at 10% per year, then it will grow 10 units during the first year and 11 units during the second year.

This basic structure of the model is in some ways reinforced and in some ways tempered by the presence of numerous positive and negative feedback loops. Positive feedback loops are those in which secondary effects tend to reinforce the basic trend. An example of a positive feedback loop is the process of capital accumulation. New investment generates greater output, which, when sold, generates profits. These profits can be used to fund additional new investments. This example suggests a manner in which the growth process is self-reinforcing.

Positive feedback loops may also be involved in global warming. Scientists believe, for example, that the relationship between emissions of methane and global warming may be described as a positive feedback loop. Since methane is a greenhouse gas, increases in methane emissions contribute to global warming. As the planetary temperature rises, however, it could release extremely large quantities of additional methane, and so on.

Human responses can intensify environmental problems. When shortages of a commodity are imminent, for example, consumers typically begin to hoard the commodity. Hoarding intensifies the shortage. Similarly, people faced with shortages of food commonly eat the seed that is the key to more plentiful food in the future. Situations giving rise to this kind of downward spiral are particularly troublesome.

A *negative feedback loop* is self-limiting rather than self-reinforcing, as illustrated by the role of death rates in limiting population growth in the model. As growth occurs, it causes larger increases in industrial output, which, in turn, cause more pollution. The increase in pollution triggers a rise in death rates, retarding population growth. From this example it can be seen that negative feedback loops can provide a tempering influence on the growth process, though not necessarily a desirable one.

Perhaps the best-known planetary-scale example of a negative feedback is provided in a theory advanced by James Lovelock, an English scientist. Called the *Gaia hypothesis* after the Greek concept for Mother Earth, this view of the world suggests that the earth is a living organism with a complex feedback system that seeks an optimal physical and chemical environment. Deviations from this optimal environment trigger natural, nonhuman response mechanisms which restore the balance. In essence, according to the Gaia hypothesis the planetary environment is a self-regulating process.

The model of the world envisioned by the Gaia hypothesis is incompatible with that envisioned by the *Limits to Growth* team. Because of the dominance of positive feedback loops, coupled with fixed limits on essential resources, the structure of the *Limits to Growth* model preordains its conclusion that human activity is on a collision course with nature. While the values assumed for various parameters (the size of the stock of depletable resources, for example) affect the timing of the various effects, they do not substantially affect the nature of the outcome.

The dynamics implied by the notion of a feedback loop is helpful in a more general sense than the specific relationships embodied in this model. As we proceed with our investigation, the degree to which our economic and political institutions serve to intensify or to limit emerging environmental problems will be a key concern.

THE BASIC OPTIMIST MODEL

Is the portrait of the fate of the world economy painted by the *Limits to Growth* model an accurate one? Because Herman Kahn and his associates did not think so, they presented an alternative vision in a book titled *The Next 200 Years: A Scenario for America and the World*.[8] This vision is an optimistic one based in large part on the continuing evolution of a form of technological progress that serves to push back the natural limits until they are no longer limiting.

Conclusions of Optimist Model

The basic conclusion reached by this study is stated in the opening pages of the book:

> ... 200 years ago almost everywhere human beings were comparatively few, poor and at the mercy of the forces of nature, and 200 years from now, we expect, almost everywhere they will be numerous, rich and in control of the forces of nature [p. 1].

The future path of population growth is expected by Kahn and his associates to approximate an S-shaped logistic curve. This image suggests that an omniscient observer during 1976 looking backward through time and then forward into the future would see rather different things. The retrospective glance would reveal a period of exponential population growth, while the glance into the future would reveal continued growth, but with steadily declining growth rates, until, at the end of the next 200-year period, growth would automatically come to a halt. By that time, however, the population would have increased four times its current level and the average person in the world economy would be earning $20,000 a year (in constant dollars)—a far cry from the 1976 average of $1300 (see Figure 1.2).

To Kahn and his associates, interference with this natural evolution of society would not only be unwarranted, it would be unethical. As they see it, tampering with the growth process would consign the residents of the poorest

---

8 Herman Kahn, William Brown, and Leon Martel, *The Next 200 Years: A Scenario for America and the World* (New York: William Morrow, 1976).

FIGURE 1.2   The Kahn perspective on prospects of humanity (in fixed 1975 dollars).

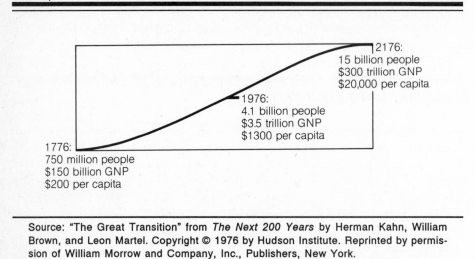

2176:
15 billion people
$300 trillion GNP
$20,000 per capita

1976:
4.1 billion people
$3.5 trillion GNP
$1300 per capita

1776:
750 million people
$150 billion GNP
$200 per capita

Source: "The Great Transition" from *The Next 200 Years* by Herman Kahn, William Brown, and Leon Martel. Copyright © 1976 by Hudson Institute. Reprinted by permission of William Morrow and Company, Inc., Publishers, New York.

developing countries—and, indeed, the poorest residents of the developed countries—to a life of poverty, a life without hope. In contrast, they see continued growth as providing continued betterment for both groups; although, due to an expected decline in the gap between the rich nations and the poor, those in the poorest nations would benefit most from continued growth.

The Nature of the Model

The Kahn model is more qualitative than the *Limits to Growth* model and therefore its structure is less specific. It is not a computer program that simulates the future. Rather, Kahn and his associates devised scenarios they believed to be plausible and then verified that the various components of these scenarios were consistent with each other. The book is filled with reasons why the chosen scenario is reasonable. These lists of reasons frequently include new technologies that, when certain limits are reached, will be introduced. These technologies effectively either remove the limit or buy time until a subsequent technology can remove the limit.

The principles underlying Kahn's work can best be illustrated through the use of two examples: food and energy. One of the sources of collapse in the *Limits of Growth* model was the inability of food supply to keep up with consumption. Kahn, by contrast, sees food production rising so rapidly as to create an eventual abundance of food. This vision, in turn, depends on some specific sources of optimism: (1) physical resources will not effectively limit production during the next 200 years, and (2) substantial increases can be expected in conventional foods produced by conventional means, conventional foods produced by unconventional means, and unconventional foods produced by unconventional means.

All of these sources of optimism are related to technological progress. The availability of physical resources can be expanded through the use of better (solar-powered, for example) irrigation systems. Conventional food production can be increased by the spread of better farming techniques and by the development of new hybrid seeds. If soils become depleted or scarce, then food can be raised with *hydroponics,* a process using no soil.[9] Finally, Kahn points to the development of a single-cell protein as a viable means of converting municipal waste into a food supplement.

A similar approach is taken when describing the world energy future. The authors of *The Next 200 Years* construct a list of technologies that can provide the transition to solar energy, making the case that solar energy can ultimately sustain a high level of economic activity. The list includes technologies that use coal, either directly or indirectly (such as gas produced from coal); those which exploit the vast world reserves of shale oil; nuclear power (fission, in the near term, replaced subsequently by fusion); and new solar technologies including windmills, photovoltaics, and ocean thermal power.

When all of these lists are combined, the prevailing message is that currently recognized technologies can overcome the limitations envisioned by the *Limits to Growth* view. *The Next 200 Years* staff, then, believes that the creators of *Limits to Growth* erred in being myopic; they were too tied to conventional technologies. When the need arises, they argue, these new technologies will be developed. The cliché, "Necessity is the mother of invention," captures the flavor of the belief of Kahn and his associates that these technologies will be developed as they are needed.

THE ROAD AHEAD

The two models used in this chapter were developed by people trained primarily in the natural, rather than social, sciences. This natural science orientation gives the models a flavor that contrasts markedly with the economic models presented in the rest of the book. The most striking difference is the central role that human

---

9 This technique grows plants in recirculating water, complemented by nutrient film. In the advanced versions of this technique, no soil at all is required even for stability. As an interesting aside, the technology is apparently sufficiently advanced that it is currently being used to grow marijuana illegally. See "Pot Growers Turn over New Leaf, Try State-of-the-Art Hydroponics," *Wall Street Journal* (January 15, 1981): 25.

behavior plays in the social science models, while it is relegated to a trivial role in natural science models.

Perhaps this distinction can best be illustrated through an analogy: When a pipe carrying water springs a leak, we plug the hole. The solution is simple, direct, and usually sufficient. However, in an economic system the most direct approach may not only be ineffective, it may be counterproductive.

Consider, for example, the manner in which the government chose to guarantee "just and reasonable" prices for natural gas, an especially important fuel. Congress imposed ceilings on the prices that pipeline companies, and ultimately producers, could charge. The evidence is now clear that this direct approach created shortages. The price ceiling lowered the quantity of natural gas available by reducing the incentives for suppliers to find new sources.[10] The failure to anticipate the effect of this policy on supplier behavior led to a situation in which the very people the law tried to protect were, instead, victimized by it. In order to gain a more complete understanding of what challenges to expect of the future, as well as possible solutions, we must consider the role of human behavior.

The Issues

Obviously these visions of the future present us with rather different conceptions of what the future holds as well as different views of what policy choices should be made. They also suggest that to act as if one vision is correct, when it is not, could prove to be a costly error. Thus, it is important to determine if one of these two views or some third view, is correct.

In order to assess any model or view, we must address the basic issues:

1. Is the problem correctly conceptualized as exponential growth with fixed, immutable resource limits? Does the earth have a finite carrying capacity?

2. If these limits do exist, have they been measured correctly or, as Kahn argues, has the *Limits to Growth* team been rather myopic in the way they treat resources? How can the carrying-capacity concept be operationalized? Do current levels of economic activity exceed the carrying capacity?

3. How does the economic system respond to scarcities? Does the process involve mainly positive feedback loops? Would it intensify or ameliorate any initial scarcities? Is the overshoot-and-collapse syndrome an accurate portrayal of the future?

---

10 Other problems were also caused by the act. See Chapter 7 for detailed examination of natural gas allocation.

4. What is the role of the political system in controlling these problems? In what circumstances is government intervention necessary? Is this intervention uniformly benign, or can it make the situation worse? What is an appropriate role for the executive, legislative, and judicial branches?

5. Many environmental problems involve a considerable degree of uncertainty about the severity of the problem and the effectiveness of possible solutions. Can our economic and political institutions respond to this uncertainty in reasonable ways?

6. Can the economic and political systems work together to eradicate poverty while respecting our obligations to future generations? Or does our obligation to future generations inevitably conflict with the desire to raise the living standards of those currently in absolute poverty? Can short-term and long-term goals be harmonized? Is sustainable development feasible? How could it be achieved? What does it imply about the future of economic activity in the industrialized nations? in the less industrialized nations?

The rest of the book uses economic analysis to suggest answers to these questions.

An Overview of the Book

In the following chapters you will study the rich and rewarding field of environmental and natural resource economics. The menu of topics is broad and varied. Economics provides a powerful analytical framework for examining the relationships between the environment, on the one hand, and the economic and political systems, on the other. The study of economics can assist in identifying circumstances that give rise to environmental problems, in discovering causes of these problems, and in searching for solutions. Each chapter is an introduction to a unique topic in environmental and natural resource economics, while our overarching focus on growth in a finite environment weaves these topics into a single theme.

We begin in Chapter 2 by comparing perspectives being brought to bear on these problems by economists and noneconomists. The manner in which scholars in various disciplines view problems and potential solutions depends on how they organize the available facts, how they interpret those facts, and what kinds of values they apply in translating these interpretations into policy. Before going into a detailed look at environmental problems, we shall compare the ideology of conventional economics to other prevailing ideologies in the natural and social sciences. This comparison not only explains why reasonable people may, upon examining the same set of facts, reach different conclusions, but it also conveys some sense of the strengths and weaknesses of economic analysis as it is applied to environmental problems.

Chapters 3 and 4 delve more deeply into the conventional economics approach. Specific evaluation criteria are defined, and examples are developed to show how these criteria can be applied to specific environmental problems.

After examining the major perspectives shaping environmental policy, we turn (Chapters 5-13) to the physical limits identified by *Limits to Growth*—to the manner in which the economic and political institutions have dealt with the resulting problems and the potential for improvement in the future. We begin our examination in Chapter 5 with an inquiry into the nature, causes, and consequences of population growth, a major factor in determining how rapidly the limits could be reached.

Chapters 6-13 deal with several topics traditionally falling within natural resource economics. Chapter 6 provides an overview of the models used to characterize the "optimal" allocation of resources over time. These models allow us to show not only how the optimal allocation depends on such factors as the cost of extraction, environmental costs, and the availability of substitutes, but also how the allocations produced by our political and economic institutions measure up against this standard of optimality. Chapter 7 discusses energy as an example of a depletable, nonrecyclable resource, and examines such topics as the role of OPEC, the balance between imports and domestic production, the role of nuclear power, and many aspects of past and present energy policy. Chapter 8 focuses on minerals to illustrate how depletable, recyclable resources are allocated over time, and to define the appropriate role for recycling. The degree to which the current situation approximates this ideal is assessed, with particular attention paid to aspects such as tax policy, disposal costs, and product durability.

Chapters 9-12 focus on renewable or replenishable resources. These chapters show that the effectiveness with which current institutions manage renewable resources depends on whether the resources are living or inanimate and whether they are treated as private or common property. In Chapter 9, the focus is on allocating water in arid regions. Water is an example of an inanimate but replenishable resource. Specific examples from the American Southwest illustrate how the political and economic institutions have coped with this form of impending scarcity. In Chapter 10, the focus is on cereal grain, an animate, private-property resource, which is the most important source of food in combating the world hunger problem, and the land on which the grain is grown. Chapter 11 deals with forestry as an example of a renewable and storable private-property resource. Managing this resource is somewhat unique in that the amount of time required to produce an efficient harvest is longer than for the other resources considered; forests are also a major source of biodiversity. In Chapter 12, fisheries are used to illustrate the problems associated with an animate, common-property resource and to explore possible means of solving these problems.

The final chapter concerned with natural resources, Chapter 13, confronts the fear that we are entering an era of generalized resource scarcity. It seeks answers to key questions: Are we in an era of increasing scarcity? How can we tell? What indicators can be used and what do they reveal? What responses should be taken given this evidence?

We then move on to an area of public policy—pollution control—which is coming to rely much more heavily on the use of economic incentives to produce the desired response. Chapter 14, an overview chapter, emphasizes not only the nature of the problems but differences among policy approaches taken to resolve them. The unique aspects of local air pollution, regional and global air pollution, automobile air pollution, water pollution, and the control of toxic substances are dealt with in the five subsequent chapters. Special attention is paid in Chapter 20 to the impacts of those policies—not only on the problems they were designed to correct, but also on other important policy concerns, such as the distribution of the benefit and cost burdens among various socioeconomic groups and geographic areas.

Following this examination of the individual environmental and natural resource problems and the policies that can be, and have been, used to ameliorate these problems, we turn to the growth process itself. Certain questions must be asked. What are the causes and consequences of economic growth? What role do natural resources and environmental control play in the growth process? What is the likely future for economic growth? Is an immediate transition to a path of zero economic growth (as suggested by *Limits to Growth*) necessary, or, if unnecessary, is it desirable?

In Chapter 23 we close by assembling the bits and pieces of evidence accumulated thus far and fusing them into an overall response to the questions posed in the chapter. The chapter also suggests some of the major unresolved issues in environmental policy that are likely to be among those commanding center stage over the next several years or decades.

SUMMARY

Is our society so myopic that it has chosen a path which can only lead to the destruction of society as we now know it? We have examined briefly two studies which provide different answers to that question. *The Limits to Growth* responds in the affirmative, while Kahn and his associates respond negatively. The pessimistic view is based upon the inevitability of exceeding the carrying capacity of the planet as the population and the level of economic activity grow. The optimistic view sees initial scarcity triggering sufficiently powerful reductions in population growth and increases in technological progress that the future brings abundance, not deepening scarcity.

Our examination of these different visions has revealed questions which must be answered if we are to assess what the future holds. Seeking the answers requires that we accumulate a much better understanding about how choices are made in economic and political systems and how those choices affect, and are affected by, the natural environment. We begin that process in Chapter 2, where the economic approach is developed in broad terms and is contrasted with other conventional approaches.

FURTHER READING

Beckerman, Wilfred. *Two Cheers for the Affluent Society: A Spirited Defense of Economic Growth* (New York: St. Martin's Press, 1974). As the title suggests, an always spirited, frequently irreverent defense of continued economic growth.

Leontief, Wassily. *The Future of the World Economy* (New York: Oxford University Press, 1977). A major empirical study led by a Nobel laureate in economics commissioned by the United Nations to examine the feasibility of closing the per capita income gap between rich and poor nations.

Pearce, David, Anil Markandya, and Edward B. Barbier. *Blueprint for a Green Economy* (London: Earthscan Publications, 1989). Originally written as a report for the British government, this document charts a course for the achievement of a more environmentally benign future for economic activity.

Simon, Julian L. *The Ultimate Resource* (Princeton, NJ: Princeton University Press, 1981). The tone of this optimistic study, conveyed by the title of his third chapter, "Can the Supply of Natural Resources Really Be Infinite? Yes!" concludes that the ultimate resource is human imagination, a resource that knows no limit.

World Commission on Environment and Development. *Our Common Future* (Oxford: Oxford University Press, 1987). An enormously influential book that has set the tone for much current environmental activity by the United Nations. Sees Third World poverty as one fundamental cause of environmental problems and a concerted effort to reduce that poverty as a necessary component of any solution.

ADDITIONAL REFERENCES

Cole, H. S. D., ed. *Models of Doom: A Critique of the Limits to Growth* (New York: Universe Books, 1973).

Council on Environmental Quality and Department of State. *The Global 2000 Report to the President of the U.S.: Entering the 21st Century,* Vols. I–III (New York: Pergamon Press, 1980).

Hughes, Barry. *World Futures: A Critical Analysis of Alternatives* (Baltimore: The Johns Hopkins University Press, 1985).

Kahn, Herman, William Brown, and Leon Martel. *The Next 200 Years: A Scenario for America and the World* (New York: William Morrow, 1976).

Meadows, Donella H., et al. *The Limits to Growth* (New York: Universe Books, 1972).

Meadows, Dennis L., et al. *Dynamics of Growth in a Finite World* (Cambridge, MA: Wright-Allen Press, 1974).

Mesarovic, Michaklo and Edward Pestel. *Mankind at the Turning Point: The Second Report to the Club of Rome* (New York: The New American Library, 1974).

Simon, Julian L. and Herman Kahn. *The Resourceful Earth: A Response to Global 2000* (New York: Blackwell, 1984).

DISCUSSION QUESTIONS

1. A central concept in the *Limits to Growth* view of the future is the finiteness of resources. In his book *The Ultimate Resource*, Julian Simon makes the point that calling the resource base "finite" is misleading. To illustrate this point he uses a yardstick, with its 1-inch markings, as an analogy. The distance between two markings is finite—1 inch—but an infinite number of points is contained within that finite space. Therefore, in one sense, what lies between the markings is finite, while in another, equally meaningful, sense it is infinite. Is the concept of a finite resource base useful or not? Why or why not?

2. This chapter contains two views of the future. Since the validity of these views cannot completely be tested until the time period covered by the forecast has past (so that predictions can be matched against actual events), how can we ever hope to establish whether one is a better view than the other? What criteria might be proposed for evaluating predictions?

3. Positive and negative feedback loops lie at the core of systematic thinking about the future. As you examine the key forces shaping the future, what examples of positive and negative feedback loops can you uncover?

CHAPTER TWO

Economics of the Environment: An Overview

When you have eliminated the impossible, whatever remains, however improbable, must be the truth.

SHERLOCK HOLMES, *From* SIR ARTHUR CONAN DOYLE'S *The Sign of Four* (1890)

INTRODUCTION

Before examining specific environmental problems and the policy responses to them, it is important that we develop and clarify the economics approach, so that we will have some sense of the forest before examining each of the trees. By having a feel for the conceptual framework, it becomes easier not only to deal with individual cases, but, perhaps more importantly, to see how they fit into a comprehensive approach.

In this chapter we develop the general conceptual framework used in economics to approach environmental problems. We begin by examining the relationship between human actions, as manifested through the economic system, and the environmental consequences of those actions. We can then establish criteria for judging the desirability of the outcomes of this relationship. These criteria provide a basis for identifying the nature and severity of environmental problems, and a foundation for designing effective policies to deal with them.

Throughout this chapter the economic point of view is contrasted with alternative points of view. These contrasts bring the economic approach into sharper focus and stimulate deeper and more critical thinking about all possible approaches.

THE HUMAN ENVIRONMENT RELATIONSHIP

The Environment as an Asset

In economics the environment is viewed as a composite asset that provides a variety of services. It is a very special asset, to be sure, since it provides the life support systems that sustain our very existence, but it is an asset nonetheless. As with other assets, we wish to prevent undue depreciation of the value of this asset so that it may continue to provide aesthetic and life-sustaining services.

The environment provides the economy with raw materials, which are transformed into consumer products by the production process, and energy, which fuels this transformation. Ultimately these raw materials and energy return to the environment as waste products (see Figure 2.1).

The environment also provides services directly to consumers. The air we breathe, the nourishment we receive from food and drink, and the protection we

FIGURE 2.1 The economic system and the environment.

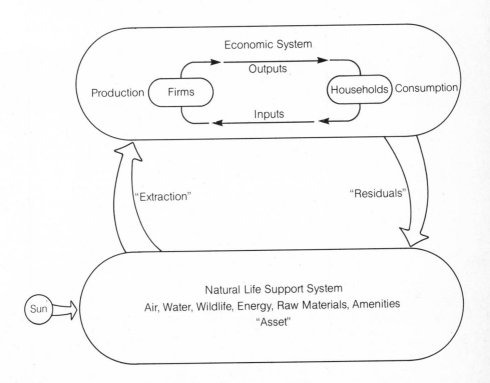

derive from shelter and clothing are all benefits we receive either directly or indirectly from the environment. In addition, anyone who has experienced the exhilaration of white-water canoeing, the total serenity of a wilderness trek, or the breathtaking beauty of a sunset will readily recognize that the environment provides us with a variety of amenities for which no substitute exists.

If the environment is defined broadly enough, the relationship between the environment and the economic system can be considered a *closed system*. For our purposes, a closed system is one in which no inputs (energy, matter, and so on) are received from outside the system and no outputs are transferred outside the system. An *open system*, by contrast, is one in which the system imports or exports matter or energy.

If we restrict our conception of the relationship in Figure 2.1 to our planet and the atmosphere around it, then clearly we do not have a closed system. We derive most of our energy from the sun, either directly or indirectly. We have also sent spaceships well beyond the boundaries of our atmosphere. Nonetheless, historically speaking, for *material* inputs and outputs (not including energy), this system can be treated as a closed system because the amount of exports (such as abandoned space vehicles) and imports (moon rocks, for example) are negligible. Whether the system remains closed depends on the degree to which space exploration opens up the rest of our solar system as a source of raw materials.

The treatment of our planet and its immediate environs as a closed system has an important implication, which is summed up in the *first law of thermodynamics*—energy and matter cannot be created or destroyed.[1] The law implies that the mass of materials flowing into the economic system from the environment has to either accumulate in the economic system or return to the environment as waste. When accumulation stops, the mass of materials flowing into the economic system is equal in magnitude to the mass of waste flowing into the environment.

Excessive wastes can, of course, depreciate the asset; when they exceed the absorptive capacity of nature, wastes reduce the services that the asset provides.[2] Examples are easy to find: air pollution can cause respiratory problems; polluted drinking water can cause cancer; smog obliterates scenic vistas.

The relationship of people to the environment is also conditioned by another physical law, the *second law of thermodynamics*. Known popularly as the *entropy*

---

1   We know, however, from Einstein's famous equation ($E=mc^2$) that matter can be transformed into energy. This transformation is the source of energy in nuclear power.

2   A detailed economic model, known as the materials balance model, has been constructed to integrate physical mass flows and the economic system. A description of this model is beyond the scope of this chapter, but can be found in Allen V. Kneese, Robert U. Ayers, and Ralph G. d'Arge, *Economics and the Environment: A Materials Balance Approach* (Washington, DC: Resources for the Future, 1970).

law, this law states that entropy increases. *Entropy* is the amount of energy not available for work.[3] Applied to energy processes, this law implies that no conversion from one form of energy to another is completely efficient and that the consumption of energy is an irreversible process. Some energy is always lost during conversion, and the rest, once used, is no longer available for further work. The second law also implies that in the absence of new energy inputs, any closed system must eventually use up its energy. Since energy is necessary for life, life ceases when energy ceases.

We should remember that our planet is not even approximately a closed system with respect to energy; we gain energy from the sun. The entropy law does suggest, however, that this flow of solar energy establishes an upper limit on the flow of energy that can be sustained. Once the stocks of stored energy (such as fossil fuels and nuclear energy) are gone, the amount of energy available for useful work will be determined solely by this flow and by the amount that can be stored (dams, trees, and so on). Thus, over the very long run, the growth process will be limited by the availability of solar energy and our ability to put it to work.

Two different types of economic analysis can be applied to increase our understanding of the relationship between the economic system and the environment: Positive economics attempts to describe *what is, what was,* or *what will be. Normative* economics, by contrast, deals with *what ought to be.* Disagreements within positive economics can usually be resolved by an appeal to the facts. Normative disagreements, however, involve value judgments.

Both branches are useful. Suppose, for example, we want to be precise about how the economic system treats the environmental asset. Positive economics would be used to describe the service flows and to show how those service flows would be affected by a change in the system (such as the discovery of a new production process). Positive analysis could not, however, be used to provide any guidance on the question of whether these service flows were optimal. That judgment would have to come from normative economics.

The essence of the normative approach in economics is to maximize the value of the asset. As long as humans exist, they cannot avoid affecting the environment. The issue, therefore, cannot be *whether* humans should have any impact on the environment; rather, the issue is to define the optimal level of impact.

Valuation of the Asset

The normative approach attempts to maximize the value of the environmental asset by creating a balance between the preservation and use of that asset. In

---

3 For a technical description of entropy and its relationship to economics, see Stuart Burness et al., "Thermodynamic and Economic Concepts as Related to Resource-Use Policies," *Land Economics* 56 (February 1980): 1-9.

order to define this balance, it is necessary to place some sort of value on the various service flows received, including the negative effects of using the environment as a receptacle for waste. In the economic point of view, this valuation is decidedly *anthropocentric*, or human-centered. Effects on the ecosphere are valued in terms of their ultimate effects on humanity. As Example 2.1 indicates, this approach is not universally accepted.

We can argue that it is appropriate to assign humans the right to govern this balance without necessarily arguing that the resulting decisions are correct. Decisions are deemed incorrect, for example, if the decision-making process leads to outcomes that are inconsistent with the collectively desired outcomes, which is precisely what the economic approach suggests. According to the economic approach, in many circumstances the individually rational choice differs from the collectively rational choice. Thus, the problem is not the *values* that are being applied to those choices but the *process* by which choices are reached.

NORMATIVE CRITERIA FOR DECISION MAKING

Since choices concerning the treatment of the environmental asset are inevitable, a criterion for judging the desirability of various options is essential. We initially consider the criterion typically used to judge resource allocations at a point in time, a useful criterion when choices in various time periods are independent. We then expand our horizons and consider criteria for making choices that have effects not only on our generation, but on subsequent generations as well.

Static Efficiency

The chief normative economic criterion for choosing among various allocations occurring at the same point in time is called static efficiency, or merely efficiency. An allocation of resources is said to satisfy the static efficiency criterion if the net benefit from the use of those resources is maximized by that allocation. The net benefit is simply the excess of benefits over costs resulting from that allocation. But how do we measure benefits and costs?

Benefits can be derived from the demand curve for the resource in question. Demand curves measure the amount of a particular good people would be willing to purchase at various prices. In a typical situation, a person will purchase less of a commodity (or environmental service) the higher is its cost. In Figure 2.2, when the price is p_0, q_0 will be purchased, but if the price rises to p_1, purchases will fall to q_1.

EXAMPLE 2.1

Nature Knows Best

The view that the environment should be managed by humans is rather controversial, particularly among ecologists. In *The Closing Circle,* Barry Commoner poses what he calls the third law of ecology: nature knows best. Commoner elaborates on this view:

> . . . living things accumulate a complex organization of compatible parts; those possible arrangements that are not compatible with the whole are screened out over the long course of evolution. Thus, the structure of a present living thing or the organization of a current natural ecosystem is likely to be "best" in the sense that it has been so heavily screened for disadvantageous components that any new one is very likely to be worse than the present one [p. 43].

Don't interfere with the ecosystem is the underlying message.

The conflict between the economic approach and that proposed by Commoner is perhaps best illustrated by the controversy over the Tellico Dam and the snail darter. The Tellico Dam was an ambitious water project on the Little Tennessee River authorized by Congress in 1967. During the summer of 1973, a Tennessee ichthyologist, Dr. David A. Etnier, Jr., discovered a previously unknown species of perch called the snail darter. During 1975, with the dam 75% complete, the Secretary of the Interior declared the snail darter an endangered species, which, under the Endangered Species Act of 1973, was sufficient to stop construction of the dam. The Supreme Court in 1978 upheld the act. The final turn of events, however, in this twisted saga came in 1979 when Congress passed, as a rider on an energy and water appropriations bill, an exemption from the Endangered Species Act for the snail darter.

The economic approach stacks up the worth of the project against the worth of the snail darter, both as a species and as a member of the larger ecological system. The principle of minimum interference suggests that regardless of the importance of the snail darter and regardless of the cost, it should be preserved. The extinction of a species is never justified regardless of the circumstances.

Ironically, this clash of principles need not have taken place. An economic analysis showed the dam to be a poor investment, and the snail darter was subsequently successfully transplanted to the nearby Hiwasee River. Nonetheless, this issue serves to illustrate that the seemingly abstract conflict between alternative sets of values can have very practical implications.

Sources: "Endangered Species Curbs," *Congressional Quarterly Almanac* 34 (1978): 707; "Public Works Energy Development Funds," *Congressional Quarterly Almanac,* 35 (1979): p. 223; "Endangered Species Act," *Congressional Quarterly Almanac,* 35 (1979): 661; Barry Commoner, *The Closing Circle* (New York: Alfred A. Knopf, 1972).

FIGURE 2.2   The individual demand curve.

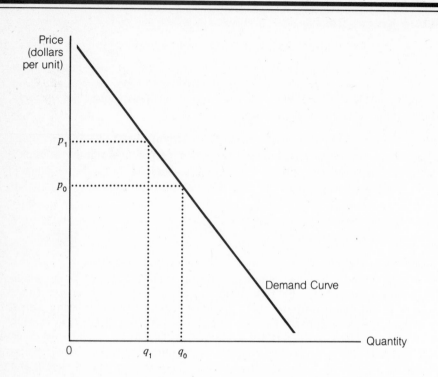

The meaning of these demand curves can be illustrated with this hypothetical experiment: suppose you were asked, "At a price of X dollars, how much commodity Y would you buy?" Your answer could be recorded as a point on a diagram, such as Figure 2.2. By repeating the question many times for different prices, we could trace out a locus of points, Connecting these points would yield an individual *demand curve*. Adding up all of the individual amounts demanded by all individuals at some stipulated price yields one point on the market demand curve. Connecting the points for various prices reveals the market demand curve.

For each quantity purchased, the corresponding point on the market demand curve represents the amount of money some person is willing to pay for the last unit of the good. The *total willingness to pay* for some quantity of this good— say, 3 units—is the sum of the willingness to pay for each of the three units. Thus the total willingness to pay for 3 units would be measured by the sum of the willingness to pay for the first, second, and third units, respectively. It is now a simple extension to determine that the total willingness to pay is the area under the continuous market demand curve to the left of the allocation in ques-

FIGURE 2.3   The relationship of demand to willingness to pay.

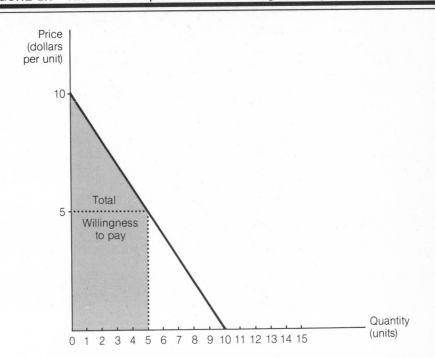

tion. For example, in Figure 2.3 the total willingness to pay for 5 units of the commodity is the shaded area.[4] Total willingness to pay is the concept we shall use to define total benefits. Thus *total benefits* are equal to the area under the market demand curve from the origin to the allocation of interest.

Measuring total costs on the same set of axes involves logic similar to measuring total benefits. It is important to stress that environmental services have costs even though they are produced without any human input. All costs should be measured as opportunity costs.

For environmental services their *opportunity cost* is the net benefit forgone because the resources providing the service can no longer be used in their next most beneficial use. Resources are not free if they can be put to alternative uses. For example, suppose a particular stretch of river can be used either for white-water canoeing or to generate electric power. Since the dam that generates the power would flood the rapids, the two uses are incom-

---

4 From simple geometry it can be noticed that for linear demand curves this area is the sum of the areas of the triangle on top plus the rectangle on the bottom. The area of a right triangle is 1/2 × base × height. Therefore, in our example this area is 1/2 × \$5 × 5 + \$5 × 5 = \$37.50.

FIGURE 2.4   The relationship of marginal cost and total cost.

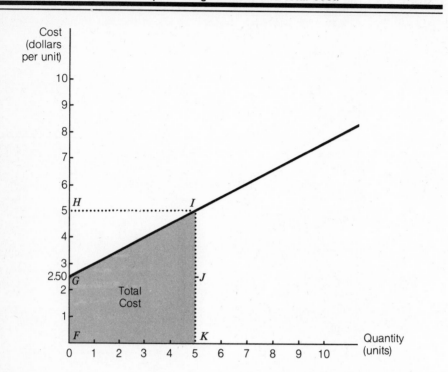

patible. The opportunity cost of saving the river for white-water canoeing is the forgone net benefit (after accounting for the cost of generation and distribution) of electricity.

In graphing costs, we shall use the marginal opportunity cost curve to correspond to the marginal willingness-to-pay function used above to graph benefits. The *marginal opportunity cost* curve defines the additional cost of producing the last unit. In purely competitive markets, the marginal opportunity cost curve is identical to the supply curve.

Total cost is simply the sum of the marginal costs.[5] The total cost of producing 3 units is equal to the cost of producing the first unit plus the cost of producing the second unit plus the cost of producing the third unit. As with total willingness to pay, the geometric representation of the sum of the individual

---

5 Strictly speaking, the sum of the marginal costs is equal to total variable cost. In the short run, this is smaller than total cost by the amount of the fixed cost. For our purposes this distinction is not important.

FIGURE 2.5   The derivation of net benefits.

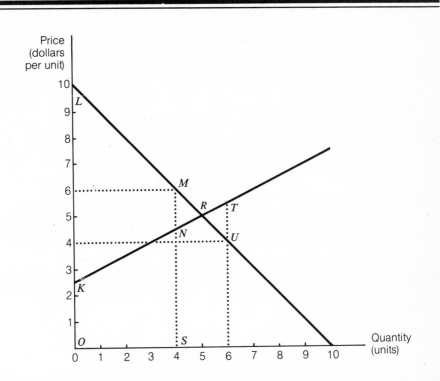

elements of a continuous marginal cost curve is the area under the marginal cost curve, as illustrated in Figure 2.4 by the shaded area *FGIJK*.[6]

Since net benefit is defined as the excess of benefits over costs, it follows that net benefit is equal to that portion of the area under the demand curve which lies above the supply curve. Consider Figure 2.5, which combines the information in Figures 2.3 and in Figure 2.4.

Our search for the efficient allocation begins by establishing the net benefit for an arbitrary production level—say, 4 units. At 4 units the total benefit is equal to *OLMNS*, and the total cost is equal to *OKNS*. Net benefit is, therefore, depicted by area *KLMN*. Is 4 units an efficient allocation? It is if it maximizes the net benefit. Do 4 units maximize the net benefit?

---

6 Notice again that this area is the sum of a right triangle and a rectangle. In Figure 2.4 the total variable cost of producing 5 units is $18.75. Why?

We can answer that question by establishing whether it is possible to increase the net benefit by producing more or less of the resource. If the net benefit can be increased, clearly the original allocation could not have maximized the net benefit and, therefore, could not have been efficient. Consider what would happen if society were to choose 5 units instead of 4. What happens to the net benefit? It *increases* by area *MNR*. Since we can find another allocation with greater net benefit, 4 units could not have been efficient. Are 5? Yes. Let's see why.

We know that 5 units convey more net benefit than 4. If this allocation is efficient, then it must also be true that the net benefit is smaller for levels of production higher than 5. Notice that the additional cost of producing the sixth unit (the area under the marginal cost curve) is *larger* than the additional benefit received from producing it (the corresponding area under the demand curve). Therefore, the triangle *RTU* represents the *reduction* in net benefit that occurs if 6 units are produced rather than 5.

Since the net benefit is reduced, both by producing less than 5 and by producing more than 5, we conclude that 5 units is the production level that maximizes net benefit. Therefore, from our definition, a level of 5 units constitutes an efficient allocation.[7] One implication of this example, which shall be very useful in succeeding chapters, is that *net benefits are maximized when the marginal benefit is equal to the marginal cost.*

The ethical basis for this criterion is derived from a concept called *Pareto optimality,* named after the Italian-born, Swiss economist Vilfredo Pareto, who first proposed it around the turn of the twentieth century. Allocations are said to be Pareto optimal if no rearrangement of that allocation could benefit some people without any deleterious effects on at least one other person. (A rearrangement of a resource allocation could involve changing the level produced or changing the shares received by each of the ultimate users of the resource.)

Allocations that do *not* satisfy this definition are suboptimal. Suboptimal allocations can always be rearranged so that some people are better off and no one is hurt by the rearrangement. In any rearrangement from a suboptimal allocation to an optimal one, the gainers would gain more than the losers lose. Therefore, the gainers could use a portion of their gains to compensate the losers sufficiently to ensure they were at least as well off as they were prior to the reallocation.

Efficient allocations are Pareto optimal. Since net benefits are maximized by an efficient allocation, it is not possible to increase the net benefit by rearranging the allocation. Without an increase in the net benefit, there is no way the gainers could sufficiently compensate the losers; the gains to the gainers would necessarily be smaller than the losses to the losers.

---

7 The monetary worth of the net benefit is the sum of two right triangles, and it equals $(1/2)(\$5)(5)$ + $(1/2)(\$2.50)(5)$ or $18.75. Why?

Inefficient allocations are judged inferior because they do not maximize the net benefit. By failing to maximize net benefit, they are forgoing an opportunity to make some people better off without harming others.

Dynamic Efficiency

The static efficiency criterion is very useful for comparing resource allocations when time is not an important factor. Yet many of the decisions made now affect the value of the asset for future generations. Time is a factor. Exhaustible energy resources, once used, are gone. Biological renewable resources (such as fisheries or forests) can be overharvested, leaving smaller and possibly weaker populations for future generations. Persistent pollutants can accumulate over time. How can we make choices when the benefits and costs may occur at different points in time?

The traditional criterion used to address this problem is called *dynamic efficiency*, a generalization of the static efficiency concept already developed. In this generalization, the criterion provides a way for thinking not only about the magnitude of benefits and costs, but also about timing. In order to incorporate timing, the criterion must provide a way to compare the net benefit received in one period with the net benefit received in another. The concept that allows this comparison is called *present value*. Therefore, before defining dynamic efficiency, we must define present value.

Present value explicitly incorporates the time value of money. A dollar today invested at 10% interest yields $1.10 a year from now (the return of the $1 principal plus $0.10 interest). The present value of $1.10 received one year from now is, therefore, $1 because, given $1 now, you can turn it into $1.10 a year from now by investing it at 10% interest. We can find the present value of any amount of money (X) received one year from now by computing $X/(1 + r)$, where r is the appropriate interest rate (10% in our above example).

What could your dollar earn in two years at r percent interest? Because of compound interest, the amount would be $\$1(1 + r)(1 + r) = \$1(1 + r)^2$. It follows then that the present value of X received two years from now is $X/(1 + r)^2$.

By now the pattern should be clear. The present value of a *one-time* net benefit received n years from now is

$$PV[B_n] = \frac{B_n}{(1 + r)^n} \ .$$

The present value of a *stream* of net benefits $\{B_0, \ldots, B_n\}$ received over a period of n years is computed as

$$PV[B_0, \ldots, B_n] = \sum_{i=0}^{n} \frac{B_i}{(1 + r)^i} \ ,$$

where r is the appropriate interest rate and B_0 is the amount of net benefits received immediately. The process of calculating the present value is called *discounting*, and the rate r is referred to as the discount rate.[8]

The number resulting from a present-value calculation has a straightforward interpretation. Suppose you were investigating an allocation that would yield the following pattern of net benefits on the last day of each of the next five years: $3000, $5000, $6000, $10,000, $12,000. If you use an interest rate of 6% (r = 0.06) and the above formula, you will discover that this stream has a present value of $29,210.

What does that number mean? If you put $29,210 in a savings account earning 6% interest and wrote yourself checks, respectively, for $3000, $5000, $6000, $10,000, and $12,000 on the last day of each of the next five years, your last check would just restore the account to a zero balance. Thus, you should be indifferent to receiving $29,210 now or in the specific five-year stream of benefits totaling $36,000; given one, you can get the other. Hence, the method is called present value because it translates everything back to its current worth.

It is now possible to define dynamic efficiency. An allocation of resources across n time periods is dynamically efficient if it maximizes the present value of net benefits that could be received from all the possible ways of allocating those resources over the n periods.

To illustrate, we can use the dynamic efficiency criterion to define an efficient allocation of a depletable, nonrecyclable resource. Dynamic efficiency assumes that society's objective is to balance the current and subsequent uses of the resources by maximizing the present value of the net benefit derived from the use of the resource. We shall demonstrate by using a very simple model, which assumes the resource can be used in only two time periods. In subsequent chapters we show how these conclusions generalize to longer times and more complicated situations.

Let's begin with a case in which the marginal cost of extracting the resource is constant, but there is a fixed supply of it to allocate between the two periods. Let's assume that demand is constant in the two periods, the marginal willingness-to-pay is given by the formula $P = 8 - 0.4q$, and marginal cost is constant at $2 per unit (see Figure 2.6). Notice that if the total supply were 30 or greater, and we were only concerned with these two periods, an efficient allocation would produce 15 units in each period, *regardless of the discount rate*. The supply is sufficient to cover the demand in both periods; the production in period 1 does

---

8 The discount rate should equal the social opportunity cost of capital. See Raymond Mikesell, *The Rate of Discount for Evaluating Public Projects* (Washington, DC: American Enterprise Institute for Public Policy Research, 1977) for detailed examination of the reasons for this choice and its implications. We examine in Chapter 3 the questions of whether private firms can be expected to use the socially correct discount rate. In Chapter 4, we discuss how the discount rate is chosen by the government.

FIGURE 2.6 The allocation of an abundant depletable resource. (a) Period 1. (b) Period 2.

not reduce the production in period 2. In this case the static efficiency criterion is sufficient, since time is not an important part of the problem.

Examine, however, what happens when the available supply is less than 30. Suppose it is equal to 20. How do we determine the efficient allocation? According to the dynamic efficiency criterion, the efficient allocation is the one that maximizes the present value of the net benefit. The present value of the net benefit for both years is simply the sum of the present values in each of the two years. To take a concrete example, consider the present value of a particular allocation: 15 units in the first period and 5 in the second. How would we compute the present value of that allocation?

The present value in the first period would be that portion of the geometric area under the demand curve which is over the supply curve— $45.00.[9] The present value in the second period is that portion of the area under the demand curve which is over the supply curve from the origin to the 5 units produced multiplied by $1/(1 + r)$. If we use $r = 0.10$, then the present value of the net benefit received in the second period is $22.73,[10] and the present value of net benefits for the two years is $67.73.

---

[9] The height of the triangle is $6 [$8 − $2] and the base is 15 units. The area is therefore $(1/2)($6)(15) = $45.

[10] The undiscounted net benefit is $25.00 (Why?) The discounted net benefit is therefore $25/1.10 = 22.73$.

FIGURE 2.7 The dynamically efficient allocation.

We now know how to find the present value of net benefits for any alloca-tion. How does one find the allocation that maximizes present value? One way, with the aid of a computer, is to try all possible combinations of q_1 and q_2, which sum to 20. The one yielding the maximum present value of net benefits can then be selected. That is tedious and, for those who have the requisite mathematics, unnecessary.

The dynamically efficient allocation of this resource has to satisfy the con-dition that the present value of the marginal net benefit from the last unit in period 1 equals the present value of the marginal net benefit in period 2 (see appendix at the end of this chapter). Even without mathematics, this principle is easy to understand, as can be demonstrated with the use of a simple graphical representation of the two-period allocation problem.[11]

Figure 2.7 depicts the present value of the marginal net benefit for each of the two periods. The net benefit curve for period 1 is to be read from left to right. The net benefit curve intersects the vertical axis at $6; demand would be zero at $8 and the marginal cost is $2, so the difference (marginal net benefit)

---

11 This type of analysis first appeared in James McInerney, "The Simple Analytics of Natural Resource Economics," *Journal of Agricultural Economics* 27 (1976): 31–52.

is \$6. The marginal net benefit for the first period goes to zero at 15 units because, at that quantity, the willingness to pay for that unit exactly equals its cost.

The only tricky aspect of drawing the graph involves constructing the curve for the present value of net benefits in period 2. Two aspects are worth noting. First, the zero axis for the period 2 net benefits is on the right, rather than the left, side. Therefore, increases in period 2 are recorded from right to left. This way, any point along the horizontal axis yields a total of 20 units allocated among the two periods. Any point on that axis picks a unique allocation between the two periods.[12]

Second, the present value of the marginal benefit curve for period 2 intersects the vertical axis at a different point than does the comparable curve in period 1. (Why?) This intersection is lower because the marginal benefits in the second period are discounted. Thus with the 10% discount rate we are using, the marginal net benefit is \$6 and the present value is \$6/\$1.10 = \$5.45. Notice that larger discount rates rotate the period 2 marginal-benefit curve around the point of zero net benefit ($q_1 = 5$, $q_2 = 15$) toward the right-hand axis. We shall use this fact in a moment.

The efficient allocation is now readily identifiable as the point where the two curves representing present value of marginal net benefit cross. The total present value of net benefits is then the area under the marginal net-benefit curve for period 1 up to the efficient allocation (labeled area *A*) plus the area under the present value of marginal net benefit curve for period 2 from the right-hand axis up to its efficient allocation (labeled area *B*). Because we have an efficient allocation, the sum of these two areas is maximized.[13]

Since we have developed our efficiency criteria independent of an institutional context, these criteria are equally appropriate for evaluating resource allocations generated by markets, government rationing, or even the whims of a dictator. While *any* efficient allocation method must take scarcity into account, the details of precisely how that is done depends on the context.

Scarcity imposes an opportunity cost that we henceforth refer to as the *marginal user cost*. When resources are scarce, greater current use diminishes future opportunities. The marginal user cost is the present value of these forgone opportunities at the margin. To be more specific, uses of those resources which would have been appropriate in the absence of scarcity may no longer be appropriate once scarcity is present. Using large quantities of water to keep lawns lush and green may be wholly appropriate for an area with sufficiently large

---

12 Note that the sum of the two allocations in Figure 2.7 is always 20. The left-hand axis represents an allocation of all 20 units to period 2, and the right-hand axis represents an allocation entirely to period 1.

13 Demonstrate by first allocating slightly more to period 2 (and therefore less to period 1) and showing that the total area decreases. Conclude by allocating slightly less to period 2 and showing that, in this case as well, total area declines.

replenishable water supplies, but quite inappropriate when it denies drinking water to future generations. Failure to take the higher scarcity value of water into account in the present will lead to an inefficiency or an extra cost to society due to the extra scarcity imposed on the future. This additional marginal value that scarcity creates is the marginal user cost.

We can illustrate how this concept is used by returning to our numerical example. With 30 or more units, each period would be allocated 15 and the type of scarcity which gives rise to the marginal user cost would not exist. With 30 or more units, therefore, the marginal user cost would be zero.

With 20 units, however, scarcity does exist. No longer can 15 units be allocated to each period; each period will have to be allocated less than would be the case without scarcity. The marginal user cost for this case is not zero. As can be seen from Figure 2.7, the present value of the marginal user cost, the additional value created by scarcity, is graphically represented by the vertical distance between the quantity axis and the intersection of the two present-value curves. It is identical to the present value of the marginal net benefit in each of the periods. This value can either be read off the graph or determined more precisely to be $1.905 from the chapter appendix.

We can make this concept even more concrete by considering its use in a market context. An efficient market would have to consider not only the marginal cost of extraction for this resource, but the marginal user cost as well. Whereas in the absence of scarcity the price would equal the marginal cost of extraction, with scarcity the price would equal the sum of marginal extraction cost and marginal user cost.

To see this, solve for the prices that would prevail in an efficient market facing scarcity over time. Inserting the efficient quantities (10.238 and 9.762, respectively) into the willingness-to-pay function ($P = 8 - 0.4q$) yields $P_1 = 3.905$ and $P_2 = 4.095$. The corresponding supply and demand diagrams are given in Figure 2.8.

In an efficient market the marginal user cost for each period is the difference between the price and the marginal cost of extraction. Notice that it takes the value $1.905 in the first period and $2.095 in the second. In both years the present value of the marginal user cost is $1.905. In the second year the actual marginal user cost is $1.905(1 + r)$. Since $r = 0.10$ in this example, the marginal user cost for the second period is $2.095.[14] Thus, while the present value of marginal user cost is equal in both periods, the actual marginal user cost rises over time.

Both the size of the marginal user cost and the allocation of the resource between the two periods is affected by the discount rate. In Figure 2.7, because of discounting, the efficient allocation allocates somewhat more to period 1 than

---

14 You can verify this by taking the present value of $2.095 and showing it to be equal to $1.905.

FIGURE 2.8 The efficient market allocation of a depletable resource: the constant-marginal-cost case. (a) Period 1. (b) Period 2.

to period 2. A discount rate larger than 0.10 would be incorporated in this diagram by rotating the period 2 curve an appropriate amount toward the right-hand axis, holding the point at which it intersects the horizontal axis fixed. The larger the discount rate is, the greater the amount of rotation required. The amount allocated to the second period would be necessarily smaller with larger discount rates. The general conclusion, which holds for all models we consider, is that higher discount rates tend to skew resource extraction toward the present because they give the future less weight in balancing the relative value of present and future resource use.

Sustainability

While no generally accepted standards of fairness or justice exist, some have more prominent support than others. One such standard concerns the treatment of future generations. What legacy should earlier generations leave to later ones? This is a particularly difficult issue because, in contrast to other groups for which we may want to ensure fair treatment, future generations cannot articulate their wishes, much less negotiate with current generations ("We'll take your radioactive wastes, if you leave us plentiful supplies of titanium.")

One starting point for intergenerational equity is provided by philosopher John Rawls in his monumental work, *A Theory of Justice*. Rawls suggests one way to derive general principles of justice is to place, hypothetically, every person in an original position behind a "veil of ignorance." This veil of ignorance would prevent them from knowing their eventual position in society. Once behind this veil, people would decide on rules to govern the society that they would, after the decision, be forced to live in.

In our context this approach would suggest a hypothetical meeting of all members of present and future generations to decide on rules for allocating resources among generations. Because these members are prevented by the veil of ignorance from knowing the generation to which they will belong, they will not be excessively conservationist (lest they turn out to be a member of an earlier generation) or excessively exploitative (lest they become a member of a later generation). What kind of rule would emerge from such a meeting? Perhaps the most common answer is known as the *sustainability criterion*. The sustainability criterion suggests that, at a minimum, future generations should be left no worse off than current generations. Allocations that impoverish future generations, in order to enrich current generations, are, according to this criterion, patently unfair.

It is also important to understand what this criterion does *not* specify. It does not say, for example, that it is unfair for current generations to enrich themselves at the expense of future generations *as long as future generations remain at least as well off as current generations.*

This distinction is important. It is sometimes argued, for example, that currently we should be depending solely on renewable resources. This argument suggests that since every unit of a depletable resource now in use is a unit unavailable for future generations, the use of depletable resources is unfair. It is not valid to conclude from the sustainability criterion that relying on depletable resources is unfair *unless the consumption of these resources causes future generations to be worse off than we are.*

Does dynamic efficiency violate the sustainability criterion? It certainly appears to. Since in our two-period numerical example more resources are allocated to the first period than to the second, net benefits in the second period appear to be lower than in the first. Sustainability does not allow earlier generations to profit at the expense of later generations, and this example certainly appears to be a case where that is happening.

Yet nothing prohibits those in the first period from saving some of the net benefits for those in the second period. If the allocation is dynamically efficient, it will always be possible to set aside sufficient net benefits accrued in the first period for those in the second period, so that those in the second period will be better off than they would have been with any other extraction profile.

Suppose, for example, you believe that setting aside half (10 units) of the available resources for each period would in your view be a better allocation than the dynamic efficient allocation. The net benefits to each period from this alternative scheme would be $40.00. (Why?)

Now let's compare this to an allocation of net benefits that could be achieved with the dynamic efficient allocation. In the dynamic efficient allocation the net benefits to the first period were 40.466, while those for the second period were

39.512.[15] Clearly if no sharing between the periods took place, this example would violate the sustainability criterion.

But suppose sharing took place. If the first generation keeps net benefits of $40.00 (thereby making it just as well off as if equal amounts were extracted in each period) and saves the extra 0.466 (the 40.466 net benefits earned during the first period in the dynamic efficient allocation minus the $40 reserved for itself) at 10% interest for those in the next period. This savings would grow to 0.513 by the second period [0.466(1.10)]. Add this to the net benefits received directly from the dynamic efficient allocation ($39.512), and the second generation would receive $40.025. Those in the second period would be better off by accepting the dynamic efficient allocation and sharing than they would if they demanded that resources be allocated equally between the two periods.

This example demonstrates that dynamic efficient allocations can be perfectly consistent with sustainability, providing that the gains are shared appropriately among generations. The possibility that the second period will be better off is not a guarantee that they will be unless the required degree of sharing takes place. Are the gains normally shared in such a way as to produce sustainable outcomes? In future chapters we provide explicit answers to this question, giving particular attention to whether our social institutions are capable of producing outcomes that are both efficient and sustainable.

SUMMARY

The relationship between humanity and the environment requires many choices. Some basis for making rational choices is absolutely necessary. If not made by design, decisions will be made by default.

The economics approach views the environment as a composite asset, supplying a variety of services to humanity. The intensity and composition of those services depend on the actions of humans as constrained by physical laws, such as the first and second laws of thermodynamics.

Economics has two rather different means of enhancing understanding of environmental and natural resource economics. Positive economics is useful in describing the actions of people and the impact of those actions on the environmental asset. Normative economics can provide guidance on how optimal service flows can be defined and achieved.

Normative economics suggests two precise criteria for judging the optimal level and composition of services: efficiency and sustainability. The former suggests maximizing the present value of net benefits to society. When the use of

---

15 The supporting calculations are (1.905)(10.238) + 0.5(4.095)(10.238) for the first period and (2.095)(9.762) + 0.5(3.095)(9.762) for the second period.

a natural resource in one period introduces scarcity or increases the degree of scarcity of that resource in subsequent periods, the efficient allocation must take the marginal user cost into account. Failure to do so would cause a smaller than efficient amount of the resource to be conserved. The sustainability criterion allows us to judge the fairness rather than the efficiency of these intertemporal allocations. Future chapters determine the degree to which our social institutions yield allocations that conform to these criteria.

FURTHER READING

Arrow, Kenneth J. *The Limits of Organization* (New York: W. W. Norton, 1974). In this short pithy book, Nobel Laureate Kenneth Arrow analyzes why, and how, human beings organize their common lives to overcome the basic economic problem of allocating scarce resources. Alternative models of achieving efficient allocations are explored, including markets and governments.

Daly, Herman E. and John B. Cobb, Jr. *For the Common Good: Redirecting the Economy toward Community, the Environment and a Sustainable Future* (Boston: Beacon Press, 1989). Written by an economist and a theologian, this powerfully argued book suggests that the world view which undergirds modern economics has some fatal flaws, and suggests some redirections in it.

Schelling, Thomas C. *Micromotives and Macrobehavior* (New York: W. W. Norton, 1978). Through familiar and readily grasped examples, Professor Schelling demonstrates how members of a society tend to be blind to the collective consequences of their separate decisions.

ADDITIONAL REFERENCES

Burness, Stuart, Ronald Cummings, Glenn Morris, and Inga Paik. "Thermodynamic and Economic Concepts as Related to Resource-Use Policies," *Land Economics* 56 (February 1980): 1-9.

Butlin, J.A., ed. *The Economics of Environmental and Natural Resource Policy* (Boulder, CO: Westview Press, 1981).

Dorfman, Robert and Nancy S. Dorfman, eds. *Economics of the Environment: Selected Readings*, 2nd ed. (New York: W. W. Norton, 1977).

Fisher, Anthony C. *Resource and Environmental Economics* (Cambridge: Cambridge University Press, 1981).

Kneese, Allen V., Robert U. Ayers, and Ralph C. d'Arge. *Economics and the Environment: A Materials Balance Approach* (Washington, DC: Resources for the Future, 1970).

Kneese, Allen V. *Economics and the Environment* (New York: Penguin Books, 1977).

Krutilla, John. "Conservation Reconsidered," *The American Economic Review* 57 (September 1968): 777-786.

Rawls, John. *A Theory of Justice* (Cambridge, MA: Harvard University Press, 1971).

Siebert, Horst. *Economics of the Environment* (Lexington, MA: Lexington Books, 1981).

DISCUSSION QUESTIONS

1. It has been suggested that we should use the "net energy" criterion to make choices among various types of energy. Net energy is defined as the total energy content in the energy source minus the energy required to extract, process, and deliver it to consumers. According to this criterion, we should use those sources with the highest net energy content first. Would the dynamic efficiency criterion and the net energy criterion be expected to yield the same choice? Why or why not?

2. The notion of sustainability is not the same in the natural sciences as in economics. In the natural sciences, sustainability frequently means maintaining a constant *physical* flow of each and every resource (e.g., fish or wood from the forest), while in economics it means maintaining the *value* of those service flows. When might the two criteria lead to different choices? Why?

PROBLEMS

1. One convenient way to express the willingness-to-pay relationship between price and quantity is to use the inverse demand function. In an inverse demand function, the price consumers are willing to pay is expressed as a function of the quantity available for sale. Suppose the inverse demand function (expressed in dollars) or a product is $P = 80 - q$, and the marginal cost (in dollars) of producing it is $MC = 1q$, where P is the price of the product and q is the quantity demanded and/or supplied. (a) How much would be supplied in a static efficient allocation? (b) What would be the magnitude of the net benefits (in dollars)?

2. In the numerical example given in the text the inverse demand function for the depletable resource is $P = 8 - 0.4q$ and the marginal cost of supplying it is $2.00. (a) If 20 units are to be allocated between two periods, in a dynamic efficient allocation how much would be allocated to the first period and how much to the second period when the discount rate is zero? (b) What would the efficient price be in the two periods? (c) What would the marginal user cost be in each period?

3. Assume the same demand conditions as stated in question 2, but for this question let the discount rate be 0.10 and the marginal cost of extraction be $4.00. How much would be produced in each period in an efficient allocation? What would the marginal user cost be in each period? Would the static and dynamic efficiency criteria yield the same answers for this problem? Why?

4. Compare two versions of the two-period depletable resource model which differ only in the treatment of marginal extraction cost. Assume that in the second version the constant marginal extraction cost is lower in the second period than the first (perhaps due to the anticipated arrival of a new, superior

extraction technology). The constant marginal extraction cost is the same in both periods in the first version and is equal to the marginal extraction cost in the first period of the second version. In a dynamic efficient allocation how would the extraction profile in the second version differ from the first? Would relatively more or less be allocated to the second period in the second version than in the first version? Would the marginal user cost be higher or lower in the second version?

The Simple Mathematics of Dynamic Efficiency*

Assume that the demand curve for a depletable resource is linear and stable over time. Thus the inverse demand curve in year t can be written as

$$P_t = a - bq_t.$$

(1)

The total benefits from extracting an amount q_t in year t is then the integral of this function (the area under the inverse demand curve):

$$(\text{Total benefits})_t = \int_0^{q_t} (a - bq)dq$$

$$= aq_t - \frac{b}{2}.$$

(2)

Further assume that the marginal cost of extracting that resource is a constant c and therefore the total cost of extracting any amount q_t in year t can be given by

$$(\text{Total cost})_t = cq_t.$$

(3)

---

* Greater detail on the mathematics of constrained optimization can be found in any standard mathematical economics text, such as Alpha Chiang, *Fundamental Methods of Mathematical Economics*, 2nd ed. (New York: McGraw-Hill, 1974).

If the total available amount of this resource is $\bar{Q}$, then the dynamic allocation of a resource over n years is the one which satisfies the maximization problem:

$$\underset{q_t}{\text{Max}} \; \sum_{i=1}^{n} \frac{aq_i - \frac{b}{2}q_i^2 - cq_i}{(1+r)^{i-1}} + \lambda\left[\bar{Q} - \sum_{i=1}^{n} q_i\right].$$

(4)

Assuming that $\bar{Q}$ is less than would normally be demanded, the dynamic efficient allocation must satisfy

$$\frac{a - bq_i - c}{(1+r)^{i-1}} - \lambda = 0, \qquad i = 1, \ldots, n,$$

(5)

$$\bar{Q} - \sum_{i=1}^{n} q_i = 0.$$

(6)

We can illustrate the use of these equations with the two-period example dealt with in the text. The following parameter values are assumed in that problem: $a = 8$, $c = \$2$, $b = 0.4$, $Q = 20$; and $r = 0.10$.
Using these, we obtain

$$8 - 0.4q_1 - 2 - \lambda = 0,$$

(7)

$$\frac{8 - 0.4q_2 - 2}{1.10} - \lambda = 0,$$

(8)

$$q_1 + q_2 = 20.$$

It is now readily verified that the solution (accurate to the third decimal place) is

$$q_1 = 10.238, \qquad q_2 = 9.762, \qquad \lambda = \$1.905$$

We can now demonstrate the propositions discussed in the text.

1. Verbally, equation (7) states that in a dynamic efficient allocation the present value of the marginal net benefit in period 1 ($8 - 0.4q_1 - 2$) has to equal λ. Equation (8) states that the present value of the marginal net benefit in period 2 should also equal λ. Therefore, they must equal each other. This demonstrates the proposition shown graphically in Figure 2.7.

2. The present value of marginal user cost is represented by λ. Thus equation (7) states that price in the first period ($8 - 0.4q_1$) should be equal to the sum of marginal extraction cost ($\$2$) and marginal user cost ($\$1.905$). Multiplying (8) by $1 + r$, it becomes clear that price in the second period ($8 - 0.4q_2$) is equal to the marginal extraction cost ($\$2$) plus the higher marginal user cost [$\lambda(1 + r) = (1.905)(1.10) = \$2.095$] in period 2. These results show why the graphs in Figure 2.8 have the properties they do. They also illustrate the point that, in this case, marginal user cost rises over time.

CHAPTER THREE

Property Rights, Externalities, and Environmental Problems

The charming landscape which I saw this morning, is indubitably made up of some twenty or thirty farms. Miller owns this field, Locke that, and Manning the woodland beyond. But none of them owns the landscape. There is a property in the horizon which no man has but he whose eye can integrate all the parts, that is, the poet. This is the best part of these men's farms, yet to this their land deeds give them no title.

RALPH WALDO EMERSON, *Nature* (1836)

INTRODUCTION

In the last chapter we developed specific normative criteria for making rational choices about the relationship between the economic system and the environment. According to those criteria, an environmental problem exists when resource allocations are either inefficient or expected to leave future generations worse off than we are.

When would breaches of efficiency or sustainability occur? Why would individual or group interests diverge from those of society at large? What circumstances give rise to this division of interests, and what can be done about it? One useful way to examine this question is based on the concept known as a *property right*. In this chapter we explore this concept and how it can be used to understand why the environmental asset can be undervalued by both the market and governmental policy. We also discuss how the government and the market can, on occasion, use knowledge of property rights and their effects on incentives to orchestrate a coordinated approach to resolving thesedifficulties.

PROPERTY RIGHTS

Property Rights and Efficient Market Allocations

The manner in which producers and consumers use environmental resources depends on the property rights governing those resources. In economics, *property right* refers to a bundle of entitlements defining the owner's rights, privileges, and limitations for use of the resource. By examining such entitlements and how they affect human behavior, we will better understand how environmental problems arise from government and market allocations.

These property rights can be vested either with individuals, as in a capitalist economy, or with the state, as in a centrally planned socialist economy. It is not uncommon to hear that the source of environmental problems in a capitalist economy is the market system itself or, more specifically, the pursuit of profits. You may have heard this point of view expressed as, "Corporations are more interested in profits than in the needs of people." Those who espouse this view look longingly at centrally planned economies as a means of avoiding environmental excess.

Simple answers rarely suffice for complex problems; environmental and natural resource problems are not an exception. Centrally planned economies, such as the Soviet Union, have not historically avoided pollution excesses (Example 3.1). On the other hand, the pursuit of profits is not inevitably inconsistent with fulfilling the needs of the people. Though the pursuit of profits may sometimes be inconsistent with fulfilling these needs, it is not always inconsistent. In fact, this pursuit is often the essential ingredient in meeting people's needs. How can we tell when the pursuit of profits is consistent with societal objectives, such as efficiency and sustainability, and when it is not?

Efficient Property Right Structures

Let's begin by describing the structure of property rights that could produce efficient allocations in a well-functioning market economy. An efficient structure has four main characteristics:

1. *Universality*—All resources are privately owned, and all entitlements completely specified.
2. *Exclusivity*—All benefits and costs accrued as a result of owning and using the resources should accrue to the owner, and only to the owner, either directly or indirectly by sale to others.

EXAMPLE 3.1

Pollution in Centrally Planned Economies

Since environmental problems are thought to be caused by a divergence between individual incentives and collective incentives, it is not uncommon to hear that centrally planned economies avoid environmental problems. Centralizing power in the state, as occurs in a centrally planned economy, is believed to allow collective decisions to be made at the outset.

Studies of air and water pollution in the Soviet Union and other Eastern European countries suggest that the problems found in market economies occur with equal intensity in the Eastern block. Copsa Mica, Romania, for example, is called Europe's most polluted urban area. Weakened by acid rain, monuments in Krakow, Poland are crumbling. Women with newborn babies in Czechoslovakia have priority access to bottled water because tap water is considered injurious to infant health.

How can this be? Goldman suggests that the centralized planning system creates different, but no less potent, divergences between individual and collective incentives. For example, as of 1970, 65% of all factories in the largest Soviet republic, the Russian Soviet Federated Socialist Republic, discharged their waste into the water without any attempt to clean it up. They did this because the managers were being judged solely in terms of output, not in terms of the harm they caused to the environment. The central plans which set the priorities to be followed by the managers very simply emphasized economic growth over the environment.

In his summary Goldman states:

> . . . not private enterprise but industrialization is the primary cause of environmental disruption. This suggests that state ownership of all the productive resources is no cure-all.

Source: Marshall I. Goldman, "The Convergence of Environmental Disruption," in *Ecology and Economics: Controlling Pollution in the 70's*, Marshall I. Goldman, ed. (Englewood Cliffs, NJ: Prentice-Hall, 1972): 211–224; D. Powell, "The Social Costs of Modernization: Ecological Problems in the USSR," *World Politics* 22 (1971): 327-334, and Marshall I. Goldman, "Economics of Environmental and Renewable Resources in Socialist Systems," in Allen V. Kneese and James L. Sweeney, eds. *Handbook of Natural Resource and Energy Economics*, Vol. II (Amsterdam: North-Holland, 1985): 725–745; Louis Berney, "Black Town of Transylvania Is Called Europe's Most Polluted," *The Boston Globe* (March 28, 1990): 2; Hilary F. French, "Industrial Wasteland," *Worldwatch* (November/December 1988): 21–30.

3. *Transferability*—All property rights should be transferable from one owner to another in a voluntary exchange.

4. *Enforceability*—Property rights should be secure from involuntary seizure or encroachment by others.

An owner of a resource with a well-defined property right (one exhibiting these four characteristics) has a powerful incentive to use that resource efficiently because a decline in the value of that resource represents a personal loss. Farmers who own the land have an incentive to fertilize and irrigate it because the resulting increased production raises income level. Similarly, they have an incentive to rotate crops when that raises the productivity of their land.

When well-defined property rights are exchanged, as in a market economy, this exchange facilitates efficiency. We can illustrate this point by examining the incentives consumers and producers face when a well-defined system of property rights is in place. Because the seller has the right to prevent the consumer from consuming the product in the absence of payment, the consumer must pay to receive the product. Given a market price, the consumer decides how much to purchase by choosing that amount which maximizes his or her individual net benefit (Figure 3.1).

FIGURE 3.1   The consumer's choice.

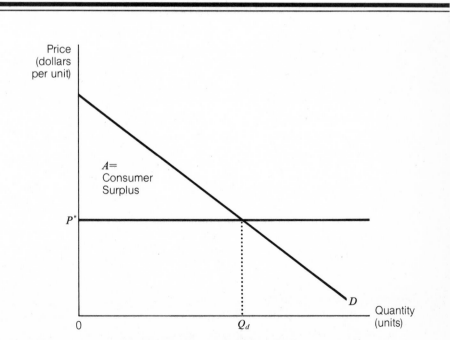

The consumer's net benefit is the area under the demand curve minus the area representing cost. The cost to the consumer is the area under the price line, since that area represents the expenditure on the commodity. Obviously, for a given price P^*, consumer net benefit is maximized by choosing to purchase Q_d units. Area A is then the geometric representation of the net benefit received, known as *consumer surplus*. It is the area under the demand curve that lies above the price, bounded from the left by the vertical axis and from the right by the quantity of the good being considered.

Meanwhile, sellers face a similar choice (Figure 3.2). Given price P^*, the seller maximizes his or her own net benefits by choosing to sell Q_s units. The net benefit received (Area B) by the seller is called *producer surplus*. It is the area under the price line that lies over the marginal cost curve, bounded from the left by the vertical axis and the right by the quantity of the good being considered.

The price level which producers and consumers face will adjust until supply equals demand, as depicted in Figure 3.3. Given that price, consumers maximize their surplus, producers maximize their surplus, and the market clears.

Is this allocation efficient? According to our definition of static efficiency from the previous chapter, it is clear the answer is yes. The net benefit is maximized by the market allocation, and, as seen in Figure 3.3, it is equal to the sum of consumer and producer surpluses. Thus, we have established a procedure for measuring net benefits, and a means of describing how the net benefits are distributed between consumers and producers.

FIGURE 3.2 The producer's choice.

FIGURE 3.3 Market equilibrium.

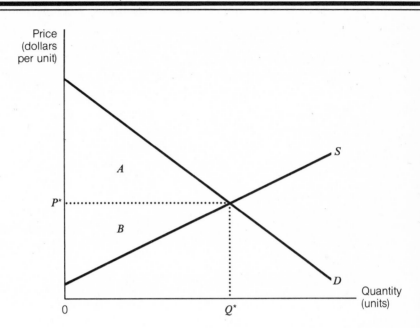

This distribution is crucially significant. Efficiency is *not* achieved because consumers and producers are seeking efficiency. They aren't! In a system with well-defined property rights and competitive markets in which to sell those rights producers try to maximize their surplus and consumers try to maximize their surplus. The price system, then, induces those self-interested parties to make choices which are efficient from the point of view of society as a whole. It channels the energy motivated by self-interest into socially productive paths.

Though familiarity may have dulled our appreciation, it is noteworthy that a system designed to produce a harmonious and congenial outcome could function effectively while allowing consumers and producers so much individual freedom in making choices. This is truly a remarkable accomplishment.

Producer's Surplus, Scarcity Rent, and Long-Run Competitive Equilibrium

Since the area under the price line is total revenue, and the area under the marginal cost curve is total variable cost, producer's surplus is related to profits. In the short run when some costs are fixed, producer's surplus is equal to profits plus fixed cost. In the long run when all costs are variable, producer surplus is equal to profits plus rent, the return to scarce inputs owned by the producer. As long as new firms can enter into an industry where profits are earned without raising the prices of purchased inputs, long-run profits will equal zero and producer surplus will equal rent.

Scarcity Rent

Most natural resource industries, however, do give rise to rent and, therefore, producer's surplus is not eliminated by competition, even with free entry. This producer's surplus which persists in long-run competitive equilibrium is called *scarcity rent.*

David Ricardo was the first economist to recognize the existence of scarcity rent. Ricardo suggested that the price of land was determined by the least fertile marginal unit of land. Since the price had to be sufficiently high to allow the poorer land to be brought into production, other, more fertile, land could be farmed at an economic profit. Competition could not erode that profit because the amount of land was limited and lower prices would serve only to reduce the supply of land below demand. The only way to expand production would be to bring additional, less fertile, land (more costly to farm) into production; consequently, additional production does not lower price, as it does in a constant-cost industry.

Other circumstances also give rise to scarcity rent for natural resources. We have already shown how the allocation of depletable resources gives rise to a positive marginal user cost. The existence of this marginal user cost implies that the efficient price will exceed the marginal cost of extraction, creating a scarcity rent for those resources as well. The first-period scarcity rent, which was computed in our two-period numerical example in the last chapter, is depicted graphically in Figure 3.4.

In this graph the marginal extraction cost is designated as *MEC* and the marginal user cost as *MUC*. A similar graph could be drawn for the second period, in which the scarcity rent would be equal to the area under the price line and above the marginal cost of extraction. This scarcity rent is appropriated by the owner of the resource and becomes part of his or her producer surplus as long as property rights are correctly defined. A similar scarcity rent would exist for scarce renewable resources.

It is important to clear up one possible source of confusion. Why is user cost included as part of producer surplus when other costs, such as extraction costs, are not? The distinction between these costs lies in whether they are actually paid. The marginal extraction cost is actually paid; it consumes resources. The marginal user cost, in contrast, is an opportunity cost, a cost that would be paid in the form of reduced profits or a reduced net benefit only if the owner of the resource would choose not to extract the last unit. When the profit-maximizing allocation is chosen, this cost is not actually borne, and, therefore, the owner of the resource appropriates it as scarcity rent. This source of producer surplus is not eliminated by competition; hence, even when time is an important considera-

FIGURE 3.4   Scarcity rent for a constant-extraction-cost depletable resource.

tion in the presence of well-defined property rights, market allocations and efficient allocations coincide.

The economic system does not always sustain efficient allocations, however, and environmental problems represent one important class of circumstances when it doesn't. If cases of inefficient depreciation of the environment are to be rectified, we must understand the circumstances which lead to inefficiency and what can be done about them.

EXTERNALITIES AS A SOURCE OF MARKET FAILURE

The Concept Introduced

Exclusivity is one of the chief characteristics of an efficient property rights structure. This characteristic is frequently violated in practice. One broad class of violations occurs when an agent making a decision does not bear all of the consequences of his or her action.

Suppose two firms are located by a river. The first produces steel, while the second, somewhat downstream, operates a resort hotel. Both use the river, though in different ways. The steel firm uses it as a receptacle for its waste, while the second uses it to attract customers seeking water recreation. If these two facilities have different owners an efficient use of the water is not likely to result. Because the steel plant does not bear the cost of reduced business at the resort resulting from waste being dumped into the river, it is not likely to be very sensitive to that cost in its decision making. As a result, it could be expected to dump too much waste into the river, and an efficient allocation of the river would not be attained.

This situation is called an externality. An *externality* exists whenever the welfare of some agent, either a firm or household, depends directly on his or her activities and on activities under the control of some other agent as well. In the example, the increased waste in the river imposed an external cost on the resort, a cost the steel firm could not be counted upon to consider appropriately in deciding the amount of waste to dump.

The effects of this external cost on the steel industry can be seen in Figure 3.5, which depicts the market for steel. Steel production inevitably involves producing pollution as well as steel. The demand for steel is shown by the demand curve D and the private marginal cost of producing the steel (exclusive of pollution control and damage) is depicted as MC_p. Because society considers both the cost of pollution and the cost of producing the steel, the social marginal cost function (MC_s) includes both of these costs as well.

If the steel industry faced no outside control on its emission levels, it would seek to produce Q_m. That choice, in a competitive setting, would maximize their private producer surplus. But that is clearly not efficient, since the net benefit is maximized at Q^* not Q_m.

With the assistance of Figure 3.5, we can draw a number of conclusions about market allocations of commodities causing pollution externalities:

1. The output of the commodity is too large.

2. Too much pollution is produced.

3. The prices of products responsible for pollution are too low.

4. As long as the costs are external, no incentives to search for ways to yield less pollution per unit of output are introduced by the market.

5. Recycling and reuse of the polluting substances are discouraged since release into the environment is so inefficiently cheap.

The effects of a market imperfection for one commodity end up affecting the demands for raw materials, labor, and so on. The ultimate effects are felt through the entire economy.

FIGURE 3.5   Market allocation with pollution.

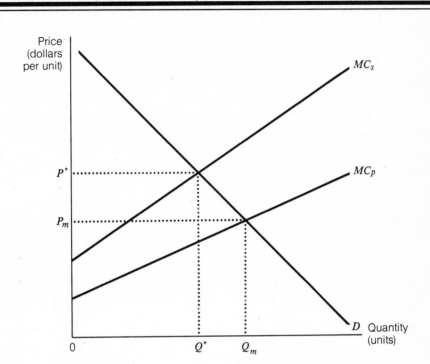

Types of Externalities

External effects can be either positive or negative. Historically, the terms *external diseconomy* and *external economy* have been used to refer, respectively, to circumstances in which the affected party is damaged or benefited by the externality. Clearly, the water-pollution example represents an external diseconomy. External economies are not hard to find, however. Private individuals who purchase a particularly scenic area provide an external economy to all who pass. Generally, when external economies are present, the market will undersupply the resources.

One other distinction is important. One class of externalities, known as *pecuniary externalities*, does not present the same kinds of problems as pollution does. Pecuniary externalities arise when the external effect is transmitted through higher prices. Suppose that a new firm moves into an area and drives up the rental price of land. That increase creates a negative effect on all those paying rent and, therefore, is an external diseconomy.

This pecuniary diseconomy, however, does not cause a market failure because the resulting higher rents are reflecting the scarcity of land. The land market provides a mechanism by which the parties can bid for land; the prices that result reflect the value of the land in its various uses. Without pecuniary externalities the price signals would fail to sustain an efficient allocation.

The pollution example is *not* a pecuniary externality because the effect is not transmitted through prices. In this example, prices do not adjust to reflect the increasing waste load. The scarcity of the water resource is not signaled to the steel firm. An essential feedback mechanism that is present for pecuniary externalities is not present for the pollution case.

The externalities concept is a broad one covering a multitude of sources of market failure. The next step is to investigate some specific circumstances which can give rise to externalities.

IMPROPERLY DESIGNED PROPERTY RIGHTS SYSTEMS

Common Property Resources

The first class of problems with market allocations occurs when the property rights to the resource lack one or more of the four characteristics described earlier. Perhaps the largest category of resources for which this is true is called common property resources. *Common property resources* are those that are not exclusively controlled by a single agent or source. If access to these resources is not restricted, the resources can be exploited on a first-come, first-served basis.

It is not difficult to derive a host of examples. Two of our important life-sustaining resources, air and water, are treated by our legal system as common property resources. Other examples include migratory wild birds, fish, and animal populations. Even oil can, under certain circumstances, become a common property resource. If a large subsurface "pool" of oil underlies property rights defined in terms of a surface area which is small in comparison to the geographic coverage of the pool, several different companies could end up tapping the same source of oil. Since none of these has exclusive control over extraction from this field, the oil in this field becomes a common property resource.

Animal populations, such as the American bison, have also been treated as common property. In the early history of the United States, bison were plentiful; that they were common property was not a problem. Frontier people who needed hides or meat could easily get whatever they needed; the aggressiveness of any one hunter did not affect the time and effort expended by other hunters. In the absence of scarcity, efficiency was not threatened by treating the herd as a common property resource.

As the years slipped by, however, the demand for bison increased and scarcity became a factor. As the number of hunters increased, the time came when every additional unit of hunting activity increased the amount of time and effort required to produce a given yield of bison.

FIGURE 3.6   Exploitation of a common property resource.

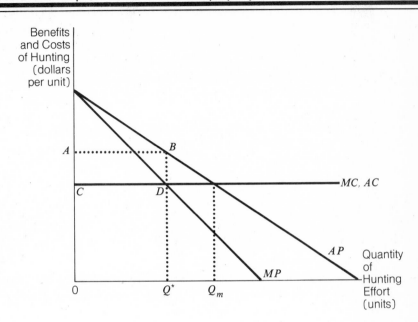

In Figure 3.6, we depict a constant marginal cost of hunting activity by portraying marginal and average cost as a horizontal line.[1] The benefits derived from this hunting activity are reflected in the *AP* (for average product) curve. This curve represents the average value of bison harvested as a function of the amount of hunting activity expended. It is calculated by multiplying, for each level of hunting activity, the (assumed constant) price of bison by the amount harvested and dividing this revenue by the number of units of hunting activity. The average product curve is downward-sloping because the greater the amount of hunting effort expended, the smaller is the resulting population size. Smaller populations support smaller harvests per unit of effort expended.

The efficient level of hunting activity in this model (*Q**) is the level where the marginal product (or, equivalently, marginal benefit) curve crosses the marginal cost curve. At this level of activity the marginal benefit would be just equal to the marginal cost, implying that net benefits are maximized. This allocation would yield society a scarcity rent equal to area *ABDC*.

With several hunters sharing nonexclusive property rights to the bison, the resulting allocation would not be efficient. No individual hunter would have an

---

1 This type of analysis was first used in H. Scott Gordon, "The Economic Theory of a Common-Property Resource: The Fishery," *Journal of Political Economy* 62 (April 1954): 124–142.

incentive to protect that scarcity rent by restricting the hunting effort. Individual hunters, without exclusive rights, would exploit the resource until their average benefit equaled average cost. This is represented by a level of effort equal to Q_m. This inefficient allocation results because individual hunters cannot appropriate the scarcity rent; therefore, they ignore it. One of the losses from further exploitation which would be incorporated by exclusive owners—the opportunity cost of overexploitation—is not part of their decision-making process as long as access is not restricted.

Two characteristics of this formulation of the common property allocation are worth noting: (1) In the presence of sufficient demand, unrestricted access will cause common property resources to be overexploited. (2) The scarcity rent is dissipated; no one appropriates the rent, so it is lost.

Why does this happen? Unlimited access destroys the incentive to conserve. A hunter who can preclude others from hunting this stock has an incentive to keep the herd at an efficient level. This restraint results in lower costs in the form of less time and effort expended to produce a given yield of bison. On the other hand, a hunter exploiting a common property resource would not have any incentive to conserve because the benefits derived from restraint would, to some extent, be captured by other hunters. Thus unrestricted access to common property resources promotes an inefficient allocation.

Public Goods

Resources known as *public goods* present a particularly complex category of environmental problems: Public goods are defined as those which exhibit consumption indivisibilities and are fully accessible to all.

Consumption is said to be *indivisible* when one person's consumption of a good does not diminish the amount available for others. Several common environmental resources are public goods, including not only the "charming landscape" referred to by Emerson, but also clean air, clean water, and biological diversity.[2] Biological diversity includes two related concepts: the amount of genetic variability among individuals within a single species and the number of species within a community of organisms. Genetic diversity, critical to species survival in the natural world, has also proved to be important in the development of new crops and livestock.[3] It enhances the opportunities for crossbreeding and, thus, the development of superior strains. The availability of different strains was the key, for example, in developing a new disease-resistant barley.

---

2 Notice that public "bads" such as dirty air and dirty water are also possible.

3 For an example of the argument that genetic diversity is important, see Norman Myers, *The Sinking Ark* (New York: Pergamon Press, 1979).

Because of the interdependence of species within ecological communities, any particular species may have a value to the community far beyond its intrinsic value. Certain species contribute balance and stability to their ecological communities by providing food sources or holding the population of the species in check.

The richness of diversity within and among species has provided new sources of food, energy, industrial chemicals, raw materials, and medicines. Yet there is considerable evidence that biological diversity is decreasing. Of the 5 to 10 million species currently existing, at least 12% of the bird and 15% of the plant species will be gone by 2000.[4] Can we rely on the private sector to produce the efficient amount of public goods such as biological diversity? Unfortunately, the answer is no! Suppose that in response to diminishing ecological diversity we decide to take up a collection to provide some means of preserving endangered species. Would the collection yield sufficient revenue to pay for an efficient level of ecological diversity? The general answer is no. Let's see why.

In Figure 3.7 we represented the demand curves for ecological diversity as determined by the preferences of two consumers, *A* and *B*. Person *A* values diversity more, in that her demand curve is represented by the *vertical* summation of the individual demand curve.[5]

This is in contrast to a market demand curve for a divisible good, which is constructed by a *horizontal* summation of the individual demand curves. The (constant) marginal cost of providing cleanup services is represented by the *MC* curve.

What is the efficient level of diversity? It can be determined by a direct application of our definition of efficiency. The efficient allocation maximizes net benefits. Net benefits, in turn, are represented geometrically by the portion of the area under the market demand curve which lies above the marginal cost curve. The allocation which maximizes net benefits is Q^*, the allocation where the demand curve crosses the marginal cost curve.

Would our collection box yield enough revenues to supply this level of diversity? No. Consider the following sequences of events: person *B* comes to the collection box first and notices nothing is in it. Therefore he chooses to contribute. How much? He contributes until his net benefits are maximized, at q_b. Not long after, person *A* comes along. She notices that person *B* has already purchased q_b. How much more will she purchase? The answer is $q_a - q_b$, because this maximizes her net benefits, given that q_b had already been purchased. The total collection, therefore, is sufficient to defray the cost of q_a units of diversity. Notice that the outcome is not efficient.

---

4 World Resources Institute and International Institute for Environment and Development, *World Resources: 1988–89* (New York: Basic Books, 1988): 92–93.

5 A vertical summation is necessary because everyone can simultaneously consume the same amount of ecological diversity. We are, therefore, able to add the amounts of money they would be willing to pay for that level of diversity.

FIGURE 3.7   Public goods and inefficiency.

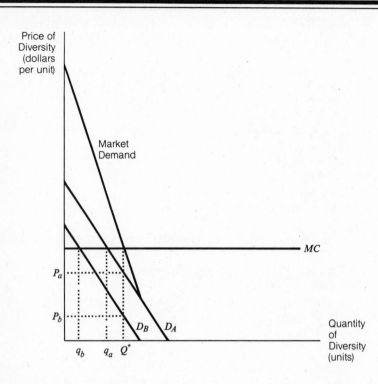

Why does this happen? Inefficiency results because each person is able to become a *free rider* on the other's contribution. Because of the consumption indivisibility and nonexcludability properties of the public good, consumers receive the benefits of any diversity purchased by other people. When this happens, it tends to diminish incentives to contribute, and the contributions are not sufficiently large to finance the efficient amount of the public good; it would be undersupplied.

Notice, however, that the privately supplied amount is not zero. Some diversity would be privately supplied. Indeed, as suggested by Example 3.2, the privately supplied amount may be considerable.

One further insight can be gained from Figure 3.7, which led to the characterization of public-good problems as "complex." The efficient market equilibrium for a public good would require different prices for each consumer. In Figure 3.7 if consumer A is charged P_a and consumer B is charged P_b then both consumers would be satisfied with the efficient allocation (the efficient allocation would have maximized their net benefits given the prices).

Furthermore, the revenue collected would be sufficient to finance the supply of the public good (since $P_b \times Q^* + P_a \times Q^* = MC \times Q^*$). Thus, while an

EXAMPLE 3.2

Public Goods Privately Provided: The Nature Conservancy

Can a demand for a public good such as biological diversity be observed in practice? Would the market respond to that demand? Apparently so, according to the existence of an organization called The Nature Conservancy.

The Nature Conservancy was born of an older organization called the Ecologist Union on September 11, 1950, for the purpose of establishing natural area reserves to preserve or aid in the preservation of areas, objects, and fauna and flora which have scientific, educational, or aesthetic significance. This organization purchases, or accepts as donations, land which has some unique ecological or aesthetic significance, to keep it from being used for other purposes. In so doing they preserve many species by preserving the habitat.

From humble beginnings, The Nature Conservancy has, as of 1988, been responsible for the preservation of 3,643,352 acres of forests, marshes, prairies, mounds, and islands. These areas serve as home to rare and endangered species of wildlife and plants. The Conservancy owns and manages some 1000 preserves, the largest privately owned nature preserve system in the world.

This approach has considerable merit. A private organization can move more rapidly than the public sector. Because it has a limited budget, the Nature Conservancy sets priorities and concentrates on acquiring the most ecologically unique areas. Yet the theory of public goods reminds us that if this were to be the sole approach to the preservation of biological diversity, it would preserve a smaller than efficient amount.

Source: *The Nature Conservancy Magazine,* Vol. 39, No. 2 (1989).

efficient pricing system exists, it is very difficult to implement. The efficient pricing system requires charging a different price to each consumer, and, in the absence of excludability, consumers may not choose to reveal the strength of their preference for this commodity. Therefore, the producer could not possibly know what prices to charge.

IMPERFECT MARKET STRUCTURES

Environmental problems also occur when one of the participants in an exchange of property rights is able to exercise an inordinate amount of power over the

FIGURE 3.8   Monopoly and inefficiency.

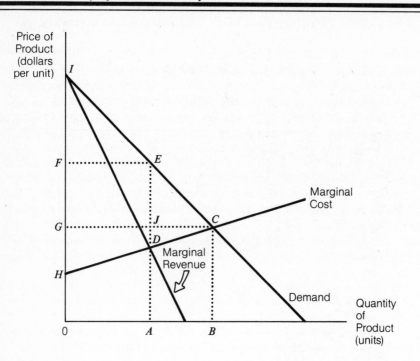

outcome. This can occur, for example, when a product is sold by a single seller, or *monopoly.*

It is easy to show that monopolies violate our definition of efficiency (Figure 3.8). According to our definition of static efficiency (Chapter 2), the efficient allocation would result when *B* is supplied. This would yield net benefits of *HIC*. The monopoly, however, would produce and sell 0*A*, where marginal revenue equals marginal cost, and would charge price 0*F*. At this point, producer's surplus is maximized, yet it is clearly inefficient because this choice causes society to lose net benefits equal to *EDC*.[6]

Imperfect markets clearly play some role in energy problems. For example, the major oil-exporting countries have formed a cartel resulting in higher than normal prices and lower than normal production. A *cartel* is a collusive agree-

---

6 Producers would lose *JDC* compared to the efficient allocation but they would gain area *FEJG,* which is much larger. Meanwhile, consumers would be worse off, since they lose area *FECJG.* Of these, *FEJG* is merely a transfer to the monopoly, but *EJC* is a pure loss to society. The total pure loss (*EDC*) is called a *deadweight* loss.

ment among producers to restrict production and raise prices. This collusive agreement allows the group to act like a monopolist.

DIVERGENCE OF SOCIAL AND PRIVATE DISCOUNT RATES

We concluded that producers, in their attempt to maximize producer surplus, also maximize the present value of net benefits under the "right" conditions, such as the absence of externalities, the presence of properly defined property rights, and the presence of competitive markets within which the property rights can be exchanged.

Now let's consider one more condition. If resources are to be allocated efficiently, firms must use the same rate to discount future net benefits as is appropriate for society at large. If firms were to use a higher rate, they would extract and sell resources faster than would be efficient. Conversely, if firms were to use a lower than appropriate discount rate, they would be excessively conservative.

Why might private and social rates differ? As stated in the previous chapter, the social discount rate is equal to the social opportunity cost of capital. This cost of capital can be separated into two components: risk-free cost of capital and the risk premium.[7] The *risk-free cost of capital* is the rate of return earned when there is absolutely no risk of earning more or less than the expected return. The *risk premium* is an additional cost of capital required to compensate the owners of this capital when the expected and actual returns may differ. Therefore, because of the risk premium, the cost of capital is higher in risky industries than in no-risk industries.

One difference between private and social discount rates may stem from a difference in social and private risk premiums. If the risk of certain private decisions is different from the risks faced by society as a whole, then the social and private risk premiums may differ. One obvious example is the risk *caused* by the government. If the firm is afraid its assets will be taken over by the government, it may choose a higher discount rate to make its profits before nationalization occurs.[8] From the point of view of society—as represented by government—this is not a risk and, therefore, a lower discount rate is appropriate. When private rates exceed social rates, current production is higher than is desirable to maximize the net benefits to society. Energy production and forestry both have to be subject to this source of inefficiency.

Though private and social discount rates do not always diverge, they may. When those circumstances arise, market decisions are not efficient.

---

7 This point is discussed in more detail in most principles of economics texts.

8 This case is described in James M. Griffin and Henry B. Steele, *Energy Economics and Policy* (New York: Academic Press, 1980): 85–86.

GOVERNMENT FAILURE

Market processes are not the only sources of inefficiency. Political processes are fully as culpable. As will become clear in the chapters which follow, some environmental problems have arisen from a failure of political rather than economic institutions. To complete our study of the ability of institutions to allocate environmental resources, we must understand this source of inefficiency as well.

Government failure shares with market failure the characteristic that improper incentives are the root of the problem. Special interest groups use the political process to engage in what has become known as *rent seeking*. Rent seeking is the use of resources in lobbying and other activities directed at securing protective legislation.[9] Successful rent-seeking activity will increase the net benefits going to the special interest group, but it will also frequently lower net benefits to society as a whole. In these instances it is a classic case of the aggressive pursuit of a larger slice of the pie leading to a smaller pie.

Why don't the losers rise up to protect their interests? One main reason is voter ignorance. It is economically rational for voters to remain ignorant on many issues simply because of the high cost of keeping informed and the low probability that any single vote will be decisive. In addition, it is difficult for diffuse groups of individuals, each of whom is affected only to a small degree, to organize a coherent, unified opposition. Successful opposition is, in a sense, a public good, with its attendant tendency for free riding on the opposition of others. Opposition to special interests would normally be underfunded.

Rent seeking can take many forms. Producers can seek protection from competitive pressures brought by imports or can seek price floors to hold prices above their efficient levels. Consumer groups can seek price ceilings or special subsidies to transfer part of their costs to the general body of taxpayers. Whatever form it takes, the existence of rent seeking provides a direct challenge to the presumption that more direct intervention by the government automatically leads to greater efficiency.

These cases illustrate the general economic premise that environmental problems arise because of a divergence between individual and collective objectives. This is a powerful explanatory device because not only does it suggest why these problems arise, but it also suggests how they might be resolved—by realigning individual incentives to make them compatible with collective objectives. As self-evident as this approach may be, it is controversial (see Example 3.3). The controversy involves whether the problem is our improper values or the improper translation of our quite proper values into action.

---

9 See Richard B. McKenzie and Gordon Tullock, "Rent Seeking," in *The New World of Economics: Explorations into the Human Experience*, 3rd ed. (Homewood, IL: Richard D. Irwin, 1981): Chapter 15.

EXAMPLE 3.3

Religion as the Source of Environmental Problems

One of the many alternative explanations of the source of environmental problems was advanced by historian Lynn White, Jr. His thesis, simply put, is that the environmental crisis is due to the teachings of Judaism and Christianity which in Western culture have created a warped view of the proper relationship between humans and their environment.

The basis for this thesis is to be found in the first book of the Old Testament:

> Then God said, "Let us make man in our image, after our likeness; and let them have dominion over the fish of the sea, and over the birds of the air, and over the cattle, and over all the earth, and over every creeping thing that creeps upon the earth" [Gen. 1:26].

Two aspects of this passage are crucial to his argument: (1) God created man in His own image, and (2) man was given dominion over the other forms of life. Both of these aspects make man the dominant force on earth and, according to White, suggest that "it is God's will that man exploit nature for his proper ends." White also makes the point that, among the world's religions, this is a rather unique view of the human-environment relationship.

His policy solution follows directly:

> More science and more technology are not going to get us out of the present ecological crisis until we find a new religion, or rethink our old one [p. 1205].

White believes that we must adopt new values which reject the primacy of humans and elevate the stature of nature.

This view provides a stark contrast to the economics approach, which suggests that the problem is neither the primacy of humans nor warped values but an imperfect translation of those values into practice.

Sources: Lynn White, Jr., "The Historical Roots of Ecologic Crisis," *Science* 155 (March 10, 1967): 1203–1207; E. F. Schumacher, "Buddhist Economics," in *Small Is Beautiful* (New York: Harper Colophon Books, 1973): 50–58; Keith Thomas, *Man and the Natural World* (New York: Knopf, 1983): 17–25.

Economists have always been reluctant to argue that values of consumers are warped because that would necessitate dictating the "correct" set of values. Both capitalism and democracy are based on the presumption that the majority knows what it is doing, whether it is casting ballots for representatives or dollar votes for goods and services. That presumption may be wrong, but history suggests it probably isn't too far off the mark.

THE PURSUIT OF EFFICIENCY

We have seen that environmental problems arise when property rights are ill-defined, when these rights are exchanged under something other than competitive conditions, and when social and private discount rates diverge. We can now use our definition of efficiency to explore possible remedies, such as private negotiation, judicial remedies, and regulation by the legislative and executive branches of government.

Private Resolution through Negotiation

The simplest means to restore efficiency occurs when the number of affected parties is small, making negotiation feasible. Suppose, for example, the noise of a stereo system shatters the tranquility of an evening. This situation is an environmental problem because the stereo owner does not exclusively bear all the costs of his or her actions. Because of the externality, an inefficiency occurs (Figure 3.9). Without considering the neighbor's welfare, the stereo owner chooses q_m decibels, a choice dictated solely by the owner's enjoyment of loud music. Meanwhile the efficient level q^* is the level which maximizes the net benefit. How can efficiency be restored in this nonmarket relationship? The first possibility is individual negotiation. The neighbor could bribe the stereo owner. Suppose, for example, the neighbor offered to pay P^* for each decibel reduced. The owner should, in that case, be willing to reduce the level to q^* decibels because of the advantages. The owner loses benefits Cq_mq^* but gains revenue equal to the rectangle CBq_mq^*, which is larger.

Meanwhile, the neighbor is also better off than before. Though he or she had to pay the bribe (CBq_mq^*), the neighbor no longer bears the cost of the loud noise (ACq^*q_m), which is greater. Notice that in equilibrium it does not pay the neighbor to offer a per unit bribe either greater than P^* or less than P^* because those bribes would, respectively, yield too much or too little reduction in noise level.

Our discussion of individual negotiations raises two questions: (1) Should the property right always belong to the person who gained or seized it first? (2) How can accident be handled where prior negotiation is clearly impractical? These questions are routinely answered by the court system.

FIGURE 3.9 Noise pollution: an example of external cost.

The Courts: Property Rules and Liability Rules

The court system can respond to environmental conflicts by imposing either property rules or liability rules. *Property rules* specify the initial allocation of the entitlement. The entitlements at conflict in our example are, on the one hand, the right to play a stereo loudly and, on the other, the right to peace and quiet. In applying property rules, the court merely decides which right is preeminent and places an injunction against violating that right. The injunction is removed only upon obtaining the consent of the party whose right was violated. Consent is usually obtained in return for an out-of-court monetary settlement.

Notice that in the absence of a court decision the entitlement is naturally allocated to the party which can most easily seize it. In our example the natural allocation would give the entitlement to the party who likes loud music. The courts must decide whether to overturn this natural allocation. How would they decide? Would the court decision be efficient? In a classic article, economist Ronald Coase (1960) held that as long as negotiation costs are negligible and affected consumers can negotiate freely with each other (when the number of affected parties is small), the court could allocate the entitlement to *either* party and an efficient allocation would result. The only effect of the court's decision is to change the distribution of costs and benefits among the affected parties. This remarkable conclusion has come to be known as the *Coase theorem*.

We have already shown (in Figure 3.9) that if the stereo owner has the property right, it is in the neighbor's interest to offer a bribe of P^* per decibel of noise reduction resulting in the desired level of q^*. Suppose, now, the neighbor had the property right instead. To play the stereo loudly, the owner must bribe the neighbor. It would be advantageous to offer the neighbor P^* per decibel allowed, and upon receiving this offer the neighbor would maximize personal net benefit by accepting q^* decibels.

The difference between these two allocations lies in how the cost of obtaining the efficient decibel level is shared between the parties. When the property right is assigned to the owner of the stereo, the cost is borne by the neighbor. When the property right is assigned to the neighbor, the cost is borne by the owner. In either case the efficient decibel level results. The Coase theorem shows that the very existence of an inefficiency triggers pressures for improvements. Furthermore, the existence of this pressure does not depend on the assignment of property rights.

This is an important point. As we shall see in succeeding chapters, private efforts triggered by inefficiency can frequently prevent the worst excesses of environmental degradation.[10] Yet the importance of this theorem should not be overstated. Both theoretical and practical objections can be raised. The chief theoretical qualification concerns the implicit assumption of zero-wealth effects. The decision to confer the property right on a particular party results in a transfer of wealth to that party. This transfer might shift the demand curve out, as long as the income elasticity of demand is not zero. Thus, giving the property right to the stereo owner in Figure 3.9 would shift the demand curve to the right, giving it to the neighbor would shift the cost curve to the left. Whenever wealth effects are significant, the type of property rule affects the outcome.

Wealth effects normally are small, so the zero-wealth-effect assumption is probably not a fatal flaw. Some serious practical flaws, however, do mar the usefulness of the Coase theorem. The first involves the incentives for noisemaking that result when the property right is assigned to the stereo owner. Since noise production would become a profitable activity with this assignment, other neighbors might be encouraged to turn their stereos up in order to earn the bribes. That certainly would not be efficient.

Negotiation is also difficult to apply when the number of people affected by the noise is large. You may have already noticed that in the presence of several

---

10 See, for example, how lobster harvesters have evolved elaborate rules to prevent this common property resource from being fished to extinction in J. M. Acheson, *The Lobster Gangs of Maine* (Hanover, NH: University Press of New England, 1988).

affected parties noise reduction is a public good.[11] The free-rider problem would make it difficult for the group to offer an efficient bribe.

When individual negotiation is not practical for one reason or another, the courts can turn to *liability rules*. These are rules which award monetary damages, after the fact, to the injured party. The amount of the award is designed to correspond to the amount of damage inflicted. Thus, returning to Figure 3.9, an efficient liability rule would impose damages equal to the area under *ECA* from *E* to the chosen decibel level. Suppose, for example, the stereo owner persisted in transmitting q_m decibels. If the court decided that damages were appropriate, it would award an amount equal to EAq_m.

The owner might initially be tempted now to play the music softer than *OE*, but, upon reflection, he would certainly resist that temptation. The owner would derive additional benefits beyond *OE* that would be greater than the costs of the damages. Knowing the damages to be paid (equal to the area formed under the line *ECA* from *E* to the chosen decibel level), the owner would choose q^*. For further reductions more benefits would be lost than would be gained in reduced damages paid. (Why doesn't he decide to increase the decibel level beyond q^*?) Thus, appropriately designed liability rules can also correct inefficiencies by forcing those who cause damage to bear the cost of that damage.

Liability rules are interesting from an economics point of view because early decisions create precedents for later ones. Imagine, for example, how the incentives to prevent oil spills facing an oil company are transformed once it has had to clean up after an oil spill and to compensate fishermen for reduced catches. It quickly becomes evident that accident prevention is cheaper than retrospectively dealing with the damage once it has occurred.

This approach, however, also has its limitations. It relies on a case-by-case determination based on the unique circumstances for each case. Administratively, such a determination is very expensive. Expenses, such as court time, lawyers' fees, and so on, fall into a category called *transaction costs* by economists. In the present context, these are the administrative costs incurred in attempting to correct the inefficiency. When the number of parties involved in a dispute is large and the circumstances are common, we are tempted to correct the inefficiency by statutes or regulations rather than court decisions.

Legislative and Executive Regulation

These remedies can take several forms. The legislature could dictate that no one should play their stereo louder than q^*. This dictum might then be backed up with sufficiently large jail sentences or fines to deter potential violators. Alter-

---

11 In this case our graph would reflect the situation by vertically summing the individual marginal cost curves to obtain a curve reflecting the total damage to all parties.

natively, the legislature could impose a tax on decibels. A per unit decibel tax of P^*, for example, would induce the stereo owner to reduce the noise to q^* (Figure 3.9).

Legislatures could also establish rules to permit greater flexibility and yet reduce damage. For example, some apartment buildings for young singles might allow louder stereos while others, catering to older folks or couples with young children needing large amounts of sleep, could enforce stricter silence standards. With this approach, those who like loud music could pick the former building and those who do not, the latter.

AN EFFICIENT ROLE FOR GOVERNMENT

While the economic approach suggests that government action could well be used to restore efficiency, it also suggests that inefficiency is not a sufficient condition to justify government intervention. Any corrective mechanism involves transaction costs. If these transaction costs are high enough, and the benefit to be derived from correcting the inefficiency small enough, then it is best simply to live with the inefficiency.

Consider, for example, the pollution problem. Wood-burning stoves, which were widely used for cooking and heat in the late 1800s in the United States, were sources of pollution, but because of the enormous capacity of the air to absorb the emissions, no regulation resulted. Today, however, the resurgence of demand for wood-burning stoves precipitated in part by high oil prices has resulted in strict regulations for wood-burning stove emissions.

As society has evolved, the scale of economic activity (and emissions) has expanded. For many air and water pollutants cities are experiencing severe problems because of the clustering of activities. Both the expansion and the clustering have increased the amount of emissions per unit volume of air or water. As a result, pollutant concentrations have caused perceptible problems with human health, vegetation growth, and aesthetics.

Historically, as incomes have risen, the demand for leisure activities has also risen. Many of these leisure activities, such as canoeing and backpacking, take place in unique, pristine environmental areas. With the number of these areas declining as a result of conversion to other uses, the value of remaining areas has increased. Thus, the benefits from protecting some areas have risen over time until they have exceeded the transaction costs of protecting them from pollution and/or development.

The level and concentration of economic activity, having increased pollution problems and driven up the demand for clean air and pristine areas, have created the preconditions for government action. Can government respond or will rent seeking prevent efficient political solutions? We devote much of this book to searching for the answer.

SUMMARY

How producers and consumers use the resources making up the environmental asset depends on the nature of the property rights governing resource use. When property right systems are universal, exclusive, transferable, and enforceable, the owner of a resource has a powerful incentive to use that resource efficiently, since the failure to do so results in a personal loss.

For scarce natural resources, the owners derive a scarcity rent. In properly specified property right systems, this rent is not dissipated by competition. It serves the social purpose of allowing owners to efficiently balance their extraction and conservation decisions.

The economic system will not always sustain efficient allocations, however. Specific circumstances which could lead to inefficient allocations include externalities, improperly defined property right systems (such as common property resources and public goods), imperfect markets for trading the property rights to the resources (monopoly), and the divergence of social and private discount rates (under the threat of nationalization). When these circumstances arise, market allocations do not maximize the present value of the net benefit.

Due to rent-seeking behavior by special interest groups or the less than perfect implementation of efficient plans, the political system can produce inefficiencies as well. Voter ignorance on many issues coupled with the public-good nature of any results of political activity tend to create a situation in which private, but not social, net benefits are maximized.

The efficiency criterion can be used to assist in the identification of circumstances in which our political and economic institutions lead us astray. It can also assist in the search for remedies by facilitating the design of regulatory, judicial, or legislative solutions.

FURTHER READING

Anderson, Terry L. and P. J. Hill. "The Evolution of Property Rights: A Study of the American West," *The Journal of Law and Economics* 18 (April 1975): 163–179. An interesting test of the proposition that as the efficiency losses from common property resources in the West rose, individuals increased the amount of time and resources devoted to definition and enforcement of rights to land, water, and livestock.

Bromley, Daniel W. "Property Rules, Liability Rules and Environmental Economics," *Journal of Economic Issues* 12 (March 1978): 43–60. An elaboration of the role of property rules and liability rules in solving environmental problems.

"Coase Theorem Symposium: Part I," *Natural Resources Journal* 13 (October 1973): 557–716; and "Coase Theorem Symposium: Part II," *Natural Resources Journal*, 14 (January 1974): 1–54. A wide ranging, penetrating series of essays on the limits and implications of the Coase theorem.

Goldfarb, Theodore D., ed. *Taking Sides: Clashing Views on Environmental Issues*, 4th ed. (Guilford, CT: Dushkin, 1991). A provocative collection of pairs of opposing views on 18 aspects of environmental policy.

Stavins, Robert N., "Harnessing Market Forces To Protect the Environment," *Environment* 31 (1989): 4–7, 28–35. An excellent, nontechnical review of the many ways in which the creative use of economic policies can produce superior environmental outcomes.

ADDITIONAL REFERENCES

Bolotin, Frederic N. *International Public Policy Sourcebook Vol. 2: Education and Environment* (Boulder, CO: Greenwood Press, 1989).

Bromley, Daniel W. *Economic Interests and Institutions: The Conceptual Foundations of Public Policy* (Oxford: Basil Blackwell, 1989).

Coase, Ronald. "The Problem of Social Cost," *The Journal of Law and Economics* 3 (October 1960): 1–44.

Johnson, Stanley P. *The Environmental Policy of the European Communities* (London: Graham & Trotman, 1989).

OECD. *Environment and Economics* (Paris: Organization for Economic Cooperation and Development, 1985).

Mercuro, Nicholas and Warren J. Samuels. "The Role and Resolution of the Compensation Principle in Society, I," in *Research in Law and Economics*, Vol. 1 (Greenwich, CT: JAI Press, 1979): 157–194 and "The Role and Resolution of the Compensation Principle, II," in *Research in Law and Economics* Vol. 2, (Greenwich, CT: JAI Press, 1980): 103–128.

Pryde, Philip R. "The 'Decade of the Environment' in the U.S.S.R.," *Science* 220 (April 15, 1983): 274–279.

Ross, Lester. *Environmental Policy in China* (Bloomington, IN: Indiana University Press, 1988).

DISCUSSION QUESTIONS

1. In a well-known legal case, *Miller v. Schoene* (287 U.S. 272), a classic conflict of property rights was featured. Red cedar trees, used only for ornamental purposes, carried a disease that could destroy apple orchards within a radius of 2 miles. There was no known way of curing the disease except by destroying the cedar trees or by ensuring that apple orchards were at least 2 miles away from the cedar trees. Apply the Coase theorem to this situation. Does it make any difference to the outcome whether the cedar tree owners are entitled to retain their trees or the apple growers are entitled to be free of them? Why or why not?

2. In primitive societies the entitlements to use land were frequently possessory rights rather than ownership rights. Those on the land could use it as they

wished, but they could not transfer it to anyone else. One could acquire a new plot by simply occupying and using it, leaving the old plot available for someone else. Would this type of entitlement system cause more or less incentive to conserve the land than an ownership entitlement? Why? Would a possessory entitlement system be more efficient in a modern society or a primitive society? Why?

PROBLEMS

1. Suppose the state is trying to decide how many miles of a very scenic river it should preserve. There are 100 people in the community, each of whom has an identical inverse demand function given by $P = 10 - 1.0q$, where q is the number of miles preserved and P is the per mile price he or she is willing to pay for q miles of preserved river. (a) If the marginal cost of preservation is $500 per mile, how many miles would be preserved in an efficient allocation? (b) How large are the net benefits?

2. (a)–Compute the consumer surplus and producer surplus if the product described by the first problem in Chapter 2 were supplied by a competitive industry. Show that their sum is equal to the efficient net benefits.
   (b)–Compute the consumer surplus and the producer surplus assuming this same product was supplied by a monopoly. (*Hint:* The marginal revenue curve has twice the slope of the demand curve.)
   (c)–Show that when this market is controlled by a monopoly, producer surplus is larger, consumer surplus is smaller, and net benefits are smaller than when it is controlled by competitive industry.

3. Suppose you were asked to comment on a proposed policy to control oil spills. Since the average cost of an oil spill has been computed as $X, the proposed policy would require any firm responsible for a spill to immediately pay the government $X. Is this likely to result in the efficient amount of precaution against oil spills? Why or why not?

CHAPTER FOUR

Regulating the Market: Information and Uncertainty

Cost-benefit analysis is valuable in regulatory decision making, but unless we recognize its shortcomings we are likely to force a superficial quantification of issues that cannot wholly be grasped by the reassuringly precise embrace of numbers. [If this technique is used inappropriately] we shall be guided by a bright light in the wrong place, and the result will be not only bad cost-benefit analysis, but bad decisions.

DOUGLAS M. COSTLE (1981),
EPA Administrator During Carter Administration

INTRODUCTION

The last chapter discussed circumstances in which markets cannot, by themselves, achieve an efficient allocation of resources. We also explored possible ways to correct this problem by realigning individual incentives through the judicial and/or legislative process. In order for this realignment to take place, however, the judges or legislators need a great deal of information on the costs and benefits of various choices they might make. This information is crucial in determining whether additional policies are needed and, if so, the types of policies which would be most efficient.

The process of regulating the market has its own transaction costs. The regulatory staffs have to be hired to draw up the regulations and administer them. Additional staff must be hired to enforce the regulations and to handle the inevitable exceptions and appeals. The firms being regulated must hire larger staffs to comply with the regulations and to fill out the reports which inevitably accompany regulation. The regulations themselves may be imperfectly designed, and the resulting loss of net benefits is an additional cost society must bear. In light of this fact, it is important to quantify the potential gains to be captured from regulation so that these may be weighed against the costs.

Quantification is not a trivial exercise. Information must be identified and structured in such a way as to allow rational decisions to be made. If this quantification is to prove useful, it must be reliable and must deal realistically with circumstances in which information is not available.

On February 17, 1981, President Reagan issued Executive Order 12291, which requires executive agencies to make more extensive use of benefit-cost analysis in defining and defending proposed regulatory changes. This decision was roundly applauded by some and, as the Costle quote suggests, severely criticized by others. In order to understand this controversy, we must delve into the procedures used to perform benefit-cost analysis and investigate what alternative forms of analysis are available to policymakers when the available information is not sufficient to allow the efficient allocation to be defined with precision.

This chapter examines the various techniques, starting with benefit-cost analysis, which seek to provide quantitative guidance to decision makers. We will be concerned specifically with the availability and reliability of information to implement these techniques, their usefulness when information is scarce or relatively untrustworthy, and the manner in which these techniques deal with uncertainty about the future. Brief summaries of case studies are presented to illustrate the principles and their applicability to actual policy situations.

BENEFIT-COST ANALYSIS

The most ambitious of the techniques is benefit-cost analysis. Though it makes the most precise statements about which policy choices are efficient, it also imposes the largest requirement for information in order to provide those statements. It is fairly easy for most people to accept the general premise that benefits and costs of actions should be weighed prior to deciding on a policy choice. The technique becomes more controversial, however, when specific numbers are attached to the anticipated benefits and costs and specific decision rules for translating these numbers into a decision are followed.

The Decision Rules

We start our investigation by discussing how the benefit and cost information is used once it is available. Three main decision rules are commonly used, and they are *not* equivalent.

The *maximum net present-value criterion* is the empirical counterpart to the present value of net-benefits criterion used to define dynamic efficiency. This criterion suggests that resources should be committed to those uses maximizing the present value of net benefits received. If accomplished properly, this analysis will correctly identify an efficient allocation.

In practice, however, two other frequently used criteria do not guarantee that the efficient allocation will be identified. These are the *benefit-cost ratio criterion* and the *positive net present-value criterion*. The decision rule for the former criterion implies that an activity should be undertaken if the ratio of the present value of benefits to the present value of costs exceeds 1.0. The decision rule for the second criterion implies that an activity should be undertaken whenever the present value of net benefits is greater than zero. While both of these techniques guarantee that no activity which confers more costs on society than benefits will be undertaken, they do not guarantee efficiency. The point can be illustrated most easily using our definition of static efficiency.

Recall from Chapter 2 that efficiency is attained when the *marginal* benefit equals the *marginal* cost. Neither a benefit-cost ratio greater than 1.0 nor a positive net benefit ensures that these marginal conditions will hold. In fact, when the benefit-cost ratio is equal to 1.0 (or, equivalently, the net benefit is equal to 0.0), this ensures that total benefit equals total cost (Figure 4.1).

The net benefit is maximized when Q_1 is supplied. At this point the marginal benefit is equal to the marginal cost, so that total benefits exceed total costs by the largest possible amount. In fact, the net benefit is equal to E, which is considerably greater than zero.[1]

At what allocation would net benefit equal zero? In Figure 4.1 the answer is Q_2. The figure is drawn such that area A equals area B. Since area B represents net cost (or, equivalently, negative net benefit) and area A represents positive net benefit, the net benefit from allocation Q_2 is zero. This implies that *average* benefits equal *average* costs, *total* benefits equal *total* costs, and the benefit-cost ratio equals 1.0.[2]

This result suggests that whenever the benefit-cost ratio or positive net present-value criteria are used, the government may choose inefficient activities. Only the maximum net present-value approach is completely compatible with efficiency.

Measuring Benefits

For many resource problems, measurement of benefits is relatively uncomplicated because the resource in question is a marketed commodity and information on prices and quantities consumed can be used to derive the demand curve. Once the demand curve is defined, it can be used to quantify the willingness to pay, the concept used to measure benefits.

---

1 Total benefits are equal to $A + C$, and total costs are equal to C.

2 Average benefits are equal to $A + C + D \div Q$, and average costs are equal to $B + C + D \div Q$. Therefore, as long as $A = B$, average benefits equal average costs.

FIGURE 4.1   Benefit-cost analysis and efficiency.

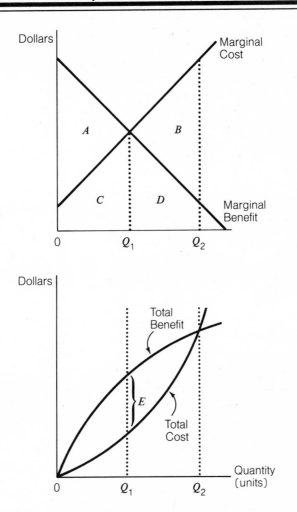

Greater difficulties are encountered when the resource in question is not handled through normal markets. One classic example arises when we compare the value of preserving an environmental resource, such as a unique canyon, with that of developing a resource, such as hydroelectric power. We must compare the recreational benefits without development to the power benefits with development.

Recreational Benefits.   Recreational benefits could be estimated from the recreational demand curve for that resource, if it were known. However, it is difficult to know what the true demand is, since visitors normally are not charged anything but nominal fees for using publicly owned recreation areas. Market prices do not prevail and demands are not revealed.

To get around this problem, a technique called the *Clawson-Knetsch method* was developed for estimating the recreational demand for a site when market prices are not available.[3] This technique uses travel costs to measure how much people would be willing to pay to come to the area.

The simplest version of the procedure is as follows:[4]

1. For a recreation site, the surrounding area is divided into concentric circular zones for the purpose of measuring the travel cost from each zone to the site and return.

2. Visitors at the site are sampled to determine their zones of origin.

3. Visitation rates defined as visitor days per capita are calculated for each zone of origin.

4. A travel cost measure is constructed to indicate the cost of travel from the origin zone to the recreation site and return.

5. Using regression analysis, one relates visitation rates to travel costs and socioeconomic variables such as average income, median educational attainment, and the like.

6. The observed total visitation for the site from all travel cost zones represents one point on the demand curve for that site—that is, the intersection of the present horizontal price line (either at a zero price or the typical nominal fee) with the true economic demand curve.

7. Other points on the demand curve are found by assuming that visitors will respond to a $1 increase in admission price in the same way that they would respond to a $1 increase in computed travel cost. To find the point on the demand curve for the site where the admission price rises by $1, we use the estimated visitation rate equation to compute visitation rates and total visits for all travel cost zones with the existing travel cost plus $1. Visits are summed across travel cost zones to determine the predicted total visitation at the higher price. These calculations

3   This is described in detail in Marion Clawson and Jack Knetsch, *Economics of Outdoor Recreation* (Baltimore: Johns Hopkins University Press for Resources for the Future, 1966); Jack L. Knetsch, "Economics of Including Recreation as a Purpose of Eastern Water Projects," *Journal of Farm Economics* 46 (December 1964): 1148–1157.

4   This description is taken from A. Myrick Freeman III, *The Benefits of Environmental Improvement: Theory and Practice* (Baltimore: The Johns Hopkins Press for Resources for the Future, 1979): 201–209. Some newer approaches are discussed in R. Mendelsohn and G. M. Brown, Jr., "Revealed Preference Approachs to Valuing Outdoor Recreation," *Natural Resources Journal* 23 (July 1983): 607–618.

are repeated for higher and higher hypothetical admission prices, and the full demand curve is traced out.

This technique is valid as long as the site is uncongested when the visitation rates are derived. Congestion serves to reduce demand artificially, and, hence, using the Clawson-Knetsch method to estimate the demand for a congested site would lead to an underestimate of the recreation benefits at that site.

The next difficulty in comparing preservation and development involves forecasting how the benefits from these alternative uses will change over time. The demand for recreational activity has a positive income elasticity, which implies that the demand curve will shift out over time as income increases. Necessarily, the benefits of the preservation alternative will increase over time as well. If benefits of preservation increase faster than costs, then the net benefits of preservation increase over time. As demonstrated by Example 4.1, preservation may be the preferred alternative, even if the benefits from preservation in the current year are lower than the benefits from development. Furthermore, as is clear from Example 4.1, the dominance of the preservation alternative may turn out to be not very sensitive to the specific estimate of recreational benefits, a comforting finding in light of the difficulty of obtaining precise estimates.

Pollution Damages and Pollution Control Benefits. Some of the most difficult problems of benefit estimation are raised by the search for an efficient level of pollution control. The benefits derived from pollution control are the damages prevented. The benefit derived from more control over pollution is the difference between the level of damage when emissions are controlled at one level and the lower level of damage which would result from greater control. Our measurement of benefits, then, depends upon our ability to estimate the damage that results from various levels of pollution.

Damage estimates have also become important in the courts in the United States. Under the Comprehensive Environmental Response, Compensation, and Liability Act, local, state, or federal governments can seek monetary compensation from responsible parties for natural resources that are injured or destroyed by spills and releases of hazardous wastes. Some basis for deciding the magnitude of the award is necessary.[5]

The damage caused by pollution can take many different forms. The first, and probably most obvious, is the effect on human health. Polluted air and water can cause disease when ingested. Other forms of damage include loss of enjoyment from outdoor activities and damage to vegetation, animals, and materials.

---

5 The rules for determing these damages are defined in Department of Interior regulations. See 40 *Code of Federal Regulations* 300.72–74.

EXAMPLE 4.1

Preservation Versus Development: The Hell's Canyon Case

Hell's Canyon, on the Snake River separating Oregon from Idaho, is the deepest canyon on the North American continent. It affords a visitor some of the most spectacular vistas in the country as well as providing a natural habitat for a variety of wildlife. It also offers one of the best remaining sites for the development of hydroelectric power.

During the 1970s a major controversy developed concerning whether a portion of this canyon should be dedicated to the production of hydroelectric power through the construction of the High Mountain Sheep Dam or preserved in its natural state. If the dam were developed, a large lake would be formed behind the dam, changing the character of the canyon.

During this controversy several economists from an organization called Resources for the Future, Inc., a respected Washington think tank, performed a benefit-cost analysis on the choice. The issues were relatively clear. As an environmental resource supporting recreational activities, this canyon was unique in the area. The demand for those activities was increasing at a very rapid rate, but the construction of the dam would diminish the value of the site for those purposes. On the other hand, the electricity produced by the dam would also be valuable.

In contrast to the use of the resource as a natural area, which, due to its uniqueness has very few substitutes, electricity could be produced by other methods. Unfortunately, these other methods would be more expensive. The benefit of the dam, then, would be the costs saved by generating electricity in this manner rather than by the next cheapest source (nuclear), while the cost would include the opportunity cost of the recreational activities forgone.

What did the analysis suggest? The authors concluded that the net benefits from preservation were rising rapidly over time and, therefore, even though current benefits from preservation were less than the current benefits from producing electricity, in present-value terms the preservation option yielded higher net benefits. The analysis indicated that if the current annual value of recreational activities exceeded $80,000, then the efficient decision would be to preserve the site. Their estimate of the current annual value of recreational activities at that site was approximately $900,000. Even though the data on which this latter estimate was based were not very solid, $900,000 is more than 10 times higher than needed to justify preservation. The likelihood that the "true" estimate would be less than $80,000, if it were known, is very low. Therefore they recommended preservation. On the basis of this recommendation and other considerations, Congress voted to prohibit further development of this section of the river.

Source: Anthony C. Fisher, John V. Krutilla, and Charles J. Chicchetti, "Alternative Uses of Natural Environments: The Economics of Environmental Modification," in *Natural Environments: Studies in Theoretical and Applied Analysis*, John V. Krutilla, ed. (Washington, DC: Johns Hopkins University Press for Resources for the Future, 1972): 18–53.

Assessing the magnitude of this damage requires (1) identifying the affected categories; (2) estimating the physical relationship between the pollutant emissions (including natural sources) and the damage caused to the affected categories; (3) estimating responses by the affected parties toward averting or mitigating some portion of the damage; and (4) placing a monetary value on the physical damages. Each step is often difficult to accomplish.

Because the experiments used to track down causal relationships are uncontrolled, identifying the affected categories is a complicated matter. Obviously we cannot run large numbers of people through controlled experiments. If people were subjected to different levels of some pollutant, such as carbon monoxide, so that we could study the short-term and long-term effects, some might become ill and even die. Ethical concern precludes human experimentation of this type.

This leaves us essentially two choices. We can try to infer the impact on humans from controlled laboratory experiments on animals,[6] or we can do an after-the-fact statistical analysis of differences in mortality or disease rates for various human populations living in polluted environments to see the extent to which they are correlated with pollution concentrations. Neither approach is completely acceptable.

Animal experiments are expensive, and, even when accomplished, the extrapolation from effects on animals to effects on humans is tenuous at best. Many of the significant effects, about which we might properly be concerned if we knew more about them, do not appear for a long time. To determine these effects in a reasonable period of time, test animals must be subjected to large doses for a relatively short period of time. The researcher then extrapolates from the results of these high-dosage, short-duration experiments to estimate the effects of lower doses over a longer period of time on a human population. Since these extrapolations move well beyond the range of experimental experience, many scientists disagree on how the extrapolations should be accomplished.

Statistical studies, on the other hand, deal with human populations subjected to low doses for long periods, but, unfortunately, they have another set of problems—correlation does not imply causation. To illustrate, the fact that death rates are higher in cities with higher pollution levels does not prove that the higher pollution *caused* the higher death rates. Perhaps those same cities averaged older populations, which would tend to lead to higher death rates. Or perhaps they had more smokers. The existing studies have been sophisticated enough to account for many of these other possible influences, but, because of the relative paucity of data, they have not been able to cover them all.

The problems discussed so far arise when identifying *whether* a particular effect results from pollution. The next step is to estimate *how strong* the relation-

---

6 Extrapolation from animal studies is used mainly in determining the toxicity of chemicals and has not been used to any appreciable degree in determining the effects of "conventional" pollutants.

ship is between the effect and the pollution concentrations. In other words, it is necessary not only to discover whether pollution causes an increased incidence of respiratory disease, but also to estimate how much reduction in respiratory illness could be expected from a given reduction in pollution. The nonexperimental nature of the data makes this a difficult task. It is not uncommon for researchers analyzing the same data to come to remarkably different conclusions.[7] Diagnostic problems are compounded when the effects are *synergistic*—that is, when the effect depends in a nonadditive way on what other elements are in the surrounding air or water at the time of the analysis.

Once physical damages have been identified, the next step is to place a monetary value on them. It is not difficult to see how complex an undertaking this is. Consider, for example, the difficulties in assigning a value to extending a human life by several years or to the pain, suffering, and grief borne by a cancer victim and his or her family.

Economists have used several different approaches to place a monetary value on reductions in physical damages. The first method, the *contingent valuation* approach, relies on surveys to ascertain how much respondents would be willing to pay to preserve the environment, to reduce the amount of injury to it caused by humans, or to lower the various types of environmental risk posed by modern industrial society. To name but a few of the large numbers of existing studies, this approach has been used to value visibility,[8] the recreational use of two rivers in Maine,[9] reductions in nuclear plant injuries,[10] and migratory waterfowl in the Pacific flyway.[11]

The major concern with the use of the contingent valuation method has been the potential for survey respondents to give biased answers. Four types of poten-

---

7 For example, economists Lester B. Lave and Eugene P. Seskin, *Air Pollution and Human Health* (Baltimore: Johns Hopkins University Press, 1977), in their often-cited study based on a large volume of data, concluded that a 50% reduction in air pollution nationally would lead to a 4.7% reduction in mortality. Working with the same data, a pair of mathematicians with General Motors Research Corporation came to the conclusion that a 50% reduction in air pollution would drop mortality by only 0.43%. This controversy is described in "New Perspective on Air Pollution," *Science News* 119 (1981): 152.

8 Robert D. Rowe and Lauraine G. Chestnut, *The Value of Visibility: Economic Theory and Applications for Air Pollution Control* (Cambridge, MA: Abt Books, 1982).

9 William O'Neil and Kristin Hallberg, *Estimating the Value of River-Related Recreational Activities: A Comparison of Two Approaches Based on Case Studies of the West Branch of the Penobscot River and the Saco River* (Orono, ME: Maine Land and Water Resources Center, 1985).

10 Patricia J. Mulligan, "Willingness-to-Pay for Decreased Risks of Nuclear Accidents," Working Paper Number 3, Energy Extension Programs (Pennsylvania State University, 1977).

11 Gardener Mallard Brown, Jr., and Judd Hammock, "A Preliminary Investigation of the Economics of Migratory Waterfowl," in *Natural Environments: Studies in Theoretical and Applied Analysis*, John V. Krutilla, ed. (Baltimore: Johns Hopkins University Press for Resources for the Future, 1972).

tial bias have been the focus of a large amount of research: (1) *strategic bias*, (2) *information bias*, (3) *starting point bias*, and (4) *hypothetical bias.*

Strategic bias arises when the respondent provides a biased answer in order to influence a particular outcome. If a decision to preserve a stretch of river for fishing, for example, depends on whether or not the survey produces a sufficiently large value for fishing, the respondents who enjoy fishing may be tempted to provide an answer that ensures a high value rather than a lower value that reflects their true valuation.

Information bias may arise whenever respondents are forced to value attributes with which they have little or no experience. For example, the valuation by a recreationist of a loss in water quality in one body of water may be based on the ease of substituting recreation on another body of water. If the respondent has no experience using the second body of water, the valuation will be based on an entirely false perception.

Starting point bias may arise in those survey instruments in which a respondent is asked to check off his or her answers from a predefined range of possibilities. How that range is defined by the designer of the survey may affect the resulting answers. A range of $0 to $100 may produce a different valuation by respondents, for example, than a range of $10 to $100, even if no bids are in the $0 to $10 range.

Hypothetical bias occurs when the respondent is being confronted by a contrived, rather than an actual, set of choices. Since he or she will not have to actually pay the estimated value, the respondent may treat the survey casually, providing ill-considered answers.

Much experimental work has been done on contingent valuation to determine how serious a problem these biases may present.[12] In general, the results seem to suggest that they can be kept acceptably small with suitably designed survey instruments.

A quite different approach involves inferring the valuation of an environmental attribute which is not directly observable from related markets where values are directly observable. Common examples include the housing and labor markets.

Housing market studies, also called property value studies, start from the presumption that the purchaser's willingness to pay for property takes the quality of the local environment into account. All other things being equal, for example, one would expect houses in neighborhoods with clean air to command higher prices than houses in neighborhoods with polluted air. By statistically comparing the market values of similar houses in neighborhoods with different levels of air

---

12 For a comprehensive survey of the state of the art, see Ronald G. Cummings, David S. Brookshire, and William D. Schulze, eds., *Valuing Environmental Goods: An Assessment of the Contingent Value Method* (Totowa, NJ: Rowman and Littlefield, 1986).

quality, these studies attempt to decompose the value of housing into its component parts. Since one of those component parts is a premium paid for clean air, this premium can serve as a measure of the value of clean air.

For labor markets the presumption is that workers facing higher levels of environmental risk (such as an exposure to a potentially hazardous substance) have to be compensated in order to accept that risk. By decomposing wages into their component parts and isolating the environmental risk premium, we can use this premium to value the benefits that would be conferred by a reduction in this risk.

In general, the statistical studies support the basic common premise behind these two approaches. Property values and wages do indeed reflect the existence of pollution as well as other forms of environmental risk, but they have also indicated that we still have a lot to learn about risk valuation. In particular, it now seems clear that environmental risk valuations are sensitive to the context in which they arise; valuations derived in one context (such as the risk of contracting lung cancer from smoking) cannot automatically be transferred to another context (such as the risk of contracting lung cancer through exposure to a radioactive substance). Furthermore, the type of risk, such as whether the exposure is voluntary or involuntary, seems to make quite a difference in the value placed on reducing that risk.[13]

Perhaps surprisingly, these rather different approaches yield quite similar valuations, as can be illustrated by an explicit comparison of the property value and contingent valuation methods for providing a measure of the benefits derived from reducing pollution in the Los Angeles area.[14] Statistical tests reveal that the two approaches yield consistent results. Considering the very different bases for deriving these numbers, this conclusion is rather striking.

One fascinating public policy area where these various approaches have been applied is in the valuation of human life. Many government programs, from those controlling hazardous pollutants in the workplace or drinking water to those improving nuclear power plant safety, are designed to save human life as well as to reduce illness. How resources should be allocated among these programs depends crucially on the value of human life. How is life to be valued?

The simple answer, of course, is that life is priceless, but that turns out to be not very helpful. Since the resources used to prevent loss of life are scarce, choices must be made. The economic approach to valuing life-saving reductions in environmental risk is to calculate the change in the probability of death resulting from the reduction in environmental risk and to place a value on the change.

---

13 See the discussion of context in environmental risk valuation in V. Kerry Smith "The Valuation of Environmental Risks Using Hedonic Wage Models," in *Horizontal Equity, Uncertainty, and Economic Well-Being*, Martin David and Timothy Smeeding, eds. (Chicago: University of Chicago Press, 1985).

14 Brookshire et al., "Valuing Public Goods: A Comparison of Survey and Hedonic Approaches," *The American Economic Review* (March 1982).

Thus it is not life itself that is being valued but a reduction in the probability that some segment of the population could be expected to die earlier than otherwise.

It is possible to translate the value derived from this procedure in an "implied value of human life." This is accomplished by dividing the amount each individual is willing to pay for a specific reduction in the probability of death by the probability reduction. Suppose, for example, that a particular environmental policy could be expected to reduce the average concentration of a toxic substance to which one million people are exposed. Suppose further that this reduction in exposure could be expected to reduce the risk of death from 1 out of 100,000 to 1 out of 150,000. This implies that the number of expected deaths would fall from 10 to 6.67 in the exposed population as a result of this policy. If each of the one million persons exposed is willing to pay $5 for this risk reduction (for a total of $5 million), then the implied value of a life is approximately $1.5 million ($5 million divided by 3.33).

What actual values have been derived from these methods? One survey of a large number of studies examining reductions in a number of life-threatening risks found that most implied values for human life clustered within one or two common ranges. The low range placed the implied value of human life between $300,000 and $600,000 (in 1981 dollars), while the high range placed it between $1,000,000 and $7,000,000.[15]

This same survey went on to suggest that the lower range should be treated as a lower bound on the value of human life. In other words, all government programs resulting in risk reductions costing less than $300,000 to $600,000 would be justified in benefit-cost terms.[16] Those costing more might or might not be justified, depending on the appropriate value of a life saved in the particular risk context being examined.

Issues in Benefit Estimation[17]

The analyst charged with the responsibility for performing a benefit-cost analysis encounters many decision points requiring judgment. If we are to understand benefit-cost analysis, the nature of these judgments must be clear in our minds.

---

15 Energy and Resource Consultants, Inc., *Valuing Reductions in Risks: A Review of the Empirical Estimates* (Washington, DC: U.S. Environmental Protection Agency, 1983): 6-2.

16 This is a controversial point. In his book *Reducing Risks to Life: Measurement of the Benefits* (Washington, DC: American Enterprise Institute for Public Policy Research, 1980), Martin Bailey argues that the lower range is the only reasonable range, not merely a lower bound.

17 This section relies heavily on Henry M. Peskin and Eugene P. Seskin, *Cost-Benefit Analysis and Water Pollution Control Policy* (Washington, DC: The Urban Institute, 1975).

Primary versus Secondary Effects. Environmental projects usually trigger both primary and secondary consequences. For example, the primary effect of cleaning a lake will be an increase in recreational uses of the lake. This primary effect will cause a further ripple effect on services provided to the increased number of users of the lake. Are these secondary benefits to be counted?

The answer depends upon the employment conditions in the surrounding area. If this increase in demand results in employment of previously unused resources, such as labor, the value of the increased employment should be counted. If, on the other hand, the increase in demand is met by a shift in previously employed resources, from one use to another, this is a different story. In general, secondary employment benefits should be counted in high unemployment areas or when the particular skills demanded are underemployed at the time the project is commenced. They should not be counted when the project simply results in a rearrangement of productively employed resources.

Tangible versus Intangible Benefits. *Tangible* benefits are those which can reasonably be assigned a monetary value. *Intangible* benefits are those which cannot be assigned a monetary value, either because data are not available or reliable enough or because it is not clear how to measure the value even with data.[18]

How are intangible benefits to be handled? One answer is perfectly clear: they should not be ignored. To ignore intangible benefits is to bias the results. That benefits are intangible does not mean they are unimportant.

Intangible benefits should be quantified to the fullest extent possible. One frequently used technique is to conduct a sensitivity analysis of the estimated benefit values derived from less than perfectly reliable data. We can determine, for example, whether or not the outcome is sensitive, within wide ranges, to the value of this benefit. If not, then very little time has to be spent on the problem. If the outcome is sensitive, the person or persons making the decision bear the ultimate responsibility for weighing the importance of that benefit.

Approaches to Cost Estimation

Estimating costs is easier, in general, than estimating benefits, but it is not easy. One major problem for both derives from the fact that benefit-cost analysis is forward-looking and thus requires an estimate of what a particular strategy *will* cost, which is much more difficult than tracking down what an existing strategy *does* cost.

---

18 The division between tangible and intangible benefits changes as our techniques improve. Recreation benefits were, until the advent of the travel cost model, treated as intangible.

Another frequent problem is posed by collecting cost information when availability of that information is controlled by a firm having an interest in the outcome. Pollution control is an obvious example. Two approaches have been used to deal with this problem.

The Survey Approach. One way to discover the costs associated with a policy is to ask those who bear the costs, and presumably know the most about them, to reveal the magnitude of the costs to policymakers. Polluters, for example, could be asked to provide control-cost estimates to regulatory bodies. The problem with this approach is the strong incentive not to be truthful. An overestimate of the costs can trigger less stringent regulation; therefore, it is financially advantageous to provide overinflated estimates.

The Engineering Approach. The engineering approach bypasses the source being regulated by using general engineering information to catalog the possible technologies which could be used to meet the objective and to estimate the costs of purchasing and using those technologies. The final step in the engineering approach is to assume that the sources would use technologies which minimize cost. This produces a cost estimate for a "typical," well-informed firm.

This approach has its own problems. The expertise needed to develop these estimates is limited. Furthermore, these estimates may not approximate the actual cost of any particular firm. Unique circumstances may cause the costs of that firm to be higher, or lower, than estimated; the firm, in short, may not be typical.

The Combined Approach. To circumvent these problems, analysts frequently use a combination of survey and engineering approaches. The survey approach collects information on possible technologies, as well as special circumstances facing the firm. Engineering approaches are used to derive the actual costs of those technologies, given the special circumstances. This combined approach attempts to balance information best supplied by the source with that best derived independently.

In the cases described so far, the costs are relatively easy to quantify and the problem is simply finding a way to acquire the best information. This is not always the case, however. Some costs are not easy to quantify, though economists have developed some ingenious ways to secure monetary estimates even for those costs.

Take, for example, a policy designed to conserve energy by forcing more people to carpool. If the effect of this is simply to increase the average time of travel, how is this cost to be measured?

Transportation analysts have, for some time, recognized that people do value their time, and quite a literature has now grown up to provide estimates of this valuation. The basis for this valuation is opportunity cost—how the time might be used if it weren't being consumed in travel. Although the results of these studies depend on the amount of time involved, individuals seem to value their time at a rate not more than half their wage rates.[19]

The Treatment of Risk

For many environmental problems, it is not possible to state with certainty what consequences a particular policy will have, because scientific estimates, themselves, often are imprecise. Determining the efficient exposure to potentially toxic substances requires obtaining results at high doses and extrapolating to low doses, as well as extrapolating from animal studies to humans. It also requires relying upon epidemiological studies which infer a pollution-induced adverse human health impact from correlations between indicators of health in human populations and recorded pollution levels.

Another illustration of the significance of scientific uncertainty is afforded by the global warming problem. Certain gases, when emitted into the atmosphere, are suspected of causing the planetary temperature to rise. If this suspicion is correct, it could have very serious implications. Among others it could trigger a rise in the sea level and could result in the deaths of large numbers of plants no longer suited for the temperatures to which they would be subjected. The conjecture that increased emissions of carbon dioxide and other greenhouse gases are causing a rise in temperature is based upon a computer model which has only partially been validated. This is a prototypical example of a problem which is poorly understood, but, if the conjectures are true, could pose significant problems in the future.

The treatment of risk in the policy process involves two major dimensions : (1) identifying and quantifying the risks; and (2) deciding how much risk is acceptable. The former is primarily scientific and descriptive, while the latter is more evaluative or normative.

Benefit-cost analysis grapples with the evaluation of risk in several ways. Suppose, for example, that we have a range of policy options *A, B, C, D* and a range of possible outcomes *E, F, G* for each of these policies depending on how the economy evolves over the future. These outcomes, for example, might depend on whether the demand growth for the resource is low, medium, or high. Thus, if we choose policy *A*, we might end up with outcomes *AE, AF,* or *AG*. Each of the other policies has three possible outcomes as well, yielding a total of 12 possible outcomes.

We could conduct a separate benefit-cost analysis for each of the 12 possible outcomes. Unfortunately, the policy which maximizes net benefits for *E* may be different from that which maximizes net benefits for *F* or *G*. Thus, if we only

---

19 See M. E. Beesley, *Urban Transport: Studies in Economic Policy* (London: Butterworth, 1973): 160, 179.

knew which outcome would prevail, we could select the policy which maximized net benefits; the problem is that we don't. Furthermore, choosing the policy which is best if outcome E prevails may be disastrous if G results instead.

When a dominant policy emerges, this problem is avoided. A *dominant policy* is one which confers higher net benefits for every outcome. In this case, the existence of risk concerning the future is not relevant for the policy choice. Though this fortuitous circumstance is exceptional rather than common, it can occur.[20]

Other options exist even when dominant solutions do not emerge. Suppose, for example, that we were able to assess the likelihood that each of the three possible outcomes would occur. Thus we might expect outcome E to occur with probability 0.5, F with probability 0.3, and G with probability 0.2. Armed with this information, we can estimate the expected present value of net benefits. The *expected present value of net benefits* for a particular policy is defined as the sum over outcomes of the present value of net benefits for that policy where each outcome is weighted by its probability of occurrence. Symbolically this is expressed as

$$EPVNB_j = \sum_{i=1}^{I} P_i \, PVNB_{ij}, \, j = 1, \ldots, J, \tag{4.1}$$

where

$$\begin{aligned}
EPVNB_j &= \text{expected present value of net benefits for policy } j \\
P_i &= \text{probability of the } i\text{th outcome occurring} \\
PVNB_{ij} &= \text{present value of net benefits for policy } j \text{ if} \\
&\quad \text{outcome } i \text{ prevails} \\
J &= \text{number of policies being considered} \\
I &= \text{number of outcomes being considered}
\end{aligned}$$

The final step is to select the policy with the highest expected present value of net benefits.

This approach has the substantial virtue that it weighs higher probability outcomes more heavily. It also, however, makes a specific assumption about society's preference for risk. This approach is appropriate if society is risk-neutral. *Risk neutrality* can be defined most easily by the use of an example. Suppose you were allowed to choose between being given a definite $50 or entering a lottery in which you had a 50% chance of winning $100 and a 50% chance

---

20 Dennis Epple and Lester Lave, "Helium: Investments in the Future," *The Bell Journal of Economics* 11 (Autumn 1980): 617–630.

of winning nothing. (Notice that the expected value of this lottery is $50 = 0.5 ($100) + 0.5 ($0).) You would be said to be risk-neutral if you would be indifferent between these two choices. If you view the lottery as more attractive, you would be exhibiting *risk-loving* behavior, while a preference for the definite $50 would suggest *risk-averse* behavior. Using the expected present value of net benefits approach implies that society is risk neutral.

Is that a valid assumption? The evidence is mixed. The existence of gambling suggests that at least some members of society are risk lovers while the existence of insurance suggests that at least for some risks others are risk-averse. Since the same people may gamble and own insurance policies, it's likely that the type of risk may be important.

Even if individuals were demonstrably risk-averse, this would not be a sufficient condition for the government to forsake risk neutrality in evaluating public investments. One famous article argues that risk neutrality is appropriate since "when the risks of a public investment are publicly borne, the total cost of risk-bearing is insignificant and, therefore, the government should ignore uncertainty in evaluating public investments."[21] The logic behind this result suggests that as the number of risk bearers (and the degree of diversification of risks) increases, the amount of risk borne by any individual diminishes to zero.

When the decision is irreversible, considerably more caution is appropriate.[22] Irreversible decisions may subsequently be regretted, but the option to change courses will be lost forever. Extra caution also affords an opportunity to learn more about alternatives to this decision and its consequences before acting. Isn't it comforting to know that procrastination can occasionally be optimal?

There is a movement in national policy in both the courts and the legislature to search for imaginative ways to define acceptable risk.[23] In general, the policy approaches reflect a case-by-case approach. We shall see that current policy reflects a high degree of risk aversion toward a number of environmental problems.

Choosing the Discount Rate

In the previous chapter we discussed how the discount rate could be defined conceptually as the social opportunity cost of capital. This cost of capital can be divided further into two components: (1) the riskless cost of capital and (2) the risk premium.

---

21 Kenneth J. Arrow and Robert C. Lind, "Uncertainty and the Evaluation of Public Investment Decisions," *American Economic Review* 60 (June 1970): 366.

22 K. J. Arrow and A. C. Fisher, "Preservation, Uncertainty, and Irreversibility," *Quarterly Journal of Economics* 87 (1974): 312–319.

23 An excellent collection of essays on this subject is contained in Theodore S. Glickman and Michael Gough, eds., *Readings in Risk* (Washington, DC: Resources for the Future, 1990).

As Example 4.2 indicates, this has been, and continues to be, an important issue. When the public sector uses a discount rate lower than that in the private sector, the public sector will find more projects with longer payoff periods worthy of authorization. And, as we have already seen, the discount rate is a major determinant of the allocation of resources among generations as well.

Traditionally, economists have used long-term interest rates on government bonds as one measure of the cost of capital, adjusted by a risk premium which would depend on the riskiness of the project considered. Unfortunately, the choice of how large an adjustment to make has been left to the discretion of the analysts. This ability to affect the desirability of a particular project or policy by the choice of discount rate led to a situation in which government agencies were using a variety of discount rates to justify programs or projects they supported. One set of hearings conducted by Congress during the 1960s discovered that, at that time, agencies were using discount rates ranging from 0% to 20%.[24]

During the early 1970s the Office of Management and Budget came out with a circular which required, with some exceptions,[25] all government agencies to use a discount rate of 10% in their benefit-cost analysis.[26] This standardization reduces biases by eliminating the agency's ability to choose a discount rate which justifies a predetermined conclusion. It also allows a project to be considered independently of fluctuations in the true social cost of capital due to cycles in the behavior of the economy. On the other hand, when the social opportunity cost of capital differs from this administratively determined level, the benefit-cost analysis will not, in general, define the efficient allocation.[27]

A Critical Appraisal

The approaches to benefit estimation are sophisticated, but most observers feel that the resulting estimates are not yet sufficiently reliable that they could be used to fine-tune policy. One well-known survey of the field, commissioned by the Council on Environmental Quality, a government body, concluded:

---

24 Senator William Proxmire, "PPB, The Agencies and the Congress," in *The Analysis and Evaluation of Public Expenditures: The PPB System*, U.S. Congress, Joint Economic Committee, Subcommittee on Economy in Government (Washington, DC: Government Printing Office, 1969): xiii.

25 The main exception involves water resources projects. The discount rates used for these projects are computed once each year by the U.S. Treasury Department and transmitted to the Water Resources Council, an independent, executive coordinating agency. See Charles W. Howe, *Natural Resources Economics: Issues, Analysis, and Policy* (New York: Wiley, 1979): 158.

26 Circular No. A-94, as revised March 27, 1972.

27 For a detailed treatment of current discounting practices in the U.S. government, see the special issue of the *Journal of Environmental Economics and Management* 18 (March 1990) which is devoted to this subject.

EXAMPLE 4.2

The Importance of the Discount Rate

For years the United States and Canada had been discussing the possibility of constructing a tidal power project in the Passamaquoddy Bay between Maine and New Brunswick. This project would have heavy initial capital costs, but low operating costs, which presumably would hold for a long time into the future. As part of their analysis of the situation, a complete inventory of costs and benefits was completed in 1959.

Using the same benefit and cost figures, Canada concluded that the project should not be built, while the United States concluded that it should. Because these conclusions were based on the same benefit-cost data, the differences can be attributed solely to the use of different discount rates. The United States used 2.5% while Canada used 4.125%. The higher discount rate makes the initial cost weigh much more heavily in the calculation, leading to the Canadian conclusion that the project yields a negative net benefit. Since the lower discount rate weights the lower future operating costs relatively more heavily, Americans saw the net benefit as positive.

There are a number of other examples, as well. During 1962, Congress authorized a number of water projects which had been justified by benefit-cost analysis using a discount rate of 2.63%. Upon examining these projects, economists Fox and Herfindahl (1964, p. 202) found that, at an 8% rate of discount, only 20% of the projects would have had favorable benefit-cost ratios.

The choice of the discount rate even played a major role during a highly publicized dispute between President Jimmy Carter and Congress. President Carter wanted to rescind authorization from many previously approved water projects that he viewed as wasteful. The president based his conclusions on a discount rate of 6.38% while Congress was using a lower one.

Far from being an esoteric subject, the choice of the discount rate is fundamentally important in defining the role of the public sector, the types of projects undertaken, and the allocation of resources across generations.

Sources: Edith Stokey and Richard Zeckhauser, *A Primer for Policy Analysis* (New York: W. W. Norton, 1978): 164–165; Raymond Mikesell, *The Rate of Discount for Evaluating Public Projects* (Washington, DC: The American Enterprise Institute for Public Policy Research, 1977): 3–5; Irving K. Fox and Orris C. Herfindahl, "Attainment of Efficiency in Satisfying Demands for Water Resources," *American Economic Review* 54 (May 1964): 202.

> This report makes two points quite clear. First, in spite of recent advances, the estimation of certain kinds of environmental benefits is still in need of much additional refinement. . . . Second, where state-of-the art analyses of environmental benefits have been undertaken—as exemplified by the studies in this report—they strongly suggest that environmental protection is good economics.[28]

While the estimates are certainly good enough to tell us that the benefits from environmental control are large and worth pursuing, they are not reliable enough to use in picking a single pollution level as the efficient one.

Similar concerns can be raised about costs. The Environmental Protection Agency (EPA) commissioned a study to examine just how accurate cost forecasts were. The study compared actual capital outlays by firms responding to the pollution control laws to the forecasts of those same costs made earlier by both the EPA and by affected industries. When issued in June 1980, the report found that "both EPA and industry forecasts tend to overestimate compliance costs more often than they underestimate these costs."[29] Further, the report found that some of these overestimates were substantial. For the oil-refining industry, for example, both EPA and the industry projected capital costs of $1.4 billion. The actual costs were around $590 million, less than half of the projected total.

We have seen that it is sometimes, though not always, difficult to estimate benefits and costs. When this estimation is difficult or unreliable, it limits the value of a benefit-cost analysis. This problem would be particularly disturbing if biases tended to systematically increase or decrease net benefits. Do such biases exist?

In the early 1970s, economist Robert Haveman did a major study which sheds some light on this question. Focusing on Army Corps of Engineers water projects, such as flood control, navigation, and hydroelectric power generation, Haveman compared the ex ante (before the fact) estimates of benefits and costs with their ex post (after the fact) counterparts. Thus he was able to address the issues of accuracy and bias. He concluded that:

> In the empirical case studies presented, *ex post* estimates of benefits often showed little relationship to their *ex ante* counterparts. On the basis of the few cases and the *a priori* analysis presented here, one could conclude that there is a serious bias incorporated into agency *ex ante* evaluation procedures, resulting in persistent overstatement of expected benefits. Similarly in the analysis of project construction costs, enormous variance was found among projects in the relationship between estimated and realized costs. Although no persistent bias in estimation was apparent, nearly 50

---

28 A. Myrick Freeman III, *The Benefits of Air and Water Pollution Control: A Review and Synthesis of Recent Estimates*, a report prepared for the Council on Environmental Quality (December 1979): xi–xii.

29 Cited in "Antipollution Costs Were Overestimated by Government and Industry, Study Says," *Wall Street Journal* (June 19, 1980) 7.

percent of the projects displayed realized costs that deviated by more than plus or minus 20 percent from *ex ante* projected costs.[30]

In the cases examined by Haveman, at least, the notion that benefit-cost analysis is purely a scientific exercise was clearly not consistent with the evidence; the biases of the analysts were merely translated into numbers.

Another shortcoming of benefit-cost analysis is that it does not really address the question of who reaps the benefits and who pays the cost. It is quite possible for a particular course of action to yield high net benefits, but to have the benefits borne by one group of society and the costs borne by another. This admittedly extreme case does serve to illustrate a basic principle—ensuring that a particular policy is efficient provides an important, but not always the sole, basis for public policy. Other aspects, such as who reaps the benefit or bears the burden, are also important.

In summary, on the positive side, benefit-cost analysis is frequently a very useful part of the policy process. Even when the underlying data are not strictly reliable, the outcomes may not be sensitive to that unreliability. In other circumstances, the data may be reliable enough to give indications of the consequences of broad policy directions, even when they are not reliable enough to fine-tune those policies. Benefit-cost analysis, when done correctly, can provide a useful complement to the other influences on the political process by clarifying what choices yield the highest net benefits to society.

On the negative side, benefit-cost analysis has been attacked as seeming to promise more than can actually be delivered, particularly in the absence of solid benefit information. There have been two responses to this kind of concern. First, regulatory processes have been developed which can be implemented with very little information and yet have desirable economic properties. The recent reforms in air pollution control provides a powerful example, which we cover in Chapter 15.

The second approach involves techniques which supply useful information to the policy process without relying on controversial techniques to monetize environmental services which are difficult to value. The rest of this chapter deals with the two most prominent of these—cost-effectiveness analysis and impact analysis.

Even when benefits are difficult or impossible to quantify, economic analysis has much to offer. Policymakers should know, for example, how much various policy actions will cost and what their impacts on society will be, even if the efficient policy choice cannot be identified with any certainty.

---

30 Robert H. Haveman, *The Economic Performance of Public Investments: An Ex Post Evaluation of Water Resources Investments* (Baltimore: Johns Hopkins University Press for Resources for the Future, 1972).

Cost-effectiveness analysis and impact analysis both respond to this need, albeit in different ways.

COST-EFFECTIVENESS ANALYSIS

The point of departure for a cost-effectiveness analysis is the realization that, without a good measure of benefits, the efficient allocation cannot be determined by the analysis. Therefore the policy objective [for example, nitrogen oxide concentrations should not exceed 100 micrograms per cubic meter ($\mu g/cm^3$) in the ambient air] must be determined on some other basis.[31] Once that objective is specified, however, the analysis can have a great deal to say about the cost consequences of choosing a means of achieving that objective.

Typically several means of achieving the specified objective are available; some will be relatively inexpensive, while others turn out to be very expensive. The problems are frequently complicated enough that identifying the cheapest manner of achieving an objective cannot be accomplished without analyzing the situation.

Cost-effectiveness analysis frequently involves an *optimization procedure*. An optimization procedure, in this context, is merely a systematic method for finding the lowest-cost means of accomplishing the objective. This procedure does not, in general, produce an efficient allocation because the predetermined objective may not be efficient. All efficient policies are cost-effective, but not all cost-effective policies are efficient.[32]

These principles can be illustrated by defining a desirable pollution control policy. Cost effectiveness can be used to find the least-cost means of meeting a particular standard and its associated cost. Using this cost as a benchmark case, we can estimate how much costs can be expected to increase from this minimum level if policies which are not cost-effective are implemented. Cost-effectiveness analysis can also be used to determine how much compliance costs can be expected to change if the EPA chooses a more stringent or less stringent standard. The case study presented in Example 4.3 not only illustrates the use of cost-effectiveness analysis, but it also shows that costs can be very sensitive to the regulatory approach chosen by the EPA.

---

31 This objective is usually specified by the political process. A survey of evidence on the physical consequences of alternatives is used to judge the "appropriate" level.

32 You may recognize an analogy from your introductory economics course. A firm which uses the cheapest possible method for producing a given output will not be maximizing profits unless the chosen output level is the one which maximizes profits. Thus profit maximization implies cost minimization, but the converse is not necessarily true.

EXAMPLE 4.3

NO$_2$ Control in Chicago: An Example of Cost-Effectiveness Analysis

As part of its mandate to implement and enforce the Clean Air Act, the Environmental Protection Agency, a part of the executive branch of the federal government, commissioned a study to examine, among other things, the cost consequences of implementing two different air quality standards by a variety of regulatory approaches. The final report, issued on September 17, 1979, shows just how sensitive costs in this area are to the regulatory approach.

The authors of the report used information on the cost of control for each of 797 stationary sources of nitrogen oxide emissions in the city of Chicago for various degrees of control. A total of 100 receptors measured the air quality at 100 different locations within the city. The relationship between ambient air quality at those receptors and emissions from the 797 sources was then modeled using mathematical equations. Once these equations were estimated, the model was calibrated to ensure that it was capable of recreating the actual situation in Chicago. Following successful calibration, this model was used to simulate what would happen if EPA were to take various regulatory actions.

The first issue addressed was, "How much would costs increase, in the least cost solution, if the ambient air quality standard were changed from 500 to 250 μ/m^3 per cubic meter?" Note that the latter implies much cleaner air than the former. The analysis indicated that the least-cost means of meeting the more stringent standard would cost about $24 million a year, while the cost of meeting the 500-μ/m^3 standard would be only $1 million. In other words, the stricter standard implies an annual cost some 24 times as high. Note that this analysis does not give any hint as to whether the additional expenditure is efficient. One would need the benefit estimates to decide that.

The second issue addressed was the sensitivity of control costs for meeting the more stringent 250-μ/m^3 standard to the regulatory approach chosen by EPA. The study considered several possibilities, two of which were (1) equal percentage reductions in all sources and (2) the least-cost solution. The results were striking. To ensure that the standard was met by all receptors under the equal-percentage reduction approach, all sources were required to cut back their emissions by 90% at an annual cost of $254 million. The least-cost solution, which targets the greatest reductions at those firms capable of achieving them most cheaply, was estimated to cost only $24 million per year.

Conclusions such as these have triggered a series of major reforms in air pollution control which are designed to reduce costs without sacrificing air quality. These reforms have reduced some of the conflict between environmentalists and industrialists. We discuss these in Chapter 15.

Source: Robert J. Anderson, Jr., Robert O. Reid, and Eugene P. Seskin, *An Analysis of Alternative Policies for Attaining and Maintaining a Short-Term NO$_2$ Standard* (Princeton, NJ: MATHTECH, 1979).

IMPACT ANALYSIS

What can be done when the information needed to perform a benefit-cost analysis or a cost-effectiveness analysis is not available? The analytical technique designed to deal with this problem is called *impact analysis*. An impact analysis, regardless of whether it focuses on economic impact or environmental impact or both, attempts to quantify the consequences of various actions.

In contrast to benefit-cost analysis, a pure impact analysis makes no attempt to convert all these consequences into a one-dimensional measure, such as dollars, to ensure comparability. In contrast to both benefit-cost analysis and cost-effectiveness analysis, impact analysis does not necessarily attempt to optimize. Impact analysis places a large amount of relatively undigested information at the disposal of the policymaker. It is up to the policymaker to assess the importance of the various consequences and act accordingly.

On January 1, 1970, President Nixon signed the National Environmental Policy Act of 1969. This act, among other things, directed all agencies of the federal government to

include in every recommendation or report on proposals for legislation and other major Federal actions significantly affecting the quality of the human environment, a detailed statement by the responsible official on—
(i) the environmental impact of the proposed action,
(ii) any adverse environmental effects which cannot be avoided
should the proposal be implemented,
(iii) alternatives to the proposed action,
(iv) the relationship between local short-term uses of man's environment and the maintenance and enhancement of long-term productivity, and
(v) any irreversible and irretrievable commitments of resources which would be involved in the proposed action should it be implemented.[33]

This was the beginning of the environmental impact statement, which is now a familiar, if controversial, part of environmental policy making.

Current environmental impact statements are more sophisticated than their early predecessors and may contain a benefit-cost analysis or a cost-effectiveness analysis in addition to other more traditional impact measurements. Historically, however, the tendency had been to issue huge environmental impact statements which are virtually impossible to comprehend in their entirety.

In response, the Council on Environmental Quality, which, by law, administers the environmental impact statement process, has set content standards that are now resulting in shorter, more concise statements. To the extent that

---

33 83 Stat. 853.

they merely quantify consequences, statements can avoid the problem of "hidden value judgments" that sometimes plague benefit-cost analysis, but they do so only by bombarding the policymakers with masses of noncomparable information. All three of the techniques discussed in this chapter are useful, but none of them can stake a claim as being universally the "best" approach. The nature of the information which is available and its reliability make a difference.

SUMMARY

We have examined the most prominent, but certainly not the only, techniques available to supply policymakers with the information needed to implement efficient policy. We have seen that benefit-cost analysis offers the most concrete guidance and is often very useful. For some functions, such as choosing the efficient level of pollution control, it is difficult to implement. Even when difficult to implement, the exercise of identifying the costs and benefits, as well as assessing their importance, is an extremely valuable part of the policy process. Unless one policy tends to so dominate the others that the outcome is not sensitive to uncertainty about possible outcomes or to a lack of reliability in the underlying data, however, we certainly have grounds to suspect any specific number or numbers which come out of that process.

Even when benefits are difficult to calculate, however, economic analysis in the form of cost effectiveness can be valuable. This technique can establish the least expensive ways to accomplish predetermined policy goals and to assess the extra costs involved when policies other than the least-cost policy are chosen. What it cannot do is answer the question of whether those predetermined policy goals are efficient.

At the end of the spectrum is impact analysis, which merely identifies and quantifies the impacts of particular policies without any pretense of optimality or even comparability of the information generated. Impact analysis does not guarantee an efficient outcome.

This chapter has examined a major issue which will reoccur throughout the book—the role of information in structuring an appropriate relationship between humankind and the environment. We have seen information problems at many levels—the absence of knowledge about the consequences of various courses of action; inability to compare different types of information in an uncontroversial way, even when we can identify impacts; and possible biases in the structuring of information, as well as in the process of transmitting it to policymakers. We must remain cognizant of these issues as we examine specific environmental problems. We begin that investigation in the next chapter with population growth, which is a major influence on both the timing and the intensity of many other environmental problems.

FURTHER READING

Ackerman, Bruce, et al. *The Uncertain Search for Environmental Quality* (New York: Free Press, 1974). An interdisciplinary team critically examines the pitfalls of incorporating complex economic analysis in the policy process, using, as a case study, water pollution control in the Delaware Estuary.

Cummings, Ronald G., David S. Brookshire, and William D. Schulze. *Valuing Environmental Goods: An Assessment of the Contingent Valuation Method* (Totowa, NJ: Rowman and Littlefield, 1986). A critical evaluation of the contingent valuation method by both practitioners and impartial reviewers.

Dixon, John A. and Maynard M. Hufschmidt. *Economic Valuation Techniques for the Environment* (Baltimore: The Johns Hopkins University Press, 1986). Several case studies on the application of valuation techniques to environmental problems in less developed countries.

Kelman, Steven. "Cost-Benefit Analysis—An Ethical Critique," *Regulation* (January/February 1981), 33–40. Kelman suggests that attempts to expand the use of benefit-cost analysis in the areas of environmental, health, and safety regulation raise troubling ethical questions.

Kneese, Allen V. *Measuring the Benefits of Clean Air and Water* (Washington, DC: Resources for the Future, 1984). An accessible introduction to a large number of studies attempting to quantify the benefits of cleaner air and water.

Lave, Lester B., ed. *Quantitative Risk Assessment in Regulation* (Washington, DC: Brookings Institution, 1982). This book examines the requirements for quantitative risk assessment and the role it has played in recent decisions of several regulatory agencies. The authors of the essays see a much larger possible role for quantitative risk assessment.

Mitchell, Robert Cameron and Richard T. Carson. *Using Surveys To Value Public Goods: The Contingent Valuation Method* (Washington: Resources for the Future, 1989). A comprehensive examination of contingent valuation research with brief summaries of representative studies.

Peskin, Henry M. and Eugene P. Seskin. *Cost-Benefit Analysis and Water Pollution Control Policy* (Washington: Urban Institute, 1975). A collection of essays by some of the foremost scholars in the field concerning the problems with and prospects for using cost-benefit analysis to guide water pollution control policy.

Smith, V. Kerry, ed. *Environmental Policy under Reagan's Executive Order: The Role of Benefit-Cost Analysis* (Chapel Hill: The University of North Carolina Press, 1984). Written by leading practitioners, this collection of essays takes stock of how President Reagan's Executive Order No. 12291 has affected the making of policy.

ADDITIONAL REFERENCES

Bailey, Martin, J. *Reducing Risks to Life: Measurement of the Benefits* (Washington, DC: American Enterprise Institute for Public Policy Research, 1980).

Boyle, Kevin J. and Richard C. Bishop. "Valuing Wildlife in Benefit-Cost Analysis: A Case Study Involving Endangered Species," *Water Resources Research* 23 (May 1987): 943-950.

Brookshire, D. S., M. A. Thayer, W. D. Schulze, and R. C. d'Arge. "Valuing Public Goods: A Comparison of Survey and Hedonic Approaches," *The American Economic Review* 72 (March 1982): 165-177.

Clawson, Marion and Jack Knetsch. *Economics of Outdoor Recreation* (Baltimore: Johns Hopkins University Press for Resources for the Future, 1966).

Fisher, Anthony C., John V. Krutilla, and Charles J. Chicchetti. "Alternative Uses of Natural Environments: The Economics of Environmental Modification," in *Natural Environments: Studies in Theoretical and Applied Analysis*, John V. Krutilla, ed. (Washington: Johns Hopkins University Press for Resources for the Future, 1972): 18-53.

Freeman, A. Myrick III. *The Benefits of Environmental Improvement: Theory and Practice* (Baltimore: Johns Hopkins University Press for Resources for the Future, 1979).

Freeman, A. Myrick III. *Air and Water Pollution Control: A Benefit-Cost Assessment* (New York: Wiley, 1982).

Freeman, A. Myrick III. *The Benefits of Air and Water Pollution Control: A Review and Synthesis of Recent Estimates*, a report prepared for the Council on Environmental Quality (December 1979).

Haveman, Robert H. *The Economic Performance of Public Investments: An Ex Post Evaluation of Water Resource Investments* (Baltimore: Johns Hopkins University Press for Resources for the Future, 1972).

Hufschmidt, Maynard, David E. James, Anton D. Meister, Blair T. Bower, and John A. Dixon. *Environment, Natural Systems, and Development: An Economic Valuation Guide* (Baltimore: Johns Hopkins University Press, 1983).

Lave, Lester B. and Eugene P. Seskin. *Air Pollution and Human Health* (Baltimore: Johns Hopkins University Press, 1977).

Mikesell, Raymond. *The Rate of Discount for Evaluating Public Projects* (Washington DC: The American Enterprise Institute for Public Policy Research, 1977).

Rowe, R. D., R. d'Arge, and D. S. Brookshire. "An Experiment on the Economic Value of Visibility," *Journal of Environmental Economics and Management* 7 (March 1980): 1-19.

Smith, V. Kerry, ed., *Environmental Resources and Applied Welfare Economics: Essays in Honor of John V. Krutilla* (Washington, DC: Resources for the Future, 1988).

DISCUSSION QUESTIONS

1. Is risk neutrality an appropriate assumption for cost-benefit analysis? Why or why not? Does it seem more appropriate for some environmental problems than others? If so, which ones? If you were evaluating the desirability of locating a hazardous waste incinerator in a particular town, would the Arrow-Lind rationale for risk neutrality be appropriate? Why or why not?

2. Was the executive order issued by President Reagan mandating a heavier use of cost-benefit analysis in regulatory rule making a step toward establishing a more rational regulatory structure, or was it a subversion of the environmental policy process? Why?

3. Certain environmental laws prohibit EPA from considering the costs of meeting various standards when the levels of the standards are set. Is this a good example of "putting first things first" or simply an unjustifiable waste of resources? Why?

PROBLEMS

1. In Mark A. Cohen, "The Costs and Benefits of Oil Spill Prevention and Enforcement," *Journal of Environmental Economics and Management* 13 (June 1986), an attempt was made to quantify the marginal benefits and marginal costs of U.S. Coast Guard enforcement activity in the area of oil spill prevention. His analysis suggests (p. 185) that the marginal per gallon benefit from the current level of enforcement activity is $7.50 while the marginal per gallon cost is $5.50. Assuming these numbers are correct, would you recommend that the Coast Guard increase, decrease, or hold at the current level their enforcement activity? Why?

2. In his book *Reducing Risks to Life: Measuring the Benefits*, Martin Bailey estimates that the cost per life saved by current government risk-reducing programs ranges from $72,000 for kidney transplants to $624,976,000 for a proposed standard to reduce occupational exposure to acrylonitrile.
   (a) Assuming these values to be correct, how might efficiency be enhanced in these two programs?
   (b) Should the government strive to equalize the marginal costs per life saved across all life-saving programs?

CHAPTER FIVE

The Population Problem

The 1990s will be a crucial decade. The choices of the next ten years will decide the speed of population growth for much of the next century; ... they will decide whether the pace of damage to the environment speeds up or slows down; ... they may decide the future of the earth as habitation for humans.

Dr. NAFIS SADIK, *Executive Director of the UN Population Fund, The State of the World Population* 1990

INTRODUCTION

In Chapter 1 we examined two strikingly different views of what the future holds for the world economic system. At the heart of those differences lie divergent views of the world population problem. Meadows and his team see population growth as continuing relentlessly, putting enormous pressure on food and environmental resources. Kahn, on the other hand, sees the world as being in a period of transition from high rates of natural increase to strikingly lower ones, culminating eventually in zero population growth. Because of abundant technological possibilities for satisfying the temporarily increasing, but eventually stable, population, Kahn's optimistic outlook is maintained.

These views are symptomatic of a debate that has deep historical roots. Thomas Malthus, a late eighteenth-century and early nineteenth-century classical economist, concluded that population growth posed a trap for nations seeking to develop. Temporary increases in income were seen as triggering increases in population until the land could no longer supply adequate food. Paul Ehrlich has brought this Malthusian argument into the twentieth century by arguing the very existence of all forms of life on the planet is jeopardized by population growth. In his provocatively titled book, *The Population Bomb*, he has argued that population is not merely *an* important problem but is *the* problem in ensuring long-term survival of the species.

Contrasting views are held by representatives of Third World countries and some prominent population economists, such as Julian Simon, who maintains that not only has Ehrlich overstated the seriousness of the problem, but also that he fails to recognize that population growth in many of the developing countries is desirable. It should be clear from this brief review that no consensus exists either on the seriousness of the problem or, indeed, whether the problem exists at all.

In this chapter we examine the macroeconomic issues relating to population and economic growth, as well as the microeconomic issues dealing with economic determinants of fertility. We briefly examine the effects that population growth and economic growth each have on the other. We then focus on a conceptual approach for understanding the demand for children, the empirical evidence which assesses the validity of this framework, and the possibilities for controlling population.

HISTORICAL PERSPECTIVE

World Population Growth

It has been estimated that at the beginning of the Christian era, A.D. 1, world population stood at about 250,000,000 people and was growing at 0.04% per year (not 4%!). When the world's population passed 4,000,000,000, it was growing at an annual rate around 2.0% per year. If that 2.0% growth rate were to continue unabated, the world's population would double in only 35 years. Since the beginning of time, the population has grown to over 4 billion people; at a 2.0% growth rate, the next 4 billion could take only 35 years.

In recent years, with the notable exception of Africa, the average rate of population growth has declined (Table 5.1). This slowdown has been experienced in both developed and less developed countries, although rates remain higher in the less developed countries.

The World Fertility Survey, a multinational survey of some 400,000 women in 61 countries, revealed a significant downward trend in fertility and birth rates during the 1970s.[1] This tendency appears in both developing and developed nations, with only African nations bucking the trend.[2] The survey found several

---

1 For an analysis of trends, see W. Parker Maudlin, "Patterns of Fertility Decline in Developing Countries, 1970-5" in *Fertility Decline in the Less Developed Countries*, Nick Eberstadt, ed. (New York: Praeger: 72-96.

2 For an analysis of the factors underlying the tendency of African nations to be experiencing increases in fertility rates, see John C. Caldwell, "Fertility in Africa," in *Fertility Decline in the Less Developed Countries*, Nick Eberstadt, ed. (New York: Praeger, 1981): 97-118.

TABLE 5.1   Annual Average Rate of World Population Growth 1965–1970, 1975–1980, 1985–1990 (percent)

	1965–70	*1975–80*	*1985–90*
World	2.04	1.75	1.63
Africa	2.62	2.97	3.02
Asia	2.43	1.86	1.63
Europe	0.64	0.42	0.27
South America	2.45	2.27	2.08
United States	1.08	1.06	0.86

Source: From *World Resources 1988–89* by The World Resources Institute. Copyright © 1988 by World Resources and the International Institute for Environment and Development in collaboration with the United Nations Environment Programme. Reprinted by permission of Basic Books, Inc., a division of HarperCollins Publishers.

apparent causes, including increased use of contraception, a growing preference for fewer children, and couples marrying later.

Although the trend toward falling birthrates is pervasive, the fact remains that most developing countries still have, and can be expected to have, substantial increases in their populations. Some 90% of the population growth between 1980 and 2000 is expected to occur in the poorer countries.

For example, in 1985–1990, Honduras, Kenya, Liberia, Zimbabwe, and Nicaragua all had annual average growth rates in excess of 3.0%. During the same period, East Germany, Italy, and Belgium all experienced annual average growth rates of less than one-tenth of 1%. Austria, Denmark, Sweden, and Germany all currently have declining populations.[3]

Population Growth in the United States

As seen in Table 5.1, population growth in the United States has followed the general declining pattern of most of the developed world, although in most periods American growth rates have exceeded the average for Europe by a substantial margin. These large reductions in American population growth rates have been due primarily to declines in the birthrate, which fell from a high of 55.2 live births per thousand population in 1820 to only 14.6 live births per thousand in 1975, the lowest recorded birthrate in the period covered by the data. By 1987 the birthrate had climbed back to 15.7 (Figure 5.1).

---

3 The comparative population growth rate figures can be found in World Resources Institute, *World Resources: 1990-91* (New York: Oxford University Press, 1990): 254-255.

FIGURE 5.1 U.S. birthrates from 1880 to 1987.

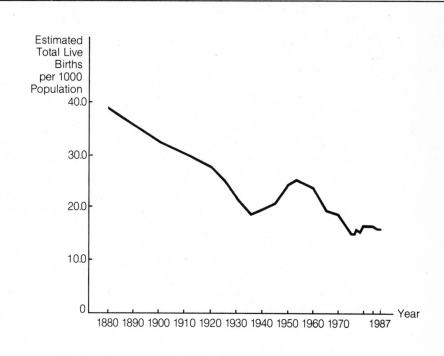

Sources: U.S. Bureau of the Census, *Historical Statistics of the United States, Colonial Times to 1970*, part 1, Series B5-B10, p. 49; *Statistical Abstract of the United States, 1989*, p. 61; and U.S. National Center for Health Statistics, *Vital Statistics of the United States*, annual, and unpublished data.

Birthrates, however, provide a rather crude measure of the underlying population trends, primarily because they do not account for age structure. To understand the effect of age structure, let's separate the birthrate experience into two components: (1) the number of persons in the childbearing years, and (2) the number of children those persons are bearing.

To quantify the second of these components, the Census Bureau uses a concept known as the *total fertility rate*, which is the number of live births an average woman has in her lifetime if, at each year of age, she experiences the average birthrates occurring in the general population of similarly aged women. This concept can be used to determine what level of fertility would, if continued, lead to a stationary population. A *stationary population* is one in which age- and sex-specific fertility rates yield a birthrate which is constant and equal to the death rate, so the growth rate is zero. The level of the total fertility rate which is compatible with a stationary population is called the *replacement rate*. Rates higher than the replacement rate would lead to population growth, while rates lower would lead to population declines. Once the replacement fertility rate is reached, the World Bank estimates that it takes approximately 25 years before the population stabilizes, due to the large numbers of families in the childbearing years. As the age structure reaches its older equilibrium, the growth rate declines until a stationary population is attained.

In the United States, the replacement rate is 2.11. The two children replace the mother and her mate, while the extra 0.11 is to compensate for those women who do not survive the childbearing years and because slightly more than 50% of births are males. The United States total fertility rate dropped below the replacement rate in 1972 and has remained below it ever since (Figure 5.2). In 1986 (the latest year for which data were available) the rate stood at 1.84. If it

FIGURE 5.2   Total U.S. fertility rate, 1940–1986.

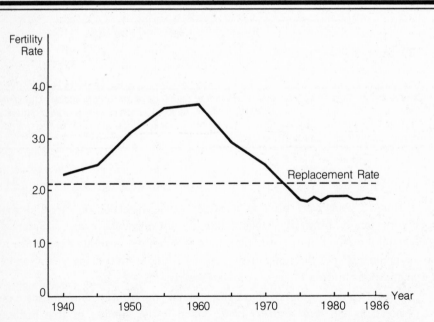

Source: U.S. Bureau of the Census, *Historical Statistics of the United States, Colonial Times to 1970*, part 1, B11, p. 50; *Statistical Abstract of the United States, 1989*, p. 64; and U.S. National Center for Health Statistics, *Vital Statistics of the United States*, annual, and unpublished data.

were to remain at this level for 25 years, the U.S. population could eventually be expected to decline at a rate of 5.2% per year.

This introduction to the population situation serves to raise two questions: (1) What is the relationship between population growth and economic growth? and (2) How can the rate of population growth be altered when alteration is appropriate? The first question lays the groundwork for considering the effect of population growth on quality of life, including the effects of a stationary population. The second allows us to consider public policies geared toward manipulating the rate of population growth when desirable.

EFFECTS OF POPULATION GROWTH ON ECONOMIC GROWTH

A number of questions guide our inquiry. Does population growth enhance or inhibit the opportunities of a country's citizens? Does the answer depend on the stage of development? Given that several countries are now entering a period of declining population growth, what are the possible effects of this decline on economic growth?

Population growth affects economic growth and, as long as each person contributes something, those effects generally are positively correlated. As long as their marginal product is positive, additional people mean additional output. Since this is not a very restrictive condition, it should usually hold true.

However, the existence of a positive marginal product is not a very appropriate test of the desirability of population growth! Perhaps a better one is to ask whether population growth positively affects the average citizen. Whenever the marginal product of an additional person is lower than the average product, adding more persons simply reduces the welfare of the average citizen. Why?

In the range of marginal productivities between zero and the average product, economic growth measured in aggregate terms would increase but measured in per capita terms would decrease. Similarly, there is a range of marginal productivities—those greater than the average product—where economic growth increases regardless of whether it is measured in aggregate or per capita terms. Whether or not the material status of the average citizen is improved by population growth becomes a question of whether the marginal product of additional people is higher or lower than the average product.

To facilitate our examination of the population-related determinants of economic growth, let's examine a rather simple definition of output:

$$O = L \cdot X \,,$$

where O is the output level, X is the output per worker, and L is the number of workers. This equation can be expressed in per capita terms by dividing both sides by population, denoted as P:

FIGURE 5.3   Age structure of two populations.

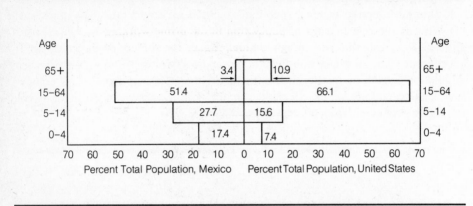

Source: Nancy Birdsall, "Population Growth and Poverty in the Developing World," *Population Bulletin* 35 (Population Reference Bureau, Washington, DC, 1980).

$$\frac{O}{P} = \frac{L}{P} \cdot X \, .$$

This equation now states that output per capita is determined by the product of two factors: the share of the population which is in the labor force and the output per worker. Each of these two factors provides a channel through which population growth affects economic growth.

The most direct effect of population growth on the percentage of the population employed, the *age structure effect*, results from induced changes in the age distribution. Suppose that we were to compare two populations, one rapidly growing and one slowly growing. The one with the rapid growth would contain a much larger percentage of younger persons (Figure 5.3).

Due to its slow growth, the U.S. population is in general older. While approximately 45% of Mexico's population is 14 years of age or younger, the comparable figure for the United States is 23%. This is reinforced at the other end of the age structure, where some 10.9% of the U.S. population is 65 or older, compared with only 3.4% in Mexico.

These differences in the age structure have mixed effects on the percentage of the labor force available to be employed. The abundance of youth in a rapidly growing population creates a large supply of people too young to work, a situation referred to as the *youth effect*. On the other hand, a country characterized by slow population growth has a rather larger percentage of persons who have reached, or are past, the traditional retirement age of 65, a situation referred to as the *retirement effect*. Some developing countries are experiencing both effects simultaneously as better public health policies reduce death rates while birthrates remain high. How do the youth and retirement effects interact to determine the percentage of the population in the labor force? Does the youth effect dominate the retirement effect?

Examine the percentage of population in the prime working ages, 15–64. As Figure 5.3 shows, this percentage is much higher for the United States. A larger percentage of the population is in the working force in the United States than in Mexico. For Mexico the youth effect dominates.

This dominance of the youth effect generalizes to other countries. For example, in 1990 the African countries had an average of 51.7% of the population in the prime working age while European countries averaged 66.9%.[4] High population growth retards per capita economic growth by decreasing the percentage of the population in the labor force.

Rapid growth also affects the percentage available to be employed through the *female availability effect*. With a slower growth rate and fewer children to care for, more women are available to join the labor force. Both the dominance of the youth effect (over the retirement effect) and the female availability effect suggest that rapid population growth reduces the percentage of the population in the labor force which, in turn, has a depressing effect on economic growth per capita.

How about possible relationships between population growth and the second factor, the amount of output produced by the average worker? The most common way to enhance productivity is through the accumulation of capital. As the capital stock is augmented (for example, through the introduction of assembly lines or production machinery), workers become more productive. Is there any connection between population growth and capital accumulation?[5]

The main connection examined by researchers has been between savings and capital accumulation. The availability of savings determines the level of additions to the capital stock. Availability of savings, in turn, is affected in part by the age structure of the population. Older populations are presumed to save more because less is spent directly on the care and nurturing of children. Therefore, all other things being equal, societies with rapidly growing populations could be expected to save proportionately less. This lowered availability of savings would lead to lower amounts of capital stock augmentation and lower productivity per worker.

A final model suggesting a negative effect of population growth on economic growth involves the presence of some fixed essential factor for which limited substitution possibilities exist (land or raw materials, for example). In this case, the *law of diminishing marginal productivity* applies. This law states that in the presence of a fixed factor (land), successively larger additions of a variable factor

---

4 World Resources Institute, *World Resources: 1990–91* (New York: Oxford University Press, 1990): 256–257.

5 This connection is clearly articulated in Ansley J. Coale and Edgar M. Hoover, *Population Growth and Economic Development in Low Income Countries* (Princeton, NJ: Princeton University Press, 1958).

(labor) will eventually lead to a decline in the marginal productivity of the variable factor. It suggests that in the presence of fixed factors successive increases in labor will drive the marginal product down. When it falls below the average product, per capita income will decline with further increases in the population.

Not all arguments suggest that growth in output per capita will be restrained by population growth. Perhaps the most compelling arguments for the view that population growth enhances per capita growth are those involving technological progress and *economies of scale* (Figure 5.4).

The vertical axis shows marginal productivity measured in units of output. The horizontal axis describes various levels of labor employed on a fixed amount of land. Population growth implies an increase in the labor force, which is recorded on the graph as a movement to the right on the horizontal axis.

The curve labeled $P(t_1)$ shows the functional relationship between the marginal product of labor and the amount of labor employed on a fixed plot of land at a particular point in time (t_1). Different curves represent different points in time because in each period of time there exists a unique state-of-the-art in the knowledge of how to use the labor most effectively. Thus, as time passes, technological progress occurs, advancing the state-of-the-art and shifting the productivity curves outward, as demonstrated by $P(t_2)$ and $P(t_3)$.

Three situations are demonstrated by Figure 5.4. At time t_1, an application of $L(t_1)$ yields a marginal product of $M(t_1)$. At times t_2 and t_3, the application of $L(t_2)$ and $L(t_3)$ units of labor respectively yield $M(t_2)$ and $M(t_3)$ marginal units of output. Marginal products have increased as larger amounts of labor were added.

Consider what would have happened, however, if the state of technical knowledge had not increased. The increase in labor from $L(t_2)$ to $L(t_3)$ would have been governed by the $P(t_1)$ curve, and the marginal product would have declined from A to B. This is precisely the result anticipated by the law of diminishing marginal productivity. Technological progress provides one means of escaping the law of diminishing marginal productivity.

The second source of increase in output per worker is economies of scale. Economies of scale occur when increases in inputs lead to a more than proportionate increase in output. Population growth, by increasing demand for output, allows these economies of scale to be exploited. In the United States, at least, this has been a potent source of growth. Edward Dennison, in a major study of U.S. economic growth, concluded that economies of scale accounted for slightly over 10% of growth in total potential national income per unit input in the 1929–69 period.[6] While it seems clear that the population level in the United States is already sufficient to exploit economies of scale, the same is not necessarily true for all developing countries.

---

6 Edward Dennison, *Accounting for United States Economic Growth, 1929–1969* (Washington, DC: Brookings Institution, 1974): 128–130.

FIGURE 5.4   Technological progress and the law of diminishing returns.

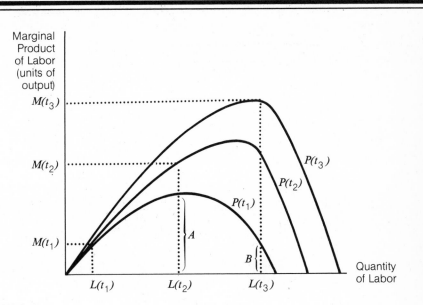

In the absense of trade restrictions, however, the relevant market now is the global market, not the domestic market. The level of domestic population has little to do with the ability to exploit economies of scale in the modern global economy unless tariffs, quotas, or other trade barriers prevent the exploitation of foreign markets. If trade restrictions are a significant barrier, the appropriate remedy would be reducing trade restrictions, not boosting the local population.

Because these a priori arguments suggest that population growth could either enhance or retard economic growth, it is necessary to rely on empirical studies to sort out the relative importance of these effects. Several researchers have attempted to validate the premise that population growth inhibits per capita economic growth. Their attempts were based on the notion that if the premise were true, one should be able to observe lower growth in per capita income in countries with higher population growth rates, all other things being equal.

A study for the National Research Council conducted an intensive review of the evidence.[7] Does the evidence support the expectations? Their major conclusions were:

---

7 Working Group on Population Growth and Economic Development, National Research Council, *Population Growth and Economic Development: Policy Questions* (Washington, DC: National Academy Press, 1986).

1. Little evidence exists to support the expectation that the average savings rate depends on growth rates or the age structure of the population.

2. Slower population growth would raise the amount of capital per worker and, hence, the productivity per worker.

3. Slower population growth is unlikely to result in a net reduction in agricultural productivity and might well raise it.

4. There is no significant relation between national population density and economies of scale.

5. Rapid population growth puts more pressure on both depletable and renewable resources.

Rapid population growth may also increase the inequality of income. Perhaps the clearest statement of this argument comes from Peter Lindert.[8] He believes that high population growth increases the degree of inequality for a variety of reasons, but the most important involve a depressing effect on the earning capacity of children and on wages.

The ability to provide for the education and training of children, given fixed budgets of time and money, is a function of the number of children in the family—the fewer the children, the higher the proportion of income (and wealth, such as land) available to develop each child's earning capacity. Since low-income families tend to have larger families than high-income families do, the offspring from low-income families are usually more disadvantaged. The result is a growing gap between the rich and the poor.

Thomas Espenshade has provided some revealing estimates of parental expenditures on child rearing in the United States that tend to confirm certain key aspects of this argument.[9] The average expenditure to raise a child to age 18 depends crucially on income level and the size of the family, ranging from an expenditure of $135,700 (in constant 1981 dollars) for high-income couples including two wage earners, and only one child, to $58,300 spent on the average child by a lower-income couple including a single wage earner and three children. Adding in college expenditures where appropriate would boost these figures considerably.

Espenshade also examines the proportion of the typical family's income spent on child rearing as well as the sensitivity of this proportion to the number of children in the family. According to his analysis, families with only one child commit about 30% of total family expenditures to their child. This percentage

---

8 Peter Lindert. *Fertility and Scarcity in America* (Princeton, NJ: Princeton University Press, 1978).

9 Thomas J. Espenshade, *Investing in Children: New Estimates of Parental Expenditures* (Washington, DC: Urban Institute Press, 1984).

rises to between 40 and 45% for two-child families and nearly 50% in three-child families. The detailed data in this study make clear that average expenditures per child consistently decline as the number of children in a family increases.

Another link between population growth and income inequality results from the effect of population growth on the labor supply. High population growth could increase the supply of labor faster than otherwise, depressing wage rates vis à vis profit rates. Since low-income groups have a higher relative reliance on wages for their income than do the rich, this effect would also increase the degree of inequality.

After an extensive review of the historical record for the United States, Lindert concludes that

> There seems to be good reason for believing that extra fertility affects the size and "quality" of the labor force in ways that raise income inequalities. Fertility, like immigration, tends to reduce the average "quality" of the labor force, by reducing the amounts of family and public school resources devoted to each child. The retardation in the historic improvement in labor force quality has in turn held back the rise in the incomes of the unskilled relative to those enjoyed by skilled labor and wealth-holders [p. 258].

Lindert's interpretation of the American historical record does seem to be valid for developing countries. The National Research Council study found that slower population growth would decrease income inequality, and it would raise the education and health levels of the children. This link between rapid population growth and income inequality provides an additional powerful motivation for controlling population. Slower population growth reduces income inequality.

On the level of individual countries some powerful evidence is beginning to emerge on the negative environmental effects of population density when coupled with poverty. In Africa, forestlands are declining as trees are cut down to provide fuel for cooking for a expanding population. Due to a shortage of land, peasants in Bangladesh settle on islands formed from the silt deposited by soil erosion. Several thousands were drowned when a cyclone hit the area in 1985. In Brazil and Southeast Asia, peasants are forced to farm marginal lands which rapidly erode and lose their nutrients. Forced to sacrifice long-term objectives merely to survive, the poor are becoming both a major source of environmental problems and the major victims of them. Population growth bears some responsibility for both the degree of poverty and the intensity of the problems it triggers.

EFFECTS OF ECONOMIC GROWTH ON POPULATION GROWTH

Up to this point, we have considered the effect of population growth on economic growth. We now have to examine the converse relationship. Does economic growth affect population growth? Table 5.1 suggests that it may, since the higher-income countries are characterized by lower population growth rates.

This suspicion is reinforced by some further evidence. Most of the industrialized countries have passed through three stages of population growth. The conceptual framework which organizes this evidence is called the *theory of demographic transition*. This theory suggests that as nations develop they eventually reach a point where birthrates fall (Figure 5.5).

During stage 1, the period immediately prior to industrialization, birthrates are stable and slightly higher than death rates, ensuring population growth. During stage 2, the period immediately following the initiation of industrialization, death rates fall dramatically with no accompanying change in birthrates. This decline in mortality results in a marked increase in life expectancy and a rise in the population growth rate. In Western Europe, stage 2 is estimated to have lasted somewhere around 50 years.

Stage 3, the period of demographic transition, involves large declines in the birthrate which exceed the continued declines in the death rate. Thus, the period of demographic transition involves further increases in life expectancy, but rather smaller population growth rates than characterized the second stage. The Chilean experience with the demographic transition is illustrated in Figure 5.6. Can you identify the stages?

The theory of demographic transition is useful because it suggests that reductions in population growth might accompany rising standards of living, at least

FIGURE 5.5   The demographic transition.

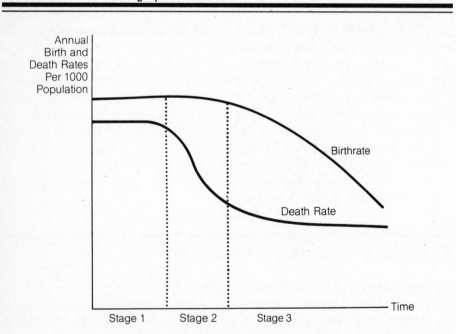

FIGURE 5.6   Annual birthrates, death rates, and rates of natural population increase in Chile, 1929–1970.

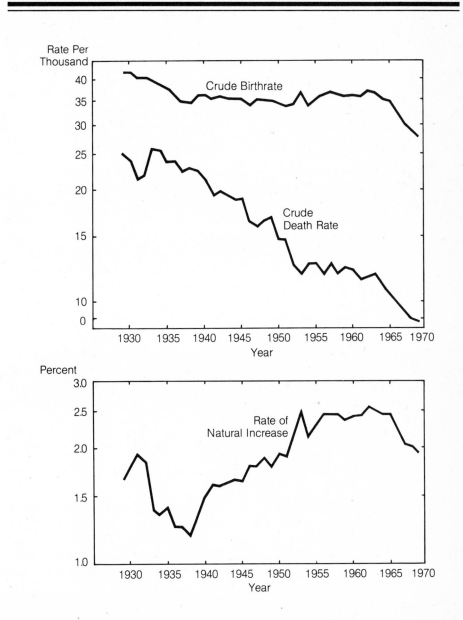

Source: Reprinted by permission of Greenwood Publishing Group, Inc., Westport CT, from *Population, Public Policy, and Economic Development*, edited by Michael C. Keeley. Copyright © 1976 by Praeger Publishers, Inc.

in the long run. However, it also leaves many questions unanswered. Why does the fall in birthrates occur? Can the process be speeded up? Will lower-income countries automatically experience demographic transition as living standards improve? Are industrialization or better designed agricultural production systems possible solutions to "the population problem"?

To answer these questions it is necessary to begin to look more deeply into the sources of change behind the demographic transition. Once these sources are identified and understood they can be manipulated in such a way as to produce the maximum social benefit.

THE ECONOMIC APPROACH TO POPULATION CONTROL

Is the current rate of population growth efficient? Is it sustainable? The issue of sustainability is most easily dealt with in specific natural resource settings (such as the ability to produce sufficient food) so intensive consideration of that question will be deferred until succeeding chapters.

The efficiency question can be attacked in two ways. The first is to conduct a benefit-cost analysis of population control to see whether some government control would maximize efficiency. Such a study was conducted by Enke and Zind (Example 5.1). Focused purely on the effects of additional population on output per capita, the study found that intensified population control measures would increase net benefits.

The demonstration that population growth reduces per capita income, however, is not sufficient to prove that an inefficiency exists. If the reduced output is borne entirely by the families of the children, this reduction may represent a conscious choice by parents to sacrifice production in order to have more children. The net benefit gained from having more children (not measured by Enke and Zind) would exceed the net benefit lost as output per person declined.

To establish whether or not population control is efficient, we must discover whether there are potential behavioral biases toward overpopulation. Will parents always make efficient childbearing decisions?

A negative response seems appropriate for several reasons. The first is derived from the previously discussed evidence that high population growth may exacerbate income inequality. Income equality is a public good.[10] The population as a whole cannot be excluded from the degree of income equality which exists. Furthermore, it is an indivisible good because, in a given society, the prevailing income distribution is the same for all the citizens of that society.

---

10 Some studies have also suggested that population pressures are a key contributor to political instability, especially in Africa and the Middle East. See Linda Feldman, "Study Correlates Population Rise, Political Instability," *The Christian Science Monitor* (June 26, 1989): 8.

EXAMPLE 5.1

The Value of an Averted Birth

If population growth tends to reduce average income, then the nation experiencing this population growth would have an incentive to spend money on population control. The determination of how much money should be spent depends on a comparison of the costs of the population control program with the value of an averted birth.

Enke and Zind developed a simulation model to assess the value of an averted birth. The model allowed for substitution among capital and labor, the restraining effect of the dependency ratio, and the effect of an age structure and income on saving. To obtain the value of averted births, they compared a scenario with no birth control to one in which a reduction in fertility over a 30-year period was compatible with 50% of all women in each age group practicing contraception. The implied terminal fertility rate was approximately 23 per 1000.

On the basis of this simulation they concluded that

A modest birth control programme, costing perhaps 30 cents a year per head of national population, can raise average income over only 15 years by almost twice the percentage that it would rise without birth control. . . . The value of permanently preventing the birth of a marginal infant is about twice an LDC's annual income per head [p. 41].

This is a controversial finding because of a lack of agreement that the simulated mechanisms approximate those which would actually prevail in developing countries, particularly if the population growth is moderate rather than rapid. Nonetheless, for those countries which are experiencing very rapid population growth it does suggest that the potential payoff to instituting means of controlling that population growth could be substantial.

Sources: S. Enke and R. Zind, "Effect of Fewer Births on Average Income," *Journal of Biosocial Science* 1 (1969): 41–55; Julian L. Simon, *The Economics of Population Growth* (Princeton, NJ: Princeton University Press, 1977).

Why should individuals care about inequality per se as opposed to simply caring about their own income? Aside from a pure humane concern for others, particularly the poor, people care about inequality because it can create social tensions. When these social tensions exist, society is a less pleasant place to live.

The demand to reduce income inequality clearly exists in modern society, as evidenced by the large number of private charitable organizations created to fulfill this demand. Yet because the reduction of income inequality is a public good, we also know that these organizations cannot be relied on to reduce inequality as much as would be socially justified. Similarly, for the same reason we know that parents will not take it sufficiently into account when they make their childbearing decisions. They will have too many children and will exacerbate income inequality in the process.

Two other externalities are apparent as well: (1) the cost of food and (2) the cost of education. It is common for developing countries to subsidize food by holding prices below market levels. Lower than normal food prices artificially lower the cost of children as long as the quantities of food available are maintained by government subsidy (we discuss this further in Chapter 10).[11]

The second area in which the costs of children are not fully borne by the parents is education. Primary education is usually state financed with the funds collected by taxes. The point is *not* that parents do not pay these costs; in part they do. The point is rather that their level of contribution is not usually sensitive to the number of children they have. The school taxes one pays are generally the same whether parents have 2 children, 10 children, or even no children. Thus the marginal educational expenditure for a parent—the additional cost of education due to the birth of a child—is certainly lower than the true social cost of educating that child.

Unfortunately, very little has been accomplished on assessing the empirical significance of these externalities. Despite this lack of evidence, the interest in controlling population is clear. The task is a difficult one. The right to bear children is considered in many countries, if not most, as an inalienable right immune to influences outside the family. Indira Gandhi, the Prime Minister of India, lost an election in the late 1970s due principally to her aggressive and direct approach to population control.[12] Though she subsequently regained her position, political figures in other democratic countries are not likely to miss the message. Dictating that no family can have more than two children is not politically palatable at this time. Such a dictum is seen as an unethical infringement on the rights of those who are mentally, physically, and monetarily equipped to care for larger families.

---

11 Notice, however, that if the food is domestically produced and the effect of price controls is to lower the prices farmers receive for their crops, the effect is to lower the demand for children in the agricultural sector. (Why?)

12 See, for example, Myron Weiner, *India at the Polls* (Washington, DC: American Enterprise Institute for Public Policy Research, 1978).

Yet population control measures can provide a higher quality of life for the smaller number of individuals born, while reducing the human impact on the planet. What, then, is a democratic country to do? How can it gain control over population growth while allowing individual families considerable flexibility in choosing their family size?

Successful population control involves two components: (1) lowering the desired family size and (2) providing sufficient access to contraceptive methods and family planning information to allow that size family to be realized.

The economic approach to population control *indirectly* controls population by lowering the desired family size. This is accomplished by identifying those factors that affect desired family size and changing those factors. To use the economic approach, we need to know how fertility decision making is affected by the economic environment experienced by the family.

The major model attempting to assess the determinants of childbirth decision making from an economic viewpoint is called the *microeconomic theory of fertility*. The point of departure for this theory is viewing children as consumer durables. The key insight is that the demand for children will, as with more conventional commodities, be downward-sloping. All other things being equal, the more expensive children become, the fewer will be demanded.

With this point of departure, childbearing decisions can be modeled within a traditional demand-and-supply framework (Figure 5.7). We shall designate the initial situation, before the imposition of any controls, as the point where demand, designated by D_1, and marginal cost, designated by MC_1, are equal. The desired number of children at this point is q_1. Notice that, according to the analysis, the desired number of children can be reduced either by an inward shift of the demand curve to D_2, or an upward shift in the marginal cost of children to MC_2, or both. What would cause these to shift?

Let's consider the demand curve. Why might it have shifted inward during the demographic transition? Several sources of this change have emerged:

1. The shift from an agricultural to an industrial economy reduces the productivity of children. In an agricultural economy, extra hands are useful, but in an industrial economy, child labor laws result in children contributing substantially less to the family. Therefore the investment demand for children is reduced.[13]

2. In countries with primitive savings systems, one of the very few ways a person can provide for old-age security is to have plenty of children

---

[13] A detailed exploration of the relationship between fertility and urbanization can be found in David Goldberg, "Residential Location and Fertility," in *Population and Development: The Search for Selective Intervention*, Ronald Ridker, ed. (Baltimore: Johns Hopkins University Press, 1976): 387–428. Urban fertility rates generally are lower.

FIGURE 5.7 The demand for children.

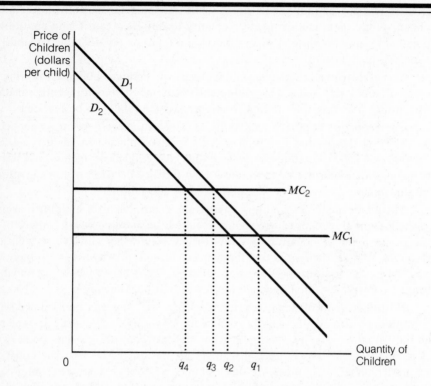

to provide for him or her in the twilight years. One would not, at first glance, think of children as social security systems, but, in many societies, they are precisely that. When alternative means of providing for old-age security are developed, the demand for children decreases.

3. In some countries a woman's status is almost exclusively defined in terms of the number of children she bears. If personal status is positively correlated with desired family size, this will increase the demand for children.

4. A decrease in infant mortality can also cause the demand curve to shift inward. When infant mortality is high, it takes many births to produce the desired number of children at the ages when they are needed. Support for this argument was obtained during an attempt to reduce infant mortality in one of the southern states of India. Apparently, this program did have the side effect of reducing the birthrate.[14]

---

14 Michael T. Kaufman, "South India Success Story: Small Families the Norm," *The New York Times* (March 6, 1980): 2.

5. Some evidence also suggests that the amount the demand curve shifts inward as a result of economic growth depends on the manner in which the increased employment associated with development is shared among the members of society. Those countries which have typically entered into a phase of sustained fertility decline in spite of low levels of average per capita income levels are usually characterized by a relatively equal distribution of income and a relatively widespread participation in the benefits of growth (Example 5.2).

Desired family size is also affected by changes in the cost of children. The costs of raising children can be changed as a means of controlling population.

1. One of the main components of the cost of children is the opportunity cost of the mother's time. By increasing the educational and labor market opportunities for women, the opportunity cost of raising children is increased. This can affect the observed fertility rate both by deferring the time of marriage and by causing a reduction in the desired number of children, once married.

2. As societies urbanize and industrialize, housing space becomes more expensive due to the concentrated demands in specific locations. Thus while the cost of extra space for children may be low in rural settings, it is much higher in urban settings.

3. The cost of children to parents may also be affected to a large extent by the cost of education. As nations struggle to improve their literacy rates by universal compulsory education, they may simultaneously raise the cost of children. These costs rise not only because of direct additional parental expenditures on education but also because of the earnings which are forgone when the children are in school rather than working.

4. As development occurs, generally parents demand more education and a higher quality education for their children. Depending on the system for financing education, providing this higher-quality education may raise the cost of every child even if the cost of a given quality of education is not rising.

All of this provides a menu of opportunities for population control. The reasons listed above represent potent forces for change. Yet these methods should be used with care. Inducing a family to have fewer children without assisting the family in satisfying the basic needs the children were fulfilling (such as old-age security) would be inequitable.

EXAMPLE 5.2

Fertility Decline in Korea: A Case Study

The dramatic fertility decline in the Republic of Korea which occurred during the period from 1960–1974 has been one of the fastest ever recorded. Therefore, it provides a unique opportunity to study the forces which led to this decline and the extent to which they might be applicable to other countries.

The period prior to the dramatic decline contained a series of shattering events, including the Korean War. Culturally homogeneous to start with, Korea emerged from this period as a relatively egalitarian society. During the fertility decline, Korea experienced very rapid economic growth stimulated to a large extent by imported capital and technology. Because the development approach focused on labor-intensive technologies, the fruits of this development were spread rather uniformly throughout the economy. Rising real wages and an expanded demand for labor served to preserve the relatively equal income distribution which had been inherited from the 1950s.

This combination of rapid economic growth and widespread participation in that growth among various sectors of the economy produced a dramatic fertility decline in almost all groups of society. Birthrates started to decline simultaneously in all regions, classes, and categories of households.

The changes in economic institutions which accompanied economic growth reinforced the tendency toward declining fertility rates. This period saw the rise, for example, of savings institutions, the widespread ownership of property (which permitted the accumulation of some wealth), and social insurance. These tended to provide alternative mechanisms for assuring old-age security.

There was also a substantial increase in the percentage of females in the labor force, resulting in an increase in the age of marriage and a reduction in the fertility rate of married women. At the same time, education levels of women rose, which also contributed to the decline.

Though the degree of income and cultural equality in Korea was unusual, many of the other factors contributing to fertility decline, such as pursuing a development plan which reduced income inequality as the nation grew, providing alternative social security systems, and ensuring expanding labor-market opportunities for women, are available to other nations.

Source: Robert Repetto, *Economic Equality and Fertility in Developing Countries* (Baltimore: Johns Hopkins University Press, 1979): 69–120.

Policies in China illustrate just how far economic incentives can be carried.[15] In announced regulations, one-child parents receive subsidized health expenditures, priority in education, health care and housing, and additional subsidized food. Meanwhile, parents who have more than two children will re-ceive a reduction of 5% in the total income for the third child (6% for the fourth, and so on). Also, families were denied access to further subsidized grain beyond that which they would already receive for their two previous children.

Initially these policies did bring about a rather dramatic fall in the birthrate in China, but recently the birth rate has taken an upturn. China's fertility rate had dipped as low as 2.1, but by 1986 it had risen to 2.4. The policies are so draconian as to precipitate a degree of resistance sufficent to undermine the effort.

Countries seeking to reduce fertility do not have to resort to extreme measures. Policies such as enhancing the status of women, providing alternative sources of old-age security, and supplying employment opportunities which equalize the income distributions are both humane and effective.

Vernon Ruttan has summarized some of the studies which have evaluated the effects of this type of approach: (a) greater family wealth sustains higher education levels and better health; (b) a rise in the value of the mother's time has a positive effect on the demand for contraceptive services and a negative effect on fertility; (c) a rise in the value of the father's earnings has a positive effect on completed family size, child health, and child education; and (d) an increase in mother's schooling has a negative effect on fertility and infant mortality and a positive effect on nutrition and children's schooling.[16]

In terms of population growth, child nutrition, and health these studies indicate a large payoff to making women fuller partners in the quest for improved living standards in the Third World. In the words of Dr. Nafis Sadik, Executive Director of the United Nations Population Fund:

> The extent to which women are free to make decisions affecting their lives may be the key to the future, not only of the poor countries, but the rich ones' too. As mothers; producers or suppliers of food, fuel and water; traders and manufacturers; political and community leaders, women are at the centre of the process of change.[17]

---

15 For a detailed investigation of China's policies, see Karen Hardee-Cleaveland and Judith Banister, "Fertility Policy and Implementation in China, 1986-88" *Population and Development Review* 14 (June 1988): 245-286.

16 Vernon W. Ruttan, "Perspectives on Population and Development," *Indian Journal of Agricultural Economics* 39 (October/December 1984): 636. Ruttan in turn credits Robert E. Evenson, "Notes on the New Home Economics," in *Home Economics and Agriculture in Third World Countries,* Miriam Seltzer, ed. (St. Paul: University of Minnesota College of Home Economics Center for Youth Development and Research, 1980).

17 Nafis Sadik, *The State of World Population 1989* (New York: UN Population Fund, 1989): 3.

The desire to reduce family size, however, is not sufficient if access to birth control information and contraceptives is inadequate. One study found that the adequacy of family planning programs varied markedly among the countries within a continent.[18] Yet where access was very good, fertility was declining, particularly when access was coupled with better education and opportunities for women.

SUMMARY

World population growth has slowed considerably in recent years, with only African nations resisting the trend. Population declines are already occurring in Germany and are expected in the near future in a number of northern European countries. The United States' total fertility rate is now below the replacement level. If maintained for a number of years, this fertility behavior would usher in an era of zero or negative population growth for the United States as well.

Those countries experiencing declines in their population growth will also experience a rise in the average age of their population. This transition to an older population should boost income per capita growth by increasing the share of the population in the labor force and by allowing more family wealth to be concentrated on the nutrition, health, and education of the children.

Slower population growth should also help to reduce income inequality. Since they typically have larger families, on average this effect will be felt most strongly in lower-income families. This tendency for incomes of lower-income families to increase faster than those of higher-income families should be reinforced by the effects on labor supply. By preventing an excess supply of labor which holds wages down, slower population growth benefits wage earners. Wages are a particularly important source of income for lower-income families.

While it is certainly premature to proclaim, as some have, an end to the population explosion,[19] it is similarly premature to label population growth as an insoluble problem. The evidence of the last few years suggests that steps to defuse *the population bomb* have been undertaken and are meeting with success.

FURTHER READING

Commission on Population Growth and the American Future, *Research Reports,* Vols I–VII, Elliot R. Morss and Richie H. Reed, eds. (Washington, DC: Government Printing

---

18 Robert J. Lapham and W. Parker Mauldin, "Contraceptive Prevalence: The Influence of Organized Family Planning Programs," *Studies in Family Planning* 16 (1985): 123–124.

19 For an articulation of this position, see Donald J. Bogue, "The End of the Population Explosion," *Public Interest* (Spring 1967): 11–20. For a critical appraisal, see Paul Demeny, "On the End of the Population Explosion," *Population and Development Review* 5 (March 1979): 141–162.

Office, 1972). An excellent survey of population issues as they relate to the American future. Volumes II and III are particularly relevant to the theme of this book.

Easterlin, Richard A. "The Economics and Sociology of Fertility: A Synthesis," in *Historical Studies of Changing Fertility*, Charles Tilly, ed. (Princeton, NJ: Princeton University Press, 1978): 57–133. One of the very few comprehensive surveys of the literature accessible to readers who are not mathematically adept.

Easterlin, Richard A., ed. *Population and Economic Change in Developing Countries* (Chicago: University of Chicago Press, 1980). An excellent collection of essays on subjects ranging from child costs and economic development to an examination of the population explosion in preindustrial England.

Kelly, Allen C., "Economic Consequences of Population Change in the Third World," *Journal of Economic Literature* 26 (December 1988): 1685–1728. Excellent review of a complex literature with a detailed bibliography.

"New Economic Approaches to Fertility," a special supplement of the *Journal of Political Economy* 81 (March/April 1973). A highly technical collection of essays that refine and test the economic theory of fertility. An excellent bibliography is included.

Schultz, T. Paul. *Economics of Population* (Reading, MA: Addison-Wesley, 1981). An intensive introduction to the field intended for undergraduates. Gives a sense of the controversies existing in the field.

Simon, Julian L. *The Economics of Population Growth* (Princeton, NJ: Princeton University Press, 1977). A comprehensive survey of the literature plus original work; proposes the idea that moderate population growth (as opposed to zero or high) may be helpful to developing countries.

ADDITIONAL REFERENCES

Becker, Gary. "An Economic Analysis of Fertility," in *Demographic and Economic Changes in Developed Countries* (Princeton, NJ: Princeton University Press, 1960): 209–231.

Davis, Kingsley, et. al. *Below Replacement Fertility in Industrial Societies: Causes, Consequences, Policies* (New York: Cambridge University Press, 1987).

Easterlin, Richard A. *Population, Labor Force and Long Swings in Economic Growth* (New York: Columbia University Press, 1968).

Eberstadt, Nick. *Fertility Decline in the Less Developed Countries* (New York: Praeger, 1981).

Johnson, D. Gale and Ronald D. Lee. *Population Growth and Economic Development: Issues and Evidence* (Madison, WI: University of Wisconsin Press, 1987).

Kuznets, Simon. *Population, Capital, and Growth: Selected Essays* (New York: W. W. Norton, 1973).

Lee, Ronald D. et al., eds. *Population, Food, and Rural Development* (New York: Oxford University Press, 1988).

Mahadevan, K. *Fertility Policies of Asian Countries* (Newbury Park, CA: Sage, 1988).

Repetto, Robert. "The Effects of Income Distribution on Fertility in Developing Countries," in *Fertility Decline in the Less Developed Countries*, Nick Eberstadt, ed. (New York: Praeger, 1981): 254–273.

Ridker, Ronald, ed. *Population and Development: The Search for Selective Interventions* (Baltimore: Johns Hopkins University Press, 1976).

Simmons, Ozzie C. *Perspectives on Development and Population* (New York: Plenum, 1988).

DISCUSSION QUESTIONS

1. Fertility rates vary widely among various ethnic groups in the United States. Black and Spanish-speaking Americans have above-average rates, for example, while Jews have below-average fertility rates. This may be due to different ethnic beliefs, but it may also be due to economic factors. How could you use economics to explain these fertility rate differences? What tests could you devise to see whether this explanation has validity?

2. The microeconomic theory of fertility provides an opportunity to determine how public policies which were designed for quite different purposes could affect fertility rates. Identify some public policies (e.g., subsidies to people who own their own home, or subsidized day care) which could have an effect on fertility rates, and describe the relationship.

PROBLEMS

1. Some education is funded by property taxes, whereas other forms of education are funded by charging each student tuition. Suppose that within a community, more money is needed for education. Assuming that they raise the same amount of revenue, would the rising cost of education have the same effect on the desired number of children regardless of whether the system was funded by property taxes or tuition? Using the microeconomic theory of fertility, trace the expected impacts.

2. Using the terminology presented in Chapter 1, is the relationship between population growth and the gap between the rich and the poor in a particular country a positive or negative feedback loop? Why?

CHAPTER SIX

The Allocation of Depletable and Renewable Resources: An Overview

The whole machinery of our intelligence, our general ideas and laws, fixed and external objects, principles, persons, and gods, are so many symbolic, algebraic expressions. They stand for experience; experience which we are incapable of retaining and surveying in its multitudinous immediacy. We should flounder hopelessly, like the animals, did we not keep ourselves afloat and direct our course by these intellectual devices. Theory helps us to bear our ignorance of fact.

GEORGE SANTAYANA, *The Sense of Beauty* (1896)

INTRODUCTION

In the *Limits to Growth* vision of the future, society's demand for resources suddenly exceeds their availability. Rather than anticipating a smooth transition to a steady state, this vision estimates that the system will overshoot the resource base, precipitating a collapse. Is this realistic? Is profit maximization inconsistent with smooth adjustments to increasing scarcity?

We approach these questions in several steps, first by defining and discussing a simple but useful *resource taxonomy* (classification system), as well as explaining the dangers of ignoring the distinctions made by this taxonomy. We begin by defining an efficient allocation of an exhaustible resource over time when no renewable substitute is available. This is accomplished by exploring the conditions any efficient allocation must satisfy and using numerical examples to illustrate the meaning of these conditions.

We begin our treatment of renewable resources with the simplest possible case—the resource is supplied at a fixed, abundant rate and can be accessed at a constant marginal cost. Solar energy and replenishable surface water are two examples that seem roughly to fit this characterization. Combining this model of renewable resource supply with our basic depletable resource model allows us to characterize efficient extraction paths for both types of resources, assuming that they are perfect substitutes. How these efficient paths are affected by changes in the nature of the cost functions is explored as is the nature of market extraction paths. Whether or not the market is capable of yielding a dynamically efficient allocation in the presence or absence of a renewable substitute provides a focal point for the analysis. Succeeding chapters will use these principles both to examine the allocation of energy, food, and water resources, and as a basis for developing more elaborate models of renewable biological populations such as fisheries and forests.

A RESOURCE TAXONOMY

Three separate concepts are used to classify the stock of depletable resources: (1) *current reserves*, (2) *potential reserves*, and (3) *resource endowment*. In the United States the Geological Survey (USGS) has the official responsibility for keeping records of the U.S. resource base, and they have developed the classification system described in Figure 6.1.

Notice the two dimensions—one economic and one geological. A movement from top to bottom represents movement from cheaply extractable resources to those extracted at substantially higher prices. By contrast, a movement from left to right represents increasing geological uncertainty about the size of the resource base.

Current reserves (shaded area in Figure 6.1) are defined as known resources that can profitably be extracted at current prices. The magnitude of these current reserves can be expressed as a number.

Potential reserves, on the other hand, are most accurately defined as a function rather than a number. The amount of reserves potentially available depends upon the price people are willing to pay for those resources—the higher the price, the larger the potential reserves. For example, Congress conducted a study on the amount of additional oil that could be recovered from existing oil fields by enhanced recovery techniques, such as injecting solvents or steam into the well to lower the density of the oil. These techniques, more expensive than conventional ones, allow greater amounts of oil to be recovered. As price is increased, the amount of oil that can be economically recovered also increases (Table 6.1).

The *resource endowment* represents the natural occurrence of resources in the earth's crust. Since prices have nothing to do with the size of the resource

FIGURE 6.1   A categorization of resources.

Total Resources

	Identified				Undiscovered	
	Demonstrated		Inferred		Hypothetical	Speculative
	Measured	Indicated				
Economic	Reserves					
Subeconomic / Paramarginal / Submarginal						

Terms

Identified resources: specific bodies of mineral-bearing material whose location, quality, and quantity are known from geological evidence, supported by engineering measurements.

Measured resources: material for which quantity and quality estimates are within a margin of error of less than 20 percent, from geologically well-known sample sites.

Indicated resources: material which quantity and quality have been estimated partly from sample analyses and partly from reasonable geological projections.

Inferred resources: material in unexplored extensions of demonstrated resources based on geological projections.

Undiscovered resources: unspecified bodies of mineral-bearing material surmised to exist on the basis of broad geological knowledge and theory.

Hypothetical resources: undiscovered materials reasonably expected to exist in a known mining district under known geological conditions.

Speculative resources: undiscovered materials that may occur either known types of deposits in favorable geological settings where no discoveries have been made, or in yet unknown types of deposits that remain to be recognized.

Source: U.S. Bureau of Mines and the U.S. Geological Survey. "Principle of the Mineral Resource Classification System of the U.S. Bureau of Mines and the U.S. Geological Survey," *Geological Survey Bulletin* 1450-A, 1976.

TABLE 6.1 Estimates of Ultimately Recoverable Oil from Enhanced Oil Recovery with 10% Minimum Rate of Return (price in constant 1976 dollars)

Price per Barrel	Ultimate Recovery (10^9 barrels)
$11.62	21.2
$13.75	29.4
$22.00	41.6
$30.00	49.2
More than $30.00	51.1

Source: U.S. Congress, Office of Technology Assessment, *Enhanced Oil Recovery Potential in the United States* (Washington, DC: OTA, 1978): 7.

endowment, it is a geological rather than an economic concept. This concept is important because it represents an upper limit on the availability of terrestrial resources.

The distinctions among these three concepts are significant. One common mistake in failing to respect these distinctions is using data on current reserves as if it represented the maximum potential reserves. As Example 6.1 indicates, this fundamental error can lead to conclusions wide of the mark.

A second common mistake is to assume that the entire resource endowment can be made available as potential reserves at some price people would be willing to pay. Clearly, if an infinite price were possible, then the entire resource endowment could be exploited. However, an infinite price is not likely.

For reasons explained in Chapter 13 certain mineral sources are so costly to extract that it is inconceivable any current or future society would be willing to pay the price necessary to extract them. Thus, it seems likely that the maximum feasible size of the potential reserves is smaller than the resource endowment. Exactly how much smaller cannot yet be determined with any degree of certainty, though Chapter 13 surveys the available evidence.

Other distinctions among resource categories are also useful. The first category includes all depletable, recyclable resources, such as copper. A *depletable resource* is one for which the natural replenishment feedback loop can safely be ignored. The rate of replenishment for these resources is so low that it does not offer a potential for augmenting the stock in any reasonable time frame.

A *recyclable resource* is one which, although currently being used for some particular purpose, exists in a form allowing its mass to be recovered once that purpose is no longer necessary or desirable. For example, copper wiring from an automobile can be recovered after the car has been shipped to the junkyard. The degree to which a resource is recycled is determined by economic conditions, a subject covered in Chapter 8.

EXAMPLE 6.1

The Pitfalls in Misusing Reserve Data

It is relatively common practice to estimate the number of years a given resource will last by computing what is known as the *static reserve index*, the ratio of current reserves to current consumption. The result of the calculation is supposed to be interpreted as the number of years remaining until the resource is exhausted. This is a correct calculation of the time to exhaustion if and only if: (1) the consumption of the resource remains at current levels until the time of exhaustion (it can neither increase nor decrease); and (2) no additions to the reserves occur in the intervening period (current reserves and potential reserves are assumed equal for the prices which can be expected to prevail).

These assumptions generally are not even approximately accurate. For example, in 1934 the static index for copper was 40, indicating the reserves would be exhausted in 40 years. In 1974, 40 years later, this index stood at 57. A similar calculation for crude oil, iron ore, and lead would reveal the same pattern; the static index tends to underestimate the time until exhaustion.

The *Limits to Growth* study used an index called the *exponential reserve index*, which tends to underestimate the time to exhaustion by an even greater amount than the static index. This index assumes that consumption will grow over time at a constant rate of growth. No correction is made for additions to reserves or for the effects of higher prices on demand. It is therefore neither very surprising, nor very interesting, that their time of exhaustion estimates are so proximate.

Sources: Paul R. Ehrlich and Anne H. Ehrlich, *Population Resources Environment*, 2nd ed. (San Francisco: W. H. Freeman, 1972): 70–72; Earl Cook, "Limits to Exploitation of Nonrenewable Resources," *Science* 191 (February 20, 1976): 667–682.

The current reserves of a depletable, recyclable resource can be augmented by economic replenishment, as well as by recycling. Economic replenishment takes many forms, all sharing the characteristic that they turn previously unrecoverable resources into recoverable ones. One obvious stimulant for this replenishment is price. As price rises, producers find it profitable to explore more widely, dig more deeply, use lower-concentration ores, and so on.

Higher prices also stimulate technological progress. Technological progress simply means an advancement in the state of knowledge which allows us to do things we were not able to do before. One profound, if controversial, example can be found in the successful harnessing of nuclear power.

The other side of the coin for depletable, recyclable resources is that their potential reserves can be exhausted. The depletion rate is affected by the demand for and the durability of the products built with the resource, and the ability to reuse the products. Except where demand is totally price inelastic (that is, insensitive to price) higher prices tend to reduce the quantity demanded. Durable products last longer, reducing the need for newer ones. Reusable products provide a substitute for new products. In the commercial sector, reusable soft-drink bottles provide one example, while flea markets (where secondhand items are sold) provide another for the household sector.

For some resources, the size of the potential reserves depends explicitly on our ability to store the resource. For example, helium generally is found commingled with natural gas in common fields. As the natural gas is extracted and stored, unless the helium is simultaneously captured and stored, it diffuses into the atmosphere. This results in such low concentrations that extraction of helium from the air is not economical at current or even likely future prices. Thus, the useful stock of helium depends crucially on how much we decide to store.

Not all depletable resources permit recycling or reuse. Depletable energy resources such as coal, oil, and gas are consumed as they are used. Once combusted and turned into heat energy, the heat dissipates into the atmosphere and becomes nonrecoverable.

The endowment of depletable resources is of finite size. Current use of depletable, nonrecyclable resources precludes future use; hence, the issue of how they should be shared among generations is raised in the starkest, least forgiving, form.

Depletable, recyclable resources raise this same issue, though somewhat less starkly. Recycling and reuse make the useful stock last longer, all other things being equal. It is tempting to suggest that depletable recyclable resources could last forever with 100% recycling, but unfortunately the physical theoretical upper limit on recycling is less than 100%—an implication of a version of the entropy law defined in Chapter 2. Some of the mass is always lost during recycling.

For example, copper pennies can be melted down to recover the copper, but the amount rubbed off during circulation would never be recovered. As long as less than 100% of the mass is recycled, the useful stock must eventually decline to zero. Even for recyclable depletable resources, the cumulative useful stock is finite, and current consumption patterns still have an effect on future generations.

Renewable resources are differentiated from depletable resources primarily by the fact that natural replenishment augments the flow of renewable resources at a nonnegligible rate. Solar energy, water, cereal grains, fish, forests, and animals are all examples of renewable resources. Thus it is possible, though not inexorable, that a flow of these resources could be maintained perpetually.[1]

---

1 Even renewable resources are ultimately finite because their renewability depends on energy from the sun and the sun is expected to serve as an energy source for only the next 5 or 6 billion years. That fact does not eliminate the need to manage resources effectively until that time. Furthermore, the finiteness of renewable resources is sufficiently far into the future to make the distinction useful.

For some renewable resources, the continuation and volume of their flow depend crucially on humans. Soil erosion and nutrient depletion reduce the flow of food. Excessive fishing reduces the stock of fish, which in turn reduces the rate of natural increase of the fish population. Newsprint can be recycled. Other examples abound. For other renewable resources, such as solar energy, the flow is independent of humans. The amount consumed by one generation does not reduce the amount that can be consumed by subsequent generations.

Some renewable resources can be stored; others cannot. For those that can, storage provides a valuable way to manage the allocation of the resource over time. We are not left simply at the mercy of natural ebbs and flows of the source. Food without proper care perishes rapidly, but with storage can be used to feed the hungry in times of famine. Unstored solar energy radiates off the earth's surface and dissipates into the atmosphere. While solar energy can be stored in many forms, the most common natural form of storage occurs when it is converted to biomass by photosynthesis.

Storage of renewable resources usually performs a different service than storage of depletable resources. Storing depletable resources extends their economic life; storing renewable resources, on the other hand, can serve as a means of smoothing out the cyclical imbalances of supply and demand. Surpluses are stored for periods when deficits may occur. Food stockpiles and the use of dams to store hydropower are two familiar examples.

Managing renewable resources presents a different challenge than managing depletable resources, though an equally significant one. The challenge for depletable resources involves allocating dwindling stocks among generations while meeting the ultimate transition to renewable resources. In contrast, the challenge for managing renewable resources involves the maintenance of an efficient sustainable flow. The next six chapters deal with how the economic and political sectors have responded to these challenges for particularly significant types of resources.

EFFICIENT INTERTEMPORAL ALLOCATIONS

If we are to judge the adequacy of market allocations, we must define what is meant by efficiency in relation to the management of depletable and renewable resource allocations. Because allocation over time is the crucial issue, dynamic efficiency becomes the core concept. The dynamic efficiency criterion assumes that society's objective is to maximize the present value of net benefits coming from the resource. For a depletable, nonrecyclable resource, this requires a balancing of the current and subsequent uses of the resource. In order to recall how the dynamic efficiency criterion defines this balance, we shall begin with an elaboration of the very simple, two-period model developed in Chapter 2. We shall show how these conclusions generalize to longer planning horizons and more complicated situations.

The Two-Period Model Revisited

In Chapter 2 we defined a situation involving the allocation over two periods of a finite resource which could be extracted at constant marginal cost. With a stable demand curve for the resource, an efficient allocation meant that more than half of the resource was allocated to the first period and less than half to the second period. This allocation was affected both by the marginal cost of extraction and by the marginal user cost.

Due to the fixed and finite supplies of depletable resources, production of a unit today precludes production of that unit tomorrow. Therefore, production decisions today must take forgone future net benefits into account. Marginal user cost is the opportunity cost measure that allows balancing to take place.

The marginal cost of extraction is assumed to be constant, but the current value of the marginal user cost rises over time. In fact, as was demonstrated mathematically in the appendix to Chapter 2, when the demand curve is stable over time and the marginal cost of extraction is constant the rate of increase in the current value of the marginal user cost is equal to r, the discount rate. Thus, in period 2, the marginal user cost would be $1 + r$ times as large as it was in period 1.[2] Marginal user cost rises at rate r in an efficient allocation in order to preserve the balance between present-versus-future production.

In summary, our two-period example suggests that an efficient allocation of a finite resource with a constant marginal cost of extraction involves rising marginal user cost and falling quantities consumed. We can now generalize to longer time periods and different extraction circumstances.

The N-Period Constant-Cost Case

We begin this generalization by retaining the constant-marginal-extraction-cost assumption while extending the time horizon within which the resource is allocated. In the numerical example shown in Figures 6.2a and 6.2b, the demand curves and the marginal cost curve from the two-period case are retained. The only changes in this numerical example from the two-period case involve spreading the allocation over a large number of years and an increase in the total recoverable supply from 20 to 40. (The mathematics behind this and subsequent examples is presented in the chapter appendix.)

Figure 6.2a demonstrates how the efficient quantity extracted varies over time, while Figure 6.2b shows the behavior of the marginal user cost and the marginal cost of extraction. Total marginal cost refers to the sum of the two. The

---

2 The condition that marginal user cost rises at rate r is true only when the marginal cost of extraction is constant. Later in this chapter, we show how the marginal user cost is affected when marginal extraction cost is not constant.

FIGURE 6.2   (a) Constant marginal extraction cost with no substitute resource: quantity profile. (b) Constant marginal extraction cost with no substitute resource: marginal cost profile.

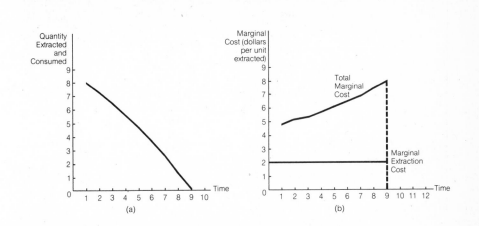

marginal cost of extraction is represented by the lower line, and the marginal user cost is depicted as the vertical distance between the marginal cost of extraction and the total marginal cost. To avoid confusion, note that the horizontal axis is defined in terms of time, not the more conventional designation, quantity.

Several trends are worth noting. First of all, in this case as in the two-period case, the efficient marginal user cost rises steadily in spite of the fact that the marginal cost of extraction remains constant. This rise in the efficient marginal user cost reflects increasing scarcity and the accompanying rise in the opportunity cost of current consumption.

In response to these rising costs over time the quantity extracted falls over time until it finally goes to zero, which occurs precisely at the moment when the total marginal cost becomes $8. At this point total marginal cost is equal to the highest price anyone is willing to pay, so demand and supply simultaneously equal zero. Thus, even in this difficult case involving no increase in the cost of extraction, an efficient allocation envisions a smooth transition to the exhaustion of a resource. The resource does not "suddenly" run out, although in this case it does run out.

Transition to a Renewable Substitute

So far we have discussed the allocation of a depletable resource when no substitute is available to take its place. Suppose, however, we consider the nature of an efficient allocation when a substitute renewable resource is available at

constant marginal cost. This case, for example, could describe the efficient allocation of oil or natural gas with a solar substitute or the efficient allocation of
exhaustible groundwater with a surface-water substitute. How could we define
an efficient allocation in this circumstance?

Since this problem is very similar to the one already discussed, we can use what
we have already learned as a foundation for mastering th₁s new situation. The
depletable resource would be exhausted in this case, just as it was in the previous case,
but that will be less of a problem, since we'll merely switch to the renewable one at
the appropriate time. For the purpose of our numerical example, assume the existence
of a perfect substitute for the depletable resource which is infinitely available at a cost
of $6 per unit. The transition from the depletable resource to this renewable resource
would ultimately transpire because its marginal cost ($6) is less than the maximum
willingness to pay ($8). (Can you figure out what the efficient allocation would be if
the marginal cost of this substitute resource was $9 instead of $6?)

The total marginal cost for the depletable resource in the presence of a $6
perfect substitute would never exceed $6, because society could always use the
renewable resource instead, whenever it was cheaper. Thus, while the maximum
willingness to pay (the *choke price*) sets the upper limit on total marginal cost
when no substitute is available, the marginal cost of extraction of the substitute
sets the upper limit when one is available at a marginal cost lower than the choke
price. The efficient path for this situation is given in Figures 6.3a and 6.3b.

FIGURE 6.3   (a) Constant marginal extraction cost with substitute resource:
quantity profile. (b) Constant marginal extraction cost with substitute resource:
marginal cost profile.

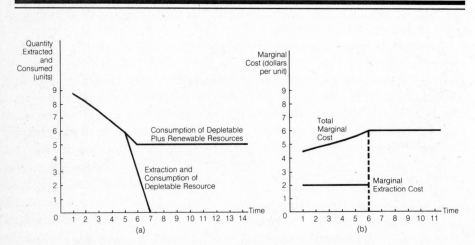

In this efficient allocation, the transition is once again smooth. Quantity extracted is gradually reduced as the marginal use cost rises until the switch is made to the substitute. No abrupt change is evident in either marginal cost or quantity profiles.

Because the renewable resource is available, more of the depletable resource would be extracted in the earlier periods than was the case in our previous numerical example without a renewable resource. As a result, the depletable resource would be exhausted sooner than it would have been without the renewable resource substitute. In this example the switch is made during the sixth period, whereas in the last example the last units were exhausted at the end of the eighth period.

At the transition point, called the switch point, consumption of the renewable resource begins. Prior to the switch point, only the depletable resource is consumed, while after the switch point only the renewable resource is consumed. This sequencing of consumption pattern results from the cost patterns. Prior to the switch point, the depletable resource is cheaper. At the switch point, the marginal cost of the depletable resource (including marginal user cost) rises to meet the marginal cost of the substitute, and the transition occurs. Due to the availability of the substitute resource, consumption never drops below 5 units in any time period. This level is maintained because 5 is the amount which maximizes the net benefit when the marginal cost equals $6 (the price of the substitute). (Convince yourself of the validity of this statement by substituting $6 into the willingness-to-pay function and solving for the quantity demanded.)

Though we shall not show the numerical example here, it is not difficult to see how an efficient allocation would be defined when the transition is from one constant marginal-cost depletable resource to another depletable resource with a constant, but higher, marginal cost (Figure 6.4). The total marginal cost of the first resource would rise over time until it equaled that of the second resource at the time of transition. In the period of time prior to transition (T^*), only the cheapest resource would be consumed; all of it would have been consumed by T^*.

A close examination of the total marginal cost path reveals two interesting characteristics worthy of our attention. First, even in this case, the transition is a smooth one; total marginal cost never jumps to a higher level. Second, the rate of increase in total marginal cost slows down after the time of transition.

The first characteristic is easy to explain. The total marginal costs of the two resources have to be equal at the time of transition. If they weren't equal, the net benefit could be increased by switching to the lower-cost resource from the more expensive resource. Total marginal costs are not equal in the other periods. In the period before transition, the first resource is cheaper and therefore used exclusively, whereas after transition the first resource is exhausted, leaving only the second resource.

The rate of increase in marginal cost is slower after transition simply because the component of total marginal cost that is growing (the marginal user cost) represents a smaller portion of the total marginal cost of the second resource

FIGURE 6.4   The transition from one constant-cost depletable resource to another.

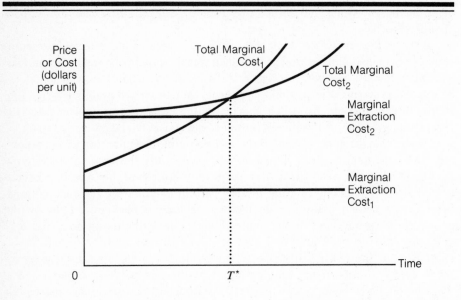

than of the first. The total marginal cost of each resource is determined by the marginal extraction cost plus the marginal user cost. In both cases the marginal user cost is increasing at rate r, and the marginal cost of extraction is constant. As seen in Figure 6.4, at the time of transition the marginal cost of extraction, which is constant, constitutes a much larger proportion of total marginal cost for the second resource than for the first. Hence, total marginal cost rises more slowly for the second resource, at least initially.

Increasing Marginal Extraction Cost

We have now expanded our examination of the efficient allocation of depletable resources to include longer time horizons and the availability of other depletable or renewable resources which could serve as perfect substitutes. As part of our trek toward increasing realism, we will next consider a situation in which the marginal cost of extracting the depletable resource rises with the cumulative amount extracted. This is commonly the case, for example, with minerals, where the higher-grade ores are extracted first, followed by an increasing reliance on lower-grade ones.

Analytically, this case is handled in the same manner as the previous case except that the function describing the marginal cost of extraction is slightly

FIGURE 6.5   (a) Increasing marginal extraction cost with substitute resource: quantity profile. (b) Increasing marginal extraction Cost with substitute resource: marginal cost profile.

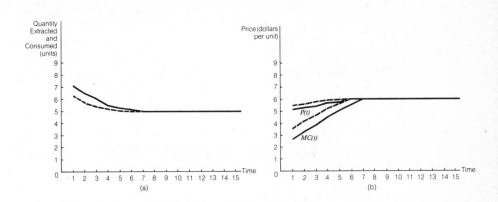

more complicated.[3] It increases with the cumulative amount extracted. The dynamic efficient allocation of this resource is found by maximizing the present value of the net benefits using this modified cost of extraction function. The results of that maximization are portrayed in Figures 6.5a and 6.5b.

The most significant difference between this case and the others lies in the behavior of marginal user cost. In the previous case we said that marginal user cost *rose* over time at rate *r*. When the marginal cost of extraction increases with the cumulative amount extracted, marginal user cost *declines* over time until, at the time of transition to the renewable resource, it goes to zero. Why is that?

Remember that marginal user cost is an opportunity cost reflecting forgone future marginal net benefits. In contrast to the constant marginal cost case, in the increasing cost case every unit extracted raises the cost of extraction. Therefore, as the current marginal cost rises over time, the sacrifice made by future generations (as an additional unit is consumed earlier) diminishes; the net benefit that would be received by a future generation if a unit of the resource were saved for them gets smaller and smaller as the marginal extraction cost of that resource gets larger and larger. By the last period the marginal extraction cost is so high

---

3   The marginal cost of extraction is $MC_t = \$2 + 0.1Q_t$, where Q_t is cumulative extraction to date. Notice how this general type of formulation could be used to characterize the data in Table 6.1.

that earlier consumption of one more unit imposes virtually no sacrifice at all. The opportunity cost of current extraction drops to zero, and total marginal cost equals the marginal extraction cost at the switch point.[4]

The increasing-cost case differs from the constant-cost case in another important way as well. In the constant-cost case, the depletable resource reserve is completely exhausted. In the increasing-cost case, however, the reserve is not exhausted; some is left in the ground because it is too expensive to take out.

Up to this point in our analysis, we have examined how an efficient allocation would be defined in a number of circumstances. First we examined a situation in which a finite amount of a resource was to be extracted at constant marginal cost. Despite the absence of increasing extraction cost, an efficient allocation involves a smooth transition to a substitute, when one is available, or to abstinence, when one is not. The complication of increasing marginal cost changes the time profile of the marginal user cost, but it does not alter the basic finding of declining consumption of depletable resources coupled with rising total marginal cost.

As a look at the historical record reveals, the consumption patterns of most depletable resources have involved increases, not decreases, in consumption over time. Is this prima facia evidence that the resources are not being allocated efficiently?

Exploration and Technological Progress

Using the historical patterns of increasing consumption to conclude that depletable resources are not being allocated efficiently would not represent a valid use of the theory of depletable resources. The models considered to this point have not yet included a consideration of the role of exploration for new resources or the role of technological progress, historically two significant factors in the determination of actual consumption paths.

The search for new resources is expensive. As easily discovered resources are exhausted, we must search in less rewarding environments, such as the bottom of the ocean or locations deep within the earth. This suggests the *marginal cost of exploration*, which is the marginal cost of finding additional units of the resource, should be expected to rise over time, just as the marginal cost of extraction does.

As the total marginal cost for a resource rises over time, society should actively explore possible new sources of that resource. The higher the marginal

---

4 Total marginal cost cannot be greater than the marginal cost of the substitute. Yet, in the increasing marginal extraction cost case, at the time of transition the marginal extraction cost also must equal the marginal cost of the substitute. If that weren't true, it would imply that some of the resource which was available at a marginal cost lower than the substitute would not be used. This would clearly be inefficient, since net benefits could be increased by simply using less of the more expensive substitute. Hence, at the switch point, in the rising marginal cost case, the marginal extraction cost has to equal total marginal cost, implying a zero marginal user cost.

cost of extraction for known sources is expected to rise, the larger is the potential increase in net benefits from exploration.

Some of this exploration would be successful; new sources of the resource would be discovered. If the marginal extraction cost of the newly discovered resources is low enough, these discoveries could lower, or at least retard, the increase in the total marginal cost of production. As a result, the new finds would tend to encourage more consumption. Compared to a situation with no exploration possible, the model with exploration would show a smaller and slower decline in consumption, while the rise in total marginal cost would be dampened.

It is also not difficult to expand our concept of efficient resource allocations to include technological progress, the general term economists give to advances in the state of knowledge. In the present context, technological progress would be manifested as reductions in the cost of extraction. For a resource which can be extracted at constant marginal cost, a one-time breakthrough lowering the marginal cost of extraction would move the time of transition further into the future. Furthermore, for an increasing-cost resource, more of the total available resource would be recovered in the presence of technological progress than would be recovered without it. (Why?)

The most pervasive effects of technological progress involve continuous downward shifts in the cost of extraction over some time period. The total marginal cost of the resource could actually fall over time if the cost-reducing nature of technological progress became so potent that, in spite of increasing reliance on inferior ore, the marginal cost of extraction decreased (Example 6.2). With a finite amount of this resource, the fall in total marginal cost would be transitory, since ultimately it would have to rise, but, as we shall see in the next few chapters, this period of transition can last quite a long time.

MARKET ALLOCATIONS

In the preceding sections we have examined in detail how the efficient allocation of substitutable depletable and renewable resources over time would be defined in a variety of circumstances. We must now address the question of whether actual markets can be expected to produce an efficient allocation. Can the private market involving millions of consumers and producers each reacting to his or her own unique preferences *ever* result in a dynamically efficient allocation? Is profit maximization compatible with dynamic efficiency?

Appropriate Property Right Structures

The most common misconception of those who believe that even a perfect market could never achieve an efficient allocation is a belief that producers want to extract and sell the resources as fast as possible, since that is how they derive

EXAMPLE 6.2

Technological Progress in the Iron Ore Industry

The term *technological progress* plays an important role in the economic analysis of mineral resources. Yet, at times, it can appear abstract, even mystical. It shouldn't! Far from being a blind faith detached from reality, technological progress refers to a host of ingenious ways in which people have reacted to impending shortages with sufficient imagination that the available supply of resources has been expanded by an order of magnitude and at reasonable cost. To illustrate how concrete a notion technological progress is, let's discuss one example of how it has worked in the past.

In 1947 the president of Republic Steel, C. M. White, calculated the expected life of the Mesabi range of northern Minnesota (the source of some 60% of iron ore consumed during World War II) as being in the range from five to seven years. By 1955, only eight years later, *U.S. News and World Report* was able to conclude that worry over the scarcity of iron ore could be forgotten. The source of this remarkable transformation of a problem of scarcity into one of abundance was the discovery of a new technique, called *pelletization*, of preparing iron ore.

Prior to pelletization, the standard ores from which iron was derived contained from 50 to more than 65% iron in crude form. There was a significant percentage of taconite ore available containing less than 30% iron in crude form, but no one knew how to produce it at reasonable cost. Pelletization is a process by which these ores are processed and concentrated at the mine sight prior to shipment to the blast furnaces. The advent of pelletization allowed the profitable use of the taconite ores.

While expanding the supply of iron ore, pelletization reduced its cost in spite of the inferior grade being used. There were several sources of the cost reduction. First, substantially *less* energy was used; the shift in ore technology toward pelletization produced net energy savings of 17% in spite of the fact that the pelletization process itself required more energy. The reduction came from the discovery that the blast furnaces could be operated much more efficiently using pelletization inputs. The process also reduced labor requirements per ton by some 8.2% while increasing the output of the blast furnaces. A blast furnace owned by Armco Steel in Middletown, Ohio, which had a rated capacity of approximately 1500 tons of molten iron per day, was able by 1960 to achieve production levels of 2700 and 2800 tons per day when fired with 90% pellets. Pellets nearly doubled the blast furnace productivity!

Sources: Peter J. Kakela, "Iron Ore: Energy Labor and Capital Changes with Technology," *Science* 202 (December 15, 1978): 1151–1157; Peter J. Kakela, "Iron Ore: From Depletion to Abundance," *Science* 212 (April 10, 1981): 132–136.

the value from the resource. This misconception makes people see markets as myopic and unconcerned about the future.

As long as the property rights governing natural resources have the characteristics of exclusivity, universality, transferability, and enforceability (Chapter 3), the markets in which those resources are bought and sold will not necessarily lead to myopic choices. When bearing the marginal user cost, the producer acts in an efficient manner. A resource in the ground has two potential sources of value to its owner: (1) a use value when it is sold (the only source considered by those diagnosing inevitable myopia), and (2) an asset value when it remains in the ground. As long as the price of a resource continues to rise, the resource in the ground is becoming more valuable. The owner of this resource accrues this capital gain, however, only if the resource is conserved. A producer who sells all resources in the earlier periods loses the chance to take advantage of higher prices in the future.

A prescient, profit-maximizing producer attempts to balance present and future production in order to maximize the value of the resource. Since higher prices in the future provide an incentive to conserve, a producer who ignores this incentive would not be maximizing the value of the resource. We would expect the resource to then be bought by someone willing to conserve and prepared to maximize its value. As long as social and private discount rates coincide, property right structures are well defined, and reliable information about future prices is available, a producer who selfishly pursues maximum profits simultaneously provides the maximum present value of net benefits for society.

The implication of this analysis is that, in prescient competitive resource markets, the price of the resource equals the total marginal cost of extracting and using the resource. Thus, Figures 6.2a through 6.5b can illustrate not only an efficient allocation but also the allocation produced by an efficient market. When used to describe an efficient market, the total marginal cost curve describes the time path that prices could be expected to follow.

Environmental Costs

One of the most important situations in which property right structures may not be well defined is that in which the extraction of a natural resource imposes an environmental cost on society not internalized by the producers. The aesthetic costs of strip mining, the health risks associated with uranium tailings, and the acids leached into streams from mine operations are all examples of associated environmental costs. Not only is the presence of environmental costs empirically important, it is also conceptually important, since it forms one of the bridges between the traditionally separate fields of environmental economics and natural resource economics.

Suppose, for example, that the extraction of the depletable resource caused some damage to the environment not adequately reflected in the costs faced by the extracting firms. This would be, in the language of Chapter 3, an external

FIGURE 6.6 (a) Increasing marginal extraction cost with substitute resource in the presence of environmental costs: quantity profile. (b) Increasing marginal extraction cost with substitute resource in the presence of environmental costs: price profile (solid line—without environmental costs; dashed line—with environmental costs).

cost. The cost of getting the resource out of the ground, as well as processing and shipping it, is borne by the resource owner and considered in the calculation of how much of the resource to extract. The environmental damage, however, is not borne by the owner and, in the absence of any outside attempt to internalize that cost, will not be part of the extraction decision. How would the market allocation, based on only the former cost, differ from the efficient allocation, which is based on both?

We can examine this issue by modifying the numerical example used earlier in this chapter. Suppose the environmental damage can be included by increasing the marginal cost by $1.00.[5] The additional dollar reflects the cost of the environmental damage caused by producing another unit of the resource. What effect do you think this would have on the efficient time profile for quantities extracted?

The answers are given in Figures 6.6a and 6.6b. The result of including environmental cost on the timing of the switch point is interesting because it involves two different effects that work in opposite directions. On the demand side, the inclusion of environmental costs results in higher prices, which tend to damp-

---

5 Including environmental damage, the marginal cost function would be raised to $3 + 0.1Q$ instead of $2 + 0.1Q$.

en demand. This lowers the rate of consumption of the resource, which, all other things being equal, would make it last longer.

All other things are not equal, however. The higher marginal cost also means that a smaller cumulative amount of the depletable resource would be extracted in an efficient allocation. (Why?) In our example depicted in Figures 6.6a and 6.6b, the efficient cumulative amount extracted would be 30 units instead of the 40 units extracted in the case where environmental costs were not included. This supply-side effect tends to hasten the time when a switch to the renewable resource is made, all other things being equal. Which effect dominates—the demand effect or the supply effect? In our numerical example the supply-side effect dominates and, as a result, the time of transition for an efficient allocation is sooner than for the market allocation. In general, the answer depends on the shape of the marginal-extraction-cost function. With constant marginal cost, for example, there would be no supply-side effect and the market would transition later. If the environmental costs were associated with the cost of the renewable resource rather than the depletable resource, the time of transition for the efficient allocation would have been later than the market allocation.

What can we learn from these graphs about the allocation of depletable resources over time when environmental side effects are not borne by the agent determining the extraction rate? The price of the depletable resource would be too low and too much of the resource would be extracted. This once again shows the interdependencies among the various decisions we have to make about the future. Environmental and natural resource decisions are intimately and inextricably linked.

SUMMARY

The efficient allocation of substitutable depletable and renewable resources depends on the circumstances. When the resource can be extracted at a constant marginal cost, the efficient quantity of the depletable resource extracted declines over time. If no substitute is available, the quantity declines smoothly to zero. If a renewable constant-cost substitute is available, the quantity of the depletable resource extracted will decline smoothly to the quantity available from the renewable resource. In both cases, all of the available depletable resource would be eventually used up and marginal user cost would rise over time, reaching a maximum when the last unit of depletable resource was extracted.

The efficient allocation of an increasing marginal cost resource is similar in that the quantity extracted declines over time, but differs with respect to the behavior of marginal user cost and the cumulative amount extracted. Whereas marginal user cost typically rises over time when the marginal cost of extraction is constant, it declines over time when the marginal cost of extraction rises. Furthermore, in the constant-cost case the cumulative amount extracted is equal to the available supply; in the increasing cost case it is less.

Introducing technological progress and exploration activity into the model tends to delay the transition to renewable resources. Exploration expands the size of current reserves while technological progress keeps marginal extraction cost from rising as much as it otherwise would. If these effects are sufficiently potent, marginal cost could actually decline for some period of time, causing the quantity extracted to rise.

Market allocations of depletable resources can, when property right structures are properly defined, be efficient. Self-interest and efficiency are not necessarily incompatible.

When the extraction of resources imposes an external environmental cost, however, market allocations will not generally be efficient. The market price of the depletable resource would be too low and too much of the resource would be extracted.

In an efficient market allocation, the transition from depletable to renewable resources is smooth and exhibits none of the overshoot and collapse characteristics of the *Limits to Growth* view of the world. Whether the actual market allocations of these various types of resources are efficient remains to be seen. To the extent they are, a laissez-faire policy would represent an appropriate response by the government. On the other hand, if the market is not capable of yielding an efficient allocation, then some form of government intervention may be necessary.

In the next few chapters we shall examine these questions for a number of different types of depletable and renewable resources. We shall then return to the issue of aggregate scarcity and a survey of the empirical evidence on whether resource scarcity in a general sense is increasing.

FURTHER READING

Bohi, Douglas R. and Michael A. Toman. *Analyzing Nonrenewable Resource Supply* (Washington, DC: Resources for the Future, 1984). A reinterpretation and evaluation of existing research which attempts to weave together theoretical, empirical, and practical insights concerning the management of depletable resources.

Chapman, Duane. "Computation Techniques for Intertemporal Allocation of Natural Resources," *American Journal of Agricultural Economics* 69 (February 1987): 134–142. Shows how to find numerical solutions for the types of depletable resource problems considered in this chapter.

Conrad, Jon M. and Colin W. Clark. *Natural Resource Economics: Notes and Problems* (Cambridge: Cambridge University Press, 1987). This book reviews techniques of dynamic optimization and shows how they can be applied to the management of various resource systems.

Fisher, Anthony C. *Resource and Environmental Economics* (Cambridge: Cambridge University Press, 1981). This volume presents a careful heuristic development of the major mathematical results in optimal resource use for depletable and renewable resources. It also has chapters on preserving natural environments and on pollution. This text is written for graduate students or upper-level undergraduates.

Toman, Michael A. " 'Depletion Effects' and Nonrenewable Resource Supply," *Land Economics* 62 (November 1986): 341–353. An excellent, non-technical discussion of the increasing cost case with and without exploration and additions to reserves.

Williams, Stephen F. "Running Out: The Problem of Exhaustible Resources," *The Journal of Legal Studies* 7 (January 1978): 165–199. An excellent, nontechnical introduction to the basic ideas contained in this chapter by a natural resource lawyer.

ADDITIONAL REFERENCES

Anders, Gerhard, W. Philip Gramm, S. Charles Maurice, and Charles W. Smithson. *The Economics of Mineral Extraction* (New York: Praeger, 1980).

Dasgupta, P. S. and G. M. Heal. *Economic Theory and Exhaustible Resources* (Cambridge: Cambridge University Press, 1979).

Dasgupta, Partha. *The Control of Resources* (Cambridge, MA: Harvard University Press, 1982).

Kneese, Allen V. and James L. Sweeney, eds. *Handbook of Natural Resource and Energy Economics*, Vol. III (Amsterdam: North-Holland, 1986).

Peterson, Frederick M. and Anthony C. Fisher. "The Exploitation of Extractive Resources: A Survey," *Economic Journal* 88 (December 1977): 681–721.

Scott, Anthony, ed. *Progress in Natural Resource Economics* (Oxford: Clarendon Press, 1985).

PROBLEMS

1. To anticipate subsequent chapters where more complicated renewable resource models are introduced, consider a slight modification of the two-period depletable resource model. Suppose a biological resource is renewable in the sense that any of it left unextracted after period one will grow at rate k. Compared to the case where the total amount of a constant-*MEC* resource is fixed, how would the efficient allocation of this resource over the two periods differ? (*Hint:* It can be shown that $MNB_1/MNB_2 = (1 + k)/(1 + r)$, where *MNB* stands for marginal net benefit.)

2. Consider an increasing marginal cost depletable resource with no effective substitute. (a) Describe in general terms how the user cost for this resource in the earlier time periods would depend on whether the demand curve for that resource was stable or shifting outward over time. (b) How would the allocation of that resource over time be affected?

3. Many states are now imposing severance taxes on resources being extracted in their states. In order to understand the effect of these on the allocation of the mineral over time, assume a stable demand curve. (a) How would the competitive allocation of an increasing marginal cost depletable resource be affected by the imposition of a per unit tax (e.g., $4.00 per ton) if there exists a constant-marginal-cost substitute? (b) Comparing the allocation without a tax to one with a tax, in general terms what are the differences in cumulative amounts extracted and the price paths?

Extensions of the Basic Depletable Resource Model

In the appendix to Chapter 2 we derived a simple model to describe the efficient allocation of a constant-marginal-cost depletable resource over time and presented the numerical solution for a two-period version of that model. In this appendix, the mathematical derivations for the Chapter 6 extension to that basic model will be documented and the resulting numerical solutions for these more complicated cases will be explained.

The N-Period, Constant-Cost, No-Substitute Case

The first extension involves calculating the efficient allocation of the depletable resource over time when the number of time periods for extraction is unlimited. This is a more difficult calculation because how long the resource will last is no longer predetermined; the time of exhaustion must be derived as well as the extraction path prior to exhaustion of the resource.

The equations describing the allocation which maximizes the present value of benefits derived in the appendix to Chapter 2 are

$$\frac{a - bq_t - c}{(1+r)^{t-1}} - \lambda = 0, \; t = 1, \ldots, T,$$

(1)

$$\sum_{t=1}^{T} q_t - \bar{Q} = 0 \; .$$

(2)

The parameter values assumed for the numerical example presented in the text are a = \$8, b = 0.4, c = \$2, $\bar{Q}$ = 40, and r = 0.10. The allocation which satisfies these conditions is

$q_1 = 8.004$	$q_4 = 5.689$	$q_7 = 2.607$	$T = 9$
$q_2 = 7.305$	$q_5 = 4.758$	$q_8 = 1.368$	$\lambda = 2.7983$
$q_3 = 6.535$	$q_6 = 3.733$	$q_9 = 0.000$	

The optimality of this allocation can be verified by substituting these values into the above equations. (Due to rounding, these add to 39.999, rather than 40.000.)

Practically speaking, solving these equations to find the optimal solution is not a trivial matter, but neither is it very difficult. One method of finding the solution involves developing a computer algorithm (computation procedure) which converges on the correct answer. One such algorithm for this example can be constructed as follows: (1) assume a value for λ; (2) using equation set (1) solve for all q's based upon this λ; (3) if the sum of the calculated q's exceeds $\bar{Q}$, adjust λ upward or if the sum of the calculated q's is less than $\bar{Q}$, adjust λ downward (the adjustment should use information gained in previous steps to ensure that the new trial will be closer to the solution value); (4) repeat steps (2) and (3) using the new λ; (5) when the sum of the q's is sufficiently close to $\bar{Q}$, stop the calculations. As an exercise, those interested in computer programming might construct a program to reproduce these results.

Constant Marginal Cost with an Abundant Renewable Substitute

The next extension assumes the existence of an abundant, renewable, perfect substitute, available in unlimited quantities at a cost of \$6 per unit. To derive the dynamically efficient allocation of both the depletable resource and its substitute, let q_t be the amount of a constant-marginal-cost depletable resource extracted in year t and q_{st} the amount used of another constant-marginal-cost resource that is perfectly substitutable for the depletable resource. The marginal cost of the substitute is assumed to be \$d.

With this change the total benefit and cost formulas become

$$\text{Total benefit} = \sum_{t=1}^{T} a(q_t + q_{st}) - \frac{b}{2}(q_t + q_{st})^2,$$

(3)

$$\text{Total cost} = \sum_{t=1}^{T} cq_t + dq_{st} .$$

(4)

The objective function is thus:

$$PVNB = \sum_{t=1}^{T} \frac{a\,(q_t + q_{st}) - \frac{b}{2}\,(q_t^2 + q_{st}^2 + 2q_t\,q_s) - cq_t - dq_{st}}{(1+r)^{t-1}},$$

(5)

subject to the constraint on the total availability of the depletable resource:

$$\bar{Q} - \sum_{t=1}^{T} q_t \geq 0 .$$

(6)

Necessary and sufficient conditions for an allocation maximizing this function are expressed in equations (7), (8), and (9).

$$\frac{a - b(q_t + q_{st}) - c}{(1 + r)^{t-1}} - \lambda \leq 0,\, t=1, \ldots, T .$$

(7)

(Any member of equation set (7) will hold as an equality when $q_t > 0$ and will be negative when

$$a - b(q_t + q_{st}) - d \leq 0, \qquad t = 1, \ldots, T .$$

(8)

Any member of equation set (8) will hold as an equality when $q_{st} > 0$ and will be negative when $q_{st} = 0$.)

$$\bar{Q} - \sum_{t=1}^{T} q_t \geq 0.$$

(9)

For the numerical example used in the test the following parameter values were assumed: $a = \$8$, $b = 0.4$, $c = \$2$, $d = \$6$, $\bar{Q} = 40$, and $r = 0.10$. It can be readily verified that the optimal conditions are satisfied by

$$q_1 = 8.798 \qquad q_3 = 7.495 \qquad q_5 = 5.919$$
$$q_2 = 8.177 \qquad q_4 = 6.744$$
$$q_{s6} = 2.137 \qquad q_{st} = \begin{cases} 5.000 \text{ for } t > 6 \\ 0 \text{ for } t < 6 \end{cases}$$
$$q_6 = 2.863$$
$$\lambda = 2.481$$

The depletable resource is used up before the end of the sixth period and the switch is made to the substitute resource at that time. From equation set (8), in competitive markets the switch occurs precisely at the moment when the resource price rises to meet the marginal cost of the substitute.

The switch point in this example is earlier than in the previous example (the sixth period rather than the ninth period). Since all characteristics of the problem except for the availability of the substitute are the same in the two numerical examples, the difference can be attributed to the availability of the renewable substitute.

Increasing Marginal Cost Case

In this case the cost function for the depletable resource differs from the previous case. Specifically, instead of $TC_t = cq_t$ the function is

$$TC_t = cq_t + (f/2) \left(\sum_{i=1}^{t} q_i \right)^2$$

prior to the switch point and $TC_1 = dq_{st}$ after. In addition, there is no availability constraint; availability in this case is determined by cost, not by a finite limit on the amount available. With this change the objective function is

$$PVNB = \sum_{t=1}^{T} \frac{a(q_t + q_{st}) - \dfrac{b}{2}(q_t^2 + q_{st}^2 + 2q_t\,q_{st}) - cq_t - dq_{st}}{(1+r)^{t-1}}$$

(10)

$$-f \sum_{t=1}^{T} \frac{\left(\sum_{i=1}^{t} q_t \right)^2}{2(1+r)^{t-1}} \; .$$

Necessary and sufficient conditions for any allocation satisfying this function are

$$\frac{a - b\,(q_t - q_{st}) - c - f\left[\sum_{i-1}^{t} q_i\right]}{(1 + r)^{t-1}} - \sum_{i=t+1}^{T} \frac{fq_i}{(1 + r)^{i-1}} \le 0, \qquad t = 1, \ldots, T.$$

(11)

(Any member of equation set (11) will hold as an equality when $q_t > 0$ and will be negative when $q_t = 0$.)

$$a - b(q_t + q_{st}) - d \le 0.$$

(12)

(Any member of equation set (12) will hold as an equality when $q_{st} > 0$ and will be negative when $q_{st} = 0$.)

In equation set (11) the term immediately before the $\le$ sign is the marginal user cost. Note that it diminishes over time as t approaches the switch point.

For the increasing-cost numerical example which ignores environmental costs the assumed parameter values were $a = \$8$, $b = 0.4$, $c = \$2$, $d = \$6$, $r = 0.10$, and $f = 0.10$. It is easily verified that the following solution satisfies the optimal conditions:

$q_1 = 7.132$	$q_3 = 6.017$	$q_5 = 5.304$	$q_7 = 4.316$
$q_2 = 6.523$	$q_4 = 5.610$	$q_6 = 5.099$	$n = 7$

$$q_{st} = \begin{cases} 0 & \text{for } t < 7 \\ 0.684 & \text{for } t = 7 \\ 5.000 & \text{for } t > 7 \end{cases}$$

All of the depletable resource that is available at a cost lower than the substitute is used up prior to the switch point, which occurs during the seventh period.

Including Environmental Cost

For the case with environmental costs all formulas are the same, and only one parameter value is changed. Specifically, the environmental cost simulation assumes $c = \$3$ rather than $c = \$2$, as had been true in the previous simulation. The difference is presumed to reflect the environmental costs associated with extracting this resource.

With this parameter change, the new solutions become:

$$q_1 = 6.297 \qquad q_3 = 5.470 \qquad q_5 = 5.048$$
$$q_2 = 5.834 \qquad q_4 = 5.207 \qquad q_6 = 2.144 \qquad \text{for } t > 6, q_{st} = 5.0$$
$$n = 6 \qquad \bar{Q} = 30 \qquad q_{s6} = 2.856 \qquad \text{for } t < 6, q_{st} = 0.00$$

CHAPTER SEVEN

Depletable, Nonrecyclable Energy Resources: Oil, Gas, Coal, and Uranium

If it ain't broke, don't fix it!

OLD MAINE PROVERB

INTRODUCTION

Energy deserves its reputation as one of our most critical resources; without it, life would cease. We derive energy from the food we eat. Through photosynthesis, the plant life we consume—both directly and indirectly when we eat meat—depends on energy from the sun. The materials we use to build our houses and produce the goods we consume are extracted from the earth's crust, then transformed into finished products with expenditures of energy.

Currently, most industrialized countries depend on oil and natural gas for most of their energy needs. In the United States, for example, these two resources together supply 67% of all energy consumed. Both are depletable, nonrecyclable sources of energy. Crude oil proven reserves peaked during the 1970s and natural gas peaked in the 1980s in the United States and Europe, and since that time, the amount extracted has exceeded additions to reserves[1] (Figures 7.1 and 7.2).

---

1 In contrast, world reserves of oil and gas have continued to increase during the 1980s. See U.S. Energy Information Administration, *International Energy Annual* (Washington, DC: Government Printing Office): various issues.

FIGURE 7.1   United States and Western Europe estimated crude oil reserves over time.

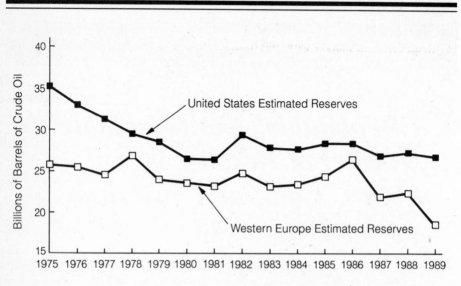

FIGURE 7.2   United States and Western Europe estimated natural gas reserves over time.

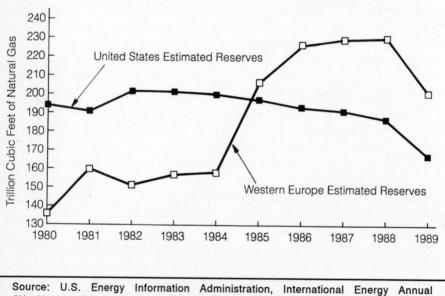

Source: U.S. Energy Information Administration, International Energy Annual (Washington, DC: Government Printing Office): annual.

According to the models in Chapter 6, oil and natural gas would be transition fuels in an efficient allocation. They would be used until the marginal cost of further use exceeded the marginal cost of substitute resources—either more abundant depletable resources, such as coal, or renewable sources, such as solar energy.[2] In an efficient market path, the transition to these alternative sources would be smooth and harmonious. Have the allocations of the last several decades been efficient or not? In a 1977 speech to the nation, President Jimmy Carter suggested that the resolve needed to solve our energy problems was "the moral equivalent of war." The existence of a crisis atmosphere suggests that the allocations have not been efficient. Why not? Is the market mechanism flawed in its allocation of depletable recyclable resources? If so, is the flaw fatal? If not, what caused the inefficient allocations? Is the problem correctable?

In this chapter we shall examine some of the major issues associated with the allocation of energy resources over time and how economic analysis can clarify our understanding of both the sources of the problems and their solutions. Because energy is too complex a subject to treat comprehensively in one chapter, however, additional references are provided.

NATURAL GAS: PRICE CONTROLS

In the United States during the winter of late 1974 and early 1975, serious shortages of natural gas developed. Customers who had contracted and were willing to pay for natural gas were unable to get as much as they wanted. The shortage (or curtailments as the Federal Energy Regulatory Commission calls them) amounted to 2.0 trillion cubic feet of natural gas in 1974–1975 which represented roughly 10% of the marketed production in 1975.[3] In an efficient allocation, shortages of that magnitude would never have happened. Why did they?

The source of the problem can be traced directly to government controls over natural gas prices. This story begins, oddly enough, with the rise of the automobile, which traditionally has not used natural gas as a fuel. The increasing importance of the automobile for transportation created a rising demand for gasoline, which in turn stimulated a search for new sources of crude oil. This exploration activity uncovered large quantities of natural gas (known as associated gas), in addition to large quantities of crude oil, which was the object of the search.

---

2 When used for other purposes, oil can be recyclable. Waste lubricating oil is now routinely recycled.

3 The curtailment figure comes from Federal Energy Administration, *National Energy Outlook* (Washington, DC, 1976): 121, and the marketed figure is from U.S. Department of Energy, *Monthly Energy Review: April 1978* (Washington, DC: Government Printing Office, 1978): 24.

As natural gas was discovered, it replaced manufactured gas—and some coal—in the geographic areas where it was found. Then, as a geographically dispersed demand developed for this increasingly available gas, a long-distance system of gas pipelines was designed and constructed. In the period following World War II, natural gas became an important source of energy for the United States.

The regulation of natural gas began in 1938 with the passage of the Natural Gas Act. This act transformed the Federal Power Commission (FPC) into a federal regulatory agency charged with maintaining "just" prices. In 1954, a Supreme Court decision in *Phillips Petroleum Co. v. Wisconsin* forced the FPC to extend their price control regulations to the producer. Prior to that time, they had merely limited their regulation to pipeline companies.

Because the process of setting price ceilings proved cumbersome, the hastily conceived initial "interim" ceilings remained in effect for almost a decade before the Commission was able to impose more carefully considered ceilings.[4] What was the effect of this regulation?

By returning to our models in the previous section, we can see the havoc this would raise. The ceiling would prevent prices from reaching their normal levels. Since price increases are the source of the incentive to conserve, the lower prices would cause more of the resource to be used in earlier years. Consumption levels in those years would be higher under price controls than without them.

Effects on the supply side are also significant. Producers would only produce the resource when they could do so profitably. Once the marginal cost rose to meet the price ceiling, no more would be produced, in spite of the large demand for the resource at that price. Thus, as long as price controls are permanent, less of the resource would be produced with controls than without. Furthermore, more of what would be produced would be used in the earlier years.

The combined impact of these demand and supply effects would be to distort the allocation significantly (Figures 7.3a and 7.3b). While a number of aspects differentiate this allocation from an efficient one, two are of particular importance: (1) the time of transition is earlier under price controls; and (2) the transition is abrupt, with prices suddenly jumping to new higher levels. Both are detrimental. The first effect means we would not be using all of the natural gas available at prices consumers were willing to pay. Among other things, this could cause a transition to the substitute before the technologies to use it were adequately developed.

The discontinuous jump to a new technology, which results from price controls, can place quite a burden on consumers. Attracted by artificially low prices,

---

4 For an excellent discussion of this period, see Stephen G. Breyer and Paul W. MacAvoy, *Energy Regulation by the Federal Power Commission* (Washington, DC: Brookings Institution, 1974).

FIGURE 7.3 (a) Increasing marginal extraction cost with substitute resource in the presence of price controls: quantity profile. (b) Increasing marginal extraction cost with substitute resource in the presence of price controls: price profile.

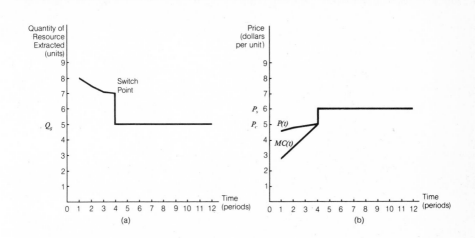

consumers would invest in equipment to use natural gas, only to discover—after the transition—that natural gas was no longer available.

One interesting characteristic of price ceilings is that they affect behavior even when they are not binding (when the market price is lower than the price ceiling, for example).[5] This effect is clearly illustrated in Figures 7.3a and 7.3b in the earlier years. Even though the price in the first year is lower than the price ceiling, it is not equal to the efficient price. The price ceiling causes a reallocation of resources toward the present, which, in turn, affects prices in the earlier years.

Price controls may cause other problems as well. Up to this point, we have discussed permanent controls. Not all price controls are permanent; they can change at the whim of the political process in unpredictable ways. The fact that prices could suddenly rise when the ceiling is lifted also creates unfortunate incentives. If producers expect a large price increase in the near future, they have an incentive to stop production and wait for the higher prices. This circumstance could cause severe problems for consumers.

For legal reasons the price controls on natural gas were placed solely on gas shipped across state lines. Gas consumed within the states where it was produced

---

5 For a complete analysis of this point, see Dwight R. Lee, "Price Controls, Binding Constraints, and Intertemporal Economic Decision Making," *Journal of Political Economy* 86 (1978): 293–301.

could be priced at what the market would bear. As a result, gas produced and sold within the state received a higher price than that sold in other states. Consequently, the share of gas in the interstate market fell over time as producers found it more profitable to commit reserve additions to the *intrastate*, rather than the *interstate*, market. In the 1964–1969 period, about 33% of the average annual reserve additions were committed to the interstate market. By 1970–1974, this commitment had fallen to a little less than 5%.

The practical effect of charging less for gas destined for the interstate market was to cause the shortages to be concentrated in states served by pipeline and dependent on the interstate shipment of gas. As a result, the damage caused was greater than it would have been if all consuming areas had shared somewhat more equitably in the shortfall. The price control system not only caused the damage, it intensified it!

Natural gas allocations not only hastened the time of transition to a substitute resource, it also caused a transition to an inefficient substitute. The reason for this substitution bias and its implications are explored in Example 7.1.

It seems fair to conclude that, by sapping the economic system of its ability to respond to changing conditions, price controls on natural gas created a significant amount of turmoil. If this kind of political control is likely to recur with some regularity, perhaps some of the *Limits to Growth* concerns may be valid, though for different reasons. The overshoot and collapse syndrome in this case would be caused by government interference rather than any pure market behavior. If so, the proverb which opens this chapter becomes particularly relevant!

Why did Congress embark on such a counterproductive policy? The answer is found in rent-seeking behavior which can be explained through the use of our consumer and producer surplus model. Let's examine the political incentives in a simple model.

Consider Figure 7.4. An efficient market allocation would result in Q^* supplied at price P^*. The net benefits received by the country would be represented by the total geometric area encompassed by the areas denoted as A and B. Of these net benefits, area A would be received by consumers as consumer surplus and B would be received by producers as a producer surplus.

Suppose now that a price ceiling were established. From the above discussion we know that this ceiling would reduce the marginal user cost because higher future prices would no longer be possible. In Figure 7.4, this has the effect for current producers of lowering the perceived supply curve, due to the lower marginal user cost. As a result of this shift in the perceived supply curve, current production would expand to Q_c and price would fall to P_c. Current consumers would unambiguously be better off, since consumer surplus would be area A + B + C instead of area A. They would have gained a net benefit equal to B + C.

It may appear that producers could also gain if $D > B$, but that is not correct. Because producers would be overproducing, they would be giving up the scarcity rent they could have gotten without price controls. Area D measures only current

EXAMPLE 7.1

Price Controls and Substitution Bias

Faced with shortages, pipeline companies looked for alternative sources of supply. Two that they discovered were liquid natural gas (LNG), shipped from abroad in pressurized ships, and synthetic natural gas (SNG), manufactured from various petroleum products. These sources were both very expensive.

Pipeline companies induced consumers to use these substitutes by using average-cost pricing. The artificially cheap natural gas was blended with the synthetic gas and sold at the average cost of the two, depending on the proportions. Thus, if they used 90% natural gas at $1 per unit and 10 percent other sources at $5 per unit, the cost of the combined gas is $1.40 per unit (0.90 × $1 + 0.10 × $5). Thus, instead of paying the high marginal cost of the substitute for additional units consumed, as efficiency would dictate, consumers paid the much lower average cost. The pricing system sent them the wrong signal.

This system of pricing created a bias toward substitutes which could be blended with natural gas and away from substitutes which could not. In this case the bias was particularly unfortunate; not only did it create additional demand for imported energy sources (LNG) at a time when the official policy was to discourage such imports, but it also encouraged lower levels of thermodynamic efficiency in the use of our diminishing oil resources. The conversion to gas caused some of the potential energy to be lost. Substitutes rendered noneconomic in certain parts of the country by this pricing system included heat pumps and residential solar space heating.

Because this system of average cost pricing encouraged pipeline companies to accept high cost sources of imported or synthetic gas that could be commingled with the artificially cheap natural gas during the 1970s, when natural gas prices began to be decontrolled in the early 1980s, the price rise was especially rapid and sharp. The large base of artificially low-cost natural gas no longer provided a cushion to counterbalance the very high cost of the new sources. Average residential prices for natural gas rose from $2.98 per thousand cubic feet in 1979 to $6.06 in 1983. Since that time they have stabilized with the 1989 price being $5.63; the excess demand in the natural gas market had been eliminated by higher prices.

Sources: Thomas H. Tietenberg, "Substitution Bias in a Depletable Resource Model with Administered Prices," in *Erschöpfbare Ressourcen* (Berlin: Duncker and Humlot, 1980): 529–552, and Energy Information Administration, *Monthly Energy Review* (January 1989): 105.

FIGURE 7.4   The effect of price controls.

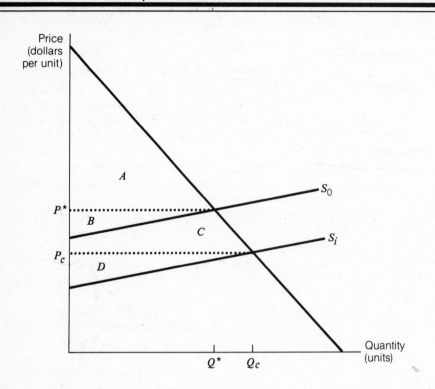

profits without considering scarcity rent. When the loss in scarcity rent is considered, producers unambiguously lose net benefits.

Some future consumers, meanwhile, are also worse off. Since the supplies are exhausted more rapidly, eventually the point will be reached when the price to consumers is higher than it would be otherwise. (Compare the prices in years 4, 5, and 6 in Figure 7.3b with the prices in the same years in Figure 6.5b.) Higher prices are experienced by future consumers in those years because the switch to the more expensive substitute is made prematurely. Future consumers who might have used natural gas had the controls not been in effect, would be forced to use the more expensive substitute. The higher price implies lower consumer surplus.

Congress may view scarcity rent as a possible source of revenue to transfer from producers to consumers. As we have seen, however, scarcity rent is an opportunity cost which serves a distinct purpose—the protection of future consumers. When a government attempts to reduce this scarcity rent through price controls, the result is an overallocation to current consumers and an underallocation to future consumers. Thus, what appears to be a transfer from producers to consumers is, in large part, also a transfer from future consumers to present consumers. Since current consumers mean current votes and future consumers may not know whom to blame by the time shortages appear, price controls are politically attractive. Unfortunately, they are also inefficient; the losses to future consumers and producers are greater than the gains to current consumers. Because they distort the allocation toward the present, controls are also unfair. Thus, markets in the presence of price controls are indeed myopic, but the problem lies with the controls, not the market.

Over the long run, price controls end up harming consumers rather than helping them. Scarcity rent plays an important role in the allocation process, and attempts to eliminate it can create more problems than are solved. After long debating the price control issue, Congress passed the Natural Gas Policy Act on November 9, 1978.[6] This act initiated the eventual phased decontrol of natural gas prices. Included among its other provisions was a movement away from the average-cost pricing of substitute gas for industrial customers and the imposition of price controls for the first time on intrastate gas, until such time as all prices are decontrolled. On July 27, 1989, President George Bush signed a bill removing in stages all remaining controls on natural gas. By January 1993, no sources of natural gas would be subject to price controls.

OIL: THE CARTEL PROBLEM

Since we have considered similar effects on natural gas, we merely note that price controls have been responsible for much mischief in the oil market as well.[7] A second source of misallocation in the oil market, however, deserves further consideration. Most of the world's oil is produced by a cartel called the Organization of Petroleum Exporting Countries (OPEC). The members of this organization collude to exercise power over oil production and prices. As established in Chapter 2, seller power over resources due to a lack of effective competition leads to an inefficient allocation. When sellers have market power, they can restrict supply and thus force prices higher than otherwise.

Though these conclusions were derived in Chapter 2 for nondepletable resources, they are valid for depletable resources as well. A monopolist can extract more scarcity rent from a depletable resource base than competitive suppliers can, simply by restricting supply. The monopolistic transition results in slower

---

6 For an excellent discussion of this complex act, see Walter J. Mead, "The Natural Gas Policy Act of 1978: An Economic Evaluation," in *Contemporary Economic Problems 1979*, William Fellner, ed. (Washington, DC: American Enterprise Institute, 1979): 325-355.

7 The price controls on oil were similar to, but not the same as, price controls on natural gas. For a discussion on the effects on those controls, see Kenneth J. Arrow and Joseph P. Kalt, *Petroleum Price Regulation: Should We Decontrol?* (Washington, DC: American Enterprise Institute, 1979).

production and higher prices.[8] The monopolistic transition to a substitute, therefore, occurs later than a competitive transition. It also reduces the net benefit
society receives from these resources.

As illustrated in Example 7.2, the cartelization of the oil suppliers was very
effective. Why? Were the conditions which made it profitable unique to oil, or
could oil cartelization be the harbinger of a wave of natural resource cartels? To
answer these questions, we must isolate those factors which make cartelization
possible. Though many factors are involved, four stand out: (1) the price elasticity of demand for OPEC oil in both the long run and the short run; (2) the
income elasticity of demand for oil; (3) the supply responsiveness of the oil producers who are not OPEC members; and (4) the compatibility of interests among
members of OPEC.

Price Elasticity of Demand

The elasticity of demand is an important ingredient because it determines how
responsive demand is to price. When demand elasticities are less than 1.0, price
increases lead to increased revenue. Exactly how much revenue would increase when
prices increase depends on the price elasticity of demand. In general, the lower the
price elasticity of demand the larger the gains to be derived from forming a cartel.

The price elasticity of demand for oil depends on the opportunities for conservation, as well as on the availability of substitutes. As storm windows cut
heat losses, the same temperature can be maintained with less heating oil. Smaller
automobiles reduce the amount of gasoline needed to travel a given distance.
The larger the set of these opportunities and the smaller the cash outlays required
to exploit them, the more price elastic the demand. This suggests that the price
elasticity of demand in the long run (when sufficient time has passed to allow
adjustments) will be greater, perhaps significantly, than in the short run.

The availability of substitutes is important because it limits the degree to
which prices can be raised by a producer cartel. Abundant quantities of substitutes available at prices not far above competitive oil prices can set an upper
limit on the cartel price. Unless OPEC controls those sources as well—and it
doesn't—any attempts to raise prices above those limits would cause the consuming nations to simply switch to these alternative sources; OPEC would have
priced itself out of the market.

---

8 The conclusion that a monopoly would extract a resource more slowly than a competitive mining
industry is not perfectly general. It is possible to construct demand curves such that the extraction
rate of the monopolist is greater than or equal to that of a competitive industry. As a practical matter,
these conditions seem unlikely. That a monopoly would restrict output, while not inevitable, is the
most likely conclusion to draw. See the discussion in Anthony C. Fisher, *Resource and Environmental
Economics* (Cambridge: Cambridge University Press, 1981): 37–39.

EXAMPLE 7.2

Optimal OPEC Pricing

In 1978 Robert Pindyck, an economist at the Massachusetts Institute of Technology, published a study of optimal OPEC pricing. His model was quite similar to that used in this book with two exceptions: (1) he chose his parameters to be consistent with current demand and reserve patterns (whereas our model is explicitly hypothetical), and (2) he incorporated into his model the fact that demand responds to higher prices slowly rather than immediately.

In this study he calculated optimal price trajectories for OPEC if it were to act competitively and if it were to act as a cartel. Each of these trajectories is calculated using two discount rates (5% and 10%). From this calculation it is possible to derive the additional gains to producers from establishing a cartel. The results are presented in the accompanying figure. As expected the monopoly prices are higher, at least in the earlier years. In the later years when the competitive allocation begins to experience more severe scarcity, competitive prices would rise above the monopoly prices. The initial dip in monopoly prices is due to the lagged response in demand. In the initial years when demand responds rather sluggishly, the price can be held high, but as demand becomes more responsive, prices have to drop to prevent too severe reductions in demand.

From: Robert S. Pindyck, "Gains to Producers from the Cartelization of Exhaustible Resources," *The Review of Economics and Statistics* 60 (May 1978): 242.

Using a 10% discount rate, Pindyck calculates that compared to a competitive allocation, the present value of producers' profits would be 1.94 times higher if the producers acted as a cartel. Most of the advantages of cartelization are accrued in the first few years. Pindyck calculates that the present value of profits accrued during the first five years in the monopoly case is 5.78 times as large as those in the competitive case. Cartelization has been extremely profitable to the producers if inefficient for the world economy.

Source: Robert S. Pindyck, "Gains to Producers from the Cartelization of Exhaustible Resources," *The Review of Economics and Statistics* 60 (May 1978): 238–251.

Alternative sources clearly exist, although they are expensive and the time of transition is long. One extensive survey of world energy resources, for example, concluded that about as much petroleum could be extracted from unconventional sources—such as deep offshore wells, wells in the polar seas, heavy oils, enhanced recovery techniques, oil shales, tar sands, and synthetic oils—as is currently available from conventional petroleum reserves. It further concludes, however, that those sources wouldn't make much of a dent in the oil market until the end of the twentieth century and then only at very high cost. This report conjectured that the high cost of these sources would confine their use to transportation and chemicals.[9] While coal is clearly a substitute for some uses and is available in large supplies, as we shall see in the next section, coal use triggers a number of environmental problems.

Clearly, the ultimate substitute is solar energy and it is the cost of solar energy that will set the long-run upper limit on the ability of OPEC to raise its prices. Since in many parts of the United States solar energy is currently cost competitive for space and hot-water heating, that limit is probably not substantially higher than recent OPEC prices. Although it will take a significant amount of time for these new technologies to get all the bugs worked out and begin to penetrate the market on a massive scale, the transition seems to be proceeding smoothly. As Example 7.3 indicates, this transition has extended to electricity production as well, which some observers felt would resist that change.

Income Elasticity of Demand

The income elasticity of oil demand is important because it indicates how sensitive oil demand is to growth in the world economy. At constant prices, as income grows, oil demand should grow. This continual increase in demand fortifies the ability of OPEC to raise its prices. High income elasticities of demand support the cartelization of oil. All other things being equal, the higher the income elasticity of demand, the higher the price would have to rise to bring demand to zero (in the absence of substitutes) or the more rapidly it would rise to the level of the substitute resource when one is available.

The income elasticity of demand is also important because it registers how sensitive demand is to the business cycle. The higher the income elasticity of demand, the more sensitive demand is. This is a major source of the weakening of the cartel which occurred during 1983. A recession caused a large reduction in the demand for oil, putting new pressure on the cartel to absorb these demand reductions.

---

9 World Energy Conference, *World Energy Resources: 1985–2020* (New York: IPC Science and Technology Press, 1978): 2–3.

EXAMPLE 7.3

Are Soft Energy Paths Doomed?

In 1976 a young physicist named Amory Lovins published an article in *Foreign Affairs* which built an immediate following for him and his ideas. His thesis, boldly stated, was that we could follow two paths to our energy future. One, dubbed by Lovins as the "hard path," consisted of an increasing reliance on large-scale, centralized technologies, while the second, the "soft path," relied more on smaller, decentralized technologies. The former is epitomized by nuclear power plants, while solar home heating, windmills, and small dams provide examples of the latter. Furthermore, Lovins argued, these paths are mutually exclusive and the existing system is biased toward the former. If valid, this argument would cast a dark shadow over any expectation that the transition to the soft path would be efficient and smooth.

Lovins suggests that the current system of relying upon centralized power has allowed the buildup of vested interests having a stake in maintaining the status quo. One way this dominance could be perpetuated is for the utilities to refuse to purchase excess power from the soft-path producers. With no market or distribution system, producers would have less incentive to produce power by these means.

Whatever validity that argument may have had at the time it was made, it has been weakened by congressional action. In 1978 Congress passed the Public Utility Regulatory Policies Act to encourage the production of electricity from renewable resources and from cogeneration systems. *Cogeneration* is the combined production of electricity and useful thermal energy. Among other provisions, this act (1) requires utilities to purchase excess power at a price equal to what it would have cost the utilities to generate the power themselves; (2) requires utilities to provide backup power to those producers at average cost (usually lower than the price utilities pay the producers for excess power); and (3) stipulates that the qualifying small-production units cannot be owned by utilities. Though this is a controversial piece of legislation, undoubtedly it is spurring the development of small, renewable, energy sources for producing electricity.

Source: Amory B. Lovins, "Energy Strategy: The Road Not Taken?" *Foreign Affairs* 55 (October 1976): 65–98. The importance of this act to potential investors in renewable resources is described in Colin Norman, "Renewable Power Sparks Financial Interest," *Science* 212 (June 26, 1981): 1479–1481.

Non-OPEC Suppliers

Another key factor in the ability of producer nations to exercise power over a natural resource market is their ability to prevent new suppliers, not part of the cartel, from entering the market and undercutting the price. Currently OPEC produces about two-thirds of the world's oil. If the remaining producers were able, in the face of higher prices, to expand their supply dramatically, they would increase the amount of oil supplied and cause the prices to fall, decreasing OPEC's market share. If this response were large enough, the allocation of oil would approach the competitive allocation.

Currently only Mexico appears to have large enough reserves to make an individual difference in the world oil market. Since both the size of its reserve and its production profile are uncertain, it is difficult to assess Mexico's ultimate impact on the future world market.

This does not mean, however, that non-OPEC members collectively do not have an impact on price. They do. The cartel must take the nonmembers into account when setting prices. Salant has proposed an interesting model of monopoly pricing in the presence of a fringe of small nonmember producers that serves as a basis for exploring this issue.[10] His model includes a number of suppliers. Some form a cartel. Others, a smaller number, form a "competitive fringe." The cartel is assumed to set the price of oil to maximize its collective profits by restricting production, taking the competitive fringe production into account. The competitive fringe cannot directly set the price, but since it is free to choose the level of production which maximizes its own profits, its output does affect the cartel's pricing strategy.

What conclusions does this model yield? The model concludes that a resource cartel would set different prices when faced with a competitive fringe than when it is not. With a competitive fringe, it would set the initial price somewhat lower and allow price to rise more rapidly than would otherwise be the case. This strategy maximizes cartel profits by forcing the competitive fringe to produce more in the earlier periods (in response to higher demand) and eventually to exhaust their supplies. After the competitive fringe has depleted its reserves, the cartel would raise the price and thereafter prices would increase much more slowly.

Thus, the optimal strategy, from the point of view of the cartel, is to hold back on its own sales during the initial period, letting the other suppliers exhaust their supplies. Sales and profits of the competitive fringe, in this optimal cartel strategy, decline over time, while sales and profits of the cartel increase over time as prices rise and the cartel captures a larger share of the market.

---

10 S. W. Salant, "Exhaustible Resources and Industrial Structure: A Nash-Cournot Approach to the World Oil Market," *Journal of Political Economy* 84 (1976): 1079–1093.

One fascinating implication of this model is that the formation of the cartel raises the present value of competitive fringe profits by an even greater percentage than the present value of cartel profits. Those without the power gain more in percentage terms than those with the power!

Though this may seem counterintuitive, it is actually easily explained. The cartel, in order to keep the price up, must cut back on its own production level. The competitive fringe, however, is under no such constraint and is free to take advantage of the high prices without cutting back its own production. Thus, the profits of the competitive fringe are higher in the earlier period. All the cartel can do is wait until the competitive suppliers become less of a force in the market. The implication of this model is that the competitive fringe is a collective force in the oil market, even if they control as little as one-third of the production.

The impact of this competitive fringe on OPEC behavior was dramatically illustrated by events in the 1985–1986 period. In 1979, OPEC accounted for approximately 50% of world oil production, while in 1986 this had fallen to approximately 30%. Taking account of the fact that total world oil production was down during this period over 10% for all producers, the pressures on the cartel mounted and prices ultimately fell. The average cost of crude oil imports in the United States fell from $36.52 per barrel in 1981 to $25.94 in January 1986. OPEC simply was not able to hold the line on prices because the necessary reductions in production were too large for the individual cartel members to sustain.

Compatibility of Member Interests

The final factor we shall consider in determining the potential for cartelization of natural resource markets is the internal cohesion of the cartel. When there is only one seller, the objective of that seller can be pursued without worrying about alienating others who could undermine the profitability of the enterprise. In a cartel composed of many sellers, that freedom is no longer as wide-ranging. The incentives of each member and the incentives of the group as a whole may diverge.

Cartel members have a strong incentive to cheat. A cheater, if undetected by the other members, could surreptitiously lower its price and steal part of the market away from the others. Formally, the price elasticity of demand facing an individual member is substantially higher than that for the group as a whole, because some of the increase in individual sales at a lower price represents sales reductions for other members. With a higher price elasticity, lower prices maximize profits. Thus, successful cartelization presupposes a means for detecting cheating and enforcing the collusive agreement.[11]

---

11 During February 1985, OPEC hired a large Dutch accounting firm to help it detect cheating among its members. See "Dutch Accountants Take On a Formidable Task: Ferreting Out 'Cheaters' in the Ranks of OPEC," *Wall Street Journal* (February 26, 1982): 39.

TABLE 7.1   The World's Largest Oil Reserves as of January 1, 1989

Country	Reserves (billions of barrels)
Saudi Arabia	255.0
Iraq	100.0
United Arab Emirates	98.1
Kuwait	94.5
Iran	92.9
U.S.S.R.	58.5
Venezuela	58.1
Mexico	54.1
United States	26.8
China	23.6

Source: *Oil and Gas Journal* (December 26, 1988): 48–49, as cited in United States: Energy Information Administration, *International Energy Annual 1988.*

In addition to cheating, however, there is another threat to the stability of cartels—the degree to which members fail to agree on pricing and output decisions. Oil provides an excellent example of how these dissensions can arise. Since the 1974 rise of OPEC as a world power, Saudi Arabia has exercised a moderating influence on the pricing decisions of OPEC. Why?

One highly significant reason is the size of Saudi Arabia's oil reserves (Table 7.1). Saudi Arabia holds approximately 33% of the OPEC proved reserves; its reserves are larger than those of any other member. Hence, Saudi Arabia has an incentive to preserve the value of those resources. It is worried about setting prices so high as to undercut the future demand for its oil. As already stated, the demand for oil in the long run is more price elastic than in the short run. Countries with smaller reserves, meanwhile, know that in the long run their reserves will be gone and are more concerned about the near future. Since alternative sources of supply are not much of a threat in the near future because of long development times, other countries want to extract as much rent as possible now.

The size of Saudi Arabia's production also gives it the potential to make its influence felt. Its capacity to produce is so large that it can unilaterally affect world prices. In January of 1981, for example, it was producing approximately 10.3 million barrels of crude oil a day—representing about 41% of all OPEC production.[12]

Cartelization is not an easy path to pursue for producers, but when possible it can be very profitable. When the resource is a strategic and pervasive raw material, cartelization can be very costly for consuming nations.

---

12 Energy Information Administration, U.S. Department of Energy, *Monthly Energy Review: May 1981* (Washington, DC: U.S. Government Printing Office, 1981): 92-93.

Strategic-material cartelization also confers on the members political, as well as economic, power. Economic power can become political power when the revenue is used to purchase weapons or the capacity to produce weapons. The producer nations can also use an embargo of the material as a lever to cajole reluctant adversaries into foreign policy concessions. When the material is of strategic importance, the potential for embargoes casts a pall over the normally clear and convincing case for free trade of raw materials among nations. What is an efficient resolution of this problem?

OIL: NATIONAL SECURITY PROBLEM

From an economic point of view, vulnerable strategic imports have an added cost which is not reflected in the marketplace. National security is a classic public good. No individual importer correctly represents our collective national security interests in making a decision on how much to import. Thus, leaving the determination of the appropriate balance between imports and domestic production to the market generally results in an excessive dependence on imports (Figure 7.5).

Three supply curves are relevant. The first S_d is the long-run domestic supply curve. Its upward slope reflects increasing availability of domestic oil at higher prices, given sufficient time to develop those resources. There are two supply curves for imported foreign oil: S_{f0} reflects the world price, and S_{f1} includes a "vulnerability premium" in addition to the world price. This premium reflects the additional national security costs caused by imports. Both curves are drawn horizontally to the axis to reflect the assumption that U.S. action on imports is unlikely to affect the world price for oil.

In Figure 7.5 the market would generally demand and receive Q_5 units of oil. Of this total amount, Q_1 would be domestically produced and $Q_5 - Q_1$ would be imported. (Why?) However, in an efficient allocation incorporating the national security costs, only Q_4 units would be consumed. Of these, Q_2 would be domestically produced and $Q_4 - Q_2$ would be imported. Notice that when national security is an issue, the market in general tends to consume too much oil and domestic production is too small. Both of these factors raise vulnerable imports above their efficient level.

What would happen during an embargo? Be careful! At first glance you would guess that we would consume Q_3 relying solely on domestic production. We may well rely solely on domestic production; yet, the amount consumed would be Q_1 and the price, P_2. Why?

Remember that S_d is the domestic supply curve, *given enough time to develop the resources*. If an embargo hits, there is not enough time to develop additional resources (six-year time lags are common). Therefore, in the short run, the supply

FIGURE 7.5   The national security problem.

curve becomes perfectly inelastic (vertical) at Q_1. The price will rise to P_2 to equate supply and demand. As the graph indicates, the loss in consumer surplus during an embargo can be very large indeed.

How can importing nations react to this inefficiency? On November 7, 1973, shortly after the embargo had been initiated, President Richard Nixon, in a nationwide address, announced Project Independence, a massive effort comparable to the Manhattan Project, designed to achieve energy self-sufficiency by the 1980s. If imports were reduced to zero, as President Nixon suggested, the vulnerability problem would disappear. Is self-sufficiency the answer?

If the situation is adequately represented by Figure 7.5, then the answer is clearly no. The net benefit from self-sufficiency (the allocation in which consumption is Q_3 and imports are zero) is clearly lower than the net benefits from the efficient allocation (Q_4). The size of the efficiency loss is indicated by the shaded area in Figure 7.5.

Why, you might ask, is self-sufficiency so inefficient when embargoes obviously impose so much damage and self-sufficiency could grant immunity from this damage? Why would we want any imports at all when national security is at stake?

The simple answer is that the vulnerability premium is lower than the cost of becoming self-sufficient, but that response merely begs the question. Why is the vulnerability premium lower? It is lower for three primary reasons: (1) embargoes are not certain events—they may never occur; (2) domestic steps can be taken to reduce vulnerability of the remaining imports; and (3) accelerating domestic production would incur a user cost by lowering the amounts available to future users.

The expected damage caused by one or more embargoes depends on the likelihood of occurrence, as well as the intensity and duration. This means that the S_{f1} curve will be lower for imports having a lower likelihood of being embargoed. Imports from countries less hostile to our interests are more secure and the vulnerability premium on those imports is smaller.[13]

For vulnerable imports, we can adopt certain contingency programs to reduce the damage an embargo would cause. The most obvious measure is to develop a domestic stockpile of oil to be used during an embargo. The United States has taken this route. The stockpile, called the *strategic petroleum reserve*, was designed to contain one billion barrels of oil. It would replace 3 million barrels a day for slightly less than one year or a larger number of barrels per day for a shorter period of time. This reserve would serve as an alternative source of supply, which, unlike our other oil resources, could be rapidly deployed on short notice. It is, in short, a form of insurance protection. The less expensive this protection is, the lower S_{f1} is and the more attractive imports are.[14]

To understand the third and final reason that paying the vulnerability premium would be less costly than self-sufficiency, we must consider vulnerability in a dynamic, rather than static, framework. Because oil is a depletable resource, there is a user cost associated with its efficient use. To reorient the extraction of that resource toward the present, as a self-sufficiency strategy would do, reduces future net benefits. Thus the self-sufficiency strategy tends to be myopic, in that it solves the short-term vulnerability problem by creating a more serious one in the future. Paying the vulnerability premium creates a more efficient balance between the present and future, as well as between current imports and domestic production.

We have established the fact that government can reduce our vulnerability to imports, which tends to keep the risk premium as low as possible. Certainly for oil, however, even after the stockpile has been established, the risk premium

---

13 It is this fact which explains the tremendous U.S. interest in Mexican oil, in spite of the fact that, historically, it has not been cheaper.

14 Economic analysis can also be used to derive the optimal-sized stockpile. The optimal stockpile is the one which minimizes the sum of expected damages plus the costs of stockpiling. This stockpile will be the one where the expected damage from not storing the last barrel of oil is equal to the cost of storing it. Larger stockpiles would cost more to establish than they would save in reduced damages. Examples of this analysis can be found in Thomas Teisberg, "A Dynamic Programming Model of the U.S. Strategic Petroleum Reserve," *The Bell Journal of Economics* 12 (Autumn 1981): 526–546, and A. L. Nicholas and R. J. Zeckhauser, "Stockpiling Strategies and Cartel Prices," *Bell Journal of Economics* 7 (Spring 1976): 66–96.

is not zero; S_{f0} and S_{f1} will not coincide.[15] Consequently, the government must also concern itself with achieving both the efficient level of consumption and the efficient share of that consumption borne by imports. Let's examine some of the policy choices.

Energy conservation is one popular approach to the problem. One way to accomplish additional conservation is by means of a tax on energy consumption, such as the widely used gasoline tax. Graphically, this approach would be reflected as a shift inward of the after-tax demand curve. Such a tax would reduce consumption (an efficient result) but would not achieve the efficient share of imports (an inefficient result). An energy tax falls on *all* energy consumption, whereas the problem involves only imports. While energy conservation may increase the net benefit, it cannot ever be the sole policy instrument used or an efficient allocation will not be attained.

Another possible strategy employs the subsidization of domestic supply. This approach was taken by Congress in establishing the Synthetic Fuel Corporation in 1980 to stimulate and subsidize the development of synthetic fuels.[16] Diagrammatically, this would be portrayed in Figure 7.5 as a shift of the domestic supply curve to the right. Notice that the effect would be to reduce the share of imports in total consumption (a desired effect) but not reduce consumption (an inefficient result). While subsidies may be better than nothing, they cannot be the sole solution to the problem, either.

A final approach would tailor the response more closely to the problem. One could use either a tariff on imports equal to the vertical distance between S_{f0} and S_{f1} or a quota on imports equal to $Q_4 - Q_2$. With either of these approaches, the price to consumers would rise to P_1, total consumption would fall to Q_4, and imports would be $Q_4 - Q_2$. In short, when either tariffs or quotas are used correctly with the contingency programs discussed earlier, an efficient allocation may be attained. As Example 7.4 makes clear, however, if these instruments are not used correctly they can cause more harm than good.[17]

---

15 Those who have examined the question of the premium are uniform in their agreement that it exists, but the estimates of how large it is vary from two times the current price to something less than the current price. See Robert Stobaugh and Daniel Yergin, eds., *Energy Future: Report of the Energy Project at the Harvard Business School* (New York: Random House, 1979): 227; Hans H. Landsberg, *Energy: The Next Twenty Years* (Cambridge, MA: Ballinger, 1979): 221; Energy Modeling Forum, *World Oil: Summary Report*, Report 6 of the Energy Modeling Forum, Stanford University (February 1982): 67–75; and E. Folkerts-Landau, "The Social Cost of Imported Oil," *Energy Journal* 5 (July 1984): 41–58.

16 During January 1986, President Reagan signed a bill abolishing the U.S. Synthetic Fuels Corporation, ending its short but turbulent history.

17 Tariffs could also be used as a weapon to slow down OPEC price increases. See, for example, the provocative proposals in A. P. Lerner, "OPEC—A Plan—If You Can't Beat Them, Join Them," *Atlantic Economic Journal* 8 (September 1980): 1–3.

EXAMPLE 7.4

The Inefficiency of the Mandatory Oil Import Program

In 1959 the Mandatory Oil Import Program was established to protect the United States from what was seen as an increasingly dangerous dependence on foreign oil. This program relied on import quotas as the sole policy measure. We know from the discussion in this chapter that this is an inefficient approach. An exclusive reliance on import quotas fails to take advantage of opportunities to import from more secure sources and it fails to use a stockpile to reduce the vulnerability of remaining imports. Import quotas leave the risk premium of imports too high. Therefore in order to produce the desired amount of safety in the absence of these complementary policies, import quotas must be more stringent (allowing fewer imports) than would normally be the case.

This is illustrated in the accompanying figure, where S_1 is the market supply curve; S_2 is the societal supply curve, which includes the risk premium after accounting for the contingency programs; and S_3 is the societal supply curve, which includes the risk premium when no contingency programs are considered. Notice that the "best" quota without the contingency programs $(Q_3 - Q_2)$ implies fewer imports and a smaller net benefit than the quota combined with other measurements $(Q_4 - Q_1)$. The white area represents the loss in net benefits from relying exclusively on import controls.

The demonstration that such losses exist does not establish that they are empirically significant. If they are not, they could be safely ignored. One set of estimates of the size of this inefficiency for the 1960–1970 period is provided by Bohi and Russell (1978). Their conclusion was that the quota was effective in reducing imports, but it accomplished this goal while wasting a significant amount of resources. Specifically, their estimated annual resource cost of the oil import program was $2.3 billion, while a combination of storage policies (sufficient to cover three-fourths of insecure imports for one year) and a tariff yielding comparable security would have cost about $965 million per year, a substantial difference.

Source: Douglas Bohi and Milton Russell, *Limiting Oil Imports: An Economic History and Analysis* (Baltimore: Johns Hopkins University Press for Resources for the Future, 1978).

The use of tariffs or quotas has some redistributive consequences. Suppose a tariff were imposed on imports equal to $P_1 - P_0$. The area *ABCD* would then represent tariff revenue collected by the government.

If a quota system were used instead of a tariff and the quotas were simply given to importers, area *ABCD* in Figure 7.5 would represent the value of those quotas to the importers, the difference between the cost of the oil and the price at which it can be sold. This explains why importers prefer this system to a tariff system.

The effect of either system on domestic producer surplus should also be noticed. Producers of domestic oil would be better off with a tariff or quota on imported oil than without it. Each raises the cost or reduces the availability of the foreign substitute, which results in higher domestic prices for the product. This result induces producers to produce more, but it also means that they earn higher profits on the oil which would have been produced anyway, echoing the premise that public policies may restore efficiency but also tend to redistribute wealth.

TRANSITION FUELS: ENVIRONMENTAL PROBLEMS

Currently the industrialized world depends on oil and gas for most of our energy. In the distant future we shall make a transition to renewable sources of energy. How about the intermediate time period?

Though some observers believe the transition to renewable sources will proceed so rapidly that no transition fuels will be necessary, most believe that transition fuels will probably play a significant role. Though there are other contenders, such as natural gas from deep wells, the fuels receiving the most attention as transition fuels are coal and uranium.

Domestic coal is abundantly available. Coal resources are approximately 22 times as large as oil and gas resources combined on a heat-equivalent basis. Neither availability nor dependency on foreign countries is an issue with coal.

Resource availability is a problem with uranium as long as we depend on conventional reactors. However, if the United States moves to the new generation of breeder reactors, which can use a wider range of fuel, availability will cease to be an important issue. On a heat-equivalent basis, domestic uranium resources are 4.2 times as great as domestic oil and gas resources if they are used in conventional reactors. With breeder reactors, the U.S. uranium base is 252 times the size of its oil and gas base.

The main issue defining the role for these two fuels involves their environmental impact. Coal's main drawback is its contribution to air pollution. Its high sulfur content makes it a potentially large source of sulfur dioxide emissions, one of the chief culprits in the acid-rain problem. It is also a major source of particulate emissions and carbon dioxide, one of the greenhouse gases implicated in global warming. Since a detailed analysis of these environmental problems follows in Chapters 15 and 16, we shall not consider them any further here except to note that if those who burn coal fail to consider these environmental costs, the market will foster an excessive reliance on coal.

The other main transition fuel, uranium, used in nuclear electrical generation stations, has its own limitations, principally safety. Two sources of concern stand out: (1) nuclear accidents, and (2) the storage of radioactive waste. Is the market likely to make the correct decisions on these questions? In both cases the answer is no, given the current decision-making environment. Let's consider these issues one by one.

The production of electricity by nuclear reactors requires radioactive elements. If these elements escape into the atmosphere and come in contact with humans in sufficient concentrations, they produce birth defects, cancer, or death. Some radioactive elements may also escape during the normal operation of a plant, but the greatest risk of nuclear power is still the threat of nuclear accidents.

Nuclear accidents may inject large doses of radioactivity into the environment. The most dangerous of these possibilities is the core meltdown. Unlike other types of electrical generation, nuclear processes continue to generate heat even after the reactor is turned off. This means that the nuclear fuel must be continuously cooled, or the heat levels will escalate beyond the design capacity of the reactor shield. If, in this case, the reactor vessel should fracture, clouds of radioactive gases and particulates would be released into the atmosphere.

For some time conventional wisdom had held that nuclear accidents involving a core meltdown were a remote possibility. On April 25, 1986, however, a serious core meltdown occurred at the Chernobyl nuclear plant in the Soviet Union. Though safety standards are generally conceded to be much higher in the Western industrialized world than in the Soviet Union, this incident has added yet another burden for an already troubled industry to bear.

Nuclear power has been beset by economic as well as political forces. New nuclear power plant construction has become much more expensive, in part due to the increasing regulatory requirements designed to provide a safer system. Its economic advantage over coal has dissipated and the demand for new nuclear plants has been eliminated. In the United States, for example, in 1973, 219 nuclear power plants were either planned or in operation. By the end of 1986 that number had fallen to 130, the difference being explained by cancellations.[18] No new applications for nuclear plants are pending.

Not all nations are making the same choice with respect to the nuclear option. Sweden not only has pledged not to build any new nuclear plants, but also plans to shut down those currently in operation early in the twenty-first century. In France and Japan, however, standardized plant design and regulatory stability have resulted in electricity generating costs for nuclear power which are lower than for coal. Both countries are expanding the role of nuclear power.[19]

---

18 Energy Information Administration, *Monthly Energy Review* (January 1986): 84.

19 For survey of the global situation for nuclear power, see Christopher Flavin, *Nuclear Power: The Market Test*, Paper No. 57 (Washington, DC: Worldwatch Institute, 1983).

An additional concern relates to storing nuclear wastes. The waste-storage issue relates to both ends of the nuclear fuel cycle—the disposal of uranium trailings from the mining process and spent fuel from the reactors, though the latter receives most of the publicity. Uranium tailings contain several elements, the most prominent being thorium-230, which decays with a half-life of 78,000 years to a radioactive, chemically inert gas, radon-222. Once formed, this gas has a very short half-life (38 days).

The spent fuel from nuclear reactors contains a variety of radioactive elements with quite different half-lives. In the first few centuries, the dominant contributors to radioactivity are fission products, principally strontium-90 and cesium-137. After approximately 1000 years, most of these elements will have decayed, leaving the transuranic elements, which have substantially longer half-lives. These remaining elements would remain a risk for up to 240,000 years. Thus, decisions made today affect not only the level of risk borne by the current generation—in the form of nuclear accidents—but also that borne by a host of succeeding generations (due to the longevity of radioactive risk from the disposal of spent fuel).

Can we expect the market to make the correct choice with respect to nuclear power? We might expect the answer for the problem of nuclear accidents to be no, because this seems to be a clear case of externalities. Third parties, those living near the reactor, would receive the brunt of the damage from a nuclear accident. Would the utility have an incentive to choose the efficient level of precaution?

If the utility had to compensate fully for all the damages caused, then the answer would be yes. To see why, consider Figure 7.6. Curve MC_a is the marginal cost of damage avoidance. The more precautions that are taken, the higher is the cost of additional measures. Curve MC_d is the marginal cost of damage, suggesting that as more precautionary measures are taken the additional reduction in damages obtained from those measures declines.

The efficient level of precaution is the one minimizing the sum of the costs of precaution and the costs of the unabated damage. In Figure 7.6 that point is $q*$, and the total cost to society from that choice is the sum of area A and area B.

Will a private utility choose $q*$? Presumably it would, if the curves it actually faces are MC_a and MC_d. The utility would be responsible for the costs of precautionary behavior, so it would face MC_a. How about MC_d? We might guess that the utility would face MC_d because people incurring damages could, through the judicial system, sue for damages. In the United States that guess is not correct for two reasons: (1) the role of the government in sharing the risk, and (2) the role of insurance.

When the government first allowed private industry to use atomic power to generate electricity, there were no takers. No utility could afford the damages if an accident occurred. No insurance company would underwrite the risk. Then in 1957, with the passage of the Price-Anderson Act, the government underwrote the liability. That act provided for a liability ceiling of $560 million (once that

FIGURE 7.6 The efficient level of precaution.

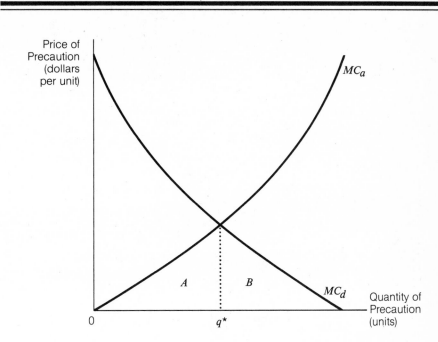

amount had been paid out no more claims would be honored), of which the government would bear $500 million. The industry would pick up the remaining $60 million. The act was originally designed to expire in 10 years, at which time the industry would assume full responsibility for the liability.

The act didn't expire, though over time a steady diminution of the government's share of the liability has occurred. Currently the liability ceiling still exists, albeit at a higher level; the amount of private insurance has increased; and a system has been set up to assess all utilities by retrospective premium, in the event an accident occurs.

The effect of the Price-Anderson Act is to shift inward the marginal damage curve that any utility faces. Both the liability ceiling and the portion of the liability borne by government reduce the potential compensation the utility would have to pay. As the industry assumes an increasing portion of the liability burden, the risk sharing embodied in the retrospective premium system (the means by which it assumes that burden) breaks the link between precautionary behavior by the individual utility and the compensation it might have to pay. Under this system, increased safety by the utility does not reduce its premiums.

The individual utilities pay into a fund that compensates victims. The important point is that the actual cost of an accident to the utility is not sensitive to the level of precautions it takes. The cost to all utilities, whether they have accidents or not, is the premium paid both before and after any accident. These premiums do not reflect the amount of precautionary measures taken by an individual plant; therefore, individual utilities have little incentive to provide an efficient amount of safety.[20]

In recognition of the utilities' lower-than-efficient concern for safety, the federal government has established the Nuclear Regulatory Commission to oversee the safety of nuclear reactors, among its other responsibilities. In the aftermath of the nuclear accident at Three Mile Island on March 28, 1979, a presidential commission was established to provide an independent evaluation of this system of safety regulation. Their final report,[21] issued on October 30, 1979, was highly critical of the existing system and made a series of recommendations to improve it. While the problem of nuclear accidents is manageable in principle, it may or may not be manageable in practice.

Both the operating safety and the nuclear waste storage issue can be viewed as a problem of determining appropriate compensation. Those who gain from nuclear power should be forced to compensate those who lose. If they can't, in the absence of externalities, the net benefits from adopting nuclear power are not positive. If nuclear power is efficient, by definition the gains to the gainers will exceed the losses to the losers. Nonetheless, it is important that this compensation actually be paid because without compensation, the losers can block the efficient allocation.

A compensation approach is already being taken in those countries still expanding the role of nuclear power. The French government, for example, has announced a policy of reducing electricity rates by roughly 15% for those living near nuclear stations. And in Japan during 1980, the Tohoku Electric Power Company paid the equivalent of $4.3 million to residents of Ojika, in northern Japan, to get them to withdraw their opposition to a nuclear power plant being built there.

This approach could also help resolve the current political controversy over the location of nuclear waste disposal sites. Most plans currently focus on burying the waste in some geologically stable formation. Current and future generations of people living near the chosen sight would have a tendency to oppose nuclear power, since the costs to them appear to outweigh the benefits. To others, however, who may enjoy nuclear-produced electricity and may live far from the sites, the benefits might exceed the costs. This rationale prompted a number of states to pass laws permitting nuclear power but prohibiting the permanent storage of waste in their state.

---

20 For further discussion of this point see Jeffrey A. Dubin and Geoffry S. Rothwell, "Subsidy to Nuclear Power through Price-Anderson Liability Limit," *Contemporary Policy Issues* 8 (July 1990): 73–79.

21 The President's Commission on the Accident at Three Mile Island, *The Need for Change: The Legacy of TMI* (New York: Pergamon Press, 1979).

Under a compensation scheme, those consuming nuclear power should be taxed to compensate those who live in the areas of the disposal site. If the compensation is adequate to induce them to accept the site, then nuclear power is a viable option and the costs of disposal are ultimately borne by the consumers. Some towns, such as Naturita, Colorado, have actively sought to become disposal sites. If taxes to obtain a sufficient number of disposal sites are so high that nuclear energy becomes noncompetitive, then nuclear energy is not an efficient source.

Are future generations adequately represented in this transaction? The quick answer is no, but that answer is not correct. Those living around the sites will experience declines in the market value of land reflecting the increased risk of living or working there. The payment system is designed to compensate those who experience the reduction, the current generation. Future generations, should they decide to live near a disposal site, would be compensated by lower land values. If the land values were not cheap enough to compensate them, they would not have to live there. As long as full information on the risks posed is available, those who do bear the cost of locating near the sites do so only if they are willing to accept the risk in return for lower land values.[22]

CONSERVATION AND LOAD MANAGEMENT

As the previous discussion indicated, environmental problems associated with the transition fuels present particular difficulties for generating electric power. While alternative fuels and solar power will eventually play an increasing role, most experts seem to feel that they will penetrate the market slowly as they become more familiar and accessible. How then is the transition to these long-term solutions to be managed by the electrical utilities sector in light of the problems associated with the transition fuels?

For a number of utilities, conservation has assumed an increasing role. To a major extent conservation has already been stimulated by market forces. High oil and natural gas prices, coupled with the rapidly increasing cost of both nuclear and coal-fired generating stations, have reduced electrical demand significantly. Yet many public utilities commissions, the state bodies charged with regulating the production, transmission, and sale of electricity, are coming to the conclusion that more conservation is needed.

---

22 For further discussion of possible compensation schemes, see Robert Cameron Mitchell and Richard T. Carson, "Property Rights, Protest, and the Siting of Hazardous Waste Facilities" and Howard Kunreuther and Paul R. Kleindorfer, "A Sealed-Bid Auction Mechanism for Siting Noxious Facilities," *American Economic Review* 76 (May 1986): 285–290, 295–299.

Perhaps the most significant role for conservation is its ability to defer capacity expansion. Each new electrical generating plant tends to cost more than the last, and frequently the cost increase is substantial. When the new plants come on line, rate increases to finance the new plant are necessary. By reducing the demand for electricity, conservation delays the date when the new capacity is needed to satisfy the higher demand. Delays in the need to construct new plants translate into delays in rate increases as well.

The dominant electricity pricing system is ill-designed to stimulate the efficient amount of conservation. Average-cost pricing is common. This pricing system implies that the new higher-cost sources are averaged in with the lower-cost sources, yielding a rate which is substantially lower than the true marginal cost of the power being generated. Thus, the consumer considering investing in conservation would save less money by conserving with average-cost pricing than would be the case if the energy saved were priced at its true marginal cost. Less than an efficient amount of conservation would be the expected outcome.

Utilities are reacting to this situation in a number of ways. One is to consider investing in conservation, rather than in new plants, when conservation is the cheaper alternative. The thrust of these programs can be illustrated by referring to a few of the programs instituted by the Pacific Gas and Electric Company (PGE), a leader in the field. PGE has established a system of rebates for residential customers to install conservation measures in their homes, has provided free home weatherization to qualified low-income homeowners, has offered owners of multifamily residential buildings incentives for installing solar water heating systems, and has provided subsidized energy audits to inform customers about money-saving conservation opportunities. Similar incentives have been provided to the commercial, agricultural, and industrial sectors. Though the costs of these investments must also be recovered from customers, PGE reports that the savings have been dramatic and customer satisfaction has been high.[23] Less power consumed means available energy supplies last longer.

The total amount of electric energy demanded in a given year is not the only concern utilities have. They are also concerned with how that energy demand is spread out over the year. The capacity of the system must be high enough to satisfy the demand even during the periods when the energy demand is highest (called peak periods). During other periods, much of the capacity remains underutilized.

Demand during the peak period imposes two rather special costs on utilities. First, the peaking units, those generating facilities fired-up only during the peak periods, produce electricity at a much higher marginal cost than do base-load plants, those fired-up virtually all the time. Typically peaking units are cheaper

---

23 Pacific Gas and Electric Company, *Report on 1984 Energy Management and Conservation Activities* (San Francisco: 1985).

to build than base-load plants, but they have higher operating costs. Second, it is the growth in peak demand that frequently triggers the need for capacity expansion. Slowing the growth in peak demand can delay the need for new expensive capacity expansion, and a higher proportion of the power needs can be met by the most efficient generating plants.

Utilities are also responding to this problem by adopting load-management techniques to produce a more balanced use of this capacity over the year. One economic load-management technique is called *peak-load pricing*. Peak-load pricing attempts to impose the full (higher) marginal cost of supplying peak power on those consuming peak power by charging higher prices during the peak period.

While many utilities have now begun to use simple versions of this approach, some are experimenting with innovative ways of implementing rather refined versions of this system. One innovative system, for example, transmits electricity prices every 5 minutes over regular power lines. In a customer's household the lines attached to one or more appliances can be controlled by switches which turn the power off any time the prevailing price exceeded a limit established by the customer. Other less sophisticated pricing systems simply inform consumers in advance the prices that will prevail in predetermined peak periods.

A study by economists at the Rand Corporation in California indicates that even the rudimentary versions of peak-load pricing work.[24] Based on the actual experience with time-of-day rates by more than 6000 commercial and industrial customers, Rand found that business customers saved themselves and utilities on average $1000 per year for an added metering cost of only $50. Working with an additional sample of over 3000, the authors found residential customers also saved by shifting some of their demand to less expensive periods. The greatest shifts were registered by the largest residential customers and those with several electrical appliances.

Interestingly, this study found the gains from peak-load pricing in the United States to be somewhat lower than those reported for European customers, who have been exposed to peak-load pricing for a longer period of time. Attributing the large European response in part to the longer time Europeans have had to adapt to this system, the authors speculate that the longer-term response by U.S. customers could turn out to be quite a bit greater than already recorded.

A third innovation in the utility sector involves procedures for internalizing the environmental costs. Those who have typically been assigned the responsibility for regulating utility prices have focused almost exclusively on holding down prices by choosing the cheapest sources of power. Unfortunately, only generating and distribution costs were considered; the damage caused by emissions

---

24 Jan Paul Acton et al., *Time-of-Day Electricity Rates for the United States, Report R-3086-HF* (Santa Monica, CA: Rand Corporation, 1983) and Rolla Edward Park and Jan Paul Acton, *Response to Time-of-Day Electricity Rates by Large Business Customers: Initial Analysis of Data from Ten U.S. Utilities, Report R-3080-HF/MD/RC* (Santa Monica, CA: Rand Corporation, 1983).

was ignored. The resulting choices turned out not to be the cheapest when all costs were considered.

To rectify this imbalance in the procedures for choosing generating sources, some states have begun explicitly incorporating environmental costs in their decision-making process. New York State, for example, adds 1.4 cents per kilowatt hour to the estimated cost of electricity produced from fossil fuel sources to account for the various negative environmental effects. By creating a more level playing field for competing sources, this technique has increased competitiveness of renewable sources such as hydro, solar, and wind.

THE LONG RUN

Ultimately our energy needs will have to be fulfilled from renewable energy sources, either because the depletable energy sources have been exhausted or, as is more likely, the environmental costs of using the depletable sources have became so high that renewable sources will be cheaper.

Depending on how the scientific uncertainty is resolved, the most compelling case for the transition may well be made by the mounting evidence that the global climate is being jeopardized by current and prospective energy consumption patterns. (A detailed analysis of this problem is presented in Chapter 16.) If the Third World were to follow the energy-intensive, fossil-fuel-based path to development pioneered by the industrialized nations, the amount of carbon dioxide emissions injected into the air would be unprecedented. Currently, half of all developing nations rely on imported oil for more than 75% of their commercial energy needs.[25] A transition away from fossil fuels to other energy forms in both the industrialized and Third World nations would be an important ingredient in any strategy to reduce carbon dioxide emissions. Can our institutions manage that transition in a timely and effective manner?

Renewable energy comes in many different forms. Hydropower can be derived from flowing water; biomass can be burned; solar energy can be used to produce heat used to drive steam turbines or converted directly into electricity by means of photovoltaics; wind energy can drive turbines; hydrogen extracted from the air by solar energy could fuel cars or furnaces; and geothermal energy can be captured from the bowels of the earth and put to useful work.

The extent to which these sources will penetrate the market will depend upon their relative cost and consumer acceptance. Relative cost will no doubt change over time as research uncovers better ways to harness the power of renewable

---

25 U.S. Agency for International Development, *Decentralized Hydropower in AID's Development Assistance Program* (Washington, DC: AID, 1986).

sources. Perhaps the best example of how research can lower costs is provided by the experience with photovoltaics.

Photovoltaics involve the direct conversion of solar energy to electricity (as opposed to indirect conversions such as when steam energy is used to drive a turbine). Anticipating a huge potential market, private industry has been very interested in photovoltaics and has poured a lot of research dollars into improving its commercial viability. The research has paid off. In 1976, the average market price for a photovoltaic module was $44 per peak watt installed, and 0.5 megawatt was sold. Only a decade later, costs were down eightfold (in constant 1986 dollars) to $5.25, and shipments had climbed to 24.7 megawatts.[26] Rural electrification projects using photovoltaics are slowly spreading into the Third World.

Somewhat lower down the scale in terms of commercial viability is using hydrogen as a fuel. If an electric current (produced by photovoltaics, for example) is conducted through a reservoir of water, the liquid splits into its constituent elements, hydrogen and oxygen. When burned with oxygen, hydrogen creates a single by-product—water that is clean enough to drink.

Hydrogen has many potential uses including serving as a fuel for automobiles. Prototype cars which use this fuel have already been built. While the costs of supplying and using this fuel have declined in response to recent research, the declines are not yet sufficiently large to make it a competitor in the near future.

Consumer acceptance is an important ingredient in the transition to any alternative source of energy. New systems are usually less reliable and more expensive than old systems. Once they become heavily used, reliability normally increases and cost declines; experience is a good teacher. Since the early consumers, the pioneers, experienced both lower reliability and higher costs, procrastination can be an optimal individual strategy. If every consumer procrastinates about switching, however, the industry will not be able to operate at a sufficient scale and will not be able to gain enough experience to produce the reliability and lower cost that will ensure a large, stable market. How can this initial consumer reluctance be overcome?

One strategy, the one used in the United States, involves using tax dollars to subsidize purchases by the pioneers. Once the market is sufficiently large that it can begin to take advantage of economies of scale and can eliminate the initial sources of unreliability the subsidies could be eliminated. The available empirical evidence suggests that the tax credit approach has significantly increased the degree of market penetration of solar equipment in the United States.[27]

---

26 Cited in Cynthia Pollock Shea, "Shifting to Renewable Energy," *State of the World: 1988* (New York: W. W. Norton, 1988): 74.

27 Catherine A. Durham, Bonnie G. Colby, and Molly Longstreth, "The Impact of State Tax Credits and Energy Prices on Adoption of Solar Energy Systems," *Land Economics* 64 (November 1988): 347–355, and Gene R. Fry, "The Economics of Home Solar Water Heating and the Role of Solar Tax Credits," *Land Economics* 62 (May 1986): 134–144.

The penetration would have been even greater if the cartel had been able to sustain the very high oil prices which were in effect at the beginning of the 1980s. As oil prices fell in real terms, both residential and commercial enthusiasm for making the transition to solar energy was undermined. Since saving money is a primary motivation for making the switch and low oil prices translate into relatively low or even negative savings, uncertainty associated with the path of future oil and natural gas prices could continue to be a barrier to the transition.

SUMMARY

We have seen that the relationship between government and the market is not always harmonious and efficient. In the past, price controls have tended to reduce energy conservation, to discourage exploration and supply, to cause biases in the substitution among fuel types to penalize future consumers, and to create the potential for abrupt, discontinuous transitions to renewable sources. This important area makes a clear case for less, not more, regulation.

This is not universally true, however. Other dimensions of the energy problem suggest the need for some government role. In particular, insecure foreign sources require tariffs and stockpiles to reduce vulnerability and to balance the true costs of imported and domestic sources. In addition, government should ensure that the costs of energy fully reflect the potentially large environmental costs and that fluctuating resource prices do not undermine the transition to energy resources that make sense in the long run. Government should also oversee nuclear reactor safety and should ensure that communities accepting nuclear waste disposal sites are fully compensated. Given the environmental difficulties with both of the traditional transition fuels (coal and uranium), conservation and load-management techniques are now playing and will continue to play a larger role in the electric utilities sector. Subsidizing conservation, where it is cheaper for the utility than capacity expansion, and peak-load pricing are two economic measures that have been instrumental in ushering in this greater role. The potential for an efficient allocation of energy resources by the economic and political institutions clearly exists, even if historically it has not always occurred.

FURTHER READING

Griffin, James M. and Henry B. Steele *Energy Economics and Policy*, 2nd ed. (New York: Academic Press, 1986). A very readable textbook on energy economics aimed at undergraduates with one course in the principles of economics. Covers OPEC, environmental issues, national security, conservation, price controls, and market structure regulations, as well as energy research and development.

Landsberg, Hans H., ed. *Energy: The Next Twenty Years* (Cambridge, MA: Ballinger, 1979). A comprehensive report combining the effort of 19 experts across the country funded by the Ford Foundation. Contains nine recommendations, including decontrol of oil and natural gas prices, development of an effective oil stockpile program, improving the acceptability of coal, vigorous pursuit of conservation, and removal of impediments to the use of solar power.

Schurr, Sam H. et al. *Energy in American's Future: The Choice Before Us* (Baltimore: Johns Hopkins University Press for Resources for the Future, 1979). A monumental, 20-chapter book attempting to synthesize what is known and not known about energy demand, supply, health, safety, and environmental issues and the process of making energy choices. Concludes "it will be possible to fulfill the expansionist requirement that enough energy will be available to support economic growth while meeting the conservationist demand that energy use be lessened substantially from what previously was thought to be the necessary minimum."

Shea, Cynthia Pollock. "Shifting to Renewable Energy," in *State of the World: 1988*, Lester R. Brown et al., eds. (New York: W. W. Norton, 1988): 62–82. A wealth of information on how the transition to renewable resources is shaping up around the world.

Stobaugh, Robert and Daniel Yergin, eds. *Energy Future: Report of the Energy Project at the Harvard Business School* (New York: Random House, 1979). A nontechnical, almost chatty collection of essays concerning the near-term energy choices for America, written by persons associated with the Harvard Business School as students or faculty. Concludes the only viable program that would politically reduce dependence on foreign oil is for the government to give financial incentives to encourage conservation and the use of solar energy.

Walton, A. L. and E. H. Warren, Jr. *The Solar Alternative: An Economic Perspective* (Englewood Cliffs, NJ: Prentice-Hall, 1982). A short, uncomplicated introduction to the economics of solar energy, including chapters on market distortions and the equity issues associated with a transition to solar power.

Webb, Michael G. and Martin J. Ricketts. *The Economics of Energy* (New York: Wiley, 1980). Written by two British economists and aimed at undergraduates who have had intermediate microeconomic theory. This textbook is particularly rich in examples drawn from the British experience.

ADDITIONAL REFERENCES

Adelman, M. A. *The World Petroleum Market* (Baltimore: Johns Hopkins University Press for Resources for the Future, 1972).

Arrow, Kenneth J. and Joseph P. Kalt. *Petroleum Price Regulation: Should We Decontrol?* (Washington, DC: American Enterprise Institute, 1979).

Bhatia, Ramesh and Armand Pereira. *Socioeconomic Aspects of Renewable Energy Technologies* (New York: Praeger, 1988).

Bohi, Douglas R. and Milton Russell. *Limiting Oil Imports: An Economic History and Analysis* (Baltimore: Johns Hopkins University Press for Resources for the Future, 1978).

Cropper, M. L. "Pollution Aspects of Nuclear Energy Use," *Journal of Environmental Economics and Management* 7 (December 1980): 334-352.

Griffin, James M. "OPEC Behavior: A Test of Alternative Hypotheses," *The American Economic Review* 75 (December 1985): 954-963.

Hall, Darwin C., ed. "Social and Private Costs of Alternative Energy Technologies," a special issue of *Contemporary Policy Issues* (July 1990).

Lerner, A. P. "OPEC—A Plan—If You Can't Beat Them, Join Them," *Atlantic Economic Journal* 8 (September 1980): 1-3.

Toman, Michael and Molly K. Macauley. "Risk Aversion and the Insurance Value of Strategic Oil Stockpiling," *Resources and Energy* 8 (1986): 151-165.

Lind, Robert C. et al. *Discounting for Time and Risk in Energy Policy* (Washington, DC: Resources for the Future, 1982).

West, Ronald E. and Frank Kreith. *Economic Analysis of Solar Thermal Energy Systems* (Cambridge, MA: MIT Press, 1988).

DISCUSSION QUESTIONS

1. Should benefit-cost analysis play the dominant role in deciding the proportion of American electric energy to be supplied by nuclear power? Why or why not?

2. Lerner (1980) proposed that the United States impose a tariff on oil imports equal to 100% of the import price. This tariff is designed to reduce dependence on foreign sources as well as to discourage OPEC from raising prices (since, due to the tariff, the delivered price would rise twice as much as the OPEC increase, causing a large subsequent reduction in consumption). Should this proposal become public policy? Why or why not?

PROBLEMS

1. During a worldwide recession in 1983 the oil cartel began to lower prices. Why would a recession make the cartel more vulnerable to price cutting? How would the reduced demand be shared between the competitive fringe and the cartel members in the absence of this price cutting?

2. Assume the demand and marginal cost conditions given in the first problem in Chapter 2 as well as a competitive market to allocate the product. In addition, assume that the government imposes a price control at $P = \$80/3$. (a) Find the consumer and producer surplus associated with the resulting allocation. (b) Compare this allocation to the monopoly allocation in the second problem in Chapter 3.

3. Recently, a conflict between a paper company and a coalition of environmental groups arose over the potential use of a Maine river for hydroelectric

power generation. As one aspect of its case for developing the dam, the paper company argued that without hydroelectric power the energy cost of operating five particular paper machines would be so high that they would have to be shut down. Environmental groups countered that the energy cost was estimated to be too high by the paper company only because it was assigning all of the high-cost (oil-fired) power to these particular machines. That was seen as inappropriate because all machines were connected to the same electrical grid and therefore drew power from all sources, not merely the high-cost sources. They suggested, therefore, that the appropriate cost to assign to the machines was the much lower average cost. Revenue from these machines was expected to be sufficient to cover this average cost. Who was right?

4. In the section of this chapter dealing with load management by the utilities, it was mentioned that peaking plants are typically cheap to build (compared to base-load plants), but that they have relatively high operating costs. Explain why it makes sense for utilities to use this lower-capital high-operating-cost type of plant for peaking and the high-capital lower-operating-cost type of plant for base load.

CHAPTER EIGHT

Recyclable Resources: Minerals, Etc.

*The Nation is in the position of a man, who, bequeathed a
fortune, has gone on spending it recklessly, never taking
the trouble to ask the amount of his inheritance, or how long
it is likely to last.*

NATIONAL CONSERVATION COMMISSION (1908)

INTRODUCTION

Once used, energy resources dissipate into heat energy. They cannot be
recycled. Other resources, in contrast, retain their basic physical and
chemical properties during use and under the proper conditions can be
recycled or reused. They therefore represent a separate category for us to
examine.

What is an efficient amount of recycling? Will the market automatically
generate this amount in the absence of government intervention? How does
the efficient allocation over time differ between recyclable and nonrecyclable resources? The phrase *planned obsolescence* is sometimes used to
suggest that industries have an incentive to produce products with a short
life span. Does the market produce an efficient level of product durability?
What impact does product durability have on the allocation of virgin and
recycled materials?

We begin our investigation by describing how an efficient market in recyclable, depletable resources would work. We then use this as a benchmark to
examine recycling in some detail. We close by relating our findings back to the
central questions of growth in a finite environment.

AN EFFICIENT ALLOCATION OF RECYCLABLE RESOURCES

Extraction and Disposal Cost

How would an efficient market, one devoid of any imperfections, allocate a recyclable depletable resource? The models developed in Chapter 6 provide a point of departure for answering this question. In the earliest periods, reliance would generally be exclusively on the virgin ore, because it is cheapest. As more concentrated ores are extracted, the mining industry would turn to the lower-graded ore and to foreign sources for higher-grade ores.

In the presence of technological progress, the increasing reliance on the lower-grade ores would not necessarily precipitate an increase in cost (as shown in Example 6.2), at least initially. Eventually, however, as the sources became increasingly difficult to extract, a point would be reached when the costs of extraction and prices of the virgin material would begin to rise.

At the same time, the costs of disposing of the products would probably rise as population density became more pronounced and wealth levels supported higher levels of waste. Over the last two centuries the world has experienced a large increase in the geographic concentration of people. The attraction of cities and exodus from rural areas led an increasingly large number of people to live in urban or near-urban environments.

This concentration creates waste disposal problems. Historically, when land was plentiful and the waste stream was less hazardous, the remnants could be buried in landfills. But as land became scarce, burial became increasingly expensive. In addition, concerns over environmental effects on water supplies and economic effects on the value of surrounding land have made buried waste less acceptable.[1]

The rising costs of virgin materials and of waste disposal increase the attractiveness of recycling. By recovering and reintroducing materials into the system, recycling provides an alternative to virgin ores and reduces the waste disposal load (Example 8.1).

Consumers, as well as manufacturers, play a role on both the demand and supply side of the market. On the demand side, consumers would find that products depending exclusively on virgin raw materials are subject to higher prices than those relying on recycled materials. Consequently, consumers would have a tendency to switch to products made with the cheaper, recycled raw

---

1 The U.S. EPA estimates that more than half of the existing landfills in the United States will reach their capacity by 1995. The New York State Legislative Commission on Solid Waste Management estimates that all landfills within its state will reach their capacity and close by 1995. Though the precision of these forecasts should be subject to the same healthy skepticism we have recommended elsewhere in this book for other forecasts, it is difficult to escape the conclusion that disposal is becoming both more expensive and more difficult.

EXAMPLE 8.1

Population Density and Recycling: The Japanese Experience

Since Japan has much greater population density than any of the other industrialized nations, it has been forced by necessity to come to grips with
its solid waste disposal problems somewhat earlier. For the Japanese the
solution of choice is recycling. In Tokyo, enterprising firms have begun tour-
ing neighborhoods, collecting newspapers, magazines, and rags in exchange for new bathroom and facial tissue. People who want quick disposal
of old refrigerators or TV sets need only to make a special call to the sanita-
tion department for a special pickup. And although a few years ago no
Japanese would touch used goods, the latest trend is garage sales and flea
markets, which give secondhand wares new life.

About 40% of solid waste is recycled, including about half the paper,
55% of glass bottles, and 66% of food and beverage cans.

Since the early 1970s, citizens have been forced to separate combus-
tible from noncombustible trash. Burnable waste, which is some 72% of the
total after recycling, is trucked to incinerators, which reduce its weight and
volume. Every Japanese community has its own incinerator, totaling some
1899 garbage burning plants (compared with 155 large plants in the United
States). Nonburnable garbage is separated, melted, and refabricated; ferrous metals are reclaimed. What's left, about 9% of the total initial waste,
is deposited in a landfill.

Some problems still exist. Concern about the toxins within the trash that
escape into the air from combustion and the water from landfills from the
ash is mounting. Furthermore, recycling has peaked at about 50% and has
even declined somewhat during the 1980s.

Source: "Teeing Off on Japan's Garbage," *Newsweek* (November 27, 1989): 70; "The
Good News: Japan Gives Trash a Second Chance," *Time* (January 2, 1989): 47.

---

materials, as long as quality is not adversely affected. This powerful incentive
is called the *composition of demand effect.*

As long as consumers bear the cost of disposal, they have the additional
incentive to return their used recyclable products to collection centers. By doing
so they avoid disposal costs, while at the same time reaping financial rewards
for supplying a product someone wants.

This highly stylized version of how the market should work has to be complemented by some hard realities that must be faced in setting up actual markets.

For the cycle to be complete it is essential that a demand exist for the recycled products. As Example 8.2 makes clear, new markets may ultimately emerge, but the transition may prove somewhat turbulent. Simply returning recycled products to the collection centers accomplishes little if they are simply dumped into a nearby landfill[2] or if the supply is increased so much by mandatory recycling laws that prices for recycled materials fall through the floor.[3] The purity of the recycled products also plays a key role in explaining the strength of demand for them. One of the reasons for the high rate of aluminum recycling and much lower rate of plastics recycling is the differential difficulty with which a high-quality product can be produced from scrap. Whereas bundles of aluminum cans have a relatively uniform quality, waste plastics tend to be highly contaminated with nonplastic substances and the plastics manufacturing process has little tolerance for impurities. Remaining contaminants in metals can frequently be eliminated by high-temperature combustion, but plastics are destroyed by high temperatures.

For some materials it is more costly for consumers to do the separation and recovery of materials and thus more efficient for municipal agencies to accomplish recycling. One example is currently operating in Saugus, Massachusetts, a North Shore suburb of Boston, processing up to 1500 tons of Boston refuse per day. From this waste, the facility annually recovers some 25,000 tons of ferrous metals and 40,000 tons of other materials suitable for use in construction. In addition, the plant is capable of producing 2 billion pounds of steam annually, which it sells to a nearby General Electric plant.

Recycling: A Closer Look

The model in the preceding section would lead us to expect that recycling would increase over time as virgin ore and disposal costs rose. This seems to be the case. Take copper, for example. During 1910, recycled copper accounted for about 18% of the total production of refined copper in the United States. By 1987, this percentage had risen to 41%.[4]

Though these percentages may seem low, in most cases recycling is not cheap. Transport and processing costs are usually significant. The sources of scrap are usually concentrated around cities, where the products are used, while for historical reasons the producing facilities are concentrated near the sources

---

2 In 1983, New York State ordered stores to charge a deposit on beverage containers. While companies were eager to use the glass and aluminum cans that were returned, few knew what to do with the recycled plastic, and most of it ended up in the landfill.

3 This has happened in the Northeast as mandatory programs to recycle newspapers produced far more than could be absorbed by the market. Falling prices undercut the incentive to recycle.

4 U.S. Department of the Interior, *Minerals Yearbook: 1987* (Washington, DC: U.S. Government Printing Office, 1987): 289.

EXAMPLE 8.2

New Markets For Trash: Tires

According to our model of the allocation of a depletable, recyclable resource over time, the demand for recycled waste products for use as raw materials in the production process should grow over time. Not only are communities willing to provide recycled waste products at a low cost merely to avoid disposal costs, but they can provide a steady supply. Is this expectation borne out by current trends?

Apparently they are. Take tires, for example. In the United States, car and truck drivers dispose of some 240 million tires per year. The current disposal cost is about 10 cents per pound when landfills will take them; many won't. Some 2 billion tires are stocked in remote locations, where they pose environmental hazards. (In October 1983 the 7-million-tire dump in Winchester, Virginia, caught fire; it finally burned itself out in June after blanketing the area in acrid smoke for the intervening eight months.)

In 1981, a research chemist named Ed Stark developed a process for coating ground-up tire particles with a polymer that "rejuvenated" the rubber, allowing it to bond together as effectively as uncured virgin material. The beauty of the process is that it makes no environmental compromises. Because it uses no water, it has no contaminated effluent to dispose of. The process does not involve combustion so the air pollutants associated with combustion are not a problem either.

This process has since formed the basis for Tirecycle, a company set up in Babbitt, Minnesota, to recycle all of Minnesota's old tires. Products made from this material include truck tire retreads, buckets, wastebaskets, gasoline tanks for lawn movers, truck bed lines, and gymnasium exercise mats, among others. The process has proved so successful, additional plants are scheduled to be opened in Massachusetts and Michigan.

Source: David Morris and Neil Seidman, "Treating Trash as a Valuable Municipal Resource," *Christian Science Monitor* (November 12, 1987): 23; Peter Tonge, "Old Tires Bounce Back as New Rubber Products," *Christian Science Monitor* (August 9, 1988): 17; and "Why Not Rubber Roadbeds?" *Christian Science Monitor* (August 9, 1988): 17.

of the virgin materials. Scrap material must first be transported to the production facility; then there are additional expenses in collecting, separating, and processing them. Even with acute scarcity, nowhere near 100% of the materials are recycled; costs don't permit it!

As recycling becomes cost competitive, rather dramatic changes occur in the manufacturing process. Not only do manufacturers rely more heavily on recycled inputs, they also begin to design their products to facilitate recycling. Facilitating recycling through product design is already important in industries where the connection between the manufacturer and disposal agent is particularly close. Aircraft manufacturers, which often are asked to scrap old aircraft, may stamp the alloy composition on parts during manufacturing to facilitate recycling.[5]

Recycling and Virgin Ore Depletion

How does the efficient allocation of a recyclable resource over time compare with that of a nonrecyclable resource? Thinking back to the models in Chapter 6, perhaps the most important difference occurs in the timing of the switch point. As long as the resource can be recycled at a marginal cost lower than that of the substitute, the market tends to rely on the recyclable resource longer than it does on a nonrecyclable resource with an identical extraction cost curve. This should not be surprising, since one effect of recycling is simply to add more of the resource.

This point can be illustrated using a simple numerical example. Suppose 100 units of a resource are contained in a product with a useful life of one year. Suppose further that 90% of the resource could be recovered and reused after one year. During the first year, the full 100 units could be used. At the end of the second year, 90% of the remaining 90 units could once again be recovered, leaving 81 units for the third year, and so on.

How much more of this resource was made available by recycling? Algebraically, if we let the original stock be A, and the recovery rate be a, then the total amount used would be an infinite sum of the form $A + Aa + Aa^2 + Aa^3$. It turns out that the sum of this series as time becomes infinitely long is $A/(1 - a)$.[6] Notice that nonrecyclable resources are represented by the special case where $a = 0$. In this case the sum of resource use equals the available stock. Whenever $a > 0$, however, as it would be when any of the resource was recycled, the sum of the resource flows exceeds the size of the stock. The closer to 1.0 a is, the larger the sum of the resource flows. For example, if $a = 0.9$, as it was in our example, the sum of the flows is 10 times the size of the stock. The effect of recycling is to increase the size of the available resources by a factor of 10.

This formulation also points out another feature of recycling. Unless the recycling rate is 100% ($a = 1.0$) the sum of the resource flows is finite. This means that while some recycled materials can be recycled forever, the amount will become infinitesimally small as time goes on.

---

5 Council on Environmental Quality, *Environmental Quality—1980* (Washington, DC: U.S. Government Printing Office, 1980): 221.

6 Note the similarity of $1/(1 - a)$ to the familiar multiplier used in introductory macroeconomics, $1/(1 - MPC)$.

An efficient economic system will orchestrate a balance between the consumption of depletable and recycled materials, between disposing of used products and recycling, and between imports and domestic production. Example 8.3 provides an example of how an efficient market can work. Mercury is an appropriate example because, according to the static reserve index, it is very scarce.

How close are we to efficiency? Have we achieved an efficient balance between imports and domestic production? Is the common pejorative notion that we are a "throwaway society" an accurate one? If so, is the market behaving efficiently—in the sense that the time for recycling has not yet come—or are there clearly identified sources of market failure, implying that the wrong price signals are being sent? The next few sections investigate these issues. Let's begin by examining the balance between domestic and foreign sources.

THE STRATEGIC-MATERIAL PROBLEM REVISITED

General Principles

Oil is not the only substance for which the United States demand has outpaced domestic supply, necessitating an increased importation. When these imports are of strategic importance in wartime situations and/or are supplied by a relatively few foreign producers, they require special treatment. As we saw in the last chapter, this situation implies that the true social cost of these resources is higher than their market price. If this divergence is large enough, some government corrective action may be appropriate.

The appropriate policy response would be to establish a tariff on imports of the strategic material and use the proceeds to finance a stockpile. This stockpile would provide a form of insurance against supply disruptions by providing a rapid-response alternative source of supply. The tariff would signal the social cost of the resources and thereby encourage domestic production and a search for substitutes. By using the tariff revenues to finance the stockpile, those who are creating the vulnerability, by demanding the resource, would pay the cost of protecting against it.

The first step in defining a list of vulnerable strategic minerals is to identify those for which foreign sources of supply are particularly important. While the specifics of this list will differ for each importing nation, some rather intense dependencies will normally emerge from any list. Figure 8.1 portrays the situation in the United States.

For the 42 most critical minerals, as defined by the government, the United States depends on foreign sources for more than 50 percent of 24 of them. Four of these—cobalt, chromium, manganese, platinum—receive the lion's share of attention. South Africa, a country with which the United States has had turbulent relations over their racial policy of apartheid, is a major supplier of three of the

EXAMPLE 8.3

Mercury Prices and Recycling

Mercury provides an interesting example of how a depletable recyclable resource can be allocated over time in a manner consistent with the principles discussed earlier in this chapter. Since the ratio of proved reserves to current consumption is quite low, scarcity should be a factor. The historical experience with mercury prices and production is presented in the accompanying figure. In the early 1850s price did not rise very much as production rose. After the peak production in the 1870s, however, prices began to rise and production began to fall.

Very little mercury was recycled initially, but the importance of recycling rose with prices. Major sources of recycled mercury were industrial and control instruments, batteries, sludges, and dental amalgams. By 1987, the domestic production of mercury was 23,488 flasks, while 11,096 flasks came from recycling. With higher prices and diminishing supplies, recycling accounted for about 47% of the total amount produced during that year. The costs of recycling prevented a larger contribution, even in the face of scarcity.

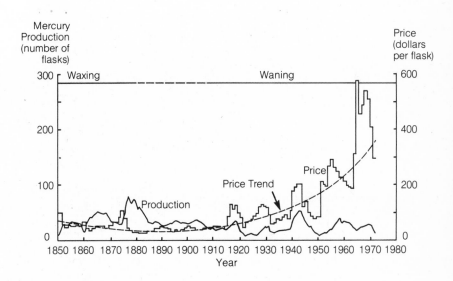

From: E. H. Bailey, A. L. Clark, and R. M. Smith, in *United States Minerals Resources*, D. A. Brobst and W. P. Pratt, eds. (U.S. Geological Survey, Washington, DC, 1973): Figure 46, p. 404.

FIGURE 8.1   Net U. S, import reliance as a percent of consumption, 1982.

Major foreign sources, 1978-81
and percent supplied, 1982

Mineral	Major foreign sources
Columbium	Brazil (73) Canada (6) Thailand (6)
Industrial diamond stones	S. Africa (61) Zaire (14) Bel-Lux (8) UK (6)
Natural Graphite	Mexico (60) Korea (12) Madagascar (5) China (5)
Mica sheet	India (83) Brazil (11) Madagascar (4)
Strontium	Mexico (99)
Ma ganese	Ore: Gabon (32) S. Africa (24) Australia (18) Brazil (15)
	Ferro Mn: S. Africa (42) France (25) Mexico (7)
Bauxite and aluminum	Jamaica (40) Guinea (28) Suriname (13)
	Alumina: Australia (76) Jamaica (15) Suriname (8)
Cobalt	Zaire (38) Zambia (13) Bel-Lux (11) Finland (6)
Tantalum	Thailand (38) Canada (11) Malaysia (8) Brazil (7)
Chromium	Chromite: S. Africa (44) USSR (18) Philippines (17)
	FeCr: S. Africa(71)Yugoslavia(11)Zimbabwe(6)Brazil(?)
Fluorspar	Mexico (60) S. Africa (30) Italy (4) Spain (3)
PGM	S. Africa (56) USSR (16) UK (11)
Nickel	Canada (44) Norway (11) Botswana (9) Australia (8)
Asbestos	Canada (97) S. Africa (3)
Tin	Malaysia (39) Thailand (21) Bolivia (17) Indonesia (?)
Ilmenite	Australia (59) Canada (34) S. Africa (6)
Potash	Canada (94) Israel (3)
Cadmium	Canada (27) Australia (18) Mexico (11) Korea (9)
Rutile	Australia (77) S. Africa (8) Siera Leone (7)
Gallium	Switzerland (65) Canada (12) Germany (10) China (?)
Silver	Canada (37) Mexico (24) Peru (23) UK (5)
Zinc	Ore & core: Canada (59) Peru (17) Mexico (8)
	Metal: Canada (51) Spain (8) Mexico (6) Australia (?)
Selerium	Canada (44) Japan (17) Germany (8) UK (8)
Tungsten	Canada (21) Bolivia (19) China (14) Thailand (7)
	Metal: Bolivia (38) China (34) Mexico (10) Belo Lux (7)
Antimony	Ore & core: Bolivia (36) Canada(19)Mexico(19)Chile(8)
	Oxide: S. Africa (44) China (15) France (14) Bolivia (11)
Mercury	Spain (34) Japan (21) Italy (12) Algeria (10)
Gold	Canada (52) USSR (20) Switzerland (17)
Iron ore	Canada (64) Venezuela (16) Brazil (9) Liberia (?)
Iron and steel	Europe (37) Japan (34) Canada (14)
Silicon	Canada (25) Norway (22) Brazil (14) S. Africa (?)
Vanadium	S. Africa (58) China (10) Canada (8)
Titanium sponge	Japan (81) China (10) USSR (8) UK (1)
Copper	Chile (32) Canada (22) Peru (14) Zambia (11)
Aluminum	Canada (62) Ghana (11) Norway (4) Japan (4)

Note: Net import reliance is figured as percent of apparent consumption. Net import = import – exports + adjustments for government and industry stock changes. Apparent consumption = U.S. primary and secondary production + net imports.

Source: *Strategic Materials: Technologies to Reduce U.S. Import Vulnerability.* Congress of the U.S.—Office of Technology Assessment (Washington, DC, 1985): 43. Original data derived from U.S. Dept. of the Interior, Bureau of Mines.

four minerals. The fourth, cobalt, comes primarily from the African nations of Zambia and Zaire. Clearly the strategic minerals problem is not a trivial one for the United States.

Government Response

How has the U.S. government reacted to this dependency? The Strategic and Critical Materials Stockpiling Act of 1946 initiated the first major government program to protect defense needs during a wartime. Since that time the program has had a checkered history. In 1954, for example, the Agricultural Trade Development and Assistance Act authorized the acquisition of strategic materials with the foreign currencies obtained from the sale of surplus agricultural commodities. This authority was subsequently revoked in 1966 by the Food for Peace Act.

The two main laws currently guiding materials policy are the Strategic and Critical Materials Stockpiling Revision Act of 1979 and the National Materials and Minerals Policy, Research and Development Act of 1980. These laws consolidated a number of separately mandated stockpiles into a single program and provided specific guidance to the president on determining the materials to be included in the stockpile and the quantities of each to be stockpiled.

The 1979 Act also created a National Defense Stockpile Transaction Fund to receive funds from sales of resources in the stockpile and to support purchases of resources for the stockpiles when actual levels fell below desired levels. Currently the national defense stockpile goals require a reserve adequate to supply the material requirements of the first three years of a conventional war, after subtracting the amounts available from domestic sources and secure foreign sources.[7]

Cobalt: A Case Study

Cobalt is an particularly interesting mineral because it is generally considered to be one of the most strategic and vulnerable of our imported minerals.[8] To what extent is government policy efficient?

Cobalt alloys are important to a number of American industries, especially aerospace and defense. Its properties make it particularly useful in high-tempera-

---

7 For more on these policies, see U.S. General Accounting Office, *Actions Needed to Promote a Stable Supply of Strategic and Critical Minerals and Materials*, Report GAO/EMD-82-69 (June 3, 1982).

8 This section was based on Richard J. Barbera, *Cobalt: Policy Options for a Strategic Mineral* (Washington, DC: Congressional Budget Office, 1982); Daniel Fine, "A Cobalt War May Endanger U.S. Security," *Business Week* (November 8, 1982): 58, 63; Cheryl Simons, "Cobalt Crusts: Deep Deposits," *Science News* 122 (October 30, 1982): 283; and "Cobalt" in Bureau of Mines, *Mineral Commodities Summaries: 1984* (Washington, DC: U.S. Department of the Interior, 1984).

ture environments such as jet engines. Short-term substitution possibilities are limited.

At present the United States produces none of its own cobalt. Therefore, all supplies come from reduction in stockpiles, recycling, or foreign producers. Currently about 16% of American consumption comes from recycling.

The supply situation has been volatile. During the 1970s, cobalt prices rose from $5.50 per pound to $25 per pound; spot prices went as high as $50 at one point. As of May 1982, the price had fallen to $12.40, and during October 1982, Zaire offered some 2000 tons at only $5.80 a pound. The price in 1987 was $6.85 a pound.

The American government responded erratically; although a cobalt stockpile has existed for some time, the appropriateness of its size has been the subject of much debate. Major purchases occurred throughout the 1950s, but in 1973, during the Nixon administration, millions of pounds of cobalt were sold from the stockpile. In late 1976 the Ford administration effectively reversed that decision, and a new goal of 85.4 million pounds was established. As of 1983 about 54% of that target level had been reached.

Subsequently, President Reagan issued a report calling for subsidies to domestic producers as another means of coping with cobalt vulnerability. Officials of the Anschutz Mining Corporation were reportedly seeking a federally guaranteed price of $28.50 per pound to open their Fredericktown, Missouri, mine while Noranda Mining sought $25 per pound to open its mine in Blackbird, Idaho. If the federal government were to purchase the approximately 40 million pounds needed to bring the stockpile up to its target level from these domestic producers at $25 a pound rather than from Zaire at $10 a pound, the additional cost would be $600 million.

That the stockpile has not reached the target level is not the only problem with current policy. As of January 1, 1987, all cobalt ores and concentrates could enter the country free of tariffs.[9] Since a tariff is an important part of an efficient policy package, we have not yet achieved an efficient allocation of this resource.

Substitution and Vulnerability

The vulnerability of a nation importing a strategic mineral depends not only on the severity of the shortfall it could experience, but also on its ability to cope with the shortfall. Coping in this context may be accomplished either by substituting other materials for the one in short supply or suffering the resulting

---

9 "Cobalt" in U. S. Department of the Interior, *Minerals Yearbook: 1987* (Washington, D.C.: U.S. Government Printing Office, 1987): 271–273.

TABLE 8.1   Mineral Supply Disruption Scenarios (cost in millions of 1974 dollars)

Shortfall (%)	Titanium	Vanadium	Cobalt	Columbium	Cadmium
5	23	19	6	6	—
15	69	38	12	11	—
25	140	98	30	35	—
35	198	159	49	46	1
50	340	21,532	25,667	17,136	2
85	33,475	80,752	74,976	78,800	4

Source: Data extracted from Michael Hazilla and Raymond J. Kopp, "Assessing U.S. Vulnerability to Raw Material Supply Disruptions: An Application to Non-fuel Minerals," *Southern Economic Journal* 52 (October 1984): Table IV, p. 351.

reduction in output. In assessing vulnerability, therefore, it is important to take the costs of both substitution and abstinence into account.

Some recent work by Hazilla and Kopp[10] attempts to accomplish this difficult task within the context of a detailed econometric model of the production process. The various production processes involving five specific strategic minerals—titanium, vanadium, cobalt, columbium, and cadmium—were modeled. These models included not only substitution possibility and their associated costs but the costs to society from any resulting reduced output as well. To quantify the degree of vulnerability, the authors estimated the total cost to the U.S. economy that would be expected to result from various levels of shortfalls of these strategic materials (Table 8.1).

Two interesting insights emerge from this information. First, small disruptions, loosely defined as those involving 35% or less of the available supply, could be handled without serious impact on the economy, but larger disruptions could be quite serious. Second, the vulnerability ranking depends on the size of the shortfall. For small shortfalls the scarcity of titanium imposes the largest cost on society. Notice, however, than when the shortage is in the range of 50%, cobalt presents a more serious problem. For shortfalls of 85%, the largest costs are imposed by shortages of vanadium. No one mineral imposes the highest cost in all shortfall scenarios.

This econometric approach has the substantial virtue that it allows the analyst to ask the kind of "what if" questions that give rise to the estimates in Table 8.1. It also has the disadvantage, however, that it is so general that the particular details of substitution are buried in the mathematics. Other authors therefore have

---

10 Michael Hazilla and Raymond J. Kopp, "Assessing U.S. Vulnerability to Raw Material Supply Disruptions: An Application to Non-fuel Minerals," *Southern Economic Journal* 52 (October 1984): 341-355.

attempted to learn more of the details by doing case studies of particular minerals.

One such study by Tilton[11] examined the substitution effects resulting from the rapid rise of tin prices during the 1970s. Three uses of tin were selected for study—beverage containers, solder, and tin-based chemicals used in manufacturing plastic pipe. Substantial substitution was uncovered. The tinplate beverage can, for example, after years of increasing its share of the market, began in the 1960s to lose market share, first to aluminum cans and ultimately to plastic bottles. As this was going on new technologies reduced the amount of tin in the average tinplate beverage can by over 93% between 1950 and 1977. Even the use of solder, thought by many to be impervious to substitution, was reduced as the introduction of low-tin alloys reduced the need for high-tin-content solder in automobile bodies. Similarly, in the plastic pipe industry, the introduction of new second- and third-generation stabilizers reduced the tin content by over 50%.

Based on this analysis, the Tilton study concluded that changes in material prices seem to have had little effect on materials usage in the short run, because producers are constrained by existing technologies and equipment. Over the long run, however, they can have a significant effect.

WASTE DISPOSAL AND POLLUTION DAMAGE

The strategic mineral problem suggests that an imperfection may arise in the way the market reacts to imports vis à vis domestically produced minerals. When the imports are critically important and come from risky sources, the market perceives a price ratio which fails to incorporate some of these social costs of imports. The result would be an inefficient and excessive reliance on imports.

Other market imperfections are apparent as well. The treatment of waste by producers and consumers can lead to biases in the market balance between recycling and the use of virgin ores. Since disposal cost is a key ingredient in determining the efficient amount of recycling, the failure of an economic agent to bear the full cost of disposal implies a bias toward virgin materials and away from recycling. We begin by considering how the method of financing the disposal of potentially recyclable waste affects the level of recycling.

---

11 John E. Tilton, ed., *Material Substitution: Lessons from Tin-Using Industries* (Washington, DC: Resources for the Future, 1985).

Disposal Cost and Efficiency

We must be clear about the relationship of the marginal disposal cost to the efficient level of recycling. Suppose, for example, it costs a community $20 per ton to recycle a particular waste product which can ultimately be sold to a local manufacturer for $10 per ton. Can we conclude that this is an inefficient recycling venture because it is losing money? No we can't! In addition to earning the $10 per ton from selling the recycled product, the town is avoiding the cost of disposing of the product. This avoided marginal cost is appropriately considered a marginal benefit from recycling. Suppose the marginal avoided disposal cost was $20 per ton. In this case the benefits to the town from recycling would be $30 per ton ($20 per ton avoided cost plus $10 per ton resale value) and the cost would be $20 per ton; this would be an efficient recycling venture. Both marginal disposal costs and the prices of recycled materials directly affect the efficient level of recycling.[12]

The Disposal Decision

Potentially recyclable waste can be divided into two types of scrap: old scrap and new scrap. *New scrap* is composed of the residual materials generated during production. For example, as steel beams are formed, the small remnants of steel left over are new scrap. *Old scrap* is recovered from products used by consumers.

To illustrate the relative importance of new scrap and old scrap, consider the aluminum industry. In 1987, a total of 2,096,071 metric tons of aluminum were recovered from scrap of both kinds. Of this, 1,165,728 metric tons came from new scrap while the rest came from old, including the recycling of some 1,002,561 metric tons of aluminum cans.[13] About 38% of the aluminum used to make aluminum products in the United States is currently being derived from scrap.

The difficulties in recycling new scrap are significantly less than those in recycling old scrap. New scrap is already at the place of production, and with most processes it can simply be reentered into the input stream without transportation costs. Transport costs tend to be an important part of the cost of using old scrap.

Equally important are the incentives involved. Since new scrap never leaves the factory, it remains under the complete control of the manufacturer. Having the joint responsibility of creating a product and dealing with the scrap, the

---

12 In 1989, Seattle, Washington found that its net recycling cost was $51.50 a ton, which was slightly higher than its avoided cost for landfill disposal, but it expected recycling to be cheaper within five years. See Jerome Richard, "Better Homes and Garbage," *The Amicus Journal* (Summer 1990): 50-51.

13 U.S. Department of the Interior, *Minerals Yearbook: 1987* (Washington, DC: U.S. Government Printing Office, 1987): 85-91.

manufacturer now has an incentive to design the product with the use of the scrap in mind. It would be advantageous to establish procedures guaranteeing the homogeneity of the scrap and minimizing the amount of processing necessary to recycle it. For all these reasons, it is likely the market for new scrap will work efficiently and effectively.

Unfortunately, the same is not true for old scrap. The market works inefficiently because the product users do not bear the full marginal social costs of disposing of their product. As a result, the market is biased away from recycling old scrap and toward the use of virgin materials.

The key to understanding why these costs are not internalized lies in the incentives facing individual product users. Suppose you had some small aluminum products which were no longer useful to you. You could either recycle them, which usually means driving to a recycling center, or you could toss them into your trash. In comparing these two alternatives, notice that recycling imposes one cost on you (transport cost), while the second imposes another (disposal cost).

It is difficult for consumers to make this comparison accurately because of the way trash collection has traditionally been financed. Urban areas have generally financed trash collection with taxes, if publicly provided, or user fees, if privately provided. Neither of these approaches directly relates the size of an individual's payment to the amount of waste. The *marginal* cost to the homeowner of throwing out one more unit of trash is negligible, even when the cost to society is not. The marginal private disposal cost and the cost to society as a whole diverge (Figure 8.2).

When the private marginal cost of disposal (MC_P) is lower than the marginal social cost of disposal (MC_s), the market level of recycling (where the marginal cost of recycling (MC_R) is equal to the marginal private disposal cost) is inefficient. Only if all social costs are included in the marginal cost of disposal will the efficient amount of recycling (Q_s) be attained.[14]

This point can be reinforced by a numerical example. Suppose your city provides trash pickup for which you pay $150 a year in taxes. Your cost will be $150 regardless (within reasonable limits) of how much you throw out. In that year your additional (marginal) cost from throwing out these items is *zero*. Certainly the marginal cost to society is *not* zero, and, therefore, the balance between these alternatives as seen by the individual homeowner is biased in favor of throwing things out.[15]

Littering is an extreme example of what we have been talking about. In the absence of some kind of government intervention the cost to society of littering

---

14 According to Figure 8.2 would 100% recycling normally be efficient? Does that conclusion make sense to you? Why or why not?

15 The problem is not that $150 is too low; indeed it may be too high! The point is that the cost of waste disposal does not increase with the amount of waste to be disposed.

FIGURE 8.2 The efficient level of recycling.

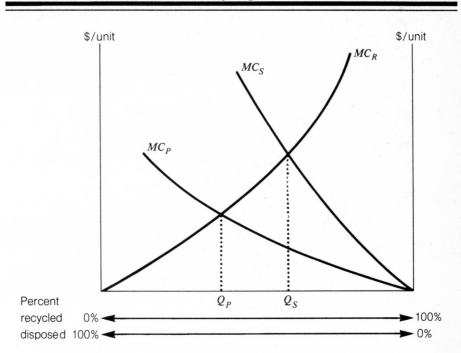

is the aesthetic loss plus the risk of damage to automobile tires and pedestrians caused by sharp edges of discarded cans or glass. Tossing used containers outside the car is relatively costless for the individual, but costly for society.[16]

Disposal Costs and the Scrap Market

How would the market respond to a policy forcing product users to bear the true marginal disposal cost? The major effect would be on the supply of materials to be recycled. Consumers would now be able to avoid disposal costs and might even be paid for discarded products. This would cause the diversion of some materials to recycling centers where they could be reintegrated into the materials process. If this expanded supply allows dealers to take advantage of previously unexploited economies of scale, this expansion

---

16 Using economic analysis, would you expect transients or residents to have a higher propensity to litter? (Why?)

FIGURE 8.3 The market response to increased disposal costs.

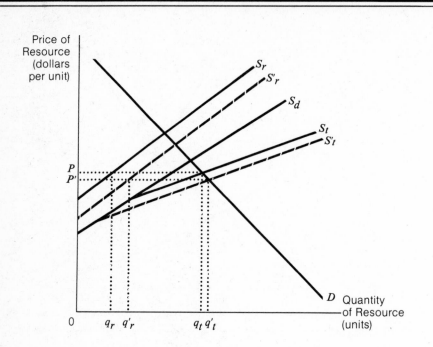

could well result in a lower average cost of processing, as well as more recycled materials.

Such a development would affect the old scrap market (Figure 8.3). S_r, S_d, and S_t represent, respectively, the supply curves for recycled old scrap, domestically supplied virgin ores, and the total supply curve (the horizontal summation of the other two) when disposal costs are not considered. S'_r and S'_t represent, respectively, the supply curves for recycled old scrap and the total supply curve when disposal costs are considered. The graph demonstrates what we stated in the previous paragraph—when disposal costs are included, the supply of recycled scrap increases. More is available at lower cost.

The effect on the market is now clearly evident. The total consumption of inputs increases from q_t to q'_t because the price falls from P to P'. The use of recycled materials increases from q_r to q'_r. The amount of virgin ore falls. Thus the correct inclusion of disposal cost would tend to increase the amount of recycling and extend the useful economic life for depletable, recyclable resources.

TABLE 8.2 Materials Being Recycled in the United States in 1986.

Material	Amount Generated (millions of tons)	Amount Recycled (millions of tons)
Paper and paperboard	64.7	14.6
Glass	12.9	1.1
Metals	13.7	1.0
Plastics	10.3	0.1
Rubber and leather	4.0	0.1
Textiles	2.8	0.0
Wood	5.8	0.0
Food waste	12.5	0.0
Yard waste	28.3	0.0
Other	2.7	0.0
Total	157.7	17.0

Source: From "Recycling in the States: Update 1989." Reprinted by permission of the National Solid Wastes Management Association.

Public Policies

As Table 8.2 indicates, the current level of recycling in the United States is rather low, particularly when judged by the standards of Japan (refer to Example 8.1). No doubt some of the responsibility for this lies in improper incentives created by inappropriate pricing. Can the misallocation resulting from inefficiently low disposal cost be corrected?

One approach would impose disposal charges reflecting the true social cost of disposal. The system in Highbridge, New Jersey, illustrates how such a scheme might work in practice.[17] In January 1988 the town replaced its flat $280 annual fee for garbage collection with a fee that varies with the amount of trash. Each 30-gallon bag or 30-gallon can set out at curbside each week must exhibit a town sticker. Each household is given 52 stickers for $140.[18] Additional stickers cost $1.25 a piece.[19]

17 Robert Hanley, "Pay-by-Bag Trash Disposal Really Pays, Town Learns," *New York Times* (November 24, 1988): B1, B7.

18 In 1989 the base sticker rate went to $200, and the cost of additional individual stickers to $1.65.

19 If you were running this program, would you allow these stickers to be freely transferable among Highbridge residents? (Why?)

What were the effects? The most obvious result was that the amount of trash went down by 25%. A number of residents began to compost food and yard wastes. Recycling programs in glass, newspapers, and cans have flourished. Neighborhood behavior has even changed as people take their trash home with them from parties or bring an extra sticker. Since disposing of large pieces of used furniture can use up four stickers, the frequency of finding new homes for them has increased.

One preimplementation concern about the program was that it might impose a hardship on the poor residents of the area. Strategies based on higher prices always raise the specter that they will end up placing an intolerable burden on the poor.

That concern apparently was misplaced. Many of the town's 4000 residents were elderly and living on relatively meager fixed incomes. Under the old system of financing trash collection, every household paid the same fee regardless of how much trash was produced. Since elderly households produce less trash, they were in effect subsidizing wealthier households under the old system. Under the new system, elderly households paid only the flat fee since they didn't need extra stickers. The expense of these stickers was less than the average cost of disposal, the basis for the previous fee. Poor households were better off, not worse off, under the new pricing system.

Seattle, Washington, has a similar system, but with higher prices. As of 1989 residents pay $13.75 for the first can of trash picked up per week and $9 for every additional can. Their experience was very similar to that in New Jersey. Trash disposal is down dramatically and recycling is up.

Another suggestion now being applied in many areas is the refundable deposit. Already widely accepted for beverage containers, such deposits could become a remedy for many other products.

A refund system is designed to accomplish two purposes: (1) the initial charge reflects the cost of disposal and produces the desired composition of demand effect; and (2) the refund, attainable upon turning the product in for recycling, helps conserve virgin materials. Such a system already is employed in Sweden and Norway to counter the problem of abandoned automobiles (Example 8.4).

The recycling of aluminum beverage cans has been one clear beneficiary of deposit refund schemes.[20] Although not all states have passed bottle bills,[21] over 50% of aluminum beverage cans are now recycled in the United States.[22] As a

---

20 A very strong demand for aluminum scrap was also influential. In fact, the price for aluminum scrap went so high in 1988 that pilferers were stealing highway signs and guardrails for their aluminum content.

21 As of 1989, only California, Connecticut, Delaware, Iowa, Maine, Massachusetts, Michigan, New York, Oregon, and Vermont had passed bottle bills.

22 In Maine, a bottle bill state, 85% of aluminum beverage cans are recycled.

EXAMPLE 8.4

Deposits as a Solution to Abandoned Automobiles

In many countries abandoned automobiles are the source of a significant visual externality. When the prices offered by junk dealers are low, for whatever reasons, discarded cars begin appearing in parking lots, meadows, forests, and even in lakes and rivers. Generally it is difficult to trace the ownership of these vehicles, so penalties are not the answer.

In Sweden a deposit-refund system was introduced in 1976 to remedy this problem. Swedish car owners who turn over their hulks to authorized junk dealers get a bonus of about $60 per car over and above whatever arrangements they could make with the junk dealer. Buyers of new cars pay a fee in the same amount. Since total deposits exceed total refunds, a surplus has accumulated. Part of this surplus has been used to finance local efforts to clean up wrecks that were abandoned before the program began.

The success of this program suggests that such an approach can work. It also suggests some pitfalls to be avoided. During the first year, a reduction in abandoned vehicles occurred. After that initial period, however, the program seemed less effective. There were two main reasons: (1) the bonus payment was eroded by high inflation and therefore provided less incentive; and (2) the bottom dropped out of the market for scrapped automobiles, so dealers began charging customers to take their hulks, rather than paying them. In some areas, even with the bonus payment, the act of turning the car in may have cost the donor additional money.

A deposit system can work, providing it is flexible enough and the refund is high enough. This seems to be the case in Norway which subsequently implemented a similar system with a higher deposit.

Source: Peter Bohm, *Deposit-Refund System: Theory and Application to Environmental, Conservation, and Consumer Policy* (Baltimore: Johns Hopkins University Press for Resources for the Future, 1981): 120–124; and J. B. Opschoor and Hans B. Vos, *Economic Instruments for Environmental Protection* (Paris: Organization for Economic Co-operation and Development, 1989).

result aluminum old scrap has become an increasingly significant component of total aluminum supplies.

Recycling aluminum saves about 95% of the energy that is needed to make new aluminum from ore. In 1987 alone, aluminum can recycling saved more than 10 billion kilowatt hours of electricity, enough to supply the residential electricity needs of New York City for more than six months. The magnitude of these energy savings has had a significant influence on the demand for recycled aluminum as cost-conscious producers search for new ways to reduce energy costs.

Beverage can recycling also reduces littering because an incentive is created to bring the bottle to a recycling center. In some cities scavenging and returning these bottles has provided a significant source of income to the homeless. One Canadian study found that recycling creates six times as many jobs as landfilling.

Deposit refund systems are also being used for batteries and tires. New Hampshire and Maine place a surcharge on new car batteries. Consumers in these states receive a rebate if they trade in their used battery for a new one. Oklahoma places a $1.00 fee on each new tire sold and then returns 50 cents to certified processing facilities for each tire handled.

The tax system can also be used to promote recycling by taxing virgin materials and by subsidizing recycling activities. The European approach to waste oil recycling, reinforced by the high cost of imported crude oil, was to require both residential and commercial users to recycle all waste oil they generate. Virgin lubricating oils are taxed, and the resulting income is used to subsidize the recycling industry. As a result, many countries collect up to 65% of the available waste oil.

In the United States, which does not subsidize waste oil recycling, the waste oil market has been rather less successful. Currently only about 15% of waste oil is recovered. The waste oil industry has been in a relative decline since World War II with the exception of the period immediately following the oil crisis during the 1970s when oil prices rose dramatically.

As described briefly in Table 8.3 many states are now using tax policy to subsidize the acquisition of recycling equipment in both the public and private sectors. Frequently taking the form of sales tax exemptions or investment tax credits to private industries or loans or grants to local communities, these approaches are designed to get recycling programs off the ground with the expectation that they will ultimately be self-sustaining. The pioneers are being subsidized.

Examining Oregon's program can serve to illustrate how a tax approach works. From 1981 to 1987, to reduce energy consumption as well as to promote recycling, the Oregon Department of Energy granted tax credits to 163 projects. Being granted this credit allows companies a five-year period in which to deduct from their taxes an amount equal to 35% of the cost of any equipment used solely for recycling. Oregon also offers a broader tax credit that covers equipment, land, and building purchases. Paper companies, the major recipients of both types of

TABLE 8.3 State Incentives for Recycling

State	Incentive
California	Recycling equipment investment tax credit for individuals and corporations. Development bonds for manufacturing products with recycled materials.
Colorado	Tax credits for investments in plastics recycling equipment.
Florida	Sales tax exemption on recycling machinery purchased after July 1, 1988.
Indiana	Property tax exemptions for buildings, equipment, and land involved in recycling operations.
Maine	Tax credit equal to 30% of the cost of equipment and machinery. Subsidies to municipalities for scrap metal transportation costs.
New Jersey	50% investment credit for recycling equipment and programs.
North Carolina	Industrial and corporate income tax credits and exemptions for equipment purchases and facilities.
Oregon	Individual and corporate income tax credits for equipment purchases and facilities.
Texas	Franchise tax exemption for sludge recycling corporations.
Wisconsin	Sales tax exemptions for equipment and facilities; business property tax exemptions for some equipment.

Source: National Solid Wastes Management Association, "Recycling in the States: Update 1989" (Washington DC).

credits, have used them to increase the capacity to use recycled newsprint and cardboard in the papermaking process. As a result, Oregon's newspaper recycling rate (65%) is twice the national average.[23]

Pollution Damage

One other situation influences the use of recycled and virgin ores. When environmental damage results from extracting and using virgin materials and not from

23 Cynthia Pollock Shea, "Building a Market for Recyclables," *Worldwatch* (May/June 1988): 12–18.

the use of recycled materials, the market allocation will be biased away from recycling. The damage might be experienced at the mine, such as the erosion and aesthetic costs of strip mining, or at the point of processing, where the ore is processed into a usable resource.

Suppose that the mining industry was forced to bear the cost of this environmental damage. What difference would the inclusion of this cost have on the scrap market? The internalizing of this cost results in a leftward shift in the supply curve for the virgin ore (S_d) in Figure 8.3. This would, in turn, cause a leftward shift in the total supply curve. The market would be using less of the resource—due to higher price—while recycling more. Thus the correct treatment of these environmental costs would share with disposal costs a tendency to increase the role for recycling.

One study by Spofford examines the significance of this cost in the context of the paper industry which, in spite of the fact it is based on a renewable resource, does rely on the recycling of used paper.[24] In his study (summarized in Figure 8.4). Spofford considers four costs: acquiring and processing virgin pulp; using scrap paper; treatment and disposal of resulting pollutants; and the external damage caused by untreated pollutants. Graphed as a function of the reuse ratio, the external damages and treatment costs are much higher with lower reuse ratios; the use of virgin materials generates most of these costs.

Spofford also differentiates the costs to society as a whole from the costs to the papermaking firm. These differ because society bears all the costs while the firm bears only the costs of acquiring and processing virgin pulp and the costs of using scrap paper. The private costs do not include either the treatment costs (in the absence of government control the firm would not choose to treat the pollutants) or the external damages. The major conclusion to be drawn is that the efficient reuse ratio (0.8) is significantly higher than what the market would automatically provide (0.55) due to its undervaluation of environmental damage.

TAX TREATMENT OF MINERALS

Built into the United States tax code is a series of special provisions for selected extractive industries. These provisions were designed to avoid taxing, as profits, the returns which really represented a liquidation of assets. The assets in this case are the reserves of natural resources being depleted. Thus these provisions,

---

24 W. O. Spofford, "Solid Residual Management: Some Economic Considerations," *Natural Resource Journal* 11 (July 1971): 561–589.

FIGURE 8.4 Optimal reuse ratio for paper residuals in the production of newsprint.

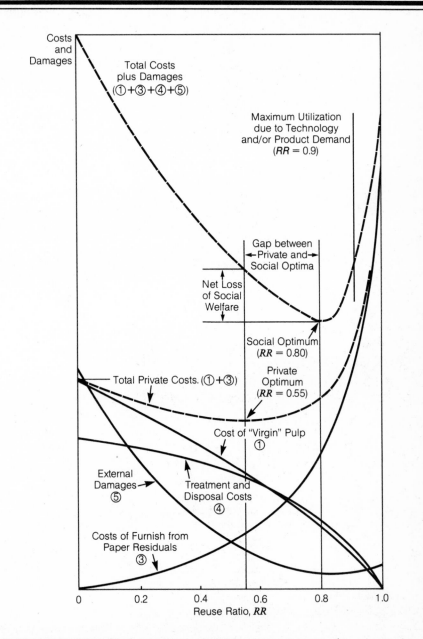

Source: Walter O. Spofford, Jr., Figure 4. Reprinted with permission from *The Natural Resources Journal* 585 (1971), published by the University of New Mexico School of Law, Albuquerque, NM.

chiefly that known as the depletion allowance, expand the conventional treatment of capital assets to include depletable resources. They stimulate the extraction of targeted minerals and fuels by providing implicit tax reduction subsidies to extractive industries. It is estimated that this subsidy amounted to over $3.5 billion during 1972.[25]

While the subsidy has taken several forms, the overall effect is to lower the after-tax cost of extraction for virgin ores. According to our models, this should have the effect of increasing the amount of virgin ore mined.

Other effects of the tax treatment of minerals can be identified as well. Because these tax breaks are accrued by some minerals, they create a bias in favor of those minerals whose lobbying groups were sufficiently strong that they were able to get favorable tax treatment. Favorable tax treatment for these minerals also creates a bias against recycling, since recycled materials are not eligible for the special tax treatment.[26]

Not all tax treatment, however, is favorable to the virgin ores. One in particular, the *severance tax*, tends to counteract these biases induced by other portions of the tax code. The severance tax is levied on minerals as they are extracted. States having severance taxes argue that the revenues compensate current citizens for localized environmental damage caused by extraction and compensate future generations for the loss of the resource by financing public investments.[27] Others suspect that states also use severance taxes to export their tax liability to consumers in other states.[28] Regardless of the reason for implementation, the rates were not designed to eliminate a bias against recycling.

In general, severance taxes are not high—except for coal, which as an energy source is not recyclable, anyway.[29] They are not levied on all minerals, nor are they levied by all states; the coverage is limited and uneven. Furthermore, there

---

25 Talbot Page, *Conservation and Economic Efficiency: An Approach to Materials Policy* (Baltimore: Johns Hopkins University Press for Resources for the Future, 1977): 109.

26 One provision, the foreign tax credit, which stipulates favorable tax treatment of foreign sources of minerals produced by U.S. corporations, may exacerbate the strategic mineral problem. This subsidy, which applies to all corporations, not merely those in the extractive industries, was estimated to be $3.7 billion in 1968. About half went to oil and gas companies. See Gerard M. Brannon, *Energy Taxes and Subsidies* (Cambridge, MA: Ballinger, 1974): 38.

27 For an example, see Arthur A. Link, "Political Constraint and North Dakota's Coal Severance Tax," *National Tax Journal* 31 (September 1978): 263-268. Link was the governor of North Dakota when this severance tax was imposed.

28 The extent to which this can be done is questionable. See, for example, the discussion of the Texas severance tax in Charles McLure, Jr., "Economic Constraint on State and Local Taxation of Energy Resources," *National Tax Journal* 31 (September 1978): 257-262.

29 On July 2, 1981, the Supreme Court ruled Montana's 30 percent severance tax on coal constitutional. The highest severance tax in the country, Montana's tax had been attacked as being "confiscatory."

is some evidence that, even for those minerals and states where the severance tax is levied, this tax has only from one-third to one-tenth the impact on market price that the depletion allowance has.[30]

While severance taxes may be useful in raising revenue for whatever purpose, they do little to correct the lack of balance between environmental and virgin resources. Furthermore, they may well make the strategic-mineral problem worse. Only domestic ore suppliers are taxed; foreign ore suppliers can avoid the tax.

DISCRIMINATION IN TRANSPORT COST

Earlier we noted that old scrap prices were generally more sensitive to transportation costs than new scrap or virgin ores. For that reason, the economic viability of old scrap is sensitive to the cost of transporting it.

For years the scrap industry has argued that the structure of transport costs discriminates unfairly against the shipments of old scrap. There are two major strands in the argument. Not only are scrap shippers believed to pay higher rates on average for a comparable shipment, but also for them freight rates constitute a larger fraction of the total value of old scrap than for virgin materials. This latter argument implies that when the rates are changed over time by equal percentage increases (historically, a common practice), it causes old scrap to become increasingly disadvantaged.

Railroad freight rates are not market-determined. They are established by a regulatory body known as the Interstate Commerce Commission (ICC). The railroads must submit any proposed rate schedules and changes in those schedules to the ICC. The ICC then holds hearings in which the affected industries participate as witnesses. At the conclusion of these hearings, the ICC renders its decision.

Are the arguments put forward by the scrap industry correct? Talbot Page, an economist with Resources for the Future, a Washington think tank, has examined this issue closely.[31] He concludes:

> . . . as one of the groups of commodities paying part of the cost of shipment of virgin materials, scrap material is paying a disproportionate share . . . [p. 76].

---

30 Robert C. Anderson, "Evaluation of Economic Benefits of Resource Conservation," U.S. Environmental Protection Agency Report EPA-60015-78-015 (September 1978): 23.

31 Talbot Page, *Conservation and Economic Efficiency: An Approach to Materials Policy* (Baltimore: Johns Hopkins University Press for Resources for the Future, 1977): 76.

He also suggests, however, that the current decisions of the ICC are moving in the direction of correcting this bias. In addition, in the current deregulation environment the ICC is leaving more and more rates to the market.[32] While a bias does seem to exist, it should diminish over time.

PRODUCT DURABILITY

In a memorable passage from *Death of a Salesman*, Willy Loman laments:

> Once in my life I would like to own something outright before it's broken! I'm always in a race with the junkyard! I just finish paying for the car and it's on its last legs. The refrigerator consumes belts like a goddamn maniac. They time those things. They time them so when you've finally paid for them, they're used up.[33]

Willy is not alone in his anguish. In the early 1960s popular author Vance Packard came out with a book called *The Waste Makers*, which suggested that Willy's plight was the product of a conscious marketing strategy by corporations. If products wear out faster, the argument goes, consumers have to buy them more often and sales are increased. Is this a valid argument? If it is, the drain on the resource base is artificially high and we have another reason for corrective measures.

Packard identifies three possible types of product obsolescence. *Functional obsolescence* occurs when a new product can perform the function in a superior manner to an older product. The vacuum tube became functionally obsolescent when it was replaced by the transistor. *Fashion obsolescence* occurs when consumers prefer a new product for reasons of taste. Wide ties and short skirts become obsolete when tastes shift to narrow ties and long skirts. *Durability obsolescence* occurs when the product can no longer perform its function because of wear and tear. A refrigerator becomes obsolete when it can no longer keep its inside temperature stable and cool. The economic implications of these three types of obsolescence are quite different.

Functional Obsolescence

Because functional obsolescence is not really a problem, we will spend little time on it. A vigorous amount of inventive activity is a natural and desirable conse-

---

32 For a description of this trend, see Thomas Gale Moore, "Rail and Trucking Deregulation," in *Regulatory Reform: What Actually Happened?* Leonard W. Weiss and Michael W. Klass, eds. (Boston: Little, Brown, 1986): 14–39.

33 Arthur Miller, *Death of a Salesman*, in *Arthur Miller's Collected Plays*, Vol. 1 (New York: Viking, 1957): 174.

quence of a market economy. Those who find better ways of doing things can become wealthy from the sales of their product, whether it be a tastier way to fry chicken or a cheaper, higher-quality method of copying documents. Far from representing a problem, functional obsolescence is the natural consequence of the successful search for better products.

Fashion Obsolescence

Fashion obsolescence is trickier. On the one hand, if fashion is a valued characteristic for consumers, then it is possible to conceive fashion obsolescence as merely a special case of functional obsolescence. New fashions replace old because they are more satisfying to the consumer. In this view there is no problem with fashion obsolescence because it is merely the result of the market continually doing a superior job of satisfying consumer preference.

The opposite point of view starts from the premise that those consumer preferences being satisfied by the market are *created* by the market.[34] If consumer preferences are created by producers, then it is appropriate to question whether consumers are legitimately being made better off or are merely being manipulated into believing they are better off.

The apparel industry is certainly one where fashion obsolescence plays a strong role. However, it is not clear that fashion obsolescence is as important for other products. The automobile has certainly had its share of fashion obsolescence, perhaps best epitomized by the era in the 1950s when pronounced tailfins were in vogue. Yet, clearly the auto industry can go only so far. It would be very difficult, for example, to explain the shift in consumer buying toward small imported automobiles in the late 1970s and early 1980s as reflecting a shift in what was fashionable.

Indeed, some observers believe that a significant portion of the malaise of the domestic auto industry in the 1980s was caused by its inability to anticipate and respond to consumer preferences. That is important because the automobile market is one in which consumer preferences were thought to be dominated by the big three American automakers.[35] Clearly that is not the case.

Even when fashion influences consumer preferences, it is not clear that taste is dictated by the manufacturer or that it relates solely to new products. Antique

---

34 For an articulation of this position, see John Kenneth Galbraith, *The Affluent Society* (Boston: Houghton Mifflin, 1958). For an opposite point of view, see F. A. Hayek, "The Non Sequitur of 'Dependence Effect'," *Southern Economic Journal* 27 (April 1961): 346-352.

35 See, for example, Vance Packard, "How to Outmode a $4,000 Vehicle in Two Years," in *The Waste Makers* (New York: David McKay, 1960).

furniture and antique cars are fashionable, but these fashions certainly are not created by manufacturers and do not help sell new cars or new furniture.

In looking at the totality of consumer decisions, we cannot conclude that consumer tastes are systematically manipulated by industry. Markets do exist for which a strong case can be made, but they seem to be isolated examples.

Durability Obsolescence

We come then to the final category, the one which triggered Willy Loman's lament. We must answer two questions: (1) What is an efficient level of durability? (2) Will the market supply that level? The *efficient level of durability* is the one which maximizes the net benefit from the product. Products that last longer confer more benefits on society, but they also cost more. Therefore, it is not obvious that the most durable product is also the most efficient. Can we trust the market to find the efficient level of durability? To examine that issue, let's look at both the demand and supply sides of the market.

On the demand side, the consumer makes his or her choices by discounting benefits and costs. The capital costs of consumer durables are borne immediately (although payments can be spread out by borrowing money), while the benefits (flow of services), as well as operating and maintenance costs, are accrued as a flow over time. He or she will purchase the commodity only if the net benefit is maximized by that level of durability (the additional cost of making a more durable commodity is justified by the additional benefit received). In performing this balancing between cost and durability, will the consumer make efficient choices or, because of lack of information or some other market imperfection, will durability be undervalued or overvalued?

One way to test this is to examine a case in which the benefits and costs are relatively easy to quantify, thereby allowing a comparison of the discount rate implied by consumer purchases of durable goods with market rates. If their individual discount rates are higher than the social opportunity cost of capital (as measured by interest rates), consumers are undervaluing durability. If they use lower discount rates, they are overvaluing it.

Jerry Hausman of MIT conducted a fascinating study which relates to this issue.[36] He was able to acquire data on individual purchases of energy-using consumer durables (room air conditioners). For each of these purchases he could calculate the benefits (longer life plus energy savings resulting from higher energy efficiency) and cost (purchase price as well as expected operating and maintenance costs). From this information he could calculate the discount rates

---

36 Jerry Hausman, "Individual Discount Rates and the Purchase and Utilization of Energy-Using Durables," *Bell Journal of Economics* 10 (Spring 1979): 33-54.

implied by the purchase made by the average consumer. High discount rates indicate a special sensitivity to the initial cost.

Interestingly, in his sample, the implied discount rates were higher than the market rates. Furthermore, Hausman found that discount rates were highest for the lowest-income people, while they approximated the efficient rates for higher income classes. This suggests that consumers—particularly low-income consumers—purchase less durability and less energy efficiency than is dictated by the dynamic efficiency criterion.[37]

To be able to structure the appropriate policy response, however, the government would have to know more about the reasons for the higher implied discount rates. If the reason is inadequate consumer information, then the appropriate policy might well be increasing the flow of reliable information through testing, labeling requirements, and so on. If it is purely that the market rate of interest is higher for low-income consumers because they have a higher probability of defaulting on loan repayments, then some means of providing easier access to capital markets might be called for. In other cases, measures such as tax subsidies or enforced standards might be appropriate.

We must also consider the supply side of the market. If they can get away with it, producers as a group have an incentive to reduce product durability below the efficient level. By doing so, they would reduce their cost per unit and they would sell many more units over time. For example a household could satisfy its demand over a 10-year period with one appliance lasting 10 years, but would have to purchase two if the appliance lasted only 5 years. As long as the profit were higher on the sale of two, rather than one (the presumption), firms would be better off with planned obsolescence.

But the key question is whether they can get away with it. As long as competitive suppliers, or even potential competitive suppliers, could enter the market to supply more durable goods, the consumer could turn to these alternative suppliers instead. In a normal market process, competition prevents individual firms from producing insufficiently durable products. Those who sell products which don't last find their markets drying up.

This market process may not work efficiently in two cases. The first case occurs when consumers are not well informed about the differences in durability, so they do not have enough information to make efficient decisions. This, remember, was one possible interpretation of the Hausman study. To the extent they face ignorant consumers, producers would have an incentive to position themselves in the lower-initial-price portion of the market by lowering the durability of their products.

---

37 These results were subsequently corroborated by a number of other authors. For a description of these, see Malcolm Gladwell, "Consumer's Choices About Money Consistently Defy Common Sense," *Washington Post* (February 12, 1990): A3.

In recognition of the importance of this information, organizations have been set up to supply it. Consumers' Union, the publisher of *Consumer Reports*, is one such organization. It performs its own independent testing and evaluating, a service which can rectify this lack of information at reasonable cost. Its chief limitation probably relates to products undergoing rapid technological change. For rapidly changing products, by the time the testing lab acquires the product, tests it, and reports the results, other untested but potentially superior products are already on the market. This flaw, however, is not fatal; it merely means the rate of adoption would be more sluggish than would be dictated by efficiency.

The second case where a firm could profit by producing a good with an inefficiently low durability is when it does not face competition. This would require either a monopoly—which is very rare—or explicit collusion to cut corners by all the members of the industry. Since competition comes from foreign, as well as domestic, firms and from potential entrants, as well as existing firms, this must be a relatively rare circumstance.

The American automobile industry provides an interesting subject for examining the hypothesis that increased competition can increase durability because that industry has faced increasingly intense foreign competition. The share of the U.S. market captured by imports rose from 14.8% in 1976 to 29.2% in 1988.[38] Did this lead to increased durability?

According to two possible measures it did. Durable cars should last longer and be safer. The average age of passenger cars increased from 6.2 years in 1976 to 7.6 years in 1988. And the deaths per 100,000,000 vehicle miles traveled decreased from 3.33 in 1976 to 2.46 in 1988. Though other factors were certainly also at work, competition probably did play a major role in increasing durability.

SUMMARY

Market mechanisms automatically create pressures for recycling and reuse which are generally in the right direction, though not always of the correct intensity. Higher disposal costs and increasing scarcity of virgin materials do create a larger demand for recycling. This is already evident for a number of products, such as those containing copper or aluminum.

Yet, there are also a number of imperfections in the market which tend to suggest the degree of recycling we are currently experiencing is less than the efficient amount. The absence of sufficient stockpiles and the absence of tariffs

---

38 The data in this and the following paragraph came from Motor Vehicles Manufacturing Association, *Motor Vehicle Facts and Figures, 1989* (Detroit: Motor Vehicles Manufacturing Association, 1989): 16, 26, and 90.

mean that our national security interests are not being adequately considered in market decisions involving strategic minerals. From the perspective of efficiency, the reliance on vulnerable imports is excessive.

Artificially low disposal costs, tax breaks for ores, and discriminatory pricing practices by the Interstate Commerce Commission all combine to depress the role which old scrap can, and should, play. Severance taxes provide a limited, if poorly targeted, redress for some minerals.

One imperfection, the supposed tendency of American manufacturers to produce products less durable than efficient, seems overstated. Yet the Hausman study indicates that some people purchase products less durable than efficient, implying that the market penetration of more energy efficient devices may be lower than efficient. This is a more limited view of product durability problems than is usually espoused by writers such as Vance Packard, but a troubling one nonetheless.

One cannot help but notice that many of these problems—such as pricing municipal disposal services, tax breaks for virgin ores, and pricing decisions of the ICC—result from government actions. It therefore appears in this area that the appropriate role for government is selective disengagement complemented by some fine-tuning adjustments.

This is not true, however, for environmental damage due to littering, air and water pollution, and strip mining. When a product is produced from virgin materials, rather than recycled or reusable materials, and the cost of any associated environmental damage is not internalized, some government action may be called for.

The selective disengagement of government in some areas must be complemented by the enforcement of programs to internalize the costs of environmental damage. The commonly heard ideological prescriptions suggesting that environmental problems can be solved either by ending government interference or by increasing the amount of government control are both inaccurate. The efficient role for government in achieving a balance between the economic and environmental systems requires less control in some areas and more in others.

FURTHER READING

Bohm, Peter. *Deposit-Refund System: Theory and Application to Environmental, Conservation, and Consumer Policy* (Baltimore: Johns Hopkins University Press for Resources for the Future, 1981). A highly readable and analytically sound exploration of the experience with and potential applications for deposit-refund systems.

Curlee, T. Randall. *The Economic Feasibility of Recycling: A Case Study of Plastic Wastes* (New York: Praeger, 1986). Analyzes in nontechnical language the incentives for, and barriers to, recycling plastics.

Manthy, Robert S. *Natural Resource Commodities—A Century of Statistics* (Baltimore: Johns Hopkins University Press for Resources for the Future, 1978). A basic reference source on natural resource prices, output, consumption, foreign trade and employment in the United States, 1870-1973. It draws no conclusions.

Roxburgh, Nigel. *Policy Responses to Resource Depletion: The Case of Mercury* (Greenwich, CT: JAI Press, 1980). An intensive examination of the depletion experience with one particular material—mercury. Includes chapters on the resource base, extractive and scrap-metal industries, and various industries which are heavy users of mercury.

ADDITIONAL REFERENCES

Banks, Ferdinand E. *Bauxite and Aluminum: An Introduction to the Economics of Non-Fuel Minerals* (Lexington, MA: Lexington Books, 1979).

Foley, Patricia T. and Joel P. Clark. "The Effects of State Taxation on United States Copper Supply," *Land Economics* 58 (May 1982): 153–180.

Gulley, D. A. "Severance Taxes and Market Failure," *Natural Resources Journal* 22 (July 1982): 597–617.

Harris, DeVerle P. *Mineral Resources Appraisal* (New York: Oxford University Press, 1984).

Kakela, Peter J. "Iron Ore: From Depletion to Abundance," *Science* 212 (April 10, 1981): 132–136.

Lee, D. R., P. E. Graves, and R. L. Sexton. "On Mandatory Deposits, Fines, and the Control of Litter," *Natural Resources Journal* 28 (Fall 1988): 837–847.

McClure, Charles and Peter Mieszkowski, eds. *Fiscal Federalism and the Taxation of Natural Resources* (Lexington, MA: Lexington Books, 1983).

Mikesell, Raymond F. *Nonfuel Minerals: Foreign Dependence and National Security* (Ann Arbor, MI: University of Michigan Press, 1987).

Peck, Merton J., ed. *The World Aluminum Industry in a Changing Energy Era* (Washington, DC: Resources for the Future, 1988).

Stollery, Kenneth R. "Mineral Depletion with Cost as the Extraction Limit: A Model Applied to the Behavior of Prices in the Nickel Industry," *Journal of Environmental Economics and Management* 10 (June 1983): 151–165.

Tilton, John E., Roderick G. Eggert, and Hans H. Landsberg, eds. *World Mineral Exploration: Trends and Economic Issues* (Washington, DC: Resources for the Future, 1988).

DISCUSSION QUESTIONS

1. Glass bottles can either be recycled (crushed and remelted) or reused. The market will tend to choose the cheapest path. What factors will tend to affect the relative cost of these options? Is the market likely to make the efficient choice? Are the "bottle bills" passed by many of the states requiring deposits on bottles a move toward efficiency? Why?

2. Many areas have attempted to increase the amount of recycled waste lubricating oil by requiring service stations to serve as collection centers or by instituting deposit-refund systems. On what grounds, if any, is government intervention called for? In terms of the effects on the waste lubrication oil

market, what differences should be noticed among those states which do nothing, those which require all service stations to serve as collection centers, and those implementing deposit-refund systems? Why?

3. What are the income distribution consequences of "fashion"? Can the need to be seen driving a new car by the rich be a boon to those with lower incomes who will utimately purchase a better, lower-priced used car as a result?

PROBLEMS

1. Suppose a product can be produced using virgin ore at a marginal cost given by $MC_1 = 0.5q_1$ and with recycled materials at a marginal cost given by $MC_2 = 5 + 0.1q_2$. (a) If the inverse demand curve were given by $P = 10 - 0.5(q_1 + q_2)$, how many units of the product would be produced with virgin ore and how many units with recycled materials? (b) If the inverse demand curve were $P = 20 - 0.5(q_1 + q_2)$, what would your answer be?

2. When the government allows private firms to extract minerals offshore or on public lands, two common means of sharing in the profits are bonus bidding and production royalties. The former awards the right to extract to the highest bidder, while the second charges a per ton royalty on each ton extracted. Bonus bids involve a single, up-front payment, while royalties are paid as long as minerals are being extracted.

(a) If the two approaches are designed to yield the same amount of revenue, will they have the same effect on the allocation of the mine over time? Why or why not?

(b) Would either or both be consistent with an efficient allocation? Why or why not?

(c) Suppose the size of the mineral deposit and the future path of prices are unknown. How do these two approaches allocate the risk between the mining company and the government?

CHAPTER NINE

Replenishable but Depletable Resources: Water

You'll never miss the water
Till your well runs dry.

WILLIAM CHRISTOPHER HANDY, *Joe Turner's Blues* (1915)

INTRODUCTION

To the red country and part of the gray country of Oklahoma, the last rains came gently, and they did not cut the scarred earth. . . . The sun flared down on the growing corn day after day until a line of brown spread along the edge of each green bayonet. The clouds appeared and went away, and in awhile they did not try anymore.[1]

With these words John Steinbeck sets the scene for his powerful novel *The Grapes of Wrath*. Drought and poor soil conservation practices combined to destroy the agricultural institutions which had provided nourishment and livelihood to Oklahoma residents since settlement in that area had begun. In desperation, those who had worked that land were forced to abandon not only their possessions, but their past. Moving to California to seek employment, they were uprooted only to be caught up in a web of exploitation and hopelessness.

Based on an actual situation, the novel demonstrates how the social fabric can tear when subject to tremendous stress, such as an inadequate availability of

---

1 John Steinbeck, *The Grapes of Wrath* (New York: Viking Press, 1939): 3.

water, and how painful those tears can be. Clearly problems such as these should be anticipated and prevented as much as possible.

Water is one of the essential elements of life. We humans depend not only on an intake of water to replace the continual loss of body fluids, but also on food sources which themselves need water to survive. This resource deserves special attention.

In this chapter we examine how our economic and political institutions have allocated this important resource in the past and how they might improve on its allocation in the future. We initiate our inquiry by examining the likelihood and severity of water scarcity. Turning to the management of our water resources, we define the efficient allocation of ground and surface water over time and compare these allocations to current practice, particularly in the United States. Finally, we examine the menu of opportunities for meaningful institutional reform.

THE POTENTIAL FOR WATER SCARCITY

The earth's renewable supply of water is governed by the hydrologic cycle, a system of continuous water circulation (Figure 9.1). Enormous quantities of water are cycled each year through this system, though only a fraction of circulated water is available each year for human use.

Available supplies are derived from two rather different sources—surface water and ground water. As the name implies, *surface water* consists of the fresh water in rivers, lakes, and reservoirs that collects and flows on the earth's surface. *Groundwater* by contrast collects in porous layers of underground rock known as aquifers. Though some groundwater is renewed by percolation of rain or melted snow, most was accumulated over geologic time and, because of its location, cannot be recharged once it is depleted. Of the 16,000 trillion gallons of groundwater estimated to be available for extraction in the United States, only about 400 trillion gallons are available on a renewable basis. The rest is a finite, depletable resource.[2]

If we were simply to add up the available supply of fresh water (total runoff) on a global scale and compare it with the demand for it, we would discover that the supply is currently about 10 times demand. Though comforting, that statistic is also misleading because it masks the impact of growing demand and the rather severe excess demand situations that already exist in certain parts of the world. Taken together, these insights suggests that in many parts of the world water scarcity is already upon us, and other areas, including several parts of the United States, can be expected to experience water scarcity in the next few decades.

---

2 Council on Environmental Quality, *Environmental Trends* (Washington, DC: Government Printing Office, 1978): 213.

FIGURE 9.1 The hydrologic cycle.

Source: Council on Environmental Quality, *Environmental Trends* (Washington, DC: Government Printing Office, 1981): 210.

The Global 2000 Report estimates that by the year 2000, worldwide available water supplies will be only 3.5 times demand because of population growth.[3] Due to the temporal and geographic variation in both water availability and population growth, some parts of the world are expected to be particularly vulnerable. Areas noted as being especially susceptible to water shortages include part of Africa, North America, the Middle East, Latin America, and South Asia.

The United States is not expected to escape water scarcity problems. The Water Resources Council estimates that "The problem of inadequate surface water supply is or will be severe by the year 2000 in 17 subregions located mainly in the Midwest and Southwest."[4] The problem with groundwater is even more severe. Groundwater levels have been declining recently in some areas of the country as a result of intensive pumping. Regionally, significant depletion of ground water supplies has occurred in three major areas—southern Arizona, the High Plains (from Nebraska to Texas), and California.[5] Kenneth Frederick of Resources for the Future, Inc. has estimated that annual withdrawals exceed recharge in Western aquifers by more than 22 million acre-feet.[6] The number is even larger in particularly dry years.

Tucson, Arizona demonstrates how western communities cope. Tucson, which averages about 11 inches of rain a year was (until the completion of the Central Arizona Project, which diverts water from the Colorado River) the largest city in the United States to rely entirely on ground water. The water levels in some wells in the Tucson area have dropped 100 feet in 10 years. Tucson annually pumped five times as much water out of the ground as nature put back in. At *current* consumption rates the aquifers supplying Tucson would have been exhausted in less than 100 years.[7] Despite the rate at which its water supplies were being depleted, Tucson continued to grow at a rapid rate. To head off this looming gap between increasing water demand and declining supply, a giant network of dams, pipelines, tunnels, and canals known as the Central Arizona Project was constructed to transfer water from the Colorado River to Tucson. Water diversion has been a common, but increasingly unavailable, policy response.

Though the discussion this far has focused on the quantity of water, that is not the only problem. Quality is also a problem. Much of the available water is

---

3 Gerald O. Barney, *The Global 2000 Report to the President of the U.S.: Entering the 21st Century, Volume 1: The Summary Report* (New York: Pergamon Press, 1980): 155.

4 U.S. Water Resources Council, *The Nation's Water Resources, 1975–2000, Volume 1* (Washington, DC: Government Printing Office, 1978): 56.

5 Council on Environmental Quality, *Environmental Quality 1983: The 14th Annual Report of the Council on Environmental Quality* (Washington, DC: Council on Environmental Quality, 1984): 86.

6 Kenneth D. Frederick, "Water Supplies" in *Current Issues in Natural Resources Policy*, Paul Portney, ed. (Washington, DC: Resources for the Future, Inc., 1982): 227.

7 David Sheridan for the Council on Environmental Quality, *Desertification of the United States* (Washington, DC: Government Printing Office, 1981): 66.

polluted with chemicals, radioactive materials, salt, or bacteria. Though we shall reserve for Chapter 16 a detailed look at the water pollution problem, it is important to keep in mind that water scarcity has an important qualitative dimension that further limits the supply of potable water.

What this brief survey of the evidence suggests is that in certain parts of the world ground water supplies are being depleted to the potential detriment of future users. Supplies, which for all practical purposes will never be replenished, are being "mined" to satisfy current needs. Once used, they are gone. Is this allocation efficient or are there demonstrable sources of inefficiency? Answering this question requires us to be quite clear about what is meant by an efficient allocation of surface water and groundwater.

THE EFFICIENT ALLOCATION OF SCARCE WATER

What efficiency means for the allocation of water depends crucially on whether surface water or groundwater is being tapped. In the absence of storage, the problem with surface water is to allocate a renewable supply among competing users. Intergenerational effects are less important as future supplies depend on natural phenomena (such as precipitation) rather than on current withdrawal practices. For groundwater, on the other hand, withdrawing water now does affect the resources available to future generations. In this case, the allocation over time is a crucial aspect of the analysis. Because it represents a somewhat simpler analytical case, we shall start by considering the efficient allocation of surface water.

Surface Water

An efficient allocation of surface water : (1) must strike a balance among a host of competing users, and (2) must supply an acceptable means of handling the year-to-year variability in surface water flow. The former issue is acute because so many different potential users have legitimate competing claims. Some withdraw the water for consumptive use (such as municipal drinking water suppliers or farmers), while others use but do not consume the water (such as swimmers or boaters). The latter challenge arises because surface water supplies are not constant from year to year or month to month. Since precipitation, runoff, and evaporation all change from year to year, in some years less water will be available to be allocated than in others. Not only must a system for allocating the average amount of water be in place, but also above-average and below-average flows must be anticipated and allocated.

With respect to the first problem, the dictates of efficiency are quite clear— the water should be allocated so that the marginal net benefit is equalized for all uses. (Remember that the marginal net benefit is the vertical distance between the demand curve for water and the marginal cost of extracting and distributing that water for the last unit of water consumed.) To demonstrate why efficiency requires equal marginal net benefits, consider a situation in which the marginal net benefits are *not* equal. We shall show that in this situation it is always possible to find some reallocation of the water which increases net benefits. Since net benefits could be increased by this reallocation, the initial allocation could not have maximized net benefits. Since an efficient allocation maximizes net benefits, any allocation which fails to equalize net benefits could not have been efficient.

If marginal net benefits have not been equalized, it is always possible to increase net benefits by transferring water from those uses with low net marginal benefits to those with higher net marginal benefits. By transferring the water to the users who value the marginal water more, the net benefits of the water use are increased; those losing water are giving up less than those receiving the additional water are gaining. When the marginal net benefits are equalized, no such transfer is possible without lowering net benefits. This can be seen in Figure 9.2.

Two individual net benefit curves (A and B) are depicted along with the aggregate net benefit curve for both individuals.[8] For supply situation S_0, the amount of water available is Q_T^0. An efficient allocation would give Q_B^0 to use *B and* Q_A^0 to use *A*. (By construction $Q_A^0 + Q_B^0 = Q_T^0$. For this allocation, notice that the marginal net benefit (MNB_0) is equal for the two uses.

Notice that the marginal net benefit for both users is positive in Figure 9.2. This implies that water sales should involve a positive marginal scarcity rent. Could we draw the diagram so that the marginal net benefit (and, hence, marginal scarcity rent) would be zero? How?

Marginal scarcity rent would be zero if water were not scarce. If the availability of water as presented by the supply curve were greater than the amount represented by the point where the aggregate marginal net benefit curve intersects the axis, water would not be scarce. Both users would get all they wanted; their demands would not be competing with each other. Their marginal net benefits would still be equal, but in this case they would both be zero.

Now let's consider the second problem—dealing with fluctuations in supply. As long as the supply level can be anticipated, the equal marginal net benefit rule still applies, but different supply levels may imply very different allocations among users. This is an important attribute of the problem because it implies that simple allocation rules, such as each user receiving a proportion of the available flow or high-priority users receiving a guaranteed amount, are not likely to be efficient.

Consider Figure 9.2 again, but this time focus on the water supply labeled S_1, a condition of restricted supply. With S_1, a very different efficient allocation

---

8 Remember that the net benefit curve for an individual would be derived by plotting the vertical distance between the demand curve and the marginal cost of getting the water to that individual.

FIGURE 9.2 The efficient allocation of surface water.

prevails; specifically, use *B* receives no water while use *A* receives it all. Why does the efficient allocation change so radically between S_0 and S_1? The answer lies in the shape of the two demand curves for water.

The demand curve for water in use *A* lies above that for *B*, implying that as supplies diminish the cost (the forgone net benefits) of doing without water is much higher for *A* than for *B*. To minimize this cost, more of the burden of the shortfall is allocated to *B* than *A*. In an efficient allocation, users who can most easily find substitutes or conserve on the use of water receive proportionately smaller allocations when supplies are diminished than those who have few alternatives.

Groundwater

Extending this analysis to encompass groundwater requires that the depletable nature of groundwater supplies be explicitly taken into account. When withdrawals exceed recharge from a particular aquifer, the resource will be mined over time until either supplies are exhausted or the marginal cost of pumping additional water becomes prohibitive. The similarity of this case to the increasing-cost, depletable-resource model discussed in Chapter 6 allows us to exploit that similarity to learn something about the efficient allocation of groundwater over time.

The first transferable implication is that a marginal user cost is associated with mining groundwater, reflecting the opportunity cost associated with the unavailability in the future of any unit of water used in the present. An efficient allocation considers this user cost.

The efficient extraction path for constant demand involves declining use of groundwater over time. The marginal extraction cost (the cost of pumping the last unit to the surface) would rise over time as the water table fell. Pumping would stop either when (1) the water table ran dry, or (2) when the marginal cost of pumping was either greater than the marginal benefit of the water or greater than the marginal cost of acquiring water from some other source.

Abundant surface water in proximity to the location of the groundwater could serve as a substitute for groundwater, effectively setting an upper bound on the marginal cost of extraction. The user would not pay more to extract a unit of groundwater than it would cost to acquire surface water. Unfortunately in many parts of the country where ground water overdrafts are particularly severe, the competition for surface water is already keen; a cheap source of surface water doesn't exist.

In efficient ground water markets, the water price would rise over time. The rise would continue until the point of exhaustion, the point at which the marginal pumping cost becomes prohibitive or when the marginal cost of pumping becomes equal to the next least expensive source of water. At that point the marginal pumping cost and the price would be equal. In all three cases the net price, the difference between the price of the water and the marginal extraction cost, would decline over time, reaching zero at the switch point (if a substitute were available) or the point of exhaustion (if it were not).[9]

THE CURRENT ALLOCATION SYSTEM

Riparian and Prior Appropriation Doctrines

Within the United States the means of allocating water differ from one geographic area to the next, particularly with respect to the legal doctrines that govern conflicts. In this section we shall focus on the allocation systems that prevail in the arid Southwest, which must cope with the most potentially serious and imminent scarcity of water.

In the earliest days of settlement in the American Southwest and West, the government had a minimal presence. Residents were pretty much on their own

---

9 This expectation of a declining net price seems consistent with the evidence. See Table 3 in L. Allen Torrell, James D. Libbin, and Michael D. Miller, "The Market Value of Water in the Ogallala Reservoir," *Land Economics* 66 (May 1990): 171.

in creating a sense of order. Property rights played a very important role in reducing conflicts in this potentially volatile situation.

As water was always a significant factor in the development of an area, the first settlements were usually oriented near bodies of water. The property rights that evolved, called *riparian rights*, allocated the right to use the water to the owner of the land adjacent to the water. This was a practical solution because by virtue of their location, these owners had easy access to the water. Furthermore, there were enough sites with access to water that virtually all who sought water could be accommodated.

With population growth and the consequent rise in the demand for land, this allocation system became less appropriate. As demand increased, the amount of land adjacent to water became scarce, forcing some spillover onto land which was not adjacent to water. The owners of this land began to seek means of acquiring water to make their land more productive.

About this time, with the discovery of gold in California, mining became an important source of employment. With the advent of mining came a need to divert water away from streams to other sites. Unfortunately, riparian property rights made no provision for water to be diverted to other locations. The rights to the water were tied to the land and could not be separately transferred.

As economic theory would predict, this situation created a demand for a change in the property right structure from riparian rights to one which was more congenial to the need for transferability. The waste resulting from the lack of transferability became so great that it outweighed any transition costs of changing the system of property rights. The evolution that took place in the mining camps became the forerunner of what has become known as the *prior appropriation* doctrine.

The miners established the custom that the first person to arrive had the superior claim on the water.[10] In practice, this severed the relationship which had existed under the riparian doctrine between the rights to land and the rights to water. As this new doctrine became adopted in legislation, court rulings, and seven state constitutions, widespread diversion of water based on prior appropriation became possible. Stimulated by the profits that could be made in shifting water to more valuable uses, private companies were formed to construct irrigation systems, and to transport water from surplus to deficit areas. Agriculture flourished.[11]

---

10 For a detailed treatment of this evolution, see Charles W. McCurdy, "Stephen J. Field and Public Land Law Development in California, 1850-1866: A Case Study of Judicial Resource Allocation in Nineteenth Century America," *Law and Society* (Winter 1976): 235-266.

11 The powerful impact of this evolution on agriculture in the West is described in Alfred G. Cuzan, "Appropriators versus Expropriators: The Political Economy of Water in the West," in *Water Rights: Scarce Resource Allocation, Bureaucracy and the Environment*, Terry L. Anderson, ed. (Cambridge, MA: Ballinger, 1983): 1920.

Although prior to 1860 the role of the government was rather minimal, after 1860 that began to change—slowly at first, but picking up momentum as the twentieth century began. The earliest incursions involved establishing the principle that the ownership of water properly belonged to the state. Claimants were accorded a right to use, known as a *usufructory right*, rather than an ownership right. The establishment of this principle of public ownership was followed in short order by the establishment of state control over the rates charged by the private irrigation companies, by imposing restrictions on the ability to transfer water out of the district, and creating a centralized bureaucracy to administer the process.

This was only the beginning. The demand for land in the arid West and Southwest was still growing, creating a complementary demand for water to make the desert bloom. The tremendous profits to be made from large-scale water diversion created the political climate necessary for the federal government to get involved.

The federal role in water resources originated in the early 1800s, largely out of concern for the nation's regional development and economic growth. Toward these ends, the federal government built a network of inland waterways to provide transportation. Since 1902, the federal government has built almost 700 dams to provide water and power to help settle the West.

To promote growth and regional development, the federal government has paid an average of 70% of the combined construction and operating costs of such projects, leaving states, localities, and private users to carry the remaining 30%. Such subsidies have even been extended to cover some of the costs of providing marketable water services. For example, the federal government pays 81% of the cost of supplying irrigation water and 64% of municipal water costs.[12]

This, in a nutshell, is the current situation for water. Both the state and federal governments play a large role. Though the prior appropriation doctrine stands as the foundation of this allocation system, it is heavily circumscribed by government regulations and direct government appropriation of a substantial amount of water.

Sources of Inefficiency

The current system is not efficient. The prime source of inefficiency involves restrictions that have been placed on water transfers, preventing their gravitation to the highest valued use, though other sources, such as charging inefficiently low prices, must bear some of the responsibility.

---

12 Kenneth Rubin, *Efficient Investments in Water Resources: Issues and Options* (Washington, DC: Congressional Budget Office, 1983): xii.

Restrictions on Transfers.[13]   To achieve an efficient allocation of water the marginal net benefits have to be equalized across all uses of the water. With a well-structured system of water property rights this equalization could be a direct result of the transferability of the rights. Users receiving low marginal net benefits from their current allocation would trade their rights to those who would receive higher net benefits. Both parties would be better off. The payment received by the seller would exceed the net benefits forgone, while the payment made by the buyer would be less than the value of the water acquired.

Unfortunately, the existing mixed system of prior appropriation rights coupled with quite restrictive regulations has diminished the degree of transferability that can take place. Diminished transferability in turn reduces the market pressures toward equalization of the marginal net benefits. By itself this indictment is not sufficient to demonstrate the inefficiency of the existing system. If it could be shown that this regulatory system was able to substitute some bureaucratic process for finding and maintaining this equalization, efficiency would still be possible. Unfortunately, that has not been the case, as can be seen by examining in more detail the specific nature of these restrictions. The allocation is inefficient.

One of the earliest restrictions required that users put their water to "beneficial use" or lose their rights to it. It is not difficult to see what this "use it or lose it" principle does to the incentive to conserve. Particularly careful users who, at their own expense, find ways to use less water would find their allocations reduced accordingly. The regulations strongly discourage conservation.

A second restriction, known as "preferential use," attempts to establish bureaucratically a value hierarchy of uses. With this doctrine, the government attempts to establish allocation priorities across categories of water. Within categories (irrigation for agriculture, for example) the priority is determined by prior appropriation ("first in time—first in right"), but among categories the preferential use doctrine governs.

The preferential use doctrine supports three rather different kinds of inefficiencies. First, it substitutes a bureaucratically determined set of priorities for market priorities, resulting in a lower likelihood that marginal net benefits would be equalized. Second, it reduces the incentive to make investments which complement water use in lower preference categories for the simple reason that their water could be involuntarily withdrawn as the needs in higher level categories grow. Finally, it allocates the risk of shortfalls in an inefficient way.

---

13 More information of the details of these restrictions can be found in Micha Gisser and Ronald N. Johnson, "Institutional Restrictions on the Transfer of Water Rights and the Survival of an Agency," in *Water Rights: Scarce Resource Allocation, Bureaucracy and the Environment,* Terry L. Anderson, ed. (Cambridge, MA: Ballinger, 1983): 137-165; and Terry L. Anderson, *Water Crisis: Ending the Policy Drought* (Washington, DC: Cato Institute, 1983): 56-62.

Although the first two inefficiencies are rather self-evident, the third merits further explanation. Because water supplies fluctuate over time, unusual scarcities can occur in any particular year. With a well-specified system of property rights, damage caused by this risk would be minimized by allowing those most damaged by a shortfall to purchase a larger share of the diminished amount of water available during a drought from those suffering the increased shortfall with smaller consequences.

By diminishing, and in some cases eliminating, the ability to transfer rights from so-called "high preferential use" categories to "lower preferential use" categories during times of acute need, the damage caused by shortfalls is higher than necessary. In essence, the preferential use doctrine fails to adequately consider the marginal damage caused by temporary shortfalls, something a well-structured system of property rights would do automatically.

Inhibiting transfers has very practical implications. Due to low energy costs and the federal subsidies, agricultural irrigation has become the dominant use of water in the West. Currently about 5 of every 6 gallons withdrawn and 9 out of every 10 gallons consumed go for the irrigation of nearly 50 million acres in 17 western states.[14] Yet the marginal net benefits from agricultural uses are lower, sometimes substantially lower, than the marginal net benefits of water use by municipalities and industry.[15] A transfer of water from irrigated agriculture to these other uses would raise net benefits, but regulatory restrictions inhibit these transfers.[16]

Federal Reclamation Projects. By providing subsidies to approved projects, Federal reclamation projects have diverted water to these projects even when the net benefits were negative. Why was this done? What motivated the construction of inefficient projects?

Some work by Howe provides a possible explanation.[17] He examined the benefits and costs of constructing the Big Thompson Project in Northeastern Colorado. With this project the water is pumped to an elevation which allows it to flow through a tunnel to the eastern side of the mountains. On that side, electric power is produced at several points. At lower elevations, the water is channeled into natural streams and feeder canals for distribution.

---

14 Kenneth D. Frederick and Allen V. Kneese, "Competition for Water" in *Water Scarcity*, Ernest A. Engelbert with Ann Foley Scheuring, eds. (Berkeley: University of California Press, 1984): 82.

15 See the estimates in Diana C. Gibbons, *The Economic Value of Water* (Washington, DC: Resources for the Future, 1986).

16 Regulatory restrictions inhibit these transfers, but they do not eliminate them. Several transfers from agricultural uses to municipalities have successfully overcome the regulatory hurdles. See Bonnie C. Saliba, "Do Water Markets 'Work'? Market Transfers and Trade-offs in the Southwestern States," *Water Resources Research* 23 (July 1987): 1117.

17 Charles W. Howe, "Project Benefits and Costs from National and Regional Viewpoints: Methodological Issues and Case Study of the Colorado-Big Thompson Project," *Natural Resources Journal* 26 (Winter 1986).

Howe calculated that the national net benefits for this project, which includes all benefits and costs, were either -$341.4 million or -$237.0, depending on the number of years included in the calculations. The project cost substantially more to construct than it returned in benefits. However, regional net benefits for the geographic region served by the facility were strongly positive ($766.9 million or $1187 million respectively). This facility was an extraordinary boon for the local area because a very large proportion of the total cost had been passed on to national taxpayers. The local political pressure was able to secure project approval despite its inherent inefficiency.

While the very existence of these facilities is a source of inefficiency, the manner in which the water is priced is another. The subsidies have been substantial. Frederick has reported on some work done by the Natural Resources Defense Council to calculate the subsidies to irrigated agriculture in the Westlands Water District, one of the world's richest agricultural areas located on the west side of California's San Joaquin Valley.[18] In recent years the Westlands Water District has paid about $10-$12 per acre-foot, less than 10% of the unsubsidized cost of delivering water to the district. (An acre-foot is the amount of water it would take to flood an acre of level land to a depth of one foot.) The resulting subsidy was estimated to be $217 per irrigated acre or $500,000 per year for the average sized farm.

Water Pricing.   Restrictions on transfer are not the only source of inefficiency in the current allocation system. The prices charged by water distribution utilities do not promote efficiency of use either.

Both the level of prices and the rate structure are at fault. In general, the price level is too low and the rate structure does not adequately reflect the costs of providing service to different types of customers.

In part, perhaps because water is considered an essential commodity, the prices charged by public water companies are too low. For surface water the rates are too low for two rather distinct reasons: (1) historic average costs are used to determine rates and (2) marginal scarcity rent is rarely included.

Efficient pricing requires the use of marginal, not average cost. In order to adequately balance conservation with use the customer should be paying the marginal cost of supplying the last unit of water. Yet these regulated utilities typically are allowed to charge prices just high enough to cover the costs of running the operation as revealed by figures from the recent past. Since average costs

---

18 The estimates are in Kenneth Frederick, "Water Resource Management and the Environment: The Role of Economic Incentives," in *Renewable Natural Resources: Economic Incentives for Improved Management* (Paris: Organization for Economic Cooperation and Development, 1989): 33. The original NRDC report was by Phillip E. LaVeen and Laura B. King, *Turning Off the Tap on Federal Water Subsidies: Vol. 1, The Central Valley Project* (San Francisco: Natural Resources Defense Council, 1985).

are lower than marginal costs and historic costs are lower than current or prospective costs, prices are understated.

The second source of the problem is the failure of regulators overseeing the operations of water distribution companies to allow a marginal user cost to be incorporated in the calculation of the appropriate price, a problem that is even more severe when groundwater is involved. One study by Martin et al. found that due to a failure to include a user cost, rates in Tucson, Arizona, were about 58% too low despite some recent increases.[19]

Both average cost pricing and ignoring the marginal user cost promote an excessive demand for water. Simple actions, such as fixing leaky faucets, are easy to overlook when water is excessively cheap. Yet in a city such as New York leaky faucets can account for a signficant amount of wasted water.

Current pricing policies also fail to provide the proper signals to migrants. New residents moving into the area are not forced to bear the full cost of their move. As a result, arid locations appear more attractive than they should. One automatic dampening mechanism that the market provides to prevent excessive population growth in water scarcity areas is thwarted.

Common Property Problems.   The allocation of groundwater must confront one additional problem. When many users tap the same aquifer, that aquifer becomes a common property resource. Tapping a common property resource will tend to deplete it too rapidly; users lose the incentive to conserve. The marginal scarcity rent will be ignored.

The incentive to conserve a groundwater resource in an efficient market is created by the desire to prevent pumping costs from rising too rapidly and the desire to capitalize on the higher prices that could reasonably be expected in the future. With common property resources, neither of these desires translates into conservation for the simple reason that water conserved by one party may simply be used by someone else because the conserver has no exclusive right to the water that is saved. Water saved by one party to take advantage of higher prices can easily be pumped out by another user before the higher prices ever materialize.

For common property resources, economic theory suggests several direct consequences. Pumping costs would rise too rapidly, initial prices would be too low, and too much water would be consumed by the earliest users. The burden of this waste would not be shared uniformly. Because the typical aquifer is bowl-shaped, users on the periphery of the aquifer would be particularly hard hit. When the water level declines, the edges go dry first, while the center can continue to supply water for substantially longer periods. Future users would also be hard hit relative to current users.

---

19 William E. Martin, Helen M. Ingram, Nancy K. Laney, and Adrian H. Griffin, *Saving Water in a Desert City* (Washington, DC: Resources for the Future, 1984).

POTENTIAL REMEDIES

Economic analysis points the way to a number of possible means of remedying the current water situation in the southwestern United States. These reforms would promote efficiency of water use while affording more protection to the interests of future generations of water users.

The first reform would reduce the number of restrictions on water transfers. The "use it or lose it" component of the beneficial use doctrine can promote the extravagant use of water and discourage conservation. Typically water saved by conservation is forfeited.[20] Allowing users to capture the value of water saved by permitting them to sell it would stimulate water conservation and allow the water to flow to higher valued uses (Example 9.1).

One serious problem with the current water use doctrine in the western and southwestern United States is that it fails to provide adequate protection for the instream uses of water, such as habitat for wildlife or for fishing and boating. As the competition for water increases, the pressure to allocate larger amounts of the stream for consumptive uses increases as well. Eventually the water level becomes too low to support aquatic life and recreation activities.

Though they do exist (Example 9.2), water rights for instream flow maintenance are few in number relative to rights for consumptive purposes. Those few instream rights that exist typically have a low priority relative to the more senior consumptive rights. As a practical matter this means that in periods of low water flow, the instream rights lose out and the water is withdrawn for consumptive uses. As long as the definition of "beneficial use" requires diversion, as it does in many states, water left for fish habitat or recreation is undervalued.

This undervaluation of instream uses is not inevitable, however, as some enterprising fishermen have discovered.[21] In the Yellowstone River Valley in Montana, several spring creeks are wholly contained within the boundaries of property owned by a single landowner. Since these creeks are not subject to the same legal restrictions as waterways crossing property boundaries, landowners can sell the daily fishing rights. The revenues from these sales provide owners with an incentive to develop spawning beds, protect the fish habitat, and in general, make the fishing experience as desirable as possible. By limiting the number of fishermen, the owners prevent overexploitation of the resource.

In England and Scotland, markets are relied upon to protect instream uses more than they are in the United States. Private angling associations have been formed to purchase fishing rights from landowners. Once these rights have been

---

20 In *Salt River User's Association v. Kavocovich* [411 P. 2d 201(1966)], the Arizona Court of Appeals ruled that irrigators who lined their ditches could not apply "saved" water to adjacent land.

21 These examples were drawn from Terry L. Anderson, *Water Crisis: Ending the Policy Drought* (Washington, DC: Cato Institute, 1983): 81–85.

EXAMPLE 9.1

Using Economic Principles to Conserve Water in California

In 1977, when California governor Jerry Brown negotiated a deal to settle one of the state's perennial water fights by building a new water diversion project, environmental groups were opposed. The opposition was expected. What was not expected was the form it took. Rather than simply block every imaginable aspect of the plan, the Environmental Defense Fund (EDF) set out to show project supporters how the water needs could be better supplied by ways that put no additional pressure on the environment.

According to this strategy, if the owners of the agricultural lands to the west of the water district seeking the water could be convinced to reduce their water use by adopting new, water saving irrigation techniques, the conserved water could be transferred to the district in lieu of the project. But the growers had no incentive to conserve because conserving the water required the installation of costly new equipment and as soon as the water was saved it would be forfeited under the "use it, or lose it" regulations. What could be done?

On January 17, 1989, largely through the efforts of EDF, an historic agreement was negotiated between the growers association, a major user of irrigation water, and the Metropolitan Water District (MWD) of California, a public agency that supplies water to the Los Angeles area. Under that agreement the MWD will bear the capital and operating costs, as well as the indirect costs (such as reduced hydro power), of a huge program to reduce seepage losses as the water is transported to the growers and to install new water-conserving irrigation techniques in the fields. In return they will get all of the conserved water. Everyone gains. The district gets the water it needs at a reasonable price; the growers retain virtually the same amount of irrigation benefits without being forced to bear large additional expenditures.

Because the existing regulatory system created a very large inefficiency, moving to a more efficient allocation of water necessarily increased the net benefits. By using those additional net benefits in creative ways, it was possible to eliminate a serious environmental threat.

Source: Robert E. Taylor, *Ahead of the Curve: Shaping New Solutions to Environmental Problems* (New York: Environmental Defense Fund, 1990).

EXAMPLE 9.2

Protecting Instream Uses through Acquiring Water Rights

Attempts by environmental groups to protect instream water uses must confront two problems. First, any acquired rights are usually public goods, implying that others can free ride on their provision without contributing to the cause. Consequently the demand for instream rights will be inefficiently low. The private acquisition of instream rights is not a sufficient remedy. Second, once the rights have been acquired, their use to protect instream flows may not be considered "beneficial use" (and therefore could be confiscated and granted to others for consumptive use) or they be so junior as to be completely ineffective in times of low flow, the times when they would most be needed.

Some movement toward protecting instream rights is occurring, however. In 1979, in what was then a precedent setting action, The Nature Conservancy, an environmental, public interest organization, applied to Arizona's Department of Water Resources for a permit for "instream flow" at the Ramsey Canyon Preserve, asking essentially for both the right to a certain amount of water and for the right to simply leave it in the stream. When the permit was approved in 1983, this was the first legal recognition in Arizona of the right to appropriate water for wildlife and recreational uses without diverting water from a streambed. As of mid-1987 over 25 minimum instream flow permit applications were pending and an Instream Task Force had been appointed to assist the Arizona authority in formulating new criteria and procedures for granting permits.

What worked at Ramsey Canyon was simple and straightforward but it is not an adequate protection device in many places. Under the prior appropriation doctrine, any rights that predate the 1983-granted instream flow right would have entitled the holder to priority for the water.

Another approach has been followed in Colorado. Several years ago a subsidiary of the Chevron corporation gave the Nature Conservancy a gift entitling it to 300 cubic feet/second flow rate of water in the Black Canyon of Colorado's Gunnison River. Because Colorado law stipulates that instream flow rights can be held only by the state, the Conservancy was faced with the "use it, or lose it" rule under the prior appropriation doctrine. Taking the only step available, a transfer of the instream flow rights to the state was negotiated.

Sources: Ken Wiley, "Untying the Western Water Knot," *The Nature Conservancy* 40 (March/April 1990): 5–13; and Bonnie Colby Saliba and David B. Bush, *Water Markets in Theory and Practice: Market Transfers and Public Policy* (Boulder, CO: Westview Press, 1987): 74–77.

acquired, the associations charge for fishing, using some of the revenues to preserve and to improve the fish habitat. Since fishing rights in England sell for as much as $220,000, the holders of these rights have a substantial incentive to protect their investments. One of the forms this protection takes is illustrated by the Anglers Cooperative Association, which has taken on the responsibility of monitoring the streams for pollution and alerting the authorities to any potential problems.

Another set of changes that would enhance efficiency involves reforming the water pricing policies followed by public water distribution utilities. The traditional practice of recovering only the costs of distributing water and treating the water itself as a free good should be abandoned in favor of a marginal cost pricing system that includes a scarcity value for water in the price. Since scarce water is not in any meaningful sense a free good, the user cost of that water must be imposed on current users. Only in this way will the proper incentive for conservation be created and the interests of future generations of water users be preserved.

Including this user cost in water prices is rather more difficult than it may first appear. Water utilities are typically regulated because they have a monopoly in the local area. One typical requirement for the rate structure of a regulated monopoly is that it earn only a "fair" rate of return. Excess profits are not permitted. Charging a uniform price for water to all users where the price includes a user cost would generate profits for the seller. (Remember the discussion of scarcity rent in Chapter 3?) The scarcity rent accruing to the seller as a result of incorporating the user cost would represent revenue in excess of operating and capital costs.

One way that water utilities are attempting to respect the rate of return requirement while promoting water conservation is though the use of an increasing block rate. Under this system the price per unit of water consumed rises as the amount consumed rises (Figure 9.3).

In this example the first ten ccf of water cost $0.70 per ccf.[22] The next 10 ccf cost .80 per ccf while the third cost .90 per ccf. A customer using 26 ccf would pay a bill for the month of $20.40 (10 × .70 + 10 × .80 + 6 × .90).

This type of structure encourages conservation by ensuring that the marginal cost of consuming additional water is high. At the margin where the consumer makes the decision of how much extra water to be used, quite a bit of money can be saved by being frugal with water use. It also, however, holds revenue down by charging a lower price for the first units consumed. This has the added virtue that those who need some water, but cannot afford the marginal price paid by more extravagant users, can have access to water without placing their budget in as much jeopardy as would be the case with a uniform price.

---

22 One ccf = 100 cubic feet = 748 gallons.

FIGURE 9.3 Increasing block rate structure.

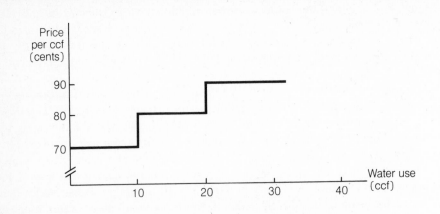

How many U.S. utilities are using increasing block pricing? As Table 9.1 indicates, not many. Some evidence from Europe suggests that increasing block pricing is not common there either.[23]

A surprisingly large number of U. S. utilities are using a flat fee, which from a scarcity point of view is the worst possible form of pricing. With a flat fee the marginal cost of additional water consumption is zero. ZERO! Water use by individual customers is not even metered.

While more complicated versions of a flat-fee system are certainly possible, they do not solve the incentive-to-conserve problem. At least up until the late 1970s Denver, Colorado, used eight different factors (including number of rooms, number of persons, number of bathrooms, etc) to calculate the monthly bill. Despite the complexity of this billing system, because the amount of the bill was unrelated to actual volume used (water use was not metered), the marginal cost of additional water consumed was still zero.

Declining block pricing, another inefficient pricing system, is much more prevalent than increasing block pricing. By charging customers a higher marginal cost for low levels of water consumption and a higher marginal cost for higher levels, regulators are placing an undue financial burden on low income people who consume little water and confronting high income people with a marginal cost that is too low to provide adequate incentives to conserve.

Other aspects of the rate structure are important as well. Efficiency dictates that prices equal the marginal cost of provision (including marginal user cost

23 Paul Harrington, *Pricing of Water Services* (Paris: Organization for Economic Cooperation and Development, 1987): 40.

TABLE 9.1 Water Rate Structures Used by U. S. Public and Private Utilities (1982)

	Number of Utilities					
	Small (500–1000)		*Medium* (25,000–50,000)		*Large* (500,000–1,000,000)	
Rate structure[a]	*Public*	*Private*	*Public*	*Private*	*Public*	*Private*
Flat fee	13	26	4	0	5	0
Flat rate	6	0	15	0	15	0
Flat fee plus flat rate	29	26	28	15	10	0
Declining block	38	22	40	64	35	43
Increasing block	4	2	4	3	0	14
Other	8	20	8	18	35	43

[a]*Flat fee*: flat fee paid monthly or annually, not based on water use.
Flat rate: constant flat rate per unit of water use.
Flat fee plus flat rate: combination of the above rate structures.
Declining block: charge per unit of water declines with increasing water use.
Increasing block: charge per unit of water increases with increasing water use.
Other: rate structures not otherwise included above. Also includes systems which have different types of rate structures for different customer classes.

Source: Congressional Budget Office from Environmental Protection Agency, Office of Drinking Water, *Survey of Operating and Financial Characteristics of Community Water Systems* (prepared by Temple, Barker, and Sloan, Inc., October 1982) as cited in Congressional Budget Office, *Financing Municipal Water Supply Systems* (May 1987): 6, 7.

when appropriate). Several practical corollaries follow from this theorem. First, prices during peak demand periods should exceed prices during off-peak periods. It is peak use which strains the capacity of the system and therefore triggers the needs for expansion. Therefore, peak users should pay the extra costs associated with system expansion by being charged higher rates. Few current water pricing systems satisfy this condition in practice.

Another corollary of the marginal cost pricing theorem is that when it costs a water utility more to serve one class of customers than another, each class of customers should bear the costs associated with its service. Typically this implies, for example, that those farther away from the source or at higher elevations (requiring more pumping) should pay higher rates. In practice utility water rates make fewer distinctions among customer classes than would be efficient. As a result, higher-cost water users are in effect subsidized; they receive too little incentive to conserve and too little incentive to locate in parts of the city that can be served at lower cost.

A somewhat more subtle, but no less important, violation of this rule occurs in rapidly expanding areas where population growth necessitates system expansion. Let's suppose, for example, that due to rapid population growth a particular city has to build a rather large water project to import water from another area. Efficiency dictates that these new users should pay higher rates to cover the additional costs of expanding the system; since, in the absence of population growth, the expansion would not be needed, existing residents should not have to foot the bill.

The efficiency condition is typically violated in practice in two different ways. First, the federal or state governments can usually be counted on to pick up a portion of the tab, so state or federal taxpayers end up paying costs that should be borne by new residents. Second, local areas often attempt to mitigate the adverse effects on growth that this system would trigger by prorating the expansion costs over all residents—existing and new. In essence, all customers pay an average cost rather than the marginal cost of supplying their water.[24]

One market-oriented way of forcing consumers to recognize the scarcity value of groundwater has been proposed by Professor Vernon L. Smith of the University of Arizona.[25] He suggests that a new system of water deeds be created to complement the system of land deeds which already exists. The two types of deeds he envisions would convey to users the rights to use predefined proportions of the available annual flow of water and the available stock of groundwater, respectively.

Professor Smith uses a case study of Tucson, Arizona, in 1976 to illustrate how his proposal would work. The first step is to select a base year (1975, in his example). During this base year each individual property deed holder, i, used some amount of water X_i. The sum of the X_i's in 1975 was 224.6 thousand acre-feet.

The first type deed conveys to the ith deedholder the right to consume r_i acre-feet of water per year in perpetuity where:

$$r_i = \frac{74.6 X_i}{224.6}.$$

The 74.6 figure represents the annual flow of renewable water available (in thousands of acre-feet) to Tucson users. The deed then allocates this renewable water among all users on the basis of their 1975 consumption of all water.

---

24 Notice the parallel between this water price problem and the synfuels price problem discussed in Example 7.1.

25 Vernon L. Smith, "Water Deeds: A Proposed Solution to the Water Valuation Problem," *Arizona Review* 26 (January 1977): 7–10.

The second deed conveys the rights to use the 30 million acre-feet of nonrenewable groundwater that are estimated to be available in the area. The *i*th property owner is allocated the same proportion of this water as surface water:

$$R_i = \frac{30X_i}{224.6} \ .$$

As long as actual consumption is less than or equal to r_i (meaning that only renewable water is consumed), the property owner does not use up any of his allocation of the nonrenewable groundwater. For every acre-foot of groundwater he uses, however, he must surrender the equivalent amount from his second water deed. In other words, if he originally was allocated 100 acre-feet and he used 3 acre-feet, he would have 97 acre-feet left. Since both types of deeds would be fully transferable, they could flow to the highest valued users. Conservation would be rewarded because excess rights could be sold. New users would have to buy the rights to water use from existing users; the impact of increased development on water scarcity would be reflected in the market price. The existence of these deeds would guarantee that the scarcity value of water would be considered. They would transform water from a free good to a valuable commodity.

Since the adoption of this type of system would represent quite a change from the existing approach, it is probably worth exploring less radical (and ultimately less efficient) alternatives. One of these would involve more widespread adoption of the principles of marginal cost pricing. More-expensive-to-serve users should pay higher prices for their water than their cheaper-to-serve counterparts. Similarly, when new, much higher cost sources of water are introduced into a water system to serve the needs of a particular category of user, those users should pay the marginal cost of that water, rather than the lower average cost of all water supplied. Finally, when a rise in the peak demand triggers a need for expanding either the water supplies or the distribution system, the peak demanders should pay the higher costs associated with the expansion.

These principles suggest a much more complicated rate structure for water than merely charging everyone the same price. As Example 9.3 demonstrates, the political consequences of introducing these changes may be rather drastic.

SUMMARY

Though on a global scale the amount of available water exceeds the demand, at particular times and in particular locations water scarcity is already a serious

EXAMPLE 9.3

Politics and the Pricing of Scarce Water

As economics can make specific recommendations about the level and structure of water prices, politics can provide insights on the implementation of those recommendations. The implementation process is not always smooth or predictable, as the people of Tucson, Arizona, found out.

In 1976, the city of Tucson faced what it perceived as a water crisis. The development of its service capacity had not kept pace with rapid population growth, and artificially low prices reduced the incentive to conserve. The groundwater supplies on which the city depended were being depleted.

The utility, assisted by a newly elected city council, instituted a new rate structure involving higher water prices overall and more attention to the cost of service in determining the rate structure. An unexpectedly dry year (creating an abnormally high demand), coupled with a newly implemented increasing block rate structure, conspired to ensure that water bills increased tremendously soon after the change. The resulting anger of the residents spawned a recall campaign in which the councillors responsible for the rate increase were retired from office.

Are major changes in prices politically infeasible? The authors of the Tucson study believe not, though they do believe that feasible increases also have to be implemented with greater care. In particular, they believe that local politicians must be willing to take risks, that local residents must be convinced that a real problem exists, and the burden of the increases must be distributed so no one group is asked to bear too large a share.

Source: William E. Martin, Helen M. Ingram, Nancy K. Laney, and Adrian H. Griffin, *Saving Water in a Desert City* (Washington, DC: Resources for the Future, 1984).

problem. In a number of locations, the current use of water exceeds replenishable supplies implying that aquifers are being irreversibly drained.

Efficiency dictates that replenishable water be allocated so as to equalize the marginal net benefits of water use even when supplies are higher or lower than normal. The efficient allocation of groundwater requires that the user cost of that depletable resource be considered. When marginal cost pricing (including marginal user cost) is used, water consumption patterns strike an efficient balance between present and future uses. Typically, the marginal pumping cost would rise over time until either it exceeded the marginal benefit received from that water or the reservoir runs dry.

In earlier times in the United States, markets played the major role in allocating water. But more recently governments have begun to play a much larger role in allocating this crucial resource.

Several sources of inefficiency are evident in the current system of water allocation in the southwestern United States. Transfers of water among various users are restricted so that the water remains in low valued uses while high valued uses are denied. Instream uses of water are actively discouraged in many western states. Prices charged for water by public suppliers typically do not cover costs and the rate structures are not designed to promote efficient use of the resource. For groundwater, user cost is rarely included and for all sources of water, the rate structure does not usually reflect the cost of service. These deficiencies combine to produce a situation in which we are not getting the most out of the water we are using and we are not conserving sufficient amounts for the future.

Reforms are possible. Allowing conservers to capture the value of water saved by selling it would stimulate conservation. Creating separate fishing rights that can be sold or allowing environmental groups to acquire and retain instream water rights would provide some incentive to protect streams as fish habitats. More utilities could adopt increasing block pricing as a means of forcing users to realize and to consider all of the costs of supplying the water. To the extent that more fundamental change is politically possible, a set of transferable water deeds can be instituted to provide for more efficiency in the consumptive uses of groundwater.

Water scarcity is not merely a problem to be faced at some distant time in the future. In many parts of the world it is already a serious problem and unless preventive measure are taken, it will get worse. The problem is not insoluble, though to date the steps necessary to solve it have not yet been taken.

FURTHER READING

Anderson, Terry L. *Water Crisis: Ending the Policy Drought* (Washington, DC: Cato Institute, 1983). A provocative survey of the political economy of water, concluding that we have to rely more on the market to solve the crisis.

Anderson, Terry L., ed. *Water Rights: Scarce Resource Allocation, Bureaucracy, and the Environment* (Cambridge, MA: Ballinger, 1983). Nine essays examining the causes, consequences, and possible solutions to water scarcity in the southwestern United States from a property rights point of view.

Gibbons, Diana. *The Economic Value of Water* (Washington, DC: Resources for the Future, 1986). A detailed survey and synthesis of existing studies on the economic value of water in various uses.

Herrington, Paul, *Pricing of Water Services* (Organization for Economic Cooperation and Development, 1987). An excellent survey of the water pricing practices in the OECD countries.

Martin, William E., Helen M. Ingram, Nancy K. Laney, and Adrian H. Griffin. *Saving Water in a Desert City* (Washington, D.C.: Resources for the Future, 1984). A detailed look at the political and economic ramifications of an attempt by Tucson, Arizona, to improve the pricing of its diminishing supply of water.

Saliba, Bonnie Colby and David B. Bush. *Water Markets in Theory and Practice: Market Transfers and Public Policy* (Boulder, CO: Westview Press, 1987): 74–77. A highly recommended, accessible study of the way western water markets work in practice in United States.

U.S. Water Resources Council. *The Nation's Water Resources 1975–2000* (Washington, DC: Government Printing Office, 1978). A multivolume series examining on a location-by-location basis the present and future supply of and demand for water.

ADDITIONAL REFERENCES

Custodio, E. and A. Gurgui, eds. *Groundwater Economics: Selected Papers from a United Nations Symposium held in Barcelona, Spain* (New York: Elsevier, 1989).

Frederick, K. D. "Water Supplies" in *Current Issues in Natural Resource Policy,* Paul R. Portney, ed. (Washington, DC: Resources for the Future, 1982): 216–252.

Frederick, K. D. *Scarce Water and Institutional Change* (Washington, DC: Resources for the Future, 1986).

Livingston, Marie L. and Thomas A. Miller. "The Impact of Instream Water Rights on Choice Domains," *Land Economics* 62 (August 1986): 269–277.

OECD. *Renewable Natural Resources: Economic Incentives for Improved Management* (Paris: Organization for Economic Cooperation and Development, 1987).

Postel, Sandra. "Saving Water for Agriculture," in *State of the World: 1990,* Lester Brown et al. (New York: W. W. Norton, 1990).

Smith, Vernon L. "Water Deeds: A Proposed Solution to the Water Valuation Problem," *Arizona Review* 26 (January 1977): 7–10.

Sheridan, David, for the Council on Environmental Quality. *Desertification of the United States* (Washington, DC: Government Printing Office, 1981).

Torell, L. Allen, James D. Libbin, and Michael D. Miller. "The Market Value of Water in the Ogallala Aquifer," *Land Economics* 66 (May 1990): 163–175.

Wahl, Richard W. *Markets for Federal Water: Subsidies, Property Rights, and the Bureau of Reclamation* (Washington, DC: Resources for the Future, 1989).

DISCUSSION QUESTIONS

1. Who stands to gain and lose compared to the current system if the Smith system of water deeds were to be instituted? Politically, where might the support for or opposition to such a proposal come from?

2. What pricing system identified in Table 9.1 best describes the pricing system used to price the water you use at your college or university? Does this pricing

system affect your behavior about water use (length of showers, etc.)? How? Could you recommend a better pricing system in this circumstance? What would it be?

3. In your home town what system is used to price the publicly supplied water? Why was that pricing system chosen?

4. Suppose you come from a part of the world that is blessed with abundant water. Demand never comes close to the available amount. Should you be careful about the amount you use or should you simply use whatever you want whenever you want it? Why?

PROBLEMS

1. Suppose that in a particular area the consumption of water varies tremendously throughout the year with average household summer use exceeding winter use by a great deal. What effect would this have on an efficient rate structure for water?

2. Is a flat rate or flat fee system more efficient for pricing scarce water? Why?

CHAPTER TEN

Reproducible Private-Property Resources: Food

The Commission's assessment of the future prospects for over-coming world hunger has led to one conclusion ... the out-come of the war on hunger, by the year 2000 and beyond, will not be determined by forces beyond human control, but, rather, by decision and actions well within the capability of nations working individually and together.

PRESIDENTIAL COMMISSION ON WORLD HUNGER,
Overcoming World Hunger: The Challenge Ahead (1980)

INTRODUCTION

In Chapter 1, food was a point of contention between Kahn and the *Limits to Growth* team. The *Limits to Growth* team foresaw the demand for food (driven by population growth) outstripping the supply (primarily due to a decline in the remaining availability of arable land), suggesting a resulting famine as one source of societal collapse. Kahn, on the other hand, foresaw population growth as diminishing, and a tremendous expansion in food supplies forthcoming from the applications of new technologies. Which vision seems more accurate?

Not long ago the World Bank concluded that somewhere in the neighborhood of one-half billion persons were subsisting on a diet not sufficient to provide adequate nutrition. Though some may quarrel with this specific number, recognition that a substantial proportion of the world's population is currently malnourished seems universal.

In its report, Overcoming World Hunger: The Challenge Ahead, the Presidential Commission on World Hunger suggests that world hunger has been transformed by inaction from a low-profile moral concern to a decisive and explosive factor in international relations. During the 1970s the rise in mutual suspicion among developed countries of the "North" and less-developed countries of the "South" made itself felt in international conferences addressing global problems. One source of apparent hostility is the fact that instead of being a problem which is faced by the citizens of all nations, malnutrition is heavily concentrated in nations of the South. Thus, allocating food is a task which will test the resilience of our political and economic systems.

Why has this situation arisen? Cereal grain, the world's chief supply of food, is a renewable private-property resource which, if managed effectively, could be sustained as long as we receive energy from the sun. Are current agricultural practices sustainable? Are they efficient? Because land is typically not a common-property resource, farmers have an incentive to invest in irrigation and other means of increasing yield because they can appropriate the additional revenues generated. On the surface, a flaw in the market process is not apparent. We must dig deeper to uncover the sources of the problem.

In this chapter we shall explore the validity of three common hypotheses used to explain widespread malnourishment: (1) a persistent global scarcity of food; (2) a maldistribution of that food both among nations and within nations; and (3) temporary shortages caused by weather or other natural causes. These hypotheses are not mutually exclusive; they could all be valid sources of a portion of the problem. As we shall see, it is important to distinguish among these sources and assess their relative importance because each implies a different policy approach.

GLOBAL SCARCITY

A number of commentators see the problem as one of absolute global scarcity—a case of too many people chasing too little food. An example of this point of view is presented by William and Paul Paddock in their provocatively titled book *Famine—1975!* Written by an agronomist and an experienced foreign-service officer, this book suggested that widespread famine would occur in 1975 causing a worldwide catastrophe of unprecedented proportions.[1] They were not alone in their general assessment of the situation, although no consensus about the timing of the anticipated widespread famines was apparent.[2]

---

1 William Paddock and Paul Paddock, *Famine—1975!* (Boston: Little, Brown, 1967).

2 See, for example, Lester R. Brown, *In the Human Interest* (New York: W. W. Norton, 1974).

To some, this onset of a food crisis suggests a need for dramatic changes in the relationship between the agricultural surplus nations and other nations. Garrett Hardin, a human ecologist, has suggested the situation is so desperate that our conventional ethics, which involve sharing the available resources, are not only insufficient but are also counterproductive. He argues we must replace these dated notions of sharing wealth with more stern "lifeboat ethics."[3]

The allegory he invokes involves a lifeboat adrift in the sea which can safely hold 50 or, at most, 60 persons. Hundreds of other persons are swimming about, clamoring to get into the lifeboat, their only chance for survival. Hardin suggests that if passengers in the boat were to follow conventional ethics and allow swimmers into the boat, it would eventually sink, taking everyone to the bottom of the sea. In contrast, he argues, lifeboat ethics would suggest a better resolution of the dilemma; the 50 or 60 should row away, leaving the others to certain death, but saving those fortunate enough to gain entry to the lifeboat. The implication is that food sharing is counterproductive. It would encourage more population growth and ultimately would cause inevitable and even more serious shortages in the future.

The existence of a global scarcity of food is the premise which underlies this view; when famine is inevitable, sharing is counterproductive. In the absence of global scarcity (the lifeboat has a large enough capacity for all), then a worldwide famine can be avoided by a sharing of resources. How accurate is the global scarcity premise?

Formulating the Global Scarcity Hypothesis

Most authorities seem to agree that an adequate amount of food is currently being produced. Studies made by the Food and Agricultural Organization of the United Nations, which report that the available supplies of food are more than adequate to supply the nutritional needs of all the world, are typical.[4]

Because this evidence is limited to a single point in time, however, it gives us no sense of whether scarcity is decreasing or increasing. If we are to identify and evaluate trends, we must develop more precise, measurable notions of how the market allocates food.

As a renewable resource, cereal grains could be produced indefinitely, if managed correctly. Yet two facets of the world hunger problem have to be taken into account. First, while population growth has slowed down, it has not stopped. Therefore, it is reasonable to expect the rising demand for food to continue. Second, the primary input for growing food is land, and land is ultimately fixed in supply. Thus, our analysis must explain how a market reacts in the presence

---

3 Garrett Hardin, "Living on a Lifeboat," *Bioscience* 24 (October 1974): 561–568.

4 The data on which this conclusion is based can be found in Table 10.1.

of rising demand for a renewable resource which is produced using a fixed factor of production!

A substantial and dominant proportion of the Western world's arable land is privately owned. Access to this land is restricted; the owners have the right to exclude others and can reap what they sow. The typical owner of farm land has sufficient control over the resource to prevent undue depreciation, but not enough control over the market as a whole to raise the specter of monopoly profits.

What kind of outcome could we expect from this market in the face of rising demand and a fixed supply of land? What do we mean by scarcity and how could we perceive its existence? The answer depends crucially on the nature of the supply curve (Figure 10.1).

Suppose the market is initially in equilibrium with quantity Q_0 supplied at price P_0. Let the passage of time be recorded as shifts outward in the demand curve. Consider what would happen in the fifth time period. If the supply curve were S_a, the quantity would rise to Q_{5a}. However, if the supply curve were S_b, the quantity supplied would only rise to Q_{5b}, but price would rise to P_{5b}.

This analysis sheds light on what is meant by scarcity in the world food market. It does not mean a shortage. Even under relatively adverse supply cir-

FIGURE 10.1   The market for food.

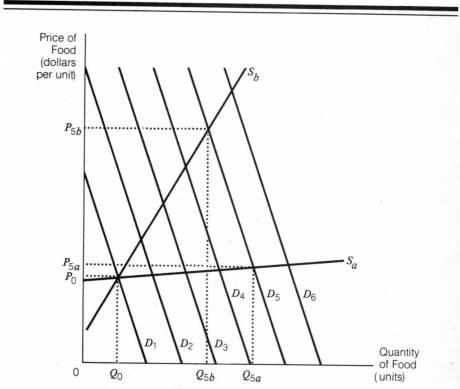

cumstances pictured by the supply curve S_b, the amount of food supplied would equal the amount demanded. As prices rose, potential demand would be choked off and additional supplies would be called forth.

Some critics argue that the demand for food is not price sensitive. Since food is a necessary commodity for survival, they say, its demand is inflexible and doesn't respond to prices. While some food is necessary, not all food fits that category. We don't have to gaze very long at an average vending machine in a developed country to conclude that some food is far from a necessity.

Examples of food purchases being price responsive abound. One occurred during the 1960s when the price of meat skyrocketed for what turned out to be a relatively short period. It wasn't long before hamburger substitute appeared in supermarkets made entirely out of soybean meal. The result was a striking reduction in meat consumption. This is a particularly important example because the raising of livestock for meat in Western countries consumes an enormous amount of grain. This evidence suggests that the balance between the direct consumption of cereal grains and the indirect consumption through meat is affected by prices.

But enough about the demand side; what do we know of the supply side? What factors would determine whether S_a or S_b is a more adequate representation of the past and the future?

While rising prices certainly stimulate a supply response, the question is, how much? As the demand for food rises, the supply can be increased either by expanding the amount of land under cultivation, or by increasing the yields on the land already under cultivation, or some combination of the two. Historically, both sources have been important.

Typically, the most fertile land is cultivated first. That land is then farmed more and more intensively until it is cheaper, at the margin, to bring additional, less fertile land into production. Because it is less fertile, the additional land is brought into production only if the prices rise enough to make farming it profitable. Thus, the supply curve for arable land (and hence for food, as long as land remains an important factor of production) can be expected to slope upward.

Two forms of the global scarcity hypothesis can be tested against the available evidence. The *strong form* suggests that per capita food production is declining. In terms of Figure 10.1, the strong form of the hypothesis would imply that the slope of the supply curve is sufficiently steep that production does not keep pace with increases in demand brought about by population growth. If the strong form is valid, we should witness declining per capita food consumption. If valid, this form could provide some support for lifeboat ethics.

The *weak form* of the global scarcity hypothesis can hold even if per capita consumption is increasing over time. It suggests that the supply curve is sufficiently steeply sloped that food prices are increasing more rapidly than other prices in general; the relative price of food is rising over time. If the weak form is valid, per capita welfare is declining, even if consumption is rising. The problem is related more to the cost of food than the availability of food; as supplies of food increase, the cost of food rises relative to the cost of other goods.

FIGURE 10.2 Index of per capita food production for the world and developing countries (1974–88).

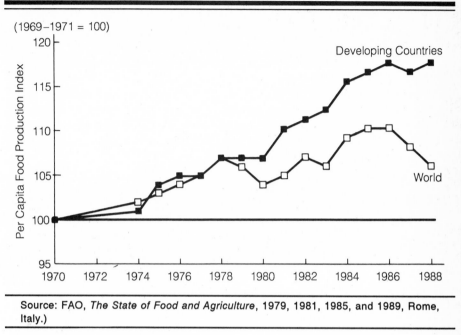

(1969–1971 = 100)

Source: FAO, *The State of Food and Agriculture*, 1979, 1981, 1985, and 1989, Rome, Italy.)

Testing the Hypothesis

Now that we have a testable hypothesis, we can assess the degree to which the historical record supports the existence of increasing global scarcity. The evidence for per capita production is clear (Figure 10.2). Food production has increased faster than population in both the developed and developing countries. Per capita production has increased, although the increase has been small. Thus, at least for the recent past, we can rule out the strong form of the global scarcity hypothesis.

How about the weak form? Have relative agricultural prices risen? Harold Barnett, a noted resource economist, published the results of a preliminary study on trends in resource prices, including agricultural prices.[5] Specifically, he examined the ratio of an index of agricultural prices to the general wholesale price index for a variety of countries over two different time periods (1950–62 and

---

5 Harold J. Barnett, "Scarcity and Growth Revisited," in *Scarcity and Growth Reconsidered*, V. Kerry Smith, ed. (Baltimore: Johns Hopkins University Press for Resources for the Future, 1979): 163–217.

1961–72). A total of 53 cases were examined. He discovered that for 23 of those cases agriculture prices rose at a statistically significant higher rate than wholesale prices in general. Using only the later time period (involving 31 countries), some 15 countries experienced rises in agricultural prices which significantly exceed rises in wholesale prices.

According to this evidence the supply curve for agricultural products is more steeply sloped than the supply curve for products in general in about half the countries. In those countries, at least, there is support for the weak form of the global-scarcity hypothesis. Since not all market prices are efficient, as we shall see later in this chapter, we must not place too much faith in these numbers. Even so, the evidence suggests that agricultural supplies have increased faster than population but at an increasing relative cost.

Outlook for the Future

What factors will influence the future relative costs of food? A continuation of past trends would suggest a major role for the developing nations to supply an increasing share of world food production to meet their increasing shares of population and also on the ability of the nations of the North to continue their role as a major food exporter. The ability of developing nations to expand their role is considered in the next section as a part of the food-distribution problem. In this section, therefore, we deal with forces affecting productivity in the industrialized nations of the North.

Rather dramatic historic increases in crop productivity were stimulated by improvements in machinery; increasing utilization of commercial fertilizers, pesticides and herbicides; developments in plant and animal breeding; expanding use of irrigation water; and adjustments in location of crop production. In the United States their combined effect doubled average yield per acre from 1910–1977.[6] Will history repeat itself?

Technological Progress.   Technological progress provides the main source of support for optimism about continued productivity increases Three techniques appear particularly promising: (1) recombinant DNA, which permits recombining genes from one species with those of another; (2) tissue culture, which allows whole plants to be grown from single cells; and (3) cell fusion, which involves uniting the cells of species that would not normally mate to create new types of plants different from "parent" cells. One knowledgeable reviewer in the field suggested several applications for these generic engineering techniques, including

---

6 Melvin L. Cotner, Nelson L. Bills, and Robert F. Boxley, "An Economic Perspective of Land Use," in *Economics, Ethics, Ecology: Roots of Productive Conservation*, Walter E. Jeske, ed. (Ankeny, IA: Soil Conservation Society of America, 1981): 31.

1. Making food crops more resistant to diseases and insect pests

2. Creating hardy new crop plants capable of surviving in marginal soils

3. Giving staple food crops such as corn, wheat, and rice the ability to make their own nitrogen-rich fertilizers by using solar energy to make ammonia from nitrogen in the air

4. Increasing crop yields by improving the way plants use the sun's energy during photosynthesis[7]

The World Bank has estimated that these techniques could increase yields at least 30% beyond those achieved with the best previously available seeds.[8]

The outlook is not uniformly bright, however. Four concerns have arisen regarding the ability of the industrial nations to achieve further productivity gains: the declining share of land allocated to agricultural use, the rising cost of energy, the rising environmental cost of traditional forms of agriculture, and the role of price distortions in agricultural policy.[9] A close examination of these concerns reveals that current agricultural practices in the industrial nations may be neither efficient nor sustainable and a transition to efficient sustainable agriculture could involve lower productivity levels.

Allocation of Agricultural Land.   During 1920 in the United States, 958 million acres were used for farming. By 1974 the comparable figure was 465 million acres.[10] Some 50% of the agricultural land in 1920 had been converted to non-agricultural purposes by 1974. A simple extrapolation of this trend would certainly raise questions about our ability to increase productivity at historical rates. Is a simple extrapolation reasonable? What determines the allocation of land between agricultural and nonagricultural uses?

Agricultural land will be converted to nonagricultural land when its profitability in nonagricultural uses is higher. If we are to explain the historical experience, we must be able to explain why the relative value of land in agriculture has declined.

Two factors stand out. First, an increasing urbanization and industrialization of society rapidly raised the value of nonagricultural land. Second, rising productivity of the remaining land allowed the smaller amount of land to produce a lot more food. Less agricultural land was needed to meet the demand for food.

---

7 Robert Cooke, "Engineering a New Agriculture," *Technology Review* 85 (May/June 1982): 24–25.

8 The World Bank, *World Development Report, 1982* (Washington, DC: International Bank for Reconstruction and Development, 1982).

9 See, for example, Lester R. Brown, "World Population Growth, Soil Erosion, and Food Security," *Science* 214 (November 1981): 995–1002.

10 See Melvin L. Cotner, Nelson L. Bills, and Robert F. Boxley, "An Economic Perspective of Land Use," in *Economics, Ethics, Ecology: Roots of Productive Conservation*, Walter E. Jeske, ed. (Ankeny, IA: Soil Conservation Society of America, 1981): 31.

It seems unlikely that simple extrapolation of the decline in agricultural land of the magnitude since 1920 would be accurate. Since the middle of the 1970s, the urbanization process has diminished to the point that many urban areas are experiencing declining population. This shift is not merely explained by suburbia spilling beyond the boundaries of what was formerly considered urban. For the first time in our history, a significant amount of population has moved from urban to rural areas.

Furthermore, as increases in food demand are accompanied by increased prices of food, the value of agricultural land should increase. Higher food prices would tend to slow conversion and possibly even reverse the trend. To make this impact even greater, several states have now allowed agricultural land to either escape the property tax (until it is sold for some nonagricultural purpose) or to pay lower rates. Confirming evidence for this generally optimistic assessment can be found in the fact that most of the conversion to nonagricultural uses actually occurred prior to World War II.[11]

Energy Costs.   Agricultural production in the industrial nations is very energy intensive. Some major portion of the productivity gains resulted from energy—using mechanization and the increased use of pesticides and fertilizers which are derived from petroleum feedstocks and natural gas. As we saw in Chapter 7, the costs of petroleum and natural gas have risen substantially and probably can be expected to continue to rise in real terms as the available supplies of fossil fuels are exhausted or global warming concerns diminish their use. To the extent that energy-intensive producers cannot develop cheaper substitutes, the supply curve must shift to the left to reflect the increasing costs of doing business.

One economist investigating this question notes that energy and capital are complements in agriculture.[12] Due to this complementary relationship, energy price increases could be expected to trigger some reduction in capital, as well as some reduction in energy on the typical energy-intensive farm, reducing the yield per acre. Furthermore, since d'Arge found that farm-wage rates have risen less rapidly than either energy costs or the costs of borrowing (as reflected by interest rates), he expects an readjustment of American agriculture in the future as labor is substituted for capital. A shift toward smaller, family-operated units would trigger a consequent reduction in the agricultural productivity growth rate.

---

11 The decline in crop land since 1949 has involved only 13 of more than 400 million acres converted since 1920. For more details on this, see Melvin L. Cotner, Nelson L. Bills, and Robert F. Boxley, "An Economic Perspective of Land Use," *Economics, Ethics, Ecology: Roots of Productive Conservation,* Walter E. Jeske, ed. (Ankeny, IA: Soil Conservation Society of America, 1981): 31–36.

12 Ralph C. d'Arge, "The Energy Squeeze and Agricultural Growth," in *Economics, Ethics, Ecology: Roots of Productive Conservation,* Walter E. Jeske, ed. (Ankeny, IA: Soil Conservation Society of America, 1981): 99–105.

Environmental Costs. A least some of the past apparent productivity gains have come by depreciating the asset. Soil erosion provides a case in point. Some soil erosion is natural, of course, and within certain tolerance limits does not harm productivity. The concern arises because some farm practices partially responsible for increasing productivity (continuous cropping rather than rotations with pasture or other soil-retaining crops) have tended to exacerbate soil erosion. The fears are further intensified by the belief that these losses are irreversible within one generation.

If increased soil erosion is taking place, why would a private property owner allow this depletion? In the past, soil conservation simply did not pay. The techniques to avoid it were expensive and the ready availability of cheap fertilizer to replace lost nutrients meant that the cost of soil depletion was low. Further, the damage caused to rivers and streams by this eroding soil was not borne by the farmers who could best control it.

The barriers that prevented erosion from being checked are now disappearing. As the level of topsoil reaches lower tolerance limits, the fertility of the land is affected. Rising cost and pollution concerns are making fertilizers a less desirable substitute for soil conservation and public policy has begun to subsidize soil erosion techniques. In 1985, the U.S. Congress authorized the Conservation Reserve Program, which was designed to reduce soil erosion and to stimulate tree planting. As of 1990 farmers had enrolled about 34 million acres of land in this program and it has become one of the largest federally sponsored tree planting programs ever. It is expected to reduce soil erosion by hundreds of millions of tons per year, to decrease sediment in reservoirs and streams, to increase the protection of recreational resources and to preserve the long-term productivity of the land.[13] In the near future we may see more soil conservation techniques practiced because they are becoming profitable.

Some past agricultural practices have caused environmental damage and the continuation of these would cause rising environmental costs. In recent years the frequency and quantity of agricultural chemicals has increased dramatically.[14] Over the past 25 years, for example, nitrogenous fertilizer use increased by 150% in the Netherlands, by 225% in Denmark, and by 300% in the United States. Serious drinking water problems have emerged. In 1979 some 179 German water authorities were supplying drinking water with nitrate concentrations exceeding the standards. Four years later the number of communities violating the standards had increased four times to 807. Some of the nutrients from fertilizers leak into lakes and stimulate the excessive growth of algae. Aside from the aesthetic cost

---

13 U.S. General Accounting Office, *1990 Farm Bill: Opportunities for Change* (Washington, DC: U.S. Government Printing Office, 1990): 23.

14 The data in this section are from M. D. Young, *Agriculture and the Environment: OECD Policy Experiences and American Opportunities* (Washington, DC: United States Environmental Protection Agency, 1990).

to a body of water choked with plant life, this nutrient excess can deprive other aquatic life forms of the oxygen they need to survive.

Pesticide use has also increased. Since 1975, for example, the quantity of pesticides used in Germany has increased by 30% and in Denmark by 69%. A great deal of pest control in the past has relied upon pesticides. Many of these persist in the environment, and some toxicity extends to species other than the target population. The herbicides and pesticides can contaminate water supplies, rendering them unfit for drinking and for supporting normal populations of fish.

Throughout all OECD countries "sustainable agriculture" is being increasingly associated with the reduced use of pesticides and mineral fertilizers. And policies have been established to facilitate the transition. Denmark and Sweden are pursuing ambitious agricultural chemical reduction targets. In Austria, Finland, the Netherlands, and Sweden a variety of input taxes and input levies have recently been reduced. The charges provide an incentive to use less agricultural chemicals while the revenue is used to ease the transition by funding research on alternative approaches and the dissemination of information. Many OECD countries expect little or no effect on crop yields.[15]

Irrigation, a traditional source of productivity growth, is running into limits as well, particularly in the western United States. Some traditionally important underground sources used to supply water are not being replenished at a rate sufficient to offset the withdrawals. Encouraged by enormous subsidies that transfer the cost to the taxpayers, these water supplies are being exhausted. Those that remain are subject to rising levels of salt. Irrigation of soils with naturally occurring salts causes a concentration of the salts near the surface. This salty soil is less productive and, in extreme cases, kills the crops.

One sign that a transition is underway is the rise of organic farming. Although at present only 1% of U.S. produce is organically grown, experts in the field predict as much as 10% by the end of the century. The transition would not be immediate or easy. It takes from one to five years to convert from conventional agriculture to organic farming. Studies comparing organic farms with comparable conventional farms have found the organic farms had lower yields, but they also had lower costs with the result that income was about the same as that for comparable conventional agriculture farms.[16]

A recent source of encouragement for organic farms has been the demonstrated willingness of consumers to pay a premium for organically grown fruits and vegetables. Since it would be relatively easy for producers to claim their produce was organically grown, even if it was not, organic growers need a

---

15   Organization for Economic Cooperation and Development, *Agriculture and Environment: Opportunities for Integration* (Paris: OECD, 1988).

16   Pierre Crosson and Janet Ekey, "Alternative Agriculture: A Review and Assessment of the Literature," Resources for the Future, Discussion Paper ENR88-01 (November 1988), and Patrick Madden, "Can Sustainable Agriculture Be Profitable?" *Environment* 29 (May 1987): 19–34.

reliable certification process to assure the consumers that they are indeed getting what they pay for. In some areas growers associations handle the testing and labeling, but in others it is handled by new organizations which have sprung up specifically to provide this service.[17] In California, where labeling of organic produce has become routine, retail sales of organics grew from $1 million in 1979 to $50 million in 1987.

In summing up our findings, it appears that agricultural productivity in the United States will rise in the future, but at lower rates. Also, energy and environmental costs will offset to some extent the expected gains from technological progress. Thus, global scarcity in its strongest form does not now exist, and in light of the declining population growth rate, is not likely to exist in the near future.

Nonetheless some changes are likely. A transition to alternative agriculture appears to be underway. What would be the effects of this transition if it were to penetrate deeply into traditional agriculture? According to a national study based upon a large model of U.S. agriculture, widespread adoption of organic farming methods in the United States would increase national net farm income, but would increase consumer food costs and decrease agricultural export levels.[18] The weak form of the global scarcity hypothesis apparently has some support.

DISTRIBUTION OF FOOD RESOURCES

The second view holds that the malnourishment problem may stem more from food distribution than from global availability. According to this outlook the basic problem is poverty. We would expect, therefore, that the poorest segments of society would be the most malnourished and the poorest countries would contain the largest proportion of malnourished people.

If accurate, this representation suggests a very different policy orientation than that suggested by global scarcity. If the problem is maldistribution, rather than shortage, the issue is how to get the food to the poorest people. The alleviation of poverty, increasing the ability to pay for food, is a strategy which could alleviate the problem. If the problem were a lack of food, this strategy would be totally ineffectual.

---

17 The first such organization, NutriClean, uses a complex evaluation procedure to establish whether the produce meets their "no detected residue" standard. If so, the produce is allowed to display the NutriClean label. The farmer pays for the service, with the fee depending on the sales volume.

18 Kent D. Olson, James Langley, and Earl O. Heady, "Widespread Adoption of Organic Farming Practices: Estimated Impacts on U.S. Agriculture," *Journal of Soil and Water Conservation* 37 (January/February 1982).

TABLE 10.1   Daily per Capita Calorie Supply as Percent of Requirements (%)

	1969–71	1974–76	1978–80	1977	1978	1979	1980
Developing market economies	95.5	95.5	99.2	96.3	99.2	99.8	98.6
Africa	93.5	93.1	93.7	94.3	93.9	93.3	94.0
Far East	92.8	90.8	95.7	91.1	96.0	96.9	94.1
Latin America	105.8	106.7	108.9	107.5	108.4	108.7	109.4
Near East	97.2	106.2	111.0	108.5	109.7	111.3	112.1
Other developing market economies	100.0	101.5	105.7	102.8	105.7	106.3	105.3
Asian centrally planned economies	90.7	97.7	104.3	99.1	101.3	105.0	106.6
Total developing countries	93.9	96.3	100.9	97.2	99.9	101.5	101.2
Least developed countries	88.3	84.1	84.1	82.9	84.3	83.1	85.0
Total developed countries	128.4	130.8	133.1	131.2	132.2	133.7	133.4
World	104.8	106.5	109.8	107.0	109.1	110.4	110.0

Source: Food and Agricultural Organization, *The State of Food and Agriculture: 1982* (Rome: United Nations, 1983), Table 1-1, p. 5.

Defining the Problem

Considerable and persuasive evidence suggests that the problem is one of distribution (Table 10.1). The information in this table is constructed by the Food and Agriculture Organization (FAO) in several steps. First, they calculated a minimum number of calories that will allow normal activity and good health in adults and will permit children to reach normal body weight and intelligence in the absence of disease. Though these vary by country, they are generally in the neighborhood of 2400 kilocalories per day.

In the second step, the FAO calculated the number of kilocalories the average citizen of that country receives from food intake. The final step involves calculating the ratio of actual intake to minimum desired intake and multiplying that ratio by 100. The results are portrayed in Table 10.1. An index equal to 100 means that the caloric intake is just sufficient for the average citizen to avoid nutritional deficiency. A number lower than 100 means the average citizen of the country is subject to nutritional deficiencies.

Though the data are far from perfect,[19] a number of interesting conclusions can be drawn. Looking at the bottom line first, we find that the average member

---

19 Dealing only with calories, these data ignore other kinds of nutritional deficiencies, such as insufficient vitamin or protein intake. By concentrating solely on the average, it ignores the nutritional problems of the very poorest citizens. Considerable hunger can exist in a country where the average citizen is well fed.

of the world population has a sufficient caloric intake. This reinforces our conclusion that the problem is not one of global scarcity. It is also clear, however, that the food is not uniformly distributed among the world's peoples. During 1979, for example, the diet of the average citizen in developing countries was barely adequate. The average diet in Africa was nutritionally deficient in every year covered by the table. For the least developed countries, the average diet contained fewer calories than the nutritional deficiency threshold. Meanwhile, nutritional levels in developed countries on average were well in excess of the minimum.

Equally interesting, however, is the trend. Clear progress is being made in the developing countries as a whole. The change from the 1966–1968 period to the 1975–1977 period is strikingly positive. These very positive results, however, are tempered considerably by the results for the least developed nations. For those countries, the average diet was woefully inadequate at the beginning of the period and the situation has deteriorated during the intervening 10 years.

Those countries which seem the most resistant to improvement in their nutritional situation seem to share two characteristics: (1) high population growth and (2) low per capita income. Of the 46 countries included in the FAO most seriously affected group, all but four have population growth rates in excess of 2.0%.[20] All but four of them had GNP per capita ratios of less than $500 per year. These figures compare with an average population growth rate of 0.7% and an average GNP per capita of $8070 in the industrialized countries.[21]

As we stated in the chapter on population growth, these characteristics may well be related. High poverty levels are generally conducive to high population growth, and high population growth rates may increase the degree of income inequality. Thus, extreme poverty may perpetuate itself. Since we have examined population-control strategies in Chapter 5, we shall now focus on strategies to increase the amount of food available to the poorest people. What can be done?

Domestic Production in LDCs

The first issue to be addressed concerns the relative merits of increasing domestic production in the less developed countries as opposed to importing more from abroad. There are several reasons for believing that many developing countries can profitably increase the percentage of their consumption domestically

---

20 Food and Agriculture Organization, *The State of Food and Agriculture: 1979* (Rome: Food and Agriculture Organization of the United Nations, 1980): 1–5.

21 The World Bank, *World Development Report, 1980* (Washington, DC: International Bank for Reconstruction and Development, 1980): 110–111, 142.

TABLE 10.2 A Hypothetical Example of the Law of Comparative Advantage

	Hours to produce one unit of textiles	*Hours to produce one unit of wheat*
Less developed country	1	3
Developed country	1	1

produced. One of the most important is that food imports use up precious foreign exchange.

Most developing countries cannot pay for imports with their own currencies. They must pay in an internationally accepted currency, such as the American dollar, earned through the sale of exports. As more foreign exchange is used for agricultural imports, less is available for imports such as capital goods, which could raise the productivity (and hence incomes) of local workers.

The lack of foreign exchange has been exacerbated by the rapid rise in oil prices. Many developing nations must spend large portions of export earnings merely to import energy. In 1986 the average low-income country spent 17% of its export earnings on energy. This was up from 7% in 1965. For some countries the situation is even more dismal. Ethiopia, for example, spent 36% of its export earnings for energy imports.[22] Little remains for capital goods or agricultural imports.

While this pressure on foreign exchange suggests a need for greater reliance on domestic agricultural production, it would be incorrect to carry that argument to its logical extreme by suggesting that all nations should become self-sufficient in food. The reason why self-sufficiency is not always efficient is suggested by *the law of comparative advantage*.

Nations are better off specializing in those products for which they have a comparative advantage. If its comparative advantage is not in food but in textiles, for example, the country would be better off by producing and exporting textiles, using the earnings to purchase food (Table 10.2). The opportunity costs of producing textiles and wheat (measured in hours of labor per unit output) are given for a hypothetical less developed country (LDC) and a developed country (DC). Suppose we are considering an eight-hour day in each country. If the average worker in each country were to spend four hours of each day on each activity, then 8 units of textile (four by the LDC and four by the DC) and 5 1/3 units of wheat (1 1/3 by the LDC and four by the DC) would be produced by the two countries each day. (Be sure you can see how these numbers can be derived from the table.)

---

22 The World Bank, *World Development Report, 1988* (Washington, DC: International Bank for Reconstruction and Development, 1988): 240.

Suppose, however, that the LDC in this case were to specialize in textiles (by allocating all 8 hours to textile production) while the DC specialized in wheat. It is easy to verify that the total world production would now be 8 units of textiles and 8 units of wheat. *When countries specialize in those products in which they have a comparative advantage, total production can increase!*

Why did this happen in our example? It happened because the opportunity cost of making textiles in LDC (in terms of forgone wheat) was lower than in DC, while the opportunity cost of growing wheat in DC (in terms of forgone textile production) was lower than that in LDC. By freeing labor in DC from making textiles, LDC would be able to reap some of the benefits of the increased wheat production.

Although this example is hypothetical, the principle it conveys is real. Total self-sufficiency in food for all nations is not an appropriate goal. Those nations with a comparative advantage in agriculture due to climate, soil type, available land, and so on, such as the United States, should be net exporters, while those nations, such as Japan, with comparative advantage in other commodities, should remain net food importers. This balance should not be allowed to get out of line, however, by creating an excessive reliance on either domestic production or imports.

Have the low-income countries as a group been reducing the share of their food consumption which comes from imports? Historically the answer was no. The World Bank (1980) computed an index of food production per capita by country. The index was constructed in such a manner that it took on the value 100 for a domestic production per capita level equal to that achieved by the country on average during the 1969–1971 period. Therefore, values of less than 100 indicated a fall in food production per capita. The average value for low-income countries for the 1976–1978 period was 97, while it was 108 for industrialized market economies. Since 1979 the low income countries have apparently barely kept pace with population growth.[23] The obvious implication was that low-income countries as a group are having trouble even keeping up with population growth, much less making headway in reducing imports.

The Undervaluation Bias

Why has food production barely kept pace with population growth for so many years? Accumulating evidence suggests that the limits to further production are primarily economic and political, not physical or biological.[24] Agriculture in the

---

23 The World Bank, *World Development Report: 1988* (Washington, DC: International Bank for Reconstruction and Development, 1988): 234.

24 For a summary of the evidence, see Sir Charles Pereira, "The Changing Patterns of Constraints on Food Production in the Third World," *Distortions of Agricultural Incentives*, Theodore W. Schultz, ed. (Bloomington, IN: Indiana University Press, 1978): 24–34.

low-income countries has been undervalued, implying that the rate of return on investment in agriculture is well below what it would be if agricultural output were allowed to receive its full social value. As a result, investments in agriculture were lower than they would otherwise have been and productivity has suffered.

Before investigating the sources and consequences of this problem, let's discuss a myth that periodically appears. According to the myth, peasant farmers do not respond to prices for cash crops because they are too ignorant, and they do not respond to prices for subsistence crops because they eat them rather than market them. Therefore, the myth concludes, supply in peasant economies is not price elastic. Population induced increases in demand would cause higher prices but not increased supplies. As one of many studies, Example 10.1 indicates this argument has one fatal flaw. It is not true!

Governments have used many mechanisms having the undesirable side effect of undervaluing agriculture and destroying incentives in the process. Two stand out—marketing boards and export taxes.

National marketing boards have been established in many developing countries for stabilizing agricultural prices and holding food prices down to protect the poor from malnutrition. Typically, a marketing board sells food at subsidized prices. As the subsidy grows, the board looks around for ways to reduce the amount of subsidy.

Two strategies regularly employed by marketing boards are the wholesale importation of artificially cheap food from the United States (available under the food aid program originally designed to get rid of wheat surpluses) and holding down prices paid to domestic farmers. Both, of course, have the long-term effect of disrupting local production. The perniciousness of this process is shown in Example 10.2.

The effects of holding prices down can be illustrated by what happened to farmers in Mali in 1979–1980. While it cost Malian farmers 83 francs per kilo to produce their irrigated rice, the government paid them only 60 francs per kilo. During that period most Malian rice was smuggled across the border to Senegal, Niger, and Upper Volta, where it received market prices. A World Bank study during the period found that farmers in 13 surveyed countries received less than half of the value of their crops.[25]

Many developing countries depend on export taxes, levied on all goods shipped abroad, as a principal source of revenue. Some of these taxes fall on cash-crop food exports (bananas, coca beans, coffee, and so on). The impact of export taxes is to raise the cost to foreign purchasers, reducing the amount of

---

25 This information came from a study by agricultural economist Carl Eicher reported in Janet Raloff, "Africa's Famine: The Human Dimension," *Science News* 127 (May 1985): 300.

EXAMPLE 10.1

The Price Responsiveness of Supply: Thailand

The market response to an increasing demand for food resulting from population growth is rising prices. This increase in prices is then presumed to call forth further increases in supply. The more price responsive is the supply, the smaller the price increases needed to satisfy a given level of demand. Therefore, the question of agricultural production responsiveness to prices is of major importance.

There is considerable debate about whether we should expect farmers to respond to prices. Those who believe that prices are important see farmers as rational, calculating individuals seizing the opportunities presented to them in the form of higher prices. The other camp generally believes that small farmers are ignorant and so set in their ways as to be oblivious to what happens in the markets for their products.

Jere Behrman, an economist on the faculty of the University of Pennsylvania, has investigated this question. He published a major empirical study assessing the price responsiveness of four major annual crop supplies in Thailand over the period 1937–63. Three (cassava, corn, and kenaf*) were cash crops while the fourth (rice) was a subsistence crop where only the surplus was marketed.

Using sophisticated econometric models, he found a substantial amount of price responsiveness in the supply of all four commodities. He notes that the substantial price responses found for kenaf are particularly noteworthy because this crop had been adopted by near-subsistence farmers who previously were, at most, marginal participants in the national market. Behrman also discovered that Thai farmers were risk averse; production could be increased by lowering the risk even if the expected price remained the same. In Thailand, at least, policies allowing prices to rise and reducing the risk have had a substantial impact. We should not sell small-scale peasant farmers short!

*Kenaf is a fiber used to manufacture gunny sacks and, to a lesser extent, rope and paper.

Source: Jere Behrman, *Supply Response in Underdeveloped Agriculture* (Amsterdam: North Holland, 1968).

EXAMPLE 10.2

Perverse Government Intervention: The Case of Colombia

The failure of the market to increase productivity in the agricultural sector, or to reduce the incidence of poverty, sometimes has been due to government policies. The experience in Colombia is relatively typical.

Marketing of wheat in Colombia is controlled by the huge Colombia Institute for Agricultural Marketing, operated by the government. In 1951–1954, wheat production averaged 140,000 metric tons a year. By 1971, this production level had fallen to 49,000 tons. During this same period, consumption of wheat in Colombia rose from 179,000 tons to 434,000 tons. The difference, of course, had to be made up by imports.

Why did this happen? There seemed to be two reasons, both of which had the effect of lowering the real price of wheat received by the Colombian farmer who, as expected, reacted by cutting production. The first reason was a massive inflow of surplus grain from the United States which was subsidized by the United States government as part of our food aid program. This artificially cheap wheat simply stole much of the market normally supplied by domestic producers.

The second cause was a decision by the marketing institute to hold wheat prices constant in the 1968–1971 period in spite of an annual inflation rate approaching 10%. The intended purpose, of course, was to hold prices down for consumers, which it temporarily did. The unintended side effect was to discourage domestic production and to increase the losses of the marketing institute which had to pay the difference between what the imported wheat cost and the lower price offered to consumers.

What is the moral to the story? The supply side has to be kept continually in mind as governments attempt to raise the nutrition levels of its citizens.

Sources: Reed Hertford, "Government Price Policies for Wheat, Rice and Tractors in Colombia," *Distortions of Agricultural Incentives*, Theodore W. Schultz, ed. (Bloomington, IN: Indiana University Press, 1978): 121–139; World Bank, *World Development Report, 1980* (Washington DC: International Bank for Reconstruction and Development, 1980): 87

demand. A reduction in demand generally means lower prices and lower incomes for the farmers. Thus, this strategy also impairs food production incentives.

Government policies in the Third World affect not only the level of agricultural production, they affect the techniques employed as well. A 1987 study by the World Bank reported that in nine developing countries pesticide subsidies ranged from 15 to 90% of full retail cost, with a median of 44%[26] Agricultural mechanization has also been stimulated by subsidies. As a result of this distortion of prices farmers have been encouraged to rely heavily on pesticides and to embrace mechanization, strategies which make little sense in the long run. Having proceeded down this path and become dependant on the subsidies, it becomes difficult for these farmers to transition to sustainable agricultural practices.

Feeding the Poor

The undervaluation bias was caused by a misguided attempt to use price controls as the way to provide the poor with access to an adequate diet. It backfired because the price controls served to reduce the availability of food. Is there a way to reduce the nutritional gap among the poor while maintaining adequate supplies of food?

Some countries such as Sri Lanka, Colombia, and the United States are using food stamp programs to subsidize food purchases by the poor. Currently, in Colombia, this is being accomplished by issuing food coupons to low-income women and children who are particularly vulnerable to nutritional deficiency. The coupons can be used by recipients to purchase a number of high-nutrition, low-cost foods. About 200,000 households were reached in 1980. By boosting the purchasing power of those with the greatest need, these programs provide access to food while protecting the incentives of farmers. Those countries lowering food prices to everyone necessitate substantially higher payments by the government to finance them. When governments search for ways to finance these subsidies, they are tempted to reduce the subsidy by paying below-market prices to farmers or to rely more heavily on artificially low-cost imported food aid. In the long run, either of these strategies can be self-defeating.

Targeting the assistance to those who need it is one strategy that works. Another approach to feeding the poor is an attempt to ensure that the income distribution effects of agricultural policies benefit the poor. One great hope associated with the "green revolution" was that new varieties of seeds produced by scientific research would expand the supply of food, holding down prices and making a better diet accessible to the poor, while at the same time providing

---

26 Development Committee, *Environment, Growth and Development* (Washington, DC: World Bank, 1987): 20.

expanding employment opportunities for the poor to supply more grain. How did it work out?

The green revolution started with maize hybrids adapted in the 1950s from the United States and Rhodesia and later spread across large parts of Central America and East Africa. Since the mid-1960s short-stalk, fertilizer-responsive varieties of rice have spread throughout East Asia and wheat have spread through Mexico, and the Indian and Pakistan Punjabs.

In many areas with access to these hybrids, productivity has doubled or tripled over a 30-year period. Short duration varieties have permitted many farmers to harvest two crops a year where only one was formerly possible. The transformation was historically unprecedented.

The effects were impressive.[27] In most areas with access to these modern varieties small farmers adopted them no less widely, intensively, or productively than others. Labor use per acre was increased with a consequent increase in the wage bill received by the poor. Poor people's consumption and nutrition were better with the new varieties than without them.

Yet the adoption of these varieties has had a darker side as well. Reliance on a few species of hybrid cereal grains increases the risk of diseases and pests. Every Wall Street portfolio manager knows that risk can be lowered by holding a diverse collection of stocks. The security offered by diversity of agricultural species has diminished as larger and larger areas are planted in these new varieties. In other areas, those without access to the new varieties have probably lost out as large quantities of new grain enter the market, eliminating by competition some of the more traditional sources. Small farmers were not always the beneficiaries of these new agricultural hybrids (Example 10.3).

We are now in a position to define the role for aid from the developed nations. Temporary food aid is helpful when traditional sources are completely inadequate (natural disasters) or when the food aid does not interfere with the earnings of domestic producers. In the long run, developed nations could provide both appropriate technologies (such as solar-powered irrigation systems) and the financial capital to get farmer-owned local cooperatives off the ground. These cooperatives would then provide some of the advantages of scale (such as risk sharing and distribution), while maintaining the existing structure of small-scale farms. Coupled with a balanced development program designed to raise the general standard of living and effective population control efforts, this approach could provide a solution to the distributional portion of the world food problem.

---

27 For the evidence, see Michael Lipton with Richard Longhurst, *New Seeds and Poor People* (Baltimore, MD: Johns Hopkins University Press, 1989).

EXAMPLE 10.3

The Distribution Dilemma: India's Green Revolution

India illustrates the trade-off between efficiency and equity sometimes faced by developing countries. India achieved substantial increases in its production of wheat (and subsequently, rice) through the introduction of new hybrid seed. Distributed through a limited budget, the new seed could either be given to small farmers in the poorer regions or to the richer Punjab area where the preconditions for rapid-yield expansion were present. India chose the latter strategy.

Several barriers to substantially increased yields existed among the poorer farmers. The smaller farmers did not have the savings or the access to capital markets to put in the complementary inputs (principally irrigation) required to gain the maximum productivity increase from the new seed. In addition, their land holdings were not typically large enough to utilize the optimum scale of the complementary inputs.

Two main developments resulted. Food products increased substantially, but the gains were captured by larger farms. Francine Frankel estimates the majority of Indian farmers experienced a relative decline in their economic position (small rice farmers received 75 to 80% of the gains received by the larger farmers), while some smaller percentage of them actually experienced an absolute decline. For this latter category, the effect of the green revolution was to make them worse off, not better off.

Source: Francine Frankel, *India's Green Revolution: Economic Gains and Political Costs* (Princeton, NJ: Princeton University Press, 1971).

FEAST AND FAMINE CYCLES

The remaining dimension of the world food problem concerns the year-to-year fluctuations in food availability caused by vagaries of weather and planting decisions. Even if the average level of food availability were appropriate, the fact that the average consists of a sequence of overproduction and underproduction years means that society as a whole can benefit from smoothing out the fluctuations.

The point is vividly depicted by an analogy. If a person were standing in two buckets of water—the first containing boiling hot water, the second, ice cold water—his misery would not be assuaged in the least by a friend telling him that

FIGURE 10.3   The cobweb model.

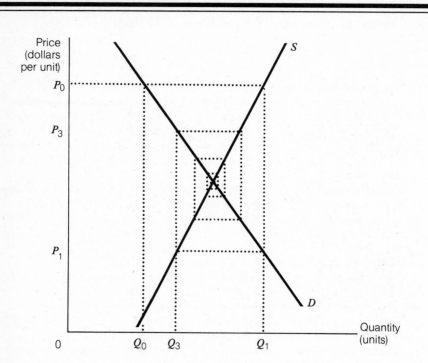

on average the temperature was perfect. The average does not tell the whole story.

The fluctuations of supplies for food seem to be rather large and the swings in prices even larger. Why? One characteristic of the farming sector suggests that farmers' production decisions may actually make the fluctuations worse or at least prolong them. This tendency is explored via the *cobweb model* (Figure 10.3). The source of the name is obvious, though no spider would own up to having created such a pathetic specimen.

Suppose, due to a weather-induced shortage, Q_0 is supplied, driving the price up to P_0. For the next growing season, farmers have to plant well in advance of harvest time. Their decisions about how much to plant will depend on the price they expect to receive. Let us suppose they use this year's price as their guess of what next year's price will be.

They will plan to supply (and in the absence of further weather aberrations *will* supply) Q_1. At price P_0, the market cannot absorb that much of the commodity so the price falls to P_1. If farmers use that price to plan the following year's crop, they will produce Q_3. This will cause the price to rise to P_3 and so on.

FIGURE 10.4 Price elasticity of demand and the size of price fluctuations.

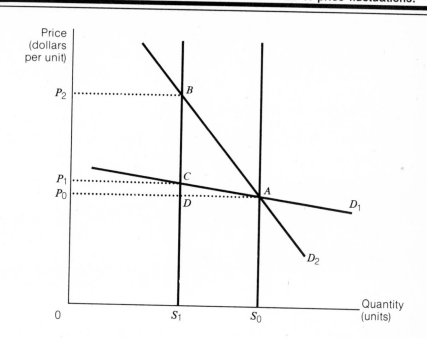

What is occurring is a *damped oscillation*. In the absence of further supply shocks, the amplitude of price and quantity fluctuations decreases over time until the equilibrium price and quantity are obtained.[28]

The demand for food tends to be price inelastic, particularly in developing countries. This has some important implications. The more price inelastic the demand curve, the higher the price has to go in order to bring the demand into line with supply when a weather-induced shortage occurs (Figure 10.4).

Figure 10.4 records an initial equilibrium situation where demand D_1 and supply S_0 are equal to point A. A supply shortfall is registered as a shift in the supply curve from S_0 to S_1. In the two demand curves shown, D_1 is the most price elastic. Notice that the more inelastic the demand curve, such as D_2, the higher the price has to go to clear the market.

Figure 10.4 also shows the effects of price shifts on producer revenues. How do supply shocks affect the incomes of farmers? At first glance the result seems ambiguous, since during shortages they get higher prices (a plus!) but have also less to sell (a minus!). Which effect dominates?

---

[28] Theoretically speaking, undamped oscillations which increase in amplitude over time are possible under certain conditions, but this pattern does not seem to characterize existing food markets.

Since producer revenue is price times quantity, it is represented as a rectangle. The size of the rectangle depends on the circumstances. Before the supply shift, revenues received are depicted by the rectangle OP_0AS_0. After the supply shift, the revenues with the elastic demand curve (D_1) are OP_1CS_1 and for the inelastic demand curve are OP_2BS_1.

Have revenues increased with the supply shift? To answer the question, we have to compare areas P_0P_1CD (the net amount gained with the elastic demand curve) or P_0P_2BD (the net amount gained with the inelastic demand curve) to DAS_0S_1 (the revenue lost due to the lower production levels).

One conclusion is immediately obvious—the more inelastic the demand curve, the more likely farmers as a group are to gain from the shortfall. As long as the demand curve is price inelastic in the relevant range (a condition commonly satisfied in the short run by food products), farmers as a group will be better off by supply shortfalls.[29]

For consumers, a quite different picture emerges. Consumers are unambiguously hurt by shortfalls and helped by situations with excess supply. The more price inelastic the demand curve, the greater the loss is in consumer surplus from shortfalls and the greater the gain in consumer surplus from excess supply.

This creates some interesting (and from the policy point of view, difficult) incentives. Producers as a group do not have any particular interest in protecting against supply shortfalls, but they have a substantial interest in protecting against excess supply. Consumers, on the other hand, have no quarrel with excess supply, but want to guard against supply shortfalls.

While society as a whole would gain from the stabilization of prices and quantities, the different segments of society have rather different views of how that stabilization should come about. Farmers would be delighted with price stabilization as long as the average price is high, while consumers would be delighted if the average price is kept low.

The main means of attempting to stabilize prices and quantities is by creating stockpiles. These can be drawn down during periods of scarcity and built up during periods of excess supply. Currently, two different types of food stockpiles exist. The first is a special internationally held emergency stockpile that would be used to alleviate the hunger caused by natural disasters (such as drought). Established in 1975 by the Seventh Special Session of the United Nations General Assembly, with an annual target of 500,000 tons, the World Emergency Stockpile has the potential to greatly reduce suffering without having any noticeable disruptive effect on the world grain market (involving some 70 million tons traded). Unfortunately, its full potential has not yet been reached. Contributions

---

29 This is not necessarily true for every farmer, of course. If the supply reduction is concentrated on a few, they will unambiguously be worse off while the remaining farmers will be better off. The point is that the revenue gains received by the latter group will exceed the losses suffered by the former group.

FIGURE 10.5   Stocks of cereals, 1971–83.

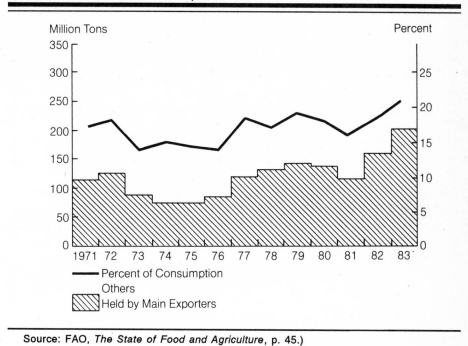

Source: FAO, *The State of Food and Agriculture*, p. 45.)

in 1979, for example, totaled 314,000 tons, considerably short of the annual target. The bulk of accumulated reserves was distributed to needy nations in that same year, leaving little in reserve.

The second kind of stockpile represents the stocks held individually by the various countries. It was hoped that these stockpiles would be internationally coordinated. Despite intensive negotiations, by 1979, the mechanism for coordinating these stocks had not yet been agreed upon, much less implemented. However, the level of the stocks was adequate. The FAO Secretariat estimates the minimum safe level of world carryover stocks for cereals to be between 17 and 18 percent of world consumption. After a rather precipitous decline in 1973, by 1977 the stocks had been rebuilt to the minimum safe levels (Figure 10.5). Almost two-thirds of the stockpile is controlled by the exporting countries.

Food stockpiles have started to increase food security on a worldwide basis but have not yet solved the problem. Significant difficult political decisions on stockpile management, such as timing purchases and sales, have yet to be agreed upon. Until that time, because the interests of producers and consumer nations are no different, it is unlikely that any uncoordinated system will be fully effective.

SUMMARY

The world hunger problem is upon us and it is real. Serious malnutrition is currently being experienced in many parts of the world. The root of the chronic problem is poverty—an inability to afford the rising costs of food. The harm caused by poverty is intensified by fluctuations in the availability of food.

These problems are not unsolvable and do not call for a massive retrenchment by the developed world. The main barriers to a solution are political and economic, rather than physical.

The FAO has concluded that developing countries *could* increase their food production by around 4% per year through the 1990s, well in excess of population growth. They conclude, however, that this will occur only if the developed nations share technology and provide the developing countries access to their markets and if the developing countries show a willingness to adopt pricing policies which do not restrict output. This can be accomplished without jeopardizing the poor by using direct food purchase subsidies (such as a food stamp program) rather than price controls.

Because a major part of the world hunger problem is poverty, it is not enough to simply produce more food. The ability of the poor to afford food has also to be improved. This is particularly important in light of the rapidly rising cost of agricultural inputs such as fertilizer. Reducing poverty can be accomplished by bolstering nonfarm employment opportunities, as well as by enhancing the returns of smaller scale farmers.

The available evidence suggests that, with respect to scale economies, there does not seem to be a trade-off between efficiency and equity; small-scale farming can compete effectively, given access to credit markets and new improved technologies.

Food stockpiles—key elements in a program to provide food security—exist but are not yet fully effective. The emergency stockpile has not achieved its designed capacity and the system of national stockpiles is large but not effectively managed. The light is visible at the end of the tunnel and the train is moving, but the journey is distressingly slow.

FURTHER READING

Crosson, Pierre R. and Sterling Brubaker. *Resource and Environmental Effects of U.S. Agriculture* (Baltimore: Johns Hopkins University Press for Resources for the Future, 1982). This book identifies the environmental costs associated with future increases in production and suggests measures to deal with them.

Meier, Gerald M. *Leading Issues in Economic Development*, 5th ed. (New York: Oxford University Press, 1989). A highly regarded extensive collection of integrated short articles on various aspects of the development process. Contains an excellent section of agricultural development with an extensive bibliography.

Presidential Commission on World Hunger. *Overcoming World Hunger: The Challenge Ahead* (Washington, DC: U.S. Government Printing Office, 1980).

Streeten, Paul. *What Price Food? Agricultural Policies in Developing Countries* (New York: St. Martin's Press, 1987). An excellent study of agricultural policies in developing countries.

ADDITIONAL REFERENCES

Alexandros, Nikos, ed. *World Agriculture: Towards 2000* (New York: New York University Press, 1988).

Browder, John O., ed. *Fragile Lands of Latin America: Strategies for Sustainable Development* (Boulder, CO: Westview Press, 1988).

Cobia, David. *Cooperatives in Agriculture* (Englewood Cliffs, NJ: Prentice-Hall, 1988).

Collins, Robert A. and J. C. Headley. "Optimal Investment to Reduce the Decay of an Income Stream: The Case of Soil Conservation," *Journal of Environmental Economics and Management* 10 (March 1983): 60-71.

Crosson, Pierre R. *The Cropland Crisis: Myth or Reality* (Washington, DC: Resources for the Future, 1982).

Crosson, Pierre R. *Productivity Effects of Cropland Erosion in the United States* (Washington, DC: Resources for the Future, 1983).

Hall, Darwin C. et al. "Organic Food and Sustainable Agriculture," *Contemporary Policy Issues* 7 (October 1989): 47-72.

Regev, Uri, Haim Shalit, and A. P. Gutteirrez. "On the Optimal Allocation of Pesticides with Increasing Resistance: The Case of Alfalfa Weevil," *Journal of Environmental Economics and Management* 10 (March 1983): 86-100.

DISCUSSION QUESTIONS

1. "By applying modern technology to agriculture, the United States has become the most productive food-producing nation in the world. The secret to solving the world food problem lies in transferring this technology to developing countries." Discuss.

2. Under Public Law 480, the United States sells surplus grains to developing countries which pay in local currencies. Since the United States rarely spends all of these currencies, much of this grain transfer is *de facto* an outright gift. Is this an equitable and efficient way for the United States to dispose of surplus grain? Why or why not?

PROBLEMS

1. The two countries Norland and Souland can produce commodities *A* and *B* per hour of labor expended according to the following table:

	Amount of A produced in one hour	Amount of B produced in one hour
Norland	4	8
Souland	2	6

Which country, if either, has the comparative advantage in producing *A*? Why?

2. "Food stamp programs only serve to drive food prices higher, not increase the quantity of food available to the poor." What would the elasticity of supply have to be for this statement to be true? What would the elasticity of supply have to be for a food stamp program to increase the availability of food to the poor with no price increase?

3. A 1985 *Wall Street Journal* article suggested that absentee landlords may be one source of soil erosion problems. (Assume for the purposes of this problem that absentee landlords rent the land to the farmer for a fixed annual price.) Use your knowledge of property rights to discuss whether or not soil erosion could be expected to be a more serious problem with absentee landlords.

CHAPTER ELEVEN

Storable, Renewable Resources: Forests

There is nothing more difficult to carry out, nor more doubtful of success, nor more dangerous to handle, than to initiate a new order of things. For the reformer has enemies in all who profit by the old order, and only lukewarm defenders in all those who would profit from the new order. The lukewarmness arises partly from fear of their adversaries who have law in their favor; and partly from the incredulity of mankind, who do not truly believe in anything new until they have had actual experience of it.

NICCOLÒ MACHIAVELLI, *The Prince* (1513)

INTRODUCTION

Forests provide a variety of products and services. The raw materials for housing and wood products are extracted from the forest. In many parts of the world wood is an important fuel. Paper products are derived from wood fiber. Trees cleanse the air by absorbing carbon dioxide and adding oxygen. Forests provide shelter and sanctuary for wildlife and they play an important role in maintaining the watersheds that supply much of our drinking water.

Although the contributions that trees make to our everyday life are easy to overlook, even the most rudimentary calculations indicate their significance. Almost one-third of the land in the United States is covered by forests, the largest category of land use with the exception of pasture and grazing land. For Maine, an example of a heavily forested state, 95% of the land area is covered by forest. In 1980, the comparable figure for the world was 31.3%.[1]

Managing these forests is no easy task. In contrast to cereal grains, which are planted and harvested on an annual cycle, trees mature very slowly. The manager must decide not only how to maximize yields on a given amount of land, but also when to harvest and replant. A delicate balance must be established among the various possible uses of forests. Since harvesting the resource diminishes other values (such as protecting the aesthetic value of forested vistas), establishing the proper balance requires some means of comparing the value of potentially conflicting uses. The efficiency criterion is one obvious method.

A glance at some of the vital signs of the forest resource do not inspire confidence that it is being managed either efficiently or sustainably. Deforestation is currently proceeding at an unprecedented rate. In 1990 the World Resources Institute reported that 40 to 50 million acres of tropical forests, an area about the size of the state of Washington, are being destroyed each year as trees are cut for timber, and for clearing land for agriculture and development.[2] This estimate, which was based upon remote sensing data from satellites, was 50 percent higher than the previous global estimate prepared by the United Nations Food and Agricultural Organization in 1980.

Deforestation is a serious problem because it has intensified global warming, has decreased biodiversity, has caused agricultural productivity to decline, has increased soil erosion and desertification, and has precipitated the decline of traditional cultures of people indigenous to the forests. Instead of forests being used on a sustainable basis to provide for the needs of subsequent generations as well as current generations, the forests are being "cashed in." According to a 1989 study for the International Tropical Timber Organization, a 69-member trade group based in Yokohama, Japan, less than 0.1% of tropical logging was done sustainably.[3] Current forestry practices seem to violate both the sustainability and efficiency criteria. Why is this occurring and what can be done about it?

In the remainder of this chapter we shall explore how economics can be combined with forest ecology to assist in efficiently managing this important

---

1 OECD, *OECD Environmental Data: Compendium 1985* (Paris: Organization for European Cooperation and Development, 1985): 103.

2 World Resources Institute and International Institute for Environment and Development, *World Resources: 1990–91* (New York: Basic Books, 1990).

3 In this context, sustainability refers to harvesting no more than would be replaced by growth; sustainable harvest would preserve the interests of future generations by assuring that the volume of remaining timber was not declining over time. This is a somewhat stronger sustainability criterion than introduced in Chapter 2, which only requires that future generations be as well off. It would conceivably be possible to make future generations better off even if the volume of wood were declining over time by providing a compensating amount of some commodity or service they value even more.

resource. We begin by characterizing what is meant by an efficient allocation of the forest resource when the value of the harvested timber is the only concern. Starting simply, we first model the efficient decision to cut a single stand or cluster of trees with a common age by superimposing economic considerations on a biological model of tree growth. This model is then refined to demonstrate how the multiple values of the forest resource should influence the harvesting decision and how the problem is altered if planning takes place over an infinite horizon, with forests being harvested and replanted in a continual sequence. Turning to matters of institutional adequacy, we shall then examine the inefficiencies that have resulted or can be expected to result from both public and private management decisions and strategies for restoring efficiency.

DEFINING EFFICIENT MANAGEMENT

Special Attributes of the Timber Resource

While timber shares many characteristics with other living resources, it also has some aspects that make it unique. Timber shares with many other animate resources the characteristic that it is both an output and a capital good. Trees, when harvested, provide a salable commodity, but left standing they are a capital good, providing for increased growth the following year. Each year, the forest manager must decide whether to harvest a particular stand of trees or to wait for the additional growth. In contrast to many other living resources, however, the time period between initial investment (planting) and recovery of that investment (harvesting) is especially long. Intervals of 25 years or more are common in forestry, but not in many other industries. Finally, forestry is unusually subject to a large variety of externalities, which are associated with either the standing timber or the act of harvesting timber. These externalities not only make it difficult to define the efficient allocation, they play havoc with incentives, reducing the ability of institutions to manage efficiently.

The Biological Dimension

Tree growth is measured on a volume basis, typically cubic feet, on a particular site. This measurement is taken of the stems, exclusive of bark and limbs, between the stump and a 4-inch top. For larger trees, the stump is 24 inches from the ground. Only standing trees are measured; those toppled by wind or age are not included. In this sense the volume is measured in net rather than gross terms.

Based on this measurement of volume, the data reveal that tree stands go through distinct growth phases. Initially, when the trees are very young, growth is rather slow in volume terms, though the tree may experience a considerable increase in height. A period of sustained, rapid growth follows with volume increasing considerably. Finally, slower growth sets in as the stand fully matures, until growth stops or even reverses.

The actual growth of a stand of trees depends on many factors, including the weather, the fertility of the soil, susceptibility to insects or disease, the type of tree, the amount of care devoted to the trees, and vulnerability to forest fire or air pollution. Thus, tree growth can vary considerably from stand to stand. Some of these growth-enhancing or growth-retarding factors are under the influence of foresters; others are not.

Abstracting from these differences, it is possible to develop a hypothetical, but realistic biological model of the growth of a stand of trees. Our model (Figure 11.1) is based on the growth of a stand of Douglas fir trees in the Pacific Northwest.[4]

Notice that the figure is consistent with the growth phases mentioned above. Following an early period of limited growth, the stand experiences rapid growth in the middle ages with growth ceasing after 135 years.

When should this stand be harvested? Foresters have come up with a calculation called the *mean annual increment* (MAI) which provides the basis for a biological approach to answering this question. Developing this concept provides a useful contrast to the economic approach which is presented in subsequent sections.

The MAI is calculated by dividing the cumulative volume of the stand at the end of each decade by the cumulative number of years the stand has been growing up to that decade. For tree growth patterns like the ones represented by Figure 11.1, the MAI rises during the early ages and then falls during the later ages (Table 11.1).

According to the biological decision rule, the forest should be harvested at the age when the MAI is maximized. For our Douglas fir example, this occurs when the stand is 100 years old. Column 4 in Table 11.1 helps us to understand what is special about this age. Annual incremental growth rises until the trees are about 70 years old, declining thereafter. The MAI rises for the first 100 years because the annual incremental growth is above the MAI during that period; it falls in the following years because the annual incremental growth is below the MAI.

The Economics of Forest Harvesting

To an economist, this biological criterion seems rather arbitrary; it fails to consider any of the factors such as the value of the timber, the time value of money,

---

4 The numerical model in the text is based loosely on the data presented in Marion Clawson, "Decision Making in Timber Production, Harvest, and Marketing," Research Paper R-4 (Washington DC: Resources for the Future, 1977): 13, Table 1. The mathematical function relating volume to age of the stand in Figure 11.1 is a third-degree polynomial of the form $v = a + bt + ct^2 + dt^3$, where v = volume in cubic feet, t = the age of the stand in years, and a, b, c, and d are parameters which take on the values 0, 40, 3.1 and -0.016, respectively.

FIGURE 11.1   Model of tree growth in a stand of Douglas fir.

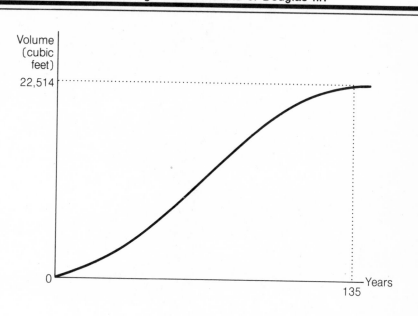

or costs associated with planting and harvesting which would play a central role in an efficient harvesting decision. It is possible, however, to use the basic biological model of growth portrayed in Figure 11.1 as the basis for an economic model of the harvesting decision.

From the definition of efficiency, the optimal time to harvest this stand would be that time which maximizes the present value of the net benefits from the wood. The size of the net benefits from the wood depends on whether the land will be perpetually committed to forestry or left to natural processes after harvest. For our first model, we will assume that the stand will be harvested once and the land will be left as is following the harvest. This model will serve to illustrate how the economic principles of forestry can be applied to the simplest case, while providing the background necessary to move to more complicated and more realistic examples.

Two costs are presumed to be important in this decision—planting costs and harvesting costs. Apart from their magnitudes, these costs differ in one significant characteristic—the time at which they are borne. Planting costs are borne immediately, while harvesting costs are borne at the time of harvest. In a present-value calculation harvesting costs are discounted (as is the value of the wood) because they are paid (received) in the future, whereas planting costs are not discounted because they are paid immediately. For the sake of our example, assume that planting this stand costs $1000 and harvesting costs $0.30 per cubic foot of wood harvested.

TABLE 11.1   The Biological Harvesting Decision: Douglas Fir

Age (years) (1)	Volume[a] (cubic feet) (2)	MAI[b] (cubic feet) (3)	Annual incremental growth[a] (cubic feet) (4)
10	694	6.9	6.9
20	1,912	95.6	121.8
30	3,558	118.6	164.6
40	5,536	138.4	198.8
50	7,750	155.0	221.4
60	10,104	168.0	235.4
70	12,502	178.6	239.8
80	14,848	185.6	234.6
90	17,046	189.4	219.8
100	19,000	190.0	195.4
110	20,614	187.4	161.4
120	21,792	181.6	117.8
130	22,438	172.6	64.6
135	22,514	166.8	11.6

[a]Calculated from the equation used to produce Figure 11.1. See footnote 4.

[b]Column 2 divided by Column 1.

[c]Change over intervening period in Column 1 divided by change in number of years in Column 1.

With these additions to the model, it is now possible to calculate the present value of net benefits that would be derived from harvesting this stand at various ages (Table 11.2). The net benefits are calculated by subtracting the present value of costs from the value of the timber at that age. Two different discount rates are used to illustrate the influence of discounting on the harvesting decision. The undiscounted calculations ($r = 0.0$) simply indicate the actual values that would prevail at each age, while the positive discount rate takes the time value of money into account.

Two interesting conclusions can be gleaned from Table 11.2. First, discounting shortens the time until the stand is harvested. Whereas the maximum undiscounted net benefits occur at 135 years, when a discount rate of only 0.02 is used, the maximum occurs at 68 years, roughly half the time of the undiscounted case. Higher discount rates would yield even shorter harvesting times. Second, the magnitude of the planting and harvesting costs do not change the optimal harvesting point. Notice that the maximum of the value of timber column and the net benefit column occur in precisely the same year for each of the discount rates. In other words, even if costs were zero, the harvesting decision would occur at the same point. Since the reasons for these conclusions are not immediately apparent, we must look deeper.

TABLE 11.2 Economic Harvesting Decision: Douglas Fir

Age (years)	Volume (cubic feet)	Undiscounted (r = 0.0)			Discounted (r = 0.02)		
		Value of timber ($)	Cost ($)	Net benefits ($)	Value of timber ($)	Cost ($)	Net benefits ($)
10	694	694	1,208	-514	567	1,171	-604
20	1,912	1,912	1,574	338	1,288	1,386	-98
30	3,558	3,558	2,067	1,491	1,964	1,589	375
40	5,536	5,536	2,661	2,875	2,507	1,752	755
50	7,750	7,750	3,325	4,425	2,879	1,864	1,015
60	10,104	10,104	4,031	6,073	3,080	1,924	1,156
68	12,023	12,023	4,607	7,416	3,128	1,938	1,190
70	12,502	12,502	4,751	7,751	3,126	1,938	1,118
80	14,848	14,848	5,454	9,394	3,046	1,914	1,132
90	17,046	17,046	6,114	10,932	2,868	1,860	1,008
100	19,000	19,000	6,700	12,300	2,623	1,787	836
110	20,614	20,614	7,184	13,430	2,334	1,700	634
120	21,792	21,792	7,538	14,254	2,024	1,607	417
130	22,438	22,438	7,731	14,707	1,710	1,513	197
135	22,514	22,514	7,754	14,760	1,449	1,466	-17

Volume of timber from Table 11.1.

Value of timber = price × volume/$(1 + r)^t$

Cost = $1000 + $0.30 × volume/$(1 + r)^t$

Net benefits = value of timber - cost

Higher discount rates imply shorter harvesting periods because they are less tolerant of the slow timber growth that occurs as the stand reaches maturity. The use of a positive discount rate implies a direct comparison between the increase in the value of the timber that occurs prior to harvesting and the increase in value that would occur if the forest were harvested and the money from the sale invested at rate r. In the undiscounted case, the opportunity cost of capital is zero, so it pays to leave the money invested in trees as long as some growth is occurring. As long as r is positive, however, the trees will be harvested as soon as the growth rate is low enough that more will be earned from financial investments.

The fact that neither harvesting nor planting costs affect the harvesting period results from the form of costs that we have used in the model. Because they are paid immediately, the present value of planting costs is equal to the actual expenditure; it does not vary with the age at which the stand is harvested. Essentially, a constant is being subtracted from the value of timber at any age. The age of the stand that maximizes the value of the timber necessarily maximizes the difference between the present value of the timber and the (constant) present value of the planting cost.

This does not imply, however, that planting costs are irrelevant to the harvesting decision. If planting costs are sufficiently high, they can exceed the maximum value of the timber. In this case, the net benefits would be negative for all possible ages and it would not be efficient to plant this type of tree for commercial harvest.

Harvesting costs are a different matter. They differ from planting costs in two respects. Not only are they borne at the time of harvest, but total harvesting costs are also proportional to the amount of timber harvested ($0.30 for each cubic foot). The present value of total harvesting cost changes with the harvesting period both because costs are discounted an amount determined by the harvesting date and because costs rise as the volume of wood to be harvested rises.

The impact of this type of cost on the harvesting decision can most easily be seen by realizing that the net benefits of a cubic foot of wood harvested at any given age is the price of that wood minus the marginal cost of harvesting that cubic foot, appropriately discounted. By assumption, the price and the marginal cost of a cubic foot of wood do not vary with age; they are constants. In the case of our numerical example this constant net value before discounting is $0.70 (the $1.00 price minus the $0.30 marginal harvest cost). If the marginal cost of harvesting were zero, this value would be $1.00. Regardless what the marginal cost of harvesting is, this net value before discounting is a constant that is multiplied by the volume of timber at each age divided by $(1 + r)^t$. Its role is merely to raise or lower the net benefits curve; it does not change its shape. Therefore the net benefits curve will reach its maximum at the same age of the stand regardless of the value of the marginal cost curve, as long as the marginal cost is less than the price received.

What would be the effect of a $0.20 tax levied on each cubic foot of wood harvested in this simple model? In essence, this type of tax would serve to raise the marginal cost of harvesting from $0.30 per cubic foot to $0.50 per cubic foot. The $0.30 would reflect the cost of the manpower and the equipment to get the timber out of the forest and to the market. The remaining $0.20 would go to the government as tax revenue.

As indicated by the analysis in the preceding sections, increasing the marginal harvesting cost in this model would not have any effect on the harvesting period. Since levying a per-unit tax has the effect of increasing marginal harvesting cost, it would have no effect on the harvesting period either.

Extending the Basic Model

Our basic model is somewhat unrealistic in several respects. Perhaps most importantly, it considers the harvest as a single event, rather than a part of an infinite sequence of harvesting and replanting. Typically in the forest industry, harvested lands are restocked and the sequence starts over again in a never-ending cycle.

At first glance it may appear that this is really no different than the case just considered. After all, can't one merely use this model to characterize the efficient interval between planting and harvest for each of the periods? The mathematics tells us that this is not the correct way to think about the problem, and with a bit of reflection it is not difficult to see why.

The single-period model we developed would be appropriate for an infinite planning period if and only if all periods were independent. If interdependencies exist among time periods, the harvesting decision must reflect those interdependencies.

Interdependencies do exist. The decision to delay a harvest imposes an additional cost on an infinite planning model that has no counterpart in our single-harvest model—the cost of delaying the onset of the next planting and harvesting cycle. In our single-harvest model the optimum time to harvest occurs when the marginal benefit of an additional year's growth equals the marginal opportunity cost of capital. When the capital gains from letting the trees grow another year become equal to the return that could be obtained from harvesting the trees and investing the gains, the stand was harvested. In the infinite-planning horizon case the opportunity cost of delaying the next cycle must also be covered by the gain in tree growth.

The effect of including this new cost can be rather profound. Assuming that all other aspects of the problem (such as planting and harvesting costs, discount rate, growth function, and price) are the same, the optimal time to harvest (called the *optimal rotation* in the infinite-planning case) is shorter in the infinite-planning case than in the single-harvest case. This follows directly from the fact that the marginal cost of a delay is higher due to the existence of the opportunity cost of starting the cycle later. The efficient forester will harvest a stand sooner when he or she is planning to replant the same area than when the plot will be left inactive after the harvest.

This more complicated model also yields some rather different conclusions than our original model, a valuable reminder of a point made in the first chapter—conclusions flow from a specific view of the world and are valid only to the extent that view captures the essence of a problem. Consider, for example, the effect of a rise in planting costs. In our single-harvest model they had no effect on the optimal time to harvest. In the infinite-planning case the optimal rotation is affected. Specifically, higher planting costs reduce the marginal opportunity cost of delaying the cycle. By doing so they allow positive net benefits to accrue from delaying the cycle, compared to the case with lower planting costs. As a result the optimal rotation (the time between planting and harvest) would increase as planting costs increase. A similar result would be obtained when harvesting costs are increased.[5] The optimal rotation period would be lengthened.

---

5 For a discussion of the results in this section and the mathematics that lies behind them, see Michael D. Bowles and John V. Krutilla, "Multiple Use Management of Public Forestlands, in *Handbook of Natural Resource and Energy Economics, Vol. II*, Allen V. Kneese and James L. Sweeney, eds. (Amsterdam: North-Holland, 1985): 534–537.

Since increased harvesting costs in the infinite-horizon model lengthen the optimal rotation period, a per-unit tax on harvested timber would lengthen the optimal rotation period in this model as well. Furthermore lengthening the rotation period implies that the harvested trees would be somewhat older and therefore each harvest would involve a somewhat larger volume of wood.

The vision of a fully regulated forest that emerges from these models involves a series of forest plots, each with trees of a different age. A sufficient number of plots would be available to provide trees at every age up to the age at which they are harvested. When the trees on a particular plot reach the age stipulated by the optimal rotation, they are harvested and the plot is restocked. The following year a different plot is harvested as its trees reach economic maturity. In this way harvesting activity can take place every year without endangering the sustainability of the forest.

Another limitation of our basic model lies in its assumption of a constant relative price for the wood over time. In fact the relative prices of timber have been rising over time. Introducing relative prices for timber that rise at a constant rate in the infinite-horizon model causes the optimal rotation period to increase.[6] In essence prices which are rising at a fixed rate act to offset the effect of discounting. Since we have already established that lower discount rates imply longer rotation periods, it immediately follows that rising prices also lead to longer efficient rotation periods.

A final concern with the models as elaborated so far is that they all are concerned solely with the sale of timber as a product. In fact, forests serve several other purposes as well, such as providing habitat for wildlife, supplying recreational opportunities, and stabilizing watersheds. For these uses additional benefits accrue to the standing timber which are lost or diminished when the stand is harvested.

It is possible to incorporate these benefits into our model to demonstrate the effect they would have on the efficient rotation.[7] Suppose that the amenity benefits conveyed by a standing forest are positively related to the age of the forest. In this case the optimal rotation would once again occur when the marginal benefit of delay equalled the marginal cost of delay. In the case being considered, the marginal benefit of delay would be higher than in the models considered above because of the additional amenity benefit. For this reason the optimal rotation would be lengthened when amenity benefits are considered. If the amenity benefits are sufficiently large, it may be efficient to delay harvest forever, leaving the forest as a wilderness area.

---

6 See the discussion in Charles W. Howe, *Natural Resource Economics: Issues, Analysis, Policy* (New York: Wiley, 1979): 238-239. If prices are rising at a rate g, then the effective discount rate becomes $r - g$.

7 The mathematics for this section of the model can be seen in R. Hartman, "The Harvesting Decision When a Standing Forest Has Value," *Economic Inquiry* 14 (1976): 52-58.

SOURCES OF INEFFICIENCY

The rather harmonious view of a regulated forest conveyed by these models contrasts rather sharply with the reality of rapid deforestation. Why are forests being harvested so rapidly, in apparent violation of both efficiency and sustainability criteria?

Global Inefficiencies

The first source of deforestation involves external costs that transcend national borders. Because the costs transcend national borders, it is unrealistic to expect national policy to solve the problem. Some international action would normally be necessary.

Biodiversity.   Due to species extinction the diversity of the forms of life that inhabit the planet is diminishing at an unprecedented rate. And the extinction of species is an irreversible process. Deforestation, particularly the destruction of the tropical rain forests, is a major source of species extinction because it destroys the most biologically active habitats. In particular, Amazonia has been characterized by Norman Myers as the "single richest region of the tropical biome."[8] The quantity of bird, fish, plant, and insect life which are unique to that region are unmatched anywhere else on the planet.

One of the tragic ironies of the situation is that these extinctions are occurring at precisely the moment in history when we would be most able to take advantage of the gene pool this biodiversity represents. Modern techniques now make it possible to transplant desirable genes from one species into another, creating species with new characteristics such as enhanced disease or pest resistance. But the gene pool must be diverse to serve as a source of donor genes. Tropical forests have already contributed genetic material to increase disease resistance of cash crops such as coffee and cocoa, and have been the source of some entirely new foods. Approximately one-quarter of all prescription drugs have been derived from substances found in tropical plants. Future discoveries, however, are threatened by deforestation's deleterious effect on habitat.

Global Warming.   Deforestation also contributes to global warming. Since trees absorb carbon dioxide, a major greenhouse gas, deforestation eliminates a potentially significant means of ameliorating the rise in carbon dioxide emissions. Furthermore, burning trees, an activity commonly associated with agricultural land

---

8 Norman Myers, *The Primary Source: Tropical Forests and Our Future* (New York: W. W. Norton, 1984): 50.

clearing, adds carbon dioxide to the air, by liberating the carbon sequestered within the trees. Why is deforestation occurring so rapidly when the benefits conferred by a standing forest are so significant by virtually anyone's reckoning? The concept of externalities provides the key to resolving this paradox. Both the global warming and biodiversity benefits are largely external to the nation containing the forest while the costs of preventing deforestation are largely internal. The loss of biodiversity precipitated by deforestation is perhaps most deeply felt by the industrialized world, not the countries that control the forests. Currently, the technologies to exploit the gene pool this diversity represents are in widest use in the industrialized countries. Similarly most of the damage from global warming would be felt outside the borders of the country being deforested. Yet stopping deforestation means giving up the jobs and income derived from harvesting the wood or harvesting the land made available by clearing the forests. It is therefore not surprising that the most vociferous opposition to the loss of biodiversity is mounted in the industrialized nations, not the tropical forest nations. With global externalities we have not only a clear rationale for market failure, but also a clear rationale for why the governments involved cannot be expected to solve the problem by themselves.

Poverty and Debt

Poverty and debt are also major sources of pressure on the forests. Peasants see unclaimed forest land as an opportunity to become landowners. Nations confronted with masses of peasants see unowned or publicly owned forests as a politically more viable source of land for the landless than taking it forcibly from the rich. Without land, peasants descend upon the urban areas in search of jobs in larger numbers than can be accommodated by urban labor markets. Politically explosive tensions, created and nourished by the resulting atmosphere of frustration and hopelessness, force governments to open up forested lands to the peasants or at least to look the other way as peasants stake their claim.

In eastern and southern Africa, positive feedback loops have created a downward cycle in which poverty and deforestation reinforce each other. Most natural forests have long since been cut down for timber, fuelwood, and cleared land for agricultural purposes. As forests disappear, the rural poor divert more time toward locating fuelwood. When fuelwood is no longer available, animal waste is burned, thereby eliminating it as a source of fertilizer to nourish depleted soils. Fewer trees hasten soil erosion. Depleted soils lead to diminished nutrition as does an inability to find or afford fuelwood or animal waste for cooking and for boiling unclean water. Lower nutrition saps energy, increases the susceptibility to disease, and reduces productivity. Survival strategies may necessarily sacrifice long-term goals simply to ward off starvation or death; the forests are typically an early casualty.

Poverty at the national level takes the form of staggering levels of debt to service in comparison to the capacity to generate foreign exchange earnings. In periods of high real interest rates, servicing these debts commands most if not all foreign exchange earnings. Using these foreign exchange earnings to service the debt eliminates the possibility of using them to finance imports for sustainable activities to alleviate poverty.

The large debts owed by many developing countries also encourage these countries to overexploit their resource endowments to raise the necessary foreign exchange. Timber exports represent a case in point. As Gus Spaeth, the president of the World Resources Institute points out, "By an accident of history and geography, half of the Third World external debt and over two-thirds of global deforestation occur in the same 14 developing countries."[9]

Perverse Incentives

Profit maximization does not produce efficient outcomes when the pattern of incentives facing decision-makers is perverse. Forestry provides an unfortunately large number of situations where perverse incentives have produced very inefficient and unsustainable outcomes.

Privately owned forests are a significant force all over the world, but in some countries, such as the United States, they are the dominant force. In the United States some 72% of forested land is privately owned. Some 15% of this forested land is owned by the forest industry, while the remaining privately owned 57% is held by farmer or other landowners. These latter parcels tend to be small in size.

Can prescient private owners be counted upon to manage efficiently? For forests dedicated to timber harvesting, profit maximization can be compatible with efficient management. As long as social and private discount rates are the same and price expectations are accurate, the rotation which maximizes profits will also maximize net benefits. Both shorter-than-efficient rotations and longer-than-efficient rotations would result in lower profits, so it is in the self-interest of the private owner to act efficiently.

Perhaps even more important are the incentives created by private ownership to increase the yield of forested lands. Since more timber means more profits, efficient techniques to boost yield become very attractive to private forest owners. A great deal of progress has been made in this area since World War II when scientific forestry began to have an impact. New strains of fast-growing, disease resistant trees have been developed. Restocking, pest control, and general management techniques have improved. In principle, markets provide a simple means to achieve efficient forest management.

In practice, however, market allocations are less than perfect, even when the sale of timber is the only objective. An analysis by Marion Clawson indicates

---

9 James Gustave Spaeth, "Coming to Terms: Toward a North-South Bargain for the Environment," *World Resources Institute Issues and Ideas* (June, 1989): 4.

that scale is an important element of achieving efficient forest management.[10] On very small holdings it does not pay for the owner to invest the time or money to become informed about good forestry practices, much less implement them. Harvesting equipment is large and expensive. Small owners may have poor access to markets due in part to their infrequent use of them. Furthermore, for many of these holdings the ownership of forest land is incidental to some other activity, so the owner has no intention of maximizing profit from timber harvest. The evidence suggests that these lands are not efficiently managed.

In the United States, plots of under 100 acres comprise about one-third of all private forests. Another third is held in plots containing from 100 to 5000 acres, considered by Clawson to have no better than fair economic prospects. Despite the amount of forested land tied up in these relatively small holdings, collectively they yield relatively little harvested timber.

In addition, the price expectations which motivate private harvesting behavior may not be accurate. To the extent that forest owners incorrectly anticipate future prices, their decisions will not be accurate.

Bearing external costs is another problem faced by private managers. Private forest decisions are plagued by externally generated costs of various types. Yields are adversely affected by externally imposed costs, such as air pollution (Example 11.1). When heavy investments in forested lands can be wiped out by factors totally out of the control of the owners, the incentive to invest is undermined.

Providing a sustainable flow of timber, however, is not the sole purpose of the forest. When the act of harvesting timber imposes costs on other valued aspects of the forest (such as watershed maintenance, prevention of soil erosion, protection of biodiversity, etc.), these may not be (and normally will not be) adequately considered in the decision.

The value of the standing forest as wildlife habitat or as a key element in the local ecosystem is one external cost that can lead to an inefficient harvesting decision. The controversy that erupted in the Pacific Northwest of the United States between environmentalists and loggers can in part be explained by the different values these two groups put on habitat destruction. This region contains a number of old-growth Douglas firs which can reach a height of 30 stories. These 200-year-old trees would be very valuable sources of timber, but they are also important components of the local ecosystem. (Among other ecosystem contributions these trees provide a home for the endangered northern spotted owl.)

---

10 Marion Clawson, *America's Land and Its Uses* (Washington, DC: Resources for the Future, 1972) and *Forests For Whom and For What?* (Washington, DC: Resources for the Future, 1975).

EXAMPLE 11.1

Externalities in Forest Management: *Waldsterben*

When the first signs of forest death began to show up in the forests of western Germany, it was widely assumed that it was the spreading of a white fir decline that had been periodically decimating fir forests in Central Europe for the past 250 years. By the late 1970s, however, when Norway spruce began dying as well, it became apparent to scientists that they were being faced with an unprecedented situation of mass devastation, a situation known in German as *Waldsterben.*

It is spreading rapidly. In 1982, the government of the Federal Republic of Germany estimated that about 8% of its forests were damaged. By 1985, a repeat survey discovered that some 52% of the stands were affected. Among white firs more than 60 years old, some 95% exhibit visible symptoms of decline. The damage is particularly acute in the Black and Bavarian Forests. In 1985, the Union of German Forest Owners estimated the annual costs of *Waldsterben* at some $1 billion a year if present trends continue as expected.

Based on the perplexing array of symptoms, as well as the rapidity with which it is moving through forests, scientists now believe that multiple causes are involved. Early speculation that it was acid rain now seems too simple to explain the magnitude of the destruction. Most current scientific hypotheses about the causes involve the interactions of several pollutants, including nitrogen and sulfur compounds, ozone, aluminum, and a variety of organic chemicals such as ethylene or aniline.

Waldsterben is a good example of the policymaker's dilemma. The destruction is widespread and increasing rapidly, but considerable scientific uncertainty exists about the specific causes. Although the costs of inaction are apparently very high, with so many suspects to choose from, it is hard to formulate an effective control strategy. Meanwhile foresters helplessly watch as their resource bases dwindle due to factors entirely beyond their control.

Source: Don Hinrichsen, "Waldsterben: Forest Death Syndrome," *The Amicus Journal* (Spring 1986): 23–27.

Perverse incentives can be created by governments as well. The rapid rate of deforestation in Brazil is in no small part due to perverse incentives created by the Brazilian government.[11]

---

11 For further details on the Brazilian situation, see Hans P. Binswanger, "Brazilian Policies That Encourage Deforestation in the Amazon," World Bank Working Paper No. 16 (April 1989) and Dennis J. Mahar, *Government Policies and Deforestation on Brazil's Amazon Region* (Washington, DC: World Bank, 1989).

The Brazilian government has reduced taxes on income derived from agriculture by as much as 90%. This tax discrimination overvalues agriculture and makes it profitable to cut down forests and convert the land to agriculture even when, in the absence of discriminatory tax relief, agriculture in these regions would not be profitable. In addition land taxes discriminate against forests. A farm containing forests is taxed at a higher rate than one containing only pastures or crop land.[12] This system of taxation encourages higher than efficient rates of conversion of land from forests to pasture or cropland and subsidizes an activity which, in the absence of tax discrimination, would not normally be economically viable. In essence, Brazilian taxpayers are subsidizing deforestation.

The system of property rights over land also is at fault. How do individuals establish a solid claim to unclaimed land in Brazil? Acquiring land by squatting has been formally recognized in Brazil since 1850. A squatter acquires a usufruct right (the right to continue using the land) by living on a plot of unclaimed public land and using it "effectively" for at least a year and a day. If the two above conditions are met for five years, the squatter acquires ownership of the land, including the right to transfer it to others. A claimant gets title for an amount of land up to three times the amount cleared of forest; the more deforestation the squatter engages in, the larger the amount of land acquired! In effect, deforestation is a necessary step for landless peasants to acquire land.

In the Far East and in the United States perverse incentives take another form. Logging is the major source of deforestation in both regions. Why don't loggers act efficiently? The sources of inefficiency can be found in the concession agreements, which define the terms under which public forests can be harvested.

To loggers existing forests have a substantial advantage over new forests; they can be harvested immediately. This advantage is reflected in the economic rent (called stumpage value in the industry) associated with a standing forest. In principle governments have a variety of policy instruments at their disposal to extract this rent from the concessionaires, but they have typically given out the concessions to harvest this timber without capturing anywhere near all of the rent.[13] The result is that the cost of harvesting is artificially reduced and loggers can afford to harvest much more forestland than would be efficient. The failure of government to capture this rent also means that the wealth tied up in these

---

12 Much of this land was apparently used to raise beef for export to the United States for use in fast-food hamburgers. For more on the hamburger connection, see J. O. Browder, "The Social Costs of Rain Forest Destruction: A Critique and Analysis of the Hamburger Debate," *InterCiencia* 13 (1988): 115–120, and C. Uhl, "Our Steak in the Jungle," *Bioscience* 35 (1986): 642.

13 One way for the government to capture this rent would be for the government to put timber concessions up for bid. Bidders would have an incentive to pay up to the stumpage value for these concessions. The more competitive the bidding was, the higher the likelihood that the government would capture all of the rent. In practice many of the concessions have been given to those with influence in the government at far below market rates. See Jeffrey R. Vincent, "Rent Capture and the Feasibility of Tropical Forest Management," *Land Economics* 66 (May 1990): 212–223.

forests has typically gone to a few, now-wealthy individuals and corporations rather than to the government to be used for the alleviation of poverty or other worthy social objectives.

Because forest concessions are typically for limited terms, the concession holders have little incentive to replant, to exercise care in their logging procedures, or even to conserve younger trees until they reach the efficient harvest age. The future value of the forest will not be theirs to capture. The resulting logging practices destroy a multiple of the number of trees represented by the high-value species due to the destruction of surrounding species by the construction of access roads, the felling and dragging of the trees, and the elimination of the protective canopy. While for many of these nations sustainable forestry would be possible, concession agreements such as these make it unlikely.[14]

The list of losers from inefficient forestry practices frequently includes indigenous peoples who have lived in and derived their livelihood from these forests for a very long time. As the loggers and squatters push deeper and deeper into forests, the indigenous people who lack the power to stem the tide are forced to relocate further and further away from their traditional lands.

IMPLEMENTING EFFICIENT MANAGEMENT

Does ownership of forest by the government provide an answer? With the large amount of resources at its disposal, plus the ability to acquire land through eminent domain proceedings, the government can achieve the efficient scale rather easily. Furthermore, since it is not obligated to maximize profits, it can more easily take external effects on wildlife or recreation into account. Unfortunately, if the U.S. experience is typical, the potential to solve these problems by public ownership is more illusory than real.

Public ownership of lands in the United States started even before the fledgling nation had a constitution. The first public land, much of it forest land, was accepted as a donation by the Confederation of Congress on October 29, 1782. Though these lands were owned by the government, they were not managed by the government until more than a century later. The forest was treated as common property.

By the second half of the nineteenth century, a number of voices began to decry the apparent wanton destruction of the forests and to call for more en-

---

14 Currently, foresters believe that the sustainable yield for closed tropical rainforests is zero, because they have not yet learned how to regenerate the species in a harvested area. Destroying the thick canopy, thereby allowing the light to penetrate, so changes the growing conditions and the nutrient levels of the soil that even replanting is unlikely to regenerate the types of trees included in the harvest.

lightened use of the resource. The first piece of legislation designed to respond to this outcry was the Forest Reserve Act of 1891, which authorized the first permanent system of forest reserves. No provision for private harvesting of trees on the forest reserves was included. It was not until 1897, with the passage of a general administration bill, that Congress provided the funds and a process to manage this system. This act authorized private harvesting on forest reserves under other restrictive conditions.

The management for these reserves was transferred in 1905 to the U.S. Department of Agriculture's Forest Service. The Weeks Act, passed in 1911, enabled the Forest Service to acquire new forest land, which ultimately became a major part of the national forests in the eastern part of the United States.

The ambitious chief of the USDA Forest Service at that time, Gifford Pinchot, was to have an enormous influence over Forest Service management for several decades. Unlike other contemporaries such as John Muir, who wanted to withdraw these lands from use, Pinchot vigorously pursued a philosophy that they should be used. Focusing first on timber production, his goal was the promotion of a sustainable level of harvest from the national forests. Concern over wildlife and recreation would come much later.

The desire for the maintenance of a sustained level of harvest gave rise to the acceptance of a number of operation procedures by the Forest Service which were explicitly biologically based. Chief among these were the maximum average annual increment described above and the requirement to keep the allowable cut on the national forests steady through time to reduce the potential instability faced by private forest owners caused by flooding the market with timber from the public lands.

Although the Forest Service had to some extent followed a multiple-use philosophy since its inception, in the period following World War II public interest in nontimber uses grew sufficiently that the rather ad hoc methods of the Forest Service for achieving a balance were no longer deemed sufficient. During the 1960s and 1970s, a significant amount of new legislation was passed (Table 11.3).

The Multiple-Use Sustained Yield Act mandated a multiple-use philosophy, without giving a lot of guidance on how to implement that philosophy. In part, this act had been sought by the Forest Service to protect its multiple-use philosophy from attack by those seeking Congressional or judicial support for single interests. Subsequent legislation, however, would force the Forest Service to be much more systematic in how it sought to define and implement a multiple-use philosophy.

The Wilderness Act set aside specific forest areas to be preserved in their pristine state. No roads were permitted and timber harvests were prohibited in wilderness areas. Although initially limited to designating specific areas that had by tradition not been harvested, the act has in fact ushered in much more wilderness land than was envisioned by those discussing it in Congress at the time the bill was passed.

TABLE 11.3   Major U.S. Forest Legislation

Date and citation	Popular name	Major provisions
March 3, 1891 26 Stat. 1095	Forest Reserve Act of 1891	Authorized first system of national permanent forest reserves.
June 12, 1960 74 Stat. 215	Multiple-Use Sustained Yield Act	Provided legislative mandate for multiple use of forestlands. No guidance on policy issues or management strategies.
Sept. 3, 1964 78 Stat. 890	The Wilderness Act of 1964	Designate initial areas to be included as wilderness areas and set stringent rules governing use.
Aug. 17, 1974 88 Stat. 476	Forest and Rangeland Renewable Resources Planning Act	A planning act, requiring an assessment of all renewable resources every 10 years and a program for the national forests every 5 years.

Though the management of public forests in the United States has been evolving since 1782, it has not yet reached the point where it yields efficient outcomes. Harvests from the public forests are subsidized by taxpayers.[15] The benefits of the forests to wildife and recreation are inadequately protected.[16] Too many political pressures influence the process. Other policy approaches offer the prospect of a more rapid transition to efficiency.

One such approach involves restoring efficient incentives. Concessionaires should pay the full cost for their rights to harvest publicly controlled lands, including compensating for damage to the forests surrounding the trees of interest. The magnitude of land transferred to squatters should not be a multiple of the amount of cleared forest. The rights of indigenous peoples should be respected.

---

15 A review of several studies estimating the size of these subsidies can be found in Robert Repetto, *The Forest for the Trees? Government Policies and the Misuse of Forest Resources* (Washington, DC: World Resources Institute, 1988): 90–98.

16 The below-cost sales of timber to harvesters is usually justified by the Forest Service in terms of the associated public benefits of harvesting (enhanced recreation opportunities and wildlife protection). This argument is difficult to accept since, as Robert Repetto puts it, "The supposed beneficiaries, including both environmental groups and fish and wildlife agencies in affected states, loudly oppose and are suing the Forest Service to stop it from providing the benefits they are allegedly receiving." (op. cit., p. 97).

Most of these changes could be implemented by individual nations to protect their own forests. And to do so would be in their interests. By definition inefficient practices cost more than the benefits received. The move to a more efficient set of policies would necessarily generate more net benefits, which could be shared in ways that build political support for the change. But what about the global inefficiencies? How can those be resolved?

Several economic strategies exist. They share the characteristic that they all involve compensating the nations conferring external benefits so as to encourage conservation actions consistent with global efficiency.

Debt-Nature Swaps. One strategy involves reducing the pressure on the forests caused by the international debt owed by many developing countries. Private banks hold most of the debt, and they are not typically motivated by a desire to protect biodiversity. Nonetheless it is possible to find some common ground for negotiating strategies to reduce the debt. Banks realize that complete repayment of the loans is probably not possible. Rather than completely write off the loans, an action which not only causes harm to the income statement but creates adverse incentives for repayment of future loans, they are willing to consider alternative strategies.

One of the more innovative policies that explores common ground in international arrangements has become known as the debt-nature swap. It is innovative in two senses: (1) the uniqueness of the policy instrument and (2) the direct involvement of nongovernmental organizations in implementing the policy. A debt-nature swap involves the purchase (at a discounted value in the secondary debt market) of a developing country debt usually by a nongovernmental environmental organization (ngo). The new holder of the debt, the ngo, offers to cancel the debt in return for an environmentally related action on the part of the debtor nation. In July 1987, for example, an American environmental organization purchased $650,000 worth of Bolivia's foreign debt from a private bank at a discounted price of $100,000. It then swapped the face value of the debt with the government of Bolivia in return for an agreement to put together a public-private partnership. This partnership would develop a program that combines ecosystem conservation and regional development planning in 3.7 million acres of designated tropical forestland. The agreement also includes a $250,000 fund in local currency for establishing and administering a system for protecting the forest reserve.

Other arrangements involving different governments and different environmental organizations have since followed this lead. The main advantage of these arrangements to the debtor nation is that a significant foreign exchange obligation can be paid off with domestic currency. Debt-nature swaps offer the realistic possibility to turn what has been a major force for unsustainable economic activity (the debt crisis) into a force for resource conservation.

Extractive Reserves. One strategy designed to protect the indigenous people of the forest as well as to prevent deforestation involves the establishment of extractive reserves. These areas would be reserved for the indigenous people to engage in the traditional hunting, gathering activities.

Extractive reserves have already been established in the Acre region of Brazil. Acre's main activity comes from the thousands of men who tap the rubber trees scattered throughout the forest, a practice dating back 100 years. Under the leadership of Chico Mendes, a leader of the tappers who was subsequently assassinated, four extractive reserves were established in June 1988 by the Brazilian government to protect the rubber tappers from encroaching development.

Establishing Conservation Easements. A common global fund could be established to receive and dispense revenue raised in the industrialized nations for the purpose of protecting biodiversity. Controlled by representatives of the signatory nations, this fund could conceivably dispense funds for acquiring conservation easements for ecologically valuable sites. Conservation easements restrict the activities which can be permitted on the land. In the context of a tropical forest, a conservation easement would allow traditional uses of the forest by indigenous people, but clear-cutting would be prohibited. The easement could be granted in perpetuity or for a very long time.

One specific proposal on how this might be accomplished has been put forward by Katzman and Cale.[17] Five characteristics undergird their proposal:

1. Tropical nations would establish a legal distinction between conservation easements and other claims of ownership to forests to ensure enforceability of the easement.

2. Industrialized nations would prioritize and evaluate habitats globally to ensure that the expended funds achieved the maximum net benefits.

3. Each tropical nation would establish an offering price for conservation easements on various habitats; in essence they would compete for the limited funds.

4. Industrialized nations would agree to a budget for the acquisition of easements and for enforcement and to a means for financing that budget.

5. A foundation would be established in each tropical nation to administer the financial transfer and to oversee the administration of the easement. (Unlike extractive reserves where the easement is implicitly held by the tropical state, the conservation easement is granted to a foundation.)

---

17 Martin T. Katzman and William G. Cale, Jr., "Harnessing Tropical Forest Preservation to Economic Incentives," *Bioscience* (Forthcoming). Also see the related proposal in I. Rubinoff, "A Strategy for Preserving Tropical Rainforests" *Ambio* 12 (1983): 255–258.

One interesting precedent which shares some, but not all, of the attributes of this proposal, is the World Heritage Convention. This convention established a World Heritage Fund, which is used to protect environments of "outstanding universal value." Each signatory is required to contribute at least 1% of its contribution to the regular budget of UNESCO to the fund every two years. In practice this means that the fund is financed almost entirely by the industrial nations, but smaller nations can tap its resources. Some 57 natural sites are currently within this system, 25 of them in the tropics.

Some 90 nations have signed this agreement, suggesting that the fund arrangements have successfully exploited some common interests. Since subscribing to the agreement apparently confers benefits on the signatories, it is essentially self-enforcing. Other groups are pursuing similar objectives (Example 11.2).

Debt-nature swaps, extractive reserves, and conservation easements all involve a recognition of the fact that resolving the global externalities component of deforestation requires a rather different approach than resolving the other aspects of the deforestation problem. In general this approach involves financial transfers from the industrialized nations to the tropical nations, transfers which are constructed so as to incorporate global interests into decisions about the future of tropical forests.

SUMMARY

Forests represent an example of a storable, renewable source. Typically tree stands go through three distinct growth phases—slow growth in volume in the early stage, followed by rapid growth in the middle years and slower growth as the stand reaches full maturity. The owner who harvests the timber receives the income from its sale, but the owner who delays harvest will receive additional growth. The amount of growth depends on the part of the growth cycle the stand is in.

From an economic point of view, the efficient time to harvest a stand of timber is when the present value of net benefits is maximized. The present value of net benefits is maximized when the marginal gain from delaying the harvest one more year is equal to the marginal cost of the delay. For longer-than-efficient delays the additional costs outweigh the increased benefits, while for earlier-than-efficient harvests more benefits (in terms of the increased value of the timber) are given up than costs saved. Typically the efficient age at harvest is 25 years or older.

The efficient harvest age depends on the circumstances the owner faces. When the plot is to be left fallow after the harvest, the efficient harvest occurs later than when the land is immediately replanted to initiate another cycle. With immediate replanting, delaying the harvest imposes an additional cost—the cost

EXAMPLE 11.2

Success Stories in Conserving Tropical Forests

It is easy to lose sight of the positive steps that are being taking while concentrating on the problem of tropical deforestation. But some success are apparent as well. Some of these include

- UNESCO's Man and Biosphere Program, which protects 244 biosphere reserves in 65 countries, 59 of them in 29 tropical countries.
- Brazil's protected area system, which includes more than 12 million hectares of parks, biological reserves, forest reserves, hunting parks, game farms, and private reserves.
- More than 500 conservation areas in Indonesia.
- Peru's system of more than 20 parks and other protected areas adding up to more than 4.3 million hectares; four of the largest conservation areas are in tropical forests.
- Private reserve systems modeled after those in the developed countries (see Example 3.2) are now beginning in several developing countries such as Venezuela, Indonesia, and Costa Rica.

Source: Laural Tangley, "Saving Tropical Forests," *Bioscience* 36 (January 1986): 4–8.

of delaying the next harvest—which, when factored into the analysis, makes it more desirable to harvest earlier.

A number of other factors affect the size of the efficient rotation as well. In general the larger the discount rate the earlier the harvest. With an infinite-planning horizon model increases in planting and harvesting costs tend to lengthen the optimal rotation, while in a single-harvest model they have no effect on the length of the efficient rotation. If the price of timber grows at a constant rate over time, the efficient rotation is longer than if prices remain constant over time. Finally if standing timber provides amenity services (such as for recreation or wildlife management) in proportion to the volume of the standing timber, the efficient rotation will be longer than it would in the absence of any amenity services.

Profit maximization can be compatible with efficient forest management under the right circumstances. In particular, profit-maximizing private owners have an incentive to adopt the efficient rotation when amenity services are small and to undertake investments which increase the yield of the forest.

In reality, not all private firms will follow efficient forest management practices because they may choose not to maximize profits, they may be operating at too small a scale of operation, or externalities may create inefficient incentives. Many forest owners are simply not acting like profit maximizers. Even if they were, small-scale plots cannot normally be operated efficiently because of the importance of economies of scale both in learning about scientific forestry and in implementing it. The costs of acquiring this knowledge and putting it into practice may be so large as to eliminate any potential benefits. Finally, when amenity values are large and not captured by the forest owner, the private rotation period may fail to consider these values, leading to an inefficiently short rotation period.

Inefficient deforestation has been encouraged by a failure to incorporate global benefits from standing forests, by concession agreements which provide incentives to harvest too much, too soon, and which fail to provide adequate incentives to protect the interests of future generations, by land property right systems that make the amount of land acquired by squatters a multiple of cleared forestland, and by tax systems which discriminate against standing forests.

Substantial strides toward restoring efficiency can be achieved simply by recognizing and correcting the perverse incentives, actions which can be and should be taken by the tropical forest nations. But these actions will not, by themselves, provide adequate protection for the global interests in the tropical forests. Three schemes designed to internalize some of these benefits—debt-nature swaps, extractive reserves, and conservation easements—have already begun to be implemented.

FURTHER READING

Bowes, Michael D. and John V. Krutilla. "Multiple Use Management of Public Forestlands," in *Handbook of Natural Resource and Energy Economics, Vol. 11*, Allen V. Kneese and James L. Sweeney, eds. (Amsterdam: North-Holland, 1985). Excellent analytical treatment of the multiple-use strategy as it applies to U.S. forest policy. Somewhat mathematical.

Clawson, Marion. *The Federal Lands Revisited* (Washington, DC: Resources for the Future, Inc., 1983). A comprehensive overview of current policy issues related to federally owned lands in the United States, including but not limited to national forests.

Clawson, Marion. "Private Forests," in *Current Issues in Natural Resource Policy*, Paul R. Portney, ed. (Washington, DC: Resources for the Future, 1982): 283-292. A short summary of the problems of and the prospects for U.S. private forests.

Deacon, R. T. "The Simple Analytics of Forest Economics," in *Forestlands: Public and Private*, R. T. Deacon and M. B. Johnson, eds. (San Francisco: Pacific Institute for Public Policy Research, 1985). An especially accessible treatment of forestry economics.

Gregory, G. Robinson. *Resource Economics for Foresters* (New York: Wiley, 1987). Undergraduate text in forest economics that could be used to go beyond the material in this chapter.

Irland, Lloyd C. *Wilderness Economics and Policy* (Lexington, MA: Lexington Books, 1979). An overview of wilderness policy in the United States and how economic analysis can contribute to a clearer understanding of the issues.

Price, Colin. *The Theory and Application of Forest Economics* (Oxford: Basil Blackwell, 1989). A text aimed at "students of forestry and of natural resource management at both undergraduate and graduate levels."

Repetto, Robert. *The Forest for the Trees? Government Policies and the Misuse of Forest Resources* (Washington, DC: World Resources Institute, 1988). A highly recommended study of forestry practices in several different countries.

ADDITIONAL REFERENCES

Berck, P. "Optimal Management of Renewable Resources with Growing Demand and Stock Externalities," *Journal of Environmental Economics and Management* 8 (1981): 105-117.

Clawson, Marion. *America's Land and Its Uses* (Washington, DC: Resources for the Future, 1972).

Clawson, Marion. "Decision-Making in Timber Production, Harvest, and Marketing," Research Paper R-4 (Washington, DC: Resources for the Future, 1977).

Clawson, Marion. *Forests For Whom and For What?* (Washington, DC: Resources for the Future, 1975).

Hartman, R. "The Harvesting Decision When a Standing Forest Has Value," *Economic Inquiry* 14 (1976): 52-58.

Hyde, William F. *Timber Supply, Land Allocation, and Economic Efficiency* (Washington, DC: Resources for the Future, 1980).

Johansson, Per-Olov. *Economics of Forestry and Natural Resources* (New York: Basil Blackwell, 1985).

Merrifield, David E. and Richard W. Hayes. "The Adjustment of Product and Factor Markets: An Application to the Pacific Northwest Forest Products Industry," *American Journal of Agricultural Economics* 66 (February 1984): 79-87.

Repetto, R. and M. Gillis, eds. *Public Policy and the Misuse of Forest Resources* (Cambridge, UK: Cambridge University Press, 1988).

Samuelson, Paul A. "Economics of Forestry in an Evolving Society," *Economic Inquiry* 14 (1976): 466-492.

DISCUSSION QUESTIONS

1. Should the U.S. national forests become "privatized" (sold to private owners)? Why or why not?

2. In his book *The Federal Land Revisited,* Marion Clawson proposed what he called the "pullback concept":

> Under the pullback concept any person or group could apply, under applicable law, for a tract of federal land, for any use they chose; but any other person or group would have a limited time between the filing of the initial application and granting other lease or the making of the sale in which to "pull back" a part of the area applied for . . . The user of the pullback provision would become the applicant for the area pulled back, required to meet the same terms applicable to the original application, . . . but the use could be what the applicant chose, not necessarily the use proposed by the original applicant (p. 216).

   Evaluate the pullback concept as a means for conservationists to prevent some mineral extraction or timber harvesting on federal lands.

PROBLEMS

1. Suppose there are two forest plots which are identical except that one will be harvested and left while the second will be cleared after the harvest and turned into a housing development. In terms of efficiency, which should have the oldest harvest age? Why?

2. In Table 11.2 when $r = 0.02$, the present value of the cost rises for 68 years and then subsequently declines. Why?

CHAPTER TWELVE

Renewable Common-Property Resources: Fisheries and Other Species

In an overpopulated (or overexploited) world, a system of the commons leads to ruin.... Even if an individual fully perceives the ultimate consequences of his actions he is most unlikely to act in any other way, for he cannot count on the restraint his conscience might dictate being matched by a similar restraint on the part of all others.

GARRETT HARDIN,
Carrying Capacity as an Ethical Concept (1967)

INTRODUCTION

Renewable resources are those for which the stock can be continually replenished. It is easy to think of renewable resources as perpetual. If this were automatically the case, we could merely assure ourselves that the market would ultimately make a smooth transition from depletable to renewable resources. But that is an overly simple view! Some renewable resources—living populations, such as plants and animals—are also exhaustible if not managed effectively. The growth or decline of these populations in general depends on the size of the population. If, through human activities, the population is drawn down beyond a critical threshold, the species can become extinct.

Extinction, though important, is not the only critical renewable resource-management issue. If it were, public policy could concentrate on avoiding ex-

TABLE 12.1   Total World Fish Catch and Per Capita Fish Catch 1960–86

	Fish catch [a] (million metric tons)	Fish catch per capita [b] (pounds)
1950	20,140	8.0
1955	27,940	10.1
1960	39,500	13.1
1965	53,700	16.1
1970	70,700	19.1
1975	71,000	17.4
1980	72,127	16.2
1985	85,686	17.7
1986	91,456	18.6

Sources: [a] Department of International Economics and Social Affairs Statistical Office, *Statistical Yearbook* (New York: Publishing Service, United Nations), various years.

[b] Calculated by author using population figures from the *Demographic Yearbook* (New York: Publishing Service, United Nations), various years.

tinction and not concern itself with any other outcome. Biological populations belong to a class of renewable resources we will call *interactive resources*, wherein the size of the resource stock (population) is determined jointly by biological considerations and by actions taken by society. The size of the population, in turn, determines the availability of the resources for the future. Thus humanity's actions determine the flow of these resources over time. Since this flow is not purely a natural phenomenon, a second crucial dimension is the optimum rate of use across time and across generations. What is the efficient rate of use of interactive renewable resources? In the absence of outside influences, can the market be relied upon to achieve and sustain this rate?

In an often-cited book published during the early 1970s, Lester Brown caught the world's attention with his statement that the world's fish catch had started to decline, thus ushering in a new age of scarcity.[1] Although this decline in total catch turned out to be temporary, during the 1970s the fish catch did not keep pace with population growth. The continuation of this trend depends on whether fisheries will be more effectively managed in the future (Table 12.1).

Fisheries are interesting not only because they are an important source of protein,[2] but also because they provide a rich and varied introduction to the problems of managing biological common-property resources. To capitalize on both the transferability of insights derived from an analysis of fisheries and the

1 Lester Brown, *In the Human Interest* (New York: W. W. Norton, 1974).

2 Some countries, such as Japan and Portugal, obtain more than half of their animal protein from fish.

wealth of analysis which already exists, we shall use the economics of fisheries management as a case study.

We begin by defining what is meant by an efficient allocation of the catch from a fishery; we can then examine how the market allocates this common-property resource and the past and potential roles for public policies in the quest for efficient and sustainable management. At the end of the chapter we briefly show how the basic analytical principles of fisheries management could be used for the management of other biological populations.

EFFICIENT ALLOCATIONS

The Biological Dimension

Like many other studies, our characterization of the fishery rests on a biological model originally proposed by Schaefer.[3] The Schaefer model posits a particular average relationship between the growth of the fish population and the size of the fish population. This is an average relationship in the sense that it abstracts from such influences as water temperature and the age structure of the population. The model therefore does not attempt to characterize the fishery on a day-to-day basis, but rather in terms of some long-term average in which these various random influences tend to counterbalance each other (Figure 12.1).

The size of the population is represented on the horizontal axis and the growth of the population on the vertical axis. The graph suggests that there is a range of population sizes ($\underline{S}$ to S^*) where population growth increases as the population increases and a range (S^* to $\overline{S}$) where initial increases in population lead to eventual declines in growth.

We can shed further light on this relationship by examining more closely the two points ($\underline{S}$ and $\overline{S}$) where the function intersects the horizontal axis and therefore growth in the stock is zero. $\overline{S}$ is known as the *natural equilibrium*, since this is population size which would persist in the absence of outside influences. Reductions in the stock due to mortality or out-migration would be exactly offset by increases in the stock due to births, growth of the fish in the remaining stock, and in-migration.

This natural equilibrium would persist because it is stable. A *stable equilibrium* is one in which movements away from this population level set forces in motion to restore it. If, for example, the stock temporarily exceeded $\overline{S}$, it would

3 M. D. Schaefer, "Some Considerations of Population Dynamics and Economics in Relation to the Management of Marine Fisheries," *Journal of the Fisheries Research Board of Canada* 14 (1957): 669–681.

FIGURE 12.1   Relationship between the fish population and growth.

be exceeding the capacity of its habitat (called carrying capacity). As a result, mortality rates or out-migration would increase until the stock was once again within the confines of the carrying capacity of its habitat at $\bar{S}$.

This tendency for the population size to return to $\bar{S}$ works in the other direction as well. Suppose the population is temporarily reduced below $\bar{S}$. Because the stock is now smaller, growth would be positive and the size of the stock would increase. Over time, the fishery would move along the curve to the right until $\bar{S}$ is reached again.

What about the other points on the curve? $\underline{S}$, known as the *minimum viable population*, represents the level of population below which growth in population is negative (deaths and out-migration exceed births and in-migration). In contrast to $\bar{S}$, this equilibrium is unstable. Population sizes to the right of $\underline{S}$ lead to positive growth and a movement along the curve to $\bar{S}$ and away from $\underline{S}$. When the population moves to the left of $\underline{S}$, the population declines until it eventually becomes extinct. In this region no forces act to return the population to a viable level.

A catch level is said to represent a *sustainable yield* whenever it equals the growth rate of the population, since it can be maintained forever. As long as the population size remains constant, the growth rate (and hence the catch) will remain constant as well.

S^* is known in biology as the *maximum sustainable yield* population, defined as that population size which yields the maximum growth; hence, the maximum sustainable yield is equal to this maximum growth and it represents the largest catch that can be perpetually sustained. If the catch is equal to the growth, the sustainable yield for any population size (between $\underline{S}$ and $\bar{S}$ can be determined by drawing a vertical line from the stock size of interest on the horizontal axis to the point where it intersects the function and the drawing a horizontal line over to the vertical axis. The sustainable yield is the growth in the biomass defined by the intersection of this line with the vertical axis. Thus, in terms of Figure 12.1, $G(S^0)$ is the sustainable yield for population size S^0. Since the catch is equal to the growth, population size (and next year's growth) remains the same.

It should now be clear why $G(S^*)$ is the maximum sustainable yield. Larger catches would be possible in the short run, but these could not be sustained; they would lead to reduced population sizes and eventually, if the population were drawn down to a level smaller than $\underline{S}$, to the extinction of the species.

Static Efficient Sustained Yield

Is the maximum sustainable yield synonymous with efficiency? The answer is no. Efficiency, it may be remembered, is associated with maximizing the net benefit from the use of the resource. If we are to define the efficient allocation, we must include the costs of harvesting as well as the benefits.

Let's begin by defining the efficient sustainable yield without worrying about discounting. The static efficient sustainable yield is the catch level which, if maintained perpetually, would produce the largest annual net benefit. We shall refer to this as the *static efficient* sustainable yield to distinguish it from the *dynamic efficient* sustainable yield, which incorporates discounting. The initial use of this static concept enables us to fix the necessary relationships firmly in mind before dealing with the more difficult role discounting plays. Subsequently, we raise the question of whether or not efficiency always dictates the choice of a sustainable yield as opposed to a catch that changes over time.

We condition our analysis on three assumptions that simplify the analysis without sacrificing too much realism: (1) the price of fish is constant and does not depend on the amount sold; (2) the marginal cost of a unit of fishing effort is constant; and (3) the amount of fish caught per unit of effort expended is proportional to the size of fish population (the smaller the population, the fewer fish caught per unit of effort).

In any sustainable yield, catches, population, effort levels, and net benefits remain constant over time. The static efficient sustainable yield allocation maximizes the constant net benefit.

In Figure 12.2, the benefits (revenues) and costs are portrayed as a function of fishing effort and can be measured in vessel years, hours of fishing, or some other convenient metric. The shape of the revenue function is dictated by the shape of the function in Figure 12.1, since the price of fish is assumed constant. To avoid confusion, notice that increasing fishing effort in Figure 12.1 would result in smaller population sizes and would be recorded as a movement from

FIGURE 12.2   Efficient sustainable yield for a fishery.

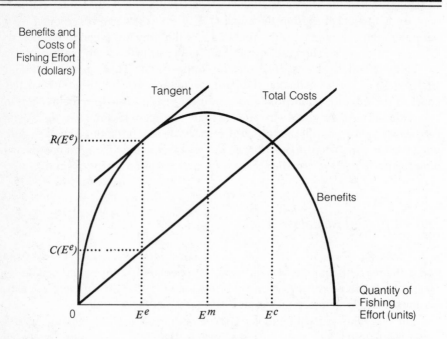

right to left. Because the variable on the horizontal axis in Figure 12.2 is effort, and not population, an increase in fishing effort is recorded as a movement from left to right.

As sustained levels of effort are increased, eventually a point is reached (E^m) where further effort reduces the sustainable catch and revenue for all years. That point, of course, corresponds to the maximum sustainable yield on Figure 12.2, which involves identical population and growth levels. Every effort level portrayed in Figure 12.2 corresponds to a population level in Figure 12.1.

The net benefit is presented in the diagram as the difference (vertical distance) between benefits (prices times the quantity caught) and costs (the constant marginal cost of effort times the units of effort expended). The efficient level of effort is E^e, that point in Figure 12.2 where the vertical distance between benefits and costs is maximized.

E^e is the efficient level of effort because it is where marginal benefit (which graphically is the slope of the total benefit curve) is equal to marginal cost (the *constant* slope of the total cost curve). Levels of effort higher than E^e are inefficient because the additional cost associated with them exceeds the value of the fish obtained. Can you see why lower levels of effort are inefficient?

Now we are armed with sufficient information to determine whether or not the maximum sustainable yield is efficient. The answer is clearly no. The maximum sustainable yield would be efficient only if the marginal cost of additional effort were zero. Can you see why? (Hint: What is the marginal benefit at the maximum sustainable yield?) Since this is not the case, the efficient level of effort is *less* than that necessary to harvest the maximum sustainable yield. Thus, the static efficient level of effort leads to a *larger* fish population than the maximum sustainable yield level of effort.

To fix these concepts firmly in mind, consider what would happen to the static efficient sustainable yield if a technological change were to occur (e.g., sonar detection) lowering the marginal cost of fishing. The lower marginal cost would result in a rotation of the total cost curve to the right. With this new cost structure, the old level of effort is no longer efficient. The marginal cost of fishing (slope of the total cost curve) is now lower than the marginal benefit (slope of the total benefit curve). Since the marginal cost is constant, the equality of marginal cost and marginal benefit can only result from a decline in marginal benefits. This implies an increase in effort. The new static efficient sustainable yield equilibrium implies more effort, a lower population level, a larger catch, and a higher net benefit for the fishery.

Dynamic Efficient Sustainable Yield

The static efficient sustainable yield turns out to be the special case of the dynamic efficient sustained yield where the discount rate is zero. It is not difficult to understand why; the static efficient sustained yield is the allocation which maximizes the (identical) net benefit in every period. Any higher effort levels than this would yield temporarily larger catches (and net benefit) but this would be more than offset by a reduced net benefit in the future as the stock reached its new lower level. Thus, the undiscounted net benefits would be reduced.

The effect of a positive discount rate for the management of a fishery is similar to its influence on the allocation of depletable resources—the higher the discount rate, the higher the cost (in terms of forgone current income) to the resource owner of maintaining any given resource stock. When positive discount rates are introduced, the efficient level of effort would be increased beyond that suggested by the static efficient sustained yield with a corresponding decrease in the equilibrium population level.

The increase in the yearly effort beyond the efficient sustained yield level would *initially* result in an increased net benefit from the increased catch. (Remember that the amount of fish caught per unit effort expended is proportional to the size of the population.) However, since this catch exceeds the sustained yield for that population size, the population of fish would be reduced and future population and catch levels would be lower. Eventually, as that level of effort is maintained, a new lower equilibrium level would be attained when the size of the catch once again equals the growth of the population. Colin Clark has shown mathematically that in terms of Figure 12.2, as the discount rate is increased, the dynamic efficient level of effort is increased until, with an infinite discount rate, it becomes equal to E^c, the point at which net benefits go to zero.[4]

It is easy to see why the use of an infinite discount rate to define the dynamic-efficient sustained yield results in allocation E^c. We have seen that interdependent allocations over time give rise to a marginal user cost measuring the opportunity cost of increasing current effort. This opportunity cost reflects the forgone future net benefits when more resources are extracted in the present. For efficient interdependent allocations, the marginal willingness to pay is equal to the marginal user cost plus the marginal cost of extraction.

With an infinite discount rate this marginal user cost is zero, because no value is received from future allocations. This implies: (1) the marginal cost of extraction equals the marginal willingness to pay, which equals the constant price, and (2) total benefits equal total costs.[5] Earlier we demonstrated that the static efficient sustained yield implies a larger fish population than the maximum sustained yield. Once discounting is introduced, it is inevitable that the dynamic efficient sustained yield would imply a smaller fish population than the static efficient sustained yield and it is possible, though not inevitable, that the sustained catch would be smaller. Can you see why? In Figure 12.2 the sustained catch clearly is lower for an infinite discount rate.

The likelihood of the population being reduced below the level supplying the maximum sustainable yield depends on the discount rate. In general, the lower the extraction costs and the higher the discount rate, the more likely it is that the dynamic efficient level of effort will exceed the level of effort associated with the maximum sustainable yield. This is not difficult to see if we remember the limiting case discussed earlier. When the marginal extraction cost is zero, the static efficient sustainable yield and the maximum sustainable yield are equal.

Thus, with zero marginal extraction costs and a positive discount rate, the dynamic efficient level of effort necessarily exceeds the static efficient level of effort and the level of effort associated with the maximum sustainable yield. Higher extraction costs reduce the static efficient sustainable yield but not the maximum sustainable yield. Higher extraction costs reduce the likelihood that discounting would cause the population to be drawn below the maximum sustainable yield level.

---

4 Colin W. Clark, *Mathematical Bioeconomics: The Optimal Management of Renewable Resources* (New York: Wiley-Interscience, 1976): 42–44.

5 This is not difficult to demonstrate mathematically. In our model, the yield (y) can be expressed as $y = qxe$, where q is the proportion of the population harvested with one unit of effort, x is the size of the population, and e is the level of effort. One of the conditions a dynamic efficient allocation has to satisfy with an infinite discount rate is $P = c/qx$, where P is the constant price, c is the constant marginal cost per unit of effort, and qx is the number of fish harvested per unit of effort. By multiplying both sides of this equation by y and collecting terms, we obtain $Py = ce$. The left-hand side is total benefits while the right is total cost, implying net benefits are zero.

Would a dynamically efficient management scheme lead to extinction of the fishery? As Figure 12.2 shows, it would not be possible under the circumstances described here because E^c is the highest dynamically efficient level possible in this model, and that level falls well short of the level needed to drive the population to extinction. It is possible under other circumstances, however.[6]

For extinction to occur under a dynamic efficient management scheme, the benefit from extracting the very last unit would have to exceed the cost of extracting that unit (including the costs on future generations). As long as the population growth rate exceeds the discount rate, this will not be the case. If, however, the growth rate is lower than the discount rate, extinction can occur in an efficient management scheme if the costs of extracting the last unit are sufficiently low.

Why does the rate of growth have anything to do with whether or not an efficient catch profile leads to extinction? Rates of growth determine the productivity of conservation efforts.[7] With high rates of growth, future generations can be easily satisfied. On the other hand, when the rate of growth is very low, it takes a large sacrifice by current generations to produce more fish for future generations. In the limiting case, where the rate of growth is zero, we have a resource with fixed supply and therefore no different from an exhaustible resource. Total depletion would occur whenever the price commanded by the resource is high enough to cover the marginal cost of extracting the last unit.

We have shown that the dynamic efficiency criterion is not automatically consistent with sustaining constant yields perpetually for an interactive renewable resource, since it is mathematically possible for an efficient allocation of a fishery to lead to extinction of the resource. How likely are these criteria to conflict in practice?

Although the information is sketchy, most empirical studies suggest that because of the importance of extraction costs, the dynamic efficient catch rate is usually smaller than the maximum sustainable yield and extinction is rarely, if ever, efficient.[8] The cost of catching the last few fish is usually well in excess of the price received for them. The two criteria are usually completely compatible, although we must bear in mind that they are not inevitably compatible.

---

6 See, for example, Juo-Shung Cheng et al., "Analysis of Modified Model for Commercial Fishing with Possible Extinctive Fishery Resources, *Journal of Environmental Economics and Management* 8 (June 1981): 151-155, for a mathematical description of sufficient conditions for extinction to occur.

7 Note the parallel with the role of the growth rate in efficient timber harvesting in the previous chapter. Note also the relevance of the two-period model in Problem 1 of Chapter Six.

8 See, for example, the discussion in Colin W. Clark, *Mathematical Bioeconomics: The Optimal Management of Renewable Resources* (New York: Wiley-Interscience, 1976): 18-21.

APPROPRIABILITY AND MARKET SOLUTIONS

We have now defined an efficient allocation of the fishery over time. The next step is to characterize the normal market allocation and to contrast these two allocations. Where they differ we can entertain the possibility of various public-policy corrective means.

Let's first consider the allocation resulting from a fishery managed by a competitive sole owner. A sole owner would have a well-defined property right to the fish. We can establish the behavior of a sole owner by elaborating on Figure 12.2, as is done in Figure 12.3. Notice that the two panels share a common horizontal axis which allows us to examine the effect of various fishing effort levels on both graphs.

A sole owner would want to maximize his or her profits. Ignoring discounting for the moment, the owner can increase profits by increasing fishing effort until marginal revenue equals marginal cost. Clearly this is effort level E^e, the static efficient sustainable yield. This will yield positive profits equal to the difference between $R(E^e)$ and $C(E^e)$.

In ocean fisheries, however, sole owners are not normal. Ocean fisheries are typically common-property resources—no one exercises complete control over them. Since the property rights to the fishery are not conveyed to any single owner, no single fisherman can exclude other from exploiting the fishery. Sometimes common-property resources can coexist in the same market as private-property fisheries (Example 12.1).

What problems arise when access to the fishery is completely unrestricted? Free-access resources create two kinds of externalities: a contemporaneous externality and an intergenerational externality. The contemporaneous externality, which is borne by the current generation, involves the overcommitment of resources to fishing—too many boats, too many fishermen, too much effort. As a result, current fishermen earn a substantially lower rate of return on their efforts. The intergenerational externality, borne by future generations, occurs because overfishing reduces the stock which, in turn, lowers future profits from fishing.[9]

We can use Figure 12.3 to see how these externalities arise.[10] Once too many fishermen have unlimited access to the same common-property fishery, the

---

[9] This will result in fewer fish for future generations as well as smaller profits if the resulting effort level exceeds that associated with the maximum sustainable yield. If the common-property effort level is lower than the maximum sustainable yield effort level (when extraction costs are very high), then reductions in stock would *increase* the growth in the stock, thus supplying more fish (albeit lower net benefits) to future generations.

[10] This type of analysis was first used in H. Scott Gordon, "The Economic Theory of a Common-Property Resource: The Fishery," *Journal of Political Economy* 62 (April 1954): 124–142.

FIGURE 12.3 Market allocation in a common-property fishery.

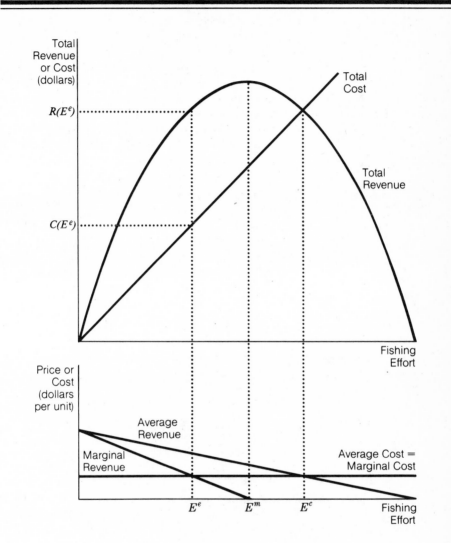

property rights to the fish are no longer efficiently defined. At the efficient level, each boat would receive a profit equal to its share of the scarcity rent. This rent, however, serves as a stimulus for new fishermen to enter, drawing up costs and eliminating the rent. Open access results in overexploitation.

The sole owner chooses not to expend more effort than E^e because to do so would reduce the profits of the fishery, resulting in a personal loss to him. When

EXAMPLE 12.1

Property Rights and Fisheries: Oysters

The oyster industry provides a unique opportunity to study the effect of property-right structures on incentives because it contains both private-property and common-property oyster beds. In some cases these private-property and common-property beds compete with each other in the same market. This allows us to compare the price and quantity behavior of markets supplied by fishermen operating under both property-right systems to markets which depend solely on one or the other.

What would we expect to find?

1. Common-property resources should be harvested earlier in the season because there is less incentive to conserve common-property resources.
2. Common-property fishermen should earn lower average incomes because the economic rent is dissipated.
3. The markets served purely by private-property fisheries should have higher prices, since private-property fishermen can respond to market conditions, whereas common-property fishermen are driven to catch and sell as many fish as early as possible.

What was revealed by examining data from Maryland, Virginia, Louisiana, and Mississippi?

1. From 1945 to 1970 the ratio of the harvest in the earlier part of the harvesting season to the later part was 1.35 for the common-property resource state (Maryland) and 1.01 for the contiguous private-property state (Virginia).
2. The average annual incomes over the period 1950–1969 of fishermen in Virginia was $2453 while that for Maryland was $1606. Another comparison revealed that fishermen in the private-property state of Louisiana earned $3207, while their counterparts in the contiguous common-property state of Mississippi earned $870.
3. Over the period 1966–1969, the mean price per pound of oysters in markets served purely by private oyster beds was $.94 while the mean price per pound for oysters from the common-property resource averaged only $.73 per pound. In addition, in a comparison of contiguous private- and common-property states, the private-property states all experienced higher prices.

Though these results do not come from carefully controlled experiments and therefore cannot be regarded as definitive, they are completely compatible with our understanding of the way in which property-right structures influence decisions.

Source: Richard J. Agnello and Lawrence P. Donnelly, "Prices and Property Rights in the Fisheries," *Southern Economic Journal* 40 (October 1979): 253–262.

access to the fishery is unrestricted, a decision to expend effort beyond E^e reduces profits to the fishery as a whole but not to that individual fisherman. Most of the decline in profits falls on the other fishermen.

In a free-access resource, the individual fisherman has an incentive to expend further effort until profits are zero. In Figure 12.3 that point is at effort level E^c, where average benefit and average cost are equal. It is now easy to see the contemporaneous externality—too much effort is being expended to catch too few fish, and the cost is substantially higher than it would be in an efficient allocation.

If this point seems abstract, it shouldn't. Many fisheries are currently plagued by precisely these problems. In a productive fishery in the Bering Sea and Aleutian Islands, for example, one study found significant over-capitalization.[11] While the efficient number of motherships (used to take on and process the catch at sea, so the catch boats do not have to return to port as often) was estimated to be 9, the current level was 140. As a result a significant amount of net benefits were lost ($124 million a year). Had the fishery been harvested more slowly, the same catch could have been achieved with fewer boats used closer to their capacity.

An intergenerational externality occurs because the size of the population is reduced, causing future profits to be lower than would otherwise be the case. As the existing population is overexploited, the free-access catch initially would be higher, but as growth rates are affected, the steady-state profit level, once attained, would be lower.

We stated in Chapter 6 that the resource owner with exclusive property rights balances the use value against the asset value. When access to the resource is unrestricted, exclusivity is lost. As a result, it is rational for a fisherman to ignore the asset value, since he or she can never appropriate it, and simply maximize the use value. In the process all the scarcity rent is dissipated. The allocation that results from allowing unrestricted access to the fishery is identical to that resulting from a dynamic efficient sustainable yield when an infinite discount rate is used.

Free access resources do not automatically lead to a stock lower than that maximizing the sustained yield. We can draw a cost function with a slope sufficiently steep that it intersects the benefit curve at a point to the left of E^m. Nonetheless, it is not unusual for mature, free-access, common-property fisheries to be exploited well beyond the point of maximum sustainable yield.

Are free-access resources and common-property resources synonymous concepts? They are not. On the one hand, governments can restrict entry, a topic we address in the next section. On the other hand, informal arrangements among

---

11 Daniel D. Huppert, *Managing Alaska's Groundfish Fisheries: History and Prospects*, University of Washington Institute for Marine Resources Working Paper (May 1990).

those harvesting the common property resource can also serve to limit access as well.[12] (Example 12.2).

Free access resources generally violate both the efficiency and sustainability criteria. If these criteria are to be fulfilled, some restructuring of the decision-making environment is necessary. How that could be done is the subject of the next section.

PUBLIC POLICY TOWARD FISHERIES

What can be done? A variety of public-policy responses are possible. Perhaps it is appropriate to start with allowing the market to work.

Aquaculture

Having demonstrated that inefficient management of the fishery results from treating it as common, rather than private, property we have one obvious solution—allowing some fisheries to be privately, rather than commonly, held. This approach can work when the fish are not very mobile, when they can be confined by artificial barriers, or when they instinctively return to their place of birth to spawn.

The advantages of such a move go well beyond the ability to preclude over-fishing. The owner is encouraged to invest in the resource and undertake measures that will increase the productivity (yield) of the fishery.[13] This movement toward controlled raising and harvesting of fish is called *aquaculture,* and there are some noteworthy examples of success.[14] Probably the highest yields ever attained through aquaculture resulted from using rafts to raise mussels. Some 300,000 kilograms per hectare of mussels, for example, have been raised in this manner in the Galician bays of Spain.[15] This productivity level approximates those achieved in poultry farming, widely regarded as one of the most successful attempts to increase the productivity of farm-produced animal protein.

In the United States, aquaculture has been thwarted by treating bodies of water as common property. This need not be the case, of course. In Example

---

12 For other examples of these arrangements, see F. Berkes, D. Feeny, B. J. McCay, and J. M. Acheson, "The Benefits of the Commons," *Nature* 340 (July 1989): 91-93.

13 For example, adding certain nutrients to the water or controlling the temperature can markedly increase the yields of some species.

14 The examples of aquaculture in this chapter are drawn from John E. Bardach, John H. Ryther, and William O. McClarney, *Aquaculture: The Farming and Husbandry of Freshwater and Marine Organisms* (New York: Wiley-Interscience, 1972).

15 A hectare is a measure of surface area equal to 10,000 square meters. It is equal to 2.471 acres.

EXAMPLE 12.2

Harbor Gangs of Maine

Unlimited access to common property resources reduces net benefits so drastically, this loss encourages those harvesting the resource to restrict access if possible. The Maine lobster fishery is one setting where informal arrangements have served to limit access.

Key among these arrangements is a system of territories which establishes boundaries between fishing areas. Particularly near the offshore islands these territories tend to be exclusively harvested by close-knit, disciplined gangs. These gangs restrict access to their territory by various covert means such as cutting the lines to lobster traps owned by new entrants, rendering them unretrievable. The income and catch levels achieved by the members of these gangs exceed those for comparable gangs lobstering less exclusive territories.

While it would be a mistake to assume that all common-property resources are characterized by unlimited access, it would also be a mistake to assume that these informal arrangement automatically provide sufficient social means for producing efficient harvests, thereby eliminating any need for public policy. The Maine lobster stock is also protected by regulations limiting the size of lobsters that can be taken and prohibiting the harvest of bearing females. Since estimates suggest that over 95% of legally harvestable lobsters are harvested, these regulations apparently afford significant protection to the stock. The main role for the informal arrangements has been to prevent the overcapitalization problem. When fewer fishermen harvest the available yield, income levels for those fishermen are higher.

Source: James M. Acheson, *The Lobster Gangs of Maine* (Hanover, NH: University Press of New England, 1988).

12.1 we saw that some oysters are raised in the United States in common-property beds and other are raised in private beds. As fish in the common-property resource become more scarce, triggering price increases, aquaculture probably would become more profitable and prevalent.

In some ways, Japan, as a densely populated country depending heavily on fish for protein, has reached the point where merely harvesting what the sea offers is no longer sufficient to satisfy the market at low cost. Consequently, Japan has become a leader in aquaculture, undertaking some of the most advanced aquaculture ventures in the world. The government has been supportive, mainly by creating private-property rights for waters formerly held common-ly. The prefecture governments (comparable to states in the United States) initiate the process by designating the areas to be used for aquaculture. The local fishermen's cooperative associations then partition these areas and al-locate the subareas to individual fishermen for exclusive use. This exclusive control allows the owner to invest in the resource and to manage it effectively and efficiently.

Another market approach to aquaculture involves fish ranching rather than fish farming.[16] Whereas fish farming involves cultivating fish over their lifetime in a controlled environment, fish ranching involves holding them in captivity only for the first few years of their lives.

Fish ranching relies on the strong homing instincts in certain fish such as Pacific salmon or ocean trout to permit their ultimate capture. The young salmon or ocean trout are hatched and confined in a convenient catch area for ap-proximately two years. When released, they migrate to the ocean. Upon reaching maturity, they return by instinct to the place of their births where they are har-vested. Brown estimates that 193,000 metric tons of salmon were harvested by the United States, the Soviet Union, and Japan in 1984.[17]

Aquaculture is certainly not the answer for all fish. Although it works well for shellfish, catfish, salmon, and some other species, some fish, such as tuna, will probably never be harvested domestically at a profit. Nonetheless, it is com-forting to note that aquaculture can provide a safety valve in some regions and for some fish.[18]

Raising the Real Cost of Fishing

Perhaps one of the best ways to illustrate the virtues of using economic analysis to help design policies is to show the harsh effects of policy approaches that ignore it. Because the earliest approaches to fishery management had a single-minded focus on attaining the maximum sustainable yield with little or no thought given to maximizing the net benefit, they provide a useful contrast.

---

16 See L. Stokes, "The Economics of Salmon Ranching," *Land Economics* 58 (November 1982): 464–477.

17 Lester R. Brown. "Maintaining World Fisheries," in *State of the World: 1985*, Lester Brown et al. (New York: W. W. Norton, 1985): 90.

18 In another example Frederick Bell shows that the social welfare losses from the overexploitation of common-property wild crawfish were reduced by an estimated $1,068,933 in 1978 by the existence of private-property crawfish farms. Without them social welfare losses would have been 4.16 times greater. See Frederick W. Bell, "Mitigating the Tragedy of the Commons," *Southern Economic Jour-nal* 52 (January 1986): 653–664.

Perhaps the best concrete example is the set of policies originally designed to deal with overexploitation of the Pacific salmon fishery in the United States.[19] The Pacific salmon is particularly vulnerable to overexploitation, and even extinction, because of its migration patterns. Pacific salmon are spawned in the gravel beds of rivers. As juvenile fish they migrate to the ocean only to return, as adults, to spawn in the rivers of their birth. After spawning, they die. When the adults swim upstream with a instinctual need to return to their native streams, they can easily be captured by traps, nets or other catching devices.

Recognizing the urgency of the problem, the government took action. To reduce the catch, they raised the cost of fishing. Initially this was accomplished by preventing the use of any barricades on the rivers and by prohibiting the use of traps (the most efficient catching devices) in the most productive areas. These measures proved insufficient, since mobile techniques (trolling, nets, and so on) proved quite capable, by themselves, of overexploiting the resource. Officials then began to close designated fishing areas and suspend fishing in other areas for certain periods of time. In Figure 12.3 these measures would be reflected as a rotation of the cost curve to the left until it intersected the benefits curve at a level of effort equal to E^e. The aggregate of all these regulations had the desired effect of curtailing the yield of salmon.

Were these policies efficient? They were not and would not have been even had they resulted in the efficient catch! This statement may seem inconsistent, but it is not. Efficiency implies not only that the catch must be at the efficient level, but it must also be extracted at the lowest possible cost. This latter condition was violated by these policies (Figure 12.4).

In Figure 12.4 are reflected the total cost in an efficient allocation (TC_1) and the total cost after these policies were imposed (TC_2). The net benefit received from an efficient policy is shown graphically as the vertical distance between total cost and total benefit. After the policy, however, the net benefit was reduced to zero; the net benefit (represented by vertical distance) was lost to society. Why?

The net benefit was squandered on the use of excessively expensive means to catch the desired yield of fish. Rather than use traps to reduce the cost of catching the desired number of fish, traps were prohibited. Larger expenditures on capital and labor were required to catch the same number of fish. This additional capital and labor represent one source of the waste.

The limitations on fishing times and fishing areas had a similar effect on cost. Rather than allowing fishermen to fish those areas and times where capital and labor would be most productively applied (while ensuring that the target

---

19 An excellent, detailed analysis of these policies can be found in J. A. Crutchfield and G. Pontecovo, *The Pacific Salmon Fisheries: A Study of Irrational Conservation* (Baltimore: Johns Hopkins University Press for Resources for the Future, 1969).

FIGURE 12.4   Effect of regulation.

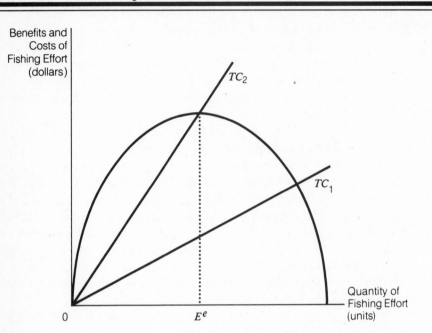

yields were not exceeded), fishermen were forced to use less productive areas and times. The additional time, energy, and equipment were also wasted resources.

Regulation imposed other costs as well. It was soon discovered that while the above regulations were adequate to protect the depletion of the fish population, they had no effect on the incentive for individual fishermen to increase their share of the take. Even though the profits would be small because of high costs, new technological change would allow adopters to increase their shares of the market and put others out of business. To protect themselves, the fishermen were successful in introducing bans on new technology. These restrictions took various forms, but two seem particularly noteworthy. The first was the banning of the use of thin-stranded, monofilament net. The course-stranded net it would have replaced was visible to the salmon in the daytime and therefore could be avoided by them. As a result, it was useful only at night. By contrast, the thinner monofilament nets could be successfully used during the daylight hours, as well as night. Monofilament nets were banned in both Canada and the United States soon after they appeared.

The most flagrantly inefficient regulation was one in Alaska which barred gill netters in Bristol Bay from using engines to propel their boats. This regulation lasted until the 1950s and heightened the public's awareness of the anachronistic nature of this regulatory approach. The world's most technologically advanced nation was reaping its harvest from the Bering Sea in sailboats, while the rest of the world—particularly Japan and the Soviet Union—was modernizing its fishing fleets at a torrid pace!

Time restriction regulations had a similar effect. Limiting fishing time provides an incentive to use that time as intensively as possible. Huge boats facilitate large harvests within the period and therefore are attractive, but are very inefficient; the same harvest could have been achieved with fewer, smaller boats used to their optimum capacity.

Guided by a narrow focus on the maximum sustainable yield which ignored costs, these policies led to a substantial loss in the net benefit received from the fishery. Costs are an important dimension of the problem and, when they are ignored, the incomes of fishermen suffer. When incomes suffer, further conservation measures become more difficult to implement and incentives to violate the regulations are intensified.

Taxes

Is it possible to provide incentives for cost reduction while assuring that the yield is reduced to the efficient level? Can a more efficient policy be devised? Economists who have studied the question believe that more efficient policies are possible.

Consider a tax on effort. In Figure 12.4 taxes on effort would also be represented as a rotation of the TC line, and the after-tax cost to the fishermen would be adequately represented by line TC_2 Since the after-tax curve coincides with TC_2, the cost curve for all those inefficient regulations, doesn't this imply that the tax system is just as inefficient? No! The key to understanding the difference is the distinction between *transfer costs* and *real-resource costs*.

Under a regulation system of the type described earlier in this chapter, all of the costs included in TC_2 are real-resource costs, which involve utilization of resources. Transfer costs, by contrast, involve transfers of resources from one part of society to another rather than their use. Transfers do represent costs to that part of society bearing them, but are exactly offset by the gain received by the recipients. Resources are not used up; they are merely transferred. Thus the calculation of the size of the net benefit should subtract real-resource costs, but not transfer costs, from benefits. For society as a whole, transfer costs are retained as part of the net benefit.

In Figure 12.3 the net benefit under a tax system is identical to that under an efficient allocation. The net benefit represents a transfer cost to the fisherman that is exactly offset by the revenues received by the tax collector. This discussion should not obscure the fact that, as far as the individual fisherman is concerned, these are very real costs. Rent normally received by a sole owner is now received by the government. Since the tax revenues involved can be substantial (Example 12.3), fishermen wishing to have the fishery efficiently managed may

EXAMPLE 12.3

Efficient Versus Market Exploitation of Lobsters

The economists Henderson and Tugwell (1979) set out to quantify the degree of overexploitation characterizing these two particular maritime Canadian common-property lobster fishing ports: Port Maitland and Miminegash. They estimated the relationship between effort and sustainable catch for each of the two fishing grounds and also the costs of various levels of fishing effort. Using these functions, they derived both the optimal and free-market solutions, which could then be compared to each other and to the maximum sustainable yield. These calculations could also be used to derive the tax required to force the market solution to converge to the efficient solution.

	Port Maitland			Miminegash		
Maximum sustainable yield stock	1,766			1,629		
Lobster price/thousand pounds	$485			$370		
Opportunity cost/hundred traps	$1,421			$950		
	Optimal solution	*Free entry*	*Actual average 1959–63*	*Optimal solution*	*Free entry*	*Actual average 1959–63*
Lobster stock (thous. lbs.)	3,050	2,490	2,467	2,450	1,125	1,273
Lobster catch (thous. lbs.)	745	1,330	1,183	801	936	1,094
Effort (100 traps)	112	454	—	122	365	—
Ratio: catch/stock	0.25	0.53	0.48	0.33	0.83	0.86
Optimal tax/thousand pounds catch	270	NA	NA	255	NA	NA
Annual resource savings: value of trap savings less value of reduced catch	$202,173	NA	NA	$180,470	NA	NA

Several features are noteworthy in this table. The "free entry" or market solutions for catch are remarkably close to the actual averages in spite of the uncertainty of estimating the underlying equations. The "free entry" catch levels are substantially greater than the optimal levels due to an inefficiently high level of effort (traps). The last entries in the table indicate that the welfare losses (compared to the optimum level) run about $202,000 in Port Maitland and $180,000 in Miminegash each year. For Port Maitland this represents a loss of some 62% of the net benefits obtainable under an efficient program!

The table also presents the optimum tax level which would cause the free access and optimum to converge. For Port Maitland this amounts to $270 per 1000 pounds of lobster, approximately 56% of the current price ($485). If this tax were levied, some fishermen would exit and the catch would rise, but the remaining fishermen would not have received higher profits. The increased net benefits would be appropriated by the government. It is not difficult to understand why fishermen do not generally support tax policies, even though these policies could prevent overexploitation.

Source: J.V. Henderson and M. Tugwell, "Exploitation of the Lobster Fishery: Some Empirical Results," *Journal of Environmental Economics and Management* 6 (December 1979): 287–296.

object to this particular way of doing it. They would prefer a policy that restricts catches while allowing them to keep the rents. Is that possible?

Individual Transferable Quotas

One policy making it possible is a properly designed quota on the number of fish that can be taken from the fishery. The "properly designed" caveat is important because there are many different types of quota schemes and not all are of equal merit. An efficient quota system has several identifiable characteristics:

1. The quotas entitle the holder to catch a specified weight of a specified type of fish;
2. The total amount of fish authorized by the quotas held by all fishermen should be equal to the efficient catch for the fishery; and
3. The quotas should be freely transferable among fishermen.

Each of these three characteristics plays an important role in obtaining an efficient allocation. Suppose, for example, the quota were defined in terms of the right to own and use a fishing boat rather than in terms of catch—not an uncommon type of quota. Such a quota is not efficient, because under this type of quota an inefficient incentive still remains for each boat owner to build larger boats, to place extra equipment on them, and to spend more time fishing. These actions would expand the capacity of each boat and cause the actual catch to exceed the target (efficient) catch. In a nutshell, the boat quota limits the number of boats fishing but does not limit the amount of fish caught by each boat. If we are to reach and sustain an efficient allocation, it is the catch which must ultimately be limited.

While the purpose of the second condition is obvious, the role of transferability deserves more consideration. With transferability, the entitlement to fish flows naturally to those gaining the most benefit from it because their costs are lower. Because it is valuable, the transferable quota commands a positive price. Those who have quotas but also have high costs find they make more money selling the quotas than using them. Meanwhile, those who have lower costs find they can purchase more quotas and still make money.

Transferable quotas also encourage technological progress. Adopters of new cost-reducing technologies can make more money on their existing quotas and make it profitable to purchase new quotas from others who have not adopted the technology. Therefore, in marked contrast to the earlier regulatory methods used to raise costs, both the tax system and the transferable quota system encourage the development of new technologies.

How about the distribution of the rent? In a quota system the distribution of the rent depends crucially on how the quotas are initially allocated. There are many possibilities with different outcomes. The first possibility is for the government to auction these quotas off. But the government would then appropriate all the rent, and the outcome would be very similar to the outcome of the tax system. If the fishermen do not like the tax system, they would not like the auction system either.

In an alternative approach, the government could give the quotas to the fishermen, say in proportion to their historical catch. The fishermen could then trade among themselves until a market equilibrium is reached. All the rent would be retained by the *current* generation of fishermen. Fishermen who might want to enter the market would have to purchase the quotas from existing fishermen. Competition among the potential purchasers would drive up the price of the transferable quotas until it reflected the market value of future rents, appropriately discounted.[20]

Thus this type of quota system allows the rent to remain with the fishermen, but only the current generation of fishermen. Future generations see little difference between this quota system and a tax system; in either case, they have to pay to enter the industry, whether it be through the tax system or by purchasing the quotas.

In 1983 a limited individual transferable quota system was established in New Zealand to protect its deepwater trawl fishery.[21] Because this fishery was newly developed, allocating the quotas proved relatively easy. The total allowable catches for the seven basic species were divided into individual transferable quotas and were allocated to existing firms on the basis of investment in harvesting equipment, investment in onshore production equipment, and recent onshore production. The rights to harvest were denominated in terms of a specific amount of fish, but were only granted for a 10-year period.

At the same time the deep-sea fishery policy was being considered, the inshore fishery began to fall on hard times. Too many participants were chasing too many fish. Some particularly desirable fish species were being seriously overfished. While the need to reduce the amount of pressure being put on the population was rather obvious, how to accomplish that reduction was not at all obvious. Although it was relatively easy to prevent new fishermen from entering the fisheries, it was harder to figure out how to reduce the pressure from those who had been fishing in the area for years or even decades. Because fishing is characterized by economies of scale, simply reducing everyone's catch proportionately wouldn't make much sense. That would simply place higher costs on everyone and waste a great deal of fishing capacity as all boats sat around idle for a sig-

---

20 This occurs because the maximum bid any potential entrant would make is the value to be derived from owning that permit. This value is equal to the present value of future rents (the difference between price and marginal cost for each unit of fish sold). Competition will force the purchaser to bid near that maximum value, lest he or she lose the quota.

21 Lee G. Anderson, "Property Rights in Fisheries: Lessons from the New Zealand Experience," Political Economy Research Center Working Paper No. 89-22 (Bozeman, MT 1989).

nificant proportion of time. A better solution would clearly be to have fewer boats harvesting the stock. That way each boat could be used closer to its full capacity without depleting the population. Which fisherman should be asked to give up their livelihood and leave the industry?

The economic incentive approach addressed this problem imposing an annual fee on fishermen for their catch quotas. The revenues derived from this fee were used to buy out fishermen who were willing to forgo any future fishing for the species in jeopardy. Essentially each fisherman stated the lowest price that he or she would accept for leaving the industry; the regulators selected those who could be induced to leave at the lowest price, paid the stipulated amount from the fee revenues, and retired their licenses to fish for this species. It wasn't long before a sufficient number of licenses had been retired and the population was protected. Because the program was voluntary, those who left the industry only did so when they felt they had been adequately compensated. Meanwhile those who paid the fee realized that this small investment would benefit them greatly in the future as the population recovered. A difficult and potentially dangerous pressure on a valuable natural resource had been avoided by the creative use of an approach that changed the economic incentives.[22]

The 200-Mile Limit

The final policy dimension concerns the international aspects of the fishery problem. Obviously the various policy approaches to effective management of fisheries requires some governing body to have jurisdiction over a fishery so that it can enforce its regulations.

This is not currently the case for many of the ocean fisheries. Much of the open water of the oceans is a common-property resource to governments, as well as to individual fishermen. No single body can exercise control over it. As long as that continues to be the case, the corrective action will be difficult to implement. In recognition of this fact there is an evolving law of the sea defined by international treaties. One of the concrete results of this law, for example, has been some limited restrictions on whaling. Whether this process ultimately yields a consistent and comprehensive system of management remains to be seen.

Countries bordering the sea have declared that their ownership rights extend some 200 miles out to sea. Within these areas, the countries have exclusive jurisdiction and can proceed to implement effective management policies. These declarations have been upheld and are now firmly entrenched in international law.

---

22 This concept is spreading to other fisheries. In the United States, for example, the Mid-Atlantic Fishery Management Council has applied it to the Atlantic surf clam and ocean quahog fishery. See *Amendment #8 Fishery Management Plan for the Atlantic Surf Clam and Ocean Quahog Fishery* (Dover, DE: Mid-Atlantic Fishery Management Council, 1989).

Thus, very rich fisheries in coastal waters can be protected, while those in the open waters await the outcome of an international negotiations process.

The Economics of Enforcement

An area which traditionally has not received much analytical treatment, but is gradually becoming recognized as a key aspect of fisheries management, is enforcement. Policies can be designed to be perfectly efficient as long as everyone voluntarily follows them, but these same policies may look rather tragic in the harsh realities of costly and imperfect enforcement.

Fisheries policies are especially difficult to enforce. Coastlines are typically long and rugged; it is not difficult for fishermen to avoid detection if they are exceeding their limits or catching species illegally.

Recognizing these realities immediately suggests two implications. First, policy design should take enforcement into consideration, and, second, what is efficient when enforcement is ignored may not be efficient once enforcement is considered.

Policies should be designed to make compliance as inexpensive as possible. Regulations which impose very high costs are more likely to be disobeyed than regulations that impose costs in proportion to the purpose. Regulations should also contain provisions for dealing with noncompliance. A common approach is to levy monetary sanctions against those failing to comply. The sanctions should be set at a high enough level as to bring the costs of noncompliance (including the sanction) into balance with the costs of compliance.

The enforcement issue points out another advantage of private-property approaches to fisheries management—they are self-enforcing. Fish farmers or fish ranchers have no incentive to deviate from the efficient scheme because they would only be hurting themselves. No enforcement activity is necessary. Noncompliance with some kind of regulatory constraint, on the other hand, could, in the absence of effective enforcement, be beneficial to those fishing in common-property resources. Mounting this enforcement effort is yet another cost associated with the public management of fisheries.

Since enforcement activity is costly, it follows that it should be figured into our definition of efficiency. How would our analysis be changed by incorporating enforcement costs? One study suggests that the incorporation of realistic enforcement cost considerations tends to reduce the efficient population below the level declared efficient in the presence of perfect, costless enforcement.[23]

---

23 Jon G. Sutinen and Peder Anderson, "The Economics of Fisheries Law Enforcement," *Land Economics* 61 (November 1985): 387–397.

The rationale is not difficult to follow. Assume that some kind of quota system is in effect to ration access. Enforcement activity would involve monitoring compliance with these quotas and assigning penalties on those found in noncompliance.[24] If the quotas are so large as to be consistent with the free-access equilibrium, enforcement cost would be zero; no enforcement would be necessary to ensure compliance. Moving the fishery away from the free-access equilibrium increases both net benefits and enforcement costs. For this model, as the steady-state population size is increased, marginal enforcement costs increase and marginal net benefits decrease. At the efficient population size (considering enforcement cost) the marginal net benefit equals the marginal enforcement cost. This necessarily involves a smaller population size than the efficient population size ignoring enforcement costs, because the latter occurs when the marginal net benefit is zero.

Extension to Other Species

Space does not permit a detailed treatment of other biological populations, but it is important to demonstrate that at least some of the principles derived from a close examination of fisheries management are transferable to other species. Examining the problems with other species using this general analytical framework should prove a rich source of student research topics.

Our examination of fisheries suggests that rearranging economic incentives can be a key to restoring efficient, sustainable management. Economic incentives are apparently also at work in Africa protecting the elephant herds in Zimbabwe.[25] African elephants have long been treated as common property. As might be expected, elephant populations are being threatened. Interestingly, however, different African countries are having rather different experiences.

The elephant populations of Zimbabwe, Botswana, Namibia, and South Africa are increasing, while those in Kenya are decreasing. The successful southern African countries all support conservation through utilization, allowing safari hunting and tourism on private, state, and communal lands, while limiting access. Hunting rights are severely limited and are granted to local communities of indigenous peoples. Since many safaris hunt with cameras, tourism can be an additional source of income without killing elephants. When animals (such as

---

24 In theory it would be possible to set the penalty so high that only a limited amount of enforcement activity would be necessary. Since large penalties are rarely imposed in practice, the model rules these out and assumes that increasing enforcement expenditures are necessary to enforce increasingly stringent quotas.

25 Randy T. Simmons and Urs P. Keuter, "Herd Mentality: Banning Ivory Sales is No Way To Save the Elephant," *Policy Review* No. 50 (Fall 1989): 46–49.

rogue elephants) are eliminated by National Parks personnel, the ivory and hides of these animals belong to the members of the local communities.

Tourism and the sale of both hunting rights and elephant products provides a significant source of income to local communities. Two dozen peasant villages in Zimbabwe earned $5 million from safari owners in 1990 by selling elephant hunting rights on their communal lands. Giving local communities a large stake in herd preservation also facilitates strict enforcement of poaching laws. Poachers are shot on sight.

Kenya, a country with large declines in its elephant population, has no such system. Whereas in Zimbabwe villagers have a very large stake in protecting the source of this income, the elephant herd, Kenyans have little stake in their protection. The potential revenue that could be used to institutionalize a protection system is enormous. Economists have estimated that some $25 million per year would be available in Kenya from tourists seeking to view and photograph elephants.[26]

One approach to the protection of biological species is to rearrange the economic incentives so that local groups have an economic interest in their preservation. Unlimited access to common-property resources undermines those incentives.

SUMMARY

We have seen that unrestricted access, common-property fisheries will not automatically be efficiently managed by markets. In general, they are overexploited and, in the case of fisheries characterized by particularly low extraction costs (the Pacific salmon fishery), extinction is a definite possibility in the absence of outside control. Where extraction costs are higher, extinction is unlikely even with unrestricted access.

Some reassuring evidence suggests that both the private and public sectors have moved to ameliorate the problems associated with past mismanagement. The reassertion of private-property rights in Japan and other countries has stimulated the development of aquaculture. Governments in Canada and the United States have moved to limit overexploitation of the Pacific salmon. International agreements have been reached to place limits on whaling. It is doubtful that these programs fully satisfy the efficiency criterion, although it does seem clear that sustainable catches will result.

An increasing reliance on individual transferable quotas, as evidenced in both New Zealand and the United States, offers the possibility to preserve stocks

---

26 Gardner Brown Jr. and Wes Henry, "The Economic Value of Elephants," London Environmental Economics Centre Working Paper #89-12 (November 1989).

without jeopardizing the incomes of those men and women currently harvesting fish from the sea. Approaches to the preservation of elephants that give local communities a stake in herd preservation similarly recognize the necessity of building political coalitions to support conservation. Creative strategies for sharing the gains from moving to an efficient level of use could prove to be a significant weapon in the arsenal of techniques design to protect biological resources from overexploitation.

It would be folly to ignore barriers to further action, such as the reluctance of individual fishermen to submit to many forms of regulation, the lack of a firm policy governing open ocean waters, and the difficulties of enforcing various approaches. Whether these barriers will fall before the pressing need for effective management remains to be seen.

FURTHER READING

Anderson, Lee G. *The Economics of Fisheries Management* (Baltimore: Johns Hopkins University Press, 1977). A highly recommended text for those wishing to go into the material in this chapter in greater depth.

Bell, Frederick W. *Food From the Sea: The Economics and Politics of Ocean Fisheries* (Boulder, CO: Westview Press, 1978). A comprehensive and comprehensible treatment of the actual and potential management of fisheries by an academic economist who was previously chief of economic research for the National Marine Fisheries Service, U.S. Department of Commerce. Full of examples of actual regulation.

Clark, Colin W. *Mathematical Bioeconomics: The Optimal Management of Renewable Resources* (New York: Wiley-Interscience, 1976). Accessible only to those with strong undergraduate backgrounds in math, this is an excellent introduction to the use of mathematics to formulate optimal management policies. Focused almost entirely on fisheries.

ADDITIONAL REFERENCES

Campbell, H. F. and R. K. Lindner. "The Production of Fishing Effort and the Economic Performance of License Limitation Programs," *Land Economics* 66 (February 1990): 56–66.

Clark, C. W. "Profit Maximization and the Extinction of Animal Species," *Journal of Political Economy* 81 (August 1973): 950–960.

Crutchfield, J.A. and G. Pontecovo. *The Pacific Salmon Fisheries: A Study of Irrational Conservation* (Baltimore: John Hopkins University Press for Resources for the Future, 1969).

Dupont, Diane P. "Rent Dissipation in Restricted Access Fisheries" *Journal of Environmental Economics and Management,* 19 (July 1990): 26–44.

Gallastegui, Carmen. "An Economic Analysis of Sardine Fishing in the Gulf of Valencia (Spain), *Journal of Environmental Economics and Management* 10 (June 1983): 138–150.

Henderson, J. V. and M. Tugwell. "Exploitation of the Lobster Fishery: Some Empirical Results," *Journal of Environmental Economics and Management* 6 (December 1979): 287–296.

Munro, G. R. "Fisheries, Extended Jurisdiction, and the Economics of Common Property Resources," *Canadian Journal of Economics* 15 (August 1982): 405–425.

Stokes, R. L. "The Economics of Salmon Ranching," *Land Economics* 58 (November 1982): 464–477.

Swanson, Timothy M. "International Regulation of the Ivory Trade," London Environmental Economics Centre Working Paper #89-04 (May 1989).

DISCUSSION QUESTIONS

1. Is the establishment of the 200-mile limit a sufficient form of government intervention to ensure that the tragedy of the commons does not occur for fisheries within the 200-mile limit? Why or why not?

2. With discounting it is possible for the efficient fish population to fall below the level required to produce the maximum sustained yield. Does this violate the sustainability criterion? Why or why not?

PROBLEMS

1. Assume that the relationship between the growth of a fish population and the population size can be expressed as $g = 4P - 0.1P^2$, where g is the growth in tons and P is the size of the population (in thousands of tons). Given a price of \$100 a ton, the marginal benefit of smaller population sizes (and hence, larger catches) can be computed as $20P - 400$. (a) Compute the population size that is compatible with the maximum sustainable yield. What would be the size of the annual catch if the population were to be sustained at this level? (b) If the marginal cost of additional catches (expressed in terms of the population size) is $MC = 2(160 - P)$, what is the population size which is compatible with the efficient sustainable yield?

2. Assume that a local fisheries council imposes an enforceable quota of 100 tons of fish on a particular fishing ground for one year. Assume further that 100 tons per year is the efficient sustained yield. Once the 100th ton has been caught, the fishery would be closed for the remainder of the year. (a) Is this an efficient solution to the common-property problem? Why or why not? (b) Would your answer be different if the 100-ton quota were divided up into 100 transferable quotas, each entitling the holder to catch one ton of fish, and distributed among the fishermen in proportion to their historical catch? Why or why not?

CHAPTER THIRTEEN

Generalized Resource Scarcity

*As a nation, we have always faced choices and always will.
What matters is the range of choice we have and the urgency
with which the need to choose is thrust upon us.*

COMMISSION ON POPULATION GROWTH AND THE AMERICAN FUTURE
(1972)

INTRODUCTION

Public concern over natural resource scarcity is not new. The National Conservation Commission, formed during the Theodore Roosevelt administration and headed by noted conservationist Gifford Pinchot, conducted the first national inventory of natural resources in 1908. This commission was established in response to a growing concern for natural resource scarcity. Its mandate was to provide data so that the situation could be assessed and appropriate public policies could be charted. This initial inquiry has been followed by a number of others with a similar focus.[1]

A number of concerns suggest the need for continued vigilance. We have seen, for example, that even though world fertility rates are now falling, the current age structure of the population creates an inertia for population growth

---

1 A detailed description of the various commissions, boards, and committees set up to advise the executive and legislative branches on resource policies can be found in Robert Cahn and Patricia L. Cahn, "Lessons from the Past," *The Global 2000 Report to the President of the U.S.: Entering the 21st Century, Vol. 1: Summary Report*, Council on Environmental Quality and Department of State (New York: Pergamon Press, 1980): 321–348.

331

EXAMPLE 13.1

Population Growth and the Demand for Resources

The demand for resources is functionally related to the level of population and per capita consumption by the identity:

$$C = C_p \times P,$$

where C is the consumption of resources, P is the population, and C_p is the per capita level of resource consumption. Both population and per capita consumption have increased the demand for resources in the past. The multiplicative nature of the formula causes demand to rise quite rapidly. For example, if population and per capita consumption were both to double, the demand for resources would be four times as high.

The Commission on Population Growth and the American Future conducted a major study to define the relationship between population growth and the demand for resources in the United States. Specifically, they analyzed the effect of two possible population growth scenarios. These scenarios differ in the number of children the average American family is assumed to contain. The first scenario assumes an average of two children per family and implies that the population would reach 300 million in the year 2015. The population in the second scenario, with its assumed three-child average family, would reach somewhat over 400 million by that same date.

The study concluded that population growth is one of the major factors affecting the demand for resources and the deterioration of the environment

which will not, even in the most optimistic projections, allow for a stable world population in the immediate future. These increases in the population will cause the demand for resources to increase faster than it would if the population were stable. The implications of this increasing growth on the demand can be profound, particularly in the industrial countries such as the United States, where per capita consumption levels are high (Example 13.1).

Previous chapters have demonstrated that while markets automatically provide some corrective responses to scarcity, market and public-policy imperfections have reduced the efficiency of these responses. These imperfections include price controls, common-property resources, externalities, and the tax treatment of resources. We were able to suggest a public-policy response to the particular resource problem under investigation. In some and that we would be considerably better off over the next 30 to 50 years if there were a prompt reduction in our population growth rate. These conclusions were drawn from a number of specific findings including

1. The *annual* consumption of minerals in the three-child scenario would be 17% higher by 2020 than in the two-child scenario.
2. The three-child scenario causes higher pressure on energy demand and results in more imports and higher prices.
3. Water shortages in the Southwest would occur under either scenario but would occur sooner (and would affect a wider geographic area) under the three-child scenario.
4. The demand for recreational facilities would be some 30% less under the two-child scenario, leading to lower levels of congestion.
5. Fifty years from now, the population resulting from the three-child average would have to pay food prices some 40% to 50% higher than the two-child average population would pay.

Because per capita consumption levels in the United States are so high, reductions in population growth have a disproportionately large impact on the global demand for resources. We would have more time to act and could reduce the strain on our institutions, as well as our resources, by holding population growth permanently in check.

Source: Commission on Population Growth and the American Future, *Population and the American Future* (New York: American Library, 1972).

cases, the appropriate response was to remove restrictions previously placed on the market.

Individual mines or wells will be exhausted in the face of this rising demand. But will these remain isolated incidents or will they add up to a pattern of generalized resource scarcity? Generalized scarcity would have a detrimental impact on the quality of life for this and succeeding generations.

Our search for evidence of generalized scarcity begins with a review and elaboration of the manner in which a market economy copes with increasing scarcity, particularly the roles of exploration and discovery, technological progress, and the substitution of abundant resources for scarce ones. We then examine how resource scarcity can be detected. What indicators can be used? What are their strengths and weaknesses? Once we have gained an appreciation for avenues of detection, we turn to the evidence revealed by these indicators and discuss how this evidence may be interpreted.

This chapter serves two purposes: an end in itself and a means to understanding more global concerns. It is an end in that the existence or nonexistence of a generalized resource scarcity is inherently important. It also represents a point of departure in the larger debate about the desirability and inevitability of future economic growth. We pursue this concern in Chapter 21, when we explore the process of economic growth in the context of limited environmental and natural resources.

FACTORS MITIGATING RESOURCE SCARCITY

The ability of a market economy to cope with pressures on the environmental asset caused by population and income growth depends on alternatives for diffusing these pressures. Three alternatives have been particularly important: (1) exploration and discovery, (2) technological process, and (3) substitution.

Exploration and Discovery

A profit-maximizing firm will undertake exploration activity until the marginal discovery cost equals the marginal scarcity rent received from a unit of the resource sold.[2] Since the marginal scarcity rent—the difference between the price received and the marginal cost of extraction—is the marginal benefit received by the firm engaging in exploration activity, to maximize profits the level of activity should be increased until this marginal benefit is equal to the marginal cost.

An understanding of this relationship between scarcity rent and marginal discovery cost allows us to think about how exploration activity would respond to population and income growth. Since both of these factors contribute to rising demand over time, they raise the marginal user cost and the scarcity rent, stimulating producers to undertake larger marginal discovery costs.

How much this demand pressure is relieved depends upon the amount of exploration activity and the amount of resources discovered per unit of exploration activity undertaken. If the marginal discovery cost curve is flat (implying a large number of relatively available resources), increases in scarcity rent can

---

2 This is strictly true only when no uncertainty is associated with exploration. Even with uncertainty, however, marginal discovery cost is highly related to scarcity rent. See Shantayanan Devarajan and Anthony C. Fisher, "Measures of Resource Scarcity under Uncertainty," *Explorations in Natural Resource Economics*, V. Kerry Smith and John V. Krutilla, eds. (Baltimore: The Johns Hopkins University Press for Resources for the Future, 1982): 332–342.

stimulate large amounts of successful exploration activity. If the marginal discovery cost curve is steeply sloped (as would be the case when exploration had to take place in increasingly hostile and unproductive environments), increases in scarcity rent stimulate less successful exploration activity.

Technological Progress

Technological progress reduces the cost of ore by discovering new ways to extract, process, and use the ore. In Chapter 6, for example, we showed the significant impact of pelletization on the cost of producing steel from iron ore. The effect was so dramatic that production costs actually fell over time in spite of the need to use a lower-grade ore.

It is important to realize that the rate and type of technological progress is influenced by the degree of resource scarcity. Rising extraction costs create new profit opportunities for the development of new technologies. These profit opportunities are largest for technologies that economize on scarce resources and utilize abundant ones. In periods when labor is scarce and capital abundant, new technologies tend to use capital and save labor. If population growth were to reverse the relative scarcity, subsequent technological progress would concentrate on using labor and saving capital. In the past when fossil-fuel energy was abundant and cheap, newly discovered technologies relied heavily on this energy source. As fossil-fuel supplies decline, technological progress could be expected to economize by increasing the amount of useful energy received per unit of fossil-fuel input and by replacing fossil-fuel energy with forms of solar energy.

Substitution

The final way in which adverse consequences of resource scarcity can be mitigated is by substituting abundant resources for scarce ones. The easier the substitution of abundant depletable or renewable resources, the smaller will be the impact of declining availability and rising costs (Figure 13.1).

In the graph three isoquants (S_1, F_1, F_2) are pictured. An *isoquant* portrays all the possible combinations of inputs that can produce a given level of output. The two right-angled isoquants $(F_1$ and $F_2)$ depict the fixed-proportions case, the case in which no input substitution is possible. The fixed-proportions isoquant nearer the original (F_2) refers to a lower output level than the other fixed-proportion isoquant (F_1). The third isoquant (S_1) does admit of some possibility for input substitution and is drawn in such a way as to produce the same output level (O_1) as F_1. Naturally it implies a different production technology or set of technologies than F_1.

We can illustrate the significance of input substitution on output using Figure 13.1. Assume that the amount of some input Y (a depletable resource) is reduced

FIGURE 13.1   Output levels and the possibilities for input substitution.

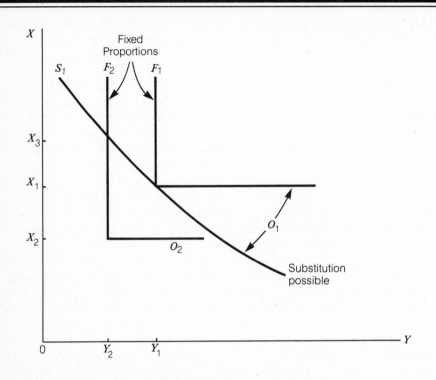

from Y_1 to Y_2. If the technology involved is characterized by S_1, the constant output level (O_1) can be maintained by increasing the amount of the other resource used from X_1 to X_3. This increase in X compensates for the reduction in Y, leaving output unaffected.

Notice what happens, however, when the production process is characterized by F_1 instead of S_1. A reduction in the availability of Y from Y_1 to Y_2 necessitates a reduction in output from O_1 to O_2. No substitution of X for Y is possible. In addition, because inputs must be used in fixed proportions, the amount of X would be reduced from X_1 to X_2. Any more X would be redundant; it would not result in any additional output.

These examples serve to illustrate a basic premise—the wider the array of substitution possibilities, the smaller the impact of resource scarcity on output. Timber scarcity illustrates an important historical example (Example 13.2) which serves to remind us that our review of the evidence must be sensitive to mitigating circumstances such as substitution possibilities and technological progress.

This short review suggests that some factors (rising population and incomes) increase the likelihood of resource scarcity, while others (exploration and dis-

EXAMPLE 13.2

Resource Scarcity in Historical Perspective: Timber

Early in our history timber was very abundant. For those who wanted to farm and had to clear the land, it was too abundant! As a result of low timber prices, Americans began to develop new technologies that relied more heavily on this vast resource. These included a whole range of woodworking machines for sawing, planing, shaping, and boring, as well as design improvements in the ax.

The use of these machines economized on labor—at that time a scarce commodity—at the cost of much wood. The saws of that period were easy to use, but they made such a wide swath that much of the log ended up as sawdust. It is interesting to note that in England, where labor was abundant and wood was scarce, the production process relied more heavily on labor and used a greater amount of the log.

When rising demand put pressure on the American forest resource base and prices began to rise, the incentive to economize on wood was created. Wood-burning stoves became increasingly popular for increasing the thermal efficiency of wood burning. Substitutes (some of superior quality) came into use. Coal replaced wood for energy. Steel began to replace wood in bridges. Concrete began to replace wood in buildings. Plastics began to replace wood in packaging and toys. New products, such as particleboard, were created to profitably use previously wasted wood by-products.

Meanwhile, other technological changes served to increase the size of the forest resource base. Forest scientists discovered a number of ways to increase the tree growth, and the lumber industry found better ways to use what was available. One example of this latter change is provided by improvements in the process of making paper during the 1920s. This process modification made possible the use of a fast-growing southern pine that previously had been unusable.

The moral of the story seems to be that technological progress has opened new avenues which previously were only dimly perceived. The development of these avenues, as well as their exploitation, was triggered by rising prices. Increasing scarcity automatically creates incentives to increase inventive activity and innovation. Whether these incentives are sufficient to call forth such timely and beneficial responses in the future remains an open question.

Source: Nathan Rosenberg, "Innovative Responses to Materials Shortages," *American Economic Review* 63 (May 1983): 111–125.

covery, technological progress, and input substitution) mitigate the seriousness of scarcity. To determine which set of factors dominates, we must examine the evidence.

DETECTING RESOURCE SCARCITY

The first step in assessing the seriousness of resource scarcity is to select a means for detecting scarcity. While this may sound like a straightforward exercise, it is not. We begin by considering what properties the ideal indicators should have and the degree to which commonly used indicators live up to these standards.

Criteria for an Ideal Scarcity Indicator

An ideal indicator would have at least the three following properties:

1. *Foresight.* The ideal indicator should be forward-looking. It should anticipate scarcity and not merely record the scarcity once it has occurred. Thus, the ideal indicator should incorporate such things as future demand patterns, alternative sources of the resource, changes in extraction cost, and so on.

2. *Comparability.* The ideal indicator should allow direct comparisons to be made among resources for the purpose of identifying the most serious problems. This comparison should facilitate an assessment not only of the degree of scarcity, but also of its seriousness. Thus the indicator should be able to incorporate such differences as the importance of the resource and the availability of substitutes.

3. *Computability.* The ideal indicator should be readily calculated from reliable, published sources of information or should depend on information that could be readily collected.

Applying the Criteria

The Physical Indicators.   Before moving on to the four types of economic indicators, let's use these criteria to evaluate the physical indices discussed in Example 6.1. Both the static and exponential versions of the reserve-to-use ratios result in a number that can be conveniently interpreted as the time until exhaustion. On the surface, this indicator appears to satisfy all three of our criteria. It is forward-looking, it allows comparisons to be made, and it is readily calculable.

This surface appearance, however, is deceiving. While reserve-to-use ratios are forward looking, their view of the future is a narrow one on several counts. Their derivation makes no provision for stock augmentation. As a result, when past predictions using these indicators are compared with the actual experience, these predictions have been uniformly and excessively pessimistic. As the little boy tending the flocks discovered, if you cry "wolf!" often when the wolf is not there, people stop listening. When the wolf actually appears, no one reacts. Thus, reserve-to-use ratios satisfy the foresight criterion only in a very limited way.

In a similar vein, reserve-to-use ratios do allow comparisons to be made, but the resulting rankings provide no guide to the seriousness of the problems. These ratios not only yield an inaccurate estimated time to exhaustion, but they also provide no estimate of how serious a matter exhaustion would be. For example, running out of an ingredient that is used solely in cosmetics and has an available substitute is less serious than running out of a substance such as helium, which is used for important scientific research and has no known substitute for that use. Reserve-to-use ratios are powerless to make this kind of crucial distinction. Therefore, the comparability which is achieved is not a very useful one for setting resource management priorities.

Reserve-to-use ratios are also powerless to draw conclusions about the seriousness of *renewable* resource scarcity. They focus on a fixed resource reserve, a concept of limited validity when applied to depletable resources that is meaningless when applied to renewable resources. As we have seen in the preceding two chapters, the problem of scarcity with renewable resources can be even more serious than that with depletable resources. Thus, the fact that this indicator allows us to draw no conclusions about scarcity in this important class of resource problems—much less integrate them into a comparable, comprehensive scheme to evaluate all resources—is a serious deficiency.

The outstanding virtue of the reserve-to-use ratio is that it is readily calculated from published data. That fact, along with its easy (but mistaken) interpretation by the general public as "time until exhaustion," probably accounts for its success.

The fact that standard physical indicators are not ideal is interesting and important, but it does not totally discredit their use unless we can show that something better exists. Does it?

Four candidate economic indictors have been suggested by the analysis in this and preceding chapters: trends in (1) resource price, (2) user cost, (3) marginal extraction cost, and (4) marginal discovery cost. To determine whether these are superior indicators, we must consider their properties in a variety of circumstances.

Resource Prices.   In previous chapters we found it useful to distinguish between efficient resource prices, which maximize the net benefits to society, and market prices, which may or may not be efficient. We shall retain that distinction here.

Efficient resource prices satisfy both the foresight and comparability criteria. Current prices are forward-looking. They are affected by such factors as rising demand, the possibilities for stock augmentation and substitution, and changes in the cost of extraction. Relative prices are also affected by the price elasticity of demand—the greater the difficulty of doing without the resource, the higher the price. Therefore, price levels and relative price changes allow us to make direct comparisons of depletable and renewable resources which reflect the seriousness of the problem.

The problem with using trends in efficient resource prices as the sole indicator is that in certain markets they are not directly observable or calculable. This occurs whenever the readily available indicator, the market price, is not equal to the efficient price. In preceding chapters we discussed cases in which these two prices might not be equal—common-property resource markets, markets with government price controls or artificial subsidies, and markets with significant externalities (such as pollution) which have not been internalized.

In these cases market price trends may not even be a valid approximation of efficient price trends. For example, take the situation with common-property resources. The problem with these resources is overexploitation in the earlier periods, followed (because the stock is so diminished) by underexploitation in the latter years. Thus, the problem is not that price would not rise to reflect scarcity. It will, eventually. The problem is that the lower earlier prices (due to the glut on the market) send a false signal of abundance. In markets where resources are treated as common property, market prices fail to exhibit the foresight property.

A similar problem occurs with uninternalized externalities. We have already seen that when the market fails to recognize these externalities, market prices are too low. And in contrast to the common-property resource problem, no automatic adjustment mechanism *ever* causes market prices to reflect this increasing scarcity. Since scarcity in this case (indicated by the rising cost of extraction and reflected in the increasing damage caused by pollution) affects non-marketed commodities (clean air and water), market prices do not signal the problem.

One further concern arises about the anticipatory role of market prices. The ability of resource markets to exhibit foresight depends, in turn, on the ability of suppliers to assess the future. If they cannot correctly anticipate future substitution possibilities, technological changes, demand patterns, and so on, market prices will fail to reflect these considerations. The information content of prices is only as rich as the information available to those who, by their collective actions, determine prices.

In conclusion, for those resources traded in efficient or nearly efficient markets, resource prices serve as a superior indicator. When markets are not efficient, the dominance of this indicator is no longer obvious. Other indicators become useful either to complement or replace resource prices in those markets.

Scarcity Rent. A second economic indicator involves trends in *scarcity rent*, the payment accruing to a resource owner when the user cost is positive. The efficient scarcity rent is forward-looking; indeed, if the future did not matter, there would be no scarcity rent! Use of scarcity rent should anticipate future increases in demand as well as changes in extraction cost as the resource is used up. Scarcity rent can be used as an indicator for both renewable and depletable resource scarcity.

As you can see, up to this point, scarcity rent trends sound roughly comparable to resource price trends as indicators. For certain types of resources, however, scarcity rent may be superior to the price of the extracted product, the most readily available price. A forestry economist, L. C. Irland, provides a case in point:[3]

> From the Civil War to about 1900, lumber prices were stable while timber prices rose. Prominent forces were the decline in transport costs and improvements in milling.

The use of *lumber* prices as a measure of timber scarcity would lead to an erroneous conclusion. The scarcity reflected in the rising price of timber was camouflaged by declining transportation and milling costs. Only the scarcity rent of the timber (called *stumpage* in the industry) correctly detected the scarcity.[4]

With respect to other resources, however, scarcity rent may well represent a less than adequate measure. As shown earlier, the scarcity rent for common-property resources is zero for all time periods. For that class of resources it is a deficient indicator of scarcity.

Even for efficient markets the relationship between scarcity rent and the degree of resource depletion is not always well defined. For depletable resources having a constant marginal cost of extraction, we expect scarcity rent to *rise* with the depletion. On the other hand, when extraction costs rise with the amount extracted, scarcity rent should *decline* with increasing scarcity. To interpret the behavior of scarcity rent, we need to know the underlying structure of extraction costs.

As a result, interpretation becomes an important problem. Declining scarcity rent could represent either increasing availability of the resource, which is desirable, or rising extraction cost, which is undesirable. Since it makes a difference which interpretation is correct, it is risky to base conclusions on this one indicator.

Marginal Discovery Cost.   Scarcity rent is not always directly observable, even in those circumstances where it might prove to be a useful indicator. Earlier we derived a relationship capable of resolving this dilemma. We noted that marginal discovery cost, which can be observed, should be equal to marginal scarcity rent. Therefore, marginal discovery cost can be used as a proxy for marginal scarcity

---

3 L. C. Irland, "Is Timber Scarce?: The Economics of a Renewable Resource," Bulletin No. 83 (New Haven, CT: Yale School of Forestry and Environmental Studies, 1974).

4 Stumpage is the price an extractor pays to the owner of forest land for the privilege of cutting and taking the timber.

rent when information on discovery cost is available and information on scarcity rent is not.

Marginal Extraction Cost.   The final indicators of resource scarcity suggested by conventional analysis are trends in the marginal cost of extraction. For a given technology of extraction, as lower-grade ores are extracted, we normally expect the marginal cost of extraction to rise. Rising marginal extraction cost should, therefore, serve as a signal of the amount of sacrifice needed to procure each unit of the resource. It is noteworthy that the usefulness of this indicator of scarcity is not undermined when the resources are treated as common property. Thus, it is perhaps the best indicator to be used for common-property resources, such as fish and whales.

Extraction cost, however, is far from a flawless indicator. Of the three economic indicators we have considered so far, extraction cost is the only one which does not fulfill the foresight criterion. Since it is based on the current cost of extraction, it provides no indication of future problems, such as rapidly rising demand or future increases in extraction cost, which may be just around the corner.[5] Business or government leaders wishing to anticipate scarcity, rather than merely react to it once it occurs, do not get much help from this indicator.

Unit extraction cost is also a difficult concept to measure precisely with published information. As a result, analysts have developed means of approximating it with available information. Perhaps the most widely cited example is the unit extraction-cost measure developed by Harold Barnett and Chandler Morse:[6]

$$C_i \quad = \quad (\alpha L_i + \beta_i K_i)/Q_i$$

where C_i =   the unit extraction cost for resource i

L_i =   labor in industry i, as measured by employment

K_i =   reproducible capital (equipment and structures)

Q_i =   net amount of the ith resource extracted

α_i, β_i =   weights used to aggregate the dissimilar capital and labor inputs

---

5 Unless all environmental costs of extraction are internalized, measured extraction cost will understate the actual cost of extraction.

6 Harold Barnett and Chandler Morse, *Scarcity and Growth: The Economics of Natural Resource Availability* (Baltimore: The Johns Hopkins University Press for Resources for the Future, 1963).

The logic behind this formulation suggests that capital and labor are primary inputs to the extraction of resources; as society begins the transition to increasingly inferior sources, larger inputs of capital and labor are required per unit of resource extracted. This is recorded as a rise in the index. Conversely, a fall over time in this index suggests either that new, low-cost sources have continually been discovered, or that technological progress has reduced the amount of capital and labor required to extract a unit of the resource to the extent of counteracting the increasing inferiority of the grades used.

Some problems with this particular specification would not arise if the true extraction-cost data were available. One of the most blatant is the omission of factors other than capital and labor that would be involved in the extraction of resources. Energy is one obvious example. If capital equipment consumed more energy over time—which is the expected response to the falling energy prices that occurred until 1974—then the Barnett-Morse measure would fail to pick one possible source of rising extraction cost: the cost of energy.[7]

The size of distortion caused by this omission is not clear. Combining this omission with the failure of this measure to include (presumably rising) environmental costs, it is, therefore, difficult to put our complete faith in this approximation until we know just how good an approximation it is.

In conclusion, no indicator of resource scarcity dominates the others in all cases. Trends in real resource prices probably dominate in efficient markets. Scarcity rent trends probably dominate in those markets, such as timber, where the common-property problem does not exist and where the values of the in situ resources are routinely collected. Marginal discovery cost trends may usefully approximate marginal scarcity rent when it is not directly observable. Trends in the cost of extraction are superior for those resources treated as common property. The moral seems to be that we cannot trust any single indicator to provide the desired information. Judgments have to be made on a case-by-case basis using a variety of indicators.

EVIDENCE ON RESOURCE SCARCITY

A number of studies have attempted to assess the degree of scarcity now facing us. Since these have relied on quite different approaches, it is not surprising to discover that they come to rather different conclusions. Our review of these studies begins with those relying mainly on the physical indicators and closes with those using economic indicators.

---

7 It would not be difficult to modify the Barnett-Morse measure to incorporate energy. The point is that they did not perform this modification, so their results must be interpreted accordingly.

Physical Indicators

To open our discussion of physical indicators, let's return to the analysis conducted by the *Limits to Growth* team, which demonstrates a typical use of physical indicators. The physical indicators computed as of 1970 are presented as Table 13.1. Of the nineteen depletable resources listed, only one (coal) could be expected to last as long as 100 years according to the exponential index. Resources that would be exhausted by the year 2000 (that is, have an exponential index of less than 30 years) include copper, gold, lead, mercury, natural gas, petroleum, silver, tin, and zinc. During the 1980s we should have already run out of gold, mercury, silver, tin, and zinc. This is a formidable list!

We know from previous discussions that a considerable degree of conservatism is built into this approach. One way to assess the depth of this conservatism is to relax some of the assumptions that went into the derivation of those numbers. One study allowing us to do this was accomplished for the United Nations by Wassily Leontief.[8]

As part of his analysis, Leontief assumed (as did the *Limits to Growth* team) that proved reserves did not change over time (no stock augmentation). In contrast to the *Limits to Growth* approach, however, his forecast of demand was sensitive to rising prices. In other words, rather than forecast a level of demand that grows at a constant exponential rate and is impervious to outside influences (as is assumed in the exponential index), Leontief calculated the effects of increasing extraction costs on resource prices and estimated the degree to which demand would respond to those higher prices. Thus, the Leontief study retains an intentionally pessimistic approach on the supply side, but allows a bit more reasonable forecast on the demand side.

After incorporating this change, the Leontief forecast finds only two minerals—lead and zinc—for which cumulated expected demand by the year 2000 expected to exceed current proven reserves. Compare this forecast to the nine minerals listed in Table 13.1 and anticipated by the *Limits to Growth* team to run out by that year. The inclusion of the demand-dampening characteristics of prices reduces the degree of expected scarcity below what the use of the pure exponential index would lead one to expect.

The key on the demand side lies in the ability to substitute renewable for depletable natural resources. One way we can assess the potential degree of substitutability between natural resources and other commodities is to estimate a construct known as the *elasticity of substitution*. The elasticity of substitution

---

8 Wassily Leontief et al., *The Future of the World Economy* (New York: Oxford University Press, 1977).

TABLE 13.1 Static and Exponential Depletion Indices (1970)

Resource	Known global reserves[a]	Static index (years)[b]	Average projected rate of growth (% per year)[c]	Exponential index (years)[d]	Resource	Known global reserves[a]	Static index (years)[b]	Average projected rate of growth (% per year)[c]	Exponential index (years)[d]
Aluminum	1.17×10^9 tons	100	6.4	31	Molybdenum	10.8×10^9 lbs	79	4.5	34
Chromium	7.75×10^8 tons	420	2.6	95	Natural gas	1.14×10^{15} cu ft	38	4.7	22
Coal	5×10^{12} tons	2300	4.1	111	Nickel	147×10^9 lbs	150	3.4	53
Cobalt	4.8×10^9 tons	110	1.5	60	Petroleum	455×10^9 bbls	31	3.9	20
Copper	308×10^6 tons	36	4.6	21	Platinum group[e]	429×10^6 troy oz	130	3.8	47
Gold	353×10^6 troy oz	11	4.1	9	Silver	5.5×10^9 troy oz	16	2.7	13
Iron	1×10^{11} tons	240	1.8	93	Tin	4.3×10^6 lg tons	17	1.1	15
Lead	91×10^6 tons	26	2.0	21	Tungsten	2.9×10^9	40	2.5	28
Manganese	8×10^8 tons	97	2.9	46	Zinc	123×10^6 tons	23	2.9	18
Mercury	3.34×10^6 flasks	13	2.6	13					

[a] U.S. Bureau of Mines, *Mineral Facts and Problems*, 1970 (Washington, DC: Government Printing Office, 1970).

[b] The number of years known global reserves will last at current global consumption. Calculated by dividing known reserves (column 2) by the current annual consumption (U.S. Bureau of Mines, *Mineral Facts and Problems*, 1970).

[c] U.S. Bureau of Mines, *Mineral Facts and Problems*, 1970.

[d] The number of years known global reserves will last with consumption growing exponentially at the average annual rate of growth. Calculated by the formula

$$\text{exponential index} = \frac{\ln((r \times s) + 1)}{r},$$

where r = average rate of growth from column 4, and s = static index from column 3.

[e] The platinum group metals are platinum, palladium, iridium, osmium, rhodium and ruthenium.

Source: From *The Limits to Growth: A Report for The Club of Rome's Project on the Predicament of Mankind*, by Donella H. Meadows, Dennis L. Meadows, Jorgen Randers, William H. Behrens, III. A Potomac Associates book published by Universe Books, N.Y., 1972. Graphics by Potomac Associates. Reprinted by permission.

(σ) is a measure of the degree to which two factor inputs complement or substitute for each other in the production process.[9]

When σ is positive, the factors are substitutes and when σ is negative they are complements.[10] The larger the positive number, the easier and more complete the substitution will be. Generally an elasticity of substitution greater than 1 indicates considerable ease in substitution. The elasticity of substitution is zero for the fixed-proportions isoquant in Figure 13.1. Though a thorough review of the voluminous literature on input substitution would carry us too far afield, it seems fair to summarize the evidence as suggesting that capital and resources are substitutes and sometimes strong substitutes.[11] The relationship between capital and energy, however, is another matter indeed.

A number of studies examining the substitutability of energy, with resources and with labor, have been accomplished for the United States and other countries.[12] Generally, the results are mixed. Energy and labor appear uniformly to be substitutes, with the size of elasticities ranging from 0.48 to 3.80, depending on the industry and country. The story about energy and capital is more complicated. Studies based on data for a single country usually find capital and energy to be complements, rather than substitutes. This is relatively easy to understand. Historically when relative energy prices were falling, the natural response by the economic system was to construct and use energy-using capital. This does not necessarily mean that capital and energy remain complements in a period when relative energy prices are rising. We discuss this further in Chapter 21.

---

9 The elasticity of substitution between two factors of production (say, X and Y) is defined as the ratio of the percentage change in the factor ratio to the percentage change in their relative prices (P_x and P_y). Thus

$$\sigma = \frac{(\Delta\, X/Y)(P_y/P_x)}{(\Delta\, P_y/P_x)(X/Y)}$$

10 Two factors are said to be complements if an increase in one leads to an increase in the other. If an increase in the first factor leads to a decrease in the second, then those factors are said to be substitutes.

11 Anyone interested in a thorough review of the state of the art in estimating input substitutability should consult Ernst R. Berndt and Barry C. Field, eds., *Modeling and Measuring Natural Resource Substitution* (Cambridge, MA: MIT Press, 1981).

12 See, for example, E. R. Berndt and D. Wood, "Technology, Prices and the Derived Demand for Energy," *Review of Economics and Statistics* 57 (August 1975): 259-268; R. Halvorsen and J. Ford, "Substitution among Energy, Capital and Labor Inputs in U.S. Manufacturing," in *Advances in the Economics of Energy and Resources*, Vol. 1, R. S. Pindyck, ed. (Greenwich, CT: JAI Press, 1978); M. Fuss, "The Demand for Energy in Canadian Manufacturing: An Example of the Estimation of Production Structures with Many Inputs," *Journal of Econometrics* 5 (January 1977): 89-116; S. E. Atkinson and R. E. Halvorsen, "Inter-fuel Substitution in Steam Electric Power Generation," *Journal of Political Economy* 84 (October 1976): 959-978; J. M. Griffen and P. R. Gregory, "An Intercountry Translog Model of Energy Substitution Process," *American Economic Review* 66 (December 1976): 845-857; Anthony C. Fisher, *Resource and Environmental Economics* (Cambridge, England: Cambridge University Press, 1981).

What can be said about substitution possibilities? In general, they seem quite good, though in particular industries problems may erupt. Both capital and labor are able to serve as substitutes for each other and for resources within reasonable limits. The complementarity of capital and energy would be troubling if it were inevitable, but this historic relationship could well be transformed to one of substitutability in the future as energy becomes much more expensive.[13]

How about the supply side and the longer term? It is not really a very damning criticism of the *Limits to Growth* to suggest that their estimates were off by 50 or more years. Massive resource scarcity in 50 years would be as deserving of our attention as that occurring sooner.

Perhaps the most searching assessment of the future long-term availability of resources was conducted by two physical scientists, Goeller and Weinberg.[14] These authors went through the entire periodic table of elements and some of the more important compounds to derive estimates of current use and future availability. Their definition of future availability was expansive, including all potential sources of supply from the atmosphere, the ocean, and the crust of the earth down to a depth of one kilometer. Essentially their estimate of supply corresponds to what we called resource endowment in Chapter 6.

Using the resource endowment as their definition of reserves, Goeller and Weinberg computed static reserve indices for each substance. The resource we would run out of first, phosphorus, according to their calculation would last another 1300 years. For most other resources their indices suggest exhaustion horizons in the millions of years. On the basis of this and a complementary analysis, Goeller and Weinberg draw two main conclusions:

1. With three exceptions—phosphorus, a few trace elements for agriculture, and energy fossil fuels—there is virtually an unlimited supply of resources.

2. The transition away from these truly limited resources can be accomplished with relatively little, if any, loss in living standards. In most cases it can be accomplished with real resource prices no more than double current levels.

If we were somehow able to peer into the future with a crystal ball, we would probably find that the actual situation would lie somewhere between the pessimism of the Meadows forecast and the optimism of the Goeller and Weinberg forecast. The conservatism of the Meadows analysis is now obvious. The op-

---

13 Consider, for example, the use of computers to control heating systems more efficiently, allowing substantial savings in energy.

14 H. E. Goeller and A. M. Weinberg, "The Age of Substitutability," *The American Economic Review* 68 (December 1978): 1–11.

timism of the Goeller and Weinberg analysis rests in part on an assumption that all of the resource endowment they identify could, in fact, be recovered and could be used without causing other environmental problems, such as changes in the climate. This expectation is fully compatible with a traditional geological view of the manner in which resources are distributed within the earth's crust. This view suggests that the lower the grade, the larger is the supply of the resource available. It posits a rather smooth supply curve, devoid of any sharp discontinuities.

Recently, however, a well-known geochemist suggested that a rather different distribution may underlie certain geochemically scarce elements in the earth's crust.[15] This analysis suggests that minerals can be classified into three groups. For the first group—iron, aluminum, titanium, magnesium, and silicon—the distribution of ores results in an inverse relationship between grade and tonnage of the ores. As grade is reduced by depleting the higher-grade ores, even larger tonnages of the lower-grade ores become available.

For the second group of resources—manganese, barium, vanadium, zirconium, sulfur, phosphorus, fluorine, and chlorine—limits to this inverse grade-tonnage relationship are present, but the supplies of ores are so great so to suggest that these limits do not constrain resource availability for the foreseeable future.

For all other metals—which Skinner calls the geochemically scarce metals, such as copper, lead, zinc, molybdenum, and gold—the distribution of ores is quite different. A comparison of the traditional view with that of Skinner is presented as Figure 13.2. The left panel presents the traditional (single-peaked) function generally found for the more abundant resources. The bimodal function is presented in the right panel.

The implication of the Skinner hypothesis is that as we mine lower grades of geochemically scarce resources, we shall find less, not more, lower-grade ore available over some considerable range of grades. Skinner further suggests the existence of a *mineralogical threshold* between the two peaks. This mineralogical threshold delineates a sharp discontinuity in the manner by which minerals are extracted to the left and to the right of this threshold. His characterization of this threshold is presented as Figure 13.3.

With abundant elements, the energy used per unit output rises smoothly as the grade of the ore is decreased. For the geochemically scarce resources, Skinner posits a sharp discontinuity in energy use when the supply of separate minerals (as represented by the smaller peak of Figure 13.2) is exhausted and the remaining sources are trapped as atomic substitutes for more abundant metals in the crystal structure of minerals.

---

15 B. J. Skinner, "A Second Iron Age Ahead?" *American Scientist* 64 (1976): 258–269.

FIGURE 13.2   Alternative views of ore distribution.

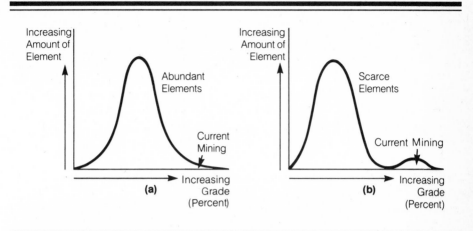

Source: B. J. Skinner, "A Second Iron Age Ahead?" *American Scientist* 64 (1976): 263.

FIGURE 13.3   Nature of the mineralogical threshold.

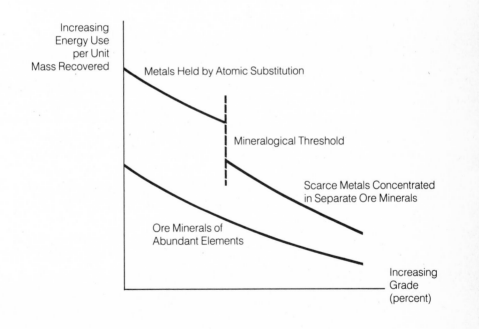

Source: B. J. Skinner, "A Second Iron Age Ahead?" *American Scientist* 64 (1976): 267.

TABLE 13.2 Energy Used To Mine and Process a Copper Ore in Which All Copper Is Present in Biotite

	Energy used (BTU/lb. Cu)		
Grade, percent Cu	0.7	0.1	0.01
Mining plus concentration	19,300	135,000	1,250,000
Preparation of a copper salt	326,858	2,288,010	22,880,100
Smelting	20,000	20,000	20,000
Total	366,158	2,443,010	24,250,100
Equivalent thermal energy in bituminous coal, in pounds of coal	28	188	1,866

Source: D. P. Harris and B. J. Skinner, "The Assessment of Long-Term Supplies of Minerals," in *Explorations in Natural Resource Economics*, V. K. Smith and J. V. Krutilla, eds. (Baltimore: Johns Hopkins University Press, 1982): 263, Table 8.3.

Traditional mineral concentration processes could no longer be used to separate these minerals. The host ore would have to be broken down in order to release the tightly bound metals. Some estimates have suggested that the successful negotiation of this transition would require energy use per unit output some 100 or 1000 times higher than current use.[16] Table 13.2 demonstrates this relationship for copper.

To the extent that the Skinner hypothesis is valid, barring the arrival of unlimited cheap energy, the Goeller and Weinberg analysis will be excessively optimistic, particularly for the geochemically scarce metals. How would the economy react to the very high prices necessary to extract these metals? Example 13.3 presents one study conducted specifically to answer this question. It seems to suggest that increasing scarcity will usher in some dramatic changes, but these changes will cushion the shock to the economy. Only the complete or near-complete disappearance of copper from the scene would cause large economic losses.

Economic Indicators

Extraction Cost. The original work that spawned serious investigation of natural resource scarcity, by Barnett and Morse in 1963, was *Scarcity and*

16 See, for example, Donald A. Brobst, "Fundamental Concepts for Analysis of Resource Availability," in *Scarcity and Growth Reconsidered*, V. Kerry Smith, ed. (Baltimore: Johns Hopkins University Press for Resources for the Future, 1979): 128.

EXAMPLE 13.3

Geochemically Scarce Metals: How Would the Economy React?

Geochemically scarce metals, such as copper, present a special challenge to the economic system as the supplies of ore decline. To understand how the economy might respond to this challenge, a team which included three economists and a geochemist constructed a model of the future copper market in the United States. This model included a wide range of current and anticipated demands for copper, a host of substitution possibilities, and estimates of supplies available from production and recycling.

From their model they draw the following conclusions:

1. The rate of extraction of copper from the earth grows rapidly over the next 100 years. Extraction peaks in about 2100 and then declines slowly. The peak extraction rate is about eight times the current rate of production of new copper.
2. The ores containing copper minerals are largely exhausted by 2070. Thereafter copper is obtained from copper rock, which has a maximum grade of 0.05%, compared with 0.5% today. Once copper is obtained from copper rock, the intrinsic scarcity of copper disappears; copper is then very expensive but no longer "scarce" in the sense of being exhaustible.
3. As times passes the services currently or historically provided by copper are progressively provided by greater amounts of substitute materials such as aluminum, titanium, stainless steel, plastics, and glass. By the end of the twenty-first century, only a handful of today's uses survive.
4. Recycling becomes big business. By the middle of next century virtually all copper available from waste is recovered and reused.
5. Copper prices rise dramatically over the next century, growing exponentially from $2 per kilogram in the early periods to $120 per kilogram when the backstop resources (common rock) are brought into play; thereafter prices remain stable in real terms.
6. Even though the price of copper metal rises 50-fold over the next century, the cost of copper-equivalent services rises only tenfold.
7. The overall cost of copper scarcity is estimated to be somewhat less than 0.5% of national income. However, the overall cost of completely doing without copper is estimated to be a whopping 22% of national income.

Source: Robert B. Gordon, Tjalling C. Koopmans, William D. Nordhaus, and Brian J. Skinner, *Toward a New Iron Age? Quantitative Modeling of Resource Exhaustion* (Cambridge, MA: Harvard University Press, 1987).

Growth: The Economics of Natural Resource Availability. This pioneering work is noteworthy both for the methodology it developed and for the conclusions it derived.

The Barnett-Morse empirical evaluations concentrated on two measures constructed using data from 1870 to 1957. The first, called the unit-cost measure, was an attempt to capture any increase in effort required to extract an output of a given quality. This measure was described in the preceding section. The second measure recorded the trends in natural resource prices relative to an index of prices for nonextractive resources. The authors made it clear that they preferred the former measure.

After examining the trends of these two indicators, Barnett and Morse conclude that, with the exception of the forestry sector, no evidence of increasing scarcity was apparent. Furthermore, they found that this conclusion was insensitive to the various subjective judgments they had been forced to make during the analysis, such as defining the weights used to combine labor and capital and the choice of indices used to capture price trends in the nonextractive sector. Different calculations based on other reasonable judgments yielded the same conclusions.

What interpretation can be placed on these results?[17] Barnett and Morse offer four explanations for the absence of any evidence of scarcity in the face of increasing demand and a finite resource base: (a) historically when higher-grade resources were exhausted, lower-grade resources became available in even greater abundance; (b) as the possibility for scarcity emerged, resource users began to switch to other less scarce resources; (c) as prices rose, exploration for new sources was encouraged and this exploration was remarkably successful; and (d) technological change reduced the costs of extraction and expanded the universe of recoverable resources. They suggest that, historically, the combined effect of these mitigating factors was so strong that they eliminated evidence of current or future scarcity, except for forest products.

This generally optimistic view of the past was complemented by an equally optimistic view of the future. They suggested:

That man will face a series of particular scarcities as the result of growth is a foregone conclusion; that these will impose general scarcity—increasing cost—is not a legitimate corollary. The twentieth century's discovery of the uniformity of energy and matter has increased the possibilities of substitution to an unimaginable degree and placed at man's disposal an indefinitely large number of alternatives from which to choose. To suppose that these alternatives must eventually become so restricted, relative to man's wants, that increasing cost will be inescapable, is not justified by

---

17 An excellent technical evaluation of this study and others with a similar focus can be found in V. Kerry Smith, "The Evaluation of Natural Resource Adequacy: Elusive Quest or Economics Analysis?" *Land Economics* 56 (August 1980): 257–298.

the evidence. An absolute limit to the possibilities of escape may exist, but it cannot be defined or specified. The finite limits of the globe, so real in their unqueried simplicity, lose definition under examination [pp. 244-245].

Skepticism may be appropriate for a sweeping conclusion like this one. One source of skepticism, the inadequacy of extraction costs as an indicator of scarcity, has been dealt with in the preceding section. Other sources include the time frame of the analysis (the Barnett-Morse data end in 1957) and a singular focus on the United States. Would studies using later data, a wider geographic frame of reference, and a richer set of indicators tend to support the Barnett-Morse conclusions?

Such studies have provided some support for at least the historical interpretation of the Barnett-Morse data. Johnson, Bell, and Bennett extended the analysis on American unit extraction costs by incorporating data through 1970 (1966 in a few cases).[18] By performing traditional hypothesis tests, they found:

1. The Barnett-Morse finding of increasing scarcity in forestry was reversed in the 1958-1970 period.

2. Of the 15 agricultural commodity groups studied, *all* had declining unit extraction cost during the 1958-1972 period. Of these, only three—food grains, oil crops, and vegetables—had smaller declines during this period than the earlier period studied by Barnett and Morse.

3. Of the eleven mineral and fuel commodity groups studied, *all* had declining unit extraction costs during the 1958-1972 period. Of these, only copper registered a smaller decline during the later period.

4. Since 1962, unit extraction costs have risen in commercial fishing. This was the only documented case of increasing scarcity that these three authors found and, after reading Chapter 12, this particular scarcity should surprise no one.

Harold Barnett, one of the authors of *Scarcity and Growth*, has also recently expanded his earlier analysis by using more recent data covering the global resource situation, rather than merely that in the United States.[19] After analyzing a wide variety of data, he found that

---

18 Manual H. Johnson, Frederick W. Bell, and James T. Bennett, "Natural Resource Scarcity: Empirical Evidence and Public Policy," *Journal of Environmental Economics and Management* 7 (September 1980): 256-271.

19 Harold J. Barnett, "Scarcity and Growth Revisited," in *Scarcity and Growth Reconsidered*, V. Kerry Smith, ed. (Baltimore: Johns Hopkins University Press for Resources for the Future, 1979): 163-217.

1. Unit extraction cost, measured as labor per unit output, declined over all time periods, all countries, and all commodities.
2. Of 20 cases examined, the unit extraction cost, measured as labor per unit output, declined more slowly in mineral industries than it did in manufacturing for only three cases.

Thus even when examination of extraction costs is expanded to include other countries and other time periods, the conclusion of declining extraction costs seems to be robust. Extraction costs are not forward looking, however, so if we are to assess future resource scarcity, we must examine the behavior of resource prices as well. Extraction costs are not enough.

Studies of Resource Price Trends.   If resource scarcity is increasing in some sense, we should be able to discover that natural resource prices are rising more rapidly than prices in general. In the Harold Barnett study mentioned earlier, resource prices were examined, as well as unit extraction costs. His price findings were that

1. Of 53 cases examined, agricultural prices rose faster than a general wholesale price index in 23 cases.
2. In West Germany over the period 1950 to 1971, prices of minerals and raw materials rose faster than prices in general in three out of the six cases studied.

This provides some evidence that prices are rising more rapidly in the natural resource sectors than in others, a finding which is compatible with projections of future increases in resource scarcity.

Recent work by V. Kerry Smith complements this study by examining more recent relative price data for the United States.[20] Using more sophisticated statistical analyses than used in other previous studies, Smith found that conclusions concerning the rise or fall of natural resource prices were very sensitive to the choice of time periods used in the analysis. Different periods yielded different results. Even so, historical decline in relative resource prices appeared to be smaller in more recent periods with some reversals (and hence, increases in prices) evident for some resources. He concluded:

---

20 V. Kerry Smith, "The Evaluation of Natural Resource Adequacy: Elusive Quest or Frontier of Economic Analysis?" *Land Economics* 56 (August 1980): 257–298; "Measuring Natural Resource Scarcity: Theory and Practice," *Journal of Environmental Economics and Management* 5 (June 1978): 150–171; "Natural Resource Scarcity: A Statistical Analysis," *Review of Economics and Statistics* 61 (August 1979): 423–427.

The analysis in this paper has raised questions as to whether the conclusions drawn from the empirical data considered by Barnett and Morse were warranted, both in terms of the inherent limitation in the use of the outcome measure and the data themselves. Our analysis with updated data indicates that this evidence alone is not sufficient to arrive at what is [*sic*] commonly accepted interpretation of Barnett and Morse—namely, there is no evidence of natural-resource scarcity [1978, p. 165].

The work described above relies upon linear functions which do not allow for relative prices to initially decline and then increase. Yet our description of the role of technological progress in Chapter 6 would lead us to expect precisely this kind of pattern. Can the presence of this nonlinear price pattern be refuted or confirmed?

Margaret Slade has specifically investigated this question for a variety of types of resources.[21] Using statistical techniques, she fitted a quadratic equation of the form

$$P_{it} = b_{0i} + b_{1i}t + b_{2i}t^2 + V_{it},$$

where P_{it} = deflated price of the ith commodity at time t

t = time measured in years (1800 = 0)

V_{it} = a random error term

The virtues of this simple approach are the use of a function that can first decline and then rise,[22] the existence of this pattern can be statistically verified,[23] and if the relationship is validated, the parameters can be used to determine the year in which the decline stopped and the increase began.[24]

In fact, Slade found that the quadratic function fit the data better than the linear function for all but one of the resources examined (lead), implying that the minimum point on the U-shaped curve had already been passed.[25] For these resources, at least, the pattern of falling, following rising, relative prices seems

---

21 Margaret E. Slade, "Trends in Natural Resource Commodity Prices: An Analysis of the Time Domain," *Journal of Environmental Economics and Management* 9 (June 1982): 122-137.

22 This pattern results when $b_0 > 0$, $b_1 < 0$, and $b_2 > 0$.

23 If $b_2 = 0$, then the equation is linear. Thus the test is to see whether $b_2 = 0$ or $b_2 > 0$.

24 Using calculus the bottom of the price decline can be found to be when $t = -b_1/2b_2$. Since $b_1 < 0$, this will be a positive number.

25 Those interested in the process by which knowledge proceeds might wish to investigate the controversy about these results. See Michael J. Mueller and Daniel R. Gorin, "Informative Trends in Natural Resource Commodity Prices: A Comment on Slade," *Journal of Environmental Economics and Management* 12 (March 1985): 89-95 and the response in Margaret E. Slade, "Noninformative Trends in Natural Resource Commodity Prices: U-Shaped Price Paths Exonerated," *Journal of Environmental Economics and Management* 12 (June 1985): 181-192.

to be the rule rather than the exception, and the turning point seems to have passed.

Slade sums up this evidence by saying: "Therefore, if scarcity is measured by relative prices, the evidence indicates that nonrenewable natural-resource commodities are becoming scarce [p. 136]."

As well done as these studies are the volatility of these prices makes it difficult to use price trends to draw firm long term conclusions about impending scarcity. The signal contains a lot of noise. During the 1970s, a period covered by the research described above, metals prices increased at least as much as inflation and in some years more. In the early 1980s, however, metals prices declined while general price indices continued to rise. During the late 1980s metals prices again began to rise.[26]

Discovery Cost.   In closing our review of the empirical evidence let's consider what information can be gleaned from an examination of discovery costs. Table 13.3 compares price information with average discovery costs in the United States for oil and gas for the years 1950–1971. All figures are expressed in constant 1947–1949 dollars. Because the preferred indicator, marginal discovery cost, was not available, average discovery cost was used instead.[27]

This table shows that over the period no real increase in crude oil prices occurred. According to that indicator, no scarcity was apparent. Yet a somewhat different picture is painted by the discovery cost data. Though the pattern is somewhat erratic, a distinct increase in discovery costs seems to characterize the later years. The message seems clear; the discovery costs were picking up an impending scarcity by the early 1970s that price information had missed. Thus, some evidence of resource scarcity on the horizon has been detected by the discovery cost indicator, as well as the relative price indicators reviewed by Slade.

SUMMARY

In view of the rapidly developing state of the art in the assessment of resource scarcity, can any concrete conclusions be drawn? Fortunately they can.

1. The problem is not whether we shall run out of resources. As the work of Goeller and Weinberg makes clear, the air, water, and crust of the

---

26 For an interesting analysis of some of the sources of this volatility, see Paul W. MacAvoy, *Explaining Metals Prices* (Boston: Academic Press, 1988).

27 When marginal discovery costs are rising (as in Table 13.3), average costs will understate marginal discovery costs.

TABLE 13.3   Constant Dollar Prices and Average Discovery Costs for Oil, 1950–1971

Year	Price per barrel[a] of crude oil	Average discovery cost for oil and gas[b]
1950	2.43	0.497
1951	2.20	0.748
1952	2.27	0.827
1953	2.43	0.692
1954	2.52	0.628
1955	2.50	1.036
1956	2.44	0.789
1957	2.63	0.653
1958	2.52	0.950
1959	2.42	1.449
1960	2.41	1.213
1961	2.42	1.509
1962	2.42	0.98
1963	2.42	1.35
1964	2.41	1.26
1965	2.35	0.98
1966	2.29	1.65
1967	2.32	1.39
1968	2.28	0.14
1969	2.30	1.78
1970	2.28	1.24
1971	2.32	1.38

[a]Prices in average 1947–1949 dollars.

[b]Dollars per equivalent barrel of oil discovered (average 1947–1949 dollars). To combine oil and gas discoveries, physical units were aggregated on the basis of market values.

Source: Anthony C. Fisher, *Resource and Environmental Economics* (New York: Cambridge University Press, 1981): 109–110, Tables 4.6, 4.7.

earth provide a storehouse of the very resources we use. For more resources, this storehouse would not be exhausted for literally millions of years. The problem is not their existence but whether we are willing to pay the price to extract and use those resources.

2. The evidence suggests the likelihood that localized (as opposed to generalized) scarcity will be experienced by some resources. For certain types of fish and for some minerals, we may, within the next 50 years, encounter extraction costs which shall cause the rate of consumption of those resources to decline.

3. Although the evidence on resource scarcity is mixed, mounting evidence suggests that for several major minerals and fuels we have

now passed the point where the prices of resources are rising more slowly than the prices of other commodities. While this evidence is not strong enough to be used to forecast generalized shortages, it does suggest that we probably are entering an age of increasing relative resource cost.

4. Our ability to detect resource scarcity is currently limited by the non-existence of an indicator which is forward-looking, comprehensive, and computable. While several indicators are currently being used, none is appropriate for all resources and all market situations.

5. One of the most serious deficiencies in both our detection system and our ability to respond to scarcity is the failure of the market system to incorporate the various environmental costs of increasing resource use, be they radiation hazards, the loss of genetic diversity or aesthetics, the pollution of the air we breathe and the water we drink, or modification of the climate. Without including these costs, our detection indicators give falsely optimistic signals and the market makes choices that put society inefficiently at risk.

To complete our examination of the *Limits to Growth*, we must determine whether these environmental costs can be included in the indicators as well as in the incentives of those who will, by their choice, define what the future holds for this generation and those which follow. The next few chapters examine this question for air pollution, water pollution, and toxic substances.

FURTHER READING

Barnett, Harold and Chandler Morse. *Scarcity and Growth: The Economics of Natural Resource Availability* (Baltimore: Johns Hopkins University Press for Resources for the Future, 1963). The pioneering book that initiated research on the use of economic indicators for assessing resource scarcity.

Leontief, Wassily et al. *The Future of the World Economy* (New York: Oxford University Press, 1977). A monumental effort led by a Nobel laureate to quantify (on a regional basis) the effects on the environment (including the natural resource base) of the world economy to the year 2000. The study also looks at how the natural resource base would affect the degree to which goals established by the United Nations for the developing nations could be met.

MacKeller, F. Landis and Daniel R. Vining, Jr. "Natural Resource Scarcity: A Global Survey," in *Population Growth and Economic Development: Issues and Evidence*, D. Gale Johnson and Ronald D. Lee, eds. (Madison, WI: University of Wisconsin Press, 1987): 259–329. Examines energy, food, and forest resources.

Portney, Paul R., ed. *Current Issues in Natural Resource Policy* (Washington, DC: Resources for the Future, 1982). An excellent collection of essays on public lands, mineral endangered species, marine fisheries, global climate, water supplies, agricultural land, and private forests. Highly recommended.

Ridker, Ronald G. and William D. Watson. *To Choose a Future: Resource and Environmental Consequences of Alternative Growth Paths* (Baltimore : Johns Hopkins University Press for Resources for the Future, 1980). This study examines, using computer simulations, various economic growth scenarios for the United States over the period 1975–2025. It concludes that, although problems will arise in the future under any of the scenarios, "the United States has the physical, technological and management capabilities to resolve them without serious losses in welfare."

Smith, V. Kerry, ed. *Scarcity and Growth Reconsidered* (Baltimore : Johns Hopkins University Press for Resources for the Future, 1979). A systematic assessment of the methodology and conclusions of the Barnett-Morse book by 12 authors aided by some 16 years of hindsight. The authors bring diverse backgrounds and viewpoints to their assessment. Most of the book is accessible to those with minimal mathematics training.

ADDITIONAL REFERENCES

Berndt, Ernst R. and Barry C. Field, eds. *Modeling and Measuring Natural Resource Substitution* (Cambridge, MA: The MIT Press, 1981).

Brown, Gardiner, Jr., and Barry Field. "The Adequacy of Measures for Signalling the Scarcity of Natural Resources," in *Scarcity and Growth Reconsidered*, V. Kerry Smith, ed. (Baltimore: Johns Hopkins University Press, 1979).

Devarajan, Shantayanan and Anthony C. Fisher. "Exploration and Scarcity," *Journal of Political Economy* 90 (December 1980): 1279–1290.

Devarajan, Shantayanan and Anthony C. Fisher. "Measures of Resource Scarcity under Uncertainty," in *Explorations in Natural Resource Economics*, V. Kerry Smith and John V. Krutilla, eds. (Baltimore: Johns Hopkins University Press for Resources for the Future, 1982): 330–343.

Manthy, Robert S. *Natural Resource Commodities—A Century of Statistics* (Baltimore: Johns Hopkins University Press for Resources for the Future, 1978).

Norgard, Richard B. "Economic Indicators of Resource Scarcity: A Critical Essay," *Journal of Environmental Economics and Management* 19 (July 1990): 19–25.

Smith, V. Kerry and John V. Krutilla, eds. *Explorations in Natural Resource Economics* (Baltimore: Johns Hopkins University Press for Resources for the Future, 1982).

CHAPTER FOURTEEN

Economics of Pollution Control: An Overview

Democracy is not a matter of sentiment, but of foresight. Any system that doesn't take the long run into account will burn itself out in the short run.

CHARLES YOST, *The Age of Triumph and Frustration*

INTRODUCTION

In Chapter 2 we introduced a schematic describing the relationship between the natural and the economic systems. One side depicted the flow of mass and energy to the economic system, while the other depicted the flow of waste products back to the environment. In the last few chapters we dealt extensively with achieving a balanced set of mass and energy flows; it now remains to discuss how a balance can be achieved in the reverse flow of waste products back to the environment. Because the waste flows are inexorably intertwined with the flow of mass and energy into the economy, establishing a balance for waste flows will have feedback effects on the input flows as well.

Two questions must be addressed: (1) What is the appropriate level of flow? (2) How should the responsibility for achieving this flow level be allocated among the various sources of the pollutant when reductions are needed?

In this chapter we lay the foundation for understanding the policy approach to controlling the flow of these waste products by developing a general framework for analyzing pollution control. This framework allows us to define efficient and cost-effective allocations for a variety of pollutant types, to compare these allocations to market allocations, and to demonstrate how efficiency and cost effectiveness can be used to formulate desirable policy responses. This overview is then followed by a series of chapters that apply these principles by ex-

FIGURE 14.1 Relationship between emissions and pollution damage.

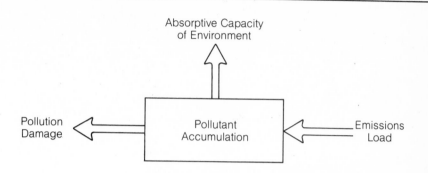

amining the policy approaches which have been taken in the United States and in the rest of the world to establish control over waste flows.

A POLLUTANT TAXONOMY

The amount of waste products emitted determines the load upon the environment. The damage done by this load depends on the capacity of the environment to assimilate the waste products (Figure 14.1). We call this ability of the environment to absorb pollutants its *absorptive capacity*. If the emissions load exceeds the absorptive capacity, then the pollutant accumulates in the environment.

Pollutants for which the environment has little or no absorptive capacity are called *stock pollutants*. Stock pollutants accumulate over time as emissions enter the environment. Examples of stock pollutants include nonbiodegradable bottles tossed by the roadside; heavy metals, such as lead, which accumulate in the soils near the emission source; and persistent synthetic chemicals such as dioxin and PCBs (polychlorinated biphenyls).

Pollutants for which the environment has some absorptive capacity are called *fund pollutants*. For these pollutants, as long as the emission rate does not exceed the absorptive capacity of the environment, the pollutants do not accumulate. Examples of fund pollutants are easy to find. Many organic pollutants injected into an oxygen-rich stream will be transformed by the resident bacteria into less harmful inorganic matter. Carbon dioxide is absorbed by plant life and the oceans.

The point is *not* that the mass is destroyed; the law of conservation of mass suggests this cannot be the case. Rather, when fund pollutants are injected into the air or water, they may be transformed into substances that are not considered harmful to people or to the ecological system, or they may be so diluted or dispersed that the resulting concentrations are not harmful.

Pollutants can also be classified by their zone of influence, defined both horizontally and vertically. The horizontal dimension deals with the domain over which damage from an emitted pollutant is experienced. The damage caused by *local* pollutants is experienced near the source of emission, while the damage from *regional* pollutants is experienced at greater distances from the source of emission. The local and regional categories are not mutually exclusive; it is possible for a pollutant to be both. Sulfur oxides and nitrogen oxides, for example, are both local and regional pollutants.

The vertical zone of influence describes whether the damage is caused mainly by ground-level concentrations of an air pollutant or by concentrations in the upper atmosphere. When the damage caused by a pollutant is determined mainly by concentrations of the pollutant near the earth's surface, it is called a *surface pollutant*. When its damage is related more to its concentration in the upper atmosphere, the substance is called a *global pollutant*.

Water pollutants are obviously surface pollutants, but air pollutants can be surface pollutants, global pollutants, or both. One common global pollutant, carbon dioxide injected into the atmosphere as a product of fossil-fuel combustion, has been implicated in raising world temperatures via the "greenhouse effect." In addition, chlorofluorocarbon emissions play a role in the destruction of the ozone layer which protects the earth's surface from harmful solar radiation. As we shall see, the appropriate policy responses for global and surface pollutants are quite different.

This taxonomy will prove useful in designing policy responses to these various types of pollution problems. Each type of pollutant requires a unique policy response. The failure to recognize these distinctions leads to counterproductive policy.

DEFINING THE EFFICIENT ALLOCATION OF POLLUTION

Pollutants are the residuals of production and consumption. These residuals must eventually be returned to the environment in one form or another. Since their presence in the environment may depreciate the service flows received, an efficient allocation of resources must take this cost into account. What is meant by the efficient allocation of pollution depends on the nature of the pollutant.

Stock Pollutants

The efficient allocation of a stock pollutant must take into account the fact that the pollutant accumulates in the environment over time and that the damage caused by its presence increases and persists as the pollutant accumulates. By their very nature, stock pollutants create an interdependency between the present and the future, since the damage imposed in the future depends on current actions.

It is not hard to establish what is meant by an efficient allocation in these circumstances.[1] Suppose, for example, that we consider the allocation of a commodity which we refer to as X. Suppose further that the production of X involves the generation of a proportional amount of a stock pollutant. The amount of this pollution can be reduced, but that takes resources away from the production of X. The damage caused by the presence of this pollutant in the environment is further assumed to be proportional to the size of the accumulated stock. As long as the stock of pollutants remains in the environment, the damage persists.

The efficient allocation, by definition, is the one which maximizes the present value of the net benefit. In this case the net benefit at any point in time t is equal to the benefit received from the consumption of X minus the cost of the damage caused by the presence of the stock pollutant in the environment.

This damage is a cost that society must bear, and in terms of its effect on the efficient allocation, this cost is not unlike that of extracting minerals or fuels. While for minerals the extraction cost rises with the cumulative amount of the depletable resource extracted, the damage cost associated with a stock pollutant rises with the cumulative amount deposited in the environment. The accretion of the stock pollutant is proportional to the production of X, which creates the same kind of linkage between the production of X and this pollution cost as exists between the extraction cost and the production of a mineral. They both rise over time with the cumulative amount produced. The one major difference is that the extraction cost is borne only at the time of extraction, while damage is borne as long as the stock pollutant exists in the environment.

We can exploit this similarity to infer the efficient allocation of a stock pollutant from our knowledge of the efficient allocation of a depletable resource with rising extraction cost. As discussed in Chapter 6, when extraction cost rises, the efficient quantity of a depletable resource extracted and consumed declines over time.

Exactly the same pattern would emerge for a commodity which is produced jointly with a stock pollutant. The efficient quantity of X (and therefore, the addition to the accumulation of this pollutant in the environment) would decline over time as the marginal cost of the damage rises. The price of X would rise over time, reflecting the rising social cost of production. To cope with the increasing marginal damage, the amount of resources committed to controlling the pollutant would increase over time. Ultimately, a steady state would be reached where additions to the amount of the pollutant in the environment would cease

---

1 The mathematically adept reader can find a formal analysis of this issue in Vernon L. Smith, "Dynamics of Waste Accumulation Versus Recycling," *Quarterly Journal of Economics* 86 (November 1972): 600–616.

and the size of the stock would stabilize. At this point all further emission of the pollutant created by the production of X would be controlled (through recycling). The price of X and the quantity consumed would remain constant. The damage caused by the stock pollutant would persist.

As was the case with rising extraction cost, technological progress could modify this efficient allocation. Specifically, technological progress could reduce the amount of pollutant generated per unit of X produced; it could create ways to recycle the stock pollutant rather than injecting it into the environment; or it could develop ways of rendering the pollutant less harmful. All of these responses would lower the marginal damage cost associated with a given level of production of X. Therefore, more of X could be produced with technological progress than without it.

Stock pollutants are, in a sense, the other side of the intergenerational equity coin from depletable resources. With depletable resources it is possible for current generations to create a burden for future generations by using up resources, thereby diminishing the remaining endowment. Stock pollutants can create a burden for future generations by passing on a damage cost which persists well after the benefits received from incurring that damage cost have been forgotten. Though neither of these situations automatically violates our sustainability criterion, they clearly require further scrutiny. We examine the relationship between stock pollutants and sustainability as well as depletable resources and sustainability in Chapter 21.

Fund Pollutants

To the extent that the emission of fund pollutants exceeds the assimilative capacity of the environment, they accumulate and share some of the characteristics of stock pollutants. When the emission rate is low enough, however, the discharges can be assimilated by the environment with the result that the link between present emissions and future damage may be broken.

When this happens, current emissions cause current damage and future emissions cause future damage, but the level of future damage is independent of current emissions. This independence of allocations among time periods allows us to explore the efficient allocation of fund pollutants using the concept of static, rather than dynamic, efficiency. Because the static concept is simpler, this affords us the opportunity to incorporate more dimensions of the problem without unnecessarily complicating the analysis.

The normal starting point for the analysis would be to maximize the net benefit from the waste flows. However, pollution is more easily understood if we deal with an equivalent formulation involving the minimization of two rather different types of costs: damage costs and control or avoidance costs.

To examine the efficient allocation graphically, we need to know something about how control costs vary with the degree of control and how the damages vary with the amount of pollution emitted. Though our knowledge in these areas is far from complete, economists generally agree on the shapes of these relationships.

Generally the marginal damage caused by a unit of pollution increases with the amount emitted. When small amounts of the pollutant are emitted, the marginal damage is quite small. However, when large amounts are emitted, the marginal unit can cause significantly more damage. It is not hard to understand why. Small amounts of pollution are easily diluted in the environment, and the body can tolerate small quantities of substances. However, as the amount in the atmosphere increases, dilution is less effective and the body is less tolerant.

Marginal control costs commonly increase with the amount controlled. For example, suppose a source of pollution tries to cut down on its particulate emissions by purchasing an electrostatic precipitator which captures 80% of the particulates as they flow past in the stack. If the source wants further control, it can purchase another precipitator and place it in the stack above the first one. This second precipitator captures 80% of the remaining 20%, or 16% of the uncontrolled emissions. Thus, the first precipitator would achieve an 80% reduction from uncontrolled emissions, while the second precipitator, which costs the same as the first, would achieve only a further 16% reduction. Obviously each unit of emission reduction costs more for the second precipitator than for the first.

In Figure 14.2 we use these two pieces of information on the shapes of the relevant curves to derive the efficient allocation. A movement from right to left refers to greater control and less pollution emitted. The efficient allocation is represented by Q^*, the point at which the damage caused by the marginal unit of pollution is exactly equal to the marginal cost of avoiding it.[2]

Greater degrees of control (points to the left of Q^*) are inefficient because the further increase in avoidance costs would exceed the reduction in damages. Hence, total costs would rise. Similarly, levels of control lower than Q^* would result in a lower cost of control, but the increase in damage costs would be even larger, yielding an increase in total cost. Either increasing or decreasing the amount controlled causes an increase in total costs. Hence Q^* must be efficient.

The diagram suggests that, under the conditions presented, the optimal level of pollution is not zero. If you find this disturbing, remember that we confront this principle every day. Take the damage caused by automobile accidents, for example. Obviously, a considerable amount of damage is caused by automobile accidents. Yet we do not reduce that damage to zero because the cost of doing so would be too high.

The point is *not* that we do not know how to stop automobile accidents. All we would have to do is eliminate automobiles! Rather, the point is since we

---

2 At this point, we can see why this formulation is equivalent to the net benefit formulation. Since the benefit is damage reduction, another way of stating this proposition is that marginal benefit must equal marginal cost. That is, of course, the familiar proposition derived by maximizing net benefits.

FIGURE 14.2   Efficient allocation of a fund pollutant.

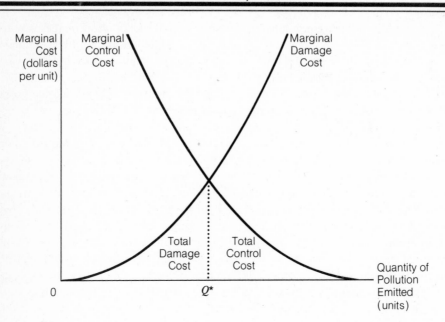

value the benefits of automobiles, we take steps to reduce accidents (using speed limits) only to the extent that the costs of accident reduction are commensurate with the damage reduction achieved. The efficient level of automobile accidents is not zero.

The second point to be made is that in some circumstances the optimal level of pollution *may* be zero or close to it. This situation occurs when the damage caused by even the first unit of pollution is so severe that it is higher than the marginal cost of controlling the last unit of pollution. This would be reflected in Figure 14.2 as a leftward shift of the damage cost curve of sufficient magnitude that its intersection with the vertical axis would lie above the point where the marginal cost curve intersects the vertical axis. This circumstance seems to characterize the treatment of highly dangerous radioactive pollutants such as plutonium.

Additional insights are easily derived from our characterization of the efficient allocation. For example, it should be clear from Figure 14.2 that the optimal level of pollution generally is not the same for all parts of the country. Areas which have higher population levels or are particularly sensitive to pollution should have lower levels, while areas which have lower population levels or are less sensitive should have more.

Examples of ecological sensitivity are not hard to find. For instance, some areas are less sensitive to acid rain than others because the local geological strata neutralize moderate amounts of the acid. Thus, the marginal damage caused by a unit of acid rain is lower in those fortunate regions than in others less tolerant. It can also be argued that pollutants affecting visibility are more damaging in national parks and other areas where visibility is an important part of the aesthetic experience than in other, more industrial, areas.

MARKET ALLOCATION OF POLLUTION

Since air and water are treated in our legal system as common-property resources, at this point in the book it should surprise no one that the market misallocates them. Our general conclusion that common-property resources are overexploited certainly applies here. Air and water resources have been overexploited as waste repositories. However, this conclusion only scratches the surface; much more can be learned about market allocations of pollution.

When firms create products, rarely does the process of converting raw material into outputs use 100% of the mass. Some of the mass, called a *residual*, is left over. If the residual is valuable, it is simply reused. However, if it is not valuable, the firm has an incentive to deal with it in the cheapest manner possible.

The typical firm has several alternatives. It can control the amount of the residual by using inputs more completely so that less is left over. It can also produce less output, so that smaller amounts of the residual are generated. Recycling the residual is sometimes a viable option, as is removing the most damaging components of the waste stream and disposing of the rest.

Because damage costs are externalities but control costs are not, what is cheapest for the firm is not always cheapest for society as a whole. When pollutants are injected into water courses or the atmosphere, they cause damages to those firms and consumers downstream or downwind of the source. These costs are *not* borne by the emitting source and hence, not considered by it, although they certainly are borne by society at large.[3] As with other services which are systematically undervalued, the disposal of wastes into the air or water becomes inefficiently attractive. As we saw in Chapter 3, inefficient pollution control choices lead to further inefficiencies in product and input markets.

In the case of stock pollutants, the problem is particularly severe. Uncontrolled markets would lead to an excessive production of X, too few resources committed to pollution control, and an inefficiently large amount of the stock

---

3 Actually the source certainly considers some of the costs if only to avoid adverse public relations. The point, however, is that this consideration is likely to be incomplete; the source is unlikely to internalize all of the damage cost.

pollutant in the environment. Thus the burden on future generations caused by the presence of this pollutant would be inefficiently large.

There are important differences between the inefficiencies associated with pollution control and the previously discussed inefficiencies associated with the extraction or production of minerals, energy, and food. For private-property resources, the market forces provide automatic signals of impending scarcity. These forces may be understated (as when the vulnerability of imports is ignored), but they operate in the correct direction. Even when some resources are treated as common property (fisheries), the possibility for a private-property alternative (fish farming) is enhanced. As we saw with Example 12.1 when private-property and common-property resources sell in the same market, the private-property owner tends to ameliorate the excesses of those who exploit common properties. Efficient firms are rewarded with higher profits.

With pollution no comparable automatic amelioration mechanism is evident.[4] Because this cost is borne partially by innocent victims, rather than producers, it does not find its way into product prices. Firms which attempt to unilaterally control their pollution are placed at a competitive disadvantage; due to the added expense, their costs of production are higher than those of their less conscientious competitors. Not only does the unimpeded market fail to generate the efficient level of pollution control, it penalizes those firms which might attempt to control an efficient amount. Hence, the case for some sort of government intervention is particularly strong for pollution control.

EFFICIENT POLICY RESPONSES

Our use of the efficiency criterion has helped in demonstrating why markets fail to produce an efficient level of pollution control and in tracing out the effects of this less than optimal degree of control on the markets for related commodities. It can also be used to define efficient policy responses.

Efficiency is achieved when the marginal cost of control is equal to the marginal damage caused by the pollution for each emitter. One way to achieve this equilibrium would be to impose a legal limit on the amount of pollution allowed by each emitter. If the limit were chosen precisely at the level of pollution where marginal control cost equals marginal damage (Q^* in Figure 14.2), efficiency would have been achieved.

An alternative approach would be to internalize the marginal damage caused by each unit of emissions by means of a tax or charge on each unit of emissions.

---

4 Affected parties do have an incentive to negotiate among themselves, a topic covered in Chapter 3. As pointed out there, however, that approach only works well in cases where the number of affected parties is small.

This per unit charge could either increase with the level of pollution (following the marginal damage curve for each succeeding unit of emission) or the tax rate could be constant as long as the rate were equal to the marginal social damage at the point where the marginal social damage and marginal control costs cross (see Figure 14.2). Since the emitter is paying the marginal social damage when confronted by these fees, pollution costs would be internalized. The efficient choice would also be the cost-minimizing choice for the emitter.[5]

However, while the efficient levels of these policy instruments can be easily defined in principle, they are very difficult to implement in practice. To implement either of these policy instruments, we must know the level of pollution at which the two marginal cost curves cross for every emitter. That is a tall order, one that imposes an unrealistically high information burden on control authorities. Control authorities typically have very poor information on control costs and little reliable information on marginal damage functions.

How can environmental authorities allocate pollution control responsibility in a reasonable manner when the information burdens are apparently so unrealistically large? One approach, the choice of several countries including the United States, is to select specific legal levels of pollution based on some other criterion such as providing adequate margins of safety for human or ecological health. Once these thresholds have been established by whatever means, only half of the problem has been resolved. The other half deals with deciding how to allocate the responsibility for meeting predetermined pollution levels among the large numbers of emitters.

This is precisely where the cost-effectiveness criterion comes in. Once the objective is stated in terms of meeting the predetermined pollution level at minimum cost, it is possible to derive the conditions that any cost-effective allocation of the responsibility must satisfy. These conditions can then be used as a basis for choosing among various kinds of policy instruments which impose more reasonable information burdens on control authorities.

COST-EFFECTIVE POLICIES FOR UNIFORMLY MIXED FUND POLLUTANTS

Defining a Cost-Effective Allocation

We begin our analysis with uniformly mixed fund pollutants, which analytically are the easiest to deal with. The damage caused by these pollutants depends on

---

5 Another policy choice is to remove the people from the polluted area. The government has used this strategy for heavily contaminated toxic waste sites such as Times Beach, Missouri, and Love Canal, New York. See Chapter 19.

the amount entering the atmosphere. In contrast to nonuniformly mixed pollutants, the damage caused by uniformly mixed pollutants is relatively insensitive to where the emissions are injected into the atmosphere. Thus, the policy can focus simply on controlling the total weight of emissions in a manner that minimizes the cost of control. What can we say about the cost-effective allocation of control responsibility for uniformly mixed fund pollutants?

Consider a simple example. Assume that there are two emission sources currently emitting a total 30 units of emissions. Assume further that the control authority determines that the environment can assimilate 15 units so that a reduction of 15 units is necessary. How should this 15-unit reduction be allocated between the two sources in order to minimize the total cost of the reduction?

With the aid of Figure 14.3 we can demonstrate the answer. Figure 14.3 is drawn by measuring the marginal cost of control for the first source from the left-hand axis (MC_1) and the marginal cost of control for the second source from the right-hand axis (MC_2). Notice that a total of 15 units reduction is achieved for every point on this graph; each point represents some different combination of reduction by the two sources. Drawn in this manner, the diagram represents all possible allocations of the 15-unit reduction between the two sources. The left-hand axis, for example, represents an allocation of the entire reduction to the second source, while the right-hand axis represents a situation in which the first source bears the entire responsibility. All points in between represent different degrees of shared responsibility. What allocation minimizes the cost of control?

In the cost-effective allocation, the first source cleans up 10 units, while the second source cleans up 5 units. The total variable cost of control for this particular assignment of the responsibility for the reduction is represented by area *A* plus area *B*. Area *A* is the cost of control for the first source; area *B* the cost of control for the second. Any other allocation would result in a higher total control cost. (Convince yourself that this is true.)

Figure 14.3 also demonstrates one of the most important propositions in the economics of pollution control. *The cost of achieving a given reduction in emissions will be minimized if and only if the marginal costs of control are equalized for all emitters.*[6] This is demonstrated by the fact that the marginal cost curves cross at the cost-effective allocation.

Cost-Effective Pollution Control Policies

This proposition can be used as a basis for choosing among the various policy instruments which the control authority might use to achieve this allocation.

---

6 This statement is true when marginal cost increases with the amount of emissions reduced (Figure 14.3). Suppose that for some pollutants the marginal cost were to decrease with the amount of emissions reduced. What would be the cost-effective allocation in that admittedly unusual situation?

FIGURE 14.3 Cost-effective allocation of a uniformly mixed pollutant.

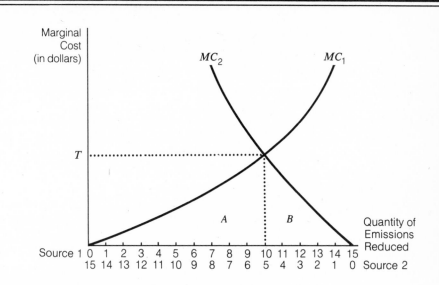

Sources have a large menu of options for controlling the amount of pollution they inject into the environment. The cheapest method of control will differ widely not only among industries but also among plants in the same industry. The selection of the cheapest method requires detailed information on the possible control techniques and their associated costs.

Generally, plant managers are able to acquire this information for their plants when it is in their interest to do so. However, the government authorities responsible for meeting pollution targets are not likely to have this information. Since the degree to which these plants would be regulated depends on cost information, it is unrealistic to expect these plant mangers to transfer unbiased information to the government. Plant managers would have a strong incentive to overstate control costs in hopes of reducing their ultimate burden.

This situation poses a difficult dilemma for control authorities. The cost of incorrectly assigning the control responsibility among various polluters is likely to be large. Yet the control authorities do not have the information at their disposal to make a correct allocation. Those who have the information—the plant managers—are not inclined to share it. Can the cost-effective allocation be found? The answer depends on the approach taken by the control authority.

Emission Standards

We start our investigation of this question by supposing that the control authority pursues a traditional legal approach by imposing a separate emission standard on each source. In the economics literature this approach is referred to as the "command-and-control" approach. An *emission standard* is a legal limit on the amount of the pollutant an individual source is allowed to emit. In our example it is clear that the two standards should add up to the allowable 15 units, but it is not clear how, in the absence of information on control costs, these 15 units are to be allocated between the two sources. The easiest method of resolving this dilemma—and the one chosen in the earliest days of pollution control—would be simply to allocate each source an equal reduction. As is clear from Figure 14.3, this strategy would not be cost-effective. While the first source would have lower costs, this cost reduction would be substantially smaller than the increase faced by the second source. Compared to a cost-effective allocation, total costs would increase if both sources were forced to clean up the same amount.

When emission standards are used, there is no reason to believe that the authority will assign the responsibility for emission reduction in a cost-minimizing way. This is probably not surprising. Who would have believed otherwise?

Surprisingly enough, however, some policy instruments do allow the authority to allocate the emission reduction in a cost-effective manner even when it has no information on the magnitude of control costs. These policy approaches rely on economic incentives to produce the desired outcome. The two most common approaches are known as emission charges and transferable emission permits.

Emission Charges

An *emission charge* is a fee, collected by the government, levied on each unit of pollutant emitted into the air or water. The total payment any source would make to the government could be found by multiplying the fee times the amount of pollution emitted. Emission charges reduce pollution because pollution costs the firm money. To save money, the source seeks ways to reduce its pollution.

How much pollution control would the firm choose to purchase? A profit-maximizing firm would control, rather than emit, pollution whenever it proved cheaper to do so. We can illustrate the firm's decision with Figure 14.4. The level of uncontrolled emission is 15 units and the emission charge is T. Thus, if the firm were to decide against controlling any emissions, it would have to pay T times 15, represented by area $OTBC$.

Is this the best the firm can do? Obviously not, since it can control some pollution at a lower cost than paying the emission charge. It would pay the firm to reduce emissions until the marginal cost of reduction is equal to the emission charge. The firm would minimize its cost by choosing to clean up 10 units of pollution and emitting 5 units. At this allocation the firm would pay control costs equal to area OAD and total emission charge payments equal to area $ABCD$ for a total cost of $OABC$. This is clearly less than $OTBC$, the amount the firm would pay if it chose not to clean up any pollution.

FIGURE 14.4   Cost-minimizing control of pollution with an emission charge.

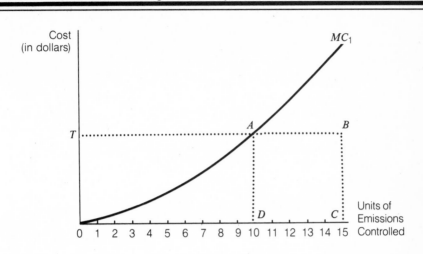

Let's carry this one step further. Suppose that we levied the same emission charge on both sources discussed in Figure 14.3. Each source would then control its emissions until its marginal control cost equaled the emission charge. (Faced with an emission charge T, the second source would clean up 5 units.) Since they both face the same emission charge, they will *independently* choose levels of control consistent with equal marginal control costs. This is precisely the condition that yields a cost-minimizing allocation.

This is a remarkable finding. We have shown that as long as the control authority imposes the same emission charge on all sources, the resulting reduction allocation *automatically* minimizes the costs of control This is true in spite of the fact that the control authority may not have any knowledge of control costs.

However, we have not yet dealt with the issue of how the appropriate level of the emission charge is determined. Each level of a charge will result in *some* level of emission reduction. Furthermore, the responsibility for meeting that reduction will be allocated in a manner that minimizes control costs. How high should the charge be set to ensure that the resulting emission reduction is the *desired* level of emission reduction?

Without knowing the cost of control, the control authority cannot establish the correct tax rate on the first try. It is possible, however, to develop an iterative, trial-and-error process to find the appropriate charge rate. This process is initiated by choosing an arbitrary charge rate and observing the amount of reduction that occurs when that charge is imposed. If the observed reduction is larger than desired, it means the charge should be lowered; if the reduction is smaller, the charge should be raised. The new reduction which results from the adjusted charge can then be observed and compared with the desired reduction. Further

FIGURE 14.5   Cost savings from technological change: charges versus standards.

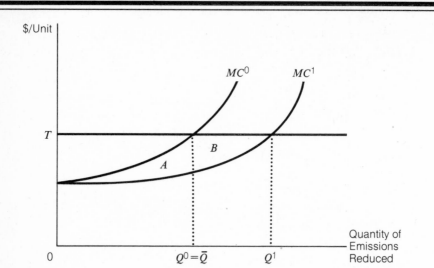

adjustments in the charge can be made as needed. This process can be repeated until the actual and desired reductions are equal. At that point the correct emission charge would have been found.

The charge system not only causes sources to choose a cost-effective allocation of the control responsibility, it also stimulates the development of newer, cheaper means of controlling emissions as well as promoting technological progress. This is illustrated in Figure 14.5.

The reason for this is rather straightforward. Control authorities base the emission standards on specific technologies. As new technologies are discovered by the control authority, the standards are tightened. These stricter standards force firms to bear higher costs. Therefore, with emissions standards, firms have an incentive to hide technological changes from the control authority.

With an emissions charge system the firm saves money by adopting cheaper new technologies. As long as the firm can reduce its pollution at a marginal cost lower than T, it pays to adopt the new technology. In Figure 14.5 the firm saves A and B by adopting the new technology and voluntarily reduces its emissions from Q^0 to Q^1.

With an emissions charge, the minimum cost allocation of meeting a predetermined emission reduction can be found by a control authority even when it has no information on control costs. An emission charge also stimulates technological advances in emission reduction. Unfortunately, the process for finding the appropriate rate takes some experimenting. During the trial-and-error period of finding the appropriate rate, sources would be faced with a volatile emission charge. Changing emission charges would make planning for the future difficult.

FIGURE 14.6 Cost effectiveness and the emission permit system.

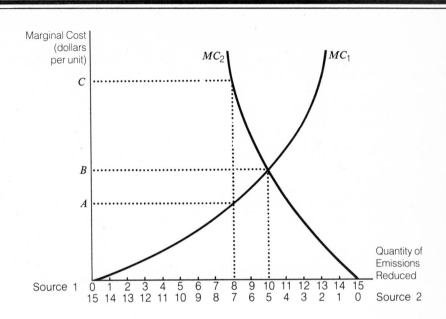

Investments that would make sense under a high emission charge might not make sense when it falls. From either a policymaker's or business manager's perspective, this process leaves much to be desired.

Transferable Emission Permits

Is it possible for the control authority to find the cost-minimizing allocation without going through a trial-and-error process? It is possible if a *transferable emission permit system* is used to control pollution. Under this system, all sources are required to have permits to emit. Each permit specifies exactly how much the firm is allowed to emit. The permits are freely transferable. The control authority issues exactly the number of permits needed to produce the desired emission level. Any emissions by a source in excess of those allowed by its permit would cause the source to face severe monetary sanctions.

Why this system automatically leads to a cost-effective allocation can be seen in Figure 14.6, which treats the same set of circumstances as Figure 14.3. Suppose that somehow the first source found itself with 7 permits. Since it has 15 units of uncontrolled emissions, this would mean it must control 8 units. Similarly, suppose that the second source has the remaining 8 permits, meaning that it would have to clean up 7 units. Notice that both firms have an incentive to trade. The marginal cost of control for the second source (C) is substantially higher than that for the first (A). The second source could lower its cost if it could buy a permit from the first source at a price lower than C. The first source, meanwhile, would be better off if it could sell a permit for a price higher than A. Since C is greater than A, grounds for trade certainly exist.

A transfer of permits would take place until the first source had only 5 permits left (and is controlling 10 units), while the second source had 10 permits (and was controlling 5 units). At this point, the permit price would equal B, since that is the marginal value of that permit to both sources, and neither source would have any incentive to trade further. The permit market would be in equilibrium.

Notice that the market equilibrium for an emission-permit system is the cost-effective allocation! Simply by issuing the appropriate number of permits (15) and letting the market do the rest, the control authority can achieve a cost-effective allocation without having even the slightest knowledge about control costs. This system allows the government to meet its policy objective while allowing greater flexibility in how that objective is met.

The incentives created by this system ensure that sources use this flexibility to achieve the objective at the lowest possible cost. As we shall see in the next two chapters, this remarkable property has been responsible for the prominence of this type of approach in current attempts to reform the regulatory process.

COST-EFFECTIVE POLICIES FOR NONUNIFORMLY MIXED SURFACE POLLUTANTS

The problem becomes more complicated when dealing with nonuniformly mixed surface pollutants rather than uniformly mixed pollutants. For these pollutants the policy must be concerned not only with the weight of emission entering the atmosphere, but also with the location of emissions. For nonuniformly mixed pollutants it is the concentration in the air, soil, and water that counts. The concentration is measured as the amount of pollutant found in a given volume of air, soil, or water at a given location and at a given point in time.

It is easy to see why pollutant concentrations are sensitive to the location of emissions. Suppose that three emission sources are clustered and emit the same amount as three separate, but otherwise identical, sources. The emissions from the clustered sources generally cause higher pollution levels because they are all entering the same volume of air or water. Because the two sets of emission do not share a common receiving volume, those from the dispersed sources result in lower concentrations. This is the main reason why cities generally face more severe pollution problems than do rural areas; urban sources tend to be more densely clustered.

Since the damage caused by nonuniformly mixed surface pollutants is related to their concentration levels in the air, soil, or water, it is natural that our search for cost-effective policies for controlling these pollutants focus on the attainment of ambient standards. *Ambient standards* are legal ceilings placed on the concentration level of specified pollutants in the air, soil, or water. They represent

FIGURE 14.7   Effect of location on local pollutant concentration.

the target concentration levels which are not to be exceeded. A cost-effective policy results in the lowest cost allocation of control responsibility consistent with ensuring that the predetermined ambient standards are met at specified locations called receptor sites.

The Single-Receptor Case

We can begin the analysis by considering a simple case in which we desire to control pollution at one, and only one, receptor location. We know that all units of emissions from sources do not have the same impact on pollution measured at that receptor. Consider, for example, Figure 14.7.

Suppose that we hypothetically allow each of the four sources individually, at different points in time, to inject 10 units of emission into the stream. Suppose further that we measured the pollutant concentration resulting from each of these injections at receptor R. In general, we would find that the emissions from A or B would cause a larger rise in the recorded concentration than would those from C and D, even though the same amount was emitted from each source. The reason for this is that the emissions from C and D would be substantially diluted by the time they arrived at R, while those from A and B would arrive in a more concentrated form.

Since emissions are what can be controlled, but the concentrations at R are the policy target, our first task must be to relate the two. This can be accomplished by using a transfer coefficient. A *transfer coefficient* (a_i) captures the constant amount the concentration at the receptor will rise if source i emits one more unit of pollution. Using this definition and the knowledge that the a_i's are constant, we can relate the concentration level at R to emissions from all sources:

$$K_R \quad = \quad \sum_{i=1}^{I} a_i E_i + B, \tag{1}$$

where K_R = concentration at the receptor
E_i = emission level of the ith source
I = total number of sources in the region
B = background concentration level (resulting from natural sources or sources outside the control region)

We are now in a position to define the cost-effective allocation of responsibility. A numerical example involving two sources is presented in Table 14.1. In that example the two sources are assumed to have the same marginal cost curves for cleaning up emissions. This assumption is reflected in the fact that the first two corresponding columns of the table for each of the two sources are identical.[7] The main difference between the two sources is their location vis-à-vis the receptor. The first source is closer to the receptor, so it has a larger transfer coefficient than the second (1.0 as opposed to 0.5).

The objective is to meet a given concentration target at minimum cost. Column 3 of the table translates emission reductions into concentration reductions for each source, while column 4 records the marginal cost of each unit of concentration reduced. The former is merely the emission reduction times the transfer coefficient, while the latter is the marginal cost of the emission reduction divided by the transfer coefficient (which translates the marginal cost of *emission* reduction into a marginal cost of *concentration* reduction).

Suppose the concentration at the receptor has to be reduced by 7.5 units in order to comply with the ambient standard. The cost-effective allocation would be achieved when the marginal costs of concentration reduction (*not* emission reduction) are equalized for all sources. In Table 14.1 this occurs when the first source reduces 6 units of emissions (and 6 units of concentration) and the second source reduces 3 units of emissions (and 1.5 units of concentration). At this allocation the marginal cost of concentration reduction is equal to $6 for both sources. By adding up all marginal costs for each unit reduced, we calculate the total variable cost of this allocation to be $27. From the definition of cost effectiveness, no other allocation resulting in 7.5 units of concentration reduction would be cheaper.

Policy Approaches. This framework can now be used to evaluate various policy approaches that the control authority might use. We begin with the *ambient charge*, the charge used to produce a cost-effective allocation of a non-uniformly mixed pollutant. This charge takes the form

$$t_i = a_i F, \tag{2}$$

---

7 This assumption has no bearing on the results we shall achieve. It serves mainly to illustrate the role location plays by eliminating control cost differences as a factor.

TABLE 14.1 Cost Effectiveness for Nonuniformly Mixed Pollutants: A Hypothetical Example

		Source 1 (a_1 = 1.0)	
Emissions units reduced	*Marginal cost of emission reduction (dollars per unit)*	*Concentration units reduced[a]*	*Marginal cost of concentration reduction (dollars per unit)[b]*
1	1	1.0	1
2	2	2.0	2
3	3	3.0	3
4	4	4.0	4
5	5	5.0	5
6	6	6.0	6
7	7	7.0	7
		Source 2 (a_2 = 0.5)	
1	1	0.5	2
2	2	1.0	4
3	3	1.5	6
4	4	2.0	8
5	5	2.5	10
6	6	3.0	12
7	7	3.5	14

[a]Computed by multiplying the emission reduction (column 1) by the transfer coefficient (a_i).
[b]Computed by dividing the marginal cost of emission reduction (column 2) by the transfer coefficient (a_i).

where t_i is the per unit charge paid by the ith source on each unit emitted, a_i is the ith source's transfer coefficient, and F is the marginal cost of a unit of concentration reduction, which is the same for all sources. In our example F is $6, so the first source would pay a per unit emission charge of $6, while the second source would pay $3. *Note that sources will, in general, pay different charges when the objective is to meet an ambient standard at minimum cost because their transfer coefficients differ.* This contrasts with the uniformly mixed pollutant case in which a cost-effective allocation required that all sources pay the same charge.

How can the cost-effective t_i be found by a control authority with no information on control costs? The transfer coefficients can be calculated using knowledge of hydrology and meteorology, but what about F? Here a striking similarity to the uniformly mixed case becomes evident. Any level of F would yield a cost-effective allocation of control responsibility for achieving *some* level of concentration reduction at the receptor. That level might not, however, be compatible with the ambient standard.

We could ensure compatibility by changing F in an iterative process until the desired concentration is achieved. If the actual pollutant concentration is below the standard, the tax could be lowered; if it is above, the tax could be raised. The correct level of F would be reached when the resulting pollution concentration is equal to the desired level. That equilibrium allocation would be the one that meets the ambient standard at minimum cost.

Table 14.1 allows us to consider another issue of significance. The cost-effective allocation of control responsibility for achieving surface-concentration targets places a larger information burden on control authorities; they have to calculate the transfer coefficients. What is lost if the simpler emission charge system (where each source faces the same charge) is used to pursue a surface-concentration target? Can location be safely ignored?

In Table 14.1 a uniform emission charge equal to $5 would achieve the desired 7.5 units of reduction (5 from the first source and 2.5 from the second). Yet the total variable cost of this allocation (calculated as the sum of the marginal costs) would be $30 ($15 paid by each source). This is $3 higher than the allocation resulting from the use of ambient charge discussed earlier. In subsequent chapters we present empirical estimates of the size of this cost increase in actual air and water pollution situations. In general, they show the cost increases to be large; location matters.

Table 14.1 also helps us understand why location matters. Notice that with a uniform emissions charge, 10 units of emission are cleaned up, whereas with the ambient charge only 8 units are cleaned up. Both achieve the concentration target, but the uniform-emission charge results in fewer emissions. The ambient charge results in a lower cost allocation than the emission charge because it results in less emission control. Those sources having only a small effect on the recorded concentration at the receptor location are forced to control less than they would with a uniform charge.

With the ambient charge, we have the same problem that we encountered with emission charges in the uniformly mixed pollutant case—the cost-effective level can only be determined by an iterative process. Can a permit system get around this problem when dealing with nonuniformly mixed pollutants?

It can by designing the permits in the correct way. An ambient permit entitles the owner to cause the concentration to rise at the receptor by a specified amount, rather than allowing the same amount of emissions to each owner. Using ΔK_R to represent this permitted rise and E to indicate the units of emissions allowed by each permit held by the ith source, we can see that from equation (1) that

$$\frac{\Delta K_R}{a_i} = \Delta E_i . \tag{3}$$

The larger the transfer coefficient (that is, the closer the source is to the receptor), the smaller is the amount of emissions legitimized by a permit. Proximate sources must purchase more permits than distant sources to legitimize a given level of emissions. In this version of the permit system the sources pay the same price for each permit, but the amount of emission allowed by each permit varies from location to location. The market automatically determines this common price, and the resulting allocation of permits is cost-effective. With respect to Table 14.1, the ambient permit price would be $6. This cost-effective system is called an *ambient permit system* to differentiate it from the *emission permit system*, which is used to achieve a cost-effective allocation of control responsibility for uniformly mixed pollutants.

We can reinforce our understanding of what is going on with the ambient permit system by examining a specific trade. Suppose our two sources in Table 14.1 want to trade permits with the first source buying from the second. To maintain the same concentration level before and after the trade, we must ensure that

$$a_1 \, \Delta E_1 = a_2 \, \Delta E_2 \, ,$$

where the subscripts refer to the first source and second source and the ΔE_i refers to a change in emissions by the ith source. Solving this for the allowable increase in emission by the buyer yields

$$\Delta E_1 = \frac{a_2}{a_1} \, \Delta E_2 \, . \tag{4}$$

For $a_2 = 0.5$ and $a_1 = 1.0$, this equation suggests that for each permit traded, the buyer (the first source) is allowed to emit only one-half the amount of emissions allowed by that same permit when it was used by the seller. After this trade, the total amount of emissions by both sources goes down.[8] This could not happen in an emissions permit system, since the design of those permits causes all trades to leave emissions (but not concentrations!) unchanged.

The Many-Receptors Case

This analysis generalizes easily to the many-receptors case. The cost-effective ambient charge paid by any source would in this case be

$$T_i = \sum_{j=1}^{J} a_{ij} F_j$$

---

8 Emissions could rise with ambient permit trades as well. This would occur whenever the transfer coefficient of the seller was larger than that of the buyer.

where T_i = charge paid by the ith source for each unit of
                emissions

a_{ij} = transfer coefficient that translates emissions by source
                i into concentration increases at the jth receptor

J = number of receptors

F_j = monetary fee associated with the jth receptor

Thus, the source has to pay a charge that incorporates its effect on all receptors. The control authority could manipulate F_j for each receptor location until the desired concentration level is achieved at that receptor.[9]

The extension of the ambient permit system to the many-receptor case requires that a separate permit market be created *for each receptor*. The price prevailing in each of these markets would reflect the difficulty of meeting the ambient standard at that receptor. All other things being equal, permit markets associated with receptors in heavily congested areas could be expected to sustain higher prices than those affected by a relatively few emitters.

Since both the ambient permit system and the ambient charge system take location into account, when these policies are chosen, the marginal cost of emission control varies from location to location. Sources located in heavily populated portions of the region pay higher marginal costs, since their emissions have a greater impact on the receptors of interest. Having control costs depend on location provides incentives for new sources to chose their location carefully. Since heavily polluted areas have high control costs, there is some incentive to locate elsewhere, even though pollution control expenditures are only part of the costs a firm considers when deciding where to locate. For nonuniformly mixed pollution problems, *where* the emissions occur is important. Therefore, it is also important that the location component of the cost be internalized by relocating sources. With the ambient permit and charge systems, this is precisely what occurs.

OTHER POLICY DIMENSIONS

Two main pollution control policy instruments rely on economic incentives—charges and transferable permits. Both of these allow the control authority to

---

9 Because any higher F_j reduces concentrations at several locations, not just at the jth receptor, not all selections of F_j which result in the ambient standards being met will result in cost-effective allocations. In the single-receptor case the charge equilibrium is unique and equal to the cost-effective one. This is a further burden on the control authority of using an emission charge system as opposed to the permit system where the equilibrium is unique and cost-effective. The permit system equilibrium is unique because all equilibria other than the cost-effective one involve higher costs and, therefore, further opportunities for trade.

distribute the responsibility for control in a cost-effective manner. The major difference between them we have discussed so far is that the appropriate charge can be determined only by an iterative trial-and-error process over time, while the permit price can be determined immediately by the market. Can other differences be identified?

One major additional difference concerns the manner in which these two systems react to changes in external circumstances in the absence of further decisions by the control authority. This is an important consideration, because bureaucratic procedures are notoriously sluggish and changes in policies are usually rendered slowly.[10] We consider three such circumstances: growth in the number of sources, inflation, and technological progress.

If the number of sources were to increase in a permit market, the demand for permits would shift to the right. Given a fixed supply of permits, the price would rise, as would the control costs, but the amount of emissions or pollution concentrations (in the case of the ambient permit system) would remain the same. If charges were being used, in the absence of additional action by the control authority the charge level would remain the same. This implies that the existing sources would control only what they would control in the absence of growth. Therefore, the arrival of new sources would cause a deterioration of air or water quality in the region. The costs of abatement would rise, since the costs of control paid by the new sources must be considered, but by a lesser amount than in a permit market, because of the lower amount of pollution being controlled. If the choice is between a fixed fee and a fixed number of permits in a growing economy, the dominance of the permit system over the fixed-fee system increases over time.[11]

With a permit system inflation in the cost of control would automatically result in higher permit prices, but with a charge system it would result in lower control. Essentially the real charge (the nominal charge adjusted for inflation) declines with inflation if the nominal charge remains the same.

We should not, however, conclude that, over time, charges always result in less control than permits. Suppose, for example, technological progress in designing pollution control equipment were to cause the marginal cost of abatement to fall. In a permit system this would result in lower prices and lower abatement costs but the same aggregate degree of control. With a charge system the amount controlled would actually increase and would, therefore, result in more control than a permit system which, prior to the fall in costs, controlled the same amount.

If the control authority were to adjust the charge in each of the above cases appropriately, the outcome would be identical to that achieved by a permit market.

---

10 This is probably particularly true when the modification involves a change in the rate at which firms are charged for their emissions.

11 See Richard V. Butler and Michael D. Maher, "The Control of Externalities in a Growing Economy," *Economic Inquiry* 20 (January 1982): 155–163.

The permit market reacts automatically to these changes in circumstances, while the charge system requires a conscious administrative act to achieve the same result.

The second major difference between permits and charges involves the cost of being wrong. Suppose that we have very imprecise information on damages caused and avoidance costs incurred by various levels of pollution and yet we have to choose either a charge level or a permit level and live with it. What can be said about the relative merits of permits versus charges in the face of this uncertainty?

The answer depends on the circumstances.[12] Permits offer a greater amount of certainty about the quantity of emissions, while charges confer more certainty about the marginal cost of control. Therefore, permits are the only system which allow an ambient standard or an aggregate emission standard to be met with certainty. In other cases, however, when the objective is to minimize total costs (the sum of damage cost and control costs), permits would be preferred when the costs of being wrong are more sensitive to changes in the quantity of emission than to change in the marginal cost of control. Charges would be preferred when control costs were more important. When would that be the case?

When the marginal damage curve is steeply sloped and the marginal cost curve is rather flat, certainty about emissions is more important than certainty over control costs. Smaller deviations of actual emissions from expected emission can cause a rather large deviation in damage costs, whereas control costs would be relatively insensitive to the degree of control. Permits would prevent large fluctuations in these damage costs and would, therefore, yield a lower cost of being wrong than charges.

Suppose, however, that the marginal control cost curve was steeply sloped, but the marginal damage curve was flat. Small changes in the degree of control would have a large effect on abatement costs but would not affect damages very much. In this case it makes sense to rely on charges to give more precise control over control costs accepting the less dire consequences from possible fluctuations in damage costs.

These cases suggest that a preference either for permits or for charges in the face of uncertainty is not universal; it depends on the circumstances. Theory is not strong enough to dictate a choice. Empirical studies are necessary to establish a preference for particular situations. Example 14.1 discusses one such empirical study.

---

12 A more formal and mathematical treatment of this issue can be found in M. Weitzman, "Prices vs. Quantities," *Review of Economic Studies* 41 (1974): 447–491. A specific application to pollution control is presented in Z. Adar and J. M. Griffin, "Uncertainty and Choice in Pollution Control Instruments," *Journal of Environmental Economics and Management* 3 (1976): 178–188.

EXAMPLE 14.1

Energy-Demand Uncertainty and the Cost of Being Wrong: Permits vs. Charges

The Four Corners area (where Utah, Arizona, New Mexico, and Colorado intersect) poses a classic confrontation between energy development and preserving the environment. Though sparsely populated, it is near several unique parks and wilderness areas and serves as the base for several large electrical generating stations which provide power to southwestern and western states.

One of the uncertainties affecting the air quality of the region is the amount that electricity demand will grow over the next several years. The higher the growth in demand, the more uncontrolled emissions. The higher the level of uncontrolled emissions, the more control that has to be placed on each source in order to preserve air quality. If, in incorrect anticipation of too high growth, the regulators impose too stringent a degree of control, then control costs will be excessively high. If controls are established at too low a level, damage costs would be too high. There are costs associated with each type of mistake.

In a doctoral dissertation submitted at Stanford, Charles Kolstad (1982) used this setting to investigate whether regulators would be better off using a permit system or an emission charge system to protect air quality in the face of this uncertainty. Capturing the control cost and damage functions in a computer simulation model, he calculated the cost of being wrong if regulators chose permits or if they chose charges. His findings were completely in accord with our analysis:

> For constant or declining marginal damage, emissions [charges] yield total costs (including damage) 5–10% lower than for [permits]. However, for even slightly upward sloping marginal damage, [permits] yield roughly 20% lower costs than emission [charges](p. 206).

Since the increasing marginal cost case is probably the most likely for sulfur oxide emissions, the use of permits in the Four Corners would seem preferable.

Source: Charles Kolstad, *Economic and Regulatory Efficiency* (Los Alamos, NM: Los Alamos National Laboratory, 1982): Report #LA-9458-T (Thesis).

SUMMARY

In this chapter we developed the conceptual framework needed to evaluate current approaches to pollution control policy. We have seen that there are many different types of pollutants, and different policy approaches are appropriate for each one.

Stock pollutants pose the most serious intertemporal problems. The efficient production of a commodity that generates a stock pollutant could be expected to decline over time. Eventually, a point would be reached when all of the pollutant would be recycled. After this point the amount of the pollutant in the environment would not increase. The amount already accumulated, however, would continue to cause damage perpetually unless some natural process could reduce the amount of the pollutant over time.

The efficient amount of a fund pollutant was defined as the amount which minimizes the sum of damage and control costs. Using this definition, we were able to derive two propositions of interest: (1) the efficient level of pollution would vary from region to region; and (2) the efficient level of pollution would not generally be zero, although in some particular circumstances it might.

Since pollution is a classic externality, markets will generally produce more than the efficient amount of both fund pollutants and stock pollutants. For both pollutants this will imply higher than efficient damages and lower than efficient control costs. For stock pollutants an excessive amount of pollution would accumulate in the environment, imposing a detrimental externality on future generations as well as on current generations.

The market would not provide any automatic ameliorating response to the accumulation of pollution as it would in the case of natural resource scarcity. Firms attempting to unilaterally control their pollution are placed at a competitive disadvantage. Hence, the case for some sort of government intervention is particularly strong for pollution control.

While policy instruments could in principle be defined to achieve an efficient level of pollution for every emitter, in practice it is very difficult because the amount of information required by the control authorities is unrealistically high.

Cost effectiveness analysis provides a way out of this dilemma. In the case of uniform mixed-fund pollutants, uniform emission charges or an emission-permit system could be used to attain the cost-effective allocation even when the control authority has no information whatsoever on either control costs or damage costs. Uniform emission standards would not, except by coincidence, be cost effective. In addition, either permits or charges would stimulate more technological progress in pollution control than would emission standards.

Policies to control nonuniformly mixed pollutants must take the location of the emissions into account as well as the amount. This can be accomplished with either an appropriately designed ambient permit system or ambient charge; either one can result in a cost-effective allocation of the control responsibility even when the control authority has no information on control costs. A policy based on emission standards cannot.

Policies ignoring these distinctions are not cost-effective. An excessively narrow focus on local pollution can make the regional pollution problem worse. Similarly, the use of a uniform emission charge or an emission permit system (which are appropriate for uniformly mixed pollutants!) to allocate the responsibility for controlling a local or regional nonuniformly mixed surface pollutant will *not* be cost effective whenever transfer coefficients differ.

The permit approach and the charge approach respond differently to growth in the number of sources, to inflation, to technological change, and to uncertainty. As we shall see in the next few chapters, some countries (primarily in Europe) have chosen to rely on emission charges, while others (primarily the United States) have chosen to rely on permits. We can now use this framework to evaluate the rather different policy approaches that have been taken toward the major sources of pollution.

FURTHER READING

Baumol, W. J. and W.E. Oates. *The Theory of Environmental Policy* (Englewood Cliffs, NJ: Prentice-Hall, 1975). A classic on the economic analysis of externalities. Accessible only to those with a thorough familiarity with multivariable calculus.

Hahn, Robert W. "Economic Prescriptions for Environmental Problems: How the Patient Followed the Doctor's Orders," *Journal of Economic Perspectives* 3 (Spring 1989): 95-114. Chronicles the experience with both marketable permits and emission charges in the United States and Europe.

Organization for Economic Cooperation and Development, *Pollution Charges in Practice* (Paris: OECD, 1980). A comprehensive survey of the application of pollution charges for air and water pollution control primarily, but not exclusively, in Western Europe.

Organization for Economic Cooperation and Development, *Economic Instruments for Environmental Protection* (Paris: OECD, 1989). A survey of how economic incentive approaches to pollution control have been used in the industrialized nations that belong to the OECD.

Portney, Paul, ed. *Public Policies for Environmental Protection* (Washington, DC: Resources for the Future, 1990). A collection of essays reviewing problems of environmental regulation from the perspective of the late 1980s.

Tietenberg, T. H. *Emissions Trading: An Exercise in Reforming Pollution Policy* (Washington, DC: Resources for the Future, 1985). An examination of the use of marketable permits to control pollution in principle and in practice.

ADDITIONAL REFERENCES

Anderson, Frederick R. et al. *Environmental Improvement through Economic Incentives* (Baltimore: Johns Hopkins University Press for Resources for the Future, 1977).

Barnett, Andy H. and Bruce Yandle, Jr. "Allocating Environmental Resources," *Public Finance* 28 (1973): 11–19.

Collinge, R. A. and W. E. Oates. "Efficiency in Pollution Control in the Short and Long Runs: A System of Rental Emission Permits," *Canadian Journal of Economics* 15 (May 1982): 347–354.

Dales, J. H. *Pollution, Property and Prices* (Toronto: Toronto University Press, 1968).

Hahn, Robert W. and Robert G. Noll. "Designing a Market for Tradable Emissions Permits," in *Reform of Environmental Regulation*, Wesley A. Magat, ed. (Cambridge, MA: Ballinger, 1982).

Kneese, Allen V. and Charles L. Schultz. *Pollution, Prices, and Public Policy* (Washington, DC: The Brookings Institution, 1975).

Lyon, R.M. "Auctions and Alternative Procedures for Allocating Pollution Rights," *Land Economics* 58 (February 1982): 16–32.

Milliman, Scott R. and Raymond Prince. "Firm Incentives to Promote Technological Change in Pollution Control," *Journal of Environmental Economics and Management* 17 (November 1989): 247–265.

Montgomery, David W. "Markets in Licenses and Efficient Pollution Control Programs," *Journal of Economic Theory* 5 (December 1982): 395–418.

Orr, Lloyd. "Incentive for Innovation as the Basis for Effluent Charge Strategy," *The American Economic Review* 66 (May 1976): 441–447.

Plourde, C. G. "A Model of Waste Accumulation and Disposal," *Canadian Journal of Economics* 5 (February 1982): 119–125.

Stavins, Robert. N. "Harnessing Market Forces To Protect the Environment," *Environment* 31 (January/February 1989): 4–7, 28–35.

Weitzman, M. "Prices vs. Quantities," *Review of Economic Studies* 41 (1974): 447–491.

DISCUSSION QUESTIONS

1. In his book *What Price Incentives?*, Steven Kelman suggests that from an ethical point of view, the use of economic incentives (such as emission charges or emission permits) in environmental policy is undesirable. He argues that transforming our mental image of the environment from a sanctified preserve to a marketable commodity has detrimental effects not only on our use of the environment but also on our attitude toward it. His point is that applying economic incentives to environmental policy weakens and cheapens our traditional values toward the environment.

(a) Consider the effects of economic incentive systems on prices paid by the poor, on employment, and on the speed of compliance with pollution control laws—as well as the Kelman arguments. Are economic incentive systems more or less ethically justifiable than the traditional regulatory approach?

(b) Kelman seems to feel that because emission permits automatically prevent environmental degradation, they are more ethically desirable than emission charges. Do you agree? Why or why not?

PROBLEMS

1. Two firms can control emissions at the following marginal costs: $MC_1 = \$200q_1$, $MC_2 = \$100q_2$, where q_1 and q_2 are, respectively, the amount of emissions reduced by the first and second firms. Assume that with no control at all, each firm would be emitting 20 units of emissions or a total of 40 units for both firms.

(a) Compute the cost-effective allocation of control responsibility if a total reduction of 21 units of emissions is necessary.

(b) Compute the cost-effective allocation of control responsibility if the ambient standard is 27 ppm, and the transfer coefficients which translate a unit of emissions into a ppm concentration at the receptor are, respectively, $a_1 = 2.0$ and $a_2 = 1.0$.

2. Assume that the control authority wanted to reach its objective in 1(a) by using an emission charge system.

(a) What per unit charge should be imposed?

(b) How much revenue would the control authority collect?

APPENDIX

The Simple Mathematics of Cost-Effective Pollution Control

Suppose that each of N polluters would emit u_n units of emission in the absence of any control. Furthermore suppose that the pollutant concentration K_R at some receptor R in the absence of control is:

$$K_R = \sum_{n=1}^{N} a_n u_n + B \tag{1}$$

where B is the background concentration and a_n is the transfer coefficient. This K_R is assumed to be greater than Φ, the legal concentration level. The regulatory problem therefore is to choose the cost-effective level of control q_n for each of the n sources. Symbolically this can be expressed as minimizing the following Lagrangian with respect to the Nq_n control variables:

$$\min \sum_{n=1}^{N} C_n(q_n) + \lambda \left[\sum_{n=1}^{N} a_n(u_n - q_n) - \Phi \right], \tag{2}$$

where $C_n(q_n)$ is the cost of achieving the q_n level of control at the nth source and λ is the Lagrangian multiplier.

The solution is found by partially differentiating (2) with respect to λ and the Nq_n's. This yields

$$\frac{\delta C_n(q_n^*)}{\delta q_n} - \lambda^* a_n \geq 0, \qquad n = 1, ..., N,$$

$$\sum_{n=1}^{N} a_n(u_n - q_n^*) + B - \Phi = 0 .$$

Solving these equations produces the N-dimensional vector q^* and the scalar λ^*.

Notice that this same formulation can be used to reflect both the uniformly mixed and nonuniformly mixed, single-receptor case. In the uniformly mixed case the a_n's all $= 1$. This immediately implies that the marginal cost of control should be equal for all emitters who are required to engage in some control. (The first N equations would hold as equalities except for any source where the marginal cost of controlling the first unit exceeded the marginal cost necessary to meet the target.) For the nonuniformly mixed, single-receptor case, in the cost-effective allocation the control responsibility would be allocated so as to ensure that the ratio of the marginal control costs for two emitters would be equal to the ratio of their transfer coefficients. For J receptors both λ^* and Φ would become J-dimensional vectors.

Policy Instruments

A special meaning can be attached to λ. If transferable permits were being used, it would be the market clearing price of a permit. In the uniformly mixed case λ would be the price of a permit to emit one unit of emission. In the nonuniformly mixed case λ would be the price of being allowed to raise the concentration at the receptor location one unit. In the case of taxes, λ represents the value of the cost-effective tax.

Notice how firms choose emissions control when permit price or tax is equal to λ. Each firm wants to minimize its costs. Assume that each firm is given permits of Ω_n, where the regulatory authority ensures that

$$\sum_{n=1}^{N} a_n \Omega_n + B = \Phi$$

for the set of all emitters. Each firm would want to

$$\min C_n(q_n) + P^*[\Omega_n - a_n(u_n - q_n)].$$

The minimum cost is achieved by choosing the value of q_n (q_n^*) that satisfies

$$\frac{\delta C_n(q_n^*)}{\delta q_n} - P^* a_n = 0.$$

This condition (marginal cost equals the price of a unit of concentration reduction) would hold for each of the N firms. Because P^* would equal λ^* and the number of permits would be chosen to ensure the ambient standard would be met, this allocation would be cost-effective. Exactly the same result is achieved by substituting T^*, the cost-effective tax rate, for P^*.

CHAPTER FIFTEEN

Stationary-Source Local Air Pollution

When choosing between two evils,
I always like to try the one I've never tried before.

MAE WEST, *Actress*

INTRODUCTION

Attaining and maintaining clean air is an exceedingly difficulty policy task. In the United States, for example, an estimated 27,000 major stationary sources of air pollution are subject to control as well as hundreds of thousands of more minor sources. Many distinct production processes emit many different types of pollutants. The resulting damages range from minimal effects on plants and vegetation to the possible modification of the earth's climate.

The policy response to this problem has been continually evolving. The U.S. experience is not atypical. Congress enacted the first legislation to grapple with these problems in 1955. Called the Air Pollution Control Act of 1955, that law mainly subsidized research into air pollution problems. The following 14 years ushered in a period of vigorous legislative activity.

Yet, the amount of legislation is a misleading indicator of what was actually accomplished. It was not until 1967 that the federal government began to play much of a role other than subsidizing research, and even the 1967 law was mainly an attempt to cajole the states into action. The common thread woven by the statutes during this period was a reliance on cooperation from the states.

By 1970 the national government had discovered that this reliance was misplaced; state cooperation was not forthcoming. Fearing that the imposition of strict controls on industrial sources would place them at a competitive disadvantage in their quest for increases in employment and taxable industrial property, states were unwilling to take the lead in air pollution control policy.

In this atmosphere of frustration, the Clean Air Act Amendments of 1970 were passed. They set a bold new direction which has been retained and refined by subsequent acts. By virtue of that act, the federal government assumed a much larger and much more vigorous direct role. The U.S. Environmental Protection Agency (EPA) was created to implement and oversee this massive attempt to control the injection of substances into our air. Individually tailored strategies were created to deal with mobile and stationary sources. These strategies depend in part on whether the type of pollutant being controlled is a "conventional" pollutant or a "hazardous" pollutant.

CONVENTIONAL POLLUTANTS

Conventional pollutants are relatively common substances, found in almost all parts of the country, and are presumed to be dangerous only in high concentrations. In the United States these pollutants are called *criteria pollutants* because the Act requires EPA to produce "criteria documents" to be used in setting acceptable standards for these pollutants. These documents summarize and evaluate all of the existing research on the various health and environmental effects associated with these pollutants. The central focus of air pollution control during the 1970s was on criteria pollutants.

The Command-and-Control Policy Framework

In Chapter 14 several possible approaches to controlling pollution were described and analyzed in theoretical terms. The historical approach to air pollution control has been based primarily on emission standards. It has been a traditional command-and-control (CAC) approach. In this section we outline the specific nature of this approach, analyze it from an efficiency and cost-effectiveness perspective, and show how a series of recent reforms based on economic incentives has worked to rectify some of these deficiencies.

For each of the conventional pollutants, the typical first step is to establish ambient air quality standards. These standards set legal ceilings on the allowable concentration of the pollutant in the outdoor air averaged over a specified time period. Many pollutants have the standard defined in terms of a long-term average (defined normally as an annual average) and a short-term average (such as a 3 hour average). These short-term averages can usually be exceeded no more than once a year. These standards have to be met everywhere, though as a practical matter they are monitored at a large number of specific locations. As Example 4.4 pointed out, control costs can be quite sensitive to the level of these short-term averages.

In the United States two ambient standards are defined.[1] The *primary stand-ard* is designed to protect human health. This is the first standard to be deter-mined, and it has the earliest deadlines for compliance. All pollutants have a primary standard. The *secondary standard* is designed to protect other aspects of human welfare from those pollutants having separate effects. Currently only sulfur oxides have separate secondary standards. Protection is afforded by the secondary standard for aesthetics (particularly visibility), physical ob-jects (houses, monuments, and so on), and vegetation. When a separate secon-dary standard exists, both it and the primary standard must be met. The existing primary and secondary standards are given in Table 15.1.

The ambient standards are required by statute to be determined without any consideration given to the costs of meeting them. They are supposed to be set at a level sufficient to protect even the most sensitive members of the population.

While EPA is responsible for defining the ambient standards, the primary responsibility for ensuring that the ambient air-quality standards are met falls on the state control agencies. They exercise this responsibility by developing and executing an acceptable state implementation plan (SIP), which must be approved by EPA. This plan divides the state into separate air quality control regions. Special procedures were developed for handling regions that cross state borders, such as metropolitan New York.

The SIP spells out for each control region the procedures and timetables for meeting local ambient standards and for abatement of the effects of locally emitted pollutants on other states. The required degree of control depends on the severity of the pollution problem in each of the control regions.

By 1975 it had become apparent that, despite some major gains in air quality, many areas had not met and would not meet the ambient standards by the statutory deadlines. Therefore, in the 1977 amendments to the Clean Air Act, Congress extended the deadline for attainment of all primary (health-related) am-bient standards to 1982 with further extensions to 1987 possible for ozone and carbon monoxide. The amendments also required EPA to designate all areas not meeting the original deadlines as *nonattainment regions*.

The areas receiving this designation were subjected to particularly stringent controls. After the 1977 Amendments were passed, all portions of state im-plementation plans applying to nonattainment regions had to be revised by the state control authorities to ensure compliance with the new deadlines. To prod

---

1 We discuss the U.S. approach in some detail to show how abstract command and control concepts can be translated into specific policy. Many industrialized countries have rather similar policies. For more detail on the environmental policies of some European countries and Japan, see Frederic N. Bolotin, ed., *International Public Policy Sourcebook, Vol. 2, Education and Environment* (Westport, CT: Greenwood Press, 1989). The Japanese approach, which is rather different, will be treated in more detail latter in the chapter.

TABLE 15.1   National Primary and Secondary Ambient Air Quality Standards

Pollutant	Primary standard[a]	Secondary standard[a]
Sulfur oxides	a. 80 µ/m³ (0.03 ppm) annual arithmetic mean	1300 µg/m³ (0.5 ppm) 3-hour concentration not to be exceeded more than once a year
	b. 365 µg/m³ (0.14 ppm) maximum 24-hour concentration not to be exceeded more than once a year	
Particulate matter[b]	a. 50 µg/m³—annual arithmetic mean	
	b. 150 µg/m³—maximum 24-hour concentration not to be exceeded more than once a year	Same as primary standard
Carbon monoxide	a. 10 mg/m³ (9 ppm) maximum 8-hour concentration not to be exceeded more than once a year	
	b. 40 mg/m³ (35 ppm) maximum 1-hour concentration not to be exceeded more than once a year	No secondary standard
Ozone	235 µg/m³ (0.12 ppm) maximum average hourly concentration not to be exceeded more than once a year	Same as primary standard
Nitrogen dioxide	100 µg/m³ (0.05 ppm) annual arithmetic mean	Same as primary standard
Lead	1.5 µg/m³ arithmetic mean averaged over a calendar quarter	Same as primary standard

[a]µg/m³ is micrograms per cubic meter; mg/m³ is milligrams per cubic meter; ppm is parts per million.
[b]TSP was the indicator pollutant for the original particulate matter standards. This standard was replaced with a new standard in 1987. The new standard tracks particles less than 10 µm in diameter as the new indicator pollutant.
Source: *Code of Federal Regulations*, Volume 40, Parts 50.4, 50.6, 50.8, 50.9, 50.11, and 50.12 (1989).

the states into action, Congress gave EPA the power to halt the construction of major new or modified pollution sources and to deny federal sewage and transportation grants for any state not submitting a plan showing precisely how and when attainment would be reached.

State implementation plans in nonattainment regions must include a permit program for newly constructed large sources or large sources that have undergone some major modification. Permits cannot be granted to these sources unless the state can demonstrate that emissions resulting from commencing or expanding operations would not jeopardize the region's progress toward attainment. The state can satisfy this requirement by controlling existing sources to a sufficiently high degree that progress can be demonstrated even with the new sources in operation.

A second condition for the permit to be issued stipulates that all major new or modified sources in nonattainment areas must also control their own emissions to the *lowest achievable emission rate* (LAER). The LAER is defined as the lowest emission rate included in any state implementation plan *whether or not any source is currently achieving that rate*. This part of the law was designed to ensure that only the most stringent controls would be used by any source locating in a nonattainment area. It is controversial because it implies that new sources could be forced to use technologies which have never been commercially tested.

Regions with air quality at least as high as the standards by the original deadline were subject to another set of controls known collectively as the PSD policy. This policy derives its name from its objective, the *prevention of significant deterioration* of the air in cleaner regions. The origin of this policy is found in the preamble to the 1970 Clean Air Act, which stated as an objective: "to protect and enhance the quality of the nation's air."

In 1972 EPA was successfully sued by the Sierra Club for promulgating regulations that did not ensure that this objective would be met. The system of ambient standards prevented the deterioration of the air *beyond* the standard, but air significantly cleaner than the standard would normally have deteriorated until it reached the standard. Following the court's decision, EPA adopted a PSD program in 1974, and the 1977 amendment to the Clean Air Act continued a modified version of that program.

The PSD regulations specify the maximum allowable increases or increments in pollution concentration beyond some baseline. To allow some variability in the size of three increments, Congress specified that PSD regions be subdivided into three types of areas with each type allowed a different increment. Class I areas include national parks and wilderness areas. The increments for these regions are the smallest. Practically any degradation in these areas is considered significant and is disallowed.

All other areas were initially designated as Class II regions, where a modest increment is allowed. States may redesignate any Class II region as a Class I region (thus allowing less future deterioration) or as a Class III region (allowing more). Class III regions are allowed the largest increment. In no case, however, can pollutant concentrations in any PSD region rise above the governing ambient standard.

New sources seeking to locate in PSD regions must secure permits. As a condition of securing their permits, these sources must install the *best available control technology* (BACT). The specific technologies that satisfy their requirement are determined by states on a case-by-case basis. Each new source permitted consumers a portion of the allowable increment. Once the increment has been completely consumed, no further deterioration of the air is allowed in that area even if the air is cleaner than required by the prevailing ambient standard. Thus, where the PSD increments are binding, for all practical purposes they define a tertiary standard varying in magnitude from region to region.

In addition to defining the ambient standards and requiring states to define BACT and LAER emission standards, the EPA itself has established national uniform emission standards for new sources of criteria pollutants or major modifications of existing sources.

The progress in defining those standards has been very slow. The standards governing new and modified sources of criteria pollutants are called the New Source Performance Standards (NSPS), and they were designed to merely serve as a floor for BACT and LAER determinations by the states. Congress wanted to ensure that all sources would have to meet a minimum standard regardless of where they were located. This was seen as a way to prevent states from caving in as industry attempted to play one state off against another in its attempt to seek the lowest possible emission standards. Neither LAER nor BACT can be lower than the new-source performance standards.

Simply stating the regulations is not enough. They must be enforced with appropriate sanctions whenever noncompliance occurs. Prior to the 1977 amendments, noncompliance was a significant problem with delays of up to six years common. Because of this situation, in 1977 Congress established the *noncompliance penalty* as a means of reducing the profitability in delaying compliance.

Without sanctions, the source benefits from delaying compliance. The equipment purchases necessary to ensure compliance are expensive and add nothing to profits. In addition, court action is slow and sometimes sympathetic toward business. The noncompliance penalty is designed to harmonize these private incentives with the social objectives pursued by the Act.

Patterned after a system first used in Connecticut, the magnitude of noncompliance penalty is determined by the economic value of delay to the source. Any economic gains received by the source as a result of noncompliance are included in the penalty and are transferred to the EPA; they no longer accrue to the source. The initial indications are that the existence of this penalty has cut delays by 30 to 40%.[2]

The final characteristic of the Clean Air Act that we shall discuss is that it rules out tailoring the degree of control to the prevailing meteorological condi-

---

2 See Sue Anne Batey Blackman and William J. Baumol, "Modified Fiscal Incentives in Environmental Policy," *Land Economics* 56 (November 1980): 419.

tions. All strategies must achieve better air quality through emission reductions stringent enough to ensure compliance in adverse conditions.

The Efficiency of the Command-and-Control Approach

Efficiency presumes that the ambient standards are set at efficient levels. To ascertain whether or not the current standards are efficient, it is necessary to inquire into five aspects of the standard-setting process: (1) the threshold concept on which the standards are based, (2) the level of the standard, (3) the choice of uniform standards over standards more tailored to the regions involved, (4) the timing of emission flows, and (5) the failure to incorporate the degree of human exposure in the standard-setting process.

The Threshold Concept.   Some basis is needed for setting the ambient standard. Since the Clean Air Act prohibits the balancing of costs and benefits, some alternative criterion must be used. For the primary (health-related) standard, this criterion is known as the *health threshold*. The standard is to be defined with a margin of safety sufficiently high that no adverse health effects would be suffered by any member of the population as long as the air quality was at least as good as the standards. This approach presumes the existence of a threshold such that concentrations above that level produce adverse health effects, but concentrations below it produce none.

If the threshold concept were valid, the marginal damage function would be zero until the threshold was reached and would be positive at higher concentrations. The belief that the actual damage function has this shape is not consistent with the evidence, because we are now learning that adverse health effects can occur at pollution levels lower than the ambient standards.[3] The standard that produces no adverse health effects among the general population (which, of course, includes especially susceptible groups) is probably zero or close to it. It is certainly lower than the established ambient standards. What the standards purport to accomplish and what they actually accomplish are rather different.

The Level of the Ambient Standard.   The absence of a defensible health threshold complicates the analysis. Some other basis must be used for determining the level at which the standard should be established. Efficiency would dic-

---

3 See, for example, the research by Lave and Seskin, which discovered a positive association between pollution and mortality even in those cities meeting the primary standards. Lester B. Lave and Eugene P. Seskin, *Air Pollution and Human Health* (Baltimore: Johns Hopkins University Press, 1977).

tate setting the standard in order to maximize the net benefit, which includes a consideration of costs as well as benefits.

The current policy explicitly excludes costs from consideration in setting the ambient standards. Costs are allowed to enter the process only when the policy instruments used to meet ambient standards are being defined. It is difficult to imagine that the process of setting the ambient standard would yield an efficient outcome when it is prohibited from considering one of the key elements of that outcome!

Unfortunately, for reasons which were discussed in some detail in Chapter 4, our current benefit measurements are not sufficiently reliable as to permit the identification of the efficient level with any confidence. Freeman, for example, in his extensive 1982 survey of the evidence concludes that the benefits (in 1978 dollars) derived from controlling stationary sources lie somewhere in the interval from $4.8 billion to $49.4 billion per year with a most likely point estimate of $21.4 billion per year.[4] This can be compared to a cost of stationary-source control of around $9.0 billion per year. These figures suggest that a high degree of confidence can be attached to the belief that government intervention is justified, but they provide no evidence whatsoever on whether current policy is efficient. A similar fate met a recent attempt to use benefit-cost analysis to ascertain the efficiency of the particulate standard (Example 15.1).

Uniformity. The same primary and secondary standards apply to all parts of the country. No account is taken of the number of people exposed, the sensitivity of the local ecology, or the costs of compliance in various areas. All of these would have some effect on the efficient standard and efficiency would, therefore, dictate different standards for different regions. In general, the evidence suggests that the inefficiencies associated with uniformity are greatest in the rural areas, but we shall leave a full description and interpretation of that evidence for Chapter 20.

The PSD program does introduce some variability by establishing more stringent standards for regions with the cleanest air. If national parks and other Class I areas are especially sensitive to pollution, that portion of the program could represent a move toward efficiency. Since states have some flexibility in choosing which portions of their area would be designated as Class II and Class III regions, it is conceivable, but by no means obvious, that they would make efficient choices.

---

4 A. Myrick Freeman III, *Air and Water Pollution Control: A Benefit-Cost Assessment* (New York: Wiley, 1982).

EXAMPLE 15.1

Net Benefit Analysis of the Particulate Ambient Standard

Although EPA is precluded from considering benefit-cost analysis in setting ambient standards, it is not precluded from having the studies done. One such study was done as part of the process of considering whether to change the stringency or the form of the particulate ambient standard.

The purpose of the study was to aggregate on a national basis estimates of various forms of damage that would be done by particulate emissions, including health effects, soiling and materials damage, and visibility effects, under various regulatory regimes. The aggregation brought together a number of different studies, each relying on different data and different valuation techniques. These aggregate benefit estimates were then combined with cost information to produce net benefit information for each of the considered options.

Aggregating these rather different studies posed some problems. First, they were not all of equal quality. Some had gone through extensive peer review, and others had not. Second, it was not clear whether estimates from the various studies could legitimately be added together without double counting some of the benefits. For example, the property and wage studies may indirectly be valuing the health effects that are more directly valued by epidemiological studies.

To grapple with these problems, Mathtech, Inc., the contractor on the study, did the net benefit analysis on a variety of regulatory options separately for each of six aggregation procedures. Unfortunately, they discovered that the

Furthermore, it remains true that no area is allowed to experience air-quality levels worse than the primary and secondary standards for any longer than necessary to reach those standards.

Timing of Emission Flows. Because concentrations are important for criteria pollutants, the timing of emissions is an important policy concern. Emissions clustered in time are as troublesome as emissions clustered in space. How do we handle those relatively rare but devastating occasions when thermal inversions prevent the normal dispersion and dilution of the pollutants? From an economic efficiency point of view, the most obvious approach is to tailor the degree of control to the circumstances. Stringent control would be exercised when meteorological conditions were relatively stagnant, and less control would be applied under normal circumstances. The strong stand against intermittent controls in the Clean Air Act, however, rules this out.

ranking of standards in terms of economic efficiency was very sensitive to the different benefit estimation procedures employed. For the most restrictive counting of benefits all changes would lead to lower net benefits than merely continuing the current policy. For less restrictive benefit aggregation procedures, net benefits were highest for much more stringent standards.

The study also compared the net benefits from some of the more restrictive ambient standards depending upon whether the implementation deadline was seven years or nine years. For this aspect the results were conclusive—the nine-year implementation period produced higher net benefits.

Two insights on the use of benefit-cost analysis can be carried away from this specific example. First, the application of benefit-cost techniques to discover the efficient set of ambient standards is subject to a large number of uncertainties; the notion that analysts can derive a single, generally agreed-upon net benefit calculation for a specific regulatory option is naive. Second, despite these uncertainties, a great deal can be learned from the analysis even if it does not produce a single definitive answer. In this specific case, not only was the evidence on the implementation deadline unambiguous, but the analysis found that some regulatory options were dominated by others. Armed with this evidence, we can focus serious consideration on the undominated options.

Source: Mathtech, Inc., "Benefit and Net Benefit Analysis of Alternative National Ambient Air Quality Standards for Particulate Matter." Volume I of a report prepared for the Benefits Analysis Program of the U.S. Environmental Protection Agency (March 1983).

It turns out that a reliance on a constant degree of control, rather than allowing intermittent controls, raises compliance costs substantially, particularly when the required degree of control is high. In perhaps the earliest empirical study soundly based on economic theory, Teller examined the costs of controlling sulfur dioxide in Nashville, Tennessee, through fuel substitution.[5] He specifically examined two strategies: constant abatement, which requires the same degree of control over time, and forecasted abatement, which allows the degree of control to be tailored to forecasted weather conditions.

5 Azriel Teller, "Air Pollution Abatement: Economic Rationality and Reality," in *America's Changing Environment*, Roger Revelle and Hans H. Landsberg, eds. (Boston: Beacon Press, 1970).

Both strategies achieve compliance with the ambient standards, but forecasted control requires less total emission reduction. His results indicate that constant abatement would be five times more expensive than forecasted abatement.

Concentration versus Exposure. Present ambient standards are defined in terms of pollutant concentrations in the outdoor air. Yet health effects are more closely related to human exposure to pollutants. (Exposure is determined both by the concentrations of air pollutants in each of the places in which people spend time and the amount of time spent in each place.) Since only about 10% of the population's person-hours are spent outdoors, indoor air becomes very important in designing strategies to improve the health risk of pollutants.[6] Recent studies have suggested that exposure to pollutants is several times higher indoors than it is outdoors.[7] To date very little attention has been focused on controlling indoor air pollution despite its apparent importance.[8]

Cost Effectiveness of the Command-and-Control Approach

Though the ambient standards are not efficient, determining the magnitude of the inefficiency is plagued by uncertainties. It is not possible to definitively state just how inefficient they are.

Cost effectiveness is based on somewhat more solid evidence. Though it does not allow us to shed any light on whether a particular ambient standard is efficient or not, cost-effectiveness studies do allow us to see whether the command-and-control policy described above has resulted in the ambient standards being met in the least costly manner possible.

The theory covered in Chapter 14 makes it clear that the CAC strategy will normally not be cost-effective. What it does not make clear, however, is the degree to which this strategy diverges from the least-cost ideal. If the divergence is small, the proponents of reform would not likely be able to overcome the inertia of the status quo. If the divergence is large, the case for reform is stronger.

The cost effectiveness of the CAC approach depends on local circumstances such as prevailing meteorology, the locational configuration of sources, stack heights, and how costs vary with the amount controlled. Several simulation models capable of dealing with these complexities have now been constructed for a number of different pollutants in a variety of airsheds (Table 15.2).

---

6 This estimate is for the United States.

7 Kirk R. Smith, "Air Pollution: Assessing Total Exposure in the United States," *Environment* 30 (October 1988): 10–15; 33–38.

8 The one major policy response to indoor air pollution has been the large number of states which have passed legislation requiring "smoke free" areas in public places to protect nonsmokers.

TABLE 15.2 Empirical Studies of Air Pollution Control

Study and year	Pollutants covered	Geographic area	CAC benchmark	Assumed pollutant type	Ratio of CAC cost to least cost
Atkinson and Lewis (1974)	Particulates	St. Louis Metropolitan Area	SIP regulations	Nonuniformly mixed	6.00
Roach et al. (1981)	Sulfur dioxide	Four Corners in Utah, Colorado, Arizona, and New Mexico	SIP regulations	Nonuniformly mixed	4.25
Hahn and Noll (1982)	Sulfates	Los Angeles	California emission standards	Nonuniformly mixed	1.07
Krupnick (1983)	Nitrogen dioxide	Baltimore	Proposed RACT regulations	Nonuniformly mixed	5.96
Seskin, Anderson, and Reid (1983)	Nitrogen dioxide	Chicago	Proposed RACT regulations	Nonuniformly mixed	14.40
McGartland (1984)	Particulates	Baltimore	SIP regulations	Nonuniformly mixed	4.18
Spofford (1984)	Sulfur dioxide	Lower Delaware Valley	Uniform percentage reduction	Nonuniformly mixed	1.78
	Particulates	Lower Delaware Valley	Uniform percentage reduction	Nonuniformly mixed	22.00
Maloney and Yandle (1984)	Hydrocarbons	All domestic DuPont plants	Uniform percentage reduction	Uniformly mixed	4.15

CAC = command and control, the traditional regulatory approach.
SIP = state implementation plan
RACT = reasonably available control technologies, a set of standards imposed on existing sources in nonattainment areas

Since for a number of reasons the estimated costs cannot be directly compared across studies, it is appropriate to develop a means of comparing costs that minimizes the comparability problems. One such technique, the one we have chosen, involves calculating the ratio of the CAC allocation costs to the lowest cost of meeting the same objective for each study. A ratio equal to 1.0 implies that the CAC allocation is cost-effective. By subtracting 1.0 from the ratio in the table, it is possible to interpret the remainder as the percentage increase in cost from the least cost ideal due to relying on the CAC system.

Of the nine reported comparisons, eight find that the CAC policy costs at least 78% more than the least-cost allocation. If we omit the Hahn and Noll (1982) study[9] (for reasons discussed in the next two paragraphs), the study involving the *smallest* cost savings (sulfur dioxide control in the Lower Delaware Valley) finds that the CAC allocation results in abatement costs that are 78% higher than necessary to meet the standards. In the Chicago study, the CAC costs are estimated to be 14 times as expensive as necessary, while in the Lower Delaware Valley they are estimated to be 22 times more expensive than necessary.

The Hahn and Noll finding that the CAC strategy was close to being cost-effective was somewhat unique in a couple of respects. Because we can learn something from this study about the conditions under which CAC policies may not be far off the mark, we study it closely.

The city studied by Hahn and Noll, Los Angeles, has a large sulfate problem, necessitating a very high degree of control. In effect, virtually every source is forced to control as much as is economically feasible. Because the menu of options in essence consists of a single feasible allocation, all policies must ultimately arrive at this allocation.[10]

Does the degree of cost excess associated with the CAC approach depend on the stringency of the ambient standard being met? The evidence seems to suggests that it does depend on the stringency, but in well-defined ways. Atkinson and Lewis (1974) find,[11] for example, that within a middle range of possible ambient standards the divergence between the CAC allocation and the least-cost allocation becomes larger as the ambient standard target becomes harder to meet. Concentrating on the most stringent range of control (as opposed to the middle

---

9 Robert W. Hahn and Roger G. Noll, "Designing a Market for Tradeable Emissions Permits," *Reform of Environmental Regulation*, Wesley A. Magat, ed. (Cambridge, MA: Ballinger, 1982).

10 Hahn and Noll also suggest that the California Air Resources Board has specifically used its multimillion dollar budget in part to promulgate cost-effective emission standards. Therefore, this board may be atypically cost-effective in its approach to a CAC strategy due to both the amount of resources at its disposal and its inclination to use them to pursue cost-effective allocations of control responsibility.

11 Scott E. Atkinson and Donald H. Lewis, "A Cost-Effective Analysis of Alternative Air Quality Control Strategies, *Journal of Environmental Economics and Management* 1 (November 1974): 237–250.

ranges of control examined by Atkinson and Lewis), however, two authors have found the relative divergence between the CAC and least-cost allocations declines as the ambient standard becomes tougher to meet. Spofford finds this to be the case for both particulates and sulfur oxides, while Maloney and Yandle find it to be true for hydrocarbon control.[12] Apparently the CAC air pollution policy approximates the least-cost allocation only at sufficiently high degrees of control that any control flexibility is effectively eliminated.

Air Quality

Despite the deficiencies of this approach, it has produced better air quality in the United States. A 1990 U.S. EPA Report reveals that since 1979 particulate emissions are down 22%, sulfur dioxide emissions by 17%, carbon dioxide emissions by 25%, nitrogen dioxide emissions by 8%, volatile organic compounds (precursors for ozone formation) by 17%, and lead by 93%.[13]

How typical has the U.S. experience been? Is pollution declining on a worldwide basis? The Global Environmental Monitoring System, operating under the auspices of the World Health Organization and the United Nations Environment Program, monitors air quality around the globe. Scrutiny of its reports reveal that the U.S. experience is typical for the industrialized nations, which have generally reduced pollution (both in terms of emissions and ambient outdoor air quality).[14] Some of the reductions achieved in countries such as Japan and Norway have been spectacular. But the air quality in most developing nations has steadily deteriorated, and the number of people exposed to unhealthy levels of pollution in those countries is frequently very high.[15] Since these countries typically are struggling merely to provide adequate employment and income to their citizens, they cannot afford to waste large sums of money on inefficient environmental policies, especially if the inefficiencies tend to subsidize the rich

---

12 See W. O. Spofford, Jr., "Efficiency Properties of Alternative Source Control Policies for Meeting Ambient Air Quality Standards: An Empirical Application to the Lower Delaware Valley," Discussion paper D-118 (Washington DC: Resources for the Future, November 1984) and M. T. Maloney and B. Yandle, "Estimation of the Cost of Air Pollution Control Regulation" *Journal of Environmental Economics and Management* 11 (1984): 244-263.

13 Office of Air Quality Planning and Standards, *National Air Quality and Emission Trends: 1988* (Raleigh, NC: U.S. Environmental Protection Agency, 1990).

14 United Nations Environment Program and the World Health Organization, "Monitoring the Global Environment: An Assessment of Urban Air Quality," *Environment* 31 (October 1989): 6-13; 26-37.

15 For sulfur oxides, for example, the GEMS study estimates that only 30% to 35% of the world's population lives in areas where air is at least as clean as that recommended by World Health Organization guidelines.

at the expense of the poor. Some cost-effective, yet fair means of improving air quality must be found.

INNOVATIVE APPROACHES

Fortunately some innovative approaches are available. Since various versions of these approaches have now been implemented around the world, we can learn from the experience gained from their implementation.

The Emissions Trading Program

Stripped to its bare essentials, the command-and-control approach toward stationary sources involves the specification of emission standards (legal ceilings) on all major emission sources. These standards are imposed on a large number of specific emission points such as stacks, vents, or storage tanks.

The emissions trading program adopted in the United States attempts to inject more flexibility into the manner in which the clean air objectives are met. Sources are encouraged to change the mix of control technologies envisioned in the standards as long as air quality is improved or at least not adversely affected by the change. The program is implemented by means of four separate policies, linked by a common element known as the emission reduction credit. The emission reduction credit is the currency used in trading among emission points, while the offset, bubble, emissions banking, and netting policies govern how the currency can be spent.[16]

The Emission Reduction Credit. Should any source decide to control any emission point to a higher degree than necessary to fulfill its legal obligations, it can apply to the control authority for certification of the excess control as an emission reduction credit. Certified credits can be banked or used in the bubble, offset, or netting programs. To receive certification, the emission reduction must be (1) surplus, (2) enforceable, (3) permanent, and (4) quantifiable.

The Offset Policy. The offset policy was established to resolve a conflict between economic growth and progress toward meeting the ambient standards in nonattainment areas. The dilemma posed by this conflict involved how new or

---

16 As described in the next chapter these policies have recently been adopted for controlling acid rain and ozone-depleting chemicals as well.

expanded sources could be accommodated while meeting the statutory require-ment that the ambient standards be met as expeditiously as possible. Since these sources would add emissions to the region, some means of offsetting them had to be found.

The offset policy allows qualified new or expanding sources to commence operations in a nonattainment area provided they acquire sufficient emission reduction credits from existing sources. Typically they must acquire credits for 20% more reductions in emissions than would be added when the new facility commences operations. By buying the credits, new sources, in effect, finance emission controls undertaken by existing sources, thereby serving as a vehicle for improved air quality. Because regional emissions would be lower after the source began operations (counting the acquired emission reduction credits) than before, economic growth became the means for achieving better air quality rather than the source of further deterioration.

Major new or modified sources are qualified to participate in this program only if they control their own emissions to the degree required by the LAER standard and all existing major sources owned or operated by the applicant in the same state as the proposed source are in compliance with their legal control responsibilities.

The Bubble Policy.   The bubble policy allows existing sources to use emission reduction credits to satisfy their SIP control responsibilities. For example, ex-isting sources in nonattainment areas can meet their assigned RACT standards either by adopting the control technology used to define the standard or by adopting some technology that emits the pollutant at a somewhat higher rate, making up the difference with acquired emission reduction credits. The sum of emission reduction credits plus actual reductions must equal the assigned reduction.

This policy derives its unusual name from its treatment of multiple emission points as if they were contained within an imaginary bubble, regulating only the amount leaving the bubble. These bubbles can be extended to include not only emission points within the same plant but emission points in plants owned by other firms as well (Example 15.2).

Netting.   Netting allows sources undergoing modification or expansion to es-cape the burden of new source review requirements so long as any net in-crease (counting the emission reduction credits) in plantwide emissions is insignificant. Traditionally, the test of whether a source was subject to the new-source review process or not was applied by calculating the expected increases in emission occurring after modernization or expansion. When these increases passed predetermined thresholds, the source was subject to review. Netting allows emission reduction credits earned elsewhere in the plant to offset the increases expected from the expanded more modernized portion in order to determine whether the threshold had been exceeded. By "netting out"

EXAMPLE 15.2

The Bubble and Offset Policies in Action

At the end of 1981, EPA had been approached by about 93 different bubble trades, and the number was growing daily. Several of these presented the prospect of saving the purchaser substantial sums of money:

1. The Narraganset Electric Company has two generating stations in Providence, Rhode Island. Under the bubble policy they were allowed to use high-sulfur oil (2.2% sulfur) at one plant when the second plant was burning natural gas or was not operating, instead of being required to burn 1% sulfur oil at both plants. This action resulted in a savings of $3 million annually, reduced the use of imported oil by 600,000 barrels per year, and reduced sulfur emissions by 30%.

2. The DuPont Corporation was allowed to control five major sources of volatile organic compounds to more than 97% efficiency in exchange for relaxed controls on more than 200 difficult-to-control sources of fugitive emissions. The expected savings include $12 million in capital costs plus several million dollars in recurring operating costs.

3. Manufacturers of cans were allowed to comply with existing regulations for each individual can-coating line by averaging emissions of volatile organic compounds on a daily basis so long as the source did not exceed the total allowable plantwide emission per day. This is expected to save the industry $107 million in capital expenditures, $28 million per year in operating costs, and 4 trillion BTUs of natural gas per year, chiefly because expensive add-on pollution control equipment which would have been energy-consuming is no longer necessary.

The exact number of offset transactions that have occurred is not known with any certainty. One search, however, uncovered hundreds.* Some ex-

of review, the facility may be exempted from the need to acquire preconstruction permits as well as from meeting the associated requirements, such as modeling or monitoring the impact of the new source on air quality, installing BACT or LAER control technology, or meeting the offset requirement; it may also avoid any applicable bans on new construction. Those facilities satisfying the significant increase threshold must still meet emission limits established by the NSPS. Emission reduction credits cannot be used to avoid this national standard.

amples serve to illustrate the flexibility this system provides:

1. A cement company in Texas entered into an agreement with another local company providing for that company to install dust collectors. The cement company paid for the equipment while the other company agreed to accept the maintenance costs, which were negligible.
2. The emissions from a 90-megawatt refuse-burning power plant to be operated by Columbus, Ohio, were offset at the city's expense by installing pollution controls at two privately owned asphalt plants and by increasing the height of a smokestack at a third company.
3. A company wanting to build an oil terminal to handle 40,000 barrels a day in Contra Costa County, California, was granted a permit when it acquired, for $250,000, an offset created when a local chemical company shut down.
4. In the mid-1970s the state of Pennsylvania created an offset by altering its road-paving practices—which served to reduce hydrocarbon emissions—and used this offset to successfully induce the Volkswagen Corporation to locate its first American production facility in a depressed region in that state.

*Jorge A. del Calvo y Gonzales, "Markets in Air: Problems and Prospects of Controlled Trading," *Harvard Environmental Law Review* 5 (1981): 401.

Source: These examples were taken from the National Commission of Air Quality, *To Breathe Clean Air* (Washington, DC: U.S. Government Printing Office, 1981): 136–137; and Richard A. Liroff, *Air Pollution Offsets: Trading, Selling and Banking* (Washington, DC: The Conservation Foundation, 1980): 13.

Banking. The banking component of the emissions trading program establishes procedures that allow firms to store emission reduction credits for subsequent use in the bubble, offset, or netting programs. States are authorized to design their own banking programs as long as the rules specify the ownership rights over the banked credits; the sources eligible to bank emission reduction credits; and the conditions governing the certification, holding, and use of these credits.

The Effectiveness of Emissions Trading

Although comprehensive data on the effects of the program do not exist because substantial proportions of it are administered by local areas and no one collects information in a systematic way, some of the major aspects of the experience are clear.[17]

The program has unquestionably and substantially reduced the costs of complying with the requirements of the Clean Air Act. Most estimates place the accumulated capital savings for all components of the program at over $10 billion. This does not include the recurring savings in operating cost. On the other hand, the program has not produced the magnitude of cost savings that was anticipated by most proponents at its inception.

The level of compliance with the basic provisions of the Clean Air Act has increased. The emissions trading program expanded the possible means for compliance and sources have responded.

Somewhere between 7000 and 12,000 trading transactions have been consummated. Each of these transactions was voluntary and for the participants represented an improvement over the traditional regulatory approach. Several of these transactions involved the introduction of innovative control technologies.

The vast majority of emissions trading transactions have involved large pollution sources trading emissions reduction credits either created by excess control of uniformly mixed pollutants (those for which the location of emission is not an important policy concern) or involving facilities in close proximity to one another. Emissions trading seems to work especially well for uniformly mixed pollutants. No diffusion modeling is necessary to establish effects on ambient concentrations and regulators do not have to worry about trades creating "hot spots" or localized areas of high pollution concentration. Trades can be on a one-to-one basis.

Emissions trading integrates particularly smoothly into any policy structure which is based either directly (through emission standards) or indirectly (through mandated technology or input limitations) on regulating emissions. In this case emission limitations embedded in the operating licenses can serve as the trading benchmark.

Because emissions trading allows the issue of who will pay for the control to be separated from who will install the control, it introduces an additional degree of flexibility. This flexibility is particularly important in nonattainment areas since marginal control costs are so high. Sources which would not normally be controlled because they could not afford to implement the con-

17 See the evaluations of this program in D. J. Dudek and J. Palmisano, "Emissions Trading: Why Is This Thoroughbred Hobbled?" *Columbia Journal of Environmental Law* 13 (1988): 217–256; R. W. Hahn, "Economic Prescriptions for Environmental Problems: How the Patient Followed the Doctor's Orders," *The Journal of Economic Perspectives* 3 (Spring 1989): 95–114; R. W. Hahn and G. L. Hester, "Where Did All the Markets Go? An Analysis of EPA's Emission Trading Program," *Yale Journal of Regulation* 6 (Winter 1989): 109–153; and T. H. Tietenberg, "Economic Instruments for Environmental Regulation," *Oxford Review of Economic Policy* 6 (Spring 1990): 17–33.

trols without going out of business can be controlled with emissions trading. The revenue derived from the sale of emission reduction credits can be used to finance the controls, effectively preventing bankruptcy.

Because it is quantity based, emissions trading also offers a unique possibility for leasing. Leasing is particularly valuable when the temporal pattern of emissions varies across sources. This appears to generally be the case with utilities. In addition when a firm plans to shut down one plant in the near future and to build a new one, leasing credits is a vastly superior alternative to the temporary installation of equipment in the old plant which would be useless when the plant was retired. The useful life of this temporary control equipment would be wastefully short.

We have also learned that ERC transactions have higher transactions costs than we previously understood. Regulators must validate every trade. When non-uniformly mixed pollutants are involved, the transaction costs associated with estimating the air quality effects are particularly high. Delegating responsibility for trade approval to lower levels of government may in principle speed up the approval process, but unless the bureaucrats in the lower level of government support the program the gain may be negligible.

Emissions trading places more importance on the operating permits and emissions inventories than other approaches. To the extent those are deficient the potential for trades that protect air quality may be lost. Firms which have actual levels of emissions substantially below allowable emissions find themselves with a trading opportunity which, if exploited, could degrade air quality. The trading benchmark has to be defined carefully.

One question that always arises about emissions trading is the degree to which market power could undermine its desirable properties. Hahn has examined the case where permits are allocated to emitters without charge (as is done in the Emissions Trading Program) rather than allocating them by an auction.[18] His most important finding was that this initial allocation could have an effect on both the final (post-trade) allocation of permits and the permit price in the presence of market power. This finding is in direct contrast to what would happen in competitive markets (as described in Chapter 14), where both the final price and the ultimate allocation of permits would be independent of the initial allocation.

It is not hard to obtain an intuitive understanding of why the initial allocation might have an effect on the potential for price-setting behavior. Whenever a single price-setting source receives an initial allocation that is either higher than or lower than its cost-effective allocation, an incentive for trading would be created. When a price-setting source receives in an initial allocation fewer permits than its cost-effective allocation, it would exercise power on the buyer's side of the market. If it received more, it would exercise power on the seller's side of the market. The farther

---

18 Robert W. Hahn, "Market Power and Transferable Property Rights," *Quarterly Journal of Economics* 99 (November 1984): 753-765.

the initial allocation diverges from the cost-effective allocation, the greater the potential for the price setter to exercise power over the market.

Is the potential for price manipulation a serious potential flaw in permit markets? Existing simulation studies suggest that it is not. Hahn found in simulating the sulfate market in Los Angeles that the total cost function was rather flat with respect to the initial allocation unless the price-setting firm receives a sufficiently large number of permits that enable it to become virtually a monopoly seller.

In another set of published data from the DuPont Corporation involving some 52 plants and 548 sources of hydrocarbons, Maloney and Yandle investigated the effects of cartelization of plants on the permit market.[19] Assuming that all sources receive a proportional initial distribution of the permits based on their uncontrolled emissions, they calculate the effects on control costs if plants collude. Their analysis allows collusion to take place separately among buyers and sellers and allows the number of colluding plants to vary from 10% to 90% of the total number of plants buying or selling.

In general, these data support the notion that high degrees of cartelization are necessary before control costs are affected to any appreciable degree and that even high degrees of cartelization do not significantly erode the large savings to be achieved from permit markets. At the 90% credit monopoly (achieved when the cartel controls 90% of all credits sold), for example, yielding a 41% increase in control costs, Maloney and Yandle point out that the cost savings from this severe market power situation, compared with command-and-control regulation, is still 66% (instead of 76%). The presence of market power does not seem to diminish the potential for cost savings very much. Even with market power, transferable permit systems seem to result in lower control costs than the command-and-control allocation.

In summary, the current regulatory reforms embodying transferable permits represent a large, but incomplete, step toward cost effectiveness.

Emission Charges

Air pollution emission charges have been implemented by France and Japan. The French air pollution charge was designed to encourage the early adoption of pollution control equipment with the revenues returned to those paying the charge as a subsidy for installing the equipment. In Japan the emission charge is designed to raise revenue to compensate victims of air pollution.

The French charge system has been in effect since 1985. Originally designed to operate until 1990, it was renewed in that year. The charge is levied on all industrial firms having a power generating capacity of 50,000 watts or more or

---

19 Michael T. Maloney and Bruce Yandle, "Estimation of the Cost of Air Pollution Control Regulation," *Journal of Environmental Economics and Management* 11 (September 1984): 244–263.

industrial firms discharging over 2500 tons or sulfur or nitrogen oxides per year. Only about 400 plants are affected. The charge is levied on the amount of actual sulfur oxides emitted. Some 90% of the charge revenue is recovered by charge payers as a subsidy for pollution control equipment, while the remaining 10% is used for new technological developments.

While data are limited, a few highlights seem clear. The charge level is too low to have any incentive impact. Total revenues are estimated to be about one-tenth of the revenue that would result from a charge sufficient to bring French industries in line with the air pollution control directives of the European Community.[20]

Economists typically envision two types of effluent or emissions charges. The first, an efficiency charge, is designed to produce an efficient outcome by forcing the polluter to compensate completely for all damage caused. The second, a cost-effective charge, is designed to achieve a predefined ambient standard at the lowest possible control cost. In practice, the French approach fits neither of these designs.

In Japan the charge takes on a different function. As a result of four important legal cases where Japanese industries were forced to compensate victims for pollution damages caused, in 1973 Japan passed the Law for the Compensation of Pollution-Related Health Injury. According to this law, victims of designated diseases, upon certification by a council of medical, legal, and other experts, are eligible for medical expenses, lost earnings, and other expenses; they are not eligible for other losses such as pain and suffering. Two classes of diseases are funded: specific diseases where the specific source is relatively clear and non-specific respiratory diseases where all polluters are presumed to have some responsibility.

This program is funded by an emissions charge on sulfur dioxides and from an automobile weight tax. The level of the tax is determined by the revenue needs of the compensation fund.

In contrast to emissions trading where ERC prices respond automatically to changing market conditions, emissions charges have to be determined by an administrative process. When the function of the charge is to raise revenue for a particular purpose, charge rates will be determined by the costs of achieving that purpose; when the costs of achieving the purpose rise, the level of the charge must rise to secure the additional revenue.[21]

Sometimes that process produces an unintended dynamic. In Japan, for example, the charge is calculated on the basis of the amount of compensation paid to victims of air pollution in the previous year. While the amount of compensa-

---

20 J. B. Opschoor and Hans B. Vos, *Economic Instruments For Environmental Protection* (Paris: Oganization for Economic Cooperation and Development, 1989): 34-5.

21 While it is theoretically possible (depending on the elasticity of demand for pollution abatement) for a rise in the tax to produce less revenue, this has typically not been the case.

tion has been increasing, the amount of emissions (the base to which the charge is applied) has been decreasing. As a result, unexpectedly high charge rates are necessary in order to raise sufficient revenue for the compensation system.

Hazardous Pollutants

Hazardous pollutants are those that pose a localized risk of severe harm to human health. They are distinguished from criteria pollutants both by the degree of harm they pose to those exposed and by the fact that emission usually occurs only at a few key locations. In recognition of these unique characteristics, the Clean Air Act sets up a special process for dealing with hazardous pollutants.

The first step in the control process involves identifying those substances which are designated as hazardous substances and therefore must receive this special treatment. The Act requires the Administrator of EPA to make and periodically update a list of hazardous pollutants. It allows a great deal of discretion in the choice of criteria to be used in distinguishing hazardous and criteria pollutants and in the length of time necessary to decide whether a substance should be listed.

Once a substance is listed, EPA must move with great speed (180 days) either to regulate emissions of the substance or to remove it from the list after finding that the evidence failed to support the tentative hazardous-substance designation. The decision to regulate a substance imposes on EPA a requirement to establish a national emission standard or workplace standard for each regulated substance. These standards must be designed to protect human health with an adequate margin of safety.

The somewhat ambiguous language in this section of the Act has led to a great deal of controversy as well as litigation concerning the meaning of this mandate. It is generally conceded that there is no safe threshold level for airborne carcinogens. Therefore, environmentalists maintain that protecting the public with an adequate margin of safety requires eliminating all exposure to listed substances. Completely eliminating emissions would, at a minimum, be very expensive and may not be possible without shutting down the operation.

EPA has reacted to this dilemma in two ways: (1) it has moved slowly in listing pollutants, and (2) it has chosen to balance costs and risks in deciding whether to list a substance. By 1989, EPA had listed only eight pollutants: asbestos (1971), beryllium (1971), mercury (1971), vinyl chloride (1975), benzene (1977), radionuclides (1979), inorganic arsenic (1980), and radon-222 (1985).[22]

In addition to moving very slowly in listing pollutants, the agency began to incorporate risk assessment and benefit-cost analysis into their decisions. The

---

22 Frustrated by a lack of action, Congress mandated controls on a large list of specific hazardous pollutants in the Clean Air Act Amendments of 1990.

first step in this process is to decide whether the risk posed by the substance is "significant." Substances which are not found to be posing significant risks are not listed. The second step, taken only for listed pollutants, involves identifying the level of control that will be required. This entails comparing the costs of various control possibilities with the damages to health prevented by adopting the controls.

Based on the work of Haigh, Harrison, and Nichols, it is possible to see how this kind of economic analysis can be applied to hazardous pollution regulation.[23] In their study, the authors applied benefit-cost analysis to three hazardous pollutants: benzene, coke oven emissions, and acrylonitrile. Benzene is a major industrial chemical, ranking among the top 15 in terms of production volume. Coke, produced by distilling coal in ovens, is essential to the production of steel. Acrylonitrile is an important industrial chemical used in the manufacture of a wide range of consumer products, including rugs, clothing, plastic pipe, and automobile hoses.

The analysis involved several steps. The amount and location of emissions had to be identified for each substance. The number of people exposed to this risk and the amount of health risk they would experience had to be calculated. Finally a dollar value had to be put on this risk so it could be directly compared with the control costs. All of these steps had to be repeated for each considered regulatory option.

Three regulatory strategies were considered for each pollutant. The first strategy was a rather stringent set of uniformly applied emission standards designed to require the use of the best available technology. (For benzene, the controls were applied to maleic anhydride plants, the largest source of emissions.) The second strategy involved a somewhat more relaxed version of the first strategy. While the standards were still applied uniformly in this second case, the level of required control was lower. The final strategy involved differential controls based on exposure. The notion of uniform controls was dropped in this case in favor of placing heavier controls on those sources posing the greatest health risk.

The authors present their results in two main forms. The first calculates the value of human life that would be needed to justify that particular regulatory option. This form of presentation allows the reader to determine whether the regulatory option is a good idea by supplying his or her own sense of what the value of human life should be. The second uses a $1 million value of human life and calculates the net benefits of each option based on that assumption.

---

23 John A. Haigh, David Harrison, Jr., and Albert L. Nichols, "Benefits Assessment and Environmental Regulation: Case Studies of Hazardous Air Pollutants," John F. Kennedy School of Government Energy and Environment Policy Center Discussion Paper E-83-07 (August 1983).

Using the $1 million figure for a human life, the results (Table 15.3) indicate that for all three pollutants the standard best available technology (BAT) strategy would yield negative net benefits. The combination of uniform standards with a very stringent level of control produces a situation where the costs exceed the benefits. A relaxed uniform standard reduces, but does not eliminate, the negative net benefits. Although lowering the uniform degree of control represents an improvement in the sense that costs are more commensurate with benefits, it still fails to target the reductions in the areas where they result in the most reduction in risk.

By configuring the controls in such a way as to target the costs on those emitters posing the greatest risk to human health (the differential strategy), we achieve a dramatic improvement in net benefits for all three pollutants. For only one, however, coke oven emissions, are the net benefits positive. For the rest even the differential strategy falls short of being justified by the benefits.

The significance of these data lie less in what they tell us about the correct regulatory option to choose for these specific pollutants than in the clues they provide concerning directions for policy to move in achieving greater efficiency in regulating hazardous pollutants in general. First, tailoring the strategy to specific circumstances can produce significant reductions in cost while achieving the same risk or much larger risk reductions for the same cost. Uniformity, in short, imposes a large cost penalty. Second, the policies being pursued in regulating hazardous pollutants imply values for human life which differ by a factor of more than 100. This finding implies that by allocating more resources to the control of those substances which can be justified with even a lower value of life and less to those which can be justified only with a high value for life, more lives could be saved with the same expenditure of money.

How can these lessons be translated into policy? One answer is to consider the adoption of a charge levied not on emission, but on exposure (Example 15.3). By forcing those emitters exposing large numbers of people to a health risk to exert greater cleanup efforts than those emitters exposing fewer people to the same health risk, we can save more lives with the same expenditure of resources. In this context, uniform exposure charges have much to recommend them.

TABLE 15.3 Net Benefits ($million/year) of Alternative Strategies for a Value of Life Saved of $1 Million

Regulatory strategy	Benzene	Coke oven emissions	Acrylonitrile
Best available technology	-2.2	-8.7	-28.8
Relaxed uniform	-1.1	-3.2	-8.0
Differential	-0.6	2.3	-4.9

Source: From "Benefits Assessment and Environmental Regulation: Case Studies of Hazardous Air Pollutants" by John A. Haigh, David Harrison, Jr., and Albert L. Nichols. John F. Kennedy School of Government Energy and Environment Policy Center Discussion Paper E-83-07 (August 1983). Reprinted by permission.

EXAMPLE 15.3

Efficient Regulation of Hazardous Pollutants: The Benzene Case

Regulatory approaches tend to emphasize uniform standards. As was clear from the discussion in the text, this can cause a particularly large deviation from efficiency when hazardous pollutants are involved, because both the control costs and damages are so localized.

Eight maleic anhydride plants in the United States emit more than half of the benzene from chemical manufacturing. From Table 15.3 we know that BAT uniform standards yield negative net benefits. Is there a more efficient approach?

The damage caused by these emissions (primarily an increase in the risk of leukemia) is a function both of the concentration level and the posed population. The highest economic marginal damage estimate found by a government agency was $1 for each person exposed continuously to a concentration of one part per billion (ppb) of benzene for one year. This corresponds to a risk of 3.4 ppb for one year and a value of $360,000 placed on each life lost.

The efficient solution would be to impose an emission charge of $1 per ppb person-year exposed since this is the (high) estimate of marginal damage. Firms would respond by choosing that level of control where their marginal cost was equal to $1 per ppb person-year exposed. Since this would guarantee the equivalence of marginal cost and marginal benefit, efficiency would be achieved.

The costs of the uniform standard were not justified by the benefits. The major problem with the proposed standard was that it did not take into account either the large differences in control costs or number of people exposed among the plants. Some plants in isolated areas exposed very few people while others in more densely populated areas clearly put more people at risk. The $1 uniform *exposure* charge solves both of these problems simultaneously. A uniform *emission* charge would take into account the differences in costs, but not the differences in exposure. Uniform emission standards take neither costs nor exposure into account and, therefore, are doubly cursed.

Source: This example is based on Albert L. Nichols, "The Importance of Exposure in Evaluating and Designing Environmental Regulations: A Case Study," *The American Economic Review* 72 (May 1982): 214–219.

SUMMARY

While air quality has improved in the industrial nations, it has deteriorated in the developing nations. Because the historical approach to air pollution control has been a traditional command-and-control approach, it has been neither efficient nor cost-effective.

The command-and-control policy has not been efficient in part because it has been based on a legal fiction, a threshold below which no health damages are inflicted on any member of the population. In fact, damages occur at levels lower than the ambient standards to especially sensitive members of the population, such as those with respiratory problems. This attempt to formulate standards without reference to control costs has been thwarted by the absence of a scientifically defensible health-based threshold. In addition, the policy fails to adequately consider the timing of emission flows. By failing to target the greatest amount of control on those periods when the greatest damage is inflicted, the current policy encourages too little control in high-damage periods and excessive control during low-damage periods. Current policy has also failed to pay sufficient attention to indoor air pollution, which may well pose larger health risks than outdoor pollution. Unfortunately, because the existing benefit estimates have large confidence intervals, the size of the inefficiency associated with these aspects of the policy has not been measured with any precision.

The policy is not cost-effective either. The allocation of responsibility among emitters for reducing pollution has resulted in control costs which are typically several times higher than necessary to achieve the air quality objective. This has been shown to be true for a variety of pollutants in a variety of geographic settings.

EPA has initiated the Emissions Trading Program, based on economic incentives, that is designed to provide more flexibility in meeting the air quality goals while reducing the cost and the conflict between economic growth and the preservation of air quality. These reforms, known as the bubble, offset, netting, and emissions banking programs, also promise to stimulate more rapid development of new control technologies than was possible under the traditional system.

France and Japan have both introduced emission charges as part of their approach to pollution control, but neither application fits the textbook model very well. In France the charge level is too low to have the appropriate incentive effects. In Japan the charge is designed mainly to raise revenue for compensating victims of respiratory damage caused by pollution. Only sulfur oxides are taxed.

The program to control hazardous pollutants is inefficient in both the speed with which the process is operating and quality of the decision being rendered. Faced with unrealistically short deadlines for publishing standards once a hazardous substance is listed, EPA has reacted by taking an excessively cautious approach to listing hazardous substances. Past decisions have resulted in the application of stringent standards that are uniformly applied to emitters. The evidence suggests that strategies tailored more closely to the risk posed (with emission posing the greatest risk being reduced more) produce substantially lower risks for the same expenditure as uniformly applied standards. One reform proposal based on this analysis would impose an exposure (as opposed to an emissions) charge on emitters which would take into account not only the concentration of the emission (and the resulting health risk to each exposed person) but also the number of people exposed.

FURTHER READING

Freeman, A. Myrick III. *Air and Water Pollution Control: A Benefit-Cost Assessment* (New York: Wiley, 1982). A detailed survey and critical evaluation of the literature on benefit-cost analysis as it applies to air and water pollution control. Contains chapters on defining and measuring benefits associated with health of humans, vegetation, and aesthetics as well as on water recreation. Calculates a range of estimates as well as the "most likely" point estimate.

Joeres, Erhard F. and Martin H. David, eds. *Buying a Better Environment: Cost Effective Regulation through Permit Trading* (Madison, WI: University of Wisconsin Press, 1983). An excellent collection of essays on aspects of permit trading including permit design, distributional matters, and dealing with uncertainty.

Nichols, Albert L. *Targeting Economic Incentives for Environmental Protection* (Cambridge, MA: MIT Press, 1984). An excellent review of the use of economic incentives to control pollution with a detailed treatment of the use of exposure charges to control airborne carcinogens.

Tietenberg, T. H. "Economic Instruments for Environmental Regulation," *Oxford Review of Economic Policy* 6 (Spring 1990): 17–33. A detailed examination of the lessons to be learned from existing applications of the economic incentives approach to pollution control.

ADDITIONAL REFERENCES

Anderson, Robert J., Jr., et al. "An Analysis of Alternative Policies for Attaining and Maintaining a Short-Term NO_2 Standard," a report prepared by MATHTECH, Inc. for the Council on Environmental Quality (September 17, 1979).

Blackman, Sue Anne Batey and William J. Baumol. "Modified Fiscal Incentives in Environmental Policy," *Land Economics* 56 (November 1980): 417–431.

Krupnick, Alan J. "Costs of Alternative Policies for the Control of NO_2 in the Baltimore Region" *Journal of Environmental Economics and Management*, 13 (June, 1986): 189–197.

Marcus, Alfred A. "Japan," in *International Public Policy Sourcebook, Vol. 2, Education and Environment*, Frederic N. Bolotin, ed. (Westport, CT: Greenwood Press, 1989): 275–291.

Maloney, M. T. and B. Yandle. "Estimation of the Cost of Air Pollution Control Regulation" *Journal of Environmental Economics and Management* 11 (November 1984):
244-263.

McGartland, Albert M. "Marketable Permit Systems for Air Pollution Control: An Empirical Study," Ph.D. dissertation, University of Maryland, 1984.

Oates, Wallace E., Paul R. Portney, and Albert M. McGartland. "The Net Benefits of Incentive-Based Regulation: A Case Study of Environmental Standard-Setting," *The
American Economic Review* 79 (December 1989): 1233-1242.

Portney, Paul R. "Air Pollution Policy," in *Public Policies for Environmental Protection*,
Paul R. Portney, ed. (Washington, DC: Resources for the Future, 1990): 27-96.

Roach, Fred, Charles Kolstad, Allen V. Kneese, Richard Tobin, and Michael Williams.
"Alternative Air Quality Policy Options in the Four Corners Region," *Southwest
Review* 1 (Summer 1981): 29-58.

Roumasset, James A. and Kirk R. Smith. "Exposure Trading: An Approach to More Efficient Air Pollution Control," *Journal of Environmental Economics and Management*
18 (May 1990): 276-291.

Seskin, Eugene P., Robert J. Anderson, and Robert O. Reid. "An Empirical Analysis of
Economic Strategies for Controlling Air Pollution," *Journal of Environmental
Economics and Management* 10 (June 1983): 112-124.

Spofford, Walter O., Jr. "Efficiency Properties of Alternative Source Control Policies for
Meeting Ambient Air Quality Standards: An Empirical Application to the Lower
Delaware Valley," unpublished Resources for the Future, Inc. discussion paper D-
1189 (February 1984).

Schelling, Thomas C. ed. *Incentives for Environmental Protection* (Cambridge, MA: MIT
Press, 1983).

DISCUSSION QUESTIONS

1. As shown in Example 15.3, the efficient regulation of hazardous pollutants
should take exposure into account—the more persons exposed to a given pollutant concentration, the larger is the damage caused by it and therefore the
smaller is the efficient concentration level, all other things being equal. An
alternative point of view would simply ensure that concentrations would be
held below a uniform threshold regardless of the number of people exposed.
For this point of view, the public-policy goal is to expose any and all people
to the same concentration level—exposure is not used to establish different
concentrations for different settings. What are the advantages and disadvantages of each approach? Which do you think represents the best approach?
Why?

2. European countries have relied to a much greater extent on emission charges
than has the United States, which seems to be moving toward a greater
reliance on transferable emission permits. From an efficiency point of view,

should the United States follow Europe's lead and shift the emphasis toward emission charges? Why or why not?

PROBLEMS

1. The marginal control cost curves for two air pollutant sources affecting a single receptor are $MC_1 = \$0.3q_1$ and $MC_2 = \$0.5q_2$, where q_1 and q_2 are controlled emissions. Their respective transfer coefficients are $a_1 = 1.5$ and $a_1 = 1.0$. With no control they would emit 20 units of emission apiece. The ambient standard is 12 ppm.

   (a) If an ambient permit system were established, how many permits would be issued and what price would prevail?

   (b) How much would each source spend on permits if they were auctioned off? How much would each source ultimately spend on permits if each source were initially given, free of charge, half of the permits?

CHAPTER SIXTEEN

Regional and Global Air Pollutants: Acid Rain and Atmospheric Modification

Everything should be made as simple as possible,
but not simpler.

ALBERT EINSTEIN

INTRODUCTION

As the zone of influence of pollutants extends beyond local boundaries, the political difficulties of implementing comprehensive, cost-effective control measures are compounded. Pollutants crossing boundaries impose external costs; neither emitters nor the nations within which they emit have the proper incentives for controlling them.

Compounding the problem of improper incentives is the scientific uncertainty which limits our understanding of most of these problems. Our knowledge about various relationships which form the basis for our understanding of the magnitude of the problems and the effectiveness of various strategies to control them is far from complete. Unfortunately, the problems are so important and the potential consequences of inaction so drastic that procrastination is not usually an optimal strategy. To avoid having to act in the future under emergency conditions when the remaining choices are few in number, strategies which have desirable properties must be formulated now on the basis of the available information, as limited as it may be. Options must be preserved.

422

The costs of inaction are not limited to the damages caused. International cooperation among such traditional allies as the United States, Mexico, and Canada and the countries of Europe has been undermined by disputes over the proper control of acid rain.

In this chapter we survey the scientific evidence on the severity of global and regional pollution and the potential effectiveness of policy strategies designed to alleviate these problems. We also consider difficulties confronted by the government in implementing solutions and the role of economic analysis in understanding how to circumvent these difficulties.

REGIONAL POLLUTANTS

The primary difference between regional pollutants and local pollutants is the distance they are transported in the air. While the damage caused by local pollutants occurs in the vicinity of emission, for regional pollutants the damage can occur at significant distances from the emission point.

The same substances can be both local pollutants and regional pollutants. Sulfur oxides, nitrogen oxides, and ozone, for example, have already been discussed as local pollutants, but they are regional pollutants as well. For example, sulfur emissions, the focal point for most acid-rain legislation, have been known to travel some 200 to 600 miles from the point of emission before returning to the earth. As the substances are being transported by the winds, they undergo a complex series of chemical reactions. Under the right conditions both sulfur and nitrogen oxides are transformed into sulfuric and nitric acids. Nitrogen oxides and hydrocarbons can combine in the presence of sunlight to produce ozone.

Acid Rain

Acid rain, the popular term for atmospheric deposition of acidic substances, is actually a misnomer. Acidic substances are deposited not only by rain and other forms of moist air but as dry particles as well. In some parts of the world, such as the southwestern United States, dry deposition is a more important source of acidity than wet deposition.

Precipitation is normally mildly acidic, with a global background pH of 5.0 (pH is the common measurement for acidity; the lower the number, the more acidic the substance, with 7.0 being the border between acidity and alkalinity). Industrialized areas commonly receive precipitation well in excess of the global background. Rainfall in eastern North America, for example, has a typical pH of 4.4. Wheeling, West Virginia, once experienced a rainstorm with a pH of 1.5. The fact that battery acid has a pH of 1.0 may help put this event into perspective.

Though natural sources of acid deposition do exist, the evidence is quite clear that anthropogenic (human-made) sources have dominated deposition in recent years. An analysis of ice cores from Greenland, for example, from 1869 to 1984, indicates that anthropogenic sulfate has dominated sulfur deposition since the early twentieth century and anthropogenic nitrate has dominated nitrogen deposition since about 1960.[1]

In 1980 the U.S. Congress funded a 10-year study (called the National Acid Rain Precipitation Assessment Program) to determine the causes and effects of acid rain and to make recommendations concerning its control. The report concluded that damage from current and historic levels of acid rain ranged from negligible (on crops) to modest (on aquatic life in some lakes and streams). Specific findings included the following:[2]

1. Most species of sport fish can tolerate pH levels above 5.5, but relatively few species can sustain populations in water with a pH below 5.0. Some 9% of the lakes in the target population have a pH $\leq$ 5.0.

2. The regions of the United States estimated to have the highest percentage of acidified lakes are the Adirondacks in New York (Example 16.1), with 14% of 1290 lakes acidified, and Florida, with 23% of 2098 lakes acidified.

3. In many national parks, fine sulfate particles formed by chemical reactions of the sulfuric acid produced from emissions of SO_2 are responsible for a 50% to 60% degradation in visibility in the East beyond that caused by natural influences.

4. No significant effect on crop growth was detected even at acidity levels 10 times the acidity now observed in the eastern United States.

5. Acidic deposition and ozone appear to intensify the effects of natural stresses upon red spruce at eastern mountain-top locations. The cumulative effects of acidic deposition may alter the chemistry of some sensitive forest soils in the lower Midwest and southeastern United States in the next 50 to 100 years, but the effect this will have on growth is unknown. The majority of American forests appear healthy.

6. Acidic deposition can increase the rate of deterioration of some construction and culturally important materials such as galvanized steel, bronze, carbonate stone, and carbonate-based paints.

---

1 P. A. Mayewski et al., *A Detailed (1869–1984) Record of Sulfate and Nitrate Concentration from South Greenland*, as cited in World Resources Institute and International Institute for Environment and Development, *World Resources: 1986* (New York: Basic Books, 1986): 169.

2 A concise summary of the findings can be found in National Acid Precipitation Assessment Program, *1989 Annual Report to the President and Congress* (Washington, DC: National Acid Precipitation Assessment Program, 1990).

EXAMPLE 16.1

Adirondack Acidification

About 180 lakes in the Adirondack Mountains of New York State, mostly at higher altitudes, which had supported natural or stocked brook trout populations in the 1930s, no longer supported these populations by the 1970s. In some cases entire communities of six or more fish species had disappeared.

The location of these lakes, some distance east of any local emission sources, makes it quite clear that most of the acid deposition is coming from outside of the region. These lakes have relatively little capacity to neutralize deposited acid because they are in areas with little or no limestone or other forms of basic rock that might serve to buffer the acid.

This is a prime recreational area, particularly for fishing. Most of the sites are within the boundary of the 6 million acre Adirondack Park, the last substantially undeveloped area of its size in the northeastern United States. Its remoteness, mountainous terrain, and multitude of lakes provide an accessible outdoor recreation experience for the 55 million people who live within a day's traveling distance.

Acidification has substantially reduced the recreational value of the area. Using a version of the travel cost method discussed in Chapter 4, Mullen and Menz conclude that the annual losses to New York resident anglers is in the neighborhood of at least $1 million in 1976 dollars.

One possibility for restoring these lakes would be to add lime (calcium carbonate) to buffer the effects of the acid. Would liming be efficient? In their investigation, Menz and Driscoll have found that a five-year lake neutralization program would cost in the neighborhood of $2–$4 million. Given the $1 million estimate of *annual* losses to recreational fishing, some neutralization would apparently be efficient. The exact number of lakes to be limed would have to be determined by comparing the marginal cost of liming each lake with the marginal gain to recreation that would result. The authors are quick to point out that while liming may be used to restore damaged lakes, it is not a substitute for controlling emissions.

Sources: Government Accounting Office, *An Analysis of Issues Concerning "Acid Rain,"* Report #GAO/RCED-85-13 (December 11, 1984): 13; John K. Mullen and Frederic C. Menz, "The Effect of Acidification Damages on the Economic Value of the Adirondack Fishery to New York Anglers," *American Journal of Agricultural Economics* 67 (February 1985): 112–119; Frederic C. Menz and Charles T. Driscoll, "An Estimate of the Costs of Liming to Neutralize Acidic Adirondack Surface Waters," *Water Resources Research* 19 (October 1983): 1139–1149.

These findings were significantly less dire than expected and provide a rather sharp contrast with findings of higher levels of damage in Europe. Studies have documented that Sweden has some 4000 highly acidified lakes; in southern Norway lakes with a total surface area of 13,000 square kilometers support no fish at all; similar reports have been received from Germany, Scotland, and Canada.[3] Furthermore, as made clear by Example 11.1, acid deposition is one of the pollution sources implicated in the massive forest death taking place in Europe.

In many countries with a federal form of government, such as the United States, the policy focus in the past has been on treating all pollutants as if they were local pollutants, overlooking the adverse regional consequences in the process. By giving local jurisdictions a large amount of responsibility for achieving the desired air quality and by measuring progress at local monitors, the stage was set for making regional pollution worse rather than better.

In the early days of pollution control local areas adopted the motto "dilution is the solution." As implemented, this approach suggested that the way to control local pollutants was to emit from tall stacks. By the time the pollutants hit the ground, the concentrations would be diluted, making it easier to meet the ambient standards at nearby monitors.

This approach had several consequences. First, it lowered the amount of emission reduction necessary to achieve ambient standards; with tall stacks any given amount of emission would produce lower ground-level concentrations than an equivalent level of emission from a shorter-stack source. Second, the ambient standards could be met at a lower cost. Using Cleveland as a case study, Atkinson has shown that control costs would be approximately 30% lower, but emissions would be two and one-half times higher if a local, rather than a regional, strategy were followed in a marketable permit system.[4] In essence, local areas would be able to lower their own cost by exporting emissions to other areas. By focusing its attention on local pollution, the Clean Air Act actually made the regional pollution problem worse.

Even by the late 1970s it had become painfully clear in the United States that the traditional approach was ill-suited to solve regional pollution problems. Therefore, a lot of attention has been focused on revamping the legislation to do a better job of dealing with regional pollutants such as acid rain.

Politically, that is a tall order. By virtue of the fact that these pollutants are transported long distances, the set of geographic areas receiving the damage is typically not the same as the set of geographic areas responsible for most of the emission causing the damage. In many cases the recipients and the emitters are even in different countries! In this political milieu, it should not be surprising

---

3 See the review in World Resources Institute and International Institute for Environment and Development, *World Resources: 1986* (New York: Basic Books, 1986): 169-170.

4 Scott E. Atkinson, "Marketable Pollution Permits and Acid Rain Externalities," *Canadian Journal of Economics* 16 (November 1983): 704-722.

that those bearing damages should call for a large, rapid reduction in emission, while those responsible for bearing the costs of that cleanup should want to proceed more slowly and with greater caution.

Economic analysis can be and has been helpful in finding a feasible path through this political thicket. In particular, a Congressional Budget Office (CBO) study helps to set the parameters of the debate by quantifying the consequences of various courses of action.[5] To analyze the economic and political consequences of various strategies designed to achieve reductions of SO_2 emissions from utilities anywhere from 8 to 12 million tons below the emission levels from those plants in 1980, the CBO used a computer-based simulation model that relates utility emissions, utility costs, and coal-market supply and demand levels to the strategies under consideration. The model, called the National Coal Model, is maintained by the Department of Energy.

The results of this modeling exercise will be presented in two segments. In the first segment we examine the basic available strategies including both a traditional command-and-control strategy which simply allocates reductions on the basis of a specific formula and an emissions charge strategy. This analysis will serve to show how sensitive costs are to various levels of emission reduction and to highlight some of the political consequences of implementing these strategies. The second segment of analysis then considers various strategies designed to mitigate the adverse political effects of the basic strategies as a means of ascertaining what is gained and lost by adopting these compromises.

In the command-and-control strategies, the emission reductions are allocated to states on the basis of what is known as the "excess emissions" formula. For each plant, this formula subtracts from actual emissions the amount of emission the plant would have been allowed to emit if it were forced to meet the 1979 NSPS sulfur standard for utilities. (Since that is a new source standard, plants built before that date are not automatically required to meet it.) The amount left, the excess emissions, are then summed over all the excess emission plants within each state and, finally, across states to get a national total. Each state is then required to meet the same share of the stipulated reduction (8, 10, or 12 million tons) that it has of the total excess emissions.

With the emission charge each utility is faced with a $600 per ton charge for all uncontrolled SO_2 emissions. The model assumes that utilities would minimize costs by cleaning up their emissions until the marginal cost of further cleanup is equal to $600. This results in a degree of emission reduction which is roughly comparable to the 10-million ton command-and-control reduction.

---

5 Congress of the United States, Congressional Budget Office, *Curbing Acid Rain: Cost, Budget, and Coal-Market Effects* (Washington, DC: U.S. Government Printing Office, 1986).

TABLE 16.1   Costs Associated with Basic Strategies to Reduce Sulfur Emissions

Strategy	Total program cost^a ($ billions)	Annual cost to utilities^b ($ billions)	Key state employment change^c (# of jobs lost)	Cost effectiveness^d ($ per ton)
8 million ton rollback	$20.4	$1.9	14,100	$270
10 million ton rollback	$34.5	$3.2	21,900	$360
12 million ton rollback	$93.6	$8.8	13,400	$779
Emission charge	$37.5	$7.7	17,900	$327

^{a}The present value (in 1985 dollars) of additional discounted utility costs incurred (over a current policy benchmark) from 1986 to 2015, using a real discount rate of 0.03. Any emission charges paid are not included.

^{b}The additional cost to utilities of this strategy over the current policy benchmark in 1995 expressed in 1985 dollars. This value includes any emissions charges paid.

^{c}The additional coal-mining job losses expected, if this strategy were implemented rather than the current policy benchmark.

^{d}The discounted program cost divided by the annual discounted SO_2 reduction measured over the 1986–2015 period.

Source: Congress of the United States, Congressional Budget Office, *Curbing Acid Rain: Cost, Budget, and Coal-Market Effects* (Washington, DC: U.S. Government Printing Office, 1986): xx, xxii, 23, 80.

The first implication of the analysis is that the marginal cost of additional control rises rapidly, particularly after 10 million tons have been reduced (Table 16.1). The cost of reducing a ton of SO_2 rises from $270 for an 8-million-ton reduction to $360 for a 10-million-ton reduction, while it rises to a rather dramatic $779 per ton for a 12-million-ton reduction. Costs would rise much more steeply as the amount of required reduction is increased because switching to low-sulfur coal—a relatively low-cost strategy—would be insufficient, by itself, to achieve the larger reductions. At stricter standards reliance on the more expensive scrubbers would become necessary. (Scrubbers involve a chemical process to extract or "scrub" sulfur gases before they escape into the atmosphere.)

The second insight, one that should be no surprise to readers of this book, is that the emissions charge would be more cost-effective than the comparable command-and-control strategy. Whereas the command-and-control strategy could secure a 10-million-ton reduction at about $360 a ton, the emission charge could do it for $327 a ton. The superiority of the emissions charge is due to the fact that it results in equalized marginal costs, a required condition for cost effectiveness.[6]

---

6 Why, the alert reader might ask, isn't location of the emissions taken into account? Since the objective was stated as securing a reduction in emissions, not achieving an ambient standard, the cost-effective allocation is achieved when marginal control costs are equalized.

A third insight is that the magnitude of the cost-effectiveness superiority of the emissions charge is not very large, especially when compared with the numbers presented in the previous chapter. In essence it appears that the "excess emissions" formula is not a particularly costly way to allocate emission reductions in this particular context.

It may seem a bit of a paradox that program costs are not minimized by an emissions charge since it is the most cost-effective strategy. The resolution of this paradox lies in the timing of the emission reductions achieved by an emissions charge strategy. Because the authors of this study chose in their analysis to impose the charge earlier than the command-and-control regulations, the utilities secure the reductions earlier with an emissions charge than with the command-and-control approach. Earlier reductions can only be achieved with earlier financial outlays, which, since all costs are discounted, causes higher program costs for the emissions charge. Unlike the program cost calculation, which gives no credit for early emission reduction, the construction of the particular cost-effectiveness measure chosen by the CBO takes the timing of the emissions reduction into account.

One of the reasons enacting acid-rain legislation in the United States took until 1990 has been expected coal industry job losses in certain key states. To the extent that coal switching becomes the utility strategy of choice, those areas producing high-sulfur coal will be hard hit, as they lose business to the low-sulfur coal-producing states. To the extent that scrubbers are adopted, however, the use of high-sulfur coal can be continued with lower employment impacts on employment in those states.

The high-sulfur coal industry is especially important in Illinois, Indiana, Ohio, and Pennsylvania (noted as key states in Table 16.1). In the absence of special acid-rain legislation, coal production in these states would be expected to be stable over time. With acid-rain legislation it is expected to decline. The size of the decline depends on the strategy chosen.

Job losses in the key high-sulfur coal states increase dramatically from 14,100 to 21,900 as the amount of required reduction is increased from 8 to 10 million tons. With a 12-million-ton reduction, they drop to 13,400. This reversal is due to the necessity of using scrubbers if this highest level of reduction is to be achieved. Once scrubbers are installed, high-sulfur coal can continue to be used and the impact on the industry is reduced.

Coal mining job losses from national acid-rain legislation are a local, not a national, problem. On a nationwide basis coal-mining employment losses would be negligible. Losses in these four key states would be counterbalanced by gains in low-sulfur coal-producing areas.

This favorable impact of higher control levels on coal-mining employment in these four key states is counterbalanced by the fact that installing scrubbers is very expensive, as can be easily seen in the program cost, annual cost to utilities, and cost-effectiveness columns (Table 16.1). One implication is that the cost to the utilities and, hence, their customers in the form of higher electricity bills, would be higher if scrubbers were installed.

The largest electricity rate increases would occur primarily in the midwestern and Appalachian states because that area is responsible for the largest share of excess emissions. Precisely these states, however, have traditionally enjoyed lower than average electricity rates, in part because they have not spent what the rest of the country has on reducing emissions. According to the CBO study, the higher electricity prices these areas might experience from almost all of the acid-rain legislation being considered would still remain below the national average.

Though the emission charge approach may be the most cost-effective policy, it is not the most popular, particularly in states with a lot of excess emissions. With an emission charge approach utilities not only have to pay the higher equipment and operating costs associated with the reductions, they also have to pay a charge on all uncontrolled emissions. As Table 16.1 indicates, the additional financial burden associated with controlling acid rain by means of an emission charge would be significant. Instead of paying the $3.2 billion for reducing 10 million tons under a command-and-control approach, utilities would be saddled with a $7.7 billion financial burden with an emissions charge. The savings from lower equipment and operating costs achieved, because the emission charge approach is more cost-effective, would be more than outweighed by the additional expense of paying the emission charges. What is least cost to society is not, in this case, least cost for the utilities.

The cost of utilities could be reduced, while retaining the cost-effectiveness properties of the straight emissions charge, by instituting a sulfur-reduction emissions permit system. In such a system the excess emissions formula would be used to allocate the initial control responsibility. Utilities would then be able to create emission reduction credits for exceeding their assigned control; other utilities could purchase these emission reduction credits to help them meet their assigned control responsibilities. Compared to an emission charge approach, this would cut the cost to utilities almost in half by eliminating the charge on uncontrolled emissions. Another study, examining the cost savings that could be achieved within a single state (Illinois), concluded that the cost of control would be approximately one-third lower if an emissions trading approach were instituted.[7] The third and most recent study makes it clear that even a severely restricted emissions trading area would yield substantial savings.[8] The larger is the area in which trading is permitted, the lower are the costs of meeting the reduction targets.

A version of the emissions trading concept is an integral part of the Clean Air Act Amendments of 1990. This approach would complement, not replace,

---

[7] Stephen L. Feldman and Robert K. Raufer, *Emissions Trading and Acid Rain: Implementing a Market Approach to Pollution Control* (Totowa, NJ: Rowman & Littlefield, 1987).

[8] One study estimates that the cost saving would be very large even if trades were limited to discharge points within the same utility. ICF Resources, Inc., "Economic, Environmental, and Coal Market Impacts of SO_2 Emissions Trading under Alternative Acid Rain Control Proposals," a report prepared for the Regulatory Innovations Staff, USEPA (March 1989).

the traditional approach which was geared to the attainment of local ambient air quality standards. As was the case with past acid-rain proposals considered by Congress, under this innovative approach more stringent emissions controls would be placed on older plants emitting precursors of acid rain as the first step. All affected utilities are given a limited number of sulfur dioxide allowances for each calendar year.[9] An allowance is a federal authorization to emit a ton of SO_2 in a specific calendar year, or subsequent year if it was banked for later use. Only the number of tons authorized by the allowances could be legally emitted. The number of allowances is limited to assure that a 10-million-ton reduction from 1980 levels was achieved. Any sources of emissions contributing to acid rain with "excess" reductions (i.e., those over and above the reductions required by law to satisfy the allowances granted) can trade their excess allowances to other utilities. These traded allowances can then be used by the purchaser to legitimize an equivalent increase in its emissions.

How tradable emission allowances facilitate achieving the environmental goal at a lower cost is not difficult to understand.[10] Achieving reductions of the magnitude envisioned by Congress would require some, but not all, utilities to adopt scrubbers. To force all older utilities to adopt scrubbers would be very expensive and unnecessary to achieve the desired reduction target. Yet it is politically and legally difficult under the traditional system to isolate only a few utilities to bear this additional burden for the greater good.

Emission allowance trading solves this problem by allowing some utilities to voluntarily accept greater control and by providing the proper incentive to assure that some do. The emission standards are stringent enough that some utilities will have to choose scrubbers or other form of overcontrol. While all utilities will face similar, if not identical, allowable emissions standards, some utilities, presumably those for whom adopting scrubbers was the cheapest alternative, will voluntarily choose to install scrubbers. This action will automatically result in their exceeding their legal emission control requirements.

By purchasing sufficient allowances to satisfy their own emission standards when combined with any other additional control, the purchasing firms would eliminate the need to install scrubbers. Sufficient, but not excessive, control will

---

9   The plan also envisions reducing NO_x emissions by 2.5 million tons per year. To keep the exposition from getting excessively complicated, only the sulfur dioxide program is discussed here.

10   See T. H. Tietenberg. "Acid Rain Reduction Credits," *Challenge* 32 (1989): 25-29. For other discussions of the use of the emissions trading concept in acid rain control, see Scott E. Atkinson, "Marketable Pollution Permits and Acid Rain Externalities," *Canadian Journal of Economics* 16 (November 1983): 704-722; Roger K. Raufer and Stephen L. Feldman, "Emissions Trading and What It May Mean for Acid Deposition," *Public Utilities Fortnightly* 114 (August 16, 1984): 17-25; Stephen L. Feldman and Robert K. Raufer, *Emissions Trading and Acid Rain: Implementing a Market Approach to Pollution Control* (Totowa, NJ: Rowman & Littlefield, 1987); and W. E. Oates et al., "The Net Benefits of Incentive-Based Regulation: The Case of Environmental Standard Setting," *American Economic Review* 79 (December 1989): 1233-1242.

result and market means of selecting those utilities to install scrubbers will have been provided. Significantly emissions trading also provides a means of sharing the costs of installing scrubbers among all utilities. Those purchasing the emission allowances will, in effect, be subsidizing a portion of the selling firm's installation of the pollution control device. Rather than isolating a few utilities to bear a disproportionate share of the control burden or requiring all utilities to bear the excessive burden of overcontrol in a misguided pursuit of fairness, emission allowance trading promotes voluntary cost sharing. Fairness and efficiency can be compatible goals with the right choice of policy instruments.

It is not difficult to imagine a similar kind of scheme operating on a regional basis to control acid rain in Europe.[11] Many of the Western European nations are at the point where further control of their own emissions is very expensive. A disproportionate share of the remaining emissions affecting Western European nations are coming from Eastern European nations. However since most of the Eastern European nations have troubled economies that can ill afford the shock of major new expenditures, they are not likely to undertake major pollution control reductions in the near future on their own. One solution to this problem is to seek agreement that all nations would implement some minimum level of control for all sources within their borders, allowing the Western industrialized nations to buy reductions above and beyond these minimum control level from the Eastern European nations.[12] In most Western countries purchasing additional pollution control from Eastern Europe would represent the cheapest means of reducing acid rain, much cheaper than controlling their own emissions to an even higher level. The Eastern European nations would then use the revenue from the sale of emission allowances to finance the installation of control equipment. In many cases this equipment would probably be produced and sold by the Western nations, an additional inducement to participate in cost sharing.

GLOBAL POLLUTANTS

Ozone Depletion

In the troposphere, the portion of the atmosphere closest to the earth, ozone (O_3) is a pollutant, and its presence has been linked to agricultural damage as well as to some adverse effects on human health. More will be said about this form of tropospheric pollution in the next chapter.

---

11 This type of market has been simulated in Karl-Goran Mäler, "International Environmental Problems," *Oxford Review of Economic Policy* 6 (Spring 1990): 80–108. The benefits from cost-effective burden sharing across borders are apparently quite large.

12 Sweden has already negotiated an agreement of this type with Poland.

However, in the stratosphere, the portion of the atmosphere lying just above the troposphere, the small amounts of ozone present have a crucial positive role to play in determining the quality of life on the planet. In particular, by absorbing the ultraviolet wavelengths, stratospheric ozone shields people, plants, and animals from harmful radiation, and by absorbing infrared radiation, it is a factor in determining the earth's climate.

Chlorofluorocarbons (CFCs) have been implicated in depleting this stratospheric ozone shield as a result of a complicated series of chemical reactions. These highly stable chemical compounds are used as aerosol propellants and in cushioning foams, packaging and insulating foams, industrial cleaning of metals and electronics components, food freezing, medical instrument sterilization, refrigeration for homes and food stores, and air conditioning of automobiles and commercial buildings.

The major known effect of the increased ultraviolet radiation resulting from ozone depletion is an increase in nonmelanoma skin cancer. Other potential effects, such as an increase in the more serious melanoma form of skin cancer, suppression of human immunological systems, damage to plants, eye cancer in cattle, and an acceleration of degradation in certain polymer materials, are suspected, but are not as well established.

On June 30, 1978, the U.S. Environmental Protection Agency promulgated a regulation banning the manufacture, processing, and distribution of any "fully halogenated chlorofluoroalkane" for those aerosol propellant uses that are subject to the Toxic Substances Control Act (which is almost all aerosol uses).[13] This ban reduced the U.S. share from about one-half to about one-third of worldwide production. Nonetheless worldwide release of the two principal chlorofluorocarbons—CFC-11 and CFC-12—continued to grow (Table 16.2).

Since further progress on this issue was going to require instituting new controls on nonaerosol uses, a group of economists from the Rand Corporation was commissioned by the U.S. EPA to model the regulatory options.[14] The resulting study collected detailed information on the costs of controlling nonaerosol applications of these gases in the United States and constructed a 10-year simulation model to capture the effects of various regulatory approaches. Because chlorofluorocarbons accumulate in the atmosphere (they are expected to remain in the atmosphere for approximately a century), the desired reductions were defined in cumulative terms over the 10-year period.

Three specific policies were considered in the analysis: (1) a system of emission standards for producers or users of these gases, which would force them to adopt specific technologies, (2) a constant-emissions charge of $0.50 (in real

---

13 This regulation can be found in 45 *Federal Register* 43721.

14 A. R. Palmer, W. E. Mooz, T. H. Quinn, and K. A. Wolf, *Economic Implications of Regulating Chlorofluorocarbon Emissions from Nonaerosol Applications*, Report #R-2524-EPA prepared for the U.S. Environmental Protection Agency by the Rand Corporation (June 1980).

TABLE 16.2   Worldwide Cumulative Release of Two Chlorofluorocarbons, Selected Years (thousands of tons)

Year	CFC-11	CFC-12
1940	0.3	7.3
1950	14.8	148.9
1960	254.4	706.3
1970	1470.2	2961.1
1980	4375.2	6685.1
1983	5176.6	7966.0
1987	6483.2	10,087.6

Sources: From *OECD Environmental Data* (Paris: OECD, 1985, 1989). Reprinted by permission of the Organisation for Economic Co-operation and Development.

terms) per pound emitted over the 10 years, and (3) a marketable permit system. In the simulation model all of the approaches were constrained to yield roughly the same cumulative level of emission reduction (Table 16.3).

Because this is an accumulating pollutant, the permits in this case would be designed to allow a one-time release, not a continuing flow as would be the case with permit systems designed to control more conventional pollutants. The holder of a permit would be entitled to emit a fixed quantity of CFCs any time during the 10-year period. By controlling the number of permits issued, the cumulative emission of CFCs would be controlled.

In this type of system, the price could be expected to rise over time as the remaining number of unused permits declined. Permit use would typically be high in the early years, while substitution options were being worked out, declining to zero at the end of the 10-year period.

Theory tells us that the constant-emission charge modeled in this study would not be fully cost effective for this problem because the modeled charge does not rise over time. A constant real-emission charge will cause marginal costs to be equated within each period, a part of a cost-effective strategy, but it will fail to signal the increasing scarcity of the allowable CFCs over time, leading to a distorted temporal pattern of permit use. To be specific, since the constant charge has to yield approximately the same cumulative level of emissions reduction as the permit system, the constant-emission charge will be higher than the cost-effective charge in the earlier years and lower than the cost-effective charge in the later years. This, in turn, implies that the constant-charge system will allow too little emission in the earlier years and too much in the later years.

The superiority of the permit system can be seen in Table 16.3. It could produce approximately the same amount of reduction as the mandatory controls at about one-half the cost. The relationship of the constant charge to the permit system is exactly as theory would have us expect. Costs are higher for the charge

TABLE 16.3 Comparisons of Alternative Policies Having Similar Cumulative Emissions Reductions

Policy design	Emissions reduction (millions of permit pounds)			Total compliance costs (millions of 1976 dollars)		
	1980	1990	Cumulative 1980–1990	1980	1990	Cumulative 1980–90[a]
Mandatory controls	54.4	102.5	812.3	20.9	37.0	185.3
Economic incentives						
Constant charge[b]	54.8	96.9	816.9	12.3	21.8	107.8
Permit System[c]	36.6	119.4	806.1	5.2	35.0	94.7

[a]Present value of annual compliance costs, discounted at 11%.
[b]Based on a constant tax rate of $0.50 from 1980 through 1990 (in 1976 dollars).
[c]Based on permit price or emissions charge rising from $0.25 in 1980 to $0.71 in 1990.
Source: Palmer, Mooz, Quinn, and Wolf (p. 225, Table 4.7).

in the earlier years (since less emission is allowed) and lower in the later years. Over the 10-year period the constant charge system results in a higher present value of costs due to this intertemporal distortion, though the increase is only about 14%.

The Rand study also studied the issue of transfer costs (the payments made to the government by the emitters for each unit of uncontrolled emissions). If an emission charge were used, firms would be faced not only with the cost of purchasing the control equipment or changing the production process, they would have to pay the charges as well. Thus, depending on the relative magnitude of the cost savings from inducing cost-effective behavior and the additional cost imposed by the charges, firms may or may not be better off under this type of economic incentive system than they are under mandatory controls. This could only be determined by discovering the magnitude of the transfer costs.

The Rand study is quite clear that for CFC control transfer costs are huge. On average, charge payments are 15 times as large as the expenditures incurred in controlling emissions. Furthermore, they would be rather unequally distributed among the various industries responsible for reducing CFC emissions (Figure 16.1).

One noteworthy aspect of Figure 16.1 is the "other" category. This category contains some product areas (rigid insulating foams, liquid fast freezing, and sterilants) where the authors found that no control methods would be introduced, even in the face of an emission charge. For these product areas, the *only* expense is the emission charge and it represents a huge outlay. The manufacturers of these product lines could be expected to be unusually vociferous in their support for a policy of no action or, if action is inevitable, for the traditional regulatory approach which, in all likelihood, would place no controls on them at all.

Responding to the ozone depletion threat, 24 nations signed the Montreal Protocol during September 1988. According to this agreement, signatory nations

Figure 16.1 Cumulative industry expenses under mandatory controls and uncompensated economic incentives. [From Adele R. Palmer et al., Economic Implications of Regulating Chlorofluorocarbon Emissions from Nonaerosol Applications, Report No. R-2524-EPA (U.S. Environmental Protection Agency, June, 1980): 23.]

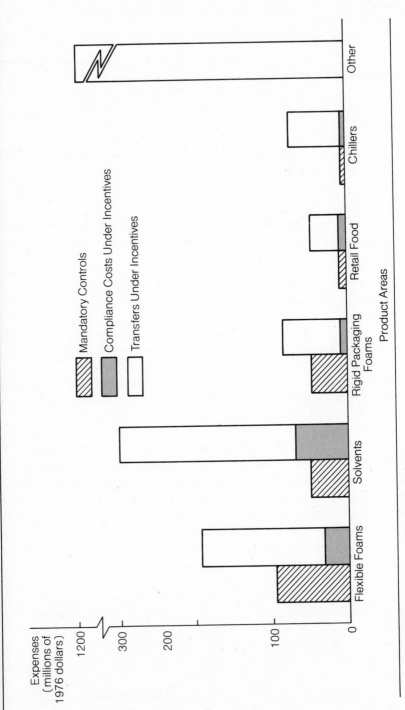

Source: Palmer, Mooz, Quinn and Wolf (1980, p. 223)

were to restrict their production and consumption of the chief responsible gases to 50% of 1986 levels by June 30, 1998. Soon after the protocol was signed, new evidence suggested that it had not gone far enough; the damage was apparently increasing more rapidly than previously thought. In response, 59 nations signed a new ozone agreement at a conference in London in July 1990. This agreement called for the complete phaseout of halons and CFCs by the end of this century. Moreover two other destructive chemicals—carbon tetrachloride and methyl chloroform—were added to the protocol and are scheduled to be eliminated by 2000 and 2005, respectively.

An important component of this new agreement was the establishment of a special $240 million fund over the next three years to help poorer countries switch from ozone-depleting chemicals to more expensive, but less harmful substitutes.[15] This was an important breakthrough because without this assistance the use of ozone-depleting chemicals was expected to rise dramatically in the developing countries.[16] In China, for example, by 1980 only 1 out of 10 households owned a refrigerator. (Refrigerators use ozone-depleting chemicals as coolants and as blowing agents in the insulating foam that makes up the walls.) The government plans for every kitchen in China to be equipped with a refrigerator by 2000.

The United States has chosen to use a tradable permit system to implement its responsibilities under the protocols. On August 12, 1988 the U.S. Environmental Protection Agency issued regulations implementing a tradable permit system to achieve the targeted reductions.[17] According to these regulations all major U.S. producers and consumers of the controlled substances were allocated baseline production or consumption allowances using 1986 levels as the basis for the proration. Each producer and consumer is allowed 100% of this baseline allowance initially, with smaller allowances being granted after predefined deadlines. These allowances are transferable within producer and consumer categories, and production allowances can be transferred across international borders to producers in other signatory nations if the transaction is approved by EPA and results in the appropriate adjustments in the buyer or seller production allowances in their respective countries. Production allowances can be augmented by demonstrating the safe destruction of an equivalent amount of

15 A panel of experts from U.S. EPA has concluded that substitutes do exist, but they would cost between $1.25 and $4.00 a pound compared to 60 to 70 cents for the traditional chemicals. *Science News* 131 (June 1987): 360.

16 Daniel F. Kohler, John Haaga, and Frank Camm, *Projections of Consumption of Products Using Chlorofluorocarbons in Developing Countries.* Rand Corporation Report N-2458-EPA (January, 1987).

17 53 *Federal Register* 30598 (August 1988). The final rules governing transfer of import and production allowances are in 54 *Federal Register* 6376 (February 1989).

controlled substances by approved means, but so far no means have been approved.

Though transfers of the production allowances are allowed, even across international borders, they are severely constrained. The regulations allow any producer to increase its production allowance by any means (including transfer of a portion of another producer's allowance) by a maximum of 10% of its apportionment before 1998 and 15% of its apportionment after that date.

Since the demand for these allowances is quite inelastic, supply restrictions increase revenue. By allocating allowances to the seven major domestic producers of CFCs and halons, EPA was concerned that its regulation would result in sizable windfall profits (estimated to be in the billions of dollars) for those producers. EPA handled this problem by imposing a tax to soak up the rents created by the regulation-induced scarcity. The Revenue Reconciliation Act of 1989 includes an excise tax imposed on all ozone-depleting chemicals sold or used by manufacturers, producers or importers of these chemicals. The tax is imposed at the time the importer sells or uses the affected chemicals. It is computed by multiplying the chemical's weight by the base tax rate and the chemical's ozone depletion factor. In addition to soaking up some of the regulation-induced scarcity rent, this tax provides incentives to switch to less harmful (and therefore untaxed) substances.

Global Warming

One class of global pollutants, the so-called greenhouse gases, absorb the long-wavelength (infrared) radiation from the earth's surface and atmosphere, trapping heat that would otherwise radiate into space. The mix and distribution of these gases within the atmosphere is in no small part responsible for both the hospitable climate on the earth and the inhospitable climate on other planets. Changing the mix of these gases can modify the climate.

Though carbon dioxide is the most abundant and the most studied of these greenhouse gases, many others have similar thermal radiation properties. These include the chlorofluorocarbons, nitrous oxide, methane, and tropospheric ozone. New evidence suggests that these gases may in the future be even more important in modifying climate than the more abundant CO_2.[18]

The current concern over the effect of this class of pollutants on climate arises because emissions of these gases are increasing over time, changing their mix in the atmosphere. Evidence is mounting that by burning fossil fuels, leveling tropical forests, and injecting more of the other greenhouse gases into the

---

18 See the description of this evidence in Michael Shepard, "The Greenhouse Effect: Earth's Climate in Transition," *EPRI Journal* 11 (June 1986): 4-15.

atmosphere, humans are creating a thermal blanket capable of trapping enough heat to raise the temperature of the earth's surface. One National Research Council report anticipates a doubling of atmospheric CO_2 during the third quarter of the next century.[19] It further suggests that this doubling of CO_2 concentrations could result in a surface air warming of between 1.5° and 4.5°C. A 1.5°C increase in the temperature within a century would produce the warmest climate in 6000 years.

The report goes on to suggest the likely consequences of this trend. For the United States as a whole, the effect on agriculture is expected to be small, as positive and negative effects largely cancel each other out. For arid parts of the country which depend on irrigation from scarce water supplies, the picture is more grim. Rising temperatures are expected to reduce the quantity and quality of available water in arid regions.

Global warming is also expected to trigger a rise in sea level. If global warming in the 3° to 4°C range were to take place over the next 100 years, the authors conclude that a global sea-level rise of about 70 centimeters would be likely. This compares with a rise of only 15 centimeters over the last century. Much larger increases (about 15–20 feet) could be expected if the warming caused the West Antarctic ice sheet to disintegrate, a low-probability event.

The effects of climate change are expected to fall unequally on the world's people. Regions with a characteristically cold climate, such as large portions of the Soviet Union, may actually benefit from this warming trend, while others that are naturally somewhat arid may see marginal agricultural land become unproductive desert, triggering a diminished capacity to raise food. These differences could prove quite divisive in the search for solutions.

Global warming poses a particularly difficult challenge for our economic and political institutions. The stratosphere is a public good. Its scarcity is not reflected in rising prices; it is not automatically rationed only to the highest-valued uses. The damage caused by greenhouse pollutants is an externality in both space and time. Emitters impose costs not only on residents of other countries, but on subsequent generations as well. Free-rider problems can be expected to undermine unilateral national attempts to respond. Market allocations can certainly be expected to violate the efficiency criterion and may well violate the sustainability criterion as well (Example 16.2).

What can be done? Four strategies have been considered: (1) climatic engineering, (2) adaptation, (3) mitigation, and (4) prevention. Climate engineering envisions taking actions such as shooting particulate matter into the atmosphere to provide compensating cooling. Adaptation refers to strategies which would allow us to function effectively in warmer temperatures. Mitigation would at-

---

19 National Research Council, *Changing Climate: Report of the Carbon Dioxide Assessment Committee* (Washington, DC: National Academy Press, 1983): 2.

EXAMPLE 16.2

Ethics, Risk Aversion, and the Greenhouse Effect

Can benefit-cost analysis be trusted to reach an optimal decision about strategies to control the greenhouse effect? Two sources of concern are paramount: (1) the long time period before the damage would be felt, and (2) the uncertainty about the ultimate size of the damage.

A complete loss of the expected world GNP 100 years from now, at current interest rates, would have a present value of about $1 million. This is trivial in comparison to the present value of potential costs of controlling the greenhouse effect because they would be spent in the near future. Due to discounting, events that happen so far in the future have little weight in decisions where costs are borne in the present. Although maximizing the present value of net benefits guarantees that the pie to be shared among generations is as large as possible, it does not automatically guarantee that the slices of pie are actually shared equitably among generations. The logical conclusion of this form of argument is that future generations may be inadequately protected from an ethical point of view by benefit/cost analysis.

A second concern deals with risk aversion. As pointed out in Chapter 4, conventional benefit-cost analysis assumes risk neutrality. Is risk neutrality a credible assumption in the face of a potential catastrophe? Common sense suggests that most people react to uncertainty by acting in a cautious, risk-averse manner. Should our governments act any differently?

Concluding that conventional benefit-cost analysis is ethically flawed when applied to the greenhouse problem, d'Arge, Schultze, and Brookshire have proposed a modest alternative. In particular, they proposed to establish whether the current generation would be willing to pay some amount of money to avoid climate modification. Relying on three samples of college students as a pilot study, they did find a willingness to spend current income to avoid an environmental catastrophe even if it would occur in all likelihood after the respondent's death. Though these samples can hardly be called representative of the population at large, the amounts per person were sufficiently large that they would justify a much larger commitment of current resources to control the problem than would be justified by a conventional benefit-cost analysis.

Sources: Ralph C. d'Arge, William D. Schultze, and David S. Brookshire, "Benefit-Cost Valuation of Long Term Effects: The Case of CO_2," a paper prepared for the "Workshop on the Methodology for Economic Impact Analysis," April 24–25, 1980, Fort Lauderdale, Florida; and Ralph C. d'Arge, William D. Schultze, and David S. Brookshire, "Carbon Dioxide and Intergenerational Choice," *The American Economic Review* 72 (May 1982): 251–256.

tempt to moderate the temperature rise by strategies designed to increase the planetary capacity to absorb greenhouse gases. Prevention refers to strategies to reduce emissions of greenhouse gases. Since only the last two of these have received serious attention in public policy arenas, we focus on those.

The most significant prevention strategy deals with our use of fossil-fuel energy. Combustion of fossil-fuel energy results in the creation of carbon dioxide. Carbon dioxide emissions can be reduced either by using less energy or by using alternative energy sources (such as wind, photovoltaics, or hydro) which produce no carbon dioxide. Since any serious reduction in carbon dioxide emissions would involve dramatic changes in our energy consumption patterns and a high economic cost, how vigorously this strategy is to be followed is a controversial public-policy issue.[20]

Since trees absorb carbon dioxide, reforestation is a commonly mentioned mitigation strategy. By decreasing the rate of deforestation and increasing the rate of reforestation, greater amounts of carbon dioxide could be absorbed.

What policy approaches are available to deal efficiently with the global warming problem? Although global warming and ozone depletion impose an environmental cost, currently that cost is not being borne, or even recognized, by those who ultimately control the magnitude of the problem. Furthermore, those choosing unilaterally to reduce their emissions expose themselves to the higher costs associated with prevention strategies.

Forcing users to bear the full cost would send a strong signal that the atmosphere is a scarce, precious resource and should be treated accordingly. Products produced by manufacturing processes which are environmentally destructive would become relatively more expensive; those produced by environmentally benign production processes would become relatively cheaper. Implementing the full-cost principle would end the implicit subsidy that all polluting activities have received since the beginning of time. When the level of economic activity was small, the corresponding subsidy was also small and therefore probably not worthy of political attention. Since the scale of economic activity has grown, however, the subsidy has become very large indeed; ignoring it leads to significant resource distortion.

What policy implications would flow from the acceptance of the full-cost principle? A first implication is that emissions of greenhouse gases should bear an emissions charge. The "carbon tax," which is currently being widely discussed in Europe and the United States, could be one component of this package.[21] Since carbon dioxide is only one of the greenhouse gases, however, taxes would neces-

---

20 According to research by William Nordhaus, a 10% to 20% reduction in carbon dioxide emissions could be achieved at a relatively low cost, but the marginal costs of larger reductions rise very rapidly. See "Greenhouse Economics: Count before You Leap," *The Economist* (July 7, 1990): 20–24.

21 As of 1989, two countries had already unilaterally levied carbon taxes. The Netherlands' carbon tax is about $2.15 per ton of carbon, while Finland's is about $5.00 per ton of carbon.

sarily be imposed on other gases as well. The appropriate level of this tax for each gas would depend upon its per unit contribution to the global warming problem; gases posing a larger per unit risk would bear higher tax rates.

Taxes on fossil fuels are not a radical concept. Gasoline taxes have routinely been levied for years. Though gasoline taxes are imposed on an input to combustion, rather than an emission rate, the administrative ease with which they can be implemented and the close relationship between the composition of the fuel and the composition of the emissions makes it a popular candidate for use as one component in a package of corrective measures to reduce global warming.

Since gasoline taxes have already been implemented by nations for their own purposes, examining the degree to which these taxes deviate from the full-cost principle provides some indication of how complex the international negotiations to reform gasoline taxes would be. To the extent that the current system of taxes approximates the ideal, conditions would appear favorable to negotiating a transition. In fact the gasoline taxes now in use around the world fail to fulfill the requirements of the full-cost principle in two main respects: the use of the revenue and the uniformity of the tax rates.

Whereas the full-cost principle requires that the tax rates reflect the damage caused by emissions, thereby fostering a reduction in emissions, current gasoline tax rates are commonly determined by the revenue needed to build more roads; added roadway capacity ultimately translates into more emissions, not fewer emissions. Because they are driven by the need to finance capacity expansion rather than to account for the environmental effects of combustion, gasoline taxes are currently not in conformance with the full-cost principle.

Although applying the full-cost principle for global warming also requires that the tax rates be uniformly applied, that condition is a far cry from actual experience. According to the Energy Information Administration publication *International Energy Prices 1980–84*, in 1984 gasoline taxes (expressed in U.S. cents per gallon) range from 21 cents in the United States to over $1.00 in the majority of European countries. When the tax rates differ by a factor of 5 or more, the allocation of control responsibility for reducing gasoline-related emissions does not fulfill the uniformity requirement.

Substances contributing to ozone depletion would also be taxed according to the full-cost principle. Since the ozone depletion tax and the global warming tax would be separately assessed, substances such as CFCs which contribute to both global warming and ozone depletion would bear both taxes.

The transition to a more sustainable economic system in atmospheric terms will depend on the development of new technologies and on much greater levels of energy efficiency than are currently being achieved. Those transitions will not occur unless the prevailing economic incentives support and encourage them. Once the greenhouse gas and ozone depletion taxes were in effect the incentives would be changed; greater energy efficiency and the development of new technologies would become top priority objectives.

Since environmental taxes would generate revenue, a common global fund could be established to receive and dispense that revenue. Controlled by representatives of the signatory nations, this fund could conceivably dispense funds for projects as diverse as reforestation or the promotion of solar-powered projects to provide income and subsistence to poor areas of the world. A fund financed by environmental taxes would help to reduce the twin causes of environmental problems: distorted market signals and poverty.

One interesting precedent for this approach is the World Heritage Convention, which established a World Heritage Fund. This fund is used to protect environments of "outstanding universal value." Each signatory is required to contribute at least 1% of its contribution to the regular budget of UNESCO to the fund every two years. In practice, this means that the fund is financed almost entirely by the industrial nations, but smaller nations can tap its resources. Some 90 nations have signed this agreement, suggesting that the fund arrangements have successfully exploited some common interests. Since subscribing to the agreement apparently confers benefits on the signatories, it is essentially self-enforcing.

Determining the appropriate rate for any per unit environmental tax would not be a trivial matter. Although to apply the full cost principle correctly the rate should be equal to the marginal social damage caused by a unit of emission, current valuation techniques would not identify that level with any reasonable degree of confidence. The high degree of scientific uncertainty associated with the magnitude of the global warming threat makes precise valuation impossible. But that may not be a fatal flaw since zero, the current rate, is not correct either. Even establishing a low tax rate would be a step in the right direction; as more information is gained the rate could be adjusted.

Making explicit environmental costs that have been hidden is only one side of the coin; the other is eliminating inappropriate subsidies. Subsidies which are incompatible with the full-cost principles should be eliminated. Implicit subsidies should be targeted as well as explicit subsidies. For example, electricity prices should not simply be determined by historic average cost; they should reflect the scarcity of the resource and the environmental costs imposed by generation.

The transition to the full-cost principle could proceed gradually, beginning in certain sectors, moving to others as greater familiarity with the approach was gained. A complete, immediate transition is not an essential ingredient of a rational approach.

The policy package should be cost-effective insofar as possible. Cost-effectiveness is an important characteristic because it can limit the amount of political backlash by limiting wasteful expenditures.

Complete acceptance and appropriate implementation of the full-cost principle would automatically produce cost effectiveness as a side benefit. Should acceptance of the full-cost principle falter, however, cost effectiveness could be elevated to a primary policy goal, worthy in its own right. It provides a desirable, if less than perfect, fallback position.

Political acceptance of the full cost principle is by no means a foregone conclusion. While taxes on greenhouse and ozone depletion gases can go a long way toward rectifying some of the current distortions in resource pricing, they will do little to reassure those whose vision of the future is defined in terms of specific limits on emissions, not correcting price distortions. It would be very difficult to establish a set of tax rates that could guarantee a specific greenhouse gas emissions target.

Establishing a limit on emissions and allocating the proposed reductions among the nations of the world would be one of the most difficult aspects of any international agreement on global warming or ozone depletion faced by this alternative approach. Fairness will no doubt be one critical aspect of the negotiations and it is likely that some form of cost sharing will result. How are the costs to be shared?

Emissions trading becomes a reasonable approach for implementing both cost-effectiveness and cost sharing. The process would be initiated by setting transferable allowances on the amounts each nation could emit on an annual basis. Nations achieving reductions of greenhouse gases greater than required by the agreement could sell excess allowances to other nations. By purchasing these allowances, the acquiring nation could increase its emissions of greenhouse gases by an equivalent amount. The total emission limit negotiated by the agreement would be binding; no trade leading to a net increase in aggregate emissions above this limit would be approved.

As long as the sum of emissions was equal to the total permitted annual emissions, cost effectiveness could be achieved regardless of how these emission allowances were initially allocated across countries. An international market in emission allowances would facilitate their movement from those countries with the capacity to create them most cheaply to those countries faced by very high costs of additional control. The capacity to achieve cost effectiveness, regardless of how the initial emission allowances are allocated, is a significant attribute of an emissions trading approach that can be exploited for developing a market approach to cost sharing.

With emission trading as the strategy of choice, those forging new international agreements have a very large latitude in attempting to establish fair and politically feasible emission limitations without jeopardizing cost effectiveness. It would be quite possible, for example, to allocate emission allowances to nations on the basis of their population in some past year, say 1986, rather than on current energy use. This particular choice, of course, would lead to many more allowances being granted to populous Third World countries and many fewer allowances being granted to the Western industrialized world. A middle ground might reserve a significant growth increment (50% of their current use, for example) for the developing countries, reducing the share going to the industrialized countries sufficiently to produce the desired target. Because of the very different current emission levels, a 50% growth increment for developing countries would necessitate a much smaller than 50% compensating reduction in the developed countries. As the Western nations acquired by purchase the necessary production allowances at market prices from those nations selling them, significant financial transfers would take place. The size of these transfers would be dictated by market forces, not by negotiation.

A precondition for the successful operation of this market is the assurance to all participants that the created production allowances or emission reduction credits are permanent, surplus, quantifiable, and enforceable. This assurance can only be given if some trusted international agency is given the power to certify these transfers on a case by case basis. While the potential trading partners would establish the price of the transfer between themselves, no transfer could take place until the international agency was satisfied that the offsetting reductions satisfied the four criteria.

The first step in attempting to chart a course for the public sector is to discover just how serious the problem is and to ascertain the costs of being wrong, either by acting too hastily or by procrastinating. Due to the rampant uncertainties in virtually every logical link in the chain from human activities to subsequent consequences, no one at this juncture can state unequivocally how serious the damage will be. We can, however, begin to elaborate the range of possibilities and see how sensitive the outcomes are to choices before us.

The risks of being wrong are clearly asymmetric. If we control more than necessary, current generations bear a larger than necessary cost. On the other hand, if the problem turns out to be as serious as the worst predictions indicate, catastrophic and largely irreversible damage to the planet would be inflicted on future generations. How can governments respond reasonably to this uncertainty? One familiar way is by acquiring some insurance against the potential harm. In this context acquiring insurance would take the form of undertaking prevention and mitigation strategies as a hedge against the consequences of global warming.

How much insurance should be purchased? One very interesting and provocative study was accomplished by William D. Nordhaus.[22] Based on a cost-benefit analysis of global warming, Nordhaus attempted to derive a reasonable level of carbon tax to deal with global warming. His estimates suggest that a tax of approximately $5 per ton of carbon (with equivalent taxes on other greenhouse gases) would be the most reasonable. A tax of this level would result in reductions of greenhouse gases of some 13% and result in net benefits of about $12 billion per year.

These results are controversial, because many believe that benefit/cost analysis has limited applicability to global warming.[23] Since the present value

---

22 William D. Nordhaus, "A Perspective on Costs and Benefits," *EPA Journal* 16 (March/April 1990): 44-45; "The Economics of the Greenhouse Effect," paper presented at MIT Workshop on Energy and Environmental Modeling and Policy Analysis (July 1989); and "Economic Policy in the Face of Global Warming" photocopy (March 9, 1990).

23 See, for example, the discussion of this controversy in Nathan J. Rosenberg and Pierre R. Crosson, "RFF Workshop on Greenhouse Warming," *Resources* (Fall 1988): 16; and Example 16.2.

component of cost-benefit analysis emphasizes short-term over long-term consequences, the application of cost-benefit analysis will weigh the current costs of controlling emissions more heavily than the distant future damages caused by global warming. Though this approach is not inherently biased against future generations, their interests will only be adequately protected if they would be willing to accept monetary compensation for a modified climate and if current generations were willing to set aside sufficient proceeds to provide this compensation. Since it is not obvious that either condition would be satisfied, the long lead times associated with this problem place the interests of future generations in maintaining a stable climate in jeopardy.

SUMMARY

Regional pollutants differ from local pollutants chiefly in the distance they are transported in the air. Whereas local pollutants damage the environment near the emission site, regional pollutants can cause damage far from the site of emission. Some substances, such as sulfur oxides, nitrogen oxides, and ozone, are both local and regional pollutants.

As the zone of influence of pollutants extends beyond local boundaries, the political difficulties of implementing comprehensive, cost-effective control measures increase. Pollutants crossing political boundaries impose external costs; neither emitters nor the nations within which they emit have the proper incentives to institute efficient control measures.

Acid rain is a case in point. Sulfate and nitrate deposition has caused problems both among regions within countries and between countries. In the United States, the Clean Air Act has had a distinctly local focus. To control local pollution problems, state governments required the installation of tall stacks to dilute the pollution before it hit ground level. In the process a high proportion of the emissions were exported to other areas, reaching the ground hundreds of miles from the point of injection. A focus on local control made the regional problem worse.

Finding solutions to the acid-rain problem has been very difficult because those bearing the costs of further control are usually different than those who will benefit from the control. In the United States, for example, opposition from the midwestern and Appalachian states has delayed action on acid-rain legislation. Stumbling blocks included the higher electricity prices that would result from the control and the employment impacts on those states which would suffer losses of jobs in the high-sulfur coal-mining industry.

Economic analysis of the policy options indicates that the cost of reducing emissions rises dramatically as the amount of reduction is increased from 10 million to 12 million tons. Economic incentive approaches, as expected from Chapter 14, would be the most cost-effective, but their superiority is not overwhelming. The command-and-control strategy, which allocates responsibility based on an excess emissions formula, is only mildly less cost-effective. All attempts to reduce the adverse impacts of control on the midwestern and Appalachian states exact a cost-effectiveness penalty. This penalty is highest for restricting coal switching and lowest for a modified version of an approach based on a charge on uncontrolled sulfur emissions coupled with capital and operating subsidies for the installation and operation of scrubbers. The rise in electricity prices that could be anticipated from the enactment of acid-rain legislation is estimated to be small; furthermore, the greatest increases would be concentrated in those states having lower than average prices.

Chlorofluorocarbons, the first of the discussed global pollutants, are a problem because they have been implicated in the destruction of the stratospheric ozone shield that protects the earth's surface from harmful ultraviolet radiation. Since this is an accumulating pollutant, an efficient response to this problem would involve declining use over time. This could be accomplished either by an emission charge on CFCs that rises over time or a permit system allowing a fixed amount of emissions. Studies of nonaerosol uses of CFCs indicate that economic incentive approaches such as these could achieve the emission target at about one-half the cost of regulatory standards. These studies also indicate, however, that an emissions charge would impose large additional financial burdens on the emitters. (The emission charge payments on uncontrolled emissions would be 15 times as large as the payments for controlling the pollution.) In part to avoid this financial burden, the United States has adopted a transferable allowance system coupled with a tax on the additional profits generated by restricting the supply.

With global warming the emitters are separated in time from the consequence of their emission. A doubling of carbon dioxide emissions is expected to occur well into the next century when virtually all of the current decision makers will have passed away. The current generation bears the cost of control while future generations would reap the benefits. Furthermore, international agreements are made more difficult by the fact that some countries may be benefited, not harmed, by global warming, diminishing even further their incentive to control.

Economic analysis of this problem suggests that it makes sense to take some action to reduce emissions of greenhouse gases to provide insurance against the adverse, irreversible consequences if the damage tends to be higher than anticipated. While the analysis suggests that drastic action is not called for yet, the next few years should be used fruitfully to ensure that energy subsidies are removed, full costs are paid, and more knowledge is gained about the problem. The transition could be facilitated by either a system of taxes on greenhouse gases or a system of transferable emission allowances for greenhouse gases. Some international cost sharing is likely to be a necessary ingredient in a successful attack on the problem. During the next few decades, options must not only be preserved, they must be enhanced.

Responding in a timely and effective fashion to global and regional pollution problems will not be easy. Our political institutions are not configured in such a way to facilitate decision making on a global scale. International organizations exist at the pleasure of the nations they serve. Only time will tell if the mechanism of international agreements will prove equal to the task.

ADDITIONAL REFERENCES

Adams, Donald D. and Walter P. Page. *Acid Deposition: Environmental, Economic, and Policy Issues* (New York: Plenum, 1985).

Bailey, Martin J. "Risks, Costs, and Benefits of Fluorocarbon Regulations," *The American Economic Review* 72 (May 1982): 247–250.

Brown, Peter G. "Policy Analysis, Welfare Economics, and the Greenhouse Effect," *Journal of Policy Analysis and Management* 7 (Spring 1988):471–475.

Croker, Thomas D., ed. *Economic Perspectives on Acid Deposition Control* (Boston: Butterworth, 1984).

Cumberland, John H. *Economics of Managing Chlorofluorocarbons: Stratospheric Ozone and Climate Issues* (Baltimore: Johns Hopkins University Press, 1982).

Feldman, Stephen L. and Robert K. Raufer. *Emissions Trading and Acid Rain: Implementing a Market Approach to Pollution Control* (Totowa, NJ: Rowman & Littlefield, 1987).

Lave, Lester B. "The Greenhouse Effect: What Government Actions Are Needed?" *Journal of Policy Analysis and Management* 7 (Spring 1988): 460–470.

Meyer, Richard and Bruce Yandle. "The Political Economy of Acid Rain," *Cato Journal* 7 (Fall 1987): 527–545.

Nordhaus, William D. "How Fast Should We Graze the Global Commons?" *The American Economic Review* 72 (May 1982): 242–246.

Nordhaus, William D. and Gary W. Yohe. "Future Paths of Energy and Carbon Dioxide Emissions," *Changing Climate: Report of the Carbon Dioxide Assessment Committee*, National Research Council (Washington, DC: National Academy Press, 1983): 87–153.

Rosenberg, Norman J., William E. Easterling III, Pierre R. Crosson, and Joel Darmstadter, eds. *Greenhouse Warming: Abatement and Adaptation* (Washington, DC: Resources for the Future, 1989).

Streets, David G. and Thomas D. Veselka. "Economic Incentives for the Reduction of Sulfur Dioxide Emissions," *Energy Systems and Policy* 11 (1987): 39–59.

Tietenberg, T. H. "Acid Rain Reduction Credits," *Challenge* 32 (March/April 1989): 25–29.

Tietenberg, T. H. "Managing the Transition: The Potential Role for Economic Policies," in *Preserving the Global Environment: The Challenge of Shared Leadership*, Jessica Mathews, ed. (New York: W. W. Norton, 1990).

PROBLEMS

1. Explain why an acid-rain policy using emissions charge revenue to provide capital and operating subsidies for scrubbers is less cost-effective than an emission charge policy alone.

2. The transfer costs associated with an emissions charge approach to controlling chlorofluorocarbon pollution are unusually large in comparison to other pollutants. What circumstances would be favorable to high transfer costs?

CHAPTER SEVENTEEN

Mobile-Source Air Pollution

There are two things you shouldn't watch being made,
sausage and law.

INTRODUCTION

Though they emit many of the same pollutants as stationary sources, mobile sources require a different policy approach. These differences arise from the mobility of the source, the number of vehicles involved, and the role of the automobile in the American lifestyle.

Mobility has two major impacts on policy. On the one hand, pollution is partly caused by the temporary location of the source—a case of being in the wrong place at the wrong time. This occurs, for example, during rush hour in metropolitan areas. Since the cars have to be where the people are, relocating them—as might be done with electric power plants—is not a viable strategy. On the other hand, it is more difficult to tailor vehicle emission rates to local pollution patterns, since any particular vehicle may end up in many different urban and rural areas during the course of its useful life.

Mobile sources are also more numerous than stationary sources. While there are approximately 27,000 major stationary sources, well over 100 million vehicles travel on American roadways. Enforcement is obviously more difficult as the number of sources being controlled increases.

Where stationary sources generally are large and run by professional managers, automobiles are small and run by amateurs. Their small size makes it more difficult to control emissions without affecting performance, while amateur ownership makes it more likely that emission control will deteriorate over time due to a lack of dependable maintenance and care.

These complications might lead us to conclude that perhaps we should ignore mobile sources and concentrate our control efforts solely on stationary sources. Unfortunately, that is not possible. Though each individual vehicle represents a miniscule part of the problem, mobile sources collectively represent a significant proportion of three criteria pollutants—ozone, carbon monoxide, and nitrogen dioxide. (Hydrocarbons and nitrogen dioxide are precursors of ozone.)

For two of these—ozone and nitrogen dioxide—the process of reaching attainment has been particularly slow. With the increased use of diesel engines, mobile sources are becoming responsible for a rising proportion of particulate emissions and vehicles which burn leaded gasoline were, until recently, a major source of airborne lead.

Since it is necessary to control mobile sources, what policy options exist? What points of control are possible and what are the advantages or disadvantages of each? In exercising control over these sources, the government must first specify the agent charged with the responsibility for the reduction. The obvious candidates are the manufacturer and the owner-driver. The balancing of this responsibility should depend on a comparative analysis of costs and benefits, with particular reference to such factors as (1) the number of agents to be regulated; (2) the rate of deterioration while in use; (3) the life expectancy of automobiles; and (4) the availability, effectiveness, and cost of programs to reduce emissions at the point of production and at the point of use.

Although automobiles are numerous and ubiquitous, they are manufactured by a small number of firms. Since it is easier and less expensive to administer a system which controls relatively few sources, regulation at the point of production has considerable appeal.

Some problems are associated with limiting controls solely to the point of production, however. If the factory-controlled emission rate deteriorates during normal usage, control at the point of production may buy only temporary emission reduction. Though the deterioration of emission control can be combatted with warranty and recall provisions, the costs of these supporting programs have to be balanced against the costs of local control.

Since automobiles are durable, *new* vehicles make up only a relatively small percentage of the total fleet of vehicles. Therefore, control at the point of production, which affects only new equipment, takes longer to produce a given reduction in aggregate emissions since newer, controlled cars replace old vehicles very slowly. Control at the point of production produces emission reductions more slowly than a program securing emission reductions from used as well as new vehicles.

Some possible means of reducing mobile-source pollution cannot be accomplished by regulating emissions at the point of production because they involve choices made by the owner-driver. The point of production strategy is oriented toward reducing the amount of emissions *per mile driven* in a particular type of car, but only the owner can decide what kind of car to drive, as well as when and where to drive it.

These are not trivial concerns. Diesel automobiles, buses, trucks, and motor-cycles emit rather different amounts of pollutants than do gasoline-powered automobiles. Changing the mix of vehicles on the road affects the amount and type of emissions even if passenger miles are not changed.

Where and when the car is driven is also important. Since clustered emissions cause higher concentration levels than dispersed emissions, driving in urban areas causes more environmental damage than driving in rural areas. Local control strategies could internalize these location costs, while a uniform national strategy focusing solely on the point of production could not.

Timing of emissions is particularly important because conventional commuting patterns lead to a clustering of emissions during the morning and evening rush hours. Indeed, plots of pollutant concentrations in urban areas during an average day typically produce a graph with two peaks corresponding to the two rush hours.[1] Since high concentrations are more dangerous than low concentrations, some spreading over the 24-hour period could also prove beneficial.

POLICY TOWARD MOBILE SOURCES

Legislative History

Concern about mobile-source pollution originated in Southern California in the early 1950s following a path-breaking study by Dr. A. J. Haagen-Smit of the California Institute of Technology. The study by Dr. Haagen-Smit identified motor vehicle emissions as a key culprit in forming the photochemical smog for which Southern California was becoming infamous.

During the early 1960s while Congress held hearings, required reports, and appointed committees, California passed legislation requiring that exhaust control devices be installed on all new cars sold in California one year after the state had certified that at least two acceptable devices were available at reasonable cost. By 1964 the state had certified four devices and exhaust control devices became mandatory for the 1966 model year.

The Clean Air Act amendments of 1965 set national standards for hydrocarbon and carbon monoxide emissions from automobiles to take effect during 1968. Interestingly, the impetus for this act came not only from the scientific data on

---

1 The exception is ozone formed by a chemical reaction involving hydrocarbons and nitrogen oxides in the presence of sunlight. Since, for the evening rush-hour emissions, too few hours of sunlight remain for the chemical reactions to be completed, graphs of daily ozone concentrations frequently exhibit a single peak.

the effects of automobile pollution, but also from the automobile industry itself. The industry saw uniform federal standards as a way to avoid a situation in which every state passed its own unique set of emission standards, something the auto industry wanted to avoid. This pressure was successful in that the law prohibits all states except California from setting their own standards.

By 1970 the slow progress being made on air pollution control in general and automobile pollution in particular created the political will to act. In a "get tough" mood as it developed the Clean Air Act amendments of 1970, Congress required new emissions standards which would reduce emissions by 90% below their uncontrolled levels. This reduction was to have been achieved by 1975 for hydrocarbon and carbon monoxide emissions and by 1976 for nitrogen dioxide. It was generally agreed at the time the Act was passed that the technology to meet the standards did not exist. By passing this tough act, Congress hoped to force the development of an appropriate technology.

It did not work out that way. The following years ushered in a series of deadline extensions. In 1972 the automobile manufacturers requested a one-year delay in the implementation of the standards. The administrator of EPA denied the request and was taken to court. At the conclusion of the litigation in April 1973, the administrator granted a one-year delay in the 1975 deadline for the hydrocarbon and carbon monoxide standards. Subsequently, in July 1973, a one-year delay was granted for nitrogen oxides as well.[2]

About this time two additional factors intervened. First, the OPEC embargo occurred, resulting in substantially higher crude oil prices. Second, Congress became aware of the trade-off between emissions control and fuel efficiency that characterized control devices at that time. In June 1974, an additional one-year delay in the enforcement of all emissions standards was granted by Congress as part of an energy bill, the Energy Supply and Coordination Act.

Meanwhile, for cars sold in California, manufacturers had begun installing catalytic converters to meet that state's stricter standards. The administrator of EPA, acting on preliminary research, feared that widespread introduction of catalytic converters would increase sulfur oxide emissions. As a result, he granted a further one-year delay for the attainment of the hydrocarbon and carbon monoxide emission standards. Though EPA subsequently concluded that the sulfur oxide problem from catalytic converters was not serious, by the time that conclusion was reached, the standards had been delayed three times and the original 1975–1976 standards were scheduled for 1978. Even that schedule was not adhered to. In the Clean Air Act Amendments of 1977, Congress granted further extensions of two years while tightening the standards.

---

2 The only legal basis for granting an extension was technological infeasibility. Only shortly before the extension was granted, the Japanese Honda CVCC engine was certified as meeting the original standards. It is interesting to speculate on what the outcome would have been if the company meeting the standards was American rather than Japanese.

Structure of the Federal Approach

The current U.S. approach to mobile-source air pollution has served as a model for mobile source control in many other countries (particularly in Europe). We therefore examine this approach in some detail.

The U.S. approach represents a blend of controlling emissions at the point of manufacture with controlling emissions from vehicles in use. New car emission standards are administered through a certification program and an associated enforcement program.

Certification Program. The certification program tests prototypes of car models for conformity to federal standards. During the test a prototype vehicle from each engine family is driven 50,000 miles on a test track or a dynamometer, following a mandated strict pattern of fast and slow driving, idling, and hot-and-cold starts. The manufacturers run the tests and record emission levels at 5000-mile intervals. If the vehicle satisfies the standards over the entire 50,000 miles, it passes the deterioration portion of the certification test.

The second step in the certification process is to apply less demanding (and less expensive) tests to three additional prototypes in the same engine family. Emission readings are taken at the 0 and 4000-mile points and then, using the deterioration rate established in the first portion of the test, are projected to the 50,000-mile point. If those projected emission levels meet the standards, then that engine family is given a certificate of conformity. Only engine families with a certificate of conformity are allowed to be sold.

Associated Enforcement Programs. The certification program is complemented by an associated enforcement program which contains assembly line testing, as well as recall and antitampering procedures and warranty provisions. To ensure that the prototype vehicles are representative, EPA tests a statistically representative sample of assembly line vehicles. If these tests reveal that more than 40% of the cars do not conform with federal standards, the certificate may be suspended or revoked.

EPA has also been given the power to require manufacturers to recall and remedy manufacturing defects that cause emissions to exceed federal standards. If EPA uncovers a defect, it usually requests the manufacturer to recall vehicles for corrective action. If the manufacturer refuses, EPA can order a recall.

The Clean Air Act also requires two separate types of warranty provisions. These warranty provisions are designed to ensure that a manufacturer will have an incentive to produce a vehicle which, if properly maintained, will meet emission standards over its useful life. The first of these provisions requires the vehicle to be free of defects that could cause the vehicle to fail to meet the standards. Any defects discovered by consumers would be fixed at the manufacturer's expense under this provision.

The second warranty provision requires the manufacturer to bring any car which fails an inspection and maintenance test (described below) during its first 24 months or 24,000 miles (whichever occurs first) into conformance with the standards. After the 24 months or 24,000 miles, the warranty is limited solely to the replacement of devices specifically designed for emission control, such as catalytic converters. This further protection lasts 60 months.

The earliest control devices used to control pollution had two characteristics that rendered them susceptible to tampering: they adversely affected vehicle performance, and they were relatively easy to circumvent. As a result, the Clean Air Act Amendments of 1970 prohibited anyone from tampering with an emission control system prior to the sale of an automobile, but, curiously, prohibited only dealers and manufacturers from tampering after the sale. The 1977 amendments extended the coverage of the postsale tampering prohibition to motor vehicle repair facilities and fleet operators.

Lead. Section 211 of the Clean Air Act provides EPA with the authority to regulate lead and any other fuel additives used in gasoline. Under this provision gasoline suppliers are required to make unleaded gasoline available. By ensuring the availability of unleaded gasoline, this regulation sought to reduce the amount of airborne lead, as well as to protect the effectiveness of the catalytic converter, which is poisoned by lead.[3] Penalties are assessed on distributors (but not individual owners) for supplying catalyst-equipped vehicles with leaded gasoline.

On March 7, 1985, EPA issued regulations imposing strict new standards on the allowable lead content in refined gasoline. This regulation required further reductions from the then existing 1.10 grams per leaded gallon (gplg) to 0.50 gplg in July 1985 and to 0.10 gplg in January 1986.[4] These actions followed a highly publicized series of medical research findings on the severe health and developmental consequences, particularly to small children, of even low levels of atmospheric lead. By 1988 unleaded gasoline accounted for 82% of the gasoline sales in the United States.

Local Responsibilities. The Clean Air Act Amendments of 1977 recognized the existence of nonattainment areas. Special requirements were placed on control authorities to bring nonattainment areas into attainment. Since many of the nonattainment areas received that designation for pollutants generated by mobile sources, local authorities in those areas were required to take further actions to reduce emissions from mobile sources.

---

3 Three tankfuls of leaded gasoline used in a car equipped with a catalytic converter produce a 50% reduction in the effectiveness of the catalytic converter.

4 These can be found in 40 CFR 80 (1990).

Measures that local authorities are authorized to use include requiring new cars registered in that area to satisfy the more stringent California standard (with EPA approval) and the development of comprehensive transportation plans. These plans could include measures such as on-street parking controls, road charges, and measures to reduce the number of vehicle miles traveled.

In nonattainment regions that could not meet the primary standard for photochemical oxidants, carbon monoxide, or both by December 31, 1982, control authorities could delay attainments until December 31, 1987, provided they agreed to a number of additional restrictions. For the purposes of this chapter, the most important of these is the requirement that each region gaining this extension must establish a vehicle inspection and maintenance (I&M) program for emissions.

The objective of the I&M program is to identify vehicles that are violating the standards and to bring them into compliance, to deter tampering and to encourage regular routine maintenance. Because the federal test procedure used in the certification process is much too expensive to use on a large number of vehicles, shorter, less expensive tests were developed specifically for the I&M programs. Because of the expense and questionable effectiveness of these programs, they are one of the most controversial components of the policy package used to control mobile-source emissions.

Alternative Fuels.   Recently the attention of policymakers has turned toward alternative fuels. In 1989, for example, the South Coast Air Quality Management District in California recommended that electric vehicles and vehicles that run on methanol be introduced into the Los Angeles area. Alternative fuels have also received prominent attention in Congress.

The attractiveness of alternative fuels is their ability to reduce emissions without dramatically affecting lifestyle. One study estimated that the widespread introduction of methane-fueled vehicles would be likely to reduce reactive hydrocarbon emissions by some 30%. If the vehicles were designed to burn 85% methanol, this same study estimated that emissions could be lowered by 50%.[5]

European Approaches

By the late 1980s emission standards patterned after the 1983 American standards were required for all new cars in Austria, Sweden, Switzerland, Norway, and

---

5 Margaret A. Walls and Alan J. Krupnick, "Cost-Effectiveness of Methanol Vehicles," *Resources* No. 100 (Summer 1990). These numbers are controversial. The American Petroleum Institute estimates that reduction would be in the neighborhood of only 24%.

Finland. West Germany, Denmark, and the Netherlands have introduced tax incentives and lower registration fees for cleaner cars.

On October 1, 1989, the European Community's 12 member nations imposed U.S. style emission standards on all new cars, starting with cars equipped with engines over 2 liters. Similar emission controls are scheduled to be extended to all engine sizes by 1993.

The Soviet Union has, in principle, agreed to follow the example of Western Europe in introducing more stringent emission controls. Since unleaded gasoline is not widely available in the Soviet Union, rapid change to catalytic converters is not expected.

The Netherlands, Norway, and Sweden are using differential tax rates to encourage consumers to purchase (and manufacturers to produce) low emitting cars before regulations take effect requiring all cars to be low-emitting.[6] Tax differentiation confers a tax advantage (and, hence, after-tax price advantage) on cleaner cars. The amount of the tax usually depends on (1) the emission characteristics of the car (heavier taxies being levied on heavily polluting cars), (2) the size of the car (in Germany heavier cars qualify for larger tax advantages to offset the relatively high control requirements placed upon them), and (3) the year of purchase (tax differential is declining since all cars will eventually have to meet the standards). It apparently works. In Sweden, 87% of the new cars sold qualified for the tax advantage, while in Germany the comparable percentage was over 90%.

AN ECONOMIC AND POLITICAL ASSESSMENT

The difficulties of controlling mobile sources are illustrated by the U.S. experience. An infeasible compliance schedule for meeting the ambient standards was established for mobile-source pollutants by the 1970 amendments to the Clean Air Act. The chief instruments to be used by local areas in meeting these standards were the new-car emission standards. Because these applied only to new cars, and because new cars make up such a small proportion of the total fleet, significant emission reductions were not experienced until well after the deadline for meeting the ambient standards. This created a very difficult situation for local areas, since they were forced to meet the ambient standards prior to the time that the emission standards (the chief sources of reduction) were having much of an impact.

---

6 For the details on these approaches see J. B. Opschoor and Hans B. Vos, *Economic Instruments for Environmental Protection* (Paris: OECD, 1989): 69–71.

The only strategy open to them was the development of local strategies to make up the difference. Recognizing the difficulties the states faced, EPA granted an extension of the deadline for submitting the transportation plans that would spell out the manner in which the standards would be reached. This extension was challenged in court by the Natural Resource Defense Council,[7] which successfully argued that EPA did not have the authority to grant the extension. Faced with the court's decision, EPA was forced to reject the state implementation plans submitted by most states as inadequate, because those plans could not ensure attainment by the deadlines. Because the law clearly states that EPA must substitute its own plan for an inadequate plan, EPA found itself thrust into the unfamiliar and unpleasant role of defining transportation control plans for states with rejected SIPs.

Two main problems with this development surfaced: EPA was not administratively equipped either in terms of staff or resources to design and implement these plans and, because of the severity of the mismatch between deadline and implementation, EPA could have done very little, even if the staff and resources had been available.

EPA made a valiant but futile attempt to meet its statutory responsibilities. It concluded that the best way to resolve its dilemma was to work backwards from the needs to the transportation plans and, once the plans were defined, to require states to implement and enforce them. To ensure state cooperation, they set up a system of civil penalties to be applied against states that failed to cooperate.

The resulting plans were virtually unenforceable because they were so severe. For example, in order to meet the ambient standard in Los Angeles by the deadline, the plan designed by EPA called for an 82% reduction in gasoline consumption in the Los Angeles basin. The reduction was to be achieved through gasoline rationing during the six months of the year when the smog problem is most severe. In publishing the plan, EPA Administrator William Ruckelshaus acknowledged that it was infeasible and would effectively destroy the economy of the state if implemented, but argued that he had no other choice under the law.

The states raised a number of legal challenges to this approach, which were never really resolved in the courts by the time Congress revised the act in 1977. The Clean Air Act Amendments of 1977 remedied the situation by extending the deadlines.

The lesson from this episode seems to be that tougher laws do not necessarily result in more rapid compliance. By creating a statutory requirement that could not be met, virtually nothing was accomplished as the various parties attempted to fashion a resolution through the courts.

---

7 475 F.2d 968 (1973).

Technology Forcing and Sanctions

This lesson was underscored by EPA's experience in gaining compliance with the national emission standards by the automobile manufacturers. The industry was able to obtain a number of delays in meeting those standards. The law was so tough that it was difficult to enforce within the time schedule envisioned by Congress.

This problem was intensified by the sanctions established by the Act to ensure compliance. They were so brutal that EPA was unwilling to use them; they did not represent a credible threat. For example, when an engine family failed the certification test, the law is quite specific in stating that vehicle classes not certified as conforming with the standards cannot be sold! Given the importance of the automobile industry in the American economy, this sanction was not likely to be applied. As a result there were considerable pressures on EPA to avoid the sanctions by defining more easily satisfied procedures for certification and by setting sufficiently flexible deadlines that no manufacturer would fail to meet them.

Differentiated Regulation

In controlling the emissions of both mobile sources and stationary sources, the brunt of the reduction effort is borne by new sources. This raises the cost of new sources, and from the purchaser's point of view, increases the attractiveness of used cars relative to new ones. The benefit from increased control is a public good and therefore cannot to be appropriated exclusively by the new-car purchasers. One result of a strategy focusing on new sources would be to depress the demand for new cars while enhancing that for used cars.

Apparently this is precisely what happened in the United States.[8] In response to the higher cost of new cars, people held onto old automobiles longer. This has produced several unfortunate side effects. Since new cars are substantially cleaner than older cars, emission reductions have been delayed. In effect, this shift in fleet composition is equivalent to a setback of three to four years in the timetable for reducing emissions.[9] Also, since older cars get worse gas mileage, gasoline consumption is higher than it would otherwise be. The focus on new sources is, to some extent, inevitable; the lesson to be drawn is that by ignoring these behavioral responses to differentiated regulation, the policymaker is likely to expect results sooner than is feasible.

---

8 See Howard K. Gruenspecht, "Differentiated Regulation: The Case of Auto Emission Standards," *The American Economic Review* 72 (May 1982): 328-331.

9 Robert W. Crandall, Howard K. Gruenspecht, Theodore E. Keeler, and Lester B. Lave, *Regulating the Automobile* (Washington, DC: Brookings Institution, 1986): 96.

EXAMPLE 17.1

Setting the National Automobile Emission Standards

A set of national emission standards provide the backbone of the 1970 Clean Air Act amendments. It is natural to imagine that these standards were set after a careful weighing of the benefits and costs of various levels, but the manner in which they were established was quite different. The analysis used to justify the standards could have been accomplished on the back of an envelope.

The basic approach was developed by D. S. Barth. His calculations relied on a rollback model that simply assumes that a linear relationship exists between emission reductions and reductions in pollutant concentrations. To initiate the analysis, he needed to pick a year in which the standards would be met—1990 was chosen. He then needed to calculate how much emissions would grow in the absence of controls and in the presence of more cars, more miles traveled, and so on. He assumed emissions would grow 2.18 times between 1967 and 1990. Finally, he needed to choose an actual air quality level in 1967. He chose the highest ambient pollution-concentration reading during the year in any city. These pieces of information were then combined in a formula:

$$DER = \left[1.00 - \frac{2.18 \times 1967\,Max - DL}{2.18 \times 1967\,Max - BL} \right] \times 1967\ rate,$$

where DER is the desired emissions rate (in grams per mile), 1967 Max is the maximum ambient concentration, DL is the desired ambient concentration, BL is the background concentration level, and 1967 rate is the actual emission rate (in grams per mile) that prevailed in 1967.

Source: This example was based on D. S. Barth, "Federal Motor Vehicle Emission Goals for CO, HC and NO_2. Based on Desired Air Quality Levels," *Air Pollution 1970, Part 5,* U.S. Senate Committee on Public Works (Washington, DC, 1970); and Eugene P. Seskin, "Automobile Air Pollution Policy," in *Current Issues in U.S. Environmental Policy,* Paul R. Portney, ed. (Baltimore: Johns Hopkins University Press, 1978): 68–104.

Uniformity of Control

With the exception of the California standards, which are more stringent, the Clean Air Act requires the same emission standards on all cars. Example 17.1 shows how these standards were established. The calculations were designed to ensure that required levels of control would be sufficient to meet the ambient standards in Los Angeles or in high-altitude cities such as Denver.[10] As a result, many of the costs borne by people in other parts of the country—particularly rural areas—do not yield much in the way of benefits.

This sounds like an inefficient policy since the severity of control is not tailored to the geographic need, and, indeed, most of the studies which have been accomplished indicate that this is so. One such study was accomplished by the U.S. Ad Hoc Committee on the Cumulative Regulatory Effects on the Cost of Automobile Transportation (known popularly as the RECAT report). The committee estimated annual benefits from the original 1975-1976 standards to be in the interval $3.5 to $9.1 billion, while the costs were estimated as $10.1 billion per year. A later report published by the National Academy of Sciences and the National Academy of Engineering estimated the discounted present value of benefits and costs over the period 1975-2101. They estimated the costs at $126 billion and the benefits at $137 billion. Thus, the first study found negative net benefits, while the latter found positive but small net benefits.

Positive net benefits, of course, are not synonymous with efficiency, although negative net benefits do imply inefficiency. One study by researchers at the General Motors Research Laboratories, attempted to use cost/benefits analysis to find the efficient levels of control. Their analysis suggested:

> One clear conclusion that emerges from the foregoing is that optimal levels, from an economic standpoint, are well below the statutory values of the amended Clean Air Act: 0.94, 0.97, 0.98 for NO_2, CO and HC, respectively. The highest level that emerges would put NO_2, CO and HC at 0.73, 0.31 and 0.82 of the 1960 values, respectively . . . . These optimal levels are relatively insensitive to the social discount rate and gasoline costs . . . . The calculated values of net benefits are dependent on the nonmarket benefits of reduced pollution levels, but the control levels are relatively insensitive.[11]

The conclusion that the costs of control exceed the benefits for automobile pollution control seems to be generally shared.[12] Large uncertainties in the benefit estimations, a theme we have explored in several previous chapters, and the failure of any of these studies to consider the role of auto emissions of carbon in global warming force us to take these results with a grain a salt. It is nonetheless interesting that because the current policy forces manufacturers to operate on a very steep portion of the marginal control cost function, benefit uncertainty

---

10 Considerable evidence suggests that in-use emission rates are substantially higher in high altitudes. See National Commission for Air Quality, *To Breathe Clean Air* (Washington, DC: U.S. Government Printing Office, 1981): 203-206.

11 Richard C. Schwing et al., "Benefit/Cost Analysis of Automotive Emission Reductions," *Journal of Environmental Economics and Management* 7 (1980): 57-58.

12 See the discussion in Robert W. Crandall, Howard K. Gruenspecht, Theodore E. Keeler, and Lester B. Lave, *Regulating the Automobile* (Washington, DC: Brookings Institution, 1986): 109-116.

TABLE 17.1 Average Lifetime (100,000 miles) Emissions of Gasoline Automobiles

Pollutant	Year model	Standard (g/ml)	Average emissions (g/ml)	Ratio of emissions to standard
Hydrocarbons	Pre-1968	None		
	1975–1976	1.5	2.41	1.6
	1977–1978	1.5	2.55	1.7
	1979	1.5	1.83	1.2
	1980	0.41	0.94	2.3
	1981	0.41	0.87	2.1
	1982	0.41	0.82	2.0
	1983	0.41	0.76	2.1
	1984+	0.41	0.79	1.9
Carbon monoxide	Pre-1968	None		
	1975–1976	15.0	29.8	2.0
	1977–1978	15.0	32.9	2.2
	1979	15.0	22.6	1.5
	1980	7.0	16.9	2.4
	1981	3.4	16.9	5.0
	1982	3.4	14.7	4.3
	1983	3.4	11.7	3.4
	1984+	3.4	12.4	3.6
Nitrogen oxides	Pre-1968	None		
	1975–1976	3.1	2.55	0.8
	1977–1979	2.0	2.10	1.1
	1980	2.0	2.10	1.0
	1981	1.0	1.34	1.3
	1982+	1.0	1.44	1.4

Source: National Commission on Air Quality, *To Breathe Clean Air* (Washington, DC: U.S. Government Printing Office, 1981): p. 199, Table 22.

does not seem to affect the conclusion that the current standards are inefficiently strict.

The Deterioration of New-Car Emission Rates

As part of its investigation of the Clean Air Act, the National Commission on Air Quality investigated the emissions of vehicles in use and compared these emission levels to the standards. Their estimates were a blend of actual measured emissions for model years already in the fleet plus forecasts for future model years based on a knowledge of the technologies to be used. The results are presented in Table 17.1. Particularly for hydrocarbons and carbon monoxide, the deterioration of emission rates in use seems pronounced.

The Commission also investigated the factors contributing to poor in-use emissions performance. It found that the principal reason for the poor performance was improper maintenance. Carburetor and ignition-timing misadjustment were key factors. Component failure and tampering were also found to affect emission levels, though to a lesser degree.

Inspection and Maintenance Programs.   The policy response to emission rate deterioration was to require I&M programs in nonattainment regions seeking extensions in the deadlines for reaching the ambient standards. There are reasons for concern, however, as to whether this is a cost-effective response.

The first concern arises out of the change taking place in emission control equipment. The new devices are becoming much more sophisticated. While they will be more difficult to tamper with than earlier devices, their malfunctions will not be detected as easily by the tests used during the inspection.[13] In addition, the costs of repair may turn out to be quite high. No longer will the turn of a carburetor screw do the trick!

A second concern arises over the timing of the program. All nonattainment regions were required to put these programs in place when seeking an extension of the deadline in meeting their ambient standards, *whether the program is necessary in meeting the standards or not.* Washington, D.C., for example, is a city which did not comply with the 1982 deadline, but was expected to meet the 1987 deadline, whether an inspection and maintenance program was in place or not.[14] Thus, for this area and others like it, the I&M program represents an additional but unnecessary expense.

An additional concern over this program questions whether this form of reduction is the cheapest way to reach the ambient standard. Apparently the cost per ton from I&M programs turns out to be two to three times higher than that for securing an equivalent reduction from stationary sources.[15] I&M programs do have merit, since they reduce other pollutants, but the current system provides little flexibility in how the program's objectives are met.

Do vehicle inspection programs yield positive net benefits? The evidence is mixed. A comparison of EPA studies on the costs of the program ($645/ton) with other EPA studies of the benefits for automotive pollutants ($260 to $721/ton)

---

13   Reitze, for example, points out that Ford relied on a fully electronic three-way catalyst system. The short emission tests used by most inspection and maintenance systems did not detect many of the major problems with this system. In Arnold W. Reitze, Jr., "Controlling Automotive Air Pollution through Inspection and Maintenance Programs," *The George Washington Law Review* 47 (May 1979): 726.

14   See Arnold W. Reitze, Jr., "Controlling Automotive Air Pollution through Inspection and Maintenance Programs," *The George Washington Law Review* 47 (May 1979): 730-731.

15   Arnold W. Reitze, Jr., "Controlling Automotive Air Pollution through Inspection and Maintenance Programs," *The George Washington Law Review* 47 (May 1979): 735.

reveals that for some geographic areas, but not all, the programs are justified. A study of the Maryland inspection program, however, suggests that the EPA cost estimates may be understated by a large amount because they do not include the costs of driver time and mileage to complete the inspection and to comply with the findings. Including these costs yields a benefit-cost ratio in the neighborhood of 0.125 for Maryland.[16]

It is easy to see why I&M programs are controversial. Requiring all nonattainment areas requesting an extension in the deadline to implement those standards is costly overkill. In areas such as Washington, D.C., the programs are simply not needed for attainment, and the associated costs are unnecessary. In other areas the desired reductions could well be obtained more cheaply from stationary sources.

Other Local Strategies. Another possible way to counter the effects of deterioration rates of new-car emissions involves the implementation of local transportation controls, such as stimulating mass-transit usage. This approach allows the highly polluted areas to tailor the degree of control to their needs. The question of interest is whether these strategies are cost-effective.

To examine this question and others, the National Science Foundation funded a multidisciplinary, multiuniversity study to examine the emissions payoff and costs of implementing various local strategies. The analysis was based on a computer model which was designed to simulate the transportation system of Boston, Massachusetts, and how that system would respond to various policies available to local authorities.

The model was based on a large amount of data on the origins and destinations of trips in the Boston area. It contained equations that simulated the choice of mode (such as bus or auto) as a function of such factors as travel time, cost, and so on. Once the travel patterns were simulated, the model projected the effects of these travel patterns on aggregate emissions and finally on the concentrations of pollutants expected in each of 123 different receptor locations in the city. With this model it was therefore possible to keep track not only of the size of the emission reductions but also of where pollutant concentrations were reduced. This latter piece of information is important because some parts of the city are more heavily polluted than others, and reductions in those areas would make a particularly valuable contribution to meeting the ambient air quality standards.

As is generally true with simulation models of this sort, an enormous amount of information was generated. A small portion of this output is presented in Table 17.2. The benchmark column represents the transportation and air quality situa-

---

16 Virginia D. McConnell, "A Social Cost/Benefit Study of the Maryland Vehicle Emissions Inspection Program," Maryland Institute for Policy Analysis and Research (1986): 41.

TABLE 17.2 Automobile Pollution Simulation

Statistic	Benchmark	Fare reduction	Transit extension	1980 emission standard
Annual vehicle miles traveled	19,818,000	19,510,000	19,799,000	19,818,000
Percent of trips originating on transit	10.37	10.78	11.92	10.37
Average length of auto trip (mi.)	9.91	9.80	10.06	9.91
Aggregate auto emissions (gr/s)				
CO	19,609	19,343	19,497	4,022
HC	2,755	2,716	2,744	485
NO_2	934	919	933	401
Annual passenger miles traveled on transit by auto users who switch to transit during trip	410,400	494,300	451,500	410,400
Annual dollar resource cost (thousands)	0	$11,517	$95,083	$120,000

Source: Frank P. Grad et al., *The Automobile and the Regulation of Its Impact on the Environment* (Norman, OK: University of Oklahoma Press, 1975): Tables 5-4, 5-5, 5-11.

tion in the Boston Air Quality Control Region in 1970. For all other simulations the population, income, and automobile fleet are assumed to be the same as for the benchmark case.

The fare reduction column portrays the effect of a 10% reduction in mass-transit fare, while the transit extension column gives the effect of a vigorous program of extending subway lines further into the suburbs. The 1980 emission standard column reflects the effect of having the degree of emission control on automobiles which should have been achieved by 1980.

The fare reduction clearly dominates the system extension on grounds of cost effectiveness, since it costs less and reduces pollution more, though neither strategy makes much of a difference. It is impossible, however, to compare the other strategies, since the 1980 emission standards are both much more expensive and much more effective (in terms of reducing pollutants).

Most of the purely local strategies considered in this study are expensive and do not have a profound impact on air quality. Therefore, heavy reliance on traditional local strategies like those covered in this study as a substitute for control over new-car emission rates would seem misguided. Yet appropriately designed, more innovative local strategies can effectively complement new-car strategies, particularly as a means to achieve the additional control needed in those areas where the new-car standards are not sufficient to meet the ambient standards.

Several Far Eastern cities have undertaken some innovative approaches. Perhaps the most innovative can be found in Singapore and Hong Kong, where the price system is used to reduce congestion. (Example 17.2)

Other, less innovative, but nonetheless interesting approaches are proliferating. Bangkok, for example, bars vehicles transporting goods from parts of the metropolitan area during various peak hours, leaving the roads to buses, cars, and motorized tricycles. In the United States reserved express bus lanes are common. (Reserved lanes for express buses lower the relative travel time for bus commuters, thereby providing an incentive for passengers to switch from cars to buses.)

Lead Banking

In the month prior to the issuance of the new, more stringent regulations on lead in gasoline, EPA announced the results of a cost-benefit analysis of their expected impact. The analysis concluded that the 0.10 gplg standard would result in $49 million in benefits (from reduced adverse health effects) at an estimated cost to the refining industry of $3.5 billion.

A main concern of EPA in issuing these regulations was the rigidity of the intermediate deadlines used to implement the phasedown. While some refineries could meet them with ease, others could do so only at a significant increase in cost. Recognizing that meeting the environmental goal did not require every refiner to meet every deadline (as long as the excess lead introduced by those complying late), EPA initiated the lead banking program to provide additional flexibility in meeting the regulations.

While not formally part of the emissions trading program discussed in the previous chapter, the lead banking program does have some design similarities to it. Under this program, refiners reducing lead more than required by the applicable standard in each quarter of the year can bank the credits for use or sale in some subsequent quarter. Banked credits are transferable among refiners.

The lead banking program eased the transition to the more stringent regulatory regime.[17] Refiners had an incentive to respond quickly because lead reductions undertaken prior to the deadlines become valuable under this new program. The availability of these credits made it possible for other refiners to comply with the deadlines even in the face of equipment failures or acts of God rather than fight the deadlines in court. Designed only as a means of facilitating

---

17 For some of the details of the program as well as a description of some of the implementation difficulties, see Robert W. Hahn and Gordon L. Hester, "Marketable Permits: Lessons for Theory and Practice," *Ecology Law Quarterly* 16 (1989): 380-391.

EXAMPLE 17.2

Innovative Mobile Pollution Control Strategies: Singapore and Hong Kong

Mobile source pollution is a function of the level of traffic congestion; the greater the congestion the greater the resulting pollutant concentrations. Reducing the level of congestion is one strategy local areas can implement to reduce peak-hour concentration levels.

Singapore has successfully reduced congestion by forcing drivers to recognize the scarcity value of congested roadways. Since 1975 cars entering the city center during the morning rush hour with fewer than four people aboard have had to display a sticker. As of 1990 the sticker cost approximately $2.60 per day. Sanctions are imposed on cars found in the designated area without a sticker.

Initially the scheme reduced the number of cars entering the restricted area by three-quarters. Though that magnitude of reduction has not been maintained, city streets remain relatively uncongested and pollution concentrations have been reduced.

To make further progress on reducing pollutant concentrations Singapore felt that it must not only limit vehicular access to certain areas during rush hours, but it must begin to reduce the total number of private vehicles. In 1990 it adopted a system whereby motorists have to bid for the right to own new cars, with the licenses going to the highest bidders. Only 22,000 new vehicles—about 4.3% of the existing car population—will be allowed on the roads in the first year of operation.

Hong Kong recently experimented with another, more precise, way of charging road users for the external costs associated with road congestion. Cars were fitted with electronic number plates that identified them to various computers strategically located around the city. Based upon these computer readings, drivers were billed, depending on the intensity, location, and time of road use. While the pilot scheme worked well, local politics prevented it from becoming permanent policy. Apparently newly elected district councils were not satisfied with the disposition of the revenue.

Source: "Traffic Jams: The City, The Commuter and The Car," *The Economist* (February 1989): 19–22; and "Driving in Singapore," *The Wall Street Journal* (February 27, 1990): A22.

the transition to the point when all refiners were in compliance with the lower standards, the lead rights program ended, as scheduled, by December 31, 1987.

Alternative Fuels

While alternative fuels have incorporated another policy option into the control picture, how effective a strategy it would be is not clear. One study examined the cost effectiveness of methanol vehicles by projecting both costs and emissions reductions for the years 2000 and 2010 and calculating a cost per ton reduced.[18]

According to these calculations, flexible-fuel vehicles would be less cost-effective than vehicles dedicated to burn either 85% methanol or 100% methanol. The cost per ton for flexible-fuel vehicles would be in the neighborhood of $66,000 per ton, while for the vehicle burning 85% methanol it would be $31,000 a ton.[19]

These numbers are very high, almost five times as high as alternative means of reducing hydrocarbon emissions. In 1989 the South Coast Air Quality Management District identified 120 options for reducing volatile hydrocarbons. The average cost effectiveness of the 68 measures proposed was $12,250 per ton. While early estimates such as these should not determine the outcome of the search for alternatives, they certainly do suggest that caution in proceeding too rapidly down this path would be appropriate.

Air Quality

Have these policies improved air quality? In this section we examine the data on three pollutants for which mobile sources are very important: ozone, carbon monoxide and lead.[20]

Ozone. Ozone continues to be the most pervasive ambient air pollution problem in the United States with 101 areas failing to meet the ozone ambient standard for 1986–1988. Some progress was made, however. Over the 1979–1988 period, exceedances decreased by some 10%. Emissions of volatile organic compounds,

---

18 Margaret A. Walls and Alan J. Krupnick, "Cost-Effectiveness of Methanol Vehicles" *Resources* No. 100 (Summer 1990).

19 Vehicles burning 100% methanol are estimated to produce reductions at $51,000 per ton.

20 In this section the data for the United States are from Office of Air Quality, *National Air Quality and Emissions Trends Report: 1988* (Washington, DC: U.S. Environmental Protection Agency, 1990), and the international data are from United Nations Environmental Program and the World Health Organization, "Monitoring the Global Environment: An Assessment of Urban Air Quality," *Environment* 31 (October 1989): 6–13, 26–37.

the precursors for ozone formation, were also down 17% during this period. Comparable data for other countries were not available.

Carbon Monoxide. In the United States carbon monoxide emissions declined by 25% over the 1979–1988 period despite a 33% increase in vehicle miles traveled. The emission reductions produced a 28% decrease in the number of sites experiencing violations of the ambient standards and an 88% decrease in the number of exceedances.

While some Western European countries have experienced stable emissions or a gradual decline, others show increased emissions. In the United Kingdom emissions rose by 7% between 1973 and 1984. In both the Netherlands and West Germany, emissions declined by 32% and 37%, respectively.

Data from Poland and Hungary suggest that CO emissions are also rising in some Eastern European countries. Experts also expect to find increasing emissions in industrializing Asian and South American countries, but current data are insufficient to confirm that conjecture.

Lead. Declines in emissions of lead in the United States have been dramatic. From 1979 to 1988 emissions of lead have dropped 93% and ambient concentrations have dropped 89%.

While relatively few countries report lead emissions, the data indicate that lead in gasoline is generally being decreased in European and Asian countries. As of 1988 it was generally not being decreased in Africa, or in South or Central America.[21]

POSSIBLE REFORMS

We have seen that the current approach has some salient weaknesses. Reliance on controlling emissions at the point of production has produced major improvements in cars leaving the assembly line, but emission rates deteriorate with use. The use of uniform standards has resulted in more control than necessary in rural areas and perhaps less than necessary in our most heavily polluted areas. Controlling mobile emissions on a per-mile basis fails to deal with emission increases caused by more vehicles and more miles driven.

Manufacturers have been able to delay implementation deadlines because the sanctions for noncompliance are so severe that EPA is reluctant to deny a certificate of conformity. Automobile users have little incentive to drive or maintain

---

[21] Gasoline in Mexico City had the highest lead content of all sites in the global monitoring network, and volunteers from that city had the highest levels of lead in their blood.

their cars in a manner that minimizes emissions. Can automobile emissions policy be reformed to make headway on these important deficiencies?

Emission Charges

A most interesting and quite detailed proposal has been suggested by Mills and White.[22] In their proposal, emission standards are replaced by emission charges designed to provide the appropriate incentives for both manufacturers and drivers.

The chief elements of the proposal include:

1. A uniform charge levied on all new cars and paid at the time the cars are sold to dealers. The size of the charge would depend on the amounts of the three major pollutants emitted by the engine class during the regular EPA test. The lower the emissions are, the smaller the tax to be paid.

2. Particularly polluted areas would be permitted to augment this basic charge with another charge to reflect the greater need for clean cars in those areas. This would induce consumers in those areas to choose cleaner cars in order to avoid paying the higher fees assessed on dirty ones. Drivers in rural areas, meanwhile, would face lower emission charges in general (because no supplemental fee would be imposed), so they would not have to buy the cars with significant control overkill as they do under current policy.

3. Manufacturers would no longer be issued a certificate of conformity. All cars could be sold. Dirtier cars would pay higher emission fees. This would eliminate the current problem with the sanctions so severe that they do not represent a credible threat, but it would provide a clear incentive for manufacturers to reduce emissions in order to hold their costs (including the charge) down.

4. An additional emission charge would be paid by drivers at their annual inspection. This fee would take into account grams per mile (as determined by the inspection) and miles driven since the last inspection. Thus a driver could reduce this fee by maintaining the car to emit less, using retrofit devices, if available, and by driving fewer miles. The incentives to keep a car clean would persist over the lifetime of the automobile and the current incentive to hold older, dirtier cars longer would no longer persist.

---

22 Edwin S. Mills and Lawrence J. White, "Government Policies toward Automobile Emissions Control," in *Approaches to Control Air Pollution*, Ann F. Friedlaender, ed. (Cambridge, MA: MIT Press, 1978): 348–402.

In Chapter 14 we developed a theorem stating that properly designed emission charges would allocate the control responsibility in a cost-minimizing way. The Mills and White proposal would appear to offer the opportunity to use this theorem as the basis for a reform of the current approach to air pollution of mobile sources.

The Two-Car Strategy

A main source of inefficiency in the current approach is the geographic uniformity of emission standards. National uniformity fails to yield enough control in the most polluted areas, and it exercises too much control in the relatively clean areas.

Recognition of this inequity has lead to a reform proposal which, although it is not nearly as comprehensive or sweeping as the emission charge proposal, does allow a more careful tailoring of the degree of control (and control costs) to the need. This proposal suggests not one emissions standard, but two. One of these would be very strict and would apply to cars destined for use in heavily polluted areas, and the other would be somewhat less strict and would apply to cars used in areas currently in compliance.

It has been estimated that only about 35% of the vehicle population needs to be made up of the low-emitting vehicles in order to meet the ambient standards for mobile-source pollutants. This means the remaining 65% are currently over-controlled.[23]

The current system involves two emissions rates—the California rate and the rate for the rest of the country. These two rates do not fill the bill, however, because both are very strict. Rather, a two-car strategy might use the California standard as the strict standard, complemented by a less strict standard.

The chief question is the administrative costs involved in implementing this strategy. Presumably, the car registration process would be used; after a certain date, cars made in a specific model year or later could be registered in nonattainment areas only if they were low-emitting vehicles. If, however, all vehicles driving in the heavily polluted urban areas are to be low-emitting, all vehicles registered in the suburbs would have to be included as well.

Where to draw the boundary between areas that require low-emitting vehicles and those that do not is not a trivial exercise. Boundaries too close to the urban areas will encourage some movement beyond the boundaries with more miles traveled (and more emissions). Expansive boundaries, on the other hand, would encompass a substantially higher proportion of the population, including many who presumably rarely drive into the heavily polluted areas. Thus, the case for

---

23 Frank P. Grad et al., *The Automobile and the Regulation of Its Impact on the Environment* (Norman, OK: University of Oklahoma Press, 1975), chap. 5.

this reform is less convincing than that for emission charges, though it has the redeeming virtue of representing a somewhat less radical departure from current policy.

Retirement Strategies

A final reform possibility involves strategies to accelerate the retirement of older, polluting vehicles. This could be accomplished either by raising the cost of holding onto older vehicles (as with higher registration fees for vehicles that pollute more) or by providing a bounty of some sort to those retiring heavily polluting vehicles early. Though probably more bureaucratically cumbersome, the bounty approach would respond to the large number of poor households who own these older vehicles and who could ill afford to pay higher registration fees.

Retirement strategies would tend to counteract the tendency for vehicles to be used longer as a result of the new source focus of current automotive regulations. By eliminating these heavily polluting vehicles from the fleet earlier than would otherwise be the case, greater emission reductions could be achieved at an earlier date. This approach could be applied selectively in those local areas for which it could make a significant difference.

SUMMARY

The current policy toward motor vehicle emissions blends point-of-production control with point-of-use control, but the existing blend seems quite removed from what efficiency or cost effectiveness would dictate. The history of legislation in this area has been a turbulent one, moving from a low federal profile— concerned mainly with studying the problem and assisting states—to a high federal profile involving a preemptive responsibility for emission controls.

In a period of frustration, Congress wrote such a tough law that little was accomplished during the early years. The ambient standards could not be met by the deadlines. The sanctions used for noncompliance were so severe that EPA was reluctant to use them. Because they were not a credible threat, the sanctions did little to alter behavior.

The focus on new source controls has caused the problem of people using older, more heavily polluting cars, delaying significant improvements in air quality. In addition, the technologies chosen by the manufacturers to meet their statutory responsibilities have failed to prevent a deterioration in operating vehicle emission rates.

The U.S. national emission standards, which represent the core of the current approach in the United States and Europe, seem inefficient for two rather different reasons: (1) according to benefit-cost calculations they are too stringent; and (2) with the exception of California, they are uniform. These two inefficiencies are somewhat related. The controls are too stringent primarily because they require cars not contributing to nonattainment to bear the same cost of controls those that do contribute. The current high standards cause these costs to be large. Thus, if uniform standards are to be retained, they probably should be lower.

Uniform emission standards, however, cannot be fully cost-effective, whatever their level. Cost effectiveness requires higher control costs in areas having real difficulty in meeting the ambient standards than in the rest of the country. Uniform emission standards are powerless to make this crucial distinction.

Likewise, local approaches relying on inspection or maintenance are not generally cost-effective. Some areas are currently required to establish these programs, whether they facilitate attainment or not. Other areas could find stationary-source control cheaper, but these areas, under current rules, are not allowed to substitute one for the other.

Despite the policy imperfections, with the exception of ozone, mobile-source pollutant concentrations and emissions have generally improved in the industrialized nations. The picture is bleaker in developing nations where control levels are low and increases in vehicle ownership are rapid.

For many nonattainment areas current policy has clearly not been enough to guarantee that the ambient standards are met. In part the emissions standards themselves are at fault. Defined in terms of emissions per mile, they are powerless to prevent increases in emissions due to growth in the number of vehicles on the road and/or growth in the number of miles driven. As the population expands, carrying with it an expansion in the number of vehicles on the road, air quality necessarily deteriorates even if every car has met the standards. As suburban communities expand farther and farther from the urban center, the average number of miles driven per driver increases. Each mile driven contributes more emissions.

Appropriate regulation of emissions from mobile sources requires a great deal more than controlling emissions at the factory. Vehicle purchases, driving behavior, fuel choice and even residential and employment locations must eventually be affected by the need to reduce mobile source emissions. The historic low cost of auto travel has led to a very dispersed pattern of development. Since dispersed patterns of development make mass transit a less viable alternative, a downward spiral of population dispersal and the decline of mass transit occurs. In the long run, part of the strategy for meeting ambient standards will necessarily involve changing land use patterns to create the kind of high-density travel corridors that are compatible with effective mass transit use. That, of course will only evolve over a long period of time, but ensuring that the true social costs of transportation are borne by those making residential location and transportation decisions will start the process moving in the right direction. Affecting the choices facing automobile owners can only happen if the economic incentives associated with those choices are structured correctly.

Innovative policies aimed specifically at restructuring these incentives may fill the bill. A manufacturer's incentive to provide new types of vehicles would be greatly affected by the anticipated size of the market and the speed with which the new vehicles would penetrate that market. In the absence of some kind of economic incentive, consumers will typically wait as long as possible to adopt new technologies because of fears about reliability and cost. Differential taxation, such as that used in Europe, can be used to speed up the rate of adoption.

Local approaches, such as those being implemented in Singapore, represent another point of departure. Using the price system to ration access to the central city forces drivers to internalize some of the costs of congestion, enhancing the attractiveness of public transit alternatives in the process.

In the case of mobile sources, however, the best strategy appears to be based on a carefully designed emission charge. This approach, if implemented, would appear to be more cost-effective and more flexible than the current approach while eliminating many of its deficiencies.

FURTHER READING

Crandall, Robert W., Howard K. Gruenspecht, Theodore E. Keeler, and Lester B. Lave. *Regulating the Automobile* (Washington, DC: Brookings Institution, 1986). An examination of the effectiveness and efficiency of the federal regulation of automobile safety, emissions, and fuel economy in the United States.

Dewees, Donald N. *Economics and Public Policy: The Auto Pollution Case* (Cambridge, MA: MIT Press, 1974). An interesting, if somewhat dated, use of economic analysis to analyze automobile air pollution. Filled with technical detail about many of the issues covered in this chapter.

Grad, Frank P. et al. *The Automobile and the Regulation of Its Impact on the Environment* (Norman, OK: University of Oklahoma Press, 1975). A comprehensive multidisciplinary, multiuniversity study of automobile pollution financed by the National Science Foundation. Includes analyses by economists, engineers, and lawyers.

Mills, Edwin S. and Lawrence J. White. "Government Policies toward Automobile Emissions Control," in *Approaches to Control Air Pollution*, Ann F. Friedlaender, ed. (Cambridge, MA: MIT Press, 1978): 348-402. A detailed, highly readable article describing the emission charge reform in detail.

ADDITIONAL REFERENCES

Gruenspecht, Howard K. "Differentiated Regulation: The Case of Auto Emission Standards," *The American Economic Review* 72 (May 1982): 328-331.

Jacoby, Henry D. et al., *Clearing the Air: Federal Policy on Automotive Emission Control* (Cambridge, MA: Ballinger Press, 1978).

National Commission on Air Quality, *To Breathe Clean Air* (Washington, DC: U.S. Government Printing Office, 1981).

Reitze, Arnold W., Jr. "Controlling Automotive Air Pollution through Inspection and Maintenance Programs," *The George Washington Law Review* 47 (May 1979): 724-736.

Seskin, Eugene P. "Automobile Air Pollution Policy," in *Current Issues in U.S. Environmental Policy*, Paul R. Portney, ed. (Baltimore: Johns Hopkins University Press, 1978): 68–104.

White, Lawrence J. "American Automotive Emissions Control Policy: A Review of the Reviews," *Journal of Environmental Economics and Management* 2 (1974): 231–246.

White, Lawrence J. "U.S. Automotive Emissions Controls: How Well Are They Working?", *The American Economic Review* 72 (May 1982): 332–335.

DISCUSSION QUESTIONS

1. When a threshold concentration is used as the basis for pollution control as it is for air pollution, one possibility for meeting the threshold at minimum cost is to spread the emissions out over time. One way to accomplish this is to establish a peak-hour pricing system in which emissions during peak periods are charged more.

   (a) Would this represent a movement toward efficiency? Why or why not?

   (b) What effects should this policy have on mass transit usage, gasoline sales, downtown shopping, and travel patterns?

2. The Mills and White emission charge discussed earlier in this chapter would, if implemented, represent quite a dramatic departure from existing policy. Discuss the desirability of implementing such a policy. What are the advantages and disadvantages of changing from the current approach to the Mills and White scheme?

CHAPTER EIGHTEEN

Water Pollution

It was the best of times, it was the worst of times, it was the age of wisdom, it was the age of foolishness, it was the epoch of belief, it was the epoch of incredulity....

CHARLES DICKENS, *A Tale of Two Cities* (1859)

INTRODUCTION

While various types of pollution share common attributes, important differences are apparent as well. These differences form the basis for the elements of policy unique to each pollutant. We have seen, for example, that although the types of pollutants emitted by mobile and stationary sources are often identical, the policy approaches differ considerably.

Water pollution control has its own unique characteristics as well. Two stand out as having particular relevance for policy:

1. Recreation benefits are much more important for water pollution control than for air pollution control.[1]

2. Large economies of scale in treating sewage and other wastes create the possibility for large, centralized treatment plants as one control strategy, while for air pollution, on-site control is the standard approach.

These characteristics create a need for yet another policy approach. In this chapter we explore the problems and prospects for controlling this unique and important form of pollution.

---

1 See Daniel Feenberg and Edwin S. Mills, *Measuring the Benefits of Water Pollution Abatement* (New York: Academic Press, 1980): 164.

476

NATURE OF WATER POLLUTION PROBLEMS

Types of Waste-Receiving Water

Two primary types of water are susceptible to contamination. The first, *surface water*, consists of the rivers, lakes, and oceans covering most of the earth's surface. Historically, policymakers have focused almost exclusively on preventing and cleaning up lake and river water pollution. Only recently has ocean pollution received the attention it deserves.

Groundwater, once considered a pristine resource, has been shown to be subject to considerable contamination from toxic chemicals. *Groundwater* is subsurface water that occurs beneath a water table in soils or rocks, or in geological formations that are fully saturated.

Groundwater is a vast natural resource. It has been estimated that the volume of groundwater is approximately 50 times the annual flow of surface water.[2] Though groundwater currently supplies only 25% of the fresh water used for all purposes in the United States, its use is increasing more rapidly than the use of surface water.

Ground water is used primarily for irrigation and as a source of drinking water. Approximately 50 percent of the population relies on ground water as the primary source of water for drinking. The proportion is even higher for rural areas.

While surface water serves as a significant source of drinking water, it has many other uses as well. Recreational benefits such as swimming, fishing, and boating are important determinants of surface water policy in areas where the water is not used for drinking.

Sources of Contamination

Contamination of groundwater occurs when polluting substances leach into a water-saturated region. Many potential contaminants are removed by filtration and adsorption as the water moves slowly through the layers of rock and soil. Toxic organic chemicals are one major example of a pollutant which may not be filtered out during migration. Once these substances enter groundwater, very little, if any, further cleansing takes place. Moreover, since the rate of replenishment for many groundwater sources, relative to the stock, is small, very little mixing and dilution of the contaminants occur (Example 18.1).

---

2 Council on Environmental Quality, *Environmental Quality—1980* (Washington, DC: U.S. Government Printing Office, 1980): 83.

EXAMPLE 18.1

Incidents of Groundwater Pollution

Traditional federal policies have paid little attention to groundwater, partly because of the high cost of testing and monitoring. Recent data, however, have shown that groundwater in many locations is contaminated by toxic chemicals. This may be posing unacceptable health risks for the public, since groundwater is widely used for drinking. Many of the chemicals now being discovered in drinking water are either known or suspected carcinogens or mutagens.

Recently discovered incidents of groundwater contamination by toxic organic substances include the following:

1. In 1979 a Massachusetts Legislative Commission on Water Supply found that at least one-third of the 351 communities in the Commonwealth were affected by chemical contamination of drinking water, and wells were restricted or closed in 22 towns.
2. All wells in Groveland and Rowley (Massachusetts) were closed because of trichloroethylene (TCE) contamination, a known carcinogen in animals.
3. In North Reading, Massachusetts, TCE concentrations exceed 90 ppb in two wells supplying 30% of the town's water. The state maximum acceptable contamination level is 10 ppb.
4. In January 1980, California public health officials closed 37 public wells that supplied water to 400,000 people in the San Gabriel Valley because of TCE contamination.
5. A New York Public Interest Research Group documented that all three major aquifers under Long Island were seriously contaminated with effluent from industrial wastes, municipal treatment plants, and runoff from highways. They also found evidence of mutagenic substances in 12 groundwater sites.

Source: Council on Environmental Quality, *Environmental Quality—1980* (Washington, DC: U.S. Government Printing Office, 1980): 81–83.

Whereas some contamination has been accidental, the product of unintended and unexpected waste migration to water supplies, a portion of the contamination was deliberate. Water courses were simply a convenient place to dump municipal or private sewage and industrial wastes. Along the shoreline of many lakes or rivers, pipes dumping human or industrial wastes directly into the water were a common occurrence before laws limiting this activity were enacted and enforced.

For lake and river pollution policy purposes it is useful to distinguish between two sources of contamination—point and nonpoint sources—even though the distinction is not always crystal clear. *Point sources* generally discharge into surface waters at a specific location through a pipe, outfall, or ditch, while *nonpoint sources* usually affect the water in a more indirect and diffuse way. From the policy point-of-view, nonpoint sources are more difficult to control and have received little legislative attention. As a result of the gains made in controlling point sources, nonpoint sources now compose over half of the waste load borne by the nation's waters.

Rivers and Lakes. The most important nonpoint sources of pollution for rivers and lakes are agricultural activity, urban storm-water runoff, silviculture, and individual disposal systems. Contamination from agriculture includes eroded topsoil, pesticides, and fertilizer. Urban storm-water runoff contains a number of pollutants, including, typically, high quantities of lead. Forestry, if not carefully done, can contribute to soil erosion and, by removing shade cover, could have a large impact on the temperature of normally shaded streams. Malfunctioning septic systems, more prevalent in rural areas, are estimated to be a major source of pollution for some 43% of the nation's river basins.

The contamination of groundwater supplies usually results from the migration of harmful substances from sites where high concentrations of chemicals can be found. These include industrial waste storage sites, landfills, and farms. Industrial wastes have been identified by EPA as the most important source of groundwater contamination.[3]

The primary point sources are industries and municipalities. As of 1980, EPA had identified 59,907 point sources. Of these, 15,395 were municipal dischargers (mostly sewage treatment plants), while industrial sources made up most of the rest. Of the 7350 "major" dischargers responsible for well over half of all discharges, municipalities and industries were about equally represented.

Ocean Pollution. The two primary sources of ocean pollution discussed in this chapter are oil spills and ocean dumping. Since a great deal of oil is transported

---

3 Council on Environmental Quality, *Environmental Quality—1980* (Washington, DC: U.S. Government Printing Office, 1980): 116-120.

TABLE 18.1 Notable Oil Spills

Source and location	Date	Tons spilled
Ixtoc I oil well, Southern Gulf of Mexico	June 3, 1979	600,000
Nowruz oil field, Persian Gulf	February, 1983	600,000 (est.)
Atlantic Express and Aegean Captain off Trinidad and Tobago	July 19, 1979	300,000
Castillo de Beliver off Cape Town, South Africa	August 6, 1983	250,000
Amoco Cadiz near Portsall, France	March 16, 1978	223,000
Torrey Canyon off Land's End, England	March 18, 1967	119,000
Sea Star Gulf of Oman	December 19, 1972	115,000
Urquiola La Coruna, Spain	May 12, 1976	100,000
Hawaiian Patriot northern Pacific	February 25, 1977	99,000
Othello Tralhavet Bay, Sweden	March 20, 1970	60,000–100,000
World Glory off South Africa	June 13, 1968	46,000
Burmah Agate Galveston Bay, Texas	November 1, 1979	36,400
Exxon Valdez Prince William Sound, Alaska	March 24, 1989	34,300

Source: From *The World Almanac & Book of Facts*, 1990 edition, copyright Pharos Books 1989, New York, NY 10166.

over the oceans and is produced from platforms exploiting fields under the ocean, oil spills have become a more common occurrence (Table 18.1). Various unwanted by-products of modern life have also been dumped in ocean waters based upon the mistaken belief that the vastness of the oceans allowed them to absorb large quantities of waste without suffering noticeable damage. Dumped materials have included sewage and sewage sludge, unwanted chemicals, trace metals, and even radioactive materials.

Types of Pollutants

For our purposes the large number of water pollutants can be usefully classified by means of the taxonomy developed in Chapter 14.

Fund Pollutants. Fund pollutants are those for which the environment has some assimilative capacity. If the absorptive capacity is high enough relative to the rate of injection, they may not accumulate at all. One type of fund water pollutant is called *degradable* because it degrades, or breaks into its component parts, within the water. Degradable wastes are normally organic residuals that are attacked and broken down by bacteria in the stream.

The process by which organic wastes are broken down into component parts consumes oxygen. The amount of oxygen consumed depends upon the magnitude of the waste load. All of the higher life forms in watercourses are *aerobic*; they require oxygen for survival. As a stream's oxygen levels fall, fish mortality increases, with the less tolerant fish becoming the first to succumb. The oxygen level can become low enough that even the aerobic bacteria die. When this happens, the stream becomes *anaerobic* and the ecology changes drastically. This is an extremely unpleasant circumstance because the stream takes on a dark hue, and the stream water stinks!

To control these waste loads, two different types of monitoring are needed: (1) monitoring the ambient conditions in the watercourse; and (2) monitoring the magnitude of emissions. One measure commonly used to keep track of ambient conditions for these conventional fund pollutants is *dissolved oxygen* (DO). The amount of dissolved oxygen in a body of water is a function of ambient conditions, such as temperature, stream flow, and the waste load.[4] The measure of the oxygen demand placed on a stream by any particular volume of effluent is called the *biochemical oxygen demand* (BOD).

Using modeling techniques, emissions (measured as BOD) at a certain point can be translated into DO measures at various receptor locations along a stream. This step is necessary in order to implement an ambient permit system or an ambient emission charge.

If we were to develop a profile of dissolved oxygen readings on a stream where organic effluent is being injected, that profile would typically exhibit one or more minimum points called oxygen sags. These *oxygen sags* represent locations along the stream where the dissolved oxygen content is lower than at other points. An ambient permit or ambient charge system would be designed to reach a desired DO level at those sag points, while an emission permit or emission charge system would simply try to hit a particular BOD reduction target. The former would take the location of the emitter into account, while the latter would not. Later in this chapter we examine studies which model these systems on particular watercourses.

A second type of fund pollutant, thermal pollution, is caused by the injection of heat into a watercourse. Typically, *thermal pollution* is caused when an industrial plant or electric utility uses surface water as a coolant, returning the heated water to the watercourse. This heat is dissipated in the receiving waters

---

4 The danger of anaerobic conditions is highest in the late summer and early fall, when temperatures are high and the stream flow is low.

by evaporation. By raising the temperature of the water near the outfall, thermal pollution lowers the dissolved oxygen content and can result in dramatic ecological changes in that area.

Yet another example is provided by a class of pollutants, such as nitrogen and phosphorus, which are plant nutrients. These pollutants stimulate the growth of aquatic plant life, such as algae and water weeds. In excess these plants can produce odor, taste, and aesthetic problems. A lake with an excessive supply of nutrients is called *eutrophic*.

The various types of fund pollutants could be ordered on a spectrum. On one end of the spectrum would be pollutants for which the environment has a very large absorptive capacity and on the other end pollutants for which the absorptive capacity is virtually nil. The limiting case, with no absorptive capacity, are stock pollutants.

Near the end of that spectrum is a class of inorganic synthetic chemicals called persistent pollutants These substances are called *persistent* because their complex molecular structures are not effectively broken down in the stream. Some degradation takes place, but so slowly that these pollutants can travel long distances in water in a virtually unchanged form.

These persistent pollutants accumulate, not only in the watercourses, but in the food chain as well. The concentration levels in the tissues of living organisms rise with the order of the species. Concentrations in lower life forms such as plankton may be relatively small, but, because small fish eat a lot of plankton and do not excrete the chemical, the concentrations in small fish would be higher. The magnification continues as large fish consume small fish; concentration levels in the larger fish would be even higher.

Because they accumulate in the food chains, persistent pollutants present an interesting monitoring challenge. The traditional approach would involve measurements of pollutant concentration in the water, but that is not the only variable of interest. The damage is related not only to its concentration in the water, but its concentration in the food chain as well. Although monitoring the environmental effects of these pollutants may be more compelling than monitoring other pollutants, it is also more difficult. Since effective monitoring is a prerequisite for successful policy, this suggests one major continuing role for EPA.

A final type of fund pollutant, infectious organisms such as bacteria and viruses, is carried into surface water and groundwater by domestic and animal wastes and by wastes from such industries as tanning and meat packing. These live organisms may either thrive and multiply in water or their population may decline over time, depending upon how hospitable or hostile the watercourse is for continued growth.

Stock Pollutants. The most troublesome cases of pollution result from *stock pollutants* which merely accumulate in the environment. No natural process removes or transforms stock pollutants; the watercourse cannot cleanse itself of them.

Inorganic chemicals and minerals comprise the main examples of stock pollutants. Perhaps the most notorious members of this group are the heavy metals, such as lead, cadmium, and mercury. Extreme examples of poisoning by these metals have occurred in Japan. One ocean dumping case was responsible for *Minamata disease*, named for the location where it occurred. Some 52 people died and 150 others suffered serious brain and nerve damage. Scientists puzzled for years over the source of the ailments until tracing them to an organic form of mercury that had accumulated in the tissues of fish eaten three times a day by local residents.

In another case in Japan, known as the *itai itai* (literally, ouch-ouch) *disease*, scientists traced the source of a previously undiagnosed, extremely painful bone disease to the ingestion of cadmium. Nearby mines were the source of the cadmium, which apparently was ingested by eating contaminated rice and soybeans.

As is typical with persistent pollutants, some of the stock pollutants are difficult to monitor. Those accumulated in the food chains give rise to the same problem as is presented by persistent pollutants. Ambient sampling must be supplemented by sampling tissues from members of the food chain. To further complicate matters, the heavy metals may sink rapidly to the bottom, remaining in the sediment. While these could be detected in sediment samples, merely drawing samples from the water itself would allow these pollutants to escape detection.

WATER POLLUTION CONTROL POLICY

United States policy for water pollution control antedates federal air pollution control by a considerable amount of time. We might suppose that the policy for water pollution control is superior, since authorities had more time to profit from early mistakes. Unfortunately, that is not the case.

Early Legislation

The first federal legislation dealing with discharge into the nation's waterways occurred when Congress passed the 1899 Refuse Act. Designed primarily to protect navigation, this act focused on preventing any discharge that would interfere with using rivers as transport links. All discharges into a river were prohibited unless approved by a permit from the Chief of the U.S. Engineers. Most permits were issued to contractors dredging the rivers, and they dealt mainly with the disposal of the removed material. This act was virtually unenforced for other pollutants until 1970, when this permit program was rediscovered and used briefly (with little success) as the basis for federal enforcement actions.

The Water Pollution Control Act of 1948 represented the first attempt by the federal government to exercise some direct influence over what previously had been a state and local function. A hesitant move, since it reaffirmed that the primary responsibility for water pollution control rested with the states, it did initiate the authority of the federal government to conduct investigations, research and surveys.

The first hints of the current approach are found in the amendments to the Water Pollution Control Act, which were passed in 1956. Two provisions of this act were especially important: (1) federal financial support for the construction of waste treatment plants and (2) direct federal regulation of waste discharges via a mechanism known as the *enforcement conference*.

The first of these provisions envisioned a control strategy based on subsidizing the construction of a particular control activity—waste treatment plants. Municipalities could receive federal grants to cover up to 55% of the construction of municipal sewage treatment plants. This approach not only lowered the cost to the local governments of constructing these facilities, it also lowered the cost to users. Since the federal government contribution was a grant, rather than a loan, the fees charged users did not reflect the federally subsidized construction portion of the cost. The user fees were set at a lower rate that was high enough to cover merely the unsubsidized portion of construction cost, as well as operating and maintenance cost.

The 1956 amendments envisioned a relatively narrow federal role in the regulation of discharges. Initially, only polluters contributing to interstate pollution were included, but subsequent laws have broadened the coverage. By 1961 discharges into all navigable water were covered.

The mechanism created by the amendments of 1956 to enforce the regulation of discharges was the enforcement conference. Under this approach the designated federal control authority could call for a conference to deal with any interstate water pollution problem or it could be requested to do so by the governor of an affected state. The fact that this authority was discretionary and not mandatory and that the control authority had very few means of enforcing any decisions reached meant that the conferences simply did not achieve the intended results.

The Water Quality Act of 1965 attempted to improve the process by establishing ambient water quality standards for interstate water courses and by requiring states to file implementation plans. This sounds like the approach currently being used in air pollution control, but there are important differences. The plans forthcoming from states in response to the 1965 Act were vague and did not attempt to link specific effluent standards on discharges to the ambient standards. They generally took the easy way out and called for secondary treatment, which removes 80-90% of BOD and 85% of suspended solids. The fact that these standards bore no particular relationship to ambient quality made them difficult to enforce in the courts, since the legal authority for them was based on this relationship.

Subsequent Legislation

Point Sources. As discussed in the preceding chapters, an air of frustration regarding pollution control pervaded Washington in the 1970s. As with air pollution legislation, this frustration led to the enactment of a very tough water control law. The tone of the act is established immediately in the preamble which calls for the achievement of two goals: (1) " . . . that the discharge of pollutants into the navigable waters be eliminated by 1985"; and (2) " . . . that wherever attainable, an interim goal of water quality which provides for the protection and propagation of fish, shellfish, and wildlife and provides for recreation in and on the water be achieved by June 1, 1983." The stringency of these goals represented a major departure from past policy.

This act also introduced new procedures for implementing the law. Permits were required of all dischargers (replacing the 1899 Refuse Act which, because of its navigation focus, was difficult to enforce). The permits would be granted only when the dischargers met certain technology-based effluent standards. The ambient standards were completely bypassed as these effluent standards were uniformly imposed and, hence, could not depend on local water conditions.[5]

According to the 1972 amendments, the effluent standards were to be implemented in two stages. By 1977 industrial dischargers, as a condition of their permit, were required to meet effluent limitations based on the "best practicable control technology currently available" (BPT). In setting these national standards, EPA was required to consider the total costs of these technologies and their relation to the benefits received, but not to consider the conditions of the individual source or the particular waters into which it was discharged. In addition, all publicly owned treatment plants were to have achieved secondary treatment by 1977. By 1983 industrial discharges were required to meet effluent limitations based on the presumably more stringent "best available technology economically achievable" (BAT) while publicly owned treatment plants were required to meet effluent limitations which depended on the "best practicable waste treatment technology."

The program of subsidizing municipal water treatment plants, begun in 1956, was continued in a slightly modified form by the 1972 Act. Whereas the 1965 Act allowed the federal government to subsidize up to 55% of the cost of construction of waste treatment plants, the 1972 Act raised the ceiling to 75%. The

---

5 Actually the ambient standards were not completely bypassed. If the uniform controls were not sufficient to meet the desired standard, the effluent limitation would have to be tightened accordingly.

1972 act also increased the funds available for this program. In 1981 the federal share was reduced to 55%.

The 1977 amendments continued this regulatory approach, but with some major modifications. This legislation drew a more careful distinction between conventional and toxic pollutants, with more stringent requirements placed on the latter, and it extended virtually all of the deadlines in the 1972 Act.

For conventional pollutants a new treatment standard was created to replace the BAT standards. The effluent limitations for these pollutants were to be based on the "best conventional technology," and the deadline for these standards was set at July 1, 1984. In setting these standards, EPA was required to consider whether the costs of adding the pollution control equipment were reasonable when compared with the improvement in water quality. For unconventional pollutants and toxics (any pollutant not specifically included on the list of conventional pollutants), the BAT requirement was retained but the deadline was shifted to 1984.

Other deadlines were also extended. The date for municipalities to meet the secondary treatment deadline moved from 1977 to 1983. Industrial compliance with the BPT standards was delayed until 1983 whenever the contemplated system had the potential for application throughout the industry.

The final modification made by the 1977 amendments involved the introduction of pretreatment standards for waste being sent to a publicly owned treatment system. These standards were designed to prevent the discharges that could inhibit the treatment process and to prevent the introduction of toxic pollutants that would not be treatment by the waste treatment facility. Existing facilities were required to meet the standards three years after the date they were published, while facilities constructed later would be required to meet the pretreatment regulations upon commencement of operations.

Nonpoint Sources.   In contrast to the control of point sources, EPA was given no specific authority to regulate nonpoint sources. This type of pollution was seen by Congress as a state responsibility.

Section 208 of the act authorized federal grants for state-initiated planning that would provide implementable plans for area wide waste treatment management. Section 208 further specified that this area wide plan must identify significant nonpoint sources of pollution, as well as procedures and methods for controlling them. The reauthorization of the Clean Water Act, passed over President Reagan's veto during February 1987, authorized an additional $400 million for a new program to help states control runoff, but it still left the chief responsibility for controlling nonpoint sources to the states.

The main federal role for controlling nonpoint sources has been the Conservation Reserve Program. Designed to remove some 40 to 45 million acres of highly erodible land from cultivation, this act provides subsidies to farmers for planting grass or trees. The Department of Agriculture expects that this act will result in a national reduction of total erosion by 8.6% and a reduction in nitrogen, phosphorus, and total suspended solid loadings by between 7.8 and 9.6%.[6]

The Safe Drinking Water Act

The 1972 policy focused on achieving water quality sufficiently high for fishing and swimming. Because that quality is not high enough for drinking water, the Safe Drinking Water Act of 1974 issued more stringent standards for community water systems. The primary drinking water regulations set maximum allowable concentration levels for bacteria, turbidity (muddiness), and chemical-radiological contaminants. National secondary drinking water regulations were also established to protect "public welfare" from odor and aesthetic problems which may cause a substantial number of people to stop using the affected water system. The secondary standards are advisory for the states; they cannot be enforced by EPA.

The 1986 amendments required EPA to issue primary standards within three years for 83 contaminants and at least 25 more by 1991, to set standards based on best available technology, and to monitor public water systems for both regulated and unregulated chemical contaminants.[7] Approximately 60,000 public water systems are subject to these regulations. Civil and criminal penalties for any violations of the standards were also increased by the amendments.

Ocean Pollution

Oil Spills. The Clean Water Act prohibits discharges of "harmful quantities" of oil into navigable waters. Since EPA regulations define "harmful" to include all discharges which "violate applicable water quality standards or cause a film or sheen upon the surface of the water," virtually all discharges are prohibited.

Industry responsibilities include complying with Coast Guard regulations (which deal with contingency planning in case of a spill and various accident avoidance requirements)[8] and assuming the financial liability for any accident. If a spill does occur, it must be immediately reported to the Coast Guard or EPA. Failure to report a spill can result in a fine up to $10,000 and/or imprisonment for not more than one year.

In addition to giving notice, the discharger must either contain the spill or pay the cost of cleanup by a responsible government agency. The discharger's

---

6 Marc O. Ribaudo, *Water Quality Benefits from the Conservation Reserve Program*, Agricultural Economic Report No. 606 (Washington, DC: U.S. Department of Agriculture, 1989).

7 The regulations and maximum contaminant levels can be found in 40 CFR 141.

8 Most of the Coast Guard regulations are authorized by the Port and Safety Tanker Act of 1978 and two international conventions on oil spills to which the United States is a party.

liability for the government's actual removal cost is limited to $50 million unless willful negligence or willful misconduct can be proved. Successful proof of willful negligence or willful misconduct eliminates the liability limit. In addition to cleanup costs, removal costs also include compensation for damages to natural resources. (Natural resource damages are defined as "any costs or expenses incurred by the federal government or any state government in the restoration or replacement of natural resources damaged or destroyed as a result of a discharge of oil . . .".)

Ocean Dumping.   Except for oil spills, which are covered by the Clean Water Act and the Oil Pollution Act of 1990, discharges to the ocean are covered by the Marine Protection Research and Sanctuaries Act of 1972. This act governs all discharges of wastes to ocean waters within U.S. territorial limits and discharges of wastes in ocean waters by U.S. vessels or persons regardless of where the dumping occurs. With only a few exceptions no ocean dumping of industrial wastes or sewer sludge is now permitted.[9] Radiological, chemical, and biological warfare agents and high-level radioactive wastes are specifically prohibited by the statute. Under the amended statute, the only ocean dumping activities permitted are the disposal of dredged soil. This dumping is subject to specific regulations and is approved on a case-by-case basis.

Citizen Suits

The degree to which environmental quality is improved by public policy depends not only on the types of policies, but also on how well those policies are enforced. Policies which initially seem to offer promise may, in the glare of hindsight, prove unsuitable if enforcement is difficult or lax.

The enforcement of the environmental statutes has long been the responsibility of state and federal environmental agencies. Enforcement at the state and federal level occurs through administrative proceedings or through civil and criminal judicial action. Since limited staff and resources do not enable these government agencies to fully enforce all of the environmental statutes, however, these methods alone do not provide the necessary level of enforcement.

During the early 1970s a pervasive recognition that the government had neither the time nor resources to provide sufficient enforcement led Congress to create a private alternative—citizen suits. Though citizen suits are now authorized by a number of different environmental statutes, the program has been particularly successful in enforcing the Clean Water Act.

---

9 Sewer sludge from New York City and its environs is the major exception, but the statute prohibits this dumping by 1991.

Empowered as private attorney generals, citizens are authorized to exercise oversight over government actions and to initiate civil proceedings against any private or public polluter violating the terms of its effluent standard. Environmental groups such as the Natural Resources Defense Council and the Sierra Club have become active participants in the process. Citizens may sue for an injunction (a court order requiring the illegal discharge to cease), but in addition are also given the power to " . . . apply any appropriate civil penalties."[10] The amount of penalty can vary between $10,000 and $25,000 per day, per violation.

EFFICIENCY AND COST EFFECTIVENESS

Ambient Standards and the Zero Discharge Goal

The 1956 amendments defined ambient standards as a means of quantifying the objectives being sought. A system of ambient standards allows the control authority to tailor the quality of a particular body of water to its use. Water used for drinking would be subject to the highest standards, swimming the next highest, and so on. Once the ambient standards are defined, the control responsibility could be allocated among sources. Greater efforts to control pollution would be expended where the gap between desired and actual water quality was the largest.

Unfortunately, the early experience with ambient standards for water was not reassuring. Rather than strengthening the legal basis for the effluent standards, while retaining their connection to the ambient standards, Congress chose to downgrade the importance of ambient standards by specifying a zero-discharge goal. Additionally, the effluent standards were given their own legal status apart from any connection with ambient standards. The wrong inference was drawn from the early lack of legislative success.

In his own inimitable style, Mark Twain put the essential point rather well:

> We should be careful to get out of an experience only the wisdom that is in it—and stop there; lest we be like the cat that sits down on a hot stove lid. She will never sit down on a hot stove lid again—and that is well; but also she will never sit down on a cold one anymore.[11]

The most fundamental problem with the current approach is that it rests on the faulty assumption that the tougher the law, the more that is accomplished. The zero-discharge goal provides one example of a case in which passing a tough

---

10 Clean Water Act, Section 505, 33 U.S.C. §1365.

11 From *Pudd'nhead Wilson*, by Mark Twain, 1897, p. 125.

standard, in the hopes of actually achieving a weaker one, can backfire. Kneese and Schultze point out that in the late 1960s the French experimented with a law that required zero discharge and imposed severe penalties for violations.[12] The result was that the law was never enforced because it was universally viewed as unreasonable. Less control was accomplished under this unenforceable law than would have been accomplished with a less stringent but enforceable one.

Is the United States case comparable? It appears to be. In 1972 EPA published an estimate of the costs of meeting a zero-discharge goal, assuming that it is feasible. They concluded that over the decade from 1971 to 1981, removing 85 to 90% of the pollutants from all industrial and municipal effluents would cost $62 billion. Removing all of the pollutants would cost $317 billion, more than five times as much, and this figure probably understates the true cost.[13]

Is this cost justified? Probably not for *all* pollutants, though for some it may be. Unfortunately, the zero-discharge goal makes no distinction among pollutant types. For some fund pollutants it seems extreme. Perhaps the legislators realized this because when the legislation was drafted, no specific timetables or procedures were established to ensure that the zero discharge goal would be met by 1985 or, for that matter, anytime.

National Effluent Standards

The first prong in the two-pronged Congressional attack on water pollution was the national effluent standards (the other being subsidies for the construction of publicly owned waste treatment facilities). Deciding on the appropriate levels for these standards for each of the estimated 60,000 sources is not a trivial task. Not surprisingly, difficulties arose.

Enforcement Problems. Soon after passage of the 1972 amendments, EPA geared up to assume its awesome responsibility. Relying on a battery of consultants, it began to study the technologies of pollution control available to each industry in order to establish reasonable effluent limits. In establishing the guidelines, EPA is required to take into account "the age of the equipment and facilities involved, the process employed, the engineering aspects of the application of various types of control techniques, process changes, nonwater quality environmental impact (including energy requirements) and such factors as the Administrator deems appropriate . . . ."

---

12 Allen V. Kneese and Charles L. Schultze, *Pollution, Prices, and Public Policy* (Washington, DC: Brookings Institution, 1975).

13 See the discussion in Allen V. Kneese and Charles L. Schultze, *Pollution, Prices, and Public Policy* (Washington, DC: Brookings Institution, 1975): 78.

It is not clear whether this provision means that individual standards should be specified for each source, or general standards for broad categories of sources. Cost effectiveness would require the former, but in a system relying on effluent standards, the transaction costs associated with that approach would be prohibitively high and the delay unacceptably long. Therefore, EPA chose the only feasible interpretation available and established general standards for broad categories of sources. While the standards could differ among categories, they were uniformly applied to the large number of sources within each category.

EPA inevitably fell behind the congressional deadlines. In fact, not one effluent standard was published within the year deadline. As the standards were published, they were immediately challenged in the courts. By 1977 some 250 cases were already pending, challenging the published standards.[14] Some of the challenges were successful, requiring EPA to revise the standards. All of this took time.

By 1977 EPA was having so much trouble defining the BPT standards that the deadlines for the BAT standards were completely unreasonable. Furthermore, for conventional pollutants, not only the deadlines but the standards themselves were irrational. Many bodies of water would have met the ambient standards without the BAT standard, while for others the effluent standards were not sufficient, particularly in areas with large nonpoint pollution problems. In addition in some cases the technologies required by BPT would not be compatible (or even necessary) once the BAT standards were in effect. The situation was in a shambles.

The 1977 amendments changed both the timing of the BAT standards (delaying the deadlines) and their focus (toward toxic pollutants and away from conventional pollutants). As a result of these amendments, EPA was required to develop industry effluent standards based on the BAT guidelines for control of 65 classes of toxic priority pollutants. In a 1979 survey EPA discovered that all primary industries regularly discharge one or more of these toxic pollutants. As of 1980 EPA had proposed BAT effluent limitations for control of toxic priority pollutants for nine primary industries.

The 1977 amendments certainly improved the situation. Because toxics represent a more serious problem, it makes sense to set stricter standards for those pollutants. Extension of the deadlines was absolutely necessary; there was no alternative.

These amendments have not, however, resulted in a cost-effective strategy. In particular, they tend to retard technological progress and to assign the responsibility for control in an unnecessarily expensive manner.

---

14 A. Myrick Freeman III, "Air and Water Pollution Policy," in *Current Issues in U.S. Environmental Policy*, Paul R. Portney, ed. (Baltimore: Johns Hopkins University Press for Resources for the Future, 1978): 46.

Allocating Control Responsibility. Because the effluent standards established by EPA are based upon specific technologies, these technologies are known to the industries. Therefore, in spite of the fact that the industry can choose any technology that keeps emissions under the limitation stated in the standard, in practice, industries tend to choose the specific equipment cited by EPA when it established the standard. This, they reason, minimizes their risk. If anything goes wrong and they are hauled into court, they can simply argue they did precisely what EPA had in mind when it set the standard.

The problem with this reaction is that it focuses too narrowly on a particular technology rather than on the real objective, emission reduction. The focus should be less on the purchase of a specific technology and more on doing what is necessary to hold emissions down, such as maintenance, process changes, and so on. In a field undergoing rapid technological change, tying all control efforts to a particular technology (which may become obsolete well before the standards are revised) is a poor strategy. Unfortunately, technological stagnation has become a routine side effect of the current policy to the detriment of securing clean water.

In allocating the control responsibility among various sources, EPA was constrained by the inherent difficulty of making unique determinations for each source and by limitations in the act itself, such as the need to apply relatively uniform standards.[15] We know from Chapter 14 that uniform effluent standards are not cost-effective, but it remains an open question whether or not the resulting increases in cost are sufficiently large to recommend an alternative approach, such as effluent charges or permits. The fact that the cost increases are large in the control of stationary-source air pollution does not automatically imply that they are large for water pollution control as well.

A number of empirical studies have investigated how closely the national effluent standards approximate the least-cost allocation (Table 18.2). These studies support the contention that the EPA standards are not cost-effective, though the degree of cost ineffectiveness is typically smaller than that associated with the standards used to control air pollution.

Perhaps the most famous study examining the cost effectiveness of uniform standards in contrast with emission and ambient charges and permits was conducted on the Delaware Estuary.[16] This river basin, though small by the standards of the Mississippi or other major basins, drains an area serving a population in excess of 6 million people. It is a highly industrial, densely populated area.

In this study a simulation model was constructed to capture the effect on ambient dissolved oxygen content of a variety of pollutants discharged by a

---

15 These limitations are spelled out in detail in C. James Koch and Robert A. Leone, "The Clean Water Act: Unexpected Impacts on Industry," *Harvard Environmental Law Review* 3 (1979): 96–104.

16 This study is described in some detail in Allen V. Kneese and Blair T. Bower, *Managing Water Quality: Economics, Technology, Institutions* (Baltimore: Johns Hopkins University Press, 1968): Chapter 11; and Allen V. Kneese, *Economics and the Environment* (New York: Penguin Books, 1977).

TABLE 18.2 Empirical Studies of Water Pollution Control

Study and year	Pollutants covered	Geographic area	CAC benchmark	DO target (mg/liter)	Ratio of CAC cost to least cost
Johnson (1967)	Biochemical oxygen demand	Delaware Estuary-86-mile reach	Equal proportional treatment	2.0 3.0 4.0	3.13 1.62 1.43
O'Neil (1980)	Biochemical oxygen demand	20-mile segment of Lower Fox River in Wisconsin	Equal proportional treatment	2.0 4.0 6.2 7.9	2.29 1.71 1.45 1.38
Eheart, Brill and Lyon (1983)	Biochemical oxygen demand	Willamette River in Oregon	Equal proportional treatment	4.8 7.4	1.12 1.19
		Delaware Estuary in PA, DE, and NJ	Equal proportional treatment	3.0 3.6	3.00 2.92
		Upper Hudson River in New York	Equal proportional treatment	5.1 5.9	1.54 1.62
		Mohawk River in New York	Equal proportional treatment	6.8	1.22

CAC = command and control, the traditional regulatory approach

DO = dissolved oxygen: higher DO targets indicate higher water quality

Source: T. H. Tietenberg, *Emissions Trading: An Exercise in Reforming Pollution Policy* (Washington, DC: Resources for the Future, 1985): 46, Table 5.

large number of polluters into the river at numerous locations. In addition, this model was capable of simulating the cost consequences of various methods used to allocate the responsibility for controlling effluent to meet dissolved oxygen standards.

Four specific methods of allocating responsibility were considered. The first was the *least-cost* (LC) method, which would correspond to an ambient charge or ambient permit system. This method takes both locations of the emissions and control costs into account.

The second method was a *uniform treatment* (UT) strategy in which all discharges were faced with an effluent standard requiring them to remove a given percentage of their waste before discharging the remainder into the river. This method mirrors, in a crude way, the current EPA strategy.

The third method simulated the allocation attained from the use of a *uniform emission charge* (UEC) or an emissions permit system. This method takes control costs but not emission locations into account. The final case simulates a *zoned effluent charge* (ZEC). For this case the river basin was subdivided into a series of zones. All dischargers within a zone would face the same emission charges, while dischargers in different zones could face different emission charges. This fourth simulation was an intermediate step between the first and third strategies. It allowed location to be more of a factor than in the third method but less of a factor than in the first method. The first simulation would be identical to the fourth if the zones were sufficiently small that each discharger was in its own unique zone; it would be identical to the third if one zone contained all sources (Table 18.3).

For control of water pollution, the UT strategy does increase the cost substantially. For either dissolved oxygen objective, the costs are roughly three times higher. Also of interest is the fact that the zonal system results in costs that are quite close to the minimum for the higher DO objective, while the UEC does not. Even rudimentary attempts to take location into account may make a big difference for water pollution just as it does for air pollution.

Despite this evidence, the regulatory reform movement that played such an important role for air pollution control has not had anywhere near the same impact in water pollution control. Aside from the Fox River in Wisconsin (Example 18.2), few examples exist.

The European Experience.   Economic incentives have been important in water pollution control in Europe, where effluent charges play a prominent role in a number of countries.[17] These charge systems take a number of forms. One common approach is illustrated by Czechoslovakia, which uses charges to achieve

---

17 For a summary of this experience, see Frederick R. Anderson et al., *Environmental Improvement through Economic Incentives* (Baltimore: Johns Hopkins University Press for Resources for the Future, 1977): 59–68; and J. B. Opschoor and Hans B. Vos, *Economic Instruments for Environmental Protection* (Paris: OECD, 1989).

TABLE 18.3 Cost of Treatment under Alternative Programs: The Delaware Estuary

DO objective	Program			
	LC	UT	UEC	ZEC
(ppm)	*(million dollars per year)*			
2	1.6	5.0	2.4	2.4
3–4	7.0	20.0	12.0	8.6

Source: From *Ecconomics and the Environment* by Allen V. Kneese. Copyright © 1977 Allen V. Kneese. Reproduced by permission of Penquin Books Ltd. and the author.

predetermined ambient standards. Others, such as West Germany, use charges mainly to encourage firms to control more than their legal requirements. A third group, illustrated by Hungary and East Germany shows, how charge systems have been combined with effluent standards.

Czechoslovakia has used effluent charges to maintain water quality at predetermined levels for more than 15 years. A basic charge is placed on BOD and suspended solids and complemented by a surcharge ranging from 10 to 100%, depending upon the contribution of the individual discharge to ambient pollutant concentrations. The basic rates can be adjusted to reflect the quality of the receiving water. This system is conceptually very close to the ambient emission charge system known to be cost-effective.

The West German charge system was announced in 1976 and implemented in 1981. The level of charge is related to the degree of compliance with the standards. Firms failing to meet their required standards pay a charge on all actual emissions. If, according to the issued permit, federal emission standards (which are separately defined for each industrial sector) are met, the charge is lowered to 50% of the base rate and is applied to the level of discharge implied by the minimum standard. If the firm can prove the discharge to be lower than 75% of minimum standards, one half of the base rate is applied to the (lower) actual discharge level. The charge is waived for three years prior to the installation of new pollution control equipment promising further reductions of at least 20%. Revenues from the charges can be used by the administering authorities for covering administrative costs and for financial assistance to public and private pollution abatement activities.

The final approach, used in Hungary and East Germany, combines effluent charges with effluent standards. The charge is levied on discharges in excess of fixed effluent limits. In the Hungarian system the level of the charge is based on the condition of the receiving waters, among other factors. Initially, the Hungarian charges had little effect, but when the charge levels were raised, a flurry of waste treatment activity resulted.

Though these European approaches differ from one to another and are not all cost effective, their existence suggests that effluent charge system are possible and practical. The German Council of Experts on Environmental Questions es-

EXAMPLE 18.2

Marketable Emission Permits on the Fox River

With the advent of the bubble and offset policies, marketable emission permits have become the centerpiece of the regulatory reform movement in air pollution control. Though no comparable scale of reform exists for control of water pollution, one attempt has been initiated in northern Wisconsin.

The Lower Fox River flows from Lake Winnebago to Green Bay, Wisconsin. Lining the banks of a key 22-mile segment of this river are 10 pulp and paper mills and four municipalities that discharge effluent into the river. During the summer the desired dissolved oxygen targets are not reached at two critical sag points, even when the industrial polluters are in compliance with BPT standards and municipal polluters are providing secondary treatment.

The Wisconsin Department of Natural Resources was faced with meeting the standards in the face of industrial resistance. To assist in choosing a policy strategy, they funded a simulation model of the river to compare traditional regulatory rules with a marketable permit system.

This model revealed significant differences among dischargers, a precondition if the market approach were to reach the environmental goals at a significantly lower cost. Transfer coefficients varied by a factor of 3 and, under traditional abatement rules, marginal abatement costs differed by a factor of 4. The study concluded that the control costs would be 40% higher if the department were to rely on traditional abatement rules. The potential annual savings realized from a permit approach were estimated at $6.7 million.

In March 1981 the department approved regulations allowing dischargers on the Lower Fox River to transfer permits by approved contracts. By 1982 the first trade had already taken place, but that also proved to be the only trade prior to 1990. The system has clearly not lived up to expectations, an experience which probably will inhibit any expansion of the concept to other geographic areas.

Source: This example was drawn from William B. O'Neil, *Pollution Permits and Markets for Water Quality*, an unpublished Ph.D. dissertation completed at the University of Wisconsin-Madison, 1980, and subsequent conversations with the author.

timated the German effluent charge policy to be about one-third cheaper for the polluters as a group than an otherwise comparable uniform treatment policy. Furthermore, it encouraged firms to go beyond the uniform standards when such effort was cost-justified.

Municipal Waste Treatment Subsidies

The second phase of the two-pronged water pollution control program involves subsidies for waste treatment plants. This program has run into problems as well, ranging from deficiencies in the allocation of the subsidies to the incentives created by the program.

The Allocation of Funds. Since the available funds were initially allocated on a first-come, first-served basis, it is not surprising that the funds were not spent in areas having the greatest impact. It was not uncommon, for example, for completed treatment plants to dump effluent that was significantly cleaner than the receiving water. Also, federal funds have traditionally been concentrated on smaller, largely suburban communities rather than the larger cities with the most serious pollution problems.[18]

The 1977 amendments attempted to deal with this problem by requiring states to set priorities for funding treatment works while giving EPA the right, after holding public hearings, to not only veto a state's priority list but to request a revised list. This tendency to ensure that the funds are allocated to the highest-priority projects was reinforced with the passage of the Municipal Wastewater Treatment Construction Grant Amendments of 1981. Under this act states are required to establish project priorities for targeting funds to projects with the most significant water quality and public health consequences.

Operation and Maintenance. The current approach subsidizes the *construction* of treatment facilities but provides no incentive to *operate* them effectively. The existence of a municipal waste treatment plant does not by itself guarantee cleaner water. EPA's annual inspection surveys of operating plants in 1976 and 1977 found only about half of the plants performing satisfactorily. More recent surveys have found that the general level of waste treatment performance has remained substantially unchanged from previous years.

When sewage treatment plants chronically or critically malfunction, EPA may take a city to court to force compliance with either a direct order or a fine. Because

---

18 An extended critical discussion of the manner in which these funds were allocated can be found in A. Myrick Freeman III and Robert H. Haveman, "Clean Rhetoric and Dirty Water," *The Public Interest* (Summer 1972).

of various constitutional legal barriers, it is very difficult to force a city to pay a fine to the federal treasury. Without an effective and credible sanction, EPA is in a difficult position to deal with municipalities. Therefore, the end of the treatment plant malfunction problem cannot yet be pronounced with any assurance.

Capital Costs. Due to the federal subsidies, local areas ended up paying only a fraction of the true cost of constructing these facilities. Since much of the money came from federal taxpayers, local communities had less incentive to hold construction costs down. One study estimated that substantially increasing the local share could reduce capital costs by as much as 30%.[19] Local areas are more careful with their own money.

Pretreatment Standards

To deal with untreatable hazardous wastes entering municipal waste treatment plants EPA has defined pretreatment standards regulating the quality of the waste water flowing into the plants. These standards suffer the same deficiencies as other effluent standards; they are not cost-effective (Example 18.3). The control over wastewater flows into treatment plants provide one more aspect of environmental policy where economic incentive approaches offer yet another opportunity to achieve equivalent results at a lower cost.

Nonpoint Pollution

The current law does little to control nonpoint pollution, which in many areas is a significant part of the total problem. In some ways the government has tried to compensate for this uneven coverage by placing more intensive controls on point sources. Is this emphasis efficient?

It could conceivably be justified on two grounds. If the marginal damages caused by nonpoint sources are significantly smaller than those of point sources, then a lower level of control could well be justified. Since in many cases nonpoint source pollutants are not the same as point source pollutants, this is a logical possibility.

Or, if the costs of controlling nonpoint sources even to a small degree are very high, this could justify benign neglect as well. Are either of these conditions met in practice?

Costs. Because research on nonpoint source pollution control is in its infancy, cost information is scarce. Of the small amount of literature available, one study can give

---

19 Congressional Budget Office, *Efficient Investments in Wastewater Treatment Plants* (Washington, DC: U.S. Congress, 1985).

EXAMPLE 18.3

Cost-Effective Pretreatment Standards

The electroplating operations of the Rhode Island jewelry industry produce high concentrations of cyanide, copper, nickel, and zinc, which are routinely discharged into municipal sewer systems. Since the treatment plants are not designed to remove these hazardous substances, EPA has defined pretreatment standards to prohibit excessive concentrations of these metals from entering the plants. These standards are financially burdensome, with some estimates suggesting that some 30 to 60% of the small firms could go out of business if the standards were imposed.

An economic analysis by Opaluch and Kashmanian (1985) of the alternatives for meeting the EPA concentration objectives concludes that the EPA pretreatment standards achieve the objective at a cost almost 50% greater than the least-cost means of achieving the same concentration objectives. An emission permit system with a permit price of $40 per pound would, after trading, achieve the target at a cost of $12.5 million. Compared to the $19.3 million the EPA proposal would cost, this represents a considerable saving.

If the permits were auctioned off, the government would collect some $5.0 million from the sale. Although the financial burden of this auction system for allocating permits would be lower on the jewelry industry as a whole than complying with the EPA proposal, even considering this $5.0 million transfer, not every segment of the industry would be better off with the auction. In particular, the permit fees paid by large firms would be sufficiently high that they would bear more financial burden under the auction scheme than with the EPA proposal. If the permits were grandfathered (allocated free of charge) rather than auctioned off, however, all existing firms would be better off under the permit system than under the EPA proposal.

Source: James J. Opaluch and Richard M. Kashmanian, "Assessing the Viability of Marketable Permit Systems: An Application in Hazardous Waste Management," *Land Economics* 61 (August 1985): 263–271.

us a sense of the economic analysis. Palmini conducted an analysis of the potential effects of agricultural nonpoint policies on two small rural counties in Illinois.[20] The specific policies he examined were designed to control nitrogen (which can cause eutrophication), sediment (soil erosion), and pesticides. His model relates these policies to the choice of various farming practices, the effects of these choices on costs, and the financial return to farmers after covering variable costs.

His results indicated that rather dramatic reduction (74%) in soil erosion could be achieved at a cost of less than 1% of the earnings after variable costs were covered. A ban on selected pesticides was predicted to cause a switch to other less damaging pesticides, which would reduce the return to farmers by 0.7%.

The major estimated economic impact came from policies designed to reduce nitrogen use. Palmini considered the effects of quantity restrictions (ceilings on amount used per acre) and the impact of taxes on nitrogen use. Quantity restrictions necessary to reduce pollution were estimated to substantially reduce revenues. Since the demand for nitrogen is price inelastic, very high rates of taxation would be needed to reduce nitrogen use very much.

The extra expense of nitrogen control would represent a large financial burden on farmers which they could only pass on in higher prices if all farmers were subjected to similar controls. This would make unilateral state control difficult because it would place the farmers in that state in jeopardy.

This study suggests that some nonpoint control can probably be reasonably undertaken, since the costs seem low. Yet it also suggests that the conclusion that all nonpoint sources can be cheaply controlled is not correct. As in other areas of environmental policy, the form and intensity of government intervention would have to be tailored to the specific problem.

The fact that point and nonpoint sources have received such different treatment from EPA suggests the possibility that costs could be lowered by a more careful balancing of these control options. One study of phosphorous control in the Dillon reservoir in Colorado by Industrial Economics, Inc. supports the validity of this suspicion.[21]

In this reservoir, four municipalities constitute the only point sources of phosphorous, while there are numerous uncontrolled nonpoint sources in the area. The combined phosphorous load on the reservoir from point and nonpoint sources was projected to exceed its assimilative capacity.

The traditional way to rescue the projected phosphorous load would be to impose even more stringent controls on the point sources. The study found, however, that by following a balanced program controlling both point and nonpoint sources,

20 Dennis J. Palmini, "The Secondary Impact of Nonpoint Pollution Controls: A Linear Programming–Input/Output Analysis," *Journal of Environmental Economics and Management* 9 (September 1982): 263–278.

21 Industrial Economics, Inc., *Case Studies on the Trading of Effluent Loads: Dillon Reservoir Final Report* (Cambridge, MA: Industrial Economics, 1984).

the desired phosphorous target could be achieved at a cost of approximately $1 million a year less than would be spent if only point sources were controlled more stringently. The more general point to be carried away from this study is that as point sources are controlled to higher and higher degrees, rising marginal control costs will begin to make controlling nonpoint sources increasingly attractive.

Oil Spills

One of the chief characteristics of the current approach to oil spills is that it depends heavily on the ability of the legal system to internalize the costs of a spill through liability law. In principle, the approach is straightforward. By forcing the owner of a vessel to pay for the costs of cleaning up the spill, including compensation for natural resource damages, a powerful incentive to exercise care is created. But is the outcome likely to be efficient in practice?

One problem with legal remedies is their high administrative cost. As Example 18.4 points out, assigning the appropriate penalties is no trivial matter. Even if the court were able to act expeditiously, the doctrines it imposes are not necessarily efficient since the financial liability for cleaning up spills is limited by statute. This point is demonstrated in Figure 18.1 which depicts the incentives of a vessel owner to take precaution. The owner will minimize costs by choosing the level of precaution which equates the marginal cost of additional precaution with the resulting reduction in the marginal expected penalty. The marginal reduction in expected penalty is a function of two factors: the likelihood of a spill and the magnitude of financial obligation it would trigger. This function slopes downward because larger amounts of precaution are presumed to yield smaller marginal reductions in both the likelihood and magnitude of resulting accidents.

The vessel owner's cost-minimizing choice with unlimited liability is depicted as Q^*. As long as the imposed penalty equaled the actual damage and the probability of having to pay the damage, once an accident occurred, was 1.0, this outcome would normally be efficient. The external costs would be internalized. The owner's private costs would be minimized by taking all possible cost-justified precaution measures to reduce both the likelihood and the seriousness of any resulting spill; taking precautions would simply be cheaper than paying for the cleanup.

Limited liability, however, produces a different outcome. With limited liability the expected penalty function rotates inward for levels of precaution lower than that level which would produce an accident resulting in damages exactly equal to the limit.[22] Lower levels of precaution imply damages which exceed the limit, but the vessel owner would not have to pay anything above the

---

22 To avoid confusion, note that the marginal expected penalty for additional precaution when the damage would exceed the liability limit is not zero. While further precaution does not lower the ultimate penalty in this range, it does lower the likelihood of an accident and, hence, the expected penalty.

EXAMPLE 18.4

Anatomy of an Oil Spill Suit: Amoco Cadiz

On March 17, 1978, the *Amoco Cadiz*, an oil transport ship traveling in a bad storm, lost steering control and, after unsuccessful towing attempts, drifted onto the rocks off the shore of Portsall, France, on the Brittany Coast. Ultimately the ship broke in two and discharged 220,000 tons of crude and 4000 tons of bunker fuels along the coast of a resort area, two months prior to the opening of the tourist season.

Before the end of the year of the grounding, a mountain of claims had been filed involving France, a consortium of resort owners and fishermen, Amoco (the owner of the vessel), Bugsier (the owner of the tug), Shell oil (the owner of the oil being carried at the time), and Astilleros Espanoles (the Spanish company that built the *Amoco Cadiz*). After extensive and expensive preparations by all parties, the trial began in May of 1982.

During March 1984 a preliminary opinion was issued finding Amoco and the shipbuilder jointly liable. The process then turned to the separate issue of the magnitude of the damages to be awarded. On February 21, 1989, a judgment of 670 million francs was levied against Amoco and Astilleros. The verdict was immediately appealed.

The trial judge, now retired from the bench, summed up the situation:

> So here we are, twelve years after the accident, eleven years after the suit was filed, with the plaintiffs in possession of an enormous judgement and subject to enormous legal fees without one cent having changed hands. The case marches onward to the Court of Appeals with each principal party expected to appeal those aspects of the final judgement with which they disagree. This raises the possibility, almost unimaginable, but very real, that the whole case could have to be tried again.

Source: Frank J. McGarr, "Inadequacy of Federal Forum for Resolution of Oil Spill Damages," a talk given at a conference on oil spills at Newport, Rhode Island, on May 16, 1990. Judge McGarr was the trial judge for the *Amoco Cadiz* case.

---

limit. (The only benefit to the vessel owner faced with limited liability of increasing precaution at lower levels of precaution is the reduction in the likelihood of a spill; in this range increasing precaution does not reduce the magnitude of the financial payment should a spill occur.) The deviation in the magnitude of the limited expected penalty function from the normal expected penalty function is greatest at lower levels of precaution; it declines

FIGURE 18.1 Oil spill liability.

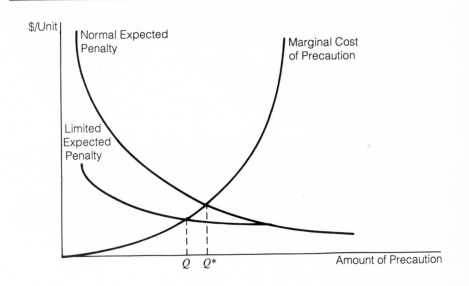

to zero at that precaution level where the expected magnitude of an accident is equal to the liability limit.

What is the effect of limited liability on the vessel owner's choice of precaution levels? As long as the liability limit is binding (which appears to routinely be the case with recent spills), the owner will chose too little precaution. (The owner's choice is depicted as *Q* in Figure 18.1.) Both the number and magnitude of resulting spills would be inefficiently large.[23]

Citizen Suits[24]

Initiated during the 1970s, citizen suits add a private enforcement alternative to public enforcement in correcting environmental market failures. Public and private enforcement are partial substitutes. If government enforcement were complete, all polluters would be in compliance and citizen suits would have no role to play. Noncompliance is a necessary condition for a successful suit. In the early

---

23 Suppose at the efficient level of precaution the magnitude of a resulting spill was less than the liability limit. How would this be depicted graphically? Would you expect the vessel owner's choice to be efficient?

24 This section benefitted from an honors research project on the economics of citizen suits completed by Wendy Naysnerski, a former undergraduate student of the author.

1980s when public enforcement decreased, private enforcement—citizen suits—increased to take up the slack. Lax public enforcement appears to have played a significant role in the rise of citizen suits.

All attorney's fees incurred by the citizen group in any successful action under the Clean Water Act must be reimbursed by the defendants. Reimbursement of attorney's fees has affected both the level and focus of litigation activity. By lowering the costs of bringing citizen suits, attorney fee reimbursement has allowed citizen groups to participate far more often in the enforcement process than otherwise would have been possible. Since courts only reimburse for appropriate claims (noncompliance claims that are upheld by the court), citizen groups are encouraged to litigate only appropriate cases.

The existence of citizen suits should affect the decision-making process of the polluting firm. Adding citizen suits to the enforcement arena increases the expected penalty to the noncomplying firm by increasing the likelihood that the firm will face an enforcement action. While this can be expected to increase the amount of precaution taken by the firm, the unavailability of compliance data makes it impossible to confirm this expectation, though participants believe compliance has increased.

While citizen suits probably do lead to greater compliance, greater compliance is not necessarily efficient. Complete compliance is not necessarily efficient if the defendant polluters face inefficiently harsh standards. If the standards are excessively high, citizen suits have the potential to promote inefficiency by forcing firms to meet standards where the marginal benefits are significantly lower than the marginal costs. However, if the effluent standards are either inefficiently low or efficient, the existence of citizen suits will necessarily create a more efficient outcome. In these cases increasing compliance is perfectly compatible with efficiency.

An Overall Assessment

Though the benefit estimates from water pollution control are subject to much uncertainty, they do exist. While being careful not to place too much reliance on them, we can see what information can be gleaned from the studies in existence.

Freeman has summarized these studies, focusing on 1985 as a target year.[25] His survey of the field suggests that the 1985 benefit (in 1984 dollars) from conventional water pollution control policy could be as low as $5.7 billion or as high as $27.7 billion with a most likely point estimate of $14.0 billion. This compares to estimated 1985 annual costs (in 1978 dollars) ranging from a low

---

25 A. Myrick Freeman III, "Water Pollution Policy," in *Public Policies for Environmental Protection,* Paul R. Portney, ed. (Washington, DC: Resources for the Future, 1990): 122–126.

of $25 billion to a high of $30 billion. Thus Freeman estimates that the net benefit from conventional control is probably negative.

Using cost-effective policies rather than the current approach, it would be possible to reduce costs substantially without affecting the benefits. Cost effectiveness would require the development of better strategies for point source control and for achieving a better balance between point and nonpoint source control. The resulting reduction in costs probably would cause net benefits to become positive. That result would not necessarily make the policy efficient, however, because the level of control might still be too high or too low. Unfortunately, the evidence is not rich enough to prove whether the overall level of control maximizes the net benefit.

In addition to promoting current cost effectiveness, economic incentive approaches would stimulate and facilitate change better than a system of rigid, technology-based standards. Russell has attempted to assess the importance of the facilitating role by simulating the effects on the allocation of pollution control responsibility in response to regional economic growth, changing technology, and changing product mix.[26] Focusing on the steel, paper and petroleum refining industries in the 11 county Delaware Estuary Region, his study estimated the change in permit use for three water pollutants (BOD, total suspended solids, and ammonia) that would have resulted if a marketable permit system were in place over the 1940–1978 period. The calculations assume that the plants existing in 1940 would have been allocated permits to legitimize their emissions at that time, that new sources would have had to purchase permits, and that plant shutdowns or contractions would free up permits for others to purchase.

This study found that for almost every decade and pollutant a substantial number of permits would have been made available by plant closing, capacity contractions, product-mix changes, and/or by the availability of new technologies. In the absence of a marketable permit program, a control authority would not only have to keep abreast of all technological developments so emission standards could be adjusted accordingly, but it would also have to ensure an overall balance between effluent increases and decreases so as to preserve water quality. This tough assignment is handled completely by the market in a marketable permit system, thereby facilitating the evolution of the economy by responding flexibly and predictably to change.

Marketable permits encourage, as well as facilitate, this evolution. Since permits have value, in order to minimize costs firms must continually be looking for new opportunities to control emissions at lower cost. This search eventually results in the adoption of new technologies and in the initiation of changes in the product-mix which result in lower amounts of emissions. The pressure on

---

26 Clifford O. Russell, "Controlled Trading of Pollution Permits," *Environmental Science and Technology* 15 (January 1981): 1–5.

sources to continually search for better ways to control pollution is a distinct advantage that economic incentive systems have over bureaucratically defined standards.

SUMMARY

Historically, policies for controlling water pollution have been concerned with conventional pollutants discharged into surface waters. More recently, concerns have shifted toward toxic pollutants, which apparently are more prevalent than previously believed; toward ground water, which traditionally was thought to be an invulnerable pristine resource; and toward the oceans, which were mistakenly considered immune from most pollution problems because of their vast size.

Early attempts at controlling water pollution followed a path similar to that of air pollution control. Legislation prior to the 1970s had little impact on the problem. Frustration then led to the enactment of a tough federal law that was so ambitious and unrealistic that little progress resulted.

There the similarity ends. Whereas in air pollution a wave of recent reforms have improved the process by making it more cost-effective, no parallel exists for control of water pollution. Current policy toward cleaning up rivers and lakes is based upon the subsidization of municipal waste treatment facilities and national effluent standards imposed on industrial sources.

The former approach has been hampered by delays, by problems in allocating funds, and by the fact that about half of the constructed plants are not performing satisfactorily. The latter approach has given rise to delays and to the need to define the standards in a series of court suits. In addition, effluent standards have assigned the control responsibility among point sources in a way that excessively raises cost. Nonpoint pollution sources have, until recently, been virtually ignored. Technological progress is inhibited rather than stimulated by the current approach. Benefit-cost analyses focusing on 1985 show the net benefit from the current approach to be negative.

This lack of progress could have been avoided. It did not result from a lack of toughness. Rather, it has resulted from a reliance on direct regulation rather than on emission charges or emission permits, which are more flexible and cost-effective in both the dynamic and static sense. In this respect the United States can perhaps take some lessons from the European experience.

The court system has assumed most of the responsibility for controlling oil spills. Those responsible for the spills are assessed the financial liability for cleaning up the site and compensating for any resulting damages to natural resources. While in principle this approach can be efficient, in practice it has been hampered by liability limitations and the huge administrative burden an oil spill trial entails.

Enforcement is always a key to successful environmental and natural resource policy. One recent innovation in enforcement involves giving private citizen groups the power to bring noncomplying firms into court. By raising the likelihood that noncomplying firms would be brought before the court and assessed penalties for noncompliance, this new system can be expected to increase compliance.

FURTHER READING

Anderson, Frederick R. et al. *Environmental Improvement through Economic Incentives* (Baltimore: Johns Hopkins University Press for Resources for the Future, 1977). This book sympathetically analyzes the political, legal, and technical problems that must be faced in a more widespread reliance on emission or effluent charges. An extensive survey of existing and proposed charge systems is included.

Freeman, A. Myrick III. "Water Pollution Policy," in *Public Policies for Environmental Protection,* Paul R. Portney, ed. (Washington, DC: Resources for the Future, 1990). An excellent, detailed analysis of control policy for water pollution, including the 1977 amendments.

Kneese, Allen V. and Blair T. Bower. *Managing Water Quality: Economics, Technology, Institutions* (Baltimore: Johns Hopkins University Press for Resources for the Future, 1968). Generally considered one of the classics in the field. Contains, among many others, chapters describing the Delaware Estuary Study and pollution-control policies in Europe.

Kneese, Allen V. and Charles L. Schultze. *Pollution, Prices, and Public Policy* (Washington, DC: Brookings Institution, 1975). A highly readable analysis of water pollution (as well as air pollution) control policy by two highly respected economists.

ADDITIONAL REFERENCES

Ashworth, John, Ivy Papps, and David Storey. "Assessing the Impact upon the British Chlor-Alkali Industry of the EEC Directive on Discharges of Mercury into Waterways," *Land Economics* 63 (February 1987): 72–78.

Bevis, Brian and Ian Dobbs. "Firm Behavior under Regulatory Control of Stochastic Environmental Wastes by Probabilistic Constraints," *Journal of Environmental Economics and Management* 14 (June 1987): 112–127.

Brown, G. Jr., and R. Johnson. "Pollution Control by Effluent Charges: It Works in the Federal Republic of Germany, Why Not in the U.S.?", *Natural Resources Journal* 24 (1984): 929–966.

Eheart, J. Wayland, E. Downey Brill, Jr. and Randolph M. Lyon. "Transferable Discharge Permits for Control of BOD: An Overview," in *Buying a Better Environment: Cost-Effective Regulation through Permit Trading,* Erhard F. Joeres and Martin H. David, eds. (Madison, WI: University of Wisconsin Press, 1983): 163–195.

Feenberg, Daniel and Edwin S. Mills. *Measuring the Benefits of Water Pollution Abatement* (New York: Academic Press, 1980).

Freeman, A. Myrick III. *Air and Water Pollution Control: A Benefit-Cost Assessment* (New York: Wiley, 1982).

Griffin, Ronald C. "Environmental Policy for Spatial and Persistent Pollutants," *Journal of Environmental Economics and Management* 14 (March 1987): 41–53.

Johnson, Edwin L. "A Study in the Economics of Water Quality Management" *Water Resources Research* 3 (Second Quarter, 1967): 291–305.

Koch, C. James and Robert A. Leone. "The Clean Water Act: Unexpected Impacts on Industry," *Harvard Environmental Law Review* 3 (1979): 84–111.

Leone, Robert A. and John E. Jackson. "The Political Economy of Federal Regulatory Activity: The Case of Water Pollution Controls," in *Studies in Public Regulation*, Gary Fromm, ed. (Cambridge, MA: MIT Press, 1981).

McConnell, Virginia D., John H. Cumberland, and Patrice L. Gordon. "Regional Marginal Costs and Cost Savings from Economies of Scale in Municipal Waste Treatment: An Application to the Chesapeake Bay" *Growth and Change* 19 (Fall 1988): 1–13.

O'Neil, William B. "Pollution Permits and Markets for Water Quality," Ph.D. dissertation (University of Wisconsin–Madison 1980).

Opaluch, James J. and Thomas A. Grigalunas. "Controlling Stochastic Pollution Events with Liability Rules: Some Evidence from OCS Leasing," *Rand Journal of Economics* 15 (1984): 142–151.

Peskin, Henry M., and Eugene P. Seskin. *Cost-Benefit Analysis and Water Pollution Control Policy* (Washington, DC: Urban Institute, 1975).

Raucher, Robert L. "The Benefits and Costs of Policies Related to Groundwater Contamination," *Land Economics* 62 (February 1986): 33–45.

Ribaudo, Marc O. "Targeting the Conservation Reserve Program to Maximize Water Quality Benefits" *Land Economics* 65 (November 1989): 320–332.

Rothfelder, M. "Reducing the Cost of Water Pollution Control under the Clean Water Act," *Natural Resources Journal* 22 (April 1982): 407–421.

Segerson, Kathleen. "Uncertainty and Incentives for Nonpoint Pollution Control" *Journal of Environmental Economics and Management* 15 (March 1988): 87–98.

Spurlock, S. R. and I.D. Clifton. "Efficiency and Equity Aspects of Nonpoint Source Pollution Controls," *Southern Journal of Agricultural Economics* 14 (December 1982): 123–129.

Walker, D. J. "A Damage Function to Evaluate Erosion Control Economics," *American Journal of Agricultural Economics* 64 (November 1982): 690–698.

DISCUSSION QUESTIONS

1. "The only permanent solution to water pollution control will occur when *all* production by-products are routinely recycled. The zero-discharge goal recognizes this reality and forces all dischargers to work steadily toward this solution. Less stringent policies are at best temporary palliatives." Discuss.

2. "In exercising its responsibility to protect the nation's drinking water, the government needs to intervene only in the case of public water supplies. Private water suppliers will be adequately protected without any government intervention." Discuss.

PROBLEMS

1. Consider the situation posed in Problem 1(a) in Chapter 12.

(a) Compute the allocation which would result if 10 emission permits were given to the second source and 9 were given to the first source. What would be the market permit price? How many permits would each source end up with after trading? What would the net permit expenditure be for each source after trading?

(b) Suppose a new source entered the area with a constant marginal cost of control equal to $1600 per unit of emission reduced. Assume further that it would add 10 units in the absence of any control. What would be the resulting allocation of control responsibility? How much would each firm clean up? What would happen to the permit price? What trades would take place?

CHAPTER NINETEEN

Toxic Substances

The fact that a problem will certainly take a long time to solve, and that it will demand the attention of many minds for several generations, is no justification for postponing the study. . . . Our difficulties of the moment must always be dealt with somehow, but our permanent difficulties are difficulties of every moment.

T. S. ELIOT, *Christianity and Culture* (1949)

INTRODUCTION

It is one of the ironies of history that the place which focused public attention in the United States on toxic substances is called the Love Canal. *Love* is not a word any impartial observer would choose to describe the relationships among the parties to that incident.

The Love Canal typifies in many ways the dilemma posed by toxic substances. Until 1953, Hooker Electrochemical (now Hooker Chemical, a subsidiary of Occidental Petroleum Corporation) dumped waste chemicals into an old abandoned waterway known as the Love Canal, near Niagara Falls, New York.[1] At the time it seemed a reasonable solution, since the chemicals were buried in what was then considered to be impermeable clay.

In 1953 Hooker deeded the Love Canal property for $1 to the Niagara Falls Board of Education, which then built an elementary school on the site. The deed specifically excused Hooker from any damages that might be caused by the chemicals. Residential development of the area around the school soon followed.

---

1 Hooker was acquired by Occidental Petroleum in 1968.

The site became the center of controversy when, in 1978, residents complained of chemicals leaking to the surface. News reports emanating from the area included stories of spontaneous fires and vapors in basements. Medical reports suggested that the residents had experienced abnormally high rates of miscarriage, birth defects, and diseases of the liver.

Similar contamination experiences befell Europe and Asia. In 1976 an accident at a F. Hoffman-La Roche & Co. plant in Sevesco spewed dioxin over the Italian countryside. More recently, explosions in a Union Carbide plant in Bhopal, India, spread deadly gases over nearby residential neighborhoods with significant loss of life, and water used to quell a warehouse fire at a Sandoz warehouse near Basel, Switzerland, carried an estimated 30 tons of toxic chemicals into the Rhine River, a source of drinking water for a number of towns in Germany.

In previous chapters we touched on a few of the policy instruments used to combat toxic substance problems. Emission standards govern the types and amounts of substances that can be injected into the air. Effluent standards regulate what can be discharged directly into water sources, and pretreatment standards control the flow of toxics into waste treatment plants. Maximum concentration levels have been established for many substances in drinking water.

This impressive array of policies is not sufficient to resolve the Love Canal problem or others having similar characteristics. When violations of the standards for drinking water are detected, for example, the water is already contaminated. Specifying maximum contaminant levels helps to identify when a problem exists, but it does nothing to prevent or contain the problem. The various standards for air and water emission that do protect against *point* sources do little to prevent contamination by *nonpoint* sources. Furthermore, most water borne toxic pollutants are stock pollutants, not fund pollutants; they cannot be absorbed by the receiving waters. Therefore, temporally constant controls on emissions (a traditional method used for fund pollutants) is inappropriate for these toxic substances since they would allow a steady rise in the concentration over time. Some additional form of control is necessary.

In this chapter we describe and evaluate the policies that deal specifically with the creation, use, transportation and disposal of toxic substances. Many dimensions will be considered. What are appropriate ways to dispose of toxic substances? How can the government ensure that all waste is appropriately disposed of? How do we prevent surreptitious dumping? Who should clean up old sites? Should victims be compensated for damages caused by toxic substances under the control of someone else? If so, by whom? What are the appropriate roles for the legislature and the judiciary in creating the proper set of incentives?

NATURE OF TOXIC SUBSTANCE POLLUTION

The main objective of the current legal system for controlling toxic substances is to protect human health, though protecting other forms of life is a secondary objective. The potential health danger depends upon the toxicity of a substance to humans and their exposure to the substance. *Toxicity* occurs when a living organism experiences detrimental effects following exposure to a substance. In normal concentrations most chemicals are not toxic. Others, such as pesticides, are toxic by design. Yet, in excess concentrations, even a benign substance such as table salt can be toxic.

A degree of risk is involved when using any chemical substance. There are benefits as well. The task for public policy is to define an acceptable risk by balancing the costs and benefits of controlling the use of chemical substances.

Health Effects

The two main health concerns associated with toxic substances are risk of cancer and effects on reproduction.

Cancer. Since the 1900s, mortality rates have fallen for most of the major causes of death. The most conspicuous exception is cancer. Even the mortality rate for heart disease, the number one killer, has declined in recent decades. Meanwhile, the mortality rate for cancer, currently the second most common cause of death, has increased steadily through this century.

While many suspect this increased mortality rate for cancer may be related to increased exposure to carcinogens, due to the latency of the disease proving or disproving this link is very difficult. *Latency* refers to the state of being concealed during the period between exposure to the carcinogen and the detection of cancer. Latency periods for cancer can run from 15 to 40 years in length, but have been known to run as long as 75 years.[2]

In the United States, part of the increase in cancer has been convincingly linked to smoking, particularly among women. The proportion of women who smoke has increased, and the incidence of lung cancer has increased as well. Smoking does not account for all of the increase in cancer, however. A smaller percentage of men smoke today than in earlier decades, and modern cigarettes contain less tar. Despite this, the incidence of lung cancer among men has increased.[3]

Though it is not entirely clear what other agents may be responsible, one suggested cause is the rise in the manufacture and use of synthetic chemicals

---

2 Paul R. Portney, "Toxic Substance Policy and the Protection of Human Health," in *Current Issues in U.S. Environmental Policy*, Paul R. Portney, ed., (Baltimore: Johns Hopkins University Press, 1978): 100.

3 Council on Environmental Quality, *Environmental Quality–1980 (Washington, DC: U.S. Government Printing Office, 1980): 194.*

since World War II.[4] A number of these chemicals have been shown in the laboratory to be carcinogenic. That does not necessarily implicate them in the rise of cancer, however, because it does not take exposure into account. The laboratory can reveal, through animal tests, the relationship between dosage and resulting effects. To track down the significance of any chemical in causing cancer in the general population would require an estimate of how large a segment of the population was exposed to various doses. Currently, our data are not extensive enough to allow these kinds of calculations to be done with any confidence.

Reproductive Effects.[5] Tracing the influence of environmental effects on human reproduction is still a new science. A growing body of scientific evidence, however, suggests that exposure to smoking, alcohol, and chemicals may contribute to infertility, may affect the viability of the fetus and the health of the infant after birth, and may cause genetic defects which can be passed on for generations.

Problems exist for both men and women. In men, exposure to toxic substances has resulted in lower sperm counts, malformed sperm, and genetic damage. In women, exposure can also result in sterility or birth defects in their children.

Policy Issues

Many aspects of the toxic substance problem make it difficult to resolve. Three important aspects are the number of substances involved, latency, and uncertainty.

Number of Substances. Of the 2 million or so known chemical compounds, approximately 70,000 are actively used in commerce. More than 30,000 of these are in substantial use. Many exhibit little or no toxicity, and even a very toxic substance represents little risk as long as it is isolated. The trick is to identify problem substances and to design appropriate policies as responses. The massive number of substances involved make that a difficult assignment. The geographic location of industrial hazardous wastes, a major component of the hazardous waste problem, is given in Table 19.1.

---

4 See, for example, Davis and Magee, who raise this possibility but who also conclude that, because of the latency period, it is too early to tell how much, if any, of the responsibility can be assigned to the increased exposure to synthetic chemicals. See Devra Lee Davis and Brian H. Magee, "Cancer and Industrial Chemical Production," *Science* 206 (December 1979): 1356–1358.

5 For an excellent summary of the literature, see Council on Environmental Quality, *Environmental Quality–1980* (Washington, DC: U.S. Government Printing Office, 1980): 199–205.

TABLE 19.1 Estimated Generation of Industrial Hazardous Waste in 1983 by State (in thousands of metric tons)

State	Quantity	Percent of national generation	State	Quantity	Percent of national generation
Alabama	6,547	2.5	Montana	662	0.2
Alaska	52	*a*	Nebraska	739	0.3
Arizona	642	0.2	Nevada	379	0.1
Arkansas	3,729	1.4	New Hampshire	431	0.2
California	17,284	6.5	New Jersey	12,948	4.9
Colorado	1,902	0.7	New Mexico	619	0.2
Connecticut	4,328	1.6	New York	9,876	3.7
Delaware	894	0.3	North Carolina	3,954	1.5
Florida	2,981	1.1	North Dakota	269	0.1
Georgia	3,338	1.3	Ohio	19,692	7.4
Hawaii	202	0.1	Oklahoma	2,673	1.0
Idaho	1,160	0.4	Oregon	969	0.4
Illinois	14,810	5.6	Pennsylvania	18,260	6.9
Indiana	10,189	3.8	Rhode Island	1,745	0.7
Iowa	1,774	0.7	South Carolina	3,669	1.4
Kansas	2,564	1.0	South Dakota	159	0.1
Kentucky	4,647	1.7	Tennessee	12,159	4.6
Louisiana	13,801	5.2	Texas	34,866	13.1
Maine	337	0.1	Utah	1,139	0.4
Maryland	2,989	1.1	Virginia	4,038	1.5
Massachusetts	4,536	1.7	Vermont	226	0.1
Michigan	12,399	4.7	Washington	5,523	2.1
Minnesota	2,212	0.8	Wisconsin	3,297	1.2
Missouri	6,046	2.3	West Virginia	5,642	2.1
Mississippi	1,816	0.7	Wyoming	572	0.2
			Total	265,595	100.0

*a*Less than one-tenth of one percent.

Projections for 1983 based on 1981 state employment shares found in Bureau of Census, U.S. Department of Commerce, *County Business Patterns 1981* (1981).

Source: Congressional Budget Office, *Hazardous Waste Management: Recent Changes and Policy Alternatives* (May 1985): 22.

Latency. The period of latency exhibited by many of these relationships compounds the problem. Two kinds of toxicity are exhibited: acute and chronic. *Acute toxicity* is present when a short-term exposure to the substance produces a detrimental effect on the exposed organisms. *Chronic toxicity* is present when the detrimental effect arises from exposure of a continued or prolonged nature.

The process of screening chemicals as potentially serious causes of chronic illness is even more complicated than that of screening for acute illness. The traditional technique for determining acute toxicity is the lethal-dose determination, a relatively quick test performed on animals that calculates the dose which results in the death of 50% of the animal population. This test is less well suited for screening substances that exhibit chronic toxicity.

The appropriate tests for discovering chronic toxicity have typically involved subjecting animal populations to sustained low-level doses of the substance over an extended period of time. These tests are very expensive and time-consuming.[6] If all proposed chemicals were subjected to such long and detailed tests, the process itself would preclude the introduction of many new chemicals. If EPA were to do the tests, given its limited resources, it could only test a few of the estimated 500 new chemicals introduced each year. If the industries were to do the tests, the expense could preclude the introduction of many potentially valuable new chemicals which have limited, specialized markets.

The EPA has attempted to respond by developing a series of screening tests that can be accomplished in a shorter period of time and at less expense. The chemicals identified by those screening tests as posing an unacceptable risk can be subjected to more expensive tests. As long as the short tests are sufficiently reliable for screening, the testing problem can be reduced to manageable proportions.

One particularly promising class of screening tests involves adding a chemical substance to a bacteria culture no longer capable of growth. If the substance is a mutagen, and therefore a likely carcinogen, the bacteria resume growth. While these tests are considerably cheaper to perform, the correlation between mutagens and carcinogens is not perfect. Benzene, a known carcinogen, is not a mutagen. Some carcinogens could slip through the mutagen screening process undetected.

Uncertainty. Another dilemma inhibiting policymakers is the uncertainty surrounding the scientific evidence on which regulation is based. Effects uncovered by laboratory studies on animals are not perfectly correlated with effects on humans. Large doses administered over a 3-year period may not produce the same effects as an equivalent amount spread over a 20-year period. Some of the effects are *synergistic*—that is, their effects are compounded by other variable factors. They are either more serious or less serious in the presence of other substances or conditions than they would be in the absence of those substances or conditions.[7] Once cancer is detected, in most

---

6 A two-year bioassay for carcinogenic effects of a single chemical would cost $1.25 million. R. C. Evans, J. Bakst, and M. Dreyfus, *An Analysis of TCSA Reauthorization Proposals* (Washington, DC: EPA Office of Pesticides and Toxic Substances, 1985).

7 For example, it has been shown that asbestos workers are 30 times more likely than their non-smoking fellow workers to get lung cancer if they smoke.

cases it does not bear the imprint of a particular source. Policymakers have to act in the face of limited information.

From an economic point of view, how the policy process reacts to this dilemma should depend on how well the market handles toxic substance problems. To the extent that the market generates the correct information and provides the appropriate incentives, policy may not be needed. On the other hand, when the government can best generate information or create the appropriate incentive, intervention may be called for. As the following pages demonstrate, the nature of the most appropriate policy response may depend crucially on the type of relationship existing between the polluter and the affected party or parties.

MARKET ALLOCATIONS AND TOXIC SUBSTANCES

Toxic substance contamination can arise in a variety of settings. In order to define the efficient policy response, we must examine what responses would be forthcoming in the normal operation of the market. Let's look at three possible relationships between the source of the contamination and the victim: employer-employee, producer-consumer, and producer–third party. The first two involve normal contractual relations among the parties, while the latter involves noncontracting parties whose connection is defined solely by the contamination.

Occupational Hazards

Many occupations involve risk, including, for some people, exposure to toxic substances. Do employers and employees have sufficient incentives to act in concert toward achieving safety in the workplace?

The caricature of the market used by the most ardent proponents of regulation suggests not. In this view the employer's desire to maximize profits precludes spending money on safety. Sick workers can simply be replaced. Therefore, the workers are powerless to do anything about it; if they complain, they are fired and replaced with others who are less vocal.

The most ardent opponents of regulation respond that this caricature omits significant market pressures and is not a particularly accurate guide. They argue that it fails to take into account employee incentives and the feedback effects of those incentives on employers.

If employees are to accept work in a potentially hazardous environment, they will do so only if appropriately compensated. Riskier occupations should call forth higher wages. The increase in wages should be sufficient to compensate them for the increased risk. These higher wages represent a real cost of the hazardous situation to the employer. They also produce an incentive to create a safer work environment, since greater safety would result in lower wages. One cost

FIGURE 19.1   Market provision of occupational safety.

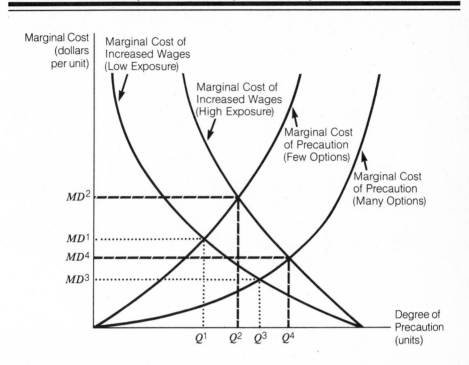

could be balanced against the other. What was spent on safety could be recovered in lower wages (Figure 19.1).

The first type of cost, the marginal increase in wages, is drawn to reflect the fact that the lower the level of precaution, the higher the wage bill. Two such curves are drawn to reflect high-exposure and low-exposure situations. The high-exposure case refers to a situation in which larger numbers of workers are exposed, while in the low-exposure case, few are exposed. The low-exposure cost curve rises more slowly because the situation is less dangerous at the margin. In the high-exposure case the sensitivity of wages to precaution is much higher because the damage caused at the margin is much larger.

The second type of curve, the marginal cost of providing precaution, is drawn to reflect increasing marginal cost. The two different curves depict different production situations. A firm with a few expensive precautionary options will face a steeply sloped marginal cost curve, while a firm with many cheaper options will face a lower marginal cost at every comparable degree of precaution chosen.

The graph depicts four possible outcomes—one for each possible combination of these four marginal cost curves. Notice that very different choices will be made, depending on the circumstances. Also notice that the level of risk chosen (as indicated by the marginal damage, labeled *MD*) and the degree of precaution are not perfectly correlated. The highest marginal risk is MD^2, but the associated level of precaution (Q^2) is not the largest. The reason, of course, is that the cost of taking precautions matters, and sometimes it is cheaper to accept the risk and compensate for it than it is to prevent it.

Because the marginal increased wages curve accurately reflects marginal damages (since the higher wages are demanded by workers to compensate them for damages), these market equilibria are also efficient. Thus, the efficient resolution of the occupational hazards problem varies not only from substance to substance, but from plant to plant as well. As long as this stylized view of the world is correct, the market will tailor the appropriate degree of precaution to the situation.

Proponents point out that this allocation would also allow more choices for workers than would, for example, a system requiring all workplaces to be equally safe. With varying occupational risk, those occupations with more risk (such as working with radioactive materials) would attract people who were less averse to risk. These workers would receive higher than average wages (to compensate them for the increased risk), but paying these higher wages would be cheaper to the firm (and hence, consumers) than producing a workplace safe enough for the average worker. The risk averse workers would be free to choose less risky occupations.

Existing empirical studies make clear that wages in risky occupations do contain a risk premium. Two conclusions about these risk premiums seem clear from these studies: (1) the willingness to pay for apparently similar risk reductions varies significantly across individuals; and (2) the revealed willingness to pay for risk reduction is substantial.[8]

What is the appropriate role for the public sector in controlling contamination in the workplace? One point raised by the court system is whether market solutions always satisfy ethical norms. For example, if the employee is a pregnant woman and the occupational hazard involves potential damage to the fetus, does the expectant mother have the right to risk the unborn child, or is some added protection for the fetus needed? Furthermore, if the lowest cost solution is to ban pregnant, or even fertile, women from a workplace that poses a risk to a fetus, is that an acceptable solution, or is it unfair discrimination against women? As Example 19.1 suggests, these are not idle concerns.

Ethical concerns are not the only challenges for market solutions. The ability of the worker to respond to a hazardous situation depends on his or her knowledge of the seriousness of the danger. With toxic substances, that knowledge is likely to be incomplete. Consequently, the marginal increased wages function may be artificially rotated toward the origin; the employer would

---

8 See the survey of this evidence in W. Kip Viscusi, *Risk by Choice: Regulating Health and Safety in the Workplace* (Cambridge, MA: Harvard University Press, 1983): 93–113.

EXAMPLE 19.1

Susceptible Populations in the Hazardous Workplace

Some employees are especially susceptible to occupational hazards. Pregnant women and women in the childbearing years are particularly vulnerable. When an employer attempts to manage a work situation that poses a hazardous threat, either the susceptible population can be separated from the hazard or the hazard can be controlled to a sufficient level that its risk is acceptable to even the most susceptible employees.

The economic aspects of this choice are easily deduced from Figure 19.1. Suppose that the firm has few control options and is on the uppermost of the two marginal cost-of-precaution curves. By removing the susceptible population, it could face the low-exposure curve. Removal of the susceptible population results in lower marginal risk to the workers, lower costs to the firm, and less precaution taken. But is it fair to those who are removed from their jobs?

This issue came to a head in 1978 when American Cyanamid decided to respond to an occupational risk by banning all fertile women from jobs in the section manufacturing lead chromate pigment at Willow Island, West Virginia. After reviewing the decision, the Occupational Safety and Health Administration (OSHA) cited the company under the general duty clause of the Occupational Safety and Health Act, which requires an employer to provide a workplace free of hazards, and fined it $10,000. That was not the last of it. In early 1980, the Oil, Chemical and Atomic Workers Union sued the company under the 1964 Civil Rights Act on the grounds that the company had discriminated unfairly against women. In March of 1991 the Supreme Court ruled that banning fertile women from any workplace posing a risk to a fetus was not an acceptable way to control risk. The hazards must be reduced.

Source: This example was taken from Council on Environmental Quality, *Environmental Quality–1980* (Washington, DC: U.S. Government Printing Office, 1980): 205.

choose too little precaution. By having access to the health records of all employees the employer may be in the best position to assess the degree of risk posed, but the employer also has an incentive to suppress that information. To publicize risk would mean demands for higher compensatory wages and possible lawsuits.

Information on the dangers posed by exposure to a particular toxic substance is a public good to employees; each employee has an incentive to be a *free rider* on the discoveries of others. Individual employees do not have an incentive to bear the cost of doing the necessary research to uncover the degree of risk. Thus, it seems neither employers nor employees can be expected to produce the efficient amount of information on the magnitude of risk.[9]

As a result, the government may play a substantial role in setting the boundaries on ethical responses, in stimulating research on the nature of hazards, and in providing for the dissemination of information to affected parties. It does not necessarily follow, however, that the government should be responsible for determining the level of safety in the workplace once this information is available and the ethical boundaries are determined.

Our analysis suggesting that the market will not provide an efficient level of information on occupational risk is consistent with recent activity in state legislatures. As of 1982, New York, California, Michigan, and five other states had already enacted "right to know" laws, while similar measures were pending in about 20 state legislatures.[10] These laws require businesses to disclose to their employees and to the public any potential health hazards associated with toxic substances used on the job. Generally employers are required to (1) label toxic substance containers, (2) inventory all toxic substances used in the workplace, and (3) provide adequate training on the handling of these substances to all affected employees.

Product Safety

Exposure to a hazardous or potentially hazardous substance can also occur as a result of using a product, as when eating food containing chemical additives or when using pesticides. Does the market efficiently supply safe products?

One view holds that the market pressures on both parties are sufficient to yield an efficient level of safety. Safer products are generally more expensive to produce and carry a higher price tag. If consumers feel that the additional safety justifies the cost, they will purchase the safer product. Otherwise they won't. Producers supplying excessively risky products will find their market drying up, because consumers will switch to competing brands that are more expensive but safer. Similarly, producers selling excessively safe products (meaning they eliminate, at great cost, risks consumers are perfectly willing to take in return

---

9 Unions would be expected to produce more efficient information flows since they represent many workers and can take advantage of economies of scale in the collection, interpretation, and dissemination of risk information. Available evidence suggests that the preponderance of wage premiums for risk have been derived from unionized workers. See W. Kip Viscusi, *Risk by Choice: Regulating Health and Safety in the Workplace* (Cambridge, MA: Harvard University Press, 1983): 55.

10 These laws are described in Frank Allen, "Battle Building Over 'Right to Know' Laws Regarding Toxic Items Used by Workers," *Wall Street Journal* (4 January 1983): 31. Significantly, proponents of these laws suggest that the targets are not the large chemical companies, which generally have excellent disclosure programs, but the smaller, largely nonunion plants.

for a lower purchase price) find their markets drying up as well. Consumers will choose the cheaper, riskier product.

This theory also suggests that the market will not (and should not) yield a uniform level of safety for all products. Different consumers will have different degrees of risk aversion. While some consumers might purchase riskier, but cheaper, products, others might prefer safer, but more expensive, products.[11]

Thus, it would be common to find products with various safety levels supplied simultaneously, reflecting and satisfying different consumer preferences for risk. Forcing all similar products to conform to a single level of risk would not be efficient. Uniform product safety is no more efficient than uniform occupational safety.

If this view of the market were completely accurate, government intervention to protect consumers would not be necessary to ensure the efficient level of risk. By the force of their collective buying habits, consumers would protect themselves.

The problem with the market's ability to provide such self-regulation is the availability of information on product safety. The consumer acquires his or her information on a product generally from personal experience. With toxic substances the latency period may be so long as to preclude any effective market reaction. Even when some damage results, it is difficult for the consumer to associate it with a particular source. While an examination of the relationships between purchasing patterns of a large number of consumers and their subsequent health might well reveal some suggestive correlations, it would be difficult for any individual consumer to deduce this correlation.

While the government may need to ensure that consumers receive adequate information on product risks, the need to dictate a prevailing level of safety is much less clear, particularly if the dictated level is uniformly applied. In situations where adequate information is available on the risks, consumers should have a substantial role in choosing the acceptable level of risk through their purchases.

Third Parties

The final case involves *third parties*, victims who have no contractual relationship to the source. When groundwater is contaminated by a neighboring waste treatment facility, by surreptitious dumping of toxic wastes, or by the improper applications of a pesticide, the victims would be third parties. In any of these situations, the affected party cannot bring any direct market pressure to bear on the source. Since these nonpoint sources are generally not controlled by the air and water regulations, the case for additional government intervention is strongest for third-party situations.

---

11 A classic example is provided by the manner in which Americans choose their automobiles. It is quite clear that many of the larger domestic cars are safer and more expensive than smaller, cheaper foreign cars. Some consumers are willing to pay for the safety, and others are not.

This does not necessarily imply, however, that executive or legislative remedies are appropriate. The most appropriate response may well come from simply requiring better information on the risk or, as discussed in Chapter 3, from using the judicial system to impose liability.

California's Proposition 65, enacted by voter initiative on November 4, 1986, provides an example of the "better information approach.[12] If a California business exposes anyone to a hazardous substance (other than through drinking water, which is handled separately), the business must provide a "clear and reasonable warning" unless the exposure poses "no signficant risk." (Generally the courts have interpreted "no significant risk" as occurring when the business is complying with an applicable standard.) As a result, signs have begun appearing in such diverse places as bars (warning about alcohol) and gas stations (warning about fumes). Here the emphasis is on educating consumers and allowing them to make the choice about the amount of risk they will accept when no applicable standard has been developed.

Liability law provides one judicial avenue for internalizing the external costs in third-party situations. If the court finds that damage occurred, that it was caused by a toxic substance, and that a particular source was responsible for the presence of the substance, the source can be forced to compensate the victim for the damages caused. Unlike regulations that are uniformly (and, hence, inefficiently) applied, a court decision can be tailored to the exact circumstances involved in the suit. Furthermore, the impact of any particular liability assignment can go well beyond the parties to that case. A decision for one plaintiff can remind other sources that they should take the efficient level of precaution now to avoid paying future damages.

In principle, liability law can force sources, including nonpoint sources, to choose efficient levels of precaution. Unlike regulation, liability law can provide compensation to the victims. How well it functions in practice remains to be seen in the rest of the chapter. Example 19.2 shows how a judicial response to one spill has transformed the way one company handles its environmental responsibilities.

CURRENT POLICY

Common Law

The common-law system is an extremely complicated approach to controlling risks. When a victim seeks recourse through the court system, a number of legal

12 David Roe, "Barking up the Right Tree: Recent Progress in Focusing the Toxics Issue," *Columbia Journal of Environmental Law* 13 (1988): 277–280.

EXAMPLE 19.2

Judicial Remedies in Toxic Substance Control: The Kepone Case

Kepone is a highly toxic substance used in the manufacture of pesticides. Kepone was produced at Hopewell, Virginia, by Life Science Products Company, a company started by former employees of Allied Chemical Corporation. The kepone produced by Life Science was sold to Allied Chemical.

Conditions at the plant and spills into the James River resulted in high contamination levels which affected workers and people eating fish taken from the river. Allied Chemical Corporation was indicted by a grand jury on criminal charges during May 1976, and was subsequently sued by various injured parties. Eventually, it paid more than $20 million in compensation, penalties, and legal fees.

As a result of the suit, Allied and a number of other companies have begun to dramatically increase expenditures on prevention. In 1977 Allied hired Arthur D. Little, a consulting firm, to develop a broad program to anticipate and prevent further accidents. By 1981 Allied had over 400 employees concerned with environmental control.

Interestingly, the staff has discovered that pollution control sometimes yields unexpected benefits. In the past Allied treated its waste, including calcium chloride, from its Baton Rouge plant and discharged it into the river. New regulations from EPA would have raised the costs of treating the waste. Allied decided to look for a market for the calcium chloride and found one, turning a liability into an asset.

The kepone suit changed this corporation's behavior, as well as the behavior of other chemical companies. They have found that anticipating can be much less costly than reacting.

Source: This example is based upon Georgette Jasen, "Like Other New-Breed Environmental Managers, Hillman of Allied Isn't Merely a Trouble Shooter," *The Wall Street Journal* (30 July 1981): 50.

grounds can be used to pursue a claim. Not all of these may be available to every plaintiff (the person initiating the suit), since the appropriate doctrine depends partially on the legal tradition in the jurisdiction where the suit is filed. Not all jurisdictions allow a plaintiff to file on all grounds. Two of the more common legal grounds are negligence and strict liability.

Negligence.   Probably the most common legal theory used by plaintiffs to pursue claims is negligence. This body of law suggests that the defendant (the party allegedly responsible for the contamination) owes a duty to the plaintiff (the affected party) to exercise due care. If that duty has been breached, the defendant is found negligent and is forced to compensate the victim for damages caused. If the defendant is found to have exercised due care and to have performed that duty to the plaintiff, no liability is assessed. Under negligence law the victim bears the liability unless it can be proven that the defendant was negligent.

Interestingly, the test conventionally applied by the courts in deciding whether the defendant has exercised due care, the Learned Hand formula, is fundamentally an economic one. Named after the judge (yes, Learned Hand!) who initially formulated it, this test suggests that the defendant is guilty of negligence if the loss caused by the contamination, multiplied by the probability of contamination, exceeds the cost of preventing the contamination.[13] When correctly applied, this is simply a version of the expected net benefit formula developed in Chapter 4.[14] The maximization of expected net benefits is efficient as long as society is risk-neutral. Therefore, the common-law approach embodied in negligence law in principle is compatible with efficiency.

Sometimes the plaintiff can prove negligence on the part of the defendant by showing that the defendant violated a statute. In many states, any related statutory violation is taken as sufficient proof of negligence.

Strict Liability.   Strict liability can be used by plaintiffs in some states and in some circumstances. Under this doctrine the plaintiff does not have to prove negligence. As long as defendant's activity causes damage, the defendant is declared liable even if the activity is completely legal and complies with all relevant laws.

Strict liability is usually applied in circumstances where the activity in question is inherently hazardous. Since the disposal of toxic substances is frequently considered such an activity, states are increasingly allowing toxic substance suits to be brought under this doctrine. In contrast to negligence, this doctrine transfers liability for damages to the source whether or not the source has exercised much care.

Strict liability can also be compatible with efficiency.[15] The agent dealing with toxic wastes must balance the costs of taking precautions with the likelihood

---

13 For a detailed discussion of this formula, see Richard A. Posner, "A Theory of Negligence," *Journal of Legal Studies* 1 (1972): 29–96.

14 For a description of necessary conditions for the formula to be applied correctly, see J. P. Brown, "Toward an Economic Theory of Liability," *Journal of Legal Studies* 2 (June 1973): 323–339.

15 One well-known case when strict liability will not be efficient is when the victims can influence the likelihood of contamination and the magnitude of the damage caused. With full compensation the victim's incentive to take precautions is undermined. In most toxic substance cases the role of the victim is minimal, so this potential source of inefficiency is not important.

of, and expected costs of, lawsuits. In cases where the precautionary expenditures are particularly high and the damages low, only limited precaution is likely to be taken. However, for truly dangerous substances it is advantageous to take extraordinary precautions and avoid large damages.

Criminal Law

Strict liability and negligence are civil law doctrines where one private party sues another. Increasingly in environmental policy, the civil law approach is being complemented by the use of criminal law in which the government serves as prosecutor, presumably acting as an agent of the people. The kepone case, described in Example 19.2, involved both civil and criminal law.

Criminal law affords regulators a different menu of remedies than available from civil law. Financial penalties imposed under criminal law cannot be covered by insurance as civil penalties can. Jail sentences may be handed out to those found breaking the law. Corporate executives, for example, could spend up to five years in jail for particularly onerous violations of the law. Fines could also be levied against guilty parties.

Several important aspects other than remedies also differentiate the civil and criminal judicial approaches to pollution control. Criminal charges can be brought against only those charged with breaking one or more specific laws, while civil suits can be brought against those causing damage, whether or not a law has been violated. The burden of proof is higher in a criminal trial. To convict a person, the state must prove the defendant is guilty "beyond a reasonable doubt," whereas, in civil trials, the decision is based merely upon the "preponderance of evidence." The presumption of innocence, an important part of criminal trials, has no counterpart in civil trials. Civil trials create no presumption in favor of either party.

The final major difference between civil liability law and criminal law is that *civil liability law compensates victims directly while criminal law does not*. Criminal law focuses on punishing the perpetrator rather than on compensating the victim.[16] Though the severity of punishment can be tailored to the amount of damage caused, the correspondence between the length of a jail sentence and the damage caused is much less indirect than forcing the defendant to pay exact monetary damages. By breaking the link between the monetary damage caused and the punishment received—the cornerstone of liability law—criminal law would be less likely to result in efficient resolu-

---

16 Criminal law remedies forcing restitution do compensate the victim, but they are the exception rather than the rule. With restitution the guilty party is forced to pay a stipulated amount of money to the victim as part of the punishment.

tions of toxic chemical contamination problems than civil law.[17] Efficiency could result, but it would be more of a coincidence than an inherent characteristic of the process.

Statutory Law

These civil and criminal common-law remedies have been accompanied by a host of legislative remedies. The statutes have evolved over time in response to particular toxic substance problems. Each time a new problem surfaced and people were able to get legislators aroused, a new law was passed to deal with it. The result is a collage of laws on the books, each with its own unique focus. We cover only the main ones here.

Federal Food, Drug, and Cosmetic Act.   The first concerns with toxic substances arose with *food additives*, since these are ingested and potentially pose a serious and immediate threat to health. Food and drug additives are regulated under the Federal Food, Drug, and Cosmetic Act of 1938, as amended in 1958. The organization administering this act is the Food and Drug Administration (FDA).

The 1938 act contained a general safety provision authorizing FDA to prohibit the sale of any food which "contains any poisonous or deleterious substance which may render it injurious to health." This provision was complemented in 1958 by a provision known as the Delaney Clause after its legislative sponsor. This provision states that no additive should be deemed safe if it was found to induce cancer in humans or animals. Coupled with the first provision, this addition prohibits any food additive determined by FDA to be a carcinogen in any dosage.

Manufacturers wishing to introduce new food additives or drugs must demonstrate the safety of their products through premarket testing. For cosmetics no premarket testing is required. For the FDA to take any action on cosmetics it must bear the burden of proof to demonstrate the product is unsafe. The burden is on the manufacturer to prove the safety of food additives and drugs.

Occupational Safety and Health Act. The 1970 Occupational Safety and Health Act created the Occupational Safety and Health Administration (OSHA)

---

17 This does not imply, however, that criminal law has no efficient role to play in enforcement. For example, falsifying official reports to EPA is appropriately a criminal offense. Without accurate reports the entire enforcement function could be undermined. Yet it would be difficult to determine the economic value of the damage caused by falsified reports, a prerequisite for assessing a financial civil penalty. In addition incarceration may be an appropriate penalty when the injurer cannot pay the fine due to insufficient assets.

and charged the agency with the regulatory responsibility for protecting workers from hazards in the workplace. The Act also created the National Institute for Occupational Safety and Health (NIOSH) which, among other responsibilities, must make recommendations for the OSHA regulatory standards.

In 1974 OSHA promulgated the first regulation establishing levels of pollutants that would be acceptable in the workplace atmosphere. The statute required the standards to be established at a level sufficiently stringent so that no employee would suffer material impairment of health, even if that employee were exposed to the substance on a regular basis throughout his or her working life. In addition, occupational standards requiring special precautions and/or protective devices have been adopted or proposed for a number of workplace contaminants.

Carcinogens are handled more severely. Once any substance is confirmed as a carcinogen, ambient workplace standards are set, rapidly followed by the imposition of special handling requirements, protective devices, and minimum contact regulations.

The approach taken by OSHA was to specify, often in excruciating detail, acceptable contaminant levels, as well as the approaches to be taken by employers to ensure the attainment of those containment levels.[18] In response to adverse public opinion about silly regulations, in 1978 OSHA revoked 928 previously promulgated regulations as unnecessary.

Federal Environmental Pesticide Control Act. The 1972 Environmental Pesticide Control Act amended the Federal Insecticide, Fungicide, and Rodenticide Act (Congress has a flair for titles!). The thrust of the legislation is to provide for the registration of all pesticides, the certification of individuals applying these pesticides, and the premarket testing of all new pesticides.

All pesticide registrations automatically expire every five years. To secure a new registration, the manufacturer must prove that the benefits derived from that pesticide will outweigh its social costs. When the evidence permits, EPA has the power to prohibit the sale of a pesticide or to restrict its use to specific applications. EPA has used this power to dramatically decrease the use of a number of pesticides, with DDT being the earliest and most publicized example.

Certification procedures for individuals applying the pesticides represent a recognition that the danger posed is to a large extent dependent on how the substances are applied. With this procedure EPA can ensure proper training for commercial applicators, and by threatening the withdrawal of certification (and the livelihood of the applicators), EPA can influence their behavior.

---

18 The humor in the situation was nicely illustrated by an ad for a political candidate opposed to OSHA. A cowboy is pictured riding off to the prairie. On the back of his horse is strapped a plastic toilet required by an OSHA regulation setting the maximum distance any employee could be from a comfort station.

Resource Conservation and Recovery Act.   To counteract the unsafe dumping of toxic wastes, Congress passed Subtitle C of the Resource Conservation and Recovery Act of 1976. This act imposes standards for handling, shipping, and disposing of toxic wastes.

The regulations implementing this act define hazardous waste and establish a cradle-to-grave management system, including standards for generators of hazardous wastes, standards for transporters, and standards and permit requirements for owners and operators of facilities that treat, store, or dispose of hazardous wastes.

The centerpiece of this rather large regulatory system is a manifest system for keeping track of the fate of the substances from their creation to their disposal. Waste generators are required to prepare a manifest for all controlled substances. If the substance is on the EPA list, it must be properly packaged and labeled, and must be delivered only to a permitted waste disposal site. Through this recording system, EPA hopes to monitor all hazardous substances and detect any surreptitious dumping. Failure to comply with the act is punishable by civil penalties and, in certain cases, by fines and imprisonment.

In 1984 this Act was amended by the Hazardous and Solid Waste Amendments of 1984. The 1984 amendments contain three major categories of changes: (1) they expanded the amount of waste covered by the regulations, (2) they limited or, in some cases, banned the use of land disposal for certain kinds of waste, and (3) they brought under regulation some activities not previously controlled, such as underground storage tanks for certain chemicals.

Toxic Substances Control Act.   The 1976 Toxic Substances Control Act was passed as a complement to the Resource Conservation and Recovery Act. Whereas the Resource Conservation and Recovery Act was designed to ensure safe handling and disposal of existing substances, the Toxic Substances Control Act was designed to provide a firmer basis for deciding which of the chemical substances not controlled by the above acts should be allowed to be commercially produced.

This act requires EPA to inventory the approximately 55,000 chemical substances in commerce; to require premanufacture notice to EPA of all new chemical substances; and to enforce recordkeeping, testing, and reporting requirements so that EPA can assess and regulate the relative risks of chemicals. At least 90 days before manufacturing or importing a new chemical, a firm must submit test results or other information to EPA showing that the chemical will not present "an unreasonable risk" to human health or the environment.

On the basis of the information in the premanufacture notification, EPA may limit the manufacture, use, or disposal of the substance. The act is significant in that it represents one of the few instances where the burden of proof is on the manufacturer to prove that the product should be marketed, rather than forcing EPA to show why it should not be marketed.

Comprehensive Environmental Response, Compensation, and Liability Act.
Known popularly as the "Superfund Act," the Comprehensive Environmental

Response, Compensation, and Liability Act of 1980 created a $1.6 billion fund to be used over a five-year period to clean up existing toxic waste sites. The revenue was derived mainly from taxes on chemical industries. It offers compensation for the loss or destruction of natural resources controlled by the state or federal government, but it does not provide any compensation for injured individuals. A $9 billion reauthorization bill was passed in 1986 significantly increasing the amount of money dedicated to the cleanup of these sites.

This act, as amended, authorized federal and state governments to respond quickly to incidents such as occurred in Times Beach, Missouri. Times Beach, a town of 2800 residents located about 30 miles southwest of St. Louis, had been contaminated by dioxin. Dioxin is a waste by-product created during the production of certain chemicals. One such chemical is Agent Orange, the defoliant used during the Vietnam War. The contamination occurred when a state oil hauler bought about 55 pounds of dioxin in 1971 from a now defunct manufacturer, mixed it with oil, and under contract with the local government, spread it on unpaved roads as a dust control measure. On December 23, 1982, after soil tests revealed dangerous levels of dioxin, the Center for Disease Control recommended total evacuation of the town.

By February 22, 1983, the federal government had authorized a transfer of some $33 million from the Superfund to cover the cost of buying out all businesses and residents and relocating them. For its part the state of Missouri has agreed to pay 10% of the $33 million cost into the Superfund, and fund representatives are free to attempt to recover damages from the responsible parties. By June 1983, all but 40 families had been relocated. By 1990 the town was now totally vacant, an eerie reminder of the tragically high human cost that can result from the improper disposal of hazardous wastes.

The existence of the Superfund allows the governments involved to move rapidly. They are not forced to wait until the outcome of court suits against those responsible to raise the money or to face the uncertainty associated with whether the suits would ultimately be successful.

This formidable list of statutory and common-law remedies embodies a variety of approaches to the resolution of toxic substance problems. The question is whether or not these approaches are efficient or cost-effective.

AN ASSESSMENT OF THE LEGAL REMEDIES

The Common Law

Judicial-Legislative Complementarity. Common law provides a potentially useful complement to statutory law for occupational, consumer product, and third-party hazards. For all three types of toxic substance problems, the market may create pressures preventing the flow of information about the dangers of these substances. The parties in the best position to transmit the information (employers or producers) to parties who can best assess the risk (employees, consumers, or third parties) are not always willing to seek or relay the information. In a market where damages are not placed on the source, sources have little incentive to uncover potential problems. Uncovering health problems will only lower sales or increase wages.

Legislative remedies such as the "right to know" laws described earlier are not sufficient if there is too little information to be shared. Because court actions that subject sources to liability for their damages make health damage information useful to the firm, they create incentives to keep good records and to analyze the results. The failure to accurately perceive a health risk could cause an enormous financial burden on the company.[19] It is cheaper to anticipate and prevent damages before the cost becomes prohibitive.

Even premarket testing of consumer products by the government is not an adequate substitute for the judicial approach. Government has neither the staff nor the financial resources to serve as the sole source of health damage information. Some substances inevitably slip through the safety net provided by government testing. It is essential that the prime responsibility for testing fall on the producer, with the costs being passed on to the consumer as part of the price of the product. The government would then bear the responsibility for ensuring the validity of the testing process.

Judicial remedies are especially important in handling third-party contamination. Without liability the incentive to exercise due care by the manufacturers, transporters, users, and disposers of these substances would be inefficiently low. The use of the court system to control the third-party problem was enhanced by the passage of the Resource Conservation and Recovery Act of 1976.

Because of the manifest system created by this act, good information is available to the courts on the types and quantities of substances which are sold or transported. It also assists in tracing responsibility so that the sources can be identified and confronted with the evidence. This recordkeeping system is immensely costly, however, and may turn out, in the glare of hindsight, to be excessively ambitious. Furthermore, hazardous wastes, which never leave the generating facility, comprise an overwhelming percentage of the total hazardous wastes, but these are not covered by the manifest system.[20] With experience, the system will hopefully evolve toward a harmonious balance between the gains from this monitoring system and the administrative burden it imposes.

---

19 During 1982, for example, the Manville Corporation faced up to $5 billion in lawsuits resulting from worker exposure to asbestos. During that same year, Monsanto was fighting a $4.7 billion class action suit for alleged prolonged worker exposure to a hazardous substance in a West Virginia plant.

20 Roger C. Dower, "Hazardous Waste," in *Public Policies for Environmental Protection,* Paul R. Portney, ed., (Washington, DC: Resources for the Future, 1990): 163.

Two additional features of judicial remedies make them a useful complement to legislative remedies. First, liability law usually provides the only way the victim of a toxic substance accident can receive compensation.[21] Even the "Superfund" bill does not compensate individuals for health-related damages. It only compensates for property damage.

The second attractive feature of judicial remedies is the degree to which they can be tailored to individual circumstances. We have seen in the chapters on air and water pollution the strong tendency for legislative remedies to be applied uniformly. We have also seen that uniform remedies are rarely efficient and that often the resulting loss of net benefits is substantial. When the courts impose the damage remedies correctly, an efficient allocation of precaution would automatically be tailored to the specific circumstances involved.

Limitations of Judicial Remedies.   The common law is far from a panacea, however. It does not cope with the largest or most complex problems, such as the emission of hazardous substances by large numbers of sources affecting large numbers of people. This was illustrated nicely in *Roger J. Diamond v. General Motors*, a California case in which the judge ruled that the court system was not the appropriate forum to resolve the Los Angeles problem of air pollution.[22] The problem was so complex and involved so many parties that it had to be resolved by the legislature.[23] Court remedies are administratively expensive and can be used efficiently only when they are used sparingly.

The common law also currently places a large, difficult-to-meet burden of proof on the plaintiff. Generally, a plaintiff must be able to (1) identify the harmful substances; (2) demonstrate that the defendant was the source of this substance; and (3) prove that identifiable damages occurred as a result of the presence of that substance. The last two steps may be difficult to establish in practice.

Suppose, for example, that a well owner who discovered a harmful substance in the well simultaneously experienced a series of illnesses for which he or she had no medical history. The owner might have discovered a source emitting the same chemical nearby, but that is not enough evidence to win a lawsuit. The

---

21   Normally workers' compensation insurance provides for claims arising from proven occupational hazards. However, a study conducted by the Labor Department during 1981 found that of the 2 million Americans who were partially or severely disabled as a result of an occupational disease, only 5% received workers' compensation. Many states have disallowed claims against workers' compensation for maladies that can take 30 years to show up.

22   97 Cal. Report 639.

23   Even when the number of sources is small, the courts can be overwhelmed if the number of plaintiffs is large. It has been estimated that asbestos suits against the Manville Corporation were being filed at the rate of 500 per month during 1982. [See "Manville May Drive Congress to Action," *Business Week* (September 13, 1982): 35.]

court would have to be convinced not only that the substance traveled from the source to the well, but also that any documented illnesses were caused by the substance and not by unrelated causes. The frequent failure to establish these links can undermine the incentive properties of common law.[24]

Japan's court system has reacted to this problem by shifting the burden of proof from the injured plaintiff to the industry. The plaintiffs in those cases have to establish the nature and cause of their diseases and the mechanism by which they were affected. To establish the link to the defendant, they were able to introduce a high statistical correlation between the defendant's activity and the incidence of the disease. Once these elements have been established, a rebuttable presumption is created that shifts the burden of proof to the defendant. The defendant is then liable unless it can be proven that its activities are not responsible for the damage.

If the American court system were to move in this direction, it would represent a radical departure from current practice.[25] The statistical approach lacks the rigor usually required by American courts because establishing a positive correlation between activity levels and the incidence of the disease does not establish causation. Other factors correlated with the activities of the defendant may be responsible.

The Japanese system does, however, effectively raise the question of who should bear the burden of proof. If the source were to bear it, nuisance suits could arise. Nuisance suits are filed mainly to harass defendants by making them spend a lot of money on defense. Such suits are without merit. As we have seen, however, if the plaintiff bears the burden of proof, the burden is particularly difficult, because the defendant generally knows so much more about the contaminating activities.

The Japanese approach gets around this problem by placing a sequential burden of proof on each party. The plaintiff is required to bear a burden sufficiently large that nuisance cases are eliminated. On the other hand, for serious cases where the plaintiff has been able to bear this initial burden of proof, the defendant (who presumably is the most knowledgeable about the subject) must then gather the information at his or her disposal.

Although we can quibble about whether the initial burden on the plaintiff is too low or too high under the Japanese system, with its inherent shared respon-

---

24 If it becomes too easy to prove these links, the defendant will be forced to pay liability even when the substance produced by the defendant did not cause the plaintiff's problem. In this case, efficiency would be lost because too much precaution would be taken.

25 Some movement in this direction is now evident. A plaintiff with asbestosis, for example, may be required to prove only that the disease is more probably than not caused by any of several asbestos manufacturers. Having met this burden of proof, the plaintiff shifts the burden to the individual manufacturer to prove, if it can, that it did not cause the plaintiff's disease. See Abel v. Eli Lilly & Co., 343 N.W. 2d 164 (1984).

sibility, this system reduces the likelihood of nuisance suits while providing incentive for the most knowledgeable party to supply the necessary information to reach a decision.

One final concern should be noted about judicial remedies. Sometimes the source of the toxic substance problem is "judgment proof" in the sense that it has no assets (or too few assets) to pay the damages. The marginal cost of additional damages to the source is zero, and profit-maximizing behavior leads the source to exercise too little precaution.

This problem is more serious for toxic substances than for conventional pollutants, because the latency of the effects means the suits must be filed much later than other kinds of suits. By this time, the source may have gone out of business or have been transformed into a different corporate entity somewhat immune from past transgressions.

Joint and Several Liability Doctrine. In interpreting the "Superfund" Act, the courts have allowed the government to sue "potentially responsible parties" (i.e., disposal site owners and operators, waste generators, and transporters) for damages and site recovery costs under the joint and several liability doctrine.[26] Reduced to its essence, the joint and several liability doctrine makes each successfully sued defendant potentially liable for an amount up to the entire damage caused, regardless of the magnitude of its individual contribution. Because of this doctrine, the government can elect to sue only a few of the wealthiest responsible parties, thereby reducing litigation costs. In one case EPA elected to sue only 10% of the responsible parties, letting the others off the hook.

Successfully sued defendants retain the right of contribution which allows parties that have made payments (either by settling out of court or in response to a court decision) to seek reimbursement from other potentially responsible parties that have not. This right of contribution can be exercised by those settling out of court as well as those assessed damages following a trial. Once a party signs a consent decree of either type, however, they cannot be sued for contribution by other parties.

The government enforces this act by seeking to encourage PRP's to initiate cleaning up the site on their own, but is prepared to initiate the investigation and even to clean up identified hazardous waste sites on its own, if necessary, financing the effort from the several billion dollar Hazardous Substance Response Trust Fund created by the Act. It then seeks reimbursement from parties who are potentially responsible for the conditions at each particular site. The potentially responsible parties are liable for any costs of restoring the site to a safe status as well as "damages for injury to, destruction of, or loss of natural resources,

---

26 Hooker Chemical, for example, was found liable for response costs at the Love Canal under the joint and several liability doctrine. See U.S. v. Hooker Chemical and Plastics Corporation 18 ELR 20580.

including the reasonable costs of assessing such injury, destruction, or loss resulting from such a release."[27]

If any liable party "fails without sufficient cause to properly provide removal or remedial action," they may be assessed punitive damages of "three times the amount of any costs incurred by the Fund as a result of such failure to take proper action.[28]

Designed primarily as a means of raising private funds to clean up hazardous waste sites, joint and several liability has not exactly worked as smoothly as expected, even as a means of collecting revenue. At least one study has put the administrative cost of litigation under Superfund at 55% of actual cleanup costs. Between 1986 and the end of 1988, EPA recovered only $166 million from private parties, or roughly 7% of the $2.4 billion spent on Superfund cleanups during the same period.[29]

Joint and several liability has also created some perverse incentives.[30] Under the joint and several liability doctrine the expected liability a potentially responsible party faces is very uncertain; it could range anywhere from 0% to 100% of the cleanup costs regardless of the degree of precaution undertaken. Since larger firms are usually targeted by EPA for Superfund suits, they have an incentive to take more than the efficient amount of precaution.[31] Meanwhile smaller firms, who may expect to get off the hook because the legal expenses of suing them exceeds the potential recovery, have little or no incentive to take appropriate precautions.

The uncertainty associated with expected damage payments has also wrecked havoc with the insurance market. Insurance companies have no idea how to set premiums and many have left the market for environmental risks entirely. Without insurance the probability of bankruptcy increases. Bankrupt firms contribute very little to the cleanup.

The Statutory Law

A commendable virtue of common law is that remedies can be tailored to the unique circumstances the parties find themselves in. But common law remedies are also expensive to impose, and they are ill-suited to solving widespread

---

27   42 U.S.C. §9607c.

28   42 U.S.C. §9607c3.

29   Roger C. Dower, "Hazardous Waste" in *Public Policies for Environmental Protection,* Paul R. Portney, ed.,   (Washington, DC: Resources for the Future, 1990): 185.

30   A formal analysis of these incentives can be found in T. H. Tietenberg, "Indivisible Toxic Torts: The Economics of Joint and Several Liability," *Land Economics* 65 (November 1989): 305–319.

31   Cleanup and litigation costs have become so high for large companies that some of the larger chemical companies have begun voluntarily cleaning up abandoned sites. See "Environmental, Industry Groups Tackle Hazardous Waste Disposal Sites," *Chemecology* (July/August): 2.

problems affecting large numbers of people. Thus, statutory law has a complementary role to play as well.

Balancing the Costs.   Statutory law, as currently structured, does not efficiently fulfill its potential as a complement to the common law due to the failure of current law to balance compliance costs with the damages being protected against.

The Delaney Clause, the most flagrant example, precludes any balancing of costs whatsoever in food additives. A substance that has been known to be carcinogenic in any dose cannot be used as a food additive even if the risk is counterbalanced by a considerable compensating benefit.[32] As Example 19.3 illustrates, a rule this stringent can lead to considerable political mischief as attempts are made to circumvent it.

The Delaney Clause is not the only culprit; other laws also fail to balance costs. The Resource Conservation and Recovery Act requires the standards imposed on waste generators, transporters, and disposal site operators to be high enough to protect human health and the environment. No mention is made of costs.

These are extreme examples, but even in less extreme cases, policymakers must face the question of how to balance costs. The Occupational Safety and Health Act, for example, requires standards that ensure "to the extent feasible that no employee will suffer material impairment of health or functional capacity. . . ." In changing the standard for the occupational exposure to benzene from 10 to 1 ppm, EPA had presented no data to show that even a 10-ppm standard causes leukemia. EPA based its decision on a series of assumptions indicating that some leukemia might result from 10 ppm, so even fewer cases might result from 1 ppm.

In a case receiving a great deal of attention, the Supreme Court set aside the new benzene standard largely on the grounds that it was based on inadequate evidence.[33] In rendering their opinion the justices stated:

the Secretary must make a finding that the workplaces in question are not safe. But "safe" is not the equivalent of "risk-free." A workplace can hardly be considered 'unsafe' unless it threatens the workers with a significant risk of harm (100 S. Ct. 2847).

In a concurring opinion that did not bind future decisions because it did not have sufficient support among the remaining justices, Justice Powell went even further:

. . . the statute also requires the agency to determine that the economic effects of its standard bear a reasonable relationship to the expected benefits (100 S. Ct. 2848).

---

32 Interestingly, a number of common foods contain natural substances that in large enough doses are carcinogenic. Radishes, for example, could probably not be licensed as a food additive because of the Delaney clause.

33 Industrial Union Department, AFL-CIO v. American Petroleum Institute et al., 100 S. Ct. 2844 (1980).

EXAMPLE 19.3

Weighing the Risks: Saccharin

Saccharin is an artificial sweetener that had been used since the early part of the twentieth century. By the 1970s, it had become the staple of the diet food industry, particularly in soft drinks.

In the late 1960s a researcher at the University of Wisconsin reported that combinations of cholesterol and saccharin injected into the urinary bladders of mice resulted in a high incidence of bladder cancer. A special research group of the National Academy of Sciences convened to investigate the safety of saccharin and a year later declared it safe.

In January 1972, however, the FDA removed saccharin from its list of additives "generally recognized as safe." This action forced food processors to list saccharin on the ingredient label and to conform to maximum recommended dosages. Following some additional Canadian tests showing a link between bladder cancer and saccharin, in 1977 the FDA proposed a ban on the use of saccharin in all foods and beverages, citing the Delaney Clause.

Since saccharin was the only approved artificial sweetener at that time, reaction was swift and vehement. Diabetics attacked the move as denying them access to any sweetener. Groups concerned with weight gain charged that this decision increased the risk of heart attacks. In April 1977 the FDA modified its proposed ban to the extent of allowing saccharin to be labeled as an over-the-counter drug (thus escaping the Delaney Clause) and sold in tablets, powder, or liquid form. It still proposed to ban saccharin from commercially prepared foods and beverages.

Since then a number of studies have appeared, some upholding the link to cancer and others disputing it. Congress reacted by passing a series of moratoriums on the banning of saccharin, thus preventing the Delaney Clause from having its intended effect. In the meantime new sweetners have been developed.

These actions strongly suggest that zero risk is usually not an appropriate policy goal. The objective should be to balance the risks. Provisions that prevent the balancing process, such as the Delaney Clause, are simply bad policy.

It seems clear that the notion of a risk-free environment has been repudiated by the high court, as it should have been. But what is meant by an *acceptable risk*? Efficiency clearly dictates that an acceptable risk is one that maximizes the net benefit. Thus the efficiency criterion would support Justice Powell in his approach to the benzene standard.

It is important to allay a possible source of confusion. The fact that it is difficult to set a precise standard using cost-benefit analysis because of the imprecision of the underlying data does not imply that some balancing of costs and benefits cannot, and should not, take place. It can and it should. While cost-benefit analysis may not be sufficiently precise and reliable to suggest, for example, that a standard of 8 ppm is efficient, it usually is reliable enough to indicate clearly that 1 ppm and 15 ppm are inefficient. By failing to consider compliance cost in defining acceptable risk, statutes are probably attempting more and achieving less than we might hope for.

Degree and Form of Intervention. The second criticism of the current statutory approach concerns both the degree of intervention and the form that intervention should take. The former issue relates to how deeply the government controls go, while the latter relates to the manner in which the regulations work.

The analysis in the second section of this chapter suggested that consumer products and labor markets require less government intervention than third-party cases. The main problem in those two areas was seen as the lack of sufficient information to allow producers, consumers, employees, and employers to make informed choices. With the Delaney Clause as an obvious exception, most consumer-product safety statutes deal mainly with research and labeling. They are broadly consistent with the results of our analysis.

This is not, however, the case with occupational exposure. Government regulations have had a major and not always beneficial effect on the workplace. By covering such a large number of potential problems, OSHA has spread itself too thin and has had too little impact on problems that really count. Selective intervention, targeted at those areas where OSHA efforts could really make a difference, would get more results.

The form the OSHA regulations have taken also causes inflexibility. Not content merely to specify exposure limits, the regulations also specify the exact precautions to be taken. The contrast between this approach and the marketable permit approach in air pollution is striking.

Under the bubble policy, EPA specifies the emission limit but allows the source great flexibility in meeting that limit. OSHA regulations, by dictating the specific activities to be engaged in or to be avoided, deny this kind of flexibility. In the face of rapid technological change, inflexibility can lead to inefficiency even if the specified activities were efficient when first required. Furthermore, having so many detailed regulations makes enforcement more difficult and probably less effective.

A serious flaw in the current approach to controlling hazardous wastes is in the insufficient emphasis placed on reducing the generation and recycling of these wastes. In order to provide additional revenue to fund the cleanup, for example, the 1980 Superfund bill imposed a tax on petroleum and chemical feedstocks. Because this tax is imposed on the front end of the production process and is not calibrated by toxicity, it does not provide the appropriate incentives to switch to less hazardous substances or to recycle the wastes.

An alternative, which is widely regarded as a superior means of raising revenue, involves the imposition of variable unit taxes (called *waste-end taxes*) on waste generated or disposed of. Waste-end taxes would not only spur industry to switch to less toxic substances and to reduce the quantity of these substances used, it would also encourage consumers to switch away from products using large amounts of hazardous materials in the production process because higher production costs would be translated into higher product prices. As of 1985, 20 states had already adopted some form of waste-end taxation. Unfortunately the Superfund Amendments and Reauthorization Act of 1986 chose to replenish the Superfund with broad-based taxes rather than taxes specifically designed to reduce the generation of toxic wastes.

Scale. The size of the hazardous waste problem dwarfs the size of the EPA staff and budget assigned to control it. The Superfund process for cleaning up existing hazardous waste sites is a good case in point. By mid-1988 EPA had placed 1177 sites (out of a total of 19,000 sites considered) on the National Priorities List for permanent cleanup. The Office of Technology Assessment (a research arm of Congress) has estimated that 10,000 sites or more will ultimately be deemed dangerous enough to be placed on the list. All agree that it is not technologically and economically feasible to permanently clean up even 2000 sites over the next few decades even with the replenishment of the Superfund voted by the U.S. Congress in 1986.

The huge scale of this undertaking has important implications for both the bureaucracy and the citizens it serves. Priorities must be established and the most serious problems attacked first. It is a fact of life that an exclusive reliance on the bureaucracy to provide complete safety is infeasible. Citizens should not abdicate their own responsibilities after being lulled into a false sense of security by the mistaken impression that the bureaucracy can and should provide adequate protection.

Assurance Bonds: An Innovative Proposal

The current control system must cope with a great deal of uncertainty about magnitude of future environmental costs associated with the disposal of hazardous waste. The costs associated with collecting funds from responsible parties through litigation are very high. Many potentially responsible parties declare bankruptcy when it is time to collect cleanup costs, thereby isolating them from their normal responsibility.

One proposed solution would require the posting of a dated assurance bond as a necessary condition for disposing of hazardous waste.[34] The amount of the

---

34 Robert Costanza and Charles Perrings, "A Flexible Assurance Bonding System for Improved Environmental Management," *Ecological Economics* 2 (1990): 57–75. A similar proposal was advanced in Clifford S. Russell, "Economic Incentives in the Management of Hazardous Waste," *Columbia Journal of Environmental Law* 13 (1988): 257–274.

required bond would be a function of the environmental authority's estimate of the costs of environmental repair or rehabilitation if the "worst-case" scenario were to come true between the posting date and the refund date. In case any site ultimately required restoration as a result of a hazardous waste leak, the funds tied up in the bond could be used to finance the work. Any unused proceeds would be redeemable at specified dates if the environmental costs turned out to be lower than predicted by the worst case.

This kind of system would create incentives for precaution; lower actual environmental costs would trigger larger refunds. Every dollar of environmental damage prevented would be a dollar earned. Assurance bonds would also make sure that the money for cleanup was readily available as soon as needed and that no lengthy and costly legal process would be necessary to secure it.

SUMMARY

The potential for contamination of the environmental asset by toxic substances is one of the most complex environmental problems. The number of potential substances that could prove toxic number literally in the millions. Some 55,000 of these are in active use.

The market provides a considerable amount of pressure toward resolving toxic substance problems as they affect employees and consumers. With reliable information at their disposal, all parties have an incentive to reduce hazards to acceptable levels. This pressure is absent, however, in cases involving third parties. Here the problem frequently takes the form of an external cost imposed on innocent bystanders.

The efficient role of government can range from ensuring the provision of sufficient information (so that participants in the market can make informed choices) to setting exposure limits on hazardous substances. Unfortunately, the scientific basis for decision making is weak. Only limited information on the effects of these substances is available, and the cost of acquiring complete information is prohibitive. Therefore, priorities must be established and tests developed to screen substances so that efforts can be concentrated on those that seem most dangerous.

In contrast to air and water pollution, the toxic substance problem is one in which the courts may play a particularly important role. Although screening tests will probably never be foolproof, and therefore some substances may slip through, they do provide a reasonable means for setting priorities. Liability law not only creates a market pressure for more and better information on potential damages associated with chemical substances, it also provides some incentives to manufacturers of substances, the generators of waste, the transporters of waste, and those who dispose of it to exercise precaution. Judicial remedies also allow the level of precaution to vary with the occupational circumstances and provide a means of compensating victims.

Judicial remedies are not sufficient, however. They are expensive and ill-suited for dealing with problems affecting large numbers of people. The burden of proof under the current American system is difficult to surmount, though in Japan some radical new approaches have been developed to deal with this problem. The joint and several liability doctrine has created some perverse incentives and has wreaked havoc on the market for environmental insurance.

The statutory responses, though clearly a positive step, seem to have gone too far in regulating behavior. The exposure standards in many cases seem excessively stringent, having been set without balancing the costs involved. Furthermore, OSHA and EPA have gone well beyond the setting of exposure limits by dictating specific activities that should be engaged in or avoided. The enforcement of these standards has proved difficult and has probably spread the available resources too thin.

Reinhold Niebuhr once said, "Democracy is finding proximate solutions to insoluble problems." That seems an apt description of the institutional response to the toxic substance problem. Our political institutions have created a staggering array of legislative and judicial responses to this problems that are neither efficient nor complete. They do, however, represent a positive first step in what must be an evolutionary process.

FURTHER READING

Crandall, Robert W. and Lester B. Lave. *The Scientific Basis of Health and Safety Regulation* (Washington, DC: Brookings Institution, 1981). For each of five health and safety regulatory actions, this book juxtaposes the views of a scientist, an economist, and a regulator on the scientific basis for the regulation and the desirability of the resulting decision. Cases considered are passive restraints in automobiles, cotton dust, saccharin, waterborne carcinogens, and sulfur dioxide.

Dower, Roger C. "Hazardous Waste," in *Public Policies for Environmental Protection*, Paul R. Portney, ed. (Washington, DC: Resources for the Future, 1990): 151–194. Examines policies related to the disposal of hazardous waste.

Graham, Jon D., Laura C. Green, and Marc J. Roberts. *In Search of Safety: Chemicals and Cancer Risk* (Cambridge, MA: Harvard University Press, 1988). A detailed examination of the attempts to regulate two suspected carcinogens, benzene and formaldehyde.

Lave, Lester B. *The Strategy of Social Regulation: Decision Frameworks for Policy* (Washington, DC: Brookings Institution, 1981). An inquiry into the ways in which the scientific foundations of regulation could be improved. Contains chapters on food additives and health, safety, and environmental regulations.

Shapiro, Michael. "Toxic Substances Policy," in *Public Policies for Environmental Protection*, Paul R. Portney, ed. (Washington, DC: Resources for the Future, 1990): 195–242. A comprehensive analysis of the statutes and implementation procedures used to combat environmental risks posed by toxic substances.

Viscusi, W. Kip. *Risk By Choice: Regulating Health and Safety in the Workplace* (Cambridge, MA: Harvard University Press, 1983). Examines the proper role for regulation of occupational risks in the market context where these policies must operate.

ADDITIONAL REFERENCES

Anderson, Frederick R. "Natural Resource Damages, Superfund, and the Courts" *Boston College Environmental Affairs Law Review* 16 (Spring 1989): 405-457.

Costanza, Robert and Charles Perrings. "A Flexible Assurance Bonding System for Improved Environmental Management," *Ecological Economics* 2 (1990): 57-75.

Dechert, W. Davis and James L. Smith. "Environmental Liability and Economic Incentives for Hazardous Waste Management," *Houston Law Review* 25 (1988): 935-942.

Doniger, David D. *The Law and Policy of Toxic Substance Control: A Case Study of Vinyl Chloride* (Baltimore: Johns Hopkins University Press for Resources for the Future, 1978).

Grigalunas, Thomas A. and James J. Opaluch. "Assessing Liability for Damages Under CERCLA: A New Approach for Providing Incentives for Pollution Avoidance," *Natural Resources Journal* 28 (1988): 509-533.

Johnson, Gary V. and Thomas S. Ulen. "Designing Public Policy Toward Hazardous Wastes: The Role of Administrative Regulations and Legal Liability Rules," *American Journal of Agricultural Economics* 68 (1986): 1266-1271.

Kopp, Raymond J. and V. Kerry Smith. "Benefit Estimation Goes to Court: The Case of Natural Resource Damage Assessments," *Journal of Policy Analysis and Management* 8 (Fall 1989): 593-612.

Lave, Lester B., ed. *Quantitative Risk Assessment in Regulation* (Washington, DC: Brookings Institution, 1982).

Mendeloff, John M. *The Dilemma of Toxic Substance Regulation* (Cambridge, MA: MIT Press, 1988).

Nichols, Albert L. "The Importance of Exposure in Evaluating and Designing Environmental Regulations: A Case Study," *The American Economic Review* 72 (May 1982): 214-219.

Russell, Clifford S. "Economic Incentives in the Management of Hazardous Waste," *Columbia Journal of Environmental Law* 13 (1988): 257-274.

Segerson, Kathleen. "Risk and Incentives in the Financing of Hazardous Waste Cleanup," *Journal of Environmental Economics and Management* 16 (January, 1989): 1-8.

Sullivan, Arthur M. "Liability Rules for Toxics Cleanup," *Journal of Urban Economics* 20 (1986), 191-204.

Tietenberg, T. H. "Indivisible Toxic Torts: The Economics of Joint and Several Liability," *Land Economics* 65 (November 1989): 305-319.

DISCUSSION QUESTIONS

1. How should the courts resolve the dilemma posed in Example 19.1? Why?

2. Over the last several decades in product liability law, there has been a movement in the court system from *caveat emptor* ("buyer beware") to *caveat venditor* ("seller beware"). The liability for using and consuming risky products has been shifted from buyers to sellers. Does this shift represent a movement toward or away from an efficient allocation of risk. Why?

CHAPTER TWENTY

Pollution Control Policy: Distributional Effects

There are many in this old world of ours who hold that things break about even for all of us. I have observed for example that we all get the same amount of ice. The rich get it in the summertime and the poor get it in the winter.

BAT MASTERSON, *Gunfighter/Newspaper Reporter*

INTRODUCTION

Environmental policy has been attacked from *both* the political left and right as being unfair. In his book *Progress and Privilege*, William Tucker portrays the environmental movement as an extension of the self-interests of the rich. Having achieved financial security, the rich protect the serenity of their surroundings to the detriment of less fortunate people. By erecting a highly bureaucratic structure to preserve and protect their privileged position under the guise of environmental policy, the rich confer benefits on themselves while imposing costs on the poor. The restitution of fairness, he believes, requires less government, and thus less environmental regulation.

This conservative critique is similar to the radical critique. Left-wing radicals believe that the government is controlled by capitalists and used to pursue their own ends. Though this left-wing view would suggest too little control (as capitalists protect their profits from regulatory erosion) rather than the excessive control decried by the conservatives, it shares with the conservative view the notion that whatever environmental control takes place primarily benefits the capitalists who are the wealthiest members of society.[1]

Taken at face value, these views raise the specter that pollution control policy may not only be unfairly implemented, but also that, given the policy-making process, this lack of fairness may be inevitable. Previous chapters have suggested that, though existing policies have not been efficient, the net benefits have, in general, been positive. While a positive net benefit implies that the gains from environmental policy have exceeded the losses for society as a whole, this may not be true for all members of society. Who are the gainers and losers? Are the net benefits fairly distributed, or is the policy biased in one way or another?

Paying attention to the benefits and costs of the policy process makes sense for two reasons—one ethical and the other pragmatic. The ethical dimension concerns whether the distribution of benefits is in accordance with the norms of social justice. The desire for just policies is a conventional complement to the desire for efficient policies. The pragmatic dimension concerns the relationship between the distributional burden, and both the likelihood that environmental legislation will pass and its ultimate form. The ability to enact legislation depends on the existence of majority support for it. Altering the form of the legislation to suit reluctant supporters is a traditional way to build majority coalitions. Knowing something about the distributional burden of environmental legislation therefore sheds some light on one aspect of the political process.

In economics, as in other disciplines, the norms of social justice are not sufficiently well defined that no norm is beyond reproach. Nonetheless, some conventional approaches have arisen which can serve to guide our inquiry. These involve two concepts known as horizontal and vertical equity.

Horizontal equity occurs when people with equal income are treated equally. (The conventional definition of "equals" in economics is based upon income levels.) With respect to pollution control, the principle of horizontal equity is satisfied if all persons with the same income level receive the same net benefit. This principle can be used to assess the geographic fairness of policy. If people with comparable income levels in different parts of the country receive different net benefits, then the horizontal equity principle is violated.

Vertical equity deals with the treatment of unequals, or, using income as a basis, with the treatment of those with different income levels. The first step in assessing whether a particular policy satisfies vertical equity is to calculate how the net benefit is distributed among income groups: *progressively, regressively,* or *proportionally.*

---

1 Gellen, for example, states, "Thus pollution control programs illustrate the ways in which government promotes the welfare of business at the expense of the taxpaying public. The nontaxpaying poor will also suffer." See Martin Gellen, "The Making of a Pollution-Industrial Complex," *Ramparts* 8 (May 1970): 27.

The distribution is said to be *proportional* if the net benefits received by various income groups are proportional to income. It is said to be *regressive* if the net benefits represent a larger proportion of the income of the rich than of the poor; it is *progressive* if, as a proportion of their income, the poor receive a larger share than the rich.[2] One implication of this definition is that a policy that confers a larger *net benefit* on the rich than the poor is not necessarily regressive. A regressive allocation occurs only if the *ratio of net benefit to income* is larger for the rich than the poor.

According to conventional practice, regressive policies violate the vertical equity principle. This practice is in line with the evident societal concern for the poor which is manifested in the health, housing, and income transfer programs that exist solely to improve their economic status. It suggests that when policies are equitable the poor get at least their share of the benefits. If environmental policies primarily benefit the rich, as argued by the two views discussed at the beginning of this chapter, then we should find that the distribution of net benefits is strongly regressive.

THE INCIDENCE OF POLLUTION CONTROL COSTS: INDIVIDUAL INDUSTRIES

The initial incidence of much of the current policy falls on industry. In order to comply with air, water, and solid-waste regulations, industries have had to invest a considerable amount of capital in equipment (Table 20.1).

The data in Table 20.1 suggest that the proportion of new plant and equipment expenditures allocated to pollution control in the average industry is large, though it has diminished since the middle 1970s. These data also suggest that, according to this way of measuring it, the distribution of the cost burden among industries in quite uneven.

The fact that the costs of pollution control may fall initially on the source of pollution does not mean that the entire burden ultimately resides there, however. In general, the ultimate incidence of pollution control costs is determined by the nature of the market. Depending on such factors as barriers to entry and elasticity of demand, these costs can be passed forward to consumers in the form of higher prices, backward to laborers in the form of lower employment and/or wages, or directly to the owners in the form of lower returns on their capital investment (or any combination of the three).

---

2 It is also possible to use these concepts to refer to the distribution of benefits or costs. Benefits are regressive if the *rich* get a larger proportional share, while costs are said to be regressive if the *poor* get a larger proportional share. The easiest way to keep these straight is to remember that progressive means beneficial to the poor.

TABLE 20.1 Percent of New Plant and Equipment Expenditures by Nonfarm Business on Pollution Control

	1975[a]	1980[b]	1981[c]	1984[c]	1987[d]
Total nonfarm business	5.8	3.1	2.8	2.1	2.1
Manufacturing	9.3	4.8	4.3	3.3	4.3
Durable goods	8.1	3.9	3.2	2.6	3.2
Primary Metals[e]	17.2	12.7	9.6	9.5	1.0
Blast furnaces, steel works	13.5	18.5	15.5	11.3	1.1
Nonferrous metals	24.1	8.7	6.6	9.9	1.1
Fabricated metals	NA	2.4	2.4	1.7	3.7
Electrical machinery	5.8	1.7	1.7	1.2	2.1
Machinery, except electrical	1.8	1.3	1.1	1.2	1.1
Transportation equipment	3.4	2.9	2.5	2.1	2.8
Motor vehicles	3.9	4.3	3.5	2.7	3.0
Aircraft	2.8	1.4	1.6	1.1	2.5
Stone, clay, and glass	14.3	6.5	5.1	4.2	5.3
Other durables[f]	5.3	2.8	2.8	1.7	1.6
Nondurable goods	10.3	5.7	5.3	3.9	5.2
Food including beverage	5.2	3.7	3.6	2.9	2.5
Textiles	4.6	4.3	3.2	2.1	2.1
Paper	16.8	5.7	5.7	7.5	5.0
Chemicals	10.9	5.8	6.5	3.8	5.2
Petroleum	11.8	8.3	6.6	5.0	1.2
Rubber	4.0	1.7	2.3	2.3	2.6
Other nondurables[g]	2.8	0.7	0.6	0.7	0.7
Nonmanufacturing	3.2	2.1	1.8	1.5	1.0
Mining	1.9	3.6	2.7	2.2	1.5
Transportation	NA	0.9	0.7	0.7	0.6
Railroad	1.4	0.9	0.9	0.7	0.7
Air	0.6	0.2	0.3	<0.1	0.3
Other	1.4	1.8	1.3	0.3	1.1
Public utilities	8.4	8.1	7.3	6.8	5.1
Electric	9.7	10.0	9.1	8.6	7.1
Gas and other	1.5	1.0	1.0	0.8	0.4
Trade and services	NA	0.2	0.1	0.2	0.2
Communication and other[h]	0.6	0.1	0.1	<0.1	<0.1

[a]*Survey of Current Business* 58 (June 1978): 34.

[b]*Survey of Current Business* 62 (June 1982): 18. Percentage was derived by dividing total pollution abatement expenditure by total new plant and equipment expenditures.

[c]*Survey of Current Business* 66 (February 1986): 41.

[d]*Survey of Current Business* 68 (February 1988): 26.

[e]Includes industries not shown separately.

[f]Consists of lumber, furniture, instruments, and miscellaneous.

[g]Consists of apparel, tobacco, leather, and printing-publishing.

[h]Consists of communication; construction; social services and membership organizations; and forestry, fisheries, and agricultural services.

FIGURE 20.1   Market reactions to pollution control costs.

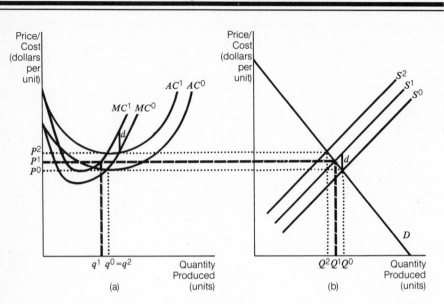

Price/
Cost
(dollars
per
unit)

AC^1 AC^0

MC^1 MC^0

d

P^2
P^1
P^0

q^1 $q^0 = q^2$ Quantity
Produced
(a)   (units)

Price/
Cost
(dollars
per
unit)

S^2
S^1
S^0

d

D

$Q^2 Q^1 Q^0$ Quantity
Produced
(b)   (units)

A Competitive Industry

Incidence.   In order to understand the conditions under which the costs can be passed forward or backward, it is necessary to be fairly specific about how an industry reacts to a change in its cost structure. To get at the essence of the problem without unnecessary detail, consider a perfectly competitive industry which is composed of identical firms. Assume that this industry is initially in long-run equilibrium (Figure 20.1). Faced with the market determined price of P^0, the representative firm maximizes its profits by producing q^0, where marginal cost equals price. Since the price is also equal to average cost at q^0, economic profits are zero. Firms have no incentive to enter or exit the industry.

Suppose now that this equilibrium is disturbed by an EPA regulation forcing each firm to reduce its pollution. Assume that the effect of this regulation on the industry can be reflected as a uniform upward shift in the marginal and average cost curves by a vertical distance d. Because the market supply curve is the sum of the marginal cost curves of the individual firms (all of which have shifted up by d), it will shift up by d as well. Therefore, the market price will rise from P^0 to P^1, an increase less than d. In the short run, price does not rise the full amount of the increase in marginal cost.

The effect on the individual firm can now be seen. The firm would maximize profits by producing the smaller amount q^1 because that is where the new marginal cost curve (MC^1) equals the new price (P^1). Notice, however, that P^1 is lower than

AC^1 when q^1 is produced so that economic profits would be negative. Therefore, firms would exit the industry until zero economic profits were restored.

This departure is reflected in market supply as a further shift leftward. The magnitude of the shift is determined by the amount of exit needed to restore the quality of price and average cost. This occurs at price P^2, which is exactly d greater than P^0. The market would produce the smaller amount Q^2, but each remaining firm would produce the same amount it did before the increase in cost.

In the short run, in response to a uniform increase in marginal cost of d, price would rise by less than d, all firms would reduce production, and negative profits would be earned. In the long run, zero profits would be restored by firms leaving the industry, but all remaining firms would produce the same amount as before the cost rise. The price would rise by the exact amount of the rise in marginal cost. Notice that in this case consumers and laborers would both bear a part of the burden. Consumers would pay higher prices for a smaller level of production, while the lower production levels would imply a lower demand for labor and, hence, lower employment and wages.

The respective burdens borne by these two segments of the population are determined to a large extent by the elasticity of demand for the product. Imagine, for example, that the demand curve for the product was perfectly inelastic (a vertical line) at Q^0. In this case the short-run price increase would be equal to d and short-run economic profits would be zero. Since the level of production and the demand for labor would be unaffected, the consumer would bear the entire burden.

At this point it should be easy to see that the more elastic the demand curve, the larger the impact on production and, hence, labor. This relationship suggests that the impact of pollution control depends not only on the degree of labor intensiveness of the industry, which determines how severely labor would be affected by declines in production, but also by the elasticity of demand, which determines how large the declines in production would be. For example, industries facing severe competition from imports not subject to the same controls would face greater threats of employment declines than those producing products with no effective substitute, domestic or foreign.

Scale Effects. In our analysis, the fact that the regulations did not affect the size distribution of firms arises from our assumptions that the cost curves shift up uniformly by d, that all firms in the industry were identical, and that the regulations affected the cost structure of every firm in the industry in exactly the same way. If the cost curves were not uniformly shifted upward, the firm would not produce the same amount after the regulation as before, because economies of scale would have been affected. In addition, because industries are not really populated by identical firms and the regulations have not been uniformly applied, both the number of firms in an industry and the size of the average firm can be affected by the regulations.

Some recent empirical studies have suggested that the air and water pollution control regulations have not been neutral with respect to the size distribution of firms, but the evidence is incomplete and not conclusive. With respect to the uniform application of regulations, Evans has found that pollution abatement costs per employee are typically smaller for small firms operated by single-plant companies than for large plants operated by multiplant companies.[3] He attributes this to "regulatory tiering," a strategy designed in part to offer special protection to small business. Under regulatory tiering small firms face less stringent standards and/or less rigorous enforcement.

Based on this evidence alone, it would be reasonable to expect that the regulatory structure might have reduced the market shares of larger firms by raising costs more for them than their smaller competitors, but that does not appear to have been the case. Pashigian, for example, found that after controlling for changes in fuel costs, market size, and other regulatory programs, industries with relatively high environmental regulatory burdens had become more capital intensive, had larger increases in mean plant size, and had larger decreases in the number of plants in the industry during the regulatory period than industries with low regulatory burdens.[4] Pittman also found for water pollution control that the regulations tended to increase the economies of scale in complying plants, resulting in an increase in the operating capacity of the optimally sized plant.[5]

On the surface the Evans evidence seems to contradict the Pashigian and Pittman evidence, but that need not be the case. First, the Pittman results deal with scale effects on complying plants, not the relationships among large and small plants per se. Second, while the regulations may well favor *existing* small plants, they may discourage potential new small plants from entering an industry. Finally, although the movement of market shares may well coincide with the peak of regulatory activity, correlation does not necessarily imply causation; the changes in the size distribution of firms could have occurred for reasons other than environmental regulations. More research may shed more light on these relationships and help us to clear away the remaining ambiguity.

New-Source Bias.   The current system of controls has another feature we have not yet considered in the analysis. Under the current regulatory approach, new sources face more stringent control requirements than existing sources, resulting in higher compliance costs. Under conditions of stable demand, no new firms would be entering, so no firms would be bearing the higher new source costs.

---

3 David B. Evans, "The Differential Effect of Regulation Across Plant Size: Comment on Pashigian," *The Journal of Law and Economics* 29 (April 1986): 187–200.

4 B. Peter Pashigian, "The Effects of Environmental Regulation on Optimal Plant Size and Factor Shares," *The Journal of Law and Economics* 28 (April 1984): 1–28.

5 Russell W. Pittman, "Issues in Pollution Control: Interplant Cost Differences and Economies of Scale," *Land Economics* 57 (February 1981): 1–17.

Differentiated regulation would not make any difference when demand is stable. However, if demand were increasing over time, then new firms would enter the market. When an industry is growing, the imposition of higher control costs on new firms, but not on old ones, would delay the entrance of new firms and would reduce their market share relative to what their share would be with regulations affecting old and new plants to the same degree.

In a study of capital turnover in the electric power industry, Maloney and Brady find that the new source bias embodied in the regulatory system has had a significant independent effect on increasing the amount of time existing facilities are operated before retirement.[6] By imposing a disproportionate share of the pollution control burden on new facilities, the desirability of investing in new plants has been diminished. Since the older plants pollute more, this reduction in the rate of capital turnover results in a delay in the amount of emission reduction achieved by any particular date.

Old plants can actually benefit from this new source bias in the regulation and could end up making positive profits. These profits would not generally be bid to zero because the normal mechanism for accomplishing that result (competition from new low-cost firms) is not allowed to work.

Since the new firms are higher-cost producers, because of higher control costs, their profits would be bid to zero. Meanwhile, existing firms receive a form of Ricardian rent. As Example 20.1 illustrates, the tissue industry has experienced precisely this kind of circumstance. This differential regulation effect makes the burden of labor in existing plants smaller than it would be if the regulations raised the costs of new and existing sources by the same amount.

Other studies have confirmed the fact that existing regulations have increased, rather than reduced, the value of existing firms by limiting competition from potential entrants. Maloney and McCormick, for example, found evidence of this in several different industries.[7]

When OSHA imposed a standard limiting the amount of cotton dust exposure for workers in textile plants, new and old firms faced very different compliance costs. An examination of stock prices revealed that a number of textile firms affected by the standard registered an increase in value at the same time that OSHA announced its proposed standards. Moreover, the value increases were positively related to the fraction of cotton used by the firms in their production.

---

6 Michael T. Maloney and Gordon L. Brady, "Capital Turnover and Marketable Pollution Rights," *Journal of Law and Economics* 31 (April 1988): 203–226.

7 Michael T. Maloney and Robert E. McCormick, "A Positive Theory of Environmental Quality Regulation," *The Journal of Law and Economics* 25 (April 1982): 99–123. A portion of this evidence has been challenged in John S. Hughes, Wesley A. Magat, and William A. Ricks, "The Economics Consequences of the OSHA Cotton Dust Standards: An Analysis of Stock Price Behavior," *The Journal of Law and Economics* 29 (April 1986): 29–59.

EXAMPLE 20.1

The Effects of Environmental Controls on the Tissue Industry

The tissue industry is made up of plants that manufacture, either from raw wood or pulp, bulk tissue for such products as facial and bathroom tissue, disposable diapers, and paper napkins. As a water polluter, it was forced to install pollution control equipment. The standards were more stringent for new sources than old.

The results of a major study to estimate the impact of these controls on the tissue industry were reported in Koch and Leone. They found:

> In the tissue industry, the imposition of water pollution controls suggested near-term price increases that would be exceeded by near-term compliance costs, thus creating substantial reductions in profits or actual losses. In the long run, however, the high costs of compliance for new facilities suggested an eventual price increase that exceeded the increases in average costs [p. 92].

In the long run, existing plants were actually *more* profitable than they would have been without the regulation, because the regulation served to diminish competition from new sources.

Koch and Leone also point out that the demand for tissue is relatively price inelastic, implying that the effect of cost increases on reductions in production would be small, and therefore the employment impact would be small. They suggest that this is likely to be true for most industries. Hence, the theory that a large number of plant closings result from environmental regulation is suspect. In the tissue industry they expect pollution controls to *reduce* the number of plant closings by conferring a competitive advantage on existing plants.

Source: James C. Koch and Robert A. Leone, "The Clean Water Act: Unexpected Impacts on Industry," *Harvard Environmental Law Review* 3 (1979): 92.

This finding suggests that the value of existing plants was increased, not reduced, by the regulation.

Maloney and McCormick also found that an increase in stock prices of companies owning smelters occurred immediately following a 1973 Supreme Court decision to uphold the Prevention of Significant Deterioration program. This decision had the effect of limiting competition from new smelters that otherwise would have located in PSD regions, increasing the value of existing firms. Clearly, environmental regulations have rather complicated effects on industries, but the notion that these regulations force many firms out of business seems clearly overstated.

Other evidence seems to confirm that few plants have been forced to close because of environmental regulations. The Economic Dislocation Early Warning System was set up by EPA to monitor plant closings and associated job losses where pollution control was alleged to be a factor in the closing. The data collected by this monitoring system from January 1971 through September 1982 suggest that a total of 154 plants were closed, involving a total of 32,749 jobs. Twenty-three percent of the plant closings and 34% of the jobs lost were in the primary metals industries. An additional 14% of the closings and 20% of the jobs were lost in the chemicals and allied products industries. From Table 20.1 it can be deduced that both of these industries are among the leaders in terms of the percentage of new plant and equipment expenditures going toward pollution control. In addition, steel, one of the primary metals industries, has faced heavy import competition, making the demand for its product more price elastic.

The adverse employment impacts have been geographically concentrated as well as sectionally concentrated. About 62% of the plant closings and 66% of the associated job losses were concentrated in the Northeast and Midwest. Over half of these were in the Midwest.

Monopoly

The effect of pollution control expenditures on any industry also depends on the market structure of that industry. In a monopoly, the entry of new firms would not occur with or without environmental controls. The absence of this pressure changes the way in which a typical firm would react to regulations.

The effect of an increase in control costs on a monopoly is shown in Figure 20.2. Initially, the monopoly is shown in a profit-maximizing equilibrium, where it produces at Q^0 and charges price P^0. If an environmental regulation forced its marginal cost to rise uniformly from MC^1 to MC^2, the firm would no longer maximize output by producing at Q^0. It must adjust its output level. At Q^0 marginal cost exceeds marginal revenue, so profits would be increased by reducing output until marginal cost once again was equal to marginal revenue. That would occur at output level Q^1. The price corresponding to this is P^1.

Some interesting differences are evident between the effect of a similar rise in control cost on a monopoly and on a competitive firm. The price, for example, does not rise as much in a monopolized industry as it would in a competitive industry. In the competitive industry, if the marginal cost curve shifts up by an amount d, the price eventually shifts up by the same amount. In a monopoly the price shifts up by less than d. This result runs contrary to a commonly preconceived notion that a monopoly would automatically pass on all costs. It would not, because it would lose profits if it did. The monopoly would not pass on all

FIGURE 20.2   Effect of pollution control costs on a monopoly.

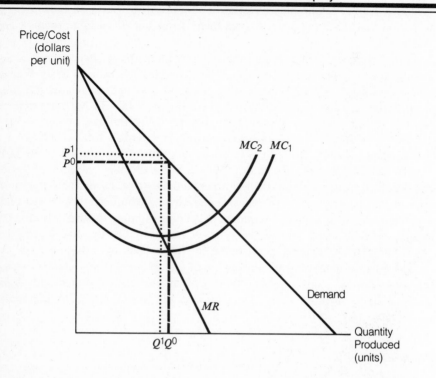

costs, because to do so would cause demand to be reduced excessively. It pays the monopolist to absorb part of the cost.

As long as the competitive industry and the monopoly face identical market demand curves, the monopoly would reduce production by a smaller amount than would the competitive industry. The effect on employment would be smaller in a monopoly than in a comparable competitive industry. To some extent, a monopolist insulates its workers from cost shocks.

THE INCIDENCE ON HOUSEHOLDS

An increase in environmental cost affects households in a number of ways. Increases in the prices of products purchased by households cause a decline in the purchasing power of a fixed income. Declines in wages or employment lead to lower incomes, as do the reduced dividends being derived from the lower earnings of industries with some market power.

These are not the only channels, however, by which households end up bearing the costs of pollution control. The money paid to municipalities to subsidize the construction of waste treatment plants is derived from tax revenues. The ultimate incidence of control costs depends not only on the nature of demand and market structure of the industries; it depends on the tax structure as well.

A number of studies have been accomplished within the last few years that trace the expenditures back through these channels of influence for the purpose of estimating the ultimate incidence of control expenditures. Because of the complexity of these relationships, the estimates are necessarily crude, but some clear insights do emerge.

Air Pollution

Households receive rather different net benefits from stationary source and mobile air pollution control because of the rather different ways in which their respective cost burdens are shared. Therefore, we need to consider each of these separately in order to assess the effects as a whole.

Automobile Control. In the early 1970s, the EPA released a study suggesting that the costs of automobile air pollution control were probably progressively distributed. In essence, the argument was that since the poor had lower rates of auto ownership, and the control policy was focused on new cars, the largest burdens would fall on the middle- and upper-income groups.

Subsequent studies have not supported that conclusion. Rather, they suggest that the problem is more complex than realized by the early EPA study. In particular, the increase in the cost of emission controls on new cars affects used-car prices.

These secondary effects create a fairly complicated incidence pattern. While new-car buyers clearly face higher prices, the owners of used cars receive a gain in the form of a higher resale value for their cars. This gain, however, is transitory. All future purchasers of automobiles will pay higher prices regardless of whether they buy new cars or used cars.

Some studies have attempted to trace these effects. Only Freeman attempts to capture the short-term effects.[8] He derives two rather interesting results: (1) the gain to used-car owners within each income group (caused by the increased resale value of the used car) is on balance larger than the loss (caused by the cost of the emission controls) to new-car owners in that same income group, and (2) the gains are progressively distributed. Thus, in the short run, the automobile pollution control costs are more than offset by used-car capital gains, and the largest capital gains are received by lower-income groups.

---

8 A. Myrick Freeman III, "The Incidence of the Cost of Controlling Automotive Air Pollution," in *The Distribution of Economic Well-Being*, F. T. Juster, ed. (Cambridge, MA: Ballinger, 1977).

As interesting as this result is, we should not make too much of it. The off-setting capital gain is a one-time benefit, not to be repeated. Furthermore, it can only be realized when the automobile is sold. And as soon as another car is purchased, the higher cost associated with the emission controls would have to be paid regardless of whether a new or used car were purchased.

For these reasons the most interesting aspect of automobile air pollution control cost incidence concerns the long run when all cars cost more. Once again, several factors should be considered: (1) the increase in cost to new-car purchasers, (2) the increase in cost to used-car purchasers, and (3) the number of new-car and used-car purchasers in each income group.

All studies have found that automobile pollution control costs are regressively distributed. Harrison has the most complete description of the incidence.[9] He finds, for example, that costs are higher in the suburbs than in the central city, and are higher in smaller cities than in larger cities. He also finds the degree of regressivity higher in the suburbs and generally in smaller cities (Los Angeles is an exception, being a large city with a highly regressive incidence.)

This evidence addresses only part of the story. In order to determine the ultimate incidence, it is necessary to complement these estimates of cost incidence with some estimate of the benefits. To complement his analysis of the distribution of the cost burden, Harrison also conducted a detailed study of the incidence of the benefits of automobile pollution control policy. Because of the difficulties of estimating a generally accepted monetary value for benefits, he measured benefits solely in terms of improvements in the concentrations of three automobile pollutants (carbon monoxide, nitrogen oxides, and ozone). These improvements were calculated for each geographic area and, using data on the income levels of people in those areas, he calculated the degree of reduced exposure experienced by each of these groups.

He found that the benefits from improvement in air quality were progressive *for those living in urban areas.* Furthermore, they were most progressively distributed in the very largest cities. This results from the disproportionate representation of the poor in the most heavily polluted areas in our largest cities.

When he combines his cost and benefit estimates for other parts of the country, Harrison concludes:

> Households living in suburban areas, small urban areas, and nonurban areas—which make up two-thirds of the United States households—do poorly under the current scheme. Households in these areas gain quite modest air-quality benefits while paying large costs. Lower income groups in these areas fare particularly poorly since the costs fall quite heavily upon them under the current scheme [p. 109].

---

9 David Harrison, Jr., *Who Pays for Clean Air: The Cost and Benefit Distribution of Automobile Emission Standards* (Cambridge, MA: Ballinger, 1975).

In a general sense the Harrison study suggests that the automobile air pollution control policy, so carefully designed to be uniformly applied, has led to a highly unbalanced distribution of the benefits. The imbalance appears both in the distribution of net benefits among geographic areas and among socioeconomic groups. Those living in rural areas, particularly the poor, seem to be relatively more burdened than other segments of society.

Stationary Source Control.   Are these results unique to automobile control? Because the programs are quite different, we cannot assume similarity without performing the analysis. Stationary source controls also result in higher prices, but the commodities affected are not the same. Furthermore, while rates of automobile ownership are quite low among the poor, particularly the urban poor, the exposure to increases in other commodity prices might well reach more of the poor.

Most studies assume that increased costs of stationary source controls are passed forward to consumers in the form of higher prices. Therefore, they affect households in proportion to what each household spends on that commodity. In general, the poor spend a higher proportion of their income on these commodities, meaning they save less. Therefore, it is not surprising that those who have derived estimates have found them to be regressively distributed.[10]

Studies of the benefits of air pollution control tell a rather different story. A study by Asch and Seneca examined how the exposure to air pollution was distributed in the United States. They wanted to know if exposure was systematically related to the economic and social characteristics of the population.[11]

To answer this question, they constructed two different samples of data. The first sample consisted of observations on the annual geometric mean concentrations of particulates taken from 284 cities. Socioeconomic variables, such as income levels, age composition, and education levels, were collected for these cities. Performing separate computations for each state, the particulate pollution levels were correlated with these socioeconomic characteristics. In virtually all states they found high pollutant concentrations in cities with higher percentages of lower-income people, higher percentages of the aged, and higher percentages of nonwhites.

They complemented this analysis with another sample which examined the intracity variation in air quality. For this second sample the exposure to three air pollutants—sulfur dioxide, nitrogen dioxides, and particulates—was correlated with socioeconomic characteristics within three cities: Chicago, Cleveland, and Nashville. Measuring pollution levels and socioeconomic characteristics at

---

10 See, for example, Robert Dorfman, "Incidence of the Benefits and Costs of Environmental Programs," *The American Economic Review* 67 (February 1977): 333–340; and L. P. Gianessi, H. M. Peskin, and Edward Wolff, "The Distributional Effects of Uniform Air Pollution Policy in the United States," *Quarterly Journal of Economics* 93 (May 1979): 281–301.

11 Peter Asch and Joseph J. Seneca, "Some Evidence on the Distribution of Air Quality," *Land Economics* 54 (August 1978): 278–297.

a number of sites within each city allowed for a much more precise link between local pollution levels and the immediately affected population to be established.

The income distribution measures consistently confirmed that the poorest residents of these cities experienced higher pollution levels. Higher pollution levels were generally found in neighborhoods with lower property values. The results for racial exposure were mixed. In Chicago higher pollution levels were found in neighborhoods with a high percentage of nonwhites, but in Cleveland the opposite was true—higher concentrations of nitrogen dioxide were found in neighborhoods containing relatively high proportions of whites.

Asch and Seneca also examined whether the improvements in air quality achieved in the early 1970s were progressively, proportionally, or regressively distributed. They found that the physical improvements were progressively distributed—the lower-income portions of the cities received the greatest reductions in pollutant concentrations. They found that many high-income areas actually became more polluted during the period. Similar results were obtained for the New York region.[12]

A Combined Assessment. The Asch-Seneca and Zupan studies deal with exposure rather than economic benefits. The two are not the same because the concept of economic benefits deals with the worth of reducing exposure, not merely the exposure reduction. Gianessi, Peskin, and Wolff attempted to bridge this gap by distributing to local areas the national damage estimates computed by the EPA and then prorating the benefits among socioeconomic groups on the basis of exposure.

Their first finding was that the variability of benefit per family estimates across regions and income groups was several times larger than the variability in costs. While the average family in large urban areas received many times the benefits from the program than did the average suburban or rural family, their costs differed by a much smaller amount. Therefore, it is not surprising that the heavily industrialized, highly populated areas of the eastern United States lead the list of the largest gainers, while the rural and agricultural areas are at the bottom of the list.

Gianessi, Peskin, and Wolff also considered the specific areas in which net benefits are positive or negative. For automobile air pollution, they found only four areas of the country (Jersey City, New York, Patterson, and Newark) enjoyed positive net benefits. For stationary source pollution, they found 61 (out of 274) areas receiving positive net benefits. When the mobile and stationary source net benefits were combined, they found 24 areas experiencing positive net benefits. These 24 areas contain approximately 28% of the population. The

---

12 Jeffrey M. Zupan, *The Distribution of Air Quality in the New York Region* (Washington, DC: Resources for the Future, 1973).

majority of the areas (and population) are paying costs for air pollution control that are higher than the benefits received.

Analyzing the distribution of net benefits among income classes, the Gianessi, Peskin, and Wolff study found the net benefit from stationary source pollution to be progressively distributed, and the net benefit from mobile-source control to be regressively distributed. The combination of policies yields ambiguous results with no clear pattern emerging. Generally, the poor and lower-middle class seem somewhat harder hit, although the poorest of the poor end up with the smallest net burden.

We probably should not make too much of any listing of areas which are not beneficiaries or net losers, such as the one described above, because the magnitude of the net benefit is subject to a great deal of uncertainty, particularly in the calculation of benefits. It does seem clear, however, that automobile air pollution control policy and, to a lesser extent, stationary-source air pollution control policy, violate both the horizontal and vertical equity dimensions. Equals in different parts of the country are not treated equally, and the net benefits of air pollution control policy are distributed in a mildly regressive manner.

Water Pollution

Water pollution presents an interesting contrast. The program of control erected to combat water pollution includes not only industrial effluent standards similar to the industrial emission standards used to combat air pollution, but it also includes federal subsidies to waste treatment plants. Since these subsidies are financed through the tax system, their impact could conceivably be quite different from measures financed chiefly by higher product prices.

Point Sources.   Three separate studies sought the distribution of costs of federal water pollution control policy for point sources.[13] All three studies came to similar conclusions.

In general, they found that the distribution of the costs was regressive. The industrial effluent standards imposed a large regressive burden, while the burden of subsidies for municipal treatment plants was progressive. Industrial standards were found to be regressive because they result in higher consumer prices. Because the poor spend a larger percentage of their income and save less, they are

---

13 Robert Dorfman, "Incidence of the Benefits and Costs of Environmental Programs," *The American Economic Review* 67 (February 1977): 333–340; and L. P. Gianessi, H. M. Peskin, and Edward Wolff, "The Distributional Effects of Uniform Air Pollution Policy in the United States," *Quarterly Journal of Economics* 93 (May 1979): 281–301; and Elizabeth Lake, William M. Hanneman, and Sharon M. Oster, *Who Pays for Clean Water? The Distribution of Water Pollution Control Costs* (Boulder, CO: Westview, 1979).

affected proportionately more. Progressiveness of the municipal waste treatment subsidies results from their major source of financing—the progressive tax system.

To place these results into perspective, Gianessi and Peskin compared the incidence of water pollution costs to the incidence of air pollution costs. They found the cost of water pollution control incidence less regressive, partly because of the manner in which municipal treatment plant subsidies are financed and partly because of the lack of any component in the water pollution policy resembling the highly regressive automobile policy.

The conclusion that the municipal waste treatment subsidies are progressive has not gone unchallenged. In an examination of the incidence of these subsidies in EPA region VII (Iowa, Missouri, Kansas, and Nebraska), Collins found that they tended to redistribute income from the middle-income classes primarily to the very rich.[14] This conclusion depends critically on one particular assumption in the analysis and characteristics that may be somewhat unique to the region studied.

This study assumes that the subsidies received by industrial users of the waste treatment plants are not passed forward to consumers in lower prices, but rather are retained by the owners. Since the owners of capital, in general, tend to be in the upper portion of the income distribution, this assumption results in a major gain by that group. If this assumption were changed to distribute the subsidy to industrial customers rather than owners, the burden of the municipal waste treatment subsidy would be quite progressive.

Assuming that the owners of capital retain the subsidy turns out to be particularly important in the Collins study, because over one-half of the subsidies in the region studied accrue to industrial users. Using exactly the same methodology as Collins to estimate the distributional burden of waste treatment subsidies within the Boston metropolitan area, Ostro found the burden to be quite progressively distributed.[15] This rather different finding results from the fact that in Boston the industrial share of the subsidy was only 7.85%, making the results less sensitive to the assumption about the incidence of the industrial subsidy.

The literature on the distribution of the benefits of water pollution control is very thin. In one study, Winston Harrington investigated the distribution of water-based recreation benefits resulting from the implementation of the BPT portion of the 1972 Water Pollution Control Amendments.[16] Using the RFF Water Network Model to simulate the effects of the policy on water quality and

---

14 Robert A. Collins, "The Distributive Effects of Public Law 92-500," *Journal of Environmental Economics and Management* 4 (December 1977): 344-354.

15 Bart D. Ostro, "The Distributional Effects of Public Law 92-500," *Journal of Environmental Economics and Management* 8 (June 1981): 196-198.

16 Winston Harrington, "The Distribution of Recreational Benefits from Improved Water Quality: A Micro Simulation, Discussion Paper D-80, Quality of the Environment Division, (Washington, DC: Resources for the Future, 1981).

an econometric model to estimate the change in recreational demand resulting from the improvement in water quality, Harrington found the benefits to be very unequally distributed. In particular, he found whites favored relative to non-whites, middle-income families favored relative to the poor, city dwellers favored relative to those living in the country, and Northeast residents favored relative to those residing in other regions.

Nonpoint Sources. The studies described above deal with pollution caused by point sources. It is now becoming clear in the United States that as point sources are becoming increasingly controlled, nonpoint sources are becoming relatively more important. The RFF Water Network Model has also been used to analyze the geographic distribution of the benefits of agricultural sediment control.[17]

The basic approach was to simulate water quality under a variety of point and nonpoint control strategies. The main conclusion derived from this exercise was that only approximately one-third of the nation's river points would experience significantly improved water quality with the adoption of cropland sediment control policy as a supplement to point-source control policy. For this reason the authors suggested that nonpoint control policies should be focused on those agricultural regions where they would make a difference. The simulations also indicated, however, that approximately one-half of the nation's rivers would still experience violations of the total phosphorus and total nitrogen standards unless more stringent controls were established for other nonpoint sources such as pastureland, rangeland, and urban runoff.

IMPLICATIONS FOR POLICY

These results suggest unambiguously that net benefits have historically been distributed in such a way as to violate both the horizontal and vertical equity criteria. The vertical equity criterion was violated because the net benefits have been disproportionately received by well-to-do people. The horizontal criterion was violated for air pollution, in part, because positive net benefits flow mainly to residents of large urban areas. Rural residents with similar incomes receive substantially smaller and possibly negative net benefits.

We must not place too much faith in these estimates. The data on which they are based are imprecise, and every step in the analysis requires some assumption capable of affecting the outcome. The simulated effects are also quite small. The most adversely affected groups are estimated to spend no more than 2% of their

---

17 Leonard P. Gianessi, and Henry M. Peskin, "Analysis of National Water Pollution Control Policies, 2: Agricultural Sediment Control," *Water Resources Research* 17 (1981): 803–821.

income to cover the costs of pollution control.[18] The degree of regressiveness of the distribution of the cost burden is roughly equal to that of a sales tax.[19] When net benefits are considered, both the degree of regressiveness and the percentage of income represented are smaller than is the case when only costs are considered.

Was this distribution inevitable or could the policies have been implemented in such a way that the horizontal and vertical equity criteria could have been satisfied without sacrificing efficiency? It was not inevitable because it is possible to pursue policies that are more efficient and more equitable. This can be illustrated by suggesting alternative approaches that could accomplish both objectives.

In the case of automobiles, generally acknowledged to be the most serious offender, one study estimated the distribution of the burden that would result if the current policies were modified in specific ways.[20] One of the modifications considered was the two-car strategy (explained in Chapter 17).

With respect to horizontal equity, the two-car strategy was found to be superior to the current policy. This result is easy to understand, since the two-car strategy allows lower costs in less polluted areas and brings the net benefits in rural areas more in line with those in urban areas. With a two-car strategy, households with comparable incomes in different geographic areas receive comparable net benefits, instead of the current situation where net benefits are disproportionately reaped in highly polluted urban areas.

This study also found that vertical equity would be improved by the adoption of a two-car strategy. By reducing control costs in medium and small cities, as well as rural areas, the burden on low-income groups is diminished more than that for higher-income groups. In contrast to large urban areas where the poor have very low rates of car ownership (presumably because of mass transit), much larger proportions of the poor own cars in smaller urban areas and rural areas. Therefore, a two-car strategy would not only be more efficient, but it would also be more equitable.

The next most regressive portion of the control package involved the controls placed on stationary sources. The cost of these controls are regressive because

---

18 See, for example, the graphs in N.S. Dorfman, "Who Will Pay for Pollution Control? The Distribution by Income of the Burden of the National Environmental Protection Program, 1972-1980," *National Tax Journal* 28 (March 1975): 101-115; and in Robert Dorfman, "Incidence of the Benefits and Costs of Environmental Programs," *The American Economic Review* 28 (March 1975): 334-340.

19 For a comparison of the regressiveness of a general sales tax with that of the costs of pollution control, see N. S. Dorfman, "Who Will Pay for Pollution Control? The Distribution by Income of the Burden of the National Environmental Protection Program, 1972-1980," *National Tax Journal* 28 (March 1975): 114.

20 David Harrison, Jr., *Who Pays for Clean Air: The Cost and Benefit Distribution of Automobile Emission Standards* (Cambridge, MA: Ballinger, 1975).

they raise the cost of goods. Since the poor spend a larger proportion of income on goods than do the rich, they are hit harder by price increases.

The magnitude of the price increases can be influenced by policy. In the second section of this chapter we demonstrated that, in the long run, the magnitude of the price increase is determined by the height of the minimum point on the long-run average cost curve. Changes in policy affecting average cost also affect prices; the larger the amount average cost is raised, the larger the impact on prices.

The transferable permit system embodied in the bubble and offset policies provides an example of how air quality objectives can be met with smaller increases in average cost than were possible prior to the adoption of these reforms. We have shown that these reforms substantially reduce compliance costs, both average and marginal, for existing sources and therefore cause smaller increases in prices. Since none of the studies described above take those reforms into account, they overstate the regressive effects of current policy.

It is also noteworthy that markets in which the permits are allocated free of charge experience smaller price increases than either an emission charge system or an auction market, where permits are purchased by sources from the government. Both the emission charge and the auction market entail an extra expense that can be avoided by existing sources with emissions trading. It is premature, however, to label the system where the permits are given away as less regressive than the other economic incentive systems until we determine definitively what is to be done with the revenue derived from the auction or the charge. If this revenue were somehow transferred to the poor, it is conceivable that other systems would be less regressive in spite of the fact that they cause larger increases in industrial prices.[21]

The general point, however is that the movement toward these economic incentive systems from the more traditional pure regulation systems can increase equity as well as efficiency. The distribution of the burden should not represent a major stumbling block to the adoption of sensible environmental policy.

Is there any evidence that the popular support for environmental policy has been weakened by the distributional patterns? The polls that have been taken suggest not. A *Business Week*/Harris National Poll, early in 1983,[22] asked the question, "Given the costs involved in cleaning up the environment, do you think Congress should make the Clean Air and Clean Water Acts stricter than they are now, keep them about the same, or ease them?" Sixty percent said they would prefer a stricter approach to water pollution control and 47% said they preferred

---

21 It is also true that *new* sources would face the same costs under any of the three economic incentive systems. Even if the permits were given away to existing sources, new sources would have to buy them. In the long run the regressiveness of the three systems is identical. Only in the short run do they differ.

22 "A Call for Tougher—Not Weaker—Antipollution Laws," *Business Week* (January 24, 1983): 87.

stricter controls for air pollution. Significantly less than 10% wanted to make either law less strict. Since this appears to be typical, it seems clear that the political support for environmental policy has not been undermined by the deficiencies in the current approaches.

Is there any evidence that regional self-interest has shaped environmental policy? Such evidence does exist and it comes in many forms. On a qualitative level, for example, it seems quite clear that the concerns of midwestern states and some of the coal-producing regions of the East have had a major effect on delaying acid-rain legislation as well as on the shape of the emerging legislation.

On a quantitative level, several studies have demonstrated strong correlations between regional voting patterns in the U.S. Congress and projected regional impacts of proposed legislation. Leone and Jackson found this to be the case for water pollution control legislation, while Crandall has suggested that votes on air quality issues are better explained by projected effects on the growth rate in income in the region than by predicted air quality effects.[23]

Relying on an econometric analysis of voting patterns for legislation establishing the PSD policy, one study found that regional economic self-interest had a strong, but not exclusive, explanatory power.[24] In particular, the author interprets his results as suggesting that a strong demand for improved air quality in the Northeast was complemented by an equally strong desire to prevent a large-scale exodus of firms from the nonattainment regions as they attempted to escape the increasingly stringent controls. According to this interpretation, the PSD policy was an attempt to assuage the fears of the Northeast, a powerful voting coalition, while continuing to give U.S. voters the improvements in air quality they so clearly wanted.

These legislators apparently acted on the presumption that the stringency of environmental regulations would be a major determinant of business location. Is it? Do businesses seek out locations where environmental regulations are more lax? Apparently not. Examining a database of new manufacturing branch plants opened by Fortune 500 companies between 1972 and 1978, one study did not find any statistically significant effect of state environmental regulations on the location of these branches.[25]

---

23 Robert A. Leone and John J. Jackson, "The Political Economy of Federal Regulatory Activity," in *Studies in Public Regulation*, Gary Fromm, ed. (Cambridge, MA: MIT Press, 1977): 231–271 and Robert W. Crandall, *Controlling Industrial Pollution* (Washington, DC: Brookings Institution, 1983).

24 B. Peter Pashigian, "Environmental Regulation: Whose Self-Interests Are Being Protected?", *Economic Inquiry* 23 (October 1985): 551–584.

25 Timothy J. Bartik, "The Effects of Environmental Regulation on Business Location in the United States," *Growth and Change* 19 (Summer 1988): 22–44.

SUMMARY

A highly debated issue is whether environmental policy is used by the rich to promote their own interests at the expense of the poor. To determine whether the net benefits are equitably distributed, two principles of equity are useful: the vertical principle and the horizontal principle.

Applying these principles requires a knowledge of how the costs and benefits are initially distributed and how these burdens can be shifted by market reactions. Beginning with the initial incidence of control costs on industries, we discovered a high degree of variability among industries. The ability of these industries to shift this burden to consumers or employees depends upon such factors as the market demand for the product, labor intensiveness of the production process, and market structure. Some industries are hit much harder than others.

The empirical evidence on the ultimate incidence suggests that the costs are regressively distributed in general for air pollution, while the benefits are progressively distributed. The evidence further suggests that net benefits are progressively distributed for stationary source controls and regressively distributed for mobile sources.

For air pollution control as a whole, net benefits are mildly regressively distributed because of the dominance of automobile pollution control. Environmental policy does not live up to the vertical equity criterion, though the degree by which it fails is small.

Current policy violates the horizontal equity principle as well. Net benefits are substantially higher for residents of large urban areas than they are for suburban or rural residents.

Less evidence is available on the distribution of water pollution control net benefits, though the evidence we have suggests they violate both the horizontal and vertical equity criteria as well. Though the costs of water pollution control are less regressive than their air pollution control counterparts, the benefits seem to be regressively distributed with a high degree of geographic variability.

While these results strongly suggest that current distribution of benefits is not as equitable as it might be, they provide little evidence of the intentional exploitation of the poor. Many parts of the control policy involve progressively distributed net benefits, particularly for the urban poor. The regressive nature of the entire package is milder than would be the case if the rich were out to exploit the poor.

These deficiencies have not apparently diminished the popular support for environmental policy to any appreciable degree. According to polls, it remains high. Regional self-interest has been a factor, however, in determining the form of environmental legislation.

Policy changes could improve the situation. Specifically, a two-car strategy for automobile pollution and transferable discharge permits for the control of stationary sources could be the basis for policies that are more efficient and equitable than those relying on pure uniform regulation.

FURTHER READING

Christiansen, G.B. and T.H. Tietenberg. "Distributional and Macroeconomic Aspects of Environmental Policy," in *Handbook of Natural Resource and Energy Economics*, Allen V. Kneese and James L. Sweeney, eds. (Amsterdam: North-Holland, 1985). A more detailed and more technical survey of the material covered in this chapter.

Elliott, Donald, Bruce A. Ackerman, and John C. Millian. "Toward a Theory of Statutory Evolution: The Federalization of Environmental Law," *Journal of Law, Economics, and Organization* 1 (Fall 1985): 313–340. An attempt to explain the economic and political forces which led to very strong U.S. environmental legislation in a period when environmental special interest groups played only a small lobbying role.

Gordon, David, ed. "Environment," in *Problems in Political Economy: An Urban Perspective* (Lexington, MA: D.C. Health, 1981). An interesting treatment of the radical, conservative, and liberal points of view on the distribution of benefits from pollution control policy. Unfortunately this discussion was dropped in the second edition.

Peskin, Henry. "Environmental Policy and the Distribution of Benefits and Costs," in *Current Issues in U.S. Environmental Policy*, Paul R. Portney, ed. (Baltimore: Johns Hopkins University Press for Resources for the Future, 1978). A more policy-oriented discussion of the distribution of the benefits and costs of the Clean Air Act Amendments of 1970 than the readings discussed in this text.

ADDITIONAL REFERENCES

Conrad, Klaus and Catherine Morrison. "The Impact of Pollution Abatement Investment on Productivity Change: An Empirical Comparison of the U. S., Germany, and Canada," *Southern Economic Journal* 55 (January 1989): 684–698.

DeMeza, David and J. R. Gould. "Free Access versus Private Property in a Resource: Income Distributions Compared," *Journal of Political Economy* 95 (December 1987): 1317–1325.

Farber, Stephen C. and Robert E. Martin. "Market Structure and Pollution Control under Imperfect Surveillance," *Journal of Industrial Economics* 35 (December 1986): 147–160.

Rose, Adam, Brandt Stevens, and Gregg Davis. *Natural Resource Policy and Income Distribution* (Baltimore: Johns Hopkins University Press, 1988).

Shortle, James S. and Keith D. Willett. "The Incidence of Water Pollution Control Costs: Partial vs. General Equilibrium Computations," *Growth and Change* 17 (April 1986): 32–43.

DISCUSSION QUESTIONS

1. "The goals of environmental policy and our concern for the poor inevitably conflict. The burden of any attempt to improve the environment necessarily falls disproportionately on the poor." Discuss.

2. "Environmental policy in the United States has been extremely fair in that it has been uniformly applied. This is evident, for example, in the uniform ambient air quality standards, uniform new-source performance standards, uniform hazardous pollutant standards, uniform new-car emission standards, and uniform discharge standards for water pollution." Does uniformity in these policies guarantee "fairness"? Defining "fairness," explain why or why not.

CHAPTER TWENTY-ONE

Growth, Poverty, and the Environment

If there is any period one would desire to be born in, is it not the age of revolution when the old and the new stand side by side and admit of being compared? When the energies of all men are searched by fear, and by hope? When the historic glories of the old can be compensated by the rich possibilities of the new era? This time, like all times, is a very good one, if we but know what to do with it.

RALPH WALDO EMERSON, *The American Scholar* (1873)

INTRODUCTION

In previous chapters we invested a considerable amount of time and effort in investigating individual environmental and natural resource problems and the policy responses that have been, and could have been, taken to solve them. In general, solutions are possible, and our economic and political institutions, with some exceptions, seem to be muddling through.

Our next step must be a consideration of the global economic system and the scale of the challenge it will face in the twenty-first century. Perhaps the major challenge is finding a way to deal effectively with global poverty without jeopardizing the environment or degrading the resource base passed on to future generations.

Poverty has emerged as a significant cause of environmental problems. The worst recorded air pollution is not found, as might be expected, in the highly industrialized cities of the high-income countries, but rather in the major cities of lower-income countries. Deforestation is caused in part by the migration of landless peasants into the forests, seeking a plot of land to work. Soil erosion is caused, in part, when the poor are driven to farm highly erodible land in an attempt to survive. Dealing effectively with these environmental problems and the human suffering that lies behind them, will require raising living standards.

Traditionally this has been accomplished through economic development.[1] One model for the development of the less industrialized countries is the path of rapid economic growth followed by the industrialized countries. How appropriate a model is this?

The two visions in Chapter 1 suggest two different answers to this question. The *Limits to Growth* view holds that exponential economic growth on a global scale will continue unabated until the physical limits are reached. At that time the global economy will overshoot its resource base and collapse. In this view economic growth is the source of the problem, not the solution. The only rational policy is to exercise direct control over the growth process itself. No other course, including the collection of individual policies discussed in the preceding chapters, would avoid the collapse.

Kahn and his associates, however, envision an automatic transition to a steady-state economy where eventually economic growth would cease, but not until all future households were significantly better off than current households. Thus, they foresee the prospect for continued development which slowly declines to zero over time. Far from being detrimental in this view, economic growth provides the vehicle for improving the welfare of future generations. As Kahn sees it, to deny that growth would consign the members of poor Third World countries to perpetual poverty. Which view of the future is correct?

Examining the appropriateness of the traditional economic growth approach to development should start by understanding that model and its success or lack of success as a means of eliminating poverty. We will begin by defining how economic growth takes place and how the growth process is affected by increasing resource scarcity and rising environmental costs. This understanding will then be used to characterize what changes in the growth process in the industrialized nations can be expected in the future.

The relationship between growth and development in the industrialized countries is then explored. Has growth increased the well-being of the average citizen in the developed countries? Or has the evident elevated consumption of material goods made possible by economic growth merely masked large offsetting problems that would cause an appropriately measured standard of living to go down, not up?

The fate of the average citizen, of course, does not always shed light on the fate of the poor. How have the poor fared in periods of rapid economic growth?

---

1 Herman Daly's useful distinction between growth and development is employed here. Development refers to a qualitative increase in well-being, while growth refers to a physical expansion in physical output of goods and services. They are related, but by no means synonymous, concepts. It is conceptually possible to have growth without development and development without growth, but historically the two have been inextricably entwined. See Herman E. Daly and John B. Cobb, Jr., *For the Common Good* (Boston: Beacon Press, 1989).

Is John Kennedy's metaphor "A rising tide lifts all ships" apt, or does a rising tide leave more people stranded?

While the historical experience in the industrialized countries is revealing, the transferability of this experience into a Third World context is by no means obvious. To what extent can economic growth provide an answer to the crushing problems of poverty that infect the Third World? What are the barriers to achieving increased standards of living for the poor in Third World countries in a finite world?

THE GROWTH PROCESS

Nature of the Process

How does economic growth occur? It occurs in two main ways: through increases in inputs such as capital, labor, energy, and other resources, or through increases in the productivity of those resources as a result of technological progress. The former source of growth involves increasingly greater outputs, given the state of the art in production, while the latter source involves improvements in the state of the art.

Increases in Inputs.   The amount of growth occurring from increases in inputs is governed by two important economic concepts: economies of scale and the law of diminishing returns. *Economies of scale* refers to the amount of increase in output obtained when all inputs are increased in the same proportion. The *law of diminishing returns* governs the relationship between inputs and output when some inputs are increased and others are held fixed.

We can add precision to these definitions by introducing a concept known as the production function. A *production function* expresses mathematically the relationship between inputs and outputs. A common general production function is expressed as

$$O = f(K, L, E, M), \tag{1}$$

where O = output, K = capital, L = labor, E = energy, and M = materials or, more generally, other resources. This equation simply states that output is functionally related to these inputs by the production function f. To know something about the growth process, we have to know more about f.

Suppose that we were to multiply the inputs by a constant (λ) and observe that output grew by another constant (θ). Thus

$$\theta O = f(\lambda K, \lambda L, \lambda E, \lambda M). \tag{2}$$

If $\lambda = \theta$, then f is said to exhibit constant returns to scale. If $\lambda < \theta$, f exhibits increasing returns to scale (a λ change in all factors leads to a change in output which is greater than λ).

The law of diminishing returns governs what happens when some, but not all, of the inputs are increased. Suppose, for example, that all the inputs are held fixed, except for capital, which increases. As constant and successive increments of capital are added to the other fixed resources, the law of diminishing returns implies that eventually a point will be reached where each increment of input will produce smaller and smaller increments of output.

Technological Progress. The final source of growth, technological progress, involves the implementation of better, less wasteful ways of doing things. With technological progress growth can occur even in the absence of increases in inputs simply because the inputs available are used more effectively. For example, with a new production technique, less energy might be wasted or fewer resources used to make a product.

Example 21.1 provides one example of a commonly used production function. It shows how these concepts of economies of scale, law of diminishing returns, and technological progress can be given specific definitions so that their importance in the growth process can be assessed.

Potential Sources of Reduced Growth

Historically, increases in factor inputs and technological progress were both important sources of growth. This does not automatically mean that they will continue to provide growth at historic levels in the future, however. A number of reasons suggest caution in extrapolating historically valid arguments into the future.

Reduced Input Flows. Not all input flows are continuing at historic levels. Population growth has slowed considerably in most countries, which causes the growth in the labor force to slow and possibly stop. The growth fed by increasing labor is diminishing and will continue to diminish in the future.

The cost of energy and raw materials seems to be rising, even in real terms. Producers respond to higher relative prices by cutting back on the use of these inputs, which diminishes their contribution to the growth process.

Capital formation has played a pivotal role in the past and is likely to continue doing so.[2] As workers were given more sophisticated capital equipment to work with, their productivity increased.

Capital has broken down the barriers imposed by human limitations. Earth moving, once limited by the strength and endurance of workers, with the advent

---

2 One of the most sophisticated studies to date on the determinants of U.S. economic growth during the period 1948–1979 finds capital formation to be the dominant force. See D. W. Jorgenson, F. M. Gollop, and B. Fraumeni, *Productivity and U. S. Economic Growth* (Cambridge, MA: Harvard University Press, 1988).

EXAMPLE 21.1

The Generalized Cobb-Douglas Production Function

In attempting to understand the effect of changes in input streams on the growth process, the notion of a production function becomes important. Several production functions have been used by economists, but perhaps one of the most powerful and yet simplest to understand is the generalized Cobb-Douglas (GCD) production function. It is useful to know this function, both to make general constructs, such as economies of scale, more concrete, and to pave the way for structuring the evidence on how the growth process could be expected to be affected by such things as slower growth in the labor force.

The GCD function is expressed as the power function:

$$Q_t = Ae^{rt}K_t^{a_1}L_t^{a_2}E_t^{a_3}M_t^{a_4},$$

where K, L, E, and M are capital, labor, energy, and materials; A, a_1, a_2, a_3, a_4, and r are constants; and t refers to the year in question. Using econometrics, the branch of economics concerned with deriving empirical estimates, actual data can be used to derive values for all constants.

Several properties in this function can be easily derived. Constant returns to scale will prevail whenever the sum of the a exponents is equal to 1.0. Most analysts find it difficult to reject the conclusion that constant returns to scale prevail for the U.S. economy as a whole.*

It can also be shown that the law of diminishing returns will apply to any factor when its associated exponent (a) is less than 1.0. Given the existing estimates, the law seems to apply to all four factors.

We can convert this equation into a rate of growth equation as follows:

$$\frac{\dot{Q}}{Q} = r + a_1\frac{\dot{K}}{K} + a_2\frac{\dot{L}}{L} + a_3\frac{\dot{E}}{E} + a_4\frac{\dot{M}}{M},$$

where the rate of growth of any variable X is denoted as $\dot{X}/X$. Thus the rate of growth of output is a weighted sum of the individual rates plus r, which is interpreted as the rate of technological progress. Notice that as long as $r > 0$ growth can continue, even in the absence of any growth in inputs.

*Ronald L. Cooper, "The Energy-Economic-Connection: 1974-1979 and Beyond," *Business Economics* 15 (September 1980): 6; E.R. Berndt and D. Wood, "Technology, Prices and the Derived Demand for Energy," *Review of Economics and Statistics* 57 (August 1975): 264.

of bulldozers, is limited no more. Size of the market, once limited by the time and effort required to transport commodities in a horse and buggy, expanded with the advent of the railroad, the truck, and the airplane. Limits on corporate controllability imposed by the size and competence of recordkeeping staffs—as they attempted to stay on top of the information and paper flows—have fallen in the face of computers providing instant access to important information compiled in the most useful format.

Although capital is a reproducible asset, some indirect limits may diminish its role in the future. These include limitations on substitutability for other factors, on the productivity of future investment, and on the incentive to invest. We consider each of these in turn.

The ability of capital to sustain historial growth rates lies in part in its ability to substitute for those factor inputs which are experiencing limits. In Chapter 13 we introduced the concept known as the elasticity of substitution and noted that when this concept takes on a value of one or greater, substitution is easy and growth should not be inhibited.[3]

The first substitution possibility to be considered is between capital and labor. As population growth dwindles, the growth rate in the supply of labor diminishes as well. Historically, the economic growth rate has exceeded the growth rate of labor supply, as capital was continually substituted for labor. Most studies of production have found capital and labor to be quite strong substitutes. When we think about the modern manufacturing sector, this seems quite reasonable. Therefore, dwindling population, by itself, doesn't seem a particularly large barrier.

Describing the substitution possibilities for other resources, however, becomes more complex. For example, while Brown and Field found capital-resource substitution elasticities to be greater than 1.0 in all four of the industries they examined, Humphrey and Moroney found capital-resource elasticities less than 1.0 in three other industries.[4] It seems clear than no general consensus has emerged concerning the degree of substitutability existing between capital and resources. This substitutability seems to depend upon the industry being considered.

---

3 For more advanced students it should be noted that the generalized Cobb-Douglas function implies substitution elasticities equal to 1.0. Therefore, the empirical work on those elasticities has relied on more general functional forms that permit different elasticities between each factor input to be estimated.

4 Gardiner Brown, Jr., and Barry Field, "The Adequacy of Measures for Signalling the Scarcity of Natural Resources, in *Scarcity and Growth Considered*, V. Kerry Smith, ed. (Baltimore: Johns Hopkins University Press, 1979); and David B. Humphrey, and J. R. Moroney, "Substitution among Capital, Labor, and Natural Resource Products in American Manufacturing, *Journal of Political Economy* 83 (February 1975): 57–82.

The relationship between capital and energy is even more puzzling. Studies of the capital-energy relationship over time in the United States find that capital and energy are complements, rather than substitutes.[5] Thus, capital and energy have together substituted for labor and other resources but not for each other. If one thinks of the tractor, the bulldozer, and the airplane, this seems like a natural finding.

The question of interest is whether capital and energy would remain complements in the future or whether substitution of capital for energy might be possible. This is an especially important question in light of the links between fossil fuel energy use and global warming. If the attack on global warming includes a reduction in the use of fossil fuel energy and capital is a complement with energy, global warming strategies would have the side effect of reducing the rate of capital formation.

In some energy uses substitution is clearly feasible because energy-saving equipment, such as computer-controlled heating and cooling, already exists. Furthermore, some capital investments will clearly hasten the transition to passive solar energy, which conserves energy by making better use of what is available.

In other sectors such as transportation, the substitution possibilities are not quite as obvious, but that does not mean they do not exist. Bicycles are used in many European countries as a substitute for automobile transportation. To some extent communication can even substitute for transportation, as more people use home-based computer terminals and phone lines to do their jobs without leaving home. While our historical experience would suggest limited substitution possibilities, it is not at all clear that experience is relevant for the future. Nonetheless, it would be premature to feel confident that the future elasticity of substitution between capital and energy will be uniformly greater than 1.0. Though it is likely that the elasticity of substitution between energy and labor is quite high, this does not offer much promise for growth in an era of declining growth in the labor force. Some drag on economic growth from higher energy prices appears likely.

The second possible source of growth drag relates to the future productivity of capital. As pollution rises, the amount of resources committed to combating it also rises. As we saw in the preceding chapter, a substantial proportion of new plant and equipment expenditures is being allocated to pollution control. Unlike conventional investments, however, these investments do not cause more goods to be produced; they produce a cleaner environment. Because the value of this cleaner environment is not usually recorded in the conventional measures of economic output, conventionally measured output should rise more slowly as a

---

5 Ernst R. Berndt and D. Wood, "Technology, Prices, and the Derived Demand for Energy, *Review of Economics and Statistics* 57 (August 1975): 259–268.

larger proportion of inputs is diverted from productivity enhancement to environmental enhancement.

The final source of drag concerns the incentive to invest. The amount of capital investment should depend upon the rate of return on that investment. The more profitable the investment is, the larger the amount undertaken. Yet we have already identified two related factors that reduce the rate of return on investments: the regulatory bias against new sources and the composition of investment. By focusing on new sources, the regulatory system diminishes the relative profitability of new investment while enhancing the profitability of existing capital stock. This new source bias diminishes the incentive to invest in new capital. Meanwhile, the large proportion of new plant and equipment expenditures going for pollution control tends to diminish the profitability of those expenditures being made, since improvements in the environment do not, in general, add to profits.

In sum, it appears that expecting increases in capital to completely compensate for reduced flows of other inputs would be risky. Some important transitions are occurring. While they do not imply a cessation of growth catastrophically or otherwise in the near future, these transitions certainly suggest some diminution in the rate of economic growth resulting from reduced factor input flows.

Limits on Technological Progress.   Can technological progress take up the slack? As is clear from Example 21.1, if technological progress is to compensate for declining input flows, an increase in the rate of technological progress must occur. Is that likely?

Some observers are beginning to suggest that the degree to which technological progress can continue to play its historic role as a growth stimulant may be limited. Some of these limits are perceived as institutional and a matter of choice, while others are perceived as natural and inexorable.

The new-source regulatory bias in pollution control policy provides on example of an institutional limit. Because most technological progress bears fruit when it is embodied in new or modified production facilities, by reducing the number of these facilities, this new-source bias inhibits technological progress.

Another institutional barrier is the decreasing commitment of resources to basic research, particularly by the public sector. Since basic research is frequently a precursor for technological progress, this trend could also diminish the rate of technological progress.

During the 1970s economic growth fell below that in earlier periods (Table 21.1). The average rates of growth in manufacturing output were down markedly, as were growth rates in labor productivity (output divided by labor input) and technological progress. Does this dramatic decline reflect the beginning of a new era?

A number of economists have tried to isolate the sources of this decline—an assignment made difficult because so many interacting variables are involved.

TABLE 21.1   Growth Rates of Output, Labor Productivity, and Technological Progress 1958–1977

Time period	Gross manufacturing output	Labor productivity	Technological progress[a]
1958–65	5.411	3.152	1.495
1965–73	3.827	2.777	0.707
1973–77	1.030	1.745	0.340

[a]Measured as growth in output minus growth in aggregate input, where aggregate input is the cost-share weighted growth of individual inputs. This is also known in the literature as the rate of growth of *total factor productivity* and would correspond to *r* in Example 21.1.

Source: Ernst R. Berndt, "Energy Price Increases and the Productivity Slowdown in United States Manufacturing," a paper presented at the Federal Reserve Bank of Boston Conference on Productivity (June 1980): Tables 2, 3.

Nonetheless, some progress has been made and is worthy of our attention. We begin with an analysis of the effects of environmental policy on growth.

Environmental Policy

We have seen that pollution control laws impose large compliance costs on industry. These should have some effect on inflation (by boosting output prices), employment, as well as on growth. The question of interest is how large those impacts have been, and could be expected to be, in the future.

One estimate by Data Resources, Inc. is typical.[6] Other estimates do not convey a significantly different impression. The impact of environmental policy on the rate of inflation (measured using the urban consumer price index) is very small, less than one half of a percentage point.

The effect on employment is particularly interesting. We suggested in the previous chapter than one effect of the new-source bias would be to diminish the adverse employment impacts on existing pollution sources. Any adverse employment impacts that occur are further offset to some degree by the gains in employment experienced by firms producing the pollution control equipment. The sales and employment in these industries would have increased as a direct result of the environmental regulations. The Data Resources results suggest that the gains to those producing the equipment more than offset the losses to those installing the equipment, resulting in more, not less, employment in the economy as a whole.

---

6 Data Resources, Inc., "The Macroeconomic Impact of Federal Pollution Control Programs, 1978 Assessment," submitted to the Environmental Protection Agency and the Council on Environmental Quality (Washington, DC: January 29, 1979).

Economist Robert Haveman has surveyed the results of a range of studies conducted around the world on the effect of pollution control expenditures on employment.[7] These studies go beyond aggregate employment effects and delve into the types of workers affected as well as into the effects of alternative ways of financing investments in pollution control. He concludes:

1. The employment demands of public sector spending for pollution control are greater than equivalent government spending for alternative purposes. About 60,000 to 70,000 jobs are created for each $1 billion of pollution control spending. For purposes of comparison, each $1 billion of GNP generates approximately 50,000 jobs on the average.

2. Changes in the composition of employment triggered by environmental policy are likely to adversely affect low-skill, low-wage workers relative to high-skill, high-wage workers.

3. In a limited number of countries, environmental policy has been employed as a demand-inducing antirecession instrument, apparently with some success. This result is in part due to the deficit public financing of the expenditures or subsidies.

4. Available evidence suggests that the adverse employment effects from plant closing attributable to environmental policy are very limited.

However, this generally positive prognosis for the impact of environmental policy on employment should not obscure the problems. Gains in employment generally benefit a different set of workers than losses do. New jobs are rarely in the same location as those lost and, as Haveman points out, rarely involve the same skill levels. Even when overall employment effects are positive, the rising costs of environmental control could cause severe localized problems.

According to the DRI simulation, the dampening effect on growth does not really begin to emerge consistently until the period following 1982. After 1982 the effect remains small (less than 1% of GNP), but the simulations suggest that the reduction in GNP grows over time. Another study using comparative data from the U.S., Canada, and West Germany found that only a small part of the slowdown in productivity growth was the result of diverting investments toward environmental control.[8] In fact, some government requirements to install cleaner

---

7 Robert H. Haveman, "The Results and the Significance of the Employment Studies, Organization for Economic Co-operation and Development, *Employment and Environment* (Paris: Organization for Economic Co-operation and Development, 1978): 48–53.

8 Catherine Morrison and Klaus Conrad, *The Impact of Pollution Abatement Investment on Productivity Change: An Empirical Comparison of the United States, Germany and Canada*, National Bureau of Economic Research Working Paper No. 1763 (1989) and Klaus Conrad and Catherine Morrison "The Impact of Pollution Abatement Investment on Productivity Change: An Empirical Comparison of the United States, Germany and Canada," *Southern Economic Journal* 55, (January 1989): 684–698.

equipment may have raised productivity by forcing firms to invest in newer and more efficient equipment. If these simulations are at all accurate, environmental policy does not bear responsibility for much of the decline in the economic growth rate in the late 1970s.

Christiansen and Haveman have pushed this analysis further by studying the effect on environmental policy on labor productivity, a major determinant of growth.[9] Their analytical approach captures, albeit crudely, the direct and indirect effects of environmental regulations. It includes whatever inhibiting effects environmental regulations may have had on capital investment and on capital-labor ratios. They conclude:

> . . . little evidence exists to suggest that as much as 15 percent of the slowdown can be attributed to them. A reasonable estimate would attribute, say 8 percent–12 percent of the slowdown in productivity growth to these regulations [p. 388].

If these estimates are accurate, environmental policy cannot escape responsibility for some portion of the decline in labor productivity, but at least the degree is small.

The final item of interest in the DRI simulations concerns the effect of environmental policy on the balance of trade. To the extent that pollution control expenditures cause prices of domestic products to rise more rapidly than prices of foreign products, some decline in exports accompanies a rise in imports. This is precisely what the DRI simulations suggest, though this effect is also small.

Energy

A second possible source of growth drag considered in the previous section was energy. Since large price increases occurred during 1973 to 1974, this period provides a unique opportunity to study the magnitude of the growth-inhibiting effects of energy.

What should we expect to find? Since energy and capital historically have been complements, we should find that price increases would slow down capital formation. At the same time the fact that energy and labor are substitutes would suggest that the use of labor should be rising, which, in turn, would cause the average productivity of labor to fall.

On a general level the evidence is consistent with this set of expectations. Investment is lower and the average productivity of labor has fallen. Work

---

9 Gregory B. Christiansen and Robert H. Haveman, "The Contribution of Environmental Regulations to the Slowdown in Productivity Growth," *Journal of Environmental Economics and Management* 8 (December 1981): 381–390.

by Jorgenson and others, such as Uri and Hassanein, confirms this impression.[10]

Focusing on 1973–1976, a period characterized by rapidly increasing energy prices, Jorgenson first examined the question of whether the decline in growth was due to declines in input growth or to declines in productivity. He found that input declines were much less significant than declines in productivity. He then attempted to discover the sources of this productivity decline by looking at the specific experience of 35 different industries.

Though a decline in economy-wide productivity could conceivably be caused either by a shift in resources from high-productivity industries to low-productivity industries or by a decline in productivity within each industry, Jorgenson found the latter to be far more important than the former. His analysis of the causes of these declines revealed that in 29 of the 35 sectors examined, technical change was biased toward the use of energy. This result suggests that in 1973–1976, productivity growth resulting from technical progress declined as energy prices rose. If this is an accurate depiction of the future, as well as the past, then this evidence provides some, albeit weak, empirical confirmation that higher energy prices might depress the rate of technological progress.

One puzzle to be explained by those who believe energy prices have already played a significant role in productivity declines is how that could be so when the energy cost share is so small. Factors with small cost shares should in general have small effects on output.

Recent work suggests a resolution to this puzzle that seems consistent with the evidence.[11] Berndt and Wood suggest that in the short run the capital services provided by the capital stock are largely fixed, as are its operating characteristics. Once the capital stock is in place, the ratio of energy to capital services actually utilized is therefore fixed. Dramatic changes in energy prices therefore affect the degree to which this capital is used, with the most energy-inefficient vintages being used least. By lowering the utilization of the existing capital stock, higher energy prices reduce total factor productivity.

In this story the lower productivity does not necessarily persist. As long as new capital can be purchased which uses less energy, utilization rates rise and productivity is restored as these new machines are installed. Once the stock of capital adjusts to the new regime of higher energy prices, productivity growth rebounds.

The key to thinking about the long run is to keep straight the differences between ex post and ex ante substitution possibilities. *Ex ante* refers to the time

10 Dale W. Jorgenson, "Energy Prices and Productivity Growth," *Scandinavian Journal of Economics* 83 (1981): 165–179; and Noel D. Uri and Saad A. Hassanein, "Energy Prices, Labour Productivity, and Causality: An Empirical Examination," *Energy Economics* 4 (April 1982): 98–104.

11 Ernst R. Berndt and David O. Wood, "Energy Price Shocks and Productivity Growth: A Survey," in *Energy: Markets and Regulation,* Richard L. Gordon, Henry D. Jacoby and Martin B. Zimmerman, eds. (Cambridge, MA: MIT Press, 1987): 305–342.

period prior to investment, while *ex post* refers to the time period after the equipment is installed. Limited ex post substitution possibilities, which seem to have played a significant role in the slowdown of productivity growth after the major energy price increases in the 1970s and early in the 1980s, do not automatically indicate that ex ante substitution possibilities will be small. It is the ex ante substitution possibilities which will determine the future of economic growth over the long run.

Our experience with higher energy prices is quite limited. Transformations of the kind envisioned by these growth models take time to unfold. New ways of doing business are not discovered immediately and old machines are not replaced instantaneously. Therefore, the estimates must be judged for what they are—an attempt to extract as much information as possible from a limited set of data.

OUTLOOK FOR THE NEAR FUTURE

Some of what the future portends for the United States and other developed countries is becoming clear. Because we are in a period of transition, some striking differences between our experiences in the recent past and what we will encounter in the near future are emerging. Though a detailed examination would be beyond the scope of our study, we will highlight some of the emerging changes.

Population Impacts

The dramatic fall in fertility rates experienced by most countries of the world will have a profound impact. Inevitably, the average age of the population will rise, putting pressure on social security systems. Since the United States relies on an unfunded social security system, current payments to retirees are financed out of current payments by workers. As long as the population is growing, the ratio of workers to retirees remains high enough to provide adequate benefit levels for retirees without putting excessive strain on current workers. When population growth declines, however, as is now happening, the ratio of workers to retirees declines as well. To keep the system solvent, benefit growth has to decline and/or worker payments have to increase.

Some studies by economists and demographers suggest that labor-market implications of declining population growth will be significant.[12] One very positive

---

12 William P. Butz et al., *Demographic Challenges in America's Future*, Report #R-2911-RC, The Rand Corporation (May 1982); Joseph M. Anderson, "An Economic-Demographic Model of the United States Labor Market," in *Research in Population Economics* 4, Julian L. Simon and Peter H. Lindert, eds. (Greenwich, CT: JAI Press, 1982).

effect will be a reduction in the unemployment rates of young adults. Because fewer young inexperienced workers will be entering the labor market, it will be easier to absorb those that do.

As a result of declines in population growth, the labor force will not grow as much as it has historically, creating some upward pressure on wages. These higher wages should reinforce and support the rising participation rates for women and should entice older workers to stay in the work force longer. These enhanced job opportunities for women should keep the fertility low, reinforcing the tendency for low rates of population growth.

The work by Lindert, studied in Chapter 5, suggested that periods of tight labor markets have an equalizing effect on the income distribution. If this model is accurate, and no countervailing tendencies develop, we should witness a trend toward greater income equality in the future as the rewards to labor rise relative to other factors.

The Information Economy

The importance of capital and resources in the American economy is a product of the Industrial Revolution. The Industrial Revolution ushered in an era of mass production where manufacturing replaced agriculture as the dominant source of employment and earnings. This transformation depended upon massive amounts of capital investment and the scale of operations it brought about consumed large amounts of resources.

It now seems clear that the economy is in the midst of an equally important transformation from an industrial society to what Daniel Bell has labeled the *post industrial society*.[13] The key elements of this transformation are a change from a goods-producing to a service economy, a rise in the importance of theoretical knowledge as a source of growth, and an increasing reliance on information processing.

In 1977 the Department of Commerce released a nine-volume study which tracked the progress of this transformation.[14] Until 1905 agricultural workers outnumbered industrial, service, and information workers. Porat defines an *information worker* as one whose income originates primarily in the manipulation of symbols or information. Industrial workers became the dominant force for the next 50 years. By 1955, information workers made up the largest category.

---

13 Daniel Bell, *The Coming of the Post-Industrial Society: A Venture in Social Forecasting* (New York: Basic Books, 1973).

14 Marc Porat, *The Information Economy: Definition and Measurement* (Washington, DC: U.S. Department of Commerce, Office of Telecommunications, 1977).

This transformation has profound implications for our society.[15] Computer-controlled robots will step in to fill the slots vacated by lower population growth in a direct substitution of capital for labor. Working at home will become possible for larger numbers of people as computer communication provides a substitute for transportation. Such changes will boost productivity while reducing pollution and our dependence on raw materials and energy. Intelligence will replace oil as the prime mover of the system.

This vision suggests that the demand for skilled labor will rise more rapidly in the future than the demand for unskilled labor. Education will, therefore, grow in importance, not only as the means of providing that skilled labor, but as the wellspring of ideas that fuel the new growth.

THE GROWTH-DEVELOPMENT RELATIONSHIP

Has economic growth historically served as a vehicle for development? Has growth really made the average person better off? Would the lowest income members of the United States and the world fare better with economic growth or without it?

These turn out to be difficult questions to answer in a way that satisfies everyone, but we must start somewhere. One appropriate point of departure is clarifying what we mean by growth. Some of the disenchantment with growth can be traced to the way that growth is measured. It is not so much that all growth is bad, but that increases in conventional indicators of growth are not always good. Some of the enthusiasm for zero economic growth stems from the fact that economic growth, as currently measured, can be shown to have several undesirable characteristics.

Conventional Measures

A true measure of development would increase whenever we, as a nation or as a world, were better off and decrease whenever we were worse off. Such a measure is called a *welfare measure* and no conventional existing measure is designed to be a welfare measure.

What we currently have are *output measures*, which attempt to indicate how many goods and services have been produced, not how well off we are. Measuring output sounds fairly simple, but it is not. The measure of economic growth

---

15 For a more detailed explanation, see Robert D. Hamrin, *Managing Growth in the 1980's: Toward a New Economics* (New York: Praeger, 1980).

with which most are familiar is based upon the GNP, or gross national product. This number represents the sum of the outputs of goods and services in any year produced by the economy. Prices are used to weight the importance of these goods and services in GNP. Conceptually, this is accomplished by adding up the value added by each sector of the production process until the product is sold.

Why weight by prices? Some means of comparing the value of extremely dissimilar commodities is needed. Prices provide a readily available system of weights that takes into account the value of those commodities to consumers. From early chapters we know that prices should reflect both the marginal benefit to the consumer and the marginal cost to the producer.

GNP is not a measure of welfare and was never meant to be one. One limitation of this indicator as a measure of welfare is that it includes the value of new machines that are replacing worn-out ones rather than increasing the size of the capital stock. To compensate for the fact that some investment merely replaces old machines and does not add to the size of capital stock, a new concept known as net national product (NNP) was introduced. *NNP* is defined as the gross national product minus depreciation.

NNP and GNP share the deficiency that they are both influenced by inflation. If the flow of all goods and services were to remain the same while prices doubled, both NNP and GNP would also double. Since neither welfare nor output would have increased, an accurate indicator should reflect that fact.

To resolve this problem, national income accountants present data on *constant-dollar GNP* and *constant-dollar NNP*. These numbers are derived by "cleansing" the actual GNP and NNP data to take out the effects of price rises. Conceptually, this is accomplished by defining a market basket of goods that stays the same over time. Each year this same basket is repriced. If the cost of the goods in the basket went up 10%, then because the quantities are held constant, we know that prices went up by 10%. This information is used to remove the effects of prices on the indicators; remaining increases should be due to an increased production of goods and services.

This correction does not solve all problems. For one thing not all components of GNP contribute equally to welfare. Probably the closest component we could use in the existing system of accounts would be *consumption*, the amount of goods and services consumed by households. It leaves out government expenditures, investments, exports, and imports.

The final correction which could easily be made to the existing accounts would involve dividing real consumption by the population to get *real consumption per capita*. This correction allows us to differentiate between rises in output needed to maintain the standard of living for an increasing population and rises indicating more goods and services consumed by the average member of that population.

Real consumption per capita is about as close as we can get to a welfare-oriented output measure using readily available data. Yet is is a far cry from being an ideal welfare indicator.

In particular, changes in real consumption per capita fail to distinguish between economic growth resulting from a true increase in income, and economic growth resulting from a depreciation in what economists have come to call "natural capital," the stock of environmentally provided assets such as the soil, the atmosphere, the forests, wildlife, and water.

The traditional definition of income was articulated by Sir John Hicks:

> The purpose of income calculations in practical affairs is to give people an indication of the amount they can consume without impoverishing themselves. Following out this idea, it would seem that we ought to define a man's income as the maximum value which he can consume during a week, and still expect to be as well off at the end of the week as he was at the beginning.[16]

While human-created capital (such as buildings, bridges, etc.) is treated in a manner consistent with this definition, natural capital is not. As human-created capital wears out, the accounts set aside an amount called depreciation to compensate for the decline in value as the equipment wears out. No increase in economic activity is recorded as an increase in income until depreciation has been subtracted from gross returns. That portion of the gains which merely serve to replace worn-out capital is not appropriately considered income.

No such adjustment is made for natural capital in the current national income accounting system. Depreciation of the stock of natural capital is incorrectly counted as income. Development strategies which "cash in" the endowment of natural resources are in these accounts indistinguishable from development strategies which do not depreciate the natural capital stock; the returns from both are treated as income.

Consider an analogy. Many high-quality private educational institutions in the United States have large financial endowments. In considering their budgets for the year, these institutions take the revenue from tuition and other fees and add in some proportion of the interest and capital gains earned from the endowment. Except in extraordinary circumstances standard financial practice, however, does not allow the institution to attack the principal. Drawing down the endowment and treating this increase in financial resources as income is not allowed.

Yet that is precisely what the national accounts allow us to do in terms of natural resources. We can deplete our soils, cut down our forests, and douse ocean coves with oil, and the resulting economic activity is treated as income, not as a decline in the endowment of natural capital.

Because the Hicksian definition is violated for natural capital, policymakers are misled. By relying upon misleading information, policymakers are more likely to undertake unsustainable development strategies.

---

16 J. R. Hicks, *Value and Capital,* 2nd ed. (Oxford: Oxford University Press, 1947): 172.

Adjusting the national income accounts to apply the Hicksian definition uniformly to human-made and natural capital could, in resource-dependent countries, make quite a difference. For example, Robert Repetto and colleagues of the World Resources Institute studied the growth rates of gross national product in Indonesia using both conventional unadjusted figures and figures adjusted to account for the depreciation of natural capital. Their study found that while the unadjusted gross national product increased at an average annual rate of 7.1% from 1971 to 1984, the adjusted estimates rose by only 4.0% per year.[17]

Motivated by a recognition of these serious flaws in the current system of accounts, a number of industrial countries have now proposed (or in a few cases have already set up) systems of adjusted accounts including Norway, France, Canada, Japan, the Netherlands, Germany, and the United States. Significant differences of opinion on such issues as whether the changes should be incorporated in a complementary system of accounts or in a complete revision of the standard accounts remain to be resolved.

Alternative Measures

Because revised accounts are not yet available, we cannot use them to assess the relationship between growth and economic well-being. But the question won't go away, so we have to do the best we can with what information is available.

Several studies have attempted to adjust real consumption per capita figures on an ad hoc basis to come up with a measure that is closer to being a welfare measure. One of the first was by Nordhaus and Tobin.[18] Their first adjustment involves an attempt to account for the amount of welfare-reducing environmental damage being inflicted by pollution. Reasoning that part of the increased wages of urban workers represents compensation for having been exposed to the higher pollution concentrations, they used a portion of the income differential between urban and rural families as their measure of the monetary value of the damage caused. This estimate is then subtracted from the real consumption data.

They then adjust the data to treat consumer durables in a different way. In conventional accounts, consumer durables are incorporated by adding in their full cost at the time of purchase, in spite of the fact that services from durable goods are received throughout their useful life. Nordhaus and Tobin subtract these durable good *purchases* and add back in an estimate of the annual *services* they provide.

---

17 Robert Repetto, "Nature's Resources as Productive Assets," *Challenge* 32 (September/October 1989): 16–20.

18 William D. Nordhaus, and James Tobin, "Is Growth Obsolete?" in *Economic Growth, Fiftieth Anniversary Colloquium*, Vol. 5 (New York: National Bureau of Economic Research, 1972): 4–17.

The final subtraction from the conventional accounts involves excluding consumer expenditures which do not seem to raise welfare. The major expenditures they excluded were the costs of commuting to and from work. While necessary expenditures, these do not themselves raise welfare.

Nordhaus and Tobin also correct for omissions that tend to bias the conventional accounts downward when interpreted in welfare terms. These include the value of leisure time and household production, neither of which is valued in conventional accounts. One benefit of growth is that productivity increases have resulted in a decline in the average workweek. This increased leisure is valued by Nordhaus and Tobin at the market wage rate that could have been earned if the time were spent working rather than in leisure activities. Household production involves the many services performed around the house. Unless there are hired servants, household production activities do not enter the conventional accounts.

The problem with the manner in which the conventional approach treats household production is nicely illustrated by an example. When a single person marries his or her housekeeper, GNP goes down, because an activity which was formerly a market activity is no longer. Yet we presume, since marriage is a voluntary arrangement, that welfare was increased. The change in the indicator sends the wrong signal. Nordhaus and Tobin correct this conventional approach by adding in an imputed value for nonmarketed household production.

Their final correction involves adding into personal consumption expenditures a value for the government services provided. Traditionally, the government sector is treated separately in the GNP and its output is valued at cost. By including this measure, Nordhaus and Tobin are correcting two problems: (1) the omission of government services from the personal consumption expenditures; and (2) valuing these services as received rather than (in the case of government durables, such as roads) at the time of purchase.

After making all these adjustments, they arrive at an indicator they call the *measure of economic welfare* (MEW). The MEW per capita rose by about 42% between 1929 and 1965. This increase was only about one-half of the 87.5% increase in real NNP per capita over the same period. According to Nordhaus and Tobin, real NNP per capita does overstate growth in economic well-being, but their estimate leaves no doubt that they believe correctly measured economic well-being has increased substantially since 1929.

Others have attempted to make different adjustments. In particular, Usher has adjusted the conventional accounts to incorporate the value of increased life expectancy and finds that this adjustment boosts the growth rate of the adjusted measure above the conventional measure.[19]

---

19 Dan Usher, *The Measurement of Economic Growth* (New York: Columbia University Press, 1980).

Zolotas performed a similar but somewhat more detailed set of calculations for the particular purpose of discovering whether the growth in well-being had declined over time.[20] The trends in his measure of welfare suggest that the additional increases in well-being are becoming smaller and smaller as growth continues. Similar results were subsequently obtained by Daly and Cobb.[21] They found that per capita welfare had increased 20% from 1951 to 1986 in the United States, but that increase was the net result of two offsetting trends. Per capita welfare had started to decline between 1970 and 1980. (Note that this is a decline in welfare, not a decline in the growth of welfare!) The estimated average annual decline during the 1970s was 0.14%, while the average annual decline during the 1980s was estimated to be 1.26%. If this evidence were ultimately confirmed by better designed accounts, the effects of economic growth on per capita well-being have been positive, but recently have turned negative. According to Daly and Cobb, further growth in the U.S. not only would not improve well-being, it would decrease it.

As the authors of the above studies would readily concede, one should be skeptical about the specific magnitude of these estimates. The procedures provide only crude approximations to those required to produce a true measure of welfare.

GROWTH AND POVERTY: THE INDUSTRIALIZED NATIONS

Conceiving of the growth-development relationship only in terms of the effects on the average citizen obscures a great deal of what may be happening in a society. Two societies may have the same per capita growth in average well-being, but if the fruits of this growth are shared uniformly in one and unequally in the second, it seems overly simplistic to argue that the increase in welfare levels would be the same in the two countries. As Example 21.2 indicates, relative income levels seem to make a difference in how well-off people feel.

While the evidence suggests that economic growth has improved the lot of the average citizen in the developed world, it tells us nothing about how the poorest members of society fared. To determine whether the poorest citizens also benefit from growth, we must dig deeper into the nature of the growth process.

One source of information about this relationship is history. To exploit that source we shall examine the data for a period of particularly high economic growth in the United States. Did it benefit the poor, or were they left behind?

---

20 Xenophon Zolotas, *Economic Growth and Declining Social Welfare* (New York: New York University, 1981).

21 Herman E. Daly and John B. Cobb, Jr., *For the Common Good* (Boston: Beacon Press, 1989): 401-455.

EXAMPLE 21.2

Does Money Buy Happiness?

In a highly subjective but interesting study, economist Richard Easterlin collected data from 30 surveys conducted in 19 developed and less developed countries that analyzed the relationship between happiness and income. In every one of these surveys, the respondents were asked to rate how happy they were feeling, using the scale "very happy," "mildly happy," "mildly unhappy," and "very unhappy." Information on respondent income levels was also collected.

In analyzing these data he found:

1. At a point in time a larger portion of high-income people are happier than low-income people, for all countries and all years.
2. The proportion of happy and unhappy in each group remained relatively constant over time in spite of generally rising incomes. For example, in the United States, roughly the same percentage of wealthy people and poor people said they were very happy in 1940 as in 1970.

The first finding suggests that higher income is positively correlated with happiness, while the second suggests that despite large increases in income, the percentage saying they were very happy did not increase. How are these apparently contradictory findings to be explained?

Easterlin explains them by suggesting that one of the components of happiness for people is their relative income. Thus, a person at the top of the heap in any particular country may be happier than he or she would be if that same income were earned in a richer country where lots of people earned that income. If this hypothesis is correct, it suggests that the average level of welfare in an economic system is an inadequate indicator of the total welfare in the society. The distribution of the fruits of economic growth makes a difference.

Source: Richard A. Easterlin, "Does Money Buy Happiness," *The Public Interest* (Winter 1973): 3–10.

The Effects on Income Inequality

Growth can help the poor, although history suggests that these beneficial effects are not inevitable. It is generally believed that income transfers are easier when the amount to be shared is growing. The donors can give up some of their gains and still be better off, while in a no-growth situation any sharing must come from a reduction in the real income of the donor.

On the surface many observers believe that growth has not, in fact, lived up to its billing as a means of alleviating poverty. Lee Rainwater, a Harvard sociologist, in his survey of the situation concluded:

It seems well established that income and wealth inequality have not declined significantly over the past half century, and probably have not declined at all in the past quarter century.[22]

The Effects on Poverty

The failure of economic growth to reduce economic inequality does not, as it might appear, imply that growth has not benefited the poor. In the first place, many of the published studies do not take into account the significant transfers to the poor that are rendered in kind (such as food stamps and Medicaid) rather than in cash. Therefore, published income levels may understate the positive effects on the poor. In addition, stating the problem in this relative form ignores the increases in absolute welfare that all persons, including the poor, derive.

With respect to the first point, it seems abundantly clear that transfers to the poor have been significant recently and have made a difference. One way to demonstrate this is to examine what has happened during recent periods of growth to the number of persons in the United States living below the poverty threshold. This threshold, which is adjusted upward each year to hold purchasing power constant in the face of rising inflation, represents the minimum income necessary to provide a person or family with the basic necessities of life.

Table 21.2 shows what has happened to the proportion of persons living below the poverty threshold with and without transfers. *Market income* shows what would have happened to the proportion if no transfers had taken place. *Census income* shows these proportions after adjusting for the major cash transfer programs, and the *adjusted income* column shows the proportion after adjusting for both cash and in-kind transfers.

Several characteristics of these data should be noticed. First, the difference between the census income and adjusted income suggests that in-kind transfer programs have had a significant impact on the poor. Studies such as those accomplished by Rainwater which do not include these in-kind transfers tend to underestimate the positive impact experienced by the poor during a growth period.

The second conclusion is that the transfers have made the difference, not growth itself. The market-income column shows that economic growth, in the absence of transfers, would not have lifted many persons from below to above

---

22 Lee Rainwater, "Equity, Income Inequality, and the Steady State," in *The Sustainable Society*, Dennis Clark Pirages, ed. (New York: Praeger, 1977): 263.

TABLE 21.2   Persons Living below Absolute Income Thresholds 1965–1980

	Census income	Adjusted income	Market income
	(%)	(%)	(%)
1965	15.6	12.1[a]	21.3
1968	12.8	10.1	18.2
1970	12.6	9.4	18.8
1972	11.9	6.2	19.2
1974	11.6	7.8	20.3
1976	11.8	6.7	21.0
1978	11.4	NA	20.2
1980	13.0	6.1	20.0
Percentage change	-16.7	-49.59	-6.10

[a]Cited in Eugene Smolensky, "Poverty in the United States: Where Do We Stand?", *University of Wisconsin-Madison Institute for Research on Poverty Focus* 5 (Winter 1981–82): 3, Table 1.

Sources: S. Danziger and R. Plotnick, "The War on Income Poverty: Achievements and Failures," in *Welfare Reform in America*, Pl. Sommers, ed. (Hingham, MA: Martinus Nijhoff, 1982). Adjusted income for 1968–1974 is from T. Smeeding, "Measuring the Economic Welfare of Low-Income Households and the Antipoverty Effectiveness of Cash and Noncash Transfer Programs" (Ph.D. diss., Department of Economics, University of Wisconsin-Madison, 1975) and "The Antipoverty Effectiveness of In-Kind Transfer," *Journal of Human Resources* 12 (1977): 360–378. Adjusted income for 1976 and 1980 are from Smeeding, "The Antipoverty Effect of In-Kind Transfers: A 'Good Idea' Gone Too Far?" *Policy Studies Journal*, forthcoming.

the poverty threshold. The linkage between growth and the poor depends more upon its affect on the willingness to transfer than on direct market effects.

By focusing on relative incomes, Rainwater was seeking to discover whether the poor are becoming better off more rapidly than the rich. His answer was no. By using an absolute standard such as the poverty threshold, however, Table 21.2 focuses on the well-being of the poor per se, without considering the rich at all. That focus suggests that the poor were made better off in terms of meeting basic needs during the 15-year period studied, even if their rate of progress did not exceed that of the rich.

To lend concreteness to the argument that the poor are better equipped during growth periods to meet basic needs, consider what has happened to one aspect of the quality of life for the poor—the desirability of their housing.

The U.S. Bureau of the Census maintains records on two indicators of poor housing quality. The *overcrowding* indicator measures the percentage of dwelling units having an average of 1.01 or more persons per room. The *substandard* indicator records the percentage of dwelling units that are considered dilapidated or are lacking complete plumbing facilities. As Table 21.3 indicates, the decline in these indicators has been strong and pervasive. The effects were felt in urban and rural areas and by both blacks and whites.

Although growth cannot be seen as a vehicle that inevitably creates equality of income among the rich and poor, the evidence shows that, in the United States

TABLE 21.3 Trends in the Condition of Urban and Rural Housing by Race of Occupant, 1950–80[a]

	All races		White[b]		Black[c]	
	Urban	Rural	Urban	Rural	Urban	Rural
Overcrowded housing (% of units occupied by 1.01 or more persons per room)						
1950	13.3	20.6	—	—	—	—
1960	10.2	15.1	8.5	12.92	24.7	40.8
1970	7.6	10.1	7.0	7.5	18.1	30.1
1980	4.5	4.7	2.7	3.6	10.3	16.8
Substandard housing (% of dilapidated or lacking complete plumbing facilities)						
1950	22.0	62.4	15.9	56.2	57.2	92.7
1960	10.5	36.0	7.4	30.3	31.8	85.6
1970	3.4	16.9	3.5	16.5	8.5	62.3
1980	1.4	4.6	1.1	3.3	3.0	22.7

[a]Data refer to combined totals for owner-occupied and renters.

[b]Figures in 1950, 1960, and 1980 include only whites; in 1970 include whites and other races except blacks.

[c]In 1950 and 1960 figures includes all non-whites; in 1970 and 1980 includes only blacks.

Sources: All information for the various years was drawn from the appropriate Census of Housing, General Housing Characteristics, United States Summary. This document is issued by the U.S. Department of Commerce, Bureau of the Census.

at least, the quality of life experienced by the poor has been improved by it. This improvement has come both from a general rising standard of living and a rise in transfers from the rich to the poor.

POVERTY IN THE LESS INDUSTRIALIZED NATIONS

Economic growth can be a vehicle for development and this form of development can benefit the poor as well as the rich according to the historical experience in the industrialized nations. Though the relationship between economic growth and poverty is neither inevitable nor universally effective, it does provide one possible path for dealing with poverty.

How relevant is this experience for the Third World? Can and should the traditional approach to economic growth serve as a model for those nations struggling to free themselves from the grip of poverty?

It would be delightful to find that the poverty problem is solving itself, but that is certainly not the case. Many of the world's poor are caught in a seamless web of deteriorating conditions.[23] According to a 1988 address by World Bank President Barber Conable: "Poverty on today's scale prevents a billion people from having even minimally acceptable standards of living. . . . In sub-Sahara Africa more than 100 million people—one in four—do not get enough to eat." Agricultural productivity per capita has been declining in Africa since 1967 and in Latin America since 1981. The World Bank reports that from 1979 to 1983 life expectancy fell in nine African countries. In Zambia twice as many children died from malnutrition in 1984 than in 1980. In its 1989 annual report the United Nations Children's Fund (UNICEF) concluded "at least half a million young children have died in the last 12 months as a result of slowing down or the reversal of progress in the developing world."

What are the trends in incomes? Many countries are actually losing ground. As Inter-American Development Bank President Enrique Iglesias said in September, 1988, "The per capita income of the average Latin American is 9 percent lower today than it was in 1980. This is average. In some countries the standard of living has slipped back to where it was 20 years ago."

The picture is not totally bleak. Success against poverty is possible. Some Asian countries have done well in the 1980s, for example. Thailand has reported a 50% decrease in its poverty rate since 1960. The Republic of Korea, Taiwan, and Singapore have all experienced rapid industrialization and rising standards of living.

Appropriateness of the Traditional Model

How appropriate is the traditional economic growth model for these countries? Does it point the way out of poverty?

Scale.   One of the first indicators that traditional models may be inappropriate derives from the ecological effects of the proposed global scale of economic activity necessary to eradicate poverty if the model of development followed by the industrialized nations of Asia, Europe, and Africa were adopted by the rest of the world. As Jim MacNeill, the former director of the World Commission on Environment and Development, has stated "If current forms of development were employed, a five to ten-fold increase in economic activity would be required over the next fifty years to meet the needs and aspirations of a population twice the size of today's 5.2 billion, as well as to begin to reduce mass poverty." Whether increases of this magnitude could be accomplished while still respecting the atmospheric and ecological systems on which all economic activity ultimately depends is not at all obvious.

---

23 The information in this paragraph and the two which follow were obtained from Alan B. Durning, *Poverty and the Environment: Reversing the Downward Spiral,* Paper No. 92 (Washington, DC: Worldwatch Institute, 1989): 15–18.

Increased energy consumption to support new industry would add greenhouse gases. Increased refrigeration would add more of the gases depleting the stratospheric ozone level. The industrialized nations have freely used the very large capacity of the atmosphere to absorb these gases. Little absorptive capacity is left. Most observers seem to believe that to meet the challenge we need to take an activist stance by controlling population, severely reducing emissions of these gases in the industrialized world, and discovering new forms of development which are sustainable.

Forms of Development. Economics can assist in the process of characterizing forms of development. Appropriate development should capitalize on local strengths and stay away from weaknesses; it should be sensitive to factor prices.

Many, if not most of the developing nations, are labor-surplus economics. It follows that their strategy for development, at least in the beginning stages should be labor-intensive. Labor-intensive processes serve the twin purposes of capitalizing on an abundant resource and providing a source of income to large numbers of people.[24]

While the forms of development in the industrialized nations are increasingly going to rely on a highly skilled labor force, that is inappropriate for countries where the educational systems may not currently be able to supply sufficient numbers of skilled workers to fill the need. By effectively utilizing the low skilled work force, developing countries can increase their incomes, decrease population growth and ultimately create the wealth needed to support a strong education a system.

Development in the industrialized countries has also been very fossil-fuel dependant. While this may be appropriate when supplies of fossil fuels are plentiful and the remaining capacity of the environment to accept the by-product gases is unlimited, it is certainly less appropriate for a future plagued by diminishing supplies and global warming.

Barriers to Development

What are the barriers to raising standards of living in the Third World? Rising populations face increasingly limited access to land, health services, education, and financial resources. Many of these problems are intensified by the current international economy. Heavy debt burdens, falling prices for their exports, and the flight of capital that could be used to create jobs and income are all significant barriers to sustainable development.

---

24 Contrast this with capital intensive processes which use much less labor and distribute more of the returns to the owners of capital, who are typically well off.

Population Growth. Poverty begets poverty. The positive feedback loop between population growth and poverty is one powerful example. Population growth rates are typically higher, substantially higher, in low income populations. High infant mortality causes parents to compensate with large numbers of births. Children provide one of the few available means of old age security. Knowledge about birth control techniques is sparse and the availability of contraceptives is limited. Women frequently have low levels of education and in some cultures large families are the only possible way for women to achieve status. Larger populations in turn tend to increase the degree of poverty by lowering wages and by spreading the family resources allocated to children over a larger number.

Population growth also puts increased pressure on the natural resource base. Pushing larger numbers of people onto marginal land increases soil erosion and deforestation. Increasing population density can cause the carrying capacity of the land to be exceeded. In parts of Africa where nomadic tribes have coexisted for centuries with a fragile ecosystem, larger populations and reduced mobility have resulted in such a serious deterioration of the ecosystem that it is no longer able to satisfy basic human needs.

Land Ownership Patterns. Pressures on the land arising from population growth are exacerbated by patterns of land ownership in many of the lower income countries. In agricultural economies access to land is a key ingredient in any attempt to eradicate poverty, but land ownership is frequently highly concentrated among a few extremely wealthy owners. Improvements in agricultural techniques can do little to raise living standards if peasants do not have access to their own land.

One common measure of the degree of inequality in land ownership is the Gini coefficient. The Gini coefficient can take on values of 0.0 (which would indicate perfect equality) to 1.0 (which would indicate perfect inequality). Perfect equality would occur if every farmer owned exactly the same amount of land. Perfect inequality would imply that all land was owned by a single farmer.

In Latin America, Gini coefficients in excess of 0.75 are common.[25] This region has the most skewed land ownership patterns on the globe, a legacy of colonial times when colonial rulers accumulated vast amounts of land. Asian nations are somewhat better with Gini coefficients ranging from 0.51 to 0.64, while in Africa, where collective tribal land ownership is common, the coefficients fall between 0.36 and 0.55.[26]

Trade Policies. Some of the barriers faced by Third World countries as they attempt to raise living standards have been erected by the industrialized nations.

---

25 The land ownership data are from Alan B. Durning, *Poverty and the Environment: Reversing the Downward Spiral*, Paper No. 92 (Washington, DC: Worldwatch Institute, 1989): 25.

26 To provide one, admittedly imperfect, basis for comparison, the 1986 U. S. Gini coefficient for the distribution of income among families was 0.389.

Trade policies are one example. The terms of trade for many Third World countries have deteriorated in the recent past.[27]

Some of the reasons for this deterioration are rather natural effects of markets rather than misguided policies. Included in this category are the import substitutions in the industrialized world (such as when optical fibers are substituted for copper in phone lines) and lower demand for Third World exports triggered by lower economic growth in the industrialized countries.

But political factors are also important. When political forces in the developed countries conspire to eliminate or substantially reduce natural markets for the developing countries, these policies not only exacerbate the poverty in the developing nations, but they have a direct degrading effect on the environment.[28]

The Multi-Fiber Arrangement, originally implemented in 1974, is a case in point. Its effect has been to severely reduce developing country exports of textiles and other products made from fibers. In developing countries fiber products are produced by labor-intensive techniques, causing the employment impact to be high. For local sustainable agriculture the opportunity to provide the fiber raw materials is another source of employment. By artificially reducing the markets for these products and the fibers from which these products are manufactured, the agreement has forced some nations to substitute resource-intensive economic activities, such as timber exports, for the more environmentally congenial fiber-based manufacturing in order to earn foreign exchange.

Agricultural trade flows not only demonstrate how price distortions can be translated into unsustainable development, but also to show how they can exacerbate poverty. In general price distortions and artificially supported exchange rates have resulted in a pattern of trade that involves excessive agricultural production in the developed world and too little in the developing world. Agriculture in the developed world is supported by a number of different subsidies. In the developing world the bias operates to promote underproduction rather than overproduction. Overvalued exchange rates increase the attractiveness of importing food and decrease the attractiveness of exporting food.

By discouraging small scale agriculture in developing countries, an activity that would provide income to a segment of the population faced with the most severe forms of poverty, biased trade flows exacerbate the poverty problem. Fur-

---

27 The terms of trade determine international purchasing power. When the terms of trade deteriorate, Third World exports purchase fewer imports. Evidence on the deteriorating terms of trade can be found in World Bank, *World Development Report 1989* (Washington, DC: Oxford University Press, 1989): 190–191, Table 14.

28 A study by the World Bank staff shows that lowering tariff barriers in the European Economic Community, the United States and Japan would permit exports from the highly indebted developing countries to increase by some $6.5 billion. World Bank, *World Debt Tables, 1988–9* (Washington, DC: World Bank, 1988): xxvii.

thermore since income increases targeted on this particular group typically lead to slower population growth, even some of the population pressures on the environment could ultimately be related to biases in current trade patterns.

One common stereotype of the difference between developed and less developed countries involves their respective supplies of minerals. According to this stereotype, less developed countries control most of the world's mineral resources, while the developed world creates the demand for them. If accurate, this view would suggest that rising mineral prices would eventually create favorable terms of trade for most developing countries.

Unfortunately, upon closer inspection this stereotype represents at best an over-simplification. While exports of minerals have increased from less-developed to developed countries, not all less developed countries share these higher export levels. A few have large reserves of petroleum or nonfuel minerals, but most do not. The benefits from increasing mineral prices tend to bypass most less developed countries.

Debt. Many Third World countries have staggering levels of debt to service. The World Bank has estimated that the total debt of all developing countries reached $1290 billion in 1989. In 1989, poor nations sent $51.6 billion more to the industrialized nations in interest and principal repayment than it received in new capital.[29] External debt is 104.1% of the gross national product of the severely indebted low-income countries. These percentages reach as high as 305.1% for Brazil and 476.0% for Guyana.[30]

Unfortunately even private capital is flowing out of the capital poor countries where it is desperately needed and into the capital rich countries. The World Bank estimates that the stock of "flight" capital held abroad by citizens of severely indebted countries equals a significant fraction of their countries' external debt.

In periods of high real interest rates servicing these debts puts a significant drain on foreign exchange earnings. Using these foreign exchange earnings to service the debt eliminates the possibility of using them to finance imports for sustainable activities to alleviate poverty. One study found that in all but one of the most indebted countries, the ratio of investment to gross domestic product was substantially lower in the 1982–1988 period (when the debt burden was heaviest) than in the previous six years.[31] In Argentina the ratio fell from 25% to 15%, while comparable figures for Venezuela indicate a fall from 33% to 18%.

---

29 Even if all official development assistance and private capital flows to the developing countries were included in the total, the net outflow would still be $9.8 billion. This evidence on the debt comes from the World Bank, *World Debt Tables 1989–90*, Vol. 1 (Washington, DC: World Bank, 1989): 1–9.

30 See World Bank, *World Debt Tables 1989–90*, Vol. 2 (Washington, DC: World Bank, 1989): 18, 58, 114.

31 "Debtors' Hangover," *The Economist* (May 20, 1989): 73.

This fall in investment has, in turn, reduced the growth of output and exports in debtor nations and thereby further undermined their ability to repay their debts.

With the notable exception of a relatively few oil-rich nations, most developing countries import a great deal of energy. Because this demand is relatively price inelastic, their expenditures on imports have risen tremendously without similar compensating increases in receipts from the sale of exports.

The situation is reversed in many of the oil-exporting countries, which are commanding abnormally high prices for their oil. Their favorable terms of trade, however, have not always insulated them from development difficulties. Nigeria is a classic example. Buoyed by oil exports the local wage structure and exchange rates ended up severely harming agricultural production. Resources flowed out of agricultural production and into oil production. Even the income distribution was adversely affected, becoming much more unequally distributed.[32]

The evidence suggests that while growth is no panacea for the problems of the developing world, it is probably better than no growth. However the traditional form of growth experienced in the industrialized countries is not likely to be the most appropriate form for the less developed countries in the future. Circumstances have changed since the Industrial Revolution. Furthermore the factor endowments in Third World countries are not the same as those in the industrialized countries. Changing circumstances call for changing approaches.

SUMMARY

Historically, increases in inputs and technological progress were important sources of economic growth in the industrialized nations. In the future some factors of production, such as labor, will not increase as rapidly as they have in the past. The effect of this decline on growth depends on the interplay among the law of diminishing marginal productivity, substitution possibilities, and technological progress. The law of diminishing marginal productivity suggests slower growth rates, while technological progress and the availability of substitution possibilities counteract this drag. One view foresees limits to technological progress imposed by the second law of thermodynamics, implying that the growth process must culminate in a steady or stationary state where growth ultimately diminishes to zero.

Our examination of empirical evidence suggests that increased environmental control has not currently had a large impact on the economy as a whole, although certain industries have been hit quite hard. Environmental policy has

32 Jan S. Hogendorn, *Economic Development*, 2nd ed. (New York: HarperCollins, 1991). My thanks to my colleague Professor Hogendorn for allowing me to refer to the typescript of his new edition.

triggered only a small rise in the rate of inflation and a mild reduction in growth. Environmental policy has apparently contributed more jobs than it has cost.

The situation is similar for energy. Though rather large increases in energy prices have occurred, the portion of the slowdown in economic growth during the 1970s attributed to these increases is not large. Some diminution of growth has certainly occurred, but it seems premature to suggest that rising energy prices have already forced a transition to a period of substantially lower growth rates.

This is not to say, however, that the economy is not being transformed. It is. Two particularly important aspects of this transformation are the decline in population growth and the rise in importance of information as a driving economic force. Both aspects tend to reduce the degree that physical limits constrain economic growth and increase the degree to which current welfare levels are sustainable.

Some crude attempts have been made to assess whether or not growth in the industrialized countries has historically made the citizens of those countries better off. Results of these studies suggest that because growth has ultimately generated more leisure, longer life expectancy, and more goods and services, it has been beneficial. But more recent studies suggest that the benefits from growth have been steadily diminishing over time. One study found that further growth in the U.S. now lowers economic well-being of the average U.S. citizen; at this stage of affluence the negative aspects were estimated to outweigh the positive aspects.

Our examination of the evidence suggests that the notion that all of the world's people are automatically benefited by economic growth is naive. Growth has demonstrably benefited the poor in the developed countries, mainly through transfers from more well-off members of society.

The outlook for the less industrialized nations is at best mixed. Solving many of their future environmental problems will require raising standards of living. However, following the path of development pioneered by the industrialized nations is probably not possible without triggering severe global environmental problems; the solution would become the problem. New forms of development will be necessary.

The less industrialized countries must overcome a number of significant barriers if development is to become a reality. At the local level, rising populations face increasingly limited access to land or productive assets. At the national level, corruption and development policies discriminate against the poor. Globally their situation is worsened by rising debt burdens, falling export prices for the products they sell, and the flight of capital that could be used to create jobs and income.

How can the barriers be overcome? What new forms of development can be introduced? By what means can they be introduced? We deal with these questions in the next chapter.

FURTHER READING

Berndt, Ernst R. and Barry C. Fields, eds. *Modeling and Measuring Natural Resource Substitution* (Cambridge, MA: MIT Press, 1981). A highly technical but insightful collection of 12 essays on the state of the art in measuring factor substitution and technical change.

Cleveland, Harlan, ed. *The Management of Sustainable Growth* (New York: Pergamon Press, 1981), and James C. Coomer, ed., *Quest for a Sustainable Society* (New York: Pergamon Press, 1981). The two volumes contain a wide-ranging multidisciplinary series of essays coming out of the third in a series of five biennial conferences dedicated to a rethinking of growth policy.

Durning, Alan B. *Poverty and the Environment: Reversing the Downward Spiral*, Paper No. 92 (Washington, DC: Worldwatch Institute, 1989). A very thorough examination of the degree of Third World poverty, the sources of that poverty, the resulting effects on the environment and some strategies to deal with these problems.

Hamrin, Robert D. *Managing Growth in the 1980's: Toward a New Economics* (New York: Praeger, 1980). Hamrin suggests that the traditional sources of economic growth can no longer support growth. He suggests new actions and policies shaped by a selective growth ethic.

Peskin, Henry M., Paul R. Portney, and Allen Kneese. *Environmental Regulation and the U.S. Economy* (Baltimore: Johns Hopkins University Press for Resources for the Future, 1981). Six essays on the effect of environmental regulations on the economy combined with an excellent introduction to the issues and summary of the implications of the evidence presented.

ADDITIONAL REFERENCES

Dasgupta, Ajit K. *Growth, Development and Welfare: An Essay on Levels of Living* (Oxford: Basil Blackwell, 1988).

Dennison, Edward. *Accounting for United States Economic Growth, 1929–1969* (Washington, DC: Brookings Institution, 1974).

Hirsh, Fred. *Social Limits to Growth* (Cambridge, MA: Harvard University Press, 1976).

Hueckel, Glenn. "A Historical Approach to Future Economic Growth," *Science* 191 (14 March 1975): 925–931.

Jorgenson, Dale W. "Energy and the Future U.S. Economy," *The Wharton Magazine* 3 (Summer 1979): 15–21.

Lindert, Peter. *Fertility and Scarcity in America* (Princeton, NJ: Princeton University Press, 1978).

Mesarovic, Michaklo and Edward Pestel. *Mankind at the Turning Point: The Second Report to the Club of Rome* (New York: New American Library, 1974).

Neary, J. Peter and Sweder Van Wijnbergen, eds. *Natural Resources and the Macroeconomy* (Cambridge, MA: MIT Press, 1986).

Perrings, Charles. *Economy and Environment: A Theoretical Essay on the Interdependence of Economic and Environmental Systems* (Cambridge: Cambridge University Press, 1987).

Peskin, Henry M. *Accounting for Natural Resource Depletion and Degradation in Developing Countries*, Working Paper No. 13, (Washington, DC: World Bank Environment Department, 1989).

Weintraub, Andrew et al., eds. *The Economic Growth Controversy* (New York: International Arts and Sciences Press, 1973).

DISCUSSION QUESTIONS

1. "Economic growth has historically provided a valuable vehicle for raising the standard of living. Now that the standard of living is so high, however, further economic growth is unnecessary. When the undesirable side effects are considered, it is probably counterproductive. Economic growth is a process that has outlived its usefulness." Discuss.

2. Is affluence part of the problem or part of the solution when it comes to environmental problems? Why?

CHAPTER TWENTY-TWO

The Quest for
Sustainable Development

*The challenge of finding sustainable development paths ought
to provide the impetus—indeed the imperative—for a renewed
search for multilateral solutions and a restructured international economic system of co-operation. These challenges cut
across the divides of national sovereignty, of limited strategies
for economic gain, and of separated disciplines of science.*

GRO HARLEM BRUNDTLAND, Prime Minister of Norway,
Our Common Future (1987)

INTRODUCTION

During May 1990, representatives from the member nations of the United Nations Economic Commission for Europe gathered in Bergen, Norway, to undertake an ambitious task. Following four previous meetings held in the United
Kingdom, Poland, Germany, and the United States, this gathering began the
process of charting a sustainable development course for the future global
economy. The fruits of this deliberation were part of the larger process of setting
an agenda for the global United Nations Conference on Environment and
Development in 1992.

What is sustainable development? According to the Brundtland Report,
which is widely credited with raising the concept to its current level of importance, "Sustainable development is development that meets the needs of the
present without compromising the ability of future generations to meet their own

needs."[1] But that is far from the only possible definition.[2] A nascent concept, sustainable development is still in the process of being refined and clarified.

Part of the widespread appeal of the concept, according to critics, is due to its vagueness. Being all things to all people can build a large following, but it also has a substantial disadvantage; close inspection may reveal the concept to be vacuous. As the emperor discovered about his new clothes, things are not always what they seem.

In this chapter we look hard at the concept of sustainable development and whether or not it is useful as a guide to the future. What are the basic principles of sustainable development? What does sustainable development imply about changes in the way our system operates? How could the transition to sustainable development be managed? Will the global economic system automatically produce sustainable development or will policy changes be needed? what policy changes?

SUSTAINABILITY OF GROWTH

Suppose we were to map out possible future trends in the long-term welfare of the average citizen. Using a time scale measured in centuries on the horizontal axis (Figure 22.1) four basic culture trends emerge, labeled *A, B, C,* and *D*, with t^0 representing the present. *D* portrays continued exponential growth in which the future becomes a simple repetition of the past. In this scenario not only would current welfare levels be sustainable, but growth in welfare would be sustainable. Our concern for intergenerational justice would lead us to favor current generations, since they would be the poorest. Worrying about future generations would be unnecessary.

The second scenario (*C*) envisions slowly diminished growth culminating in a steady state where growth diminishes to zero. The welfare of each future generation is at least as well off as all previous generations. Current welfare levels are sustainable, though current levels of welfare growth would not be. Since the level of welfare of each generation is sustainable, artificial constraints on the process would be unnecessary. To constraint growth would injure all subsequent generations.

The third scenario (*B*) is similar in that it envisions initial growth followed by a steady state, but with an important difference—those generations between

1 The World Commission on Environment and Development, *Our Common Future* (Oxford: Oxford University Press, 1987): 43.

2 One search for definitions produced 61, though many were very similar. See John Pezzey, *Economic Analysis of Sustainable Growth and Sustainable Development*, Working Paper No. 15, (Washington, DC: World Bank Environmental Department, 1989).

FIGURE 22.1   Possible alternative futures.

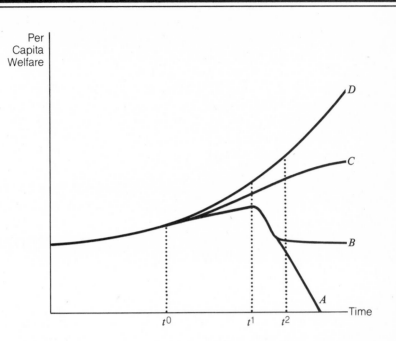

t^1 and t^2 are worse off than the generations preceding them. This is the type of scenario anticipated by Meadows and his colleagues. Neither growth nor welfare levels are sustainable at current levels, and the sustainability criterion would call for an immediate transition to sustainable welfare levels.

The final scenario (A) denies the existence of sustainable per-capita welfare levels, suggesting that the only possible sustainable level is zero. All consumption by the current generation serves simply to hasten the end of civilization.

These scenarios suggest that three dimensions of the sustainability issue are important: (1) the existence of a positive sustainable level of welfare; (2) the magnitude of the ultimate sustainable level of welfare vis à vis current welfare levels; and (3) the sensitivity of the future level of welfare to actions by previous generations. The first dimension is important because if positive sustainable levels of welfare are possible, scenario A, which in some ways is the most philosophically difficult, is ruled out. The second is important because, if the ultimately sustainable welfare level is higher than the current level, radical surgery to cut current living standards is not necessary. The final dimension raises the issue of whether the ultimate sustainable level of welfare can be increased or reduced by the actions of current generations. If so, the sustainability criterion would suggest taking these impacts into account, lest future generations be unnecessarily impoverished by involuntary wealth transfers to previous generations.

The first dimension is relatively easy to dispense with. The existence of positive sustainable welfare levels is guaranteed by the existence of renewable resources, particularly solar energy, as well as by nature's ability to assimilate a certain amount of waste.[3] Therefore we can rule out scenario A.

No one knows exactly what level of economic activity can ultimately be sustained, but the prediction of early societal collapse certainly seems grossly exaggerated. Since growth is slowing as a natural process, the most serious excesses of unregulated growth (such as pollution) are being mitigated, and solar energy is abundant, scenario *C* seems likely, though with current levels of information no one can completely rule out *B*.

Current generations can affect the sustainable welfare levels of future generations both positively and negatively. We could use our resources to accumulate a capital stock, providing future generations with shelter, productivity, and transportation, but our decaying inner cities illustrate that machines and buildings do not last forever. Even capital that physically stands the test of time may become economically obsolete by being ill-suited to the needs of subsequent generations.

Our most lasting contribution to future generations would probably come from what economists call human capital—investments in people. Though the people who receive education and training are mortal, the ideas they bring forth are not. Knowledge endures.[4]

Current actions could also reduce future welfare levels, however. Fossil-fuel combustion could modify the climate to the detriment of future agriculture. Current chlorofluorocarbon emissions might, by depleting the atmosphere's ozone, raise the incidence of skin cancer. The storage of radioactive wastes could increase the likelihood of genetic damage in the future. The reduction of genetic diversity in the stock of plants and animals could well reduce future medical discoveries.

Suppose that high levels of sustainable welfare are feasible. Would our economic system automatically choose a growth path that produces sustainable welfare levels, or could it choose one that enriches current generations at the expense of future generations?

---

3   One study has estimated that humans are currently using approximately 19% to 25% of the renewable energy available from photosynthesis. On land the estimate is more like 40%. See Peter M. Vitousek, et. al. "Human Appropriation of the Products of Photosynthesis," *BioScience* 36 (June 1986): 368–373.

4   While it is true that ideas can last forever, the value of those ideas may decline with time as they are supplanted by new ideas. The person who conceived of horseshoes made an enormous contribution to society at the time, but the value of that insight to society has diminished along with our reliance on horses for transportation.

Market Allocations

Market imperfections, including intertemporal externalities, free-access resources and market power, play havoc with the ability of a market to achieve sustainable outcomes. They create incentives that can interfere in important ways with the quest for sustainable development.

Allowing free access to resources promotes unsustainable allocations. Because free-access resources are overexploited by current generations, diminished stocks are left for the future. In the extreme it is even possible that the species would become extinct.

Intertemporal externalities also undermine the ability of the market to produce sustainable outcomes. Emissions of greenhouse gases impose a cost on future generations which is external to current generations. Current actions to reduce the gases will cost this generation money, but the benefits would not be felt until significantly later. Economic theory clearly forecasts that too many greenhouse gas emissions would be forthcoming for the sustainability criterion to be satisfied.

The general conclusion that market imperfections exacerbate the problem of unsustainability, however, would not be correct. For example, the existence of an oil cartel holding up prices serves to retard demand and conserve more for future generations than would otherwise be the case.

Markets can sometimes provide a safety valve to ensure sustainability when the supply of a renewable resource is threatened. Fish farming is one example where declining supplies of a renewable resource trigger the availability of an alternative renewable substitute. Even when the government intervenes detrimentally in a way that benefits current generations at the expense of future generations, as it did with natural gas, the market can limit the damage. The market for solar energy still exists as a substitute for natural gas, so the effect of the government regulation was to make the transition significantly less smooth than it might have been, rather than preventing the transition.

The notion that left to their own devices markets would automatically provide for the future is naive, despite their apparent success in providing for generations in the past.

Efficiency and Sustainability

Suppose future governments were able to eliminate all market imperfections, restoring efficiency to the global economic system. In this idealized world, intertemporal and contemporaneous externalities would be reduced to efficient levels. Access to common resources would be restricted to efficient levels and harvesting excess capacity would be eliminated. Competition would be restored to previously cartelized natural resource markets. Would this package of policies be sufficient to achieve sustainability, or is something more required?

One way to examine this question is to examine a number of different models which capture the essence of intertemporal resource allocation. For each model the question becomes, "Will efficient markets automatically produce sustainable development?" The conclusion to be drawn from these models is very clear; restoring efficiency is not sufficient to produce sustainability.

Take the allocation of depletable resources over time. Imagine a simple economy where the only activity is the extraction and consumption of a single depletable resource. Even when the population is constant and demand curves are stable, the efficient quantity profiles show declining consumption over time. In this hypothetical world, later generations would be unambiguously worse off unless current generations transferred some of the net benefits into the future. Even an efficient market allocation would not be sustainable in the absence of transfers.

The existence of an abundant renewable backstop resource would not solve the problem; even in this more congenial set of circumstances, the quantity profile of the depletable resource would still involve declining consumption until the backstop was reached. In the absence of compensating transfers even efficient markets would use depletable resources to support a higher current standard of living than could ultimately be supported.

Dasgupta and Heal find a similar result for a slightly more realistic model.[5] They assume an economy where a single consumption good is produced (using a Cobb-Douglas type of production function) by combining capital with a depletable resource. The finite supply of the depletable resource can be used to produce capital as well as be used in combination with capital to produce the consumption good. The more capital produced, the higher is the marginal product of the remaining depletable resource.

They prove that a sustainable constant consumption level exists in this model. The rising capital stock (implying a rising marginal product for the depletable resource) would compensate for the declining availability of the depletable resource. They also prove, however, that the use of any positive discount rate would necessarily result in declining consumption levels, a violation of the sustainability criterion. Discounting, of course, is an inherent component of dynamically efficient allocations.

In all of these models sustainable development is possible, but it is not the choice made by efficient markets. Why not? What would it take to ensure sustainable allocations? Hartwick shows that the achievement of a constant per capita consumption path (which would satisfy our definition of sustainability) results when all scarcity rent is invested in capital. None of it should be consumed by current generations.[6]

---

5 P. S. Dasgupta and G. M. Heal, *Economic Theory and Exhaustible Resources* (Cambridge: Cambridge University Press, 1979): 299.

6 J. M. Hartwick, "Intergenerational Equity and the Investing of Rents from Exhaustible Resources," *American Economic Review* 67 (December 1977): 972–974.

Would all scarcity rent be invested? With a positive discount rate, some of the scarcity rent is consumed, violating the Hartwick rule. The point is profound. Restoring efficiency will typically represent a move toward sustainability, but it will not, by itself, be sufficient. Further policies must be implemented to guarantee sustainable outcomes.

Another study by Howarth and Norgard comes to a similar conclusion from a different perspective.[7] They derive competitive resource allocations across generations assuming that each generation is assigned a specific share of the available depletable resources. This share is then varied and a new allocation calculated for each to reveal the effect of this intertemporal assignment of property rights to resources among generations. For our purposes two of their conclusions are relevant: (1) the resulting allocations are sensitive to the initial allocation of the resource rights across generations; and (2) assigning all of the rights to the first generation would not produce a sustainable outcome. Efficient allocations of depletable resources do not necessarily produce sustainable development.

How about with renewable resources? At least renewable-resource flows could, in principle, endure forever. Are efficient market allocations of renewable resources compatible with sustainable development? John Pezzey has examined the sustainability of an allocation of a single renewable resource (such as corn) over time.[8] Sustained growth of welfare can occur in this model, but only if two conditions both hold: (1) the resource growth rate exceeds the sum of the discount rate and the population growth rate; (2) and the initial food supply is sufficient for the existing population. The first condition is sometimes difficult to meet, particularly with rapid population growth and slow-growing biological resources. Sustainable development of renewable resources is very much harder in the presence of rapid population growth rates because the pressure to exceed sustainable harvest rates becomes irresistible.

Global climate change presents a different example where efficiency may not be sufficient for sustainability. Since the present-value component of dynamic efficiency emphasizes short-term over long-term consequences, the current costs of controlling emissions would be weighed more heavily than the distant future damages caused by global warming. Though this approach is not inherently biased against future generations, their interests would only be adequately protected if they would be willing to accept monetary compensation for a modified climate and if current generations were willing to set aside sufficient proceeds to provide this compensation. Since it is not obvious that either condition would be satisfied in practice, the long lead times associated with this par-

---

7 Richard B. Howarth and Richard B. Norgard, "Intergenerational Resource Rights," *Land Economics* 66 (February 1990): 1–11.

8 John Pezzey, *Economic Analysis of Sustainable Growth and Sustainable Development*, Working Paper No. 15 (Washington, DC: World Bank Environment Department, 1989): 43–46.

ticular problem place in jeopardy the interests of future generations in maintaining a stable climate.

Efficient allocations can also violate the notion of sustainability in a deeper sense. Because our definition of sustainability is based on nondeclining aggregate welfare levels, it does not require the preservation of individual resources. Harvesting fish stocks to extinction, for example, would be compatible with our definition of sustainability as long as future generations were sufficiently compensated.

But we don't really know how much they would value the continued existence of those fish stocks. Not only is our knowledge about the ultimate ecosystem effects of the extinction of any species extremely limited, we have no idea how valuable those fish would be to future generations. It is possible that they would value the continued existence of the population substantially more than we. Not only would the appropriate amount of the compensation be difficult to determine (since we don't know their preferences), but compensating future generations would be silly if they value the continued existence of the population more than any compensation (including accrued interest) we could pay.

One straightforward way to deal with this uncertainty is to include in the definition of sustainability some protection of the resources themselves. According to this logic since it is impossible to know the value future generations place on specific renewable resources, we can only preserve their options by guaranteeing access to the resources. Efficiency would certainly not guarantee this outcome.

We must be careful to distinguish between what has been said and what has not been said. We have shown that efficient markets would not always achieve sustainable development paths. This does not mean that they would never, or even normally, result in sustainable allocations! Indeed, the historical record reviewed in the previous chapter suggests that the incompatibility of the efficiency criterion and the sustainability criterion has been the exception, not the rule. Capital accumulation and technological progress have expanded the ways in which resources could be used and have increased subsequent welfare levels in spite of a declining resource base. Nonetheless, the two criteria are not inevitably compatible. As resource bases diminish and global externalities increase, the conflict can be expected to become more important.

A MENU OF OPPORTUNITIES

Is sustainable development just an unrealistic attempt to provide optimism in the face of a bleak future? Human nature being what it is we need to have hope. When the situation is hopeless, the natural human tendency is to create scenarios that offer the illusion of hope. Is sustainable development one of those illusions? Or can reasonable, skeptical people find grounds for believing in the existence of new forms of development that can raise living standards while respecting both the environment and the rights of future generations?

While it is not possible in the space we have to go into detail about the various techniques that fulfill this vision, it is possible to convey a flavor.[9] Hopefully this flavor will be sufficient to demonstrate that sustainable development is a pragmatic possibility, not merely an illusion.

Agriculture

Most experts believe that food supply can be expanded to meet the forecasted increases in population, but sustainable development requires this expansion to take place in a way that does not destroy the natural environment. What are the prospects?

Multiple cropping, which includes crop rotations, intercropping (sometimes with trees and annual crops sharing the same fields), overseeding legumes into cereals, and double cropping, is one technique that offers the potential for reduced agricultural chemicals, increased productivity, less erosion, and more effective use of water. The concept is not new. A system employed in central America since pre-Columbian times intermixes maize, beans, and squash. The maize provides a trellis for the beans; the beans enrich the soil with nitrogen; and the squash provides ground cover, reducing erosion, soil compactation, and weed growth.

Trees can be used in multiple cropping. In West Africa, leaf litter from the *Acacia alba* enriches the soil for the benefit of various grain and vegetable crops grown between them.

In the American Midwest, farmers are experimenting with growing corn with other, low-growing plants. In one experiment in Nebraska, two-row corn windbreaks were spaced every 15 rows through a field of sugar beets. The wind shelter provided by the corn increased sugar production by 11%. The greater access to sunlight and carbon dioxide increased corn yields by 150%.

In Montana tall wheatgrass, a perennial, has been used to protect winter wheat. In winter wheatgrass barriers capture snow, forming a uniform layer which insulates dormant plants from the effects of extremely low temperatures. In spring the snow melts, providing the moisture winter wheat needs for early growth. Once the winter wheat begins to grow, the wheatgrass serves as a wind barrier.

---

9 The material in this section comes mainly from three excellent articles: Pierre R. Crosson and Norman J. Rosenberg, "Strategies for Agriculture"; John H. Gibbons, Peter D. Blair, and Holly L. Gwin, "Strategies for Energy Use"; and Robert A. Frosch and Nicholas E. Gallopoulos, "Strategies for Manufacturing." All can be found in *Scientific American* 261 (September 1989). Readers interested in more detail should consult those articles and the references at the end of each article.

Multiple cropping can reduce the need for pesticides. In fields where crops are rotated regularly, pests (weeds, insects, and pathogens) cannot adapt themselves to a single set of environmental conditions and therefore do not increase as quickly.

Biotechnology and new irrigation techniques also offer prospects for reduced fertilizer and water use. Developing plants that "fix" nitrogen in the soil would lessen the demand for nitrogen fertilizer, while incorporating genes from pest-resistant plants into commercial crops could reduce the need for pesticides. Trickle (or drip) irrigation systems would reduce the amount of water needed by increasing the efficiency of the water used. Already widely used in Israel and part of the United States, trickle irrigation can also reduce the problems associated with salt buildup.

Energy

Prior to the 1970s, increases in the gross national product were always accompanied by proportionate increases in energy consumption. This relationship proved so stable that it was used for forecasting energy consumption. Some observers at the time took this relationship as evidence that proportionate increases in energy would be a necessary condition for growth.

Following the oil embargo and the accompanying increases in prices during the 1970s, it became clear that growth and energy consumption did not have to move in lockstep. The industrialized world's energy intensity—the amount of energy used to produce one unit of gross national product—fell by one-fifth between 1973 and 1985. In the United States, gross national product grew 40% while energy consumption remained constant during this period.

Energy efficiency is the short-run key to sustainable development because it offers the opportunity to increase living standards without increasing energy consumption. Enhanced energy efficiency, which can stretch energy supplies, slow climate changes, and buy time to develop alternative energy resources, can be achieved in a variety of ways. Some of the possibilities are presented in Table 22.1.

Consider one possibility in more detail. Advanced building materials can sharply reduce loss of heat through windows, doors, and walls. In "superinsulated" homes, where normal insulation is doubled and a liner forms an airtight seal in walls, heat radiating from people, lights, stoves, and other appliances alone can warm the house. In comparison with the average home built in the United States, some superinsulated homes in Minnesota require 68% less heat; for some residences in Sweden the saving is 89%. Similar savings would be possible in lighting, transportation, and manufacturing.

TABLE 22.1 Opportunities for Greater Energy Efficiency

	Car miles per gallon (mpg)	Home (thousand joules per square meter)	Refrigerator (kilowatt-hours per day)	Gas furnace joules (million per day)	Air conditioner (kilowatt-hours per day)
Model average	18	190	4	210	10
New model	27	110	3	180	7
Best model	50	68	2	140	5
Best prototype	77	11	1	110	3

Source: From "Strategies for Energy Use" by John H. Gibbons, Peter D. Blair, and Holly L. Gwin in *Scientific American*, Vol. 261, No. 3 (September 1989). Copyright © 1989 by Scientific American, Inc. All rights reserved. Reprinted by permission.

Waste Reduction

Sustainable development involves a more integrated approach to production than traditionally practiced in order to reduce raw material demands and waste discharge. In such an integrated system the consumption of energy and materials is optimized; waste generation is minimized; and the effluents of one process—whether they are spent catalysts from petroleum refining, fly and bottom ash from electric-power generators, or discarded plastic containers from consumer products—serve as raw materials for another process.

As the costs of waste disposal rise and the regulations dealing with hazardous waste disposal become more strict, examples of industries adopting this type of integrated approach become more prevalent. Meridian National, a midwestern steel processing company, now reprocesses the sulfuric acid with which it removes scale from steel sheets and slabs, reuses the acid, and sells ferrous sulfate compounds to magnetic tape manufacturers.

At the Atlantic Richfield Company's Los Angeles refinery complex, a series of relatively low-cost changes have reduced waste volumes from about 12,000 tons a year during the early 1980s to about 3400 tons by the end of the decade. Since disposal costs were about $300 a ton, the company saved over $2 million a year in disposal costs alone.

Markets have been found for much of Atlantic Richfield's former waste, adding further revenue. The company sells its spent alumina catalysts to Allied Chemical and its spent silica catalysts to cement makers. Alkaline carbonate sludge from a water-softening operation at the refinery goes to a sulfuric acid manufacturer a few miles away, where it neutralizes acidic wastewater.

Sustainable development frequently requires changes in the way economic activities are conducted. Some of those changes are already occurring (Example 22.1). Others await additional policy changes.

EXAMPLE 22.1

Sustainable Development: Three Success Stories

In Kenya 83% of the urban population and 17% of rural households use charcoal stoves known as *jikos*. A household in Nairobi with one wage earner typically spends more than one-fifth of its income on charcoal. The typical *jiko* is very energy inefficient; it represents an unnecessary drain on both income and the forests which supply the wood for charcoal.

In 1981 the government of Kenya and a local nongovernmental organization began a project disseminating a new, more energy-efficient stove. By 1985 the new stove had captured 10% of the market. Nationwide savings on fuel were in the neighborhood of $2 million annually.

Much of Central America is faced with declining soil fertility due to soil erosion and monocropping. Guinope, Honduras, was not an exception. Farmers were migrating out of the area, and those remaining were plagued by low incomes.

In 1981, World Neighbors, a private voluntary organization, introduced a sustainable agriculture program which relied on soil conservation practices in use elsewhere in Central America. The program included constructing drainage ditches, planting grass barriers, erecting rock walls, training farmers in fertilization methods using chicken manure, intercropping leguminous plants, and some chemical fertilizers. Significantly no subsidies were involved at all. All costs were borne by the farmers.

In the first year the yields tripled, in some cases quadrupled. Nearby villages have requested training, and the program is spreading rapidly.

In Brazil some 500,000 rubber tappers (*seringueiros*) have made their living from the Amazon since the late 1800s. Recently their livelihood was threatened by the migration of large numbers of people to the forests seeking land. Encouraged by government subsidies, these migrants ultimately discovered the land to be unsuited for agriculture once the forest canopy has been removed. One sustainable form of land used was being jeopardized by another unsustainable land use.

On June 30, 1987, the Brazilian government created an extractive reserve for the rubber tappers and in the process provided protection for the countless genetic species found in the forest. The extractive reserve allows continued extraction of rubber (as well as nuts and other renewable products), but protects the forest and its people from the ravages of deforestation.

Source: Walter V. C. Reid, "Sustainable Development: Lessons from Success," *Environment* 31 (May 1989): 7–9, 29–35.

MANAGING THE TRANSITION

If, in fact, sustainable development is possible and unfettered markets are not capable, by themselves, of managing the transition, what can be done? How can the transition to sustainable development be accomplished?

Our situation is similar to that of the thoroughly disoriented tourist, a central character in Maine folklore. Enticed by unusually brilliant fall foliage, a tourist forsook the security of the well-marked main highways for some less traveled country roads. After an hour of driving, he was no longer sure he was even headed in the right direction. Seeing a Maine native mending a fence, he pulled over to the side of the road to seek assistance. After hearing the tourist's destination, the native sadly shook his head and in his best Maine accent responded "If I was goin' they-uh, I sure wouldn't start from he-uh!"

Had we known long ago that human activities could seriously impact environmental life support systems and could deny future generations the quality of life to which our generation has become accustomed, we might have chosen a different, more sustainable, path for improving human welfare. The fact that we did not have that knowledge and therefore did not make that choice years ago means that current generations are faced with making more difficult choices with fewer options. These choices will test the creativity of our solutions and the resilience of our social institutions.

The task of managing the transition to sustainable development is made all the more difficult by the fact that some entrenched development paths are not only themselves unsustainable, but they have so dominated sustainable strategies that switching from one to the other has become very difficult.

Southern California represents a case in point. In the Los Angeles air basin the ambient air quality standards, designed to protect human health, are currently violated on the order of 150 out of the 365 days a year. Due to the way the city has developed, regulators in Los Angeles now face a very difficult problem. As a prime example of an automobile city, population growth in Los Angeles has spawned land use patterns which accommodate the automobile and are, in turn, accommodated by the automobile. Responding to a massive program of highway construction and low gasoline prices, the city has become very spread out with highly dispersed residential and employment locations. Since the efficient use of mass transit requires the existence of high-density travel corridors, an effective public transit alternative is now difficult to implement, though it could have been quite possible before the highly dispersed land use patterns became so firmly entrenched. The options left open to these regulators have steadily diminished over time. The entire fabric of life in the Los Angeles area is so interwoven with automobile access that the problem cannot be solved without envisioning fairly radical changes in life-style.

To meet the challenges of the next century it will be necessary to foster and to support institutional change by being somewhat more creative in the way that we deal with environmental policy. One key to exploiting these opportunities involves harnessing the power of the marketplace and focusing that power on the reduction, or hopefully even eradication, of poverty in an environmentally sound manner.

Prospects for International Cooperation

As the scale of economic activity has proceeded steadily upward, the scope of environmental problems triggered by that activity has transcended both geographic and generational boundaries. Whereas the nation state used to be a sufficient form of political organization for resolving environmental problems, that may no longer the case. Whereas each generation of humans once had the luxury of being able to satisfy its own needs without worrying about the needs of those generations to come, that is no longer the case either. Solving problems such as poverty, global warming, ozone depletion, and the loss of biodiversity require international cooperation. Ideally the search for solutions would also involve intergenerational cooperation, but, of course, that is not possible. Future generations cannot speak for themselves; we must speak for them. Our policies must incorporate our obligation to future generations, however difficult or imperfect that incorporation might prove to be.

International cooperation is by no means a foregone conclusion. Global environmental problems can trigger very different effects on the countries that will sit around the negotiating table. While low-lying countries could be completely submerged by the sea-level rise predicted by some global warming models, or arid nations could see their marginal agricultural lands succumb to desertification, other nations may see agricultural productivity rise as warmer climates support longer growing seasons in traditionally intemperate climates.

Countries which unilaterally set out to improve the global environmental situation run the risk of making their businesses vulnerable to competition from less conscientious nations. Industrialized countries that undertake stringent environmental policies may not suffer greatly at the national level (due to offsetting employment and income increases in the industries producing pollution control equipment), but some individual industries facing the stringent regulations will face higher costs than their competitors, and can be expected to suffer accordingly. Declining market share and employment in industries confronted by especially stringent regulations are powerful political weapons that can be used to derail efforts to implement an aggressive environmental policy. The search for solutions must accommodate these concerns.

Forging new international agreements is not enough. To produce the desired effect, the agreements must be enforceable. Enforceability will be a difficult criterion to satisfy as long as the agreements infringe upon significant segments of society with legitimate claims to an alternative future. The most legitimate claim is perhaps advanced by those currently in abject poverty.

Many individuals and institutions currently have a large stake in maintaining the status quo. Fishermen harvesting their catch from an overexploited fishery are loathe to undertake any reduction in harvests, even if the reduction is necessary to conserve the stock and return the population to a healthy level. Farmers who have come to depend on fertilizer and pesticide subsidies will be reluctant to give them up. The principle of inertia applies to politics as fully as to physical bodies; a body at rest will tend to stay at rest unless a significant outside force is introduced. Changing economic incentives can provide that force.

Opportunities for Cooperation

While this list of barriers to international cooperation is certainly imposing, the new global environmental problems also offer new opportunities for cooperation, opportunities that in some ways are unprecedented. Although the degree to which various nations are affected by these problems differ, a point made above, it is also true that some potential common ground exists.

One important foundation for this common ground is the inefficiency of many current economic activities. In many cases these inefficiencies are very large indeed; resources are being wasted. Whenever resources are wasted, much more environmental improvement could be obtained for current expenditures or the same improvement could be realized with a much smaller commitment of resources. By definition moving from an inefficient policy to an efficient one creates gains to be shared. Agreements on how these gains should be shared among the cooperating parties can be used to build coalitions.

The level and form of any such cost-sharing arrangements, however, are usually not clearly specified. By the appropriate choice of policy instruments, much of this cost sharing could be handled by normal market forces.

The natural reluctance of nations to impose increasingly stringent environmental policies within their borders can be diminished by ensuring that the policies imposed are cost effective. We live in an age when the call for tighter environmental controls intensifies with each new discovery of yet another injury modern society is inflicting on the planet. But resistance to additional controls is also growing with the recognition that the cost of compliance is growing as all the easy techniques become used up. By choosing cost-effective and flexible policy instruments, the potential for backlash can be reduced.

Policy instrument choice can also affect enforceability. In developing countries local communities typically have the greatest accessibility to and knowledge about local biological resources. As these countries have undergone a centralization of political power, including the power to control these resources, some of the local commitment to them has been lost. Policy instruments which reestablish this commitment by offering these local communities a stake in the preservation of the resource can enhance enforceability. Subsequent sections present some specific examples of how this can be accomplished.

By being creative in the design of policy instruments, the incentives of local and global communities can become compatible. In some cases being creative requires the use of conventional economic instruments in unconventional ways, but in others it requires the use of unconventional instruments in unconventional ways.

Unconventional approaches are not pipe dreams. Most of them have been successfully employed in one form or another in local communities around the globe. The experience with these instruments in their current setting provides a model for their use on an international level. How well this model fits remains an open question, but it is better to sit down for a dinner with a full menu offering some novel, but interesting, choices rather than one offering only a limited selection of familiar, unappetizing fare.

Restructuring Incentives

How can economic incentives be used to provide the kinds of signals that will make sustainable development possible? Perhaps the best way to begin to answer this question is to recall a few examples of how this approach has worked in practice.

The first application involves the use of an economic incentives approach to reduce the stress on an already overexploited New Zealand fishery. Due to their desirability and the traditional open access to the fishery, the populations of several species of fish off the coast of New Zealand were being depleted. While the need to reduce the amount of pressure being put on the population was rather obvious, how to accomplish that reduction was not at all obvious. Although it was relatively easy to prevent new fishermen from entering the fisheries, it was harder to figure out how to reduce the pressure from those who had been fishing in the area for years or even decades. Because fishing is characterized by economies of scale, simply reducing everyone's catch proportionately wouldn't make much sense. That would simply place higher costs on everyone and waste a great deal of fishing capacity as all boats sat around idle for a significant proportion of time. A better solution would clearly be to have fewer boats harvesting the stock. That way each boat could be used closer to its full capacity without depleting the salmon population. Which fisherman should be asked to give up their livelihood and leave the industry?

The economic incentive approach addressed this problem by imposing transferable catch quotas on all fish harvested from the fishery. Revenues derived from the annual fee charged for renewing these quotas were used to buy out fishermen who were willing to forgo any future fishing for the relevant species. Essentially each fisherman stated the lowest price that he or she would accept for leaving the industry; the regulators selected those who could be induced to leave at the lowest price, paid the stipulated amount from the tax revenues, and retired their catch quotas for the affected species. It wasn't long before a sufficient number of licenses had been retired and the population was protected. Because the program was voluntary, those who left the industry only did so when they felt they had been adequately compensated. A difficult and potentially dangerous pressure on a valuable natural resource had been avoided by the creative use of an approach that changed the economic incentives.

As the offset policy makes clear, economic incentives can not only be used to reduce the conflict between economic development and environmental protection, they can make economic development the vehicle by which greater environmental protection is achieved. Under this U.S. policy, firms already established in nonattainment areas that chose to voluntarily control their emissions more than required under the prevailing regulations would be allowed to have those excess emission reductions certified as "emission reduction credits." Once certified, their operating permits would be tightened to ensure that the reductions were permanent. These emission reduction credits could then be sold to new firms seeking to move into the nonattainment area provided that the acquiring firm bought 1.2 emission reduction credits for each 1.0 units of emissions added by the new plant. Air quality improved every time a new firm moved into the area. With this policy the confrontation between economic growth and environmental protection was diffused. New firms were not only allowed to move into polluted cities, but they became one of the main vehicles for improving the quality of the air. Economic development facilitated, rather than blocked, air quality improvement.

It now remains only to show how the entire menu of economic incentive policies can be woven together in a manner that facilitates international cooperation in the resolution of international environmental problems. Economic analysis suggests four principles which can provide the foundation for this approach.

The Full-Cost Principle. According to full cost principle, all users of environmental resources should pay their full cost. Those using the environment as a waste repository, for example, would be presumed responsible not only for controlling pollution to the full extent required by the law, but also for restoring environmental resources damaged beyond some de minimus amount and for compensating those suffering damage.

This principle is based upon the presumption that humanity has a right to a reasonably safe and healthy environment. Since this right has been held in common for the stratosphere and the international sections of the oceans, no administrative body has either the responsibility or the authority for protecting that right. As a result it has been involuntarily surrendered on a first-come, first-served basis without compensation.

Although global warming and ozone depletion impose both an international and intergenerational environmental cost, currently that cost is not being borne, or even recognized, by those who ultimately control the magnitude of the problem. Furthermore, those choosing unilaterally to reduce their emissions expose themselves to the higher costs associated with mitigating strategies. Applying the full-cost principle would send a strong signal to all users of the environment that the atmosphere is a scarce, precious resource and should be treated accordingly. Products produced by manufacturing processes which are environmentally destructive would become relatively more expensive; those produced by environmentally benign production processes would become relatively cheaper. Implementing the full-cost principle would end the implicit subsidy that all polluting activities have received since the beginning of time. When the level of economic activity was small, the corresponding subsidy was also small and therefore probably not worthy of political attention. Since the scale of economic activity has grown, however, the subsidy has become very large indeed; ignoring it leads to significant resource distortion.

What policy implications would flow from the acceptance of the full-cost principle? A first implication is that emissions of harmful substances should bear an emission charge. For the global warming problem, this could take the form of a tax on all greenhouse gases emitted into the atmosphere. The "carbon tax," which is currently being widely discussed in Europe and the United States, could be one component of this package. Since carbon dioxide is only one of the greenhouse gases, however, taxes would necessarily be imposed on other gases as well. The appropriate level of this tax for each gas would depend on its per unit contribution to the global warming problem; gases posing a larger per unit risk would bear higher tax rates.[10]

Substances contributing to ozone depletion would also be taxed according to the full-cost principle. Since the ozone depletion tax and the global warming tax would be separately assessed, substances such as CFCs, which contribute to both global warming and ozone depletion, would bear both taxes.

The transition to a more sustainable economic system will depend on the development of new technologies and upon much greater levels of energy efficiency than are currently being achieved. Those transitions will not occur unless the prevailing economic incentives support and encourage them. Once the greenhouse gas and ozone depletion taxes were in effect, the incentives would be changed; greater energy efficiency and the development of new technologies would become top-priority objectives.

Since environmental taxes would generate revenue, a common global fund could be established to receive and dispense that revenue. An appropriately designed fund financed by environmental taxes could help to reduce the twin causes of environmental problems: distorted market signals and poverty.[11]

Determining the appropriate rate for any per unit environmental tax would not be a trivial matter. Although to apply the full-cost principle correctly the rate should be equal to the marginal social damage caused by a unit of emission, current valuation techniques would not identify that level with any reasonable

---

10 See the discussion of this point in Chapter 16.

11 One interesting precedent for this approach is the World Heritage Fund. See the discussion of this Fund in Chapter 16.

degree of confidence. The high degree of scientific uncertainty associated with the magnitude of the global warming threat makes precise valuation impossible. But that may not be a fatal flaw since zero, the current rate, is not correct either. Even establishing a low tax rate would be a step in the right direction; as more information is gained, the rate could be adjusted.

Implications for the legal system would flow from the full-cost principle as well. For example international laws should permit full recovery for damage caused by oil spills or other environmental incidents. Not only should the contaminated site be restored insofar as possible, but those suffering demonstrable losses should be fully compensated.

Making explicit environmental costs that have been hidden is only one side of the coin; the other is eliminating inappropriate subsidies. Subsidies which are incompatible with the full-cost principle should be eliminated. Implicit subsidies should be targeted as well as explicit subsidies. For example, when the pricing of environmental resources is subject to government regulation (such as water in the American Southwest), prices should not simply be determined by historic average cost; they should reflect the scarcity of the resource.

Incremental block pricing provides a practical means of implementing this recommendation without jeopardizing the traditional legal constraint that water distribution utilities can earn no more than a fair rate of return. With incremental block pricing the price of additional water consumed rises with the amount consumed per unit time. While the first units consumed per month up to some predetermined threshold would be relatively cheap, units consumed beyond the threshold would face a much higher price that truly reflects the scarcity of the resource. By ensuring that the marginal units consumed were priced at full cost, adequate incentives to conserve would be introduced.

The transition to the full-cost principle could proceed gradually, beginning in certain sectors, moving to others as greater familiarity with the approach was gained. A complete, immediate transition is not an essential ingredient of a rational approach.

The Cost-Effectiveness Principle.   A policy is cost-effective if it achieves the policy objective at the lowest possible cost. Cost effectiveness is an important characteristic because it can diminish political backlash by limiting wasteful expenditures.

Appropriate implementation of the full-cost principle would automatically produce cost effectiveness as a side benefit. Should acceptance of the full-cost principle falter, however, cost effectiveness could be elevated to a primary policy goal, worthy in its own right. It provides a desirable, if less than perfect, fallback position.

Political acceptance of the full cost principle is by no means a forgone conclusion. While taxes on greenhouse and ozone depletion gases can go a long way toward rectifying some of the current distortions in resource pricing, they will do little to reassure those whose vision of the future is defined in terms of specific limits on emissions, not correcting price distortions. It would be very difficult to establish a set of tax rates that could guarantee a specific emissions target.

If international agreements were to proceed by establishing global limits for greenhouse gases (the approach taken for ozone depleting gases), allocating the proposed reductions among the nations of the world would be one of the most difficult aspects of this alternative approach. Fairness will no doubt be one critical aspect of the negotiations and it is likely that some form of cost sharing will result. How are the costs to be shared?

Emissions trading becomes a reasonable approach for implementing the cost effectiveness principle while providing opportunities for cost sharing. The process of establishing emissions trading in greenhouse gases would be initiated by setting transferable limits on the amounts each nation could emit on an annual basis. Nations achieving reductions greater than required by the agreement could receive transferable emission reduction credits that could be sold to other nations. By purchasing these credits, the acquiring nation could increase its quota by the amount covered by the emission reduction credits.

An international market in emission reduction credits would facilitate the movement of credits from those countries with the capacity to create them most cheaply to those countries faced by very high costs of additional control. The capacity to achieve cost effectiveness regardless of how the initial emission allowances are allocated, is a significant attribute of an emissions trading approach that could be exploited for developing a market approach to cost sharing. With emission trading as the strategy of choice, those forging new international agreements would have a very large latitude in attempting to establish emission limitations that are fair and politically feasible without jeopardizing cost effectiveness. As the Western nations acquired by purchase the necessary production allowances at market prices from those nations selling them, significant financial transfers would take place. The size of these transfers would be dictated by market forces, not by negotiation.

The Property Rights Principle.   Part of the evident loss of efficiency in modern environmental problems involves misspecified property rights which create perverse incentives. According to the property right principle, local communities should have a property right over flora and fauna within their border. This property right would entitle the local community to share in any benefits created by preserving the species. Ensuring that local property rights over genetic resources are defined and respected would give local communities a much larger stake in some of the global benefits to be derived from the use of those resources and would enhance the prospects for effective enforcement.

Consider the problem of stemming the decline in the elephant population as an example. Insofar as permitted by the migratory nature of the herd, the property rights principle would confer the right to harvest a fixed number of elephants to the indigenous peoples who live in the elephant's native habitat. Ownership of harvesting rights and the possibility of continued employment as long as the herd was preserved would ensure an income to the local community, giving it a stake in preserving the herd. Preventing poaching would become easier because poachers would become a threat to the local community, not merely a threat to a distant national government which inspires little allegiance.

A somewhat related application of the property rights principle could provide an additional means of resolving the diminishing supply of biologically rich tropical rain forests. One of the arguments for preserving biodiversity is that it offers a valuable gene pool for the development of future products such as medicines or food crops. Typically, however, the nations which govern the forestland containing this biologically rich gene pool have not shared in the wealth created by the products derived from it. One solution to this problem is to establish the principle that the nations which contain these biologically rich resources within their borders would be entitled to a stipulated royalty on any and all products developed from the genes obtained from these preserves.

Currently nations cutting down their tropical forests have little incentive to protect the gene pool harbored within those forests because they are unlikely to reap any of the rewards than will ultimately result. Exploitation of the gene pool and the economic rewards that result from it typically accrue only to those nations and to those companies that can afford the extensive research. By establishing the principle that stipulated royalty payments would accrue to the nation from which the original genes were extracted, local incentives would become more compatible with global incentives.

Implementing this recommendation would not be trivial. Though it is not hard to envision licenses being required of all those conducting research or collecting specimens of local flora or fauna, it is more difficult to imagine a process which would guarantee royalty payments on every new derivative genetic discovery. For Third World countries to be aware of new discoveries would be difficult enough, but the need to enforce the terms of the license on a company which is physically located in another country could prove inordinately time-consuming and expensive.

The Sustainability Principle. According to the sustainability principle all resources should be used in a manner which respects the needs of future generations. Adopting the foregoing three principles would go a long way toward restoring efficiency. And restoring efficiency would set in motion the transition toward producing sustainable outcomes. As we have seen, however, restoring efficiency would not be sufficient. Other policies would be needed to satisfy the sustainability principle.

Restoring intergenerational fairness in the use of depletable resources might be an appropriate place to start. As the economic models have made clear, current incentives for sharing the wealth from the use of depletable resources are biased toward the present, even in efficient markets. Clearly this could be rectified by transferring some of the created wealth into the future, but how much?

Salah El Serafy has developed an ingenious, practical way to answer this question.[12] Calculate the present value of the net benefits received from the extraction of a depletable resource over its useful life. This becomes the wealth to be shared. Using standard annuity tables calculate the constant annual payments that could be made from this fund forever. (In essence, these payments represent the dividends and interest derived from the wealth; the principle would be left intact.) This constant annual payment is what can be consumed from the wealth created from the depletable resources. Receipts in excess of this amount (in the years the resource is being extracted and sold) must be paid into the fund. All succeeding generations receive the same annual payment; the payments continue forever.

The payments could be invested in research rather than in instruments producing a financial return. Such a strategy might envision, for example, setting aside through taxation a certain proportion of all proceeds from depletable resources for funding research on substitutes likely to be used by future generations. In the case of fossil fuels, for example, one might subsidize research into fusion power or solar energy so that as fossil fuels are depleted, future generations would have the ability to switch to alternative sources easily without diminishing living standards in the process.

Another adjustment would confront the possibility of species extinction. Compensating future generations for extinct species (the implicit strategy in an efficient allocation) may not be adequate. Not only do we not know the appropriate level of compensation, but it is possible that the preferences of future generations would be such the value of the preserved species would exceed any possible compensation our generation would be willing to offer. Given this uncertainty about their preferences one strategy would be to incorporate species preservation into our definition of sustainability to allow future generations to make their own valuations. With this approach strategies which lead to species extinction would simply be infeasible, regardless of the net benefit calculations. The interests of future generations would be protected by preserving their options rather than by attempting to second-guess their preferences.

Adjusting the national income accounts would be another immediate implication of the sustainability principle. The income accounts must conform with the Hicksian definition of income. All of the costs, including the depreciation of natural capital, should be subtracted from the gross receipts in producing a national income figure. Failure to do this, as is the current practice, provides very misleading signals to the public sector. These misleading signals provide powerful incentives for public figures to engage in economic activities which violate the sustainability principle.

---

12 Salah El Serafy, "Absorptive Capacity, the Demand for Revenue, and the Supply of Petroleum, *The Journal of Energy and Development* 7 (Autumn 1981): Appendix A.

Adopting the sustainability principle could also have consequences for the conduct of trade policy. Trade in commodities produced in violation of the principle could be prohibited or subject to trade sanctions.

The process to implement this change in policy is already in place. Under the General Agreement on Trade and Tariffs (GATT) current trade practices are scrutinized to ferret out those that are unfair. Dumping, defined as selling abroad at a price below the home market, is one trading practice that currently receives that scrutiny. Under U.S. antidumping statutes, when dumping is proved the U.S. Department of Commerce applies an antidumping duty as an offset and adds on a penalty. Nonsustainability could become another of the practices receiving such scrutiny without altering the current process by which the GATT agreement is enforced.

Less targeted trade sanctions could also be used to make both signing an agreement and fulfilling its terms more attractive to reluctant signatories. The Packwood-Magnuson Amendment to the U.S. Fishery Conservation and Management Act (1976) requires the United States to retaliate whenever foreign nationals undermine the effectiveness of the International Whaling Convention. Specifically an offending nation automatically loses half of its allocation of fish products derived from U.S. waters. Continued disregard of the convention by the foreign national leads to revocation of the right to fish in U.S. waters.

FORCED TRANSITION

Suppose that current levels of welfare were shown to be unsustainable and that an immediate transition to a new, lower standard of living were necessary to protect future generations. Suppose further that a "guided forced transition" would be less painful than a laissez-faire forced transition. How could that more abrupt transition be negotiated?

The most concrete proposals for a forced transition to the steady state come from Herman Daly, an economist with the World Bank.[13] Daly is very sympathetic with the goal of a rapid transition to sustainable development and has spent a good deal of his professional life looking into the best way to achieve that objective. We will focus on his proposals in examining how an economy might be forced to this new sustainable path more rapidly than would normally be the case.

---

13 Herman E. Daly, *Steady-State Economics* (San Francisco: W. H. Freeman, 1977). Expanded edition forthcoming from Island Press, 1991.

Defining the Target

Daly begins by attempting to define the steady state, the target of his approach, and how we know when it is achieved. His definition is couched in physical, rather than value, terms. For Daly the *steady-state economy* is characterized by constant stocks of people and physical wealth maintained at some chosen, desirable level by a low rate of *throughput*. This throughput—flow of resources and energy—provides direct consumption benefits (such as food and shelter) and investment, insofar as necessary to counteract depreciation of the capital stock.

Conceiving of the steady state in physical rather than value terms is significant because it forms an important difference between Daly and others who see the steady state as simply the absence of any development. Daly recognizes that some development would and should occur even in the steady state in spite of a constant stock of people and physical wealth. For example, as society learned more efficient ways to use energy, the value derived from the flow of energy may increase, even when the flow itself does not. Due to technological progress, the value of the services received can grow, even if the physical stocks and flows are unchanging. *The steady state and zero economic growth are not necessarily the same thing.*

Institutional Structure

Daly sees three institutional modifications as necessary for the rapid attainment of the steady state:

1. An institution for stabilizing population
2. An institution for stabilizing the stock of physical wealth and throughput
3. An institution to ensure that the stocks and flows are distributed fairly among the population

Allocation among alternative uses is handled by the market. Collective decisions are made on scale and distribution, but allocation remains with the market. Daly argues that the questions of scale, distribution, and allocation involve three separate policy goals and cannot all be served by the single instrument of prices. Market prices achieve the goal of efficient allocation; the other insitutions are designed to achieve an optimal (sustainable) scale and an optimal (fair) distribution.

Population Stabilization. According to the Daly proposals, population would be stabilized over the long run using an idea first put forth by Kenneth Boulding.[14] In this scheme each individual would be given the inalienable right to

---

14   Kenneth E. Boulding, *The Meaning of the Twentieth Century* (New York: Harper and Row, 1964).

produce one (and only one!) child. Because this scheme over a generation allows each member of the current population to replace himself or herself, births would necessarily equal deaths and population stability would be achieved.

This scheme would award each person a certificate entitling the holder to have one child. Couples could pool their certificates to have two. Every time a child was born a certificate would be surrendered. Failure to produce a certificate would cause the child to be put up for adoption.

Certificates would be fully transferable. Families who placed a particularly high value on children could purchase extra certificates, while those who viewed parenting with something less than enthusiasm could sell certificates. As one of its virtues, this system would ensure that the overall objective of population stability would be achieved, but no family would be required to maintain a particular family size. Though every couple would be guaranteed the right to have two children, they could choose to have fewer or more than two.

Stock and Throughput Stabilization.   Daly suggests that throughput should be held at some minimum level using depletion quotas for all depletable resources. These quotas would define the amount of the resource which could be extracted and used. Any extraction and use in excess of this quota would be illegal.

The size of these quotas would be determined by bureaucrats, but according to Daly, these bureaucrats would follow a specific rule. The quotas would be set at a level sufficiently stringent that the price of the resource in question would equal the price of the closest renewable substitute. When no close renewable substitute was available, the bureaucrats would be empowered to decide the most ethical level. Because the quotas would be auctioned off by the government, the government would extract all of the scarcity rent associated with the depletable resources. The quota prices would equal the scarcity rent of the covered resources.

Ensuring Distributional Fairness.   Daly also sees a need to override the normal channels for distributing income in the steady-state economy. In a growth economy, tensions between the rich and poor can be ameliorated by the opportunities for social and economic mobility that a growth economy provides. In a steady-state economy those opportunities are diminished as the number of new jobs created is smaller.

To alleviate these tensions, Daly proposes the establishment of a maximum and minimum income level, as well as a maximum limit on wealth. The minimum income level would be financed in part by progressive taxes with 100% marginal rates above the maximum income and wealth limits. Since these 100% tax rates would presumably yield very little revenue (the incentive to earn more having been eliminated), most of the revenue would come from the sale of depletion quotas and from lower tax rates on income levels between the minimum and maximum.

Administration

The Daly system would be expensive to implement. Large bureaucratic staffs would be needed to define the quotas, run the auctions, and ensure compliance. In an age where public sentiment seems to be for decreasing rather than increasing bureaucracy, this proposal would buck the trend. A universal quota system for depletable and renewable resources, in addition to being bureaucratically cumbersome, holds the potential to disrupt a smoothly operating institutional structure. Historically the only time a system such as this has been acceptable is during a war.[15]

Child certificates would also be administratively cumbersome and, in most of the industrialized world, unnecessary. In addition, child certificates raise moral questions. For example, this system tends to preserve the existing racial status quo. To minority groups with above-average birth rates and below-average incomes, this looks like a policy to limit their proportion in the population. Even though that is clearly not the intended result, the suspicions raised create unnecessary tensions.

SUMMARY

Sustainable development refers to a process for providing for the needs of the present generation (particularly those in poverty) without compromising the ability of future generations to meet their own needs.

Market imperfections frequently make sustainable development less likely. Intergenerational externalities such as climate modification impose excessive costs on future generations. Free access to biological common property resources can lead to excessive exploitation and even extinction of the species.

Even efficient markets do not necessarily produce sustainable development. Restoring efficiency is a desirable and helpful, but insufficient means for producing sustainable welfare levels. While in principle dynamically efficient allocations produce extraction profiles for depletable resources that are compatible with the interests of future generations, in practice this is not necessarily the case. Guaranteeing sustainability frequently requires compensation from the present to future generations, but profit-maximizing behavior produces compensation levels that are too low. Furthermore, adequate compensation levels may be difficult to define at best and it is not clear that financial payments can ade-

---

15 In a personal communication honoring my request that he review this chapter and the one which precedes it, Herman Daly responded, "In my view the real threat to freedom and stimulus to bureaucratic control is *crisis* and avoidance of crisis with a bit of collective action now seems a good strategy for maximizing freedom over the long run."

quately compensate future generations for all of the options they might be asked to forego.

New sustainable forms of development are possible, but they will not automatically be adopted. Economic incentive policies can be used to manage the transition from current practices to these new forms of development. These approaches work best in managing a transition to higher standards of living.

If it turns out that universally higher standards of living are not possible without exceeding the carrying capacity of the planet, a rapid transition to a new steady state involving levels of welfare lower than current levels would be needed. To examine how this might occur we considered the proposals of economist Herman Daly. He sees three institutional modifications as necessary: (1) a new mechanism to control the distribution of income and wealth; (2) a system of annual quotas to govern the rate of consumption of both depletable and renewable resources; and (3) a plan to control population. The institutional modifications suggested by Daly would be implemented at a very high cost.

The search for solutions must recognize that market forces are extremely powerful. Attempts to negotiate agreements which seek to block those forces or to meet them head on are probably doomed to failure. Nonetheless it is possible to negotiate agreements which harness those forces and channel them in directions which enhance the possibilities of international cooperation. To take these steps will require thinking and acting in somewhat unconventional ways. Whether the world community is equal to the task remains to be seen.

FURTHER READING

Battie, Sandra S. "Sustainable Development: Challenges to the Agricultural Economics Profession," *American Journal of Agricultural Economics* 71 (December 1989): 1083–1101. Contrasts the viewpoints of "deep ecology" sustainable development advocates with those of traditional economists and suggests some things each can learn from the other.

Costanza, Robert et al. *The Ecological Economics of Sustainability: Making Local and Short-Term Goals Consistent with Global and Long-Term Goals*, Working Paper No. 32 (Washington, DC: World Bank Environment Department, 1990). A catalogue containing abstracts of nearly 200 works in ecological economics presented at a 1990 conference on sustainability in Washington.

Pearce, David, Anil Markandya, and Edward B. Barbier. *Blueprint for a Green Economy* (London: Earthscan, 1989). Seeks to answer the question "If we accept sustainable development as a working idea, what does it mean for the way we manage a modern economy?"

Pirages, Dennis Clark, ed. *The Sustainable Society* (New York: Praeger, 1977). A multidisciplinary series of essays on the transition to a steady state.

Weiss, Edith Brown. "In Fairness to Future Generations," *Environment* 32 (April 1990): 7–11, 30–31. A lawyer proposes a new doctrine to protect the interests of future generations and a set of principles and procedures for implementing that doctrine.

ADDITIONAL REFERENCES

Aniansson, Britt and Uno Svedin. *Towards an Ecological Sustainable Economy* (Stockholm: Swedish Council for Planning and Coordination of Research, 1990).

Baumol, William J. "On the Possibility of Continuing Expansion of Finite Resources," *Kyklos* 39 (1986): 167–179.

Becker, Robert A. "Intergenerational Equity: The Capital-Environment Trade-Off," *Journal of Environmental Economics and Management* 9 (June 1982): 165–185.

Brown, Lester R., Christopher Flavin, and Sandra Postel. "Picturing a Sustainable Society," in *State of the World: 1990*, Lester R. Brown et. al (New York: W. W. Norton, 1990): 173–190.

Daly, Herman E. "The Economic Growth Debate: What Some Economists Have Learned but Many Have Not," *Journal of Environmental Economics and Management* 14 (December 1987): 323–336.

McNeeley, Jeffrey A. et al. "Strategies for Conserving Biodiversity," *Environment* 32 (April 1990): 16–20, 36–40.

Redclift, Michael. *Sustainable Development: Exploring the Contradictions* (New York: Methuen, 1987).

Turner, R. Kerry. *Sustainable Environmental Management: Principles and Practice* (Boulder, CO: Westview Press, 1988).

World Resources Institute. *Natural Endowments: Financing Resource Conservation for Development* (Washington, DC: World Resources Institute, 1989).

DISCUSSION QUESTIONS

1. Discuss the mechanism favored by Daly to control population growth. What are its advantages and disadvantages? Would it be appropriate to implement this policy now in the United States? For those who believe that it would, what are the crucial reasons? For those who believe it is not appropriate, are there any circumstances in any countries where it might be appropriate? Why or why not?

2. "Every molecule of a nonrenewable resource used today precludes its use by future generations. Therefore, the only morally defensible policy for any generation is to use only renewable resources." Discuss.

3. "Future generations can cast neither votes in current elections nor dollars in current market decisions. Therefore, it should not come as a surprise to anyone that the interests in future generations are ignored in a market economy." Discuss.

CHAPTER TWENTY-THREE

Visions of the Future Revisited

*Mankind was destined to live on the edge of perpetual
disaster. We are mankind because we survive.
We do it in a half-assed way, but we do it.*

PAUL ADAMSON, *a fictional character in*
JAMES A. MICHENER'S *Chesapeake* (1978)

We have now come full circle. Having begun our study with two lofty visions
of the future, we proceeded to dissect the details of the various components of
these visions—population, the management of depletable and renewable resources, pollution, and the growth process itself. During these inquiries a number of
useful insights were gained about individual environmental and natural resource
problems. Now it is time to step back and coalesce those insights into a systematic assessment of the two visions.

ADDRESSING THE ISSUES

In Chapter 1 we posed a number of questions to serve as our focus for the overarching issue of growth in a finite environment. Those questions addressed three
major issues: (1) How is the problem correctly conceptualized? (2) Can our
economic and political institutions respond in a timely and democratic fashion
to the challenges presented? (3) Can the needs of the present generation be met
without compromising the ability of future generations to meet their own needs?
Can short-term and long-term goals be harmonized? The next three segments of
this section summarize and interpret the evidence uncovered.

Conceptualizing the Problem

At the beginning of this book we suggested that if the *Limits to Growth* team had correctly conceptualized the problem, theirs was the only conclusion that could be drawn. An exponential growth in demand coupled with a finite supply of resources implies that the resources must eventually be exhausted. If those resources are essential, society will collapse when the resources are exhausted.

We have seen that this is an excessively harsh characterization. The growth in the demand for resources is not insensitive to their scarcity. Though the rise in energy prices was triggered more by politics than by scarcity, it is possible to use higher energy prices as an example of how the economic system reacts.

The growth in demand following the increase in prices fell dramatically, with petroleum experiencing the largest reductions. In the United States, for example, total energy consumption in 1981 (73.8 quadrillion BTUs) was lower than it was in 1973 (74.6 quadrillion BTUs), despite increases in income and population. Petroleum consumption went from 34.8 quadrillion BTUs in 1973 to 32.0 quadrillion BTUs in 1981. Though some of this reduction was caused by sluggishness of the economy, price certainly played a major role.

Price is not the only factor which retards demand growth. Declines in population growth also play a significant role. Since the developed nations appropriate a disproportionate share of the world's resources, the dramatic declines in population growth in those countries has had a disproportionate effect on slowing the demand for resources.

Characterizing the resource base as finite—the second aspect of the model— is also excessively harsh: (1) this characterization ignores the existence of a substantial renewable resource base; (2) it focuses attention on the wrong issue; and (3) it supports ill-conceived attempts to measure the size of the resource base. We consider each problem in turn.

In a very real sense the resource base is not finite. Plentiful supplies of renewable resources including, significantly, energy are available. The normal reaction to increasing scarcity of depletable resources is to switch to renewable resources. That is clearly happening. The most dramatic examples can be found in the transition to solar energy in its various forms.

Labeling the resource base as finite is also misleading because it suggests that our concern should be "running out." In fact, for most resources we shall never run out. Millions of years of finite resources are left at current consumption rates. The rising cost of extracting and using those resources, not the potential for exhausting them, is the chief threat to future standards of living. The limits on our uses of these resources are not determined by their scarcity in the crust of the earth, but rather by what we would have to sacrifice to extract and process the ores. The work by Skinner and others suggests that we may not be willing to pay the price required to extract some of the lower-grade sources of those minerals.

Ignorance of this basic point has led to a number of ill-fated attempts to measure the size of this finite resource base. The timing of the societal collapse in the *Limits to Growth* forecast was quite sensitive to the techniques used to forecast resource exhaustion. Conventional physical indicators, such as the static and the exponential reserve indices, are excessively pessimistic because they fail to take into account possibilities for expanding current reserves. Historically, no forecast based on these techniques has stood the test of time. There is no reason to expect any similar forecast to do so in the future. They are convenient since they can be readily calculated and easily interpreted, but they are also usually dead wrong.

Current reserves can be expanded in many ways. These include finding new sources of conventional materials, as well as discovering new uses for unconventional materials, including what was previously considered waste. We can also stretch the useful life of these reserves by reducing the amount of materials needed to produce the products. Striking examples include the diminishing size of a typical computer system needed to process a given amount of information and the substantially diminished amount of energy needed to heat a superinsulated home.

Although our ability to assess what is happening to cost is far from perfect, two things seem clear. Historically, very little, if any, evidence supports a fear of impending scarcity of minerals. Our ability to develop lower-cost technologies for processing resources dominated the necessity to extract lower-grade sources. As a result, in real terms, extraction costs have fallen, rather than risen, over time. The most recent evidence suggests, however, that for a number of minerals a turning point has been reached in the last few years. For those resources evidence of scarcity, in the form of rising relative prices and increased exploration activity, has appeared.

Not all errors in resource-base measurement have been committed by those having a tendency to understate the adequacy of the resource base. Errors in the other direction are committed by those who point to the abundance in the earth's crust and atmosphere of almost all substance on which we depend. While the abundance of those substances may be supported by the evidence, the amounts we actually use will no doubt fall far short of the amounts available.

Paradoxically some of the most obvious cases where limits are being approached and the carrying capacity concept has the most validity, involve renewable resources rather than depletable resources. Population growth is a key contributor to this phenomenon. Expanding populations force the cultivation of marginal lands and the deforestation of large biologically rich tracts. The erosion of overworked soils diminishes their fertility and ultimately their productivity. Biological resources such as fisheries can be overexploited, even to the point of extinction. The problem with these resources is not their finiteness, but the way in which they have been managed.

Correct conceptualization of the resource scarcity problem suggests that both extremely pessimistic and extremely optimistic views are wrong. Impenetrable proximate physical limits on resource availability are typically not the problem; improper incentives and inadequate information are frequently much more serious. But believing in unlimited amounts of all resources that could support continued economic growth at current rates forever is equally naive. Plenty of resources are available if we are willing to pay the price, but that price is now rising. Transitions to renewable resources, recycled resources, and less costly depletable resources have already begun.

Institutional Responses

One of the keys to understanding how society will cope with increasing resource scarcity and environmental damage lies in understanding how social institutions will react. Are market systems, with their emphasis on decentralized decision making, and democratic political systems, with their commitment to public participation and majority rule, equal to the challenge?

Our examination of the record seems to suggest that while our economic and political systems are far from infallible and some rather glaring deficiencies have become evident, no fatal flaws have become evident.

On the positive side, markets have responded swiftly and automatically to deal with those resources experiencing higher prices. Demand has been reduced and substitution encouraged. Markets for recycling are growing and consumer habits are changing. No one has had to oversee these responses to make sure they occur. As long as property rights are well defined, the market system provides incentives for consumers and producers to respond to scarcity in a variety of useful ways. This characteristically rapid and smooth response illustrates none of the overshoot and collapse behavior anticipated by the *Limits to Growth* team.

As compelling as the evidence is for this point of view, it does not support the conclusion that, left to itself, the market would automatically choose a dynamically efficient or a sustainable path for the future. Market imperfections frequently make sustainable development less likely. The most serious limitations of the market become evident in how it treats common property resources, such as the fish we eat, the air we breathe, and the water we drink. Left to its own devices, a market will overexploit common property resources, substantially lowering the net benefits received by future generations. Such overexploitation could, if not compensated for by sufficient increases in net benefits elsewhere in the economy, result in a violation of the sustainability criterion.

Even efficient markets do not necessarily produce sustainable development. Restoring efficiency is a desirable, but insufficient, means for producing sustainable welfare levels. While in principle dynamically efficient allocations produce extraction profiles for depletable resources that are compatible with the interests of future generations, in practice this is not necessarily the case. Guaranteeing sustainability in the face of declining supplies of depletable resources requires compensation from present to future generations, but profit-maximizing behavior produces compensation levels that are too low. Furthermore, adequate compensation levels may be difficult to define at best, and it is not clear that financial payments could adequately compensate future generations for the options they might be asked to forgo.

The market has some capacity for self-correction. The decline of common-property fish catches, for example, has led to the rise of private-property fish farming. The artificial scarcity created by imperfectly defined property rights gives rise to incentives for the development of a private-property substitute.

This capacity of the market for self-healing, while comforting, is not always adequate. In some cases cheaper, more effective solutions (such as preventing the deterioration of the original natural resource base) are available. Preventive medicine is frequently superior to corrective surgery. In other cases, such as when our air is polluted, no good private substitutes are available. To provide an adequate response, it is sometimes necessary to complement market decisions with political ones.

The need for government intervention is particularly acute in controlling pollution. Uncontrolled markets not only produce too much pollution, but they also tend to underprice commodities that contribute to pollution either when produced or consumed. Firms which unilaterally attempt to control their pollution run the risk of pricing themselves out of the market. Government intervention is needed to ensure that firms which neglect environmental damage in their operating decisions do not thereby gain a competitive edge.

Significant progress has been made in reducing the amount of pollution, particularly conventional air pollution. Recently, regulatory innovations, such as the bubble and offset policies, represent major steps toward the development of a flexible but potential framework for controlling air pollutants. By making it less costly to achieve environmental goals, these reforms have limited the potential for a backlash against the policy. They have brought perceived costs more in line with perceived benefits. Emission charges have played a similar role for water pollution control in Europe.

It would be a great mistake, however, to assume that government intervention has been uniformly benign. The acid-rain problem was almost certainly made worse by a policy structure that focused on local rather than regional pollution problems. Requiring scrubbers for all new coal-fired electrical generating stations was done for purely political reasons and served to raise the cost of compliance unnecessarily.

One aspect of the policy process that does not seem to have been handled well is the speed with which improvement has been sought. Public opinion polls have unambiguously shown that the general public supports environmental protection even when it raises costs and lowers employment. Policy makers have reacted to this resolve by writing very tough legislation designed to force rapid technological development.

Common sense suggests that tough legislation with early deadlines can achieve environmental goals more rapidly than weaker legislation with less tight deadlines. Common sense is frequently wrong. Writing tough legislation with early deadlines can have the opposite effect. Unreasonably tough regulations are virtually impossible to enforce. Recognizing this, polluters have repeatedly sought (and received) delays in compliance. It has frequently been better, from the polluter's point of view, to spend resources to change the regulations than to comply with them. This would not have been the case with less stringent regulations, since the firms would have had no legally supportable grounds for delay.

Perhaps the most flagrant examples of counterproductive government intervention are to be found in treatment of energy and water resources. By imposing price ceilings on natural gas and oil, the government removed much of the normal resiliency of the economic system. With price controls the incentives for expanding the supply are reduced and the time profile of consumption is tilted toward the present. As was the case with natural gas, these controls can even cause biases that interfere with the transition to renewable resources. By holding water prices below the marginal cost of supply, water authorities have subsidized excess use. Resources which in a normal market would have been conserved for future generations are, with price controls, consumed by the current generation. When price controls are placed on normal market transactions, the overshoot syndrome anticipated by the *Limits to Growth* team can occur. The smooth transition to renewable resources that characterizes the normal market allocation is eliminated by price controls; shortages can arise.

Price controls are also playing a key role in the world hunger problem. By controlling the price of food, many developing countries have undervalued domestic agriculture. The long-run effect of these controls has been to increase their reliance on food imports at a time when foreign exchange to pay for those imports is becoming increasingly scarce. Whereas developed countries have gone substantially down the road to price decontrol, less developed countries have not yet been able to extricate themselves to a similar degree.

In summary, the record compiled by our economic and political institutions has been mixed. It seems clear that simple prescriptions such as "leave it to the market" or "more government intervention" simply do not bear up under a close scrutiny of the record. The relationship between the economic and political sectors has to be one of selective engagement, complemented in some areas by selective disengagement. Each problem has to be treated on a case-by-case basis. As we have seen in our examination of a variety of environmental and natural resource problems, the efficiency and sustainability criteria allow such distinctions to be drawn and they serve as a basis for policy reform.

Sustainable Development

Historically, increases in inputs and technological progress have been important sources of economic growth in the industrialized nations. In the future some factors of production, such as labor, will not increase as rapidly as they have in the past. The effect of this decline on growth depends on the interplay among the law of diminishing marginal productivity, substitution possibilities, and technological progress. The law of diminishing marginal productivity suggests slower growth rates, while technological progress and the availability of substitution possibilities counteract this drag. One view foresees limits to technological progress imposed by the second law of thermodynamics, implying that the growth process must culminate in a steady or stationary state where growth ultimately diminishes to zero.

Our examination of empirical evidence suggests that increased environmental control has not currently had a large impact on the economy as a whole, although certain industries have been hit quite hard. Environmental policy has triggered only a small rise in the rate of inflation and a mild reduction in growth. Environmental policy has apparently contributed more jobs than it has cost. The notion that respecting the environment is incompatible with a healthy economy is demonstrably wrong.

The situation is similar for energy. Though rather large increases in energy prices have occurred, the portion of the slowdown in productivity growth during the 1970s attributed to these increases is not large. Some diminution of growth has certainly occurred, but it seems premature to suggest that rising energy prices have already forced a transition to a period of substantially lower productivity growth.

The economy is being transformed, however. It is not business as usual. Two particularly important aspects of this transformation are the decline in population growth and the rise in importance of information as a driving economic force. Both aspects tend to reduce the degree that physical limits constrain economic growth and increase the degree to which current welfare levels would be sustainable.

Recognizing that conventional measures of economic growth shed little light on the question, some crude attempts have been made to estimate whether or not growth in the industrialized countries has historically made the citizens of those countries better off. Results of these studies suggest that because growth has ultimately generated more leisure, longer life expectancy, and more goods and services, it has been beneficial. But more recent studies suggest that the benefits from growth have been steadily diminishing over time. One study found that further growth in the United States now lowers economic well-being of the average U.S. citizen; at this stage of affluence the negative aspects were estimated to outweigh the positive aspects.

Our examination of the evidence suggests that the notion that all of the world's people are automatically benefited by economic growth is naive. Growth has demonstrably benefited the poor in the developed countries, but mainly through transfers from more well-off members of society, not from the direct effects of growth.

The future outlook for the less industrialized nations is at best mixed. Solving many of their future environmental problems will require raising standards of living. However, following the path of development pioneered by the industrialized nations is probably not possible without triggering severe global environmental problems; the solution would become the problem. New forms of development will be necessary.

The less industrialized countries must overcome a number of significant barriers if development is to become a reality. At the local level, rising populations face increasingly limited access to land or productive assets. At the national level corruption and development policies discriminate against the poor. Globally their situation is worsened by rising debt burdens, falling prices for exports, and the flight of capital that could be used to create jobs and income.

New sustainable forms of development are possible and desirable, but they will not automatically be adopted in either the high-income or the low-income nations. Are cooperative solutions possible? Can any common ground be established?

The experience in the United States suggests that cooperative solutions may be possible even among traditional adversaries. Environmental regulators and lobbying groups with a special interest in environmental protection in the United States have traditionally looked upon the market system as a powerful and potentially dangerous adversary. That the market unleashed powerful forces was widely recognized and that those forces clearly acted to degrade the environment was widely lamented. Meanwhile development proponents have traditionally seen environmental concerns as blocking projects that had the potential to raise living standards significantly. Conflict and confrontation became the modus operandi for dealing with this clash of objectives.

The climate for dealing effectively with both concerns has improved dramatically within the last few years. Not only have development proponents learned that in many cases short-term wealth enhancement projects which degrade the environment are ultimately counterproductive, but environmental groups have come to realize that poverty itself is a major threat to environmental protection. No longer are economic development and environmental protection seen as an "either-or" proposition. Rather the focus has shifted toward the identification of policies or policy instruments which can promote the alleviation of poverty while protecting the environment.

The economic incentives approach to environmental and natural resource regulation has, in the last decade or so, become a significant component of environmental and natural resource policy. Instead of mandating prescribed actions, such as requiring the installation of a particular piece of pollution control equipment, this approach achieves environmental objectives by changing the economic incentives of those doing the polluting. Incentives can be changed by fees or charges, transferable permits, or even liability law. By changing the incentives an individual agent faces, that agent can use his or her typically superior information to select the best means of meeting his or her assigned responsibility. When it is in the interest of individuals to change to new forms of development, the transformation can be amazingly rapid.

Public policy and sustainable development must proceed in a mutually supportive relationship. The government must ensure that the market is sending the right signals to all participants so the sustainable outcome is compatible with other business objectives. Economic incentive approaches are a means of establishing that kind of compatibility. The experience with the various versions of this approach used in the United States, Europe, and Asia since the mid-1970s suggests that economic approaches in general are both feasible and effective.

How about global environmental problems? As the scale of economic activity has proceeded steadily upward, the scope of environmental problems triggered by that activity has transcended both geographic and generational boundaries. Whereas the nation state used to be a sufficient form of political organization for resolving environmental problems, that may no longer the case. Whereas each generation of humans used to have the luxury of being able to satisfy its own needs without worrying about the needs of those generations to come, that is no longer the case either. Solving problems such as poverty, global warming, ozone depletion, and the loss of biodiversity require international cooperation.

By being creative in the design of policy instruments, the incentives of local and global communities can become compatible. Whenever resources are wasted, much more environmental improvement could be obtained for current expenditures or the same improvement could be realized with a much smaller commitment of resources. By definition, moving from an inefficient policy to an efficient one creates gains to be shared. Agreements on how these gains should be shared among the cooperating parties can be used to build coalitions.

Economic incentives approaches could be helpful here as well. Emissions trading facilitates cost sharing among participants while ensuring cost-effective responses to the need for additional control. By separating the question of what control is undertaken from the question of who ultimately pays for it, the government widens the control possibilities significantly. Conferring property rights for biological populations on local communities provides an incentive for those communities to protect the populations. Strategies for reducing debt can diminish the pressure on forests and other natural resources that may be "cashed in" to pay off the debt.

The courts are beginning to use economic incentives as well; judicial remedies for environmental problems are beginning to take their place alongside regulatory remedies. Take, for example, the problem of cleaning up already closed toxic waste sites. Current U.S. law allows the government to sue all potentially responsible parties who contributed to the contaminated site (such as waste generators or disposal site operators). These suits accomplish a double purpose: (1) they ensure that the financial responsibility for contaminated sites is borne by those who directly caused the problem, and (2) they encourage those who are currently using those sites to exercise great care, least they be forced to bear a large financial burden in the event of an incident. The traditional remedy of going to the taxpayers would have resulted in less revenue raised, fewer sites restored, and less adequate incentives for users to exercise care.

Europe has tended to depend more on another type of economic incentive, the effluent or emission charge. This approach places a per unit fee on each unit of pollution discharged. Faced with the responsibility for paying for the damage caused by their pollution, firms recognize it as a controllable cost of doing business. This recognition triggers a search for possible ways to reduce the damage, including changing inputs, changing the production process, transforming the residuals to less harmful substances, and recycling by-products. The experience in the Netherlands, a country where the fees are higher than in most other countries, suggests that the effects can be dramatic.

Fees also raise revenue. Successful development, particularly sustainable development, requires a symbiotic partnership between the public and private sectors. To function as an equal partner, the public sector must be adequately funded. If it fails to raise adequate revenue, the public sector becomes a drag on the growth process, but if it raises revenue in ways that distort incentives that, too, can act as a drag on development. Effluent or emission charges offer the realistic opportunity to raise revenue for the public sector without producing inefficient incentives. Whereas other types of taxation discourage growth by penalizing legitimate development incentives, emission or effluent charges provide incentives for sustainable development. Some work from the United States suggests that the drag on development avoided by substituting effluent or emission charges for more traditional revenue raising devices such as capital gains, income, and sales taxes could be significant.

Incentives for forward-looking public action are as important as those for private action. The current national income accounting system provides an example of a perverse economic incentive. Though national income accounts were never intended to function as a device for measuring the welfare of a nation, in practice that is how they are used. National income per capita is a common metric for evaluating how well off a nation's people are. Yet the current construction of those accounts sends the wrong signals.

Rather than recognizing the recent *Exxon Valdez* spill for what it was, namely a decline in the value of the endowment of natural resources in the area, it is recorded as an increase in the national income. The spill boosted GNP! All the cleanup expenditures served to increase national income, but no account was taken of the consequent depreciation of the natural environment. Under the current system the accounts make no distinction between growth that is occurring because a country is damaging its natural resource endowment with a consequent irreversible decline in its value, and sustainable growth where the value of the endowment remains. Only when suitable corrections are made to these accounts will governments be judged by the appropriate standards.

The power of economic incentives is certainly not inevitably channeled toward the achievement of sustainable growth. They can be misapplied as well as appropriately applied. Tax subsidies to promote cattle ranching on the fragile soil in the Brazilian rain forest stimulated an unsustainable activity, which has done irreparable damage to an ecologically significant area.

The search for solutions to environmental and natural resource problems must recognize that market forces are extremely powerful. Attempts to negotiate agreements which seek to block those forces or to meet them head on are probably doomed to failure. Nonetheless it is possible to negotiate agreements which harness those forces and channel them in directions which enhance the possibilities for cooperative solutions. To take these steps would require thinking and acting in somewhat unconventional ways.

UNRESOLVED ISSUES

The jury is still out on a number of issues. The evidence is not yet strong enough for us to discern whether or how these issues will be resolved. Though others may have a legitimate claim for our attention, these are of particular importance.

Transboundary Pollutants

Global air pollutants remain in the atmosphere for sustained periods of time. They are not cleansed by gravity or rain. Their presence in the atmosphere alters its chemical composition. This altered chemistry can modify the climate, or it can attack the shield of ozone that protects us from harmful radiation from the sun.

Regional pollutants are generally removed from the atmosphere, but usually not until they have traveled long distances. As a result, they share with global pollutants a propensity to cross political borders.

Since solving pollution problems requires a creative partnership between the government and the economic system, the success of this partnership has traditionally depended on whether the boundaries of the problem match those of the government's jurisdiction. When the damage caused by pollution is confined to a relatively small geographic area around the source, the geographic jurisdiction of the government coincides with the boundaries of the problem. Both the sources of the pollution and those affected by it fall under a single government's purview. Achieving a balance between these conflicting interests has not always been easy, but it has been possible.

As the damage from pollution becomes more regional or global in scope, it becomes more difficult for governments to handle. Pollution that crosses state or national boundaries creates the potential for political externalities. A government concerned with balancing the benefits and costs within its jurisdiction may pay insufficient attention to costs and benefits received by those outside its borders.

Acid rain provides a good example of the problems created by a transboundary regional pollutant. Canada and the United States are currently grappling with this issue, as are a number of European countries.

Though the resolution of these disputes will prove much harder than resolving disputes that fall within the confines of a single nation's borders, the prerequisites for a successful resolution seem present. The parties to the dispute are readily identified. Though there are unresolved scientific issues, the research currently underway should help clear up these issues. Finally, and perhaps most important, the number of countries involved is not sufficiently large to preclude bilateral or multilateral negotiations.

While, as described in the preceding section, some policy approaches to solve the problems in a reasonable manner do exist, the case for successful implementation of these policies is by no means clear. One obvious solution, a world government, does not exist; the United Nations does not have sufficient power at this point to implement this kind of program. International agreements are one promising avenue, particularly in light of the successful agreement to eliminate ozone depleting gases, but how even this forward-looking agreement will work out in practice remains to be seen. Whether our existing social institutions will prove equal to the challenge remains an open question.

Scientific Uncertainty

The ability of the policy process to reach decisions about the appropriate level of use of the environmental asset presumes the existence of solid scientific information. Only when the physical consequences of various courses of action are understood can the task of weighing the costs and benefits begin. In many significant areas we simply do not have solid scientific information on which to base decisions. Making a wrong choice based on incomplete or misleading information could prove very costly.

Reflecting on the previous chapters, it is not difficult to identify a number of areas of environmental concern where better scientific evidence is needed. What is happening to stratospheric ozone and why? What are the dynamics of the greenhouse effect? To what extent will climate ultimately be modified? What are the exact causes of forest death in Germany? Can simple, accurate, inexpensive tests be developed to predict which new substances will prove toxic? Will fusion energy live up to the potential foreseen by its supporters?

Though far from complete, this list is sufficient to suggest that the reduction of uncertainty should play an important role in any long range plan to assure harmony between the economic and ecological systems. Furthermore the scientific findings have to be presented in such a way that those in a position to implement policy can understand both the nature of the evidence and its policy implications. Although the increasing complexity of the problems at hand makes this a tall order, expanding the frontiers of knowledge and integrating the new findings into the policy process will be essential.

Siting Hazardous Waste Facilities

As the furor over the siting of waste disposal facilities has demonstrated, another key unresolved issue is how to site hazardous waste facilities. Simply put, the "not in my backyard, you don't!" philosophy is able to mobilize a substantial amount of local sentiment in opposition to facilities which from some larger geographic perspective may make good sense. Unfortunately, virtually every potential site is in someone's backyard.

The solution to this issue may at first seem rather simple—don't produce hazardous wastes! Certainly we can do more in this regard. In the preceding chapters we have discussed some possible means of reducing the quantity of hazardous waste. Yet this view neglects the fact that many hazardous substances are involved in some valuable social functions (medical uses, for example) that would exact a very high cost if terminated. The conclusion that some hazardous substances will continue to be produced seems inescapable.

Better processes of identifying suitable sites and for securing the acquiescence of local residents must be developed. Economists naturally feel that compensation provides the key to solving the acquiescence issue, but implementing this abstract idea is far from trivial. How much compensation is to be awarded? Who is entitled to receive it? How much should each recipient receive? Establishing a framework for answering these questions and a process for implementing this framework remains a pressing need.

Controlling Toxic Substances

Regulating the amount and type of toxic substances introduced into the economic system is another of the most difficult issues to confront our social institutions. As if the latency of the damage caused by toxic substances and the scientific uncertainty about the relationships involved were not enough, the number of potential toxic substances involved is staggering.

Our society is currently evolving a complementary relationship among the economic system, the court system, and the legislative and executive branches of government which holds promise. We are, however, not yet out of the woods. More reliable, inexpensive screening devices need to be developed. Courts must develop procedures for handling liability in cases where the damage causing activities took place many years earlier and where the causal chain from activity to damage is less than completely proven. Significantly, the public must learn that part of the risk is theirs. The government cannot and should not provide a risk-free environment.

The toxic substance problem provides an excellent opportunity to reassess the contrast between the role of values and the role of process in environmental decision making. By this point it should be clear that process bears a major share of the responsibility for our environmental problems. Persons who yearn for efficient allocations may find themselves in circumstances where, as individuals, they are powerless to achieve the desired outcome. Allocations can occur that virtually no one would find desirable.

Yet it would be a mistake to say that all values are equally acceptable, leaving it up to the government to produce harmony. The plain fact of the matter is that not all behavior can be regulated. It costs too much to catch every offender. Our law enforcement system works because most people obey the law, whether anyone is watching or not. A high degree of voluntary compliance is essential if the system is to work smoothly.

The best resolution of the toxic substance problem is undoubtedly for all makers of potentially toxic substances to be genuinely concerned about the safety of their products and to bite the bullet whenever their research raises questions. The ultimate responsibility for developing an acceptable level of risk must rest on the integrity of those who make, use, transport, and dispose of the substances. The government can assist by penalizing and controlling those few who fail to exhibit this integrity, but it can never substitute for integrity on a large scale. We cannot and should not depend purely upon altruism to solve these problems, but we should not underestimate its importance either.

The notion that we are at the end of an era may well be true. But we are also at the beginning of a new one. What the future holds is not the decline of civilization, but its transformation. As the opening quote to this chapter suggests, the road may be strewn with obstacles and our social institutions may deal with those obstacles with less grace and less finesse than we might hope, but we are unquestionably making progress.

PROBLEM SET ANSWERS

Chapter 2

1. (a) Net benefits are maximized where the demand curve intersects the marginal curve-cost curve. Therefore, the efficient q would occur when $80 - 1q = 1q$. Thus the efficient q = 40 units.

    (b) Draw the diagram. Draw a horizontal line from the place where the demand curve intersects the marginal cost curve to the vertical axis. This intersection will take place at a price of $40. The net benefits can now be computed as the sum of the upper right triangle (the area under the demand curve and over this line) and the lower right triangle (the area under the demand curve and over this line). The area of a right triangle is 1/2 × base × height. Therefore, the net benefits are 1/2 × $40 × 40 + 1/2 × $40 × 40 = $1600.

2. (a) Ten units would be allocated to each period.

    (b) $P = \$8 - 0.4q = \$8 - \$4 = \$4$

    (c) User cost $= P - MC = \$4 - \$2 = \$2$

3. Because in this example the static allocations to the two periods (those which ignore the effects on the other period) are feasible within the 20 units available, the marginal user cost would be zero. With a marginal cost of $4.00, the net benefits in each period would independently be maximized by allocating 10 units to each period. In this example no intertemporal scarcity is present, so price would equal $4.00 marginal cost.

4. Refer to Figure 2.7. In the second version of the model the lower marginal extraction cost in the second period would raise the marginal net benefit curve in that period (since marginal net benefit is the difference between the unchanged demand curve and the lower MC curve). This would be reflected in Figure 2.7 as a parallel leftward shift out of the the curve labeled "present value of marginal net benefits in period 2." This shift would immediately have two consequences: it would move the intersection to the left (implying relatively more would be extracted in the second period), and the intersection would take place at a higher vertical distance from the horizontal axis (implying that the marginal user cost would have risen).

Chapter 3

1. (a) This is a public good, so add the 100 demand curves vertically. This yields $P = 1000 - 100q$. This demand curve would intersect the marginal cost curve when $P = 500$, which occurs when $q = 5$ miles.

    (b) The net benefits are represented by a right triangle where the height of the triangle is $500 ($1000, the point where the demand curve crosses the vertical axis, minus $500, the marginal cost) and the base is 5 miles. The area of a right triangle is $1/2 \times$ base $\times$ height $= 1/2 \times \$500 \times 5 = \$1250$.

2. (a) Consumer surplus $= \$800$. Producer surplus $= \$800$. Consumer surplus plus producer surplus $= \$1600 =$ net benefits.

    (b) The marginal revenue curve has twice the slope of the demand curve, so $MR = 80 - 2q$. Setting $MR = MC$ yields $q = 80/3$ and $P = 160/3$. Using Figure 3.8, producer surplus is the area under the price line *(FE)* and over the marginal cost line *(DH)*. This can be computed as the sum of a rectangle (formed by *FED* and a horizontal line drawn from *D* to the vertical axis) and a triangle (formed by *DH* and the point created by the intersection of the horizontal line drawn from *D* with the vertical axis).

    The area of any rectangle is base $\times$ height. The base $= 80/3$ and the

    $$\text{Height} = P - MC = \frac{160}{3} - \frac{80}{3} = \frac{80}{3}.$$

    Therefore, the area of the rectangle is 6400/9. The area of the right triangle is

    $$\frac{1}{2} \times \frac{80}{3} \times \frac{80}{3} = \frac{3200}{9}.$$

    $$\text{Producer surplus} = \frac{3200}{9} + \frac{6400}{9} = \frac{\$9600}{9}.$$

    $$\text{Consumer surplus} = \frac{1}{2} \times \frac{80}{3} \times \frac{80}{3} = \frac{\$32000}{9}.$$

    (c) 1. $\dfrac{\$9600}{9} > \$800$ 2. $\dfrac{\$3200}{9} < \$800$ 3. $\dfrac{\$12800}{9} < \$1600$

3.   The policy would not be consistent with efficiency. As the firm considers measures to reduce the magnitude of any spill, it would compare the marginal costs of those measures with the expected marginal reduc-

tion in its liability from reducing the magnitude of the spill. Yet the expected marginal reduction in liability would be zero. Firms would pay $X regardless of the size of the spill. Since the amount paid cannot be reduced by controlling the size of the spill, the incentive to take precautions which reduce the size of the spill will be inefficiently low.

Chapter 4

1.   In order to maximize net benefits, Coast Guard oil spill prevention enforcement activity should be increased until the marginal benefit of the last unit equals the marginal cost of providing that unit. Efficiency requires that the level of the activity be chosen so as to equate marginal benefit with marginal cost. When marginal benefits exceeds marginal cost (as in this example), the activity should be expanded.

2. (a) According to the figures given, the per life cost of kidney transplants lies well under the implied value of life estimates given in the chapter, while per life cost implied by the proposed standard for acrylonitrile lies well over those estimates. In benefit-cost terms the allocation of resources to kidney transplants should be increased, while the acrylonitrile standard should be relaxed somewhat to bring the costs back into line with the benefits.

   (b) Efficiency requires that the marginal benefit of a life saved in government programs (as determined by the implied value of a human life in that context) should be equal to the marginal cost of saving that life. Since the data given in the problem indicate that the marginal costs would be beneficial, should all marginal costs be equal? Only if the marginal benefits are equal and, as we saw in the chapter, risk valuations (and hence the implied value of human life) depend on the risk context, so it is unlikely they are equal across all government programs.

Chapter 5

1.   According to the microeconomic theory of fertility, the impact would be greater for tuition-funded education. With tuition funding, the cost of education for an additional child would be the present value of all tuitions paid. With property tax funding, the cost of education for an additional child would be miniscule; the amount the family would pay would depend on the value of their property, not on the number of children in the family. Hence, the marginal cost of an additional child is higher with tuition funding, so the impact on the desired number of children would be larger.

2.   It is a positive feedback loop. The rich typically have low fertility rates, while the poor typically have high fertility rates. High fertility rates among the poor tend to widen the gap between rich and poor by increasing the supply of labor (placing downward pressure on wages, particularly unskilled wages) and by reducing the amount of resources committed to each child (thereby limiting future earning capacity).

Chapter 6

1.   From the hint, $MNB_1/MNB_2 = (1 + k)/(1 + r)$. Notice that when $k = 0$, this reduces to $MNB_2 = MNB_1(1 + r)$, the case we have already considered. When $k = r$, then $MNB_1 = MNB_2$; the effect of stock growth exactly offsets the effect of discounting, and both periods extract the same amount. If $r > k$, then $MNB_2 > MNB_1$. If $r < k$, then $MNB_2 < MNB_1$.

2. (a) With a demand curve shifting out over time, the marginal net benefits from a given future allocation increase over time. This raises the marginal user cost (since it is the opportunity cost of using the resource now) and, hence, the total marginal cost. Thus, the initial user cost would be higher.

   (b) Less of the resource would be consumed in the present; more would be saved for the future.

3. (a) This turns out to have the same effect as the environmental cost pictured in Figures 6.6a and 6.6b. The tax serves to raise the total marginal cost and, hence, the price. This tends to lower the amount consumed in all periods compared to a competitive allocation.

   (b) The tax also serves to reduce the cumulative amount extracted because it raises the marginal cost of each unit extracted. Some resources which would have been extracted without the tax would not be extracted with the tax; their after-tax cost to the producer exceeds the cost of the substitute. The price would be higher with the tax in all periods prior to the without-tax switch point. After that time the price would be equal to the price of the substitute with or without the tax.

Chapter 7

1.   During a recession the demand curve shifts inward. If price is held constant, then the quantity demanded is reduced. Since the burden of holding the price up falls on the cartel, while the competitive fringe can

keep on producing, the demand reduction causes production to fall most heavily in OPEC nations. This causes the cartel market share to fall. To protect their individual market shares, members start cutting prices. In growing markets cartel market shares can be protected without cutting prices.

2. (a) Producer surplus = $\dfrac{\$3200}{9}$ $\quad P = MC = \dfrac{\$80}{3}$

Consumer surplus = $\dfrac{\$9600}{9}$ $\quad q = \dfrac{80}{3}$

(b) This is the mirror image of the monopoly allocation. The net benefits are identical in the two allocations, but they are distributed among producers and consumers rather differently. With this form of price control, the consumer surplus is larger and the producer surplus is smaller than the corresponding concepts when the allocation is governed by a monopoly. Essentially, the rectangle discussed in the answer to part (b) of the second problem in Chapter 3 goes to consumers with price ceilings and to producers in a monopoly.

3. The paper company. The high-cost energy is appropriately assigned to the five paper machines because that is the energy cost that would be eliminated if the machines were shut down. The company would not shut down all energy sources in proportion; it would shut down the most expensive sources. In making a shutdown decision, therefore, it is essential that the machines in question cover the cost of the energy which would be saved if the machines were shut down; otherwise the company is losing money.

4. Peaking plants run only a small percentage of the time, so the capital expenditures remain unused most of the time. Operating costs are incurred only when they are needed. It makes sense, therefore, for utilities to design peaking plants so as to keep capital costs as low as possible, even if it means incurring higher operating cost. Base-load plants, on the other hand, run almost continuously, so the capital costs are prorated over a very large number of kilowatt-hours and therefore are less of a burden.

Chapter 8

1. (a) Assume that only virgin ores are used. In this case $P = MC_1$, so $10 - 0.5q_1 = 0.5q_1$ or $q_1 = 10$. This implies $MC_1 = 5$. The marginal cost of producing any units using recycled products is clearly higher than 5, so none will be used. Therefore, 10 units would be produced, and all of them would be produced using virgin ores.

(b) With the higher demand curve the price will be high enough to stimulate the producer to make some of the product with recycled materials. The key to solving this problem is provided by Figure 8.4, where it can be seen that the producer will equate the marginal costs of products made with recycled materials and those made with virgin ores. Using this fact, we can set $0.5q_1 = 5 + 0.1q_2$ or $q_1 = 10 + 0.2 \, q_2$. Substituting this into the demand function yields

$$P = 20 - 0.5(10 + 0.2q_2 + q_2) \qquad \text{or} \qquad P = 15 - 0.6q_2.$$

Solving for $P = MC$ yields

$$15 - 0.6q_2 = 5 + 0.1q_2 \qquad \text{or} \qquad q_2 = \frac{100}{7}$$

and

$$q_1 = 10 + 0.2 \, (\frac{100}{7}) = \frac{90}{7}.$$

The solution can be verified by showing $P = MC_1 = MC_2 = \frac{45}{7}$.

2. (a) They will not have the same effect. Because the royalty is a per-ton fee, it raises the marginal cost of extraction to the firm, but the bonus bid, which does not affect the marginal cost of extraction, does not. If the mineral has an increasing marginal cost of extraction, less will be extracted with a royalty system than with a bonus bid system because the marginal cost of extraction (including the royalty payment) will hit the backstop price at a smaller cumulative amount extracted.

(b) The bonus bid is consistent with efficiency because it does not distort the allocation over time. The allocation which maximized firm profits before the bonus bid will still maximize it after the bonus bid. While the government shares the profits, it does so without distorting incentives. By raising the marginal cost of extraction, royalty schemes distort incentives.

(c) With a bonus bid scheme the firm bears the risk. The government gets a fixed payment. The firm can either win big or lose big, depending on how valuable the deposit turns out to be. With the royalty scheme, the risk is shared. If the mine turns out to be very valuable, profits and government fees both go up. If the deposit turns out not to be very valuable, the firm gains little but so does the government.

Chapter 9

1. Since the amount of capacity needed would depend on the maximum flow during the year, the extra cost of expanding capacity during this high-flow period should be reflected in higher prices charged to users during these periods.

2. Assuming the rate was correct, the flat rate would be more efficient because it would confront the user with a positive marginal cost of further consumption. The marginal cost of further consumption with a flat fee is zero.

Chapter 10

1. Norland has the comparative advantage in producing *A*. For every unit of *A* it produces, Norland gives up 2 units of *B*. This is a lower opportunity cost than incurred by Souland, which gives up 3 units of *B* for each unit of *A* produced. Souland has a comparative advantage in producing *B*.

2. Food stamp programs give the poor more money to spend on food, thus shifting their demand curve for food to the right. Only if supply is perfectly inelastic would this shift in demand increase prices without increasing quantity sold. On the other hand, prices would normally rise somewhat unless the supply curve was perfectly elastic. In general, the more elastic the supply curve, the larger would be the increase in quantity sold and the smaller would be the increase in prices for a given shift in demand.

3. Soil erosion diminishes future productivity, but its prevention requires current outlays. If the renter has a long-term lease, and hence would be able to recoup the investment, he or she might well take efforts to prevent soil erosion. If, however, the renter has a short-term lease, he or she would not be likely to prevent soil erosion. The losses would accrue to the absentee landlord, who would be less knowledgeable about the extent of the problem.

Chapter 11

1. The plot being turned into a housing development would have the shortest rotation period because the cost of delaying the harvest would be

greatest in this case. It would include an additional cost—the cost of delaying the construction of the housing development—that would have to be factored in, causing net benefits to be maximized at an earlier harvest age.

2.   The cost trend is the result of two offsetting trends. Harvesting cost is a function of the volume of wood, so it increases as the volume of wood increases. Since these costs are discounted, however, costs further in the future are discounted more. When the tree growth gets small enough, the discounting effect dominates the growth effect and the present values of the costs decline.

Chapter 12

1. (a) The maximum sustainable yield is obtained when the marginal benefit of an additional reduction in the population size is zero: $20P - 400 = 0$ or $P = 20,000$ tons. The maximum sustainable yield can then be calculated using the g equation: $g = 4(20) - 0.1(20)^2 = 40$ tons.

   (b) The efficient sustained yield can be found by setting marginal cost equal to marginal benefit: $20P - 400 = 2(160 - P)$; therefore, $P = 32.7$, which is a larger population than that which would produce the maximum sustainable yield.

2. (a) No, despite the fact that this approach yields the efficient sustainable yield, this is not an efficient solution. Net benefits would not be maximized because costs would be too high. Everyone would have an incentive to capture as large a share of the quota for themselves as quickly as possible. This would lead to excessively large boats and would not guarantee that the fishermen who could catch the fish most cheaply would do the harvesting. The net benefits would be smaller than possible.

   (b) Yes, this would be efficient. This quota system creates exclusive property rights and, therefore, eliminate the need to catch as much as possible as soon as possible. Each fisherman can proceed on the most individually appropriate schedule because his or her share of the catch is guaranteed. Since the need to rush harvesting is eliminated, the need for excessively large boats is also eliminated. Fishermen with high harvesting costs would find it in their interest to sell their quotas to fishermen with low harvesting costs in order to maximize their return from their quota. These transfers guarantee that the fish are caught by those with the lowest harvesting costs, so net benefits are maximized.

Chapter 14

1. (a) In a cost-effective allocation of emission reduction, the marginal control costs should be equal. So $200q_1$ = $100 q_2. Furthermore, the total reduction is 21 units, so $q_1 + q_2 = 21$. Solving the first of these equations for q_1 yields $q_1 = 0.5 q_2$. Substituting this into the second yields $0.5q_2 + q_2 = 21$. Solving this for q_2 results in $q_2 = 14$ and $q_1 = 7$.

    (b) From the text we know that in a cost-effective allocation with a single receptor

    $$\frac{MC_1}{a_1} = \frac{MC_2}{a_2}.$$

    Therefore,

    $$\frac{\$200q_1}{2} = \frac{\$100q_2}{1}.$$

    Furthermore,

    $$a_1(20 - q_1) + a_2(20 - q_2) = 27 \quad \text{or} \quad 2(20 - q_1) + (20 - q_2) = 27.$$

    From the first equation it is clear that in a cost-effective allocation $q_1 = q_2$. It remains to derive the total amount of control using the second equation: $2(20 - q_1) + (20 - q_1) = 27$ so $q_1 = 11$ and $q_2 = 11$.

2. (a) From the text we know $T = MC_1 = MC_2$. From Problem 1(a) we know $MC_1 = MC_2 = \$1400$. Therefore $T = \$1400$.

    (b) Revenue $= T(20 - q_1) + T(20 - q_2) = \$1400(13) + \$1400(6) = \$26,600$.

Chapter 15

1. (a) There would be 12 permits issued, each worth 1 ppm. The price of the permit will be that price which will clear the market; that is

    $$\frac{MC_1}{a_1} = \frac{MC_2}{a_2} = P.$$

    We know that in equilibrium, $\dfrac{0.3q_1}{1.5} = \dfrac{0.5q_2}{1.0}$, or $q_1 = 2.5q_2$.

Further,

$$a_1(20 - q_1) + a_2(20 - q_2) = 12 \quad \text{or} \quad 1.5(20 - 2.5q_2) + 1.0(20 - q_2) = 12.$$

Solving this equation yields $q_2 = 9$ and $q_1 = 20$. So,

$$P = \frac{0.3(20)}{1.5} = \frac{0.5(8)}{1.0} = \$4 \text{ per ppm.}$$

(b) Permits auctioned off

First source$=P(20 - q_1)a_1 = \$4(20 - 20)1.5 = \$0,$

Second source$=P(20 - q_2)a_2 = \$4(20 - 8)1.0 = \$48.$

The six permits are worth \$24, so the first source would sell all its permits for a gain of \$24. The second source would keep its initial allocation of six permits and would buy six more at a cost of \$24. The cost to the second source exactly balances the gain to the first.

Chapter 16

1.   The emission charge equalizes marginal cost, a required condition for cost effectiveness. The subsidies include utilities to choose options with a higher marginal cost. By equalizing their after-subsidy marginal costs, utilities will minimize their outlays. This will not minimize total costs of control, since a greater reliance on scrubbers will result than would be cost-effective.

2.   High transfer costs in this context arise from a combination of high charges and large amounts of uncontrolled emissions. This circumstance arises when the marginal cost of control function rises steeply at relatively low levels of control. Since the charge is equal to the marginal cost of control, high marginal control costs imply a high charge rate. Furthermore, if the function rises steeply at relatively low levels of control, then there are large amount of emissions to which this high rate of charge is applied. Multiplying a high charge times a large amount of uncontrolled emissions yields high transfer costs.

Chapter 18

1. (a) This allocation would be similar to that in Problem 2(a) in Chapter 14. The price would be \$1400. In the final allocation the first source would

control 7 units and would hold 13 permits, where the second source would control 14 units and hold 6 permits. The first source would have to purchase 4 permits—the 13 it needs to minimize cost minus the 9 it was initially given—at a total cost of $5600. The second source would sell 4 permits, thereby moving from the 10 held initially to the 6 it needs to minimize costs, so it would gain $5600 from the sale.

(b) We know that in the final equilibrium the marginal control costs will be equal. Since for the third source the marginal control cost is constant at $1600, this will determine the final marginal control cost. The final permit price will be $1600. The control allocation can be found for the first and second sources by choosing that level of control which yields a marginal control cost equal to $1600. Thus $1600 = $200q_1$, so q_1 = 8 and $1600 = $100q_2$, so q_2 = 16.

The third source will have to clean up sufficient additional emissions to meet the target. Uncontrolled emissions were stated to be equal to 50. The first two sources would clean up 24 units, leaving 26 units uncontrolled. Since the target emission level is stated as 19 units, the third source would have to clean up the remaining 7 units (q_3 = 7). The third source would have to purchase three permits since it received no initial allocation. Two would be purchased from the second source, and one would be purchased from the first.

Name Index

Subject Index

676   Subject Index

Singapore, methods to reduce traffic, 466, 467
Skin cancer, ozone depletion, 433
Snail darter, 23
Solar energy
cost factors, 164
technologies related to, 11
South Africa, mineral supply, 194, 197
South Coast Air Quality Management District, 456, 468
Speculative resources, 127
Starting point bias, 81
State implementation plan, 394, 395
Static efficiency, 22, 24–29
demand curves, 22, 24–25
fisheries, 307–309
marginal opportunity cost curve, 26
opportunity costs, 25–26
Pareto optimality, 28
total cost, 26–28
Static reserve index, 129
Stationary source controls, effect on households, 555–556
Statistical studies, to assess pollution damage, 81–82
Statutory law, 535, 537
and cost balancing, 535–537
and degree and form of intervention, 537–538
legislative remedies for toxic substances pollution, 526–529
and scale of hazardous waste problem, 538
Steady-state economy, 622–623
Stockpiles
cobalt, 198
food, 272–273
minerals, 194, 197, 198
strategic petroleum reserve, 171
Stock pollutants, 361, 362–364, 482–483
efficient allocation of, 363–364
inorganic chemicals as, 483
Storage, of renewable resources, 131
Strategic and Critical Minerals Stockpiling Act of 1946, 197
Strategic bias, 81
Strategic minerals problem, 194–200
Strategic petroleum reserve, 171
Strict liability, toxic substances claims, 524–525
Substandard indicator, housing quality, 588
Substitution
elasticity of, 344, 346, 571

ex ante and ex post substitution, 577
illustration of effects of, 335–336
and resource scarcity, 335–336
Substitution bias, and price controls, 159
Substitution effects, minerals, 200
Sulfur oxides, 395, 413, 423
Superfund Act, 528–529, 529, 531, 533, 538
Superfund Amendments and Reauthorization Act of 1986, 538
Supply curve, 31
for oil, 169–170
Surface pollutants, 361
Surface water, 223
efficient allocation of, 226–228
Surplus
consumer, 48
producer, 48
Survey approach, cost estimation, 85
Sustainability, 35–37
criterion, 36
and dynamic efficiency, 36–37
Sustainability principle, 619–621
implementation of, 621
implications of, 620
nature of, 619
and trade policy, 621
Sustainable development
and agriculture, 607–608
definition of, 599–600
and efficiency, 603–606
and energy, 608
future view, 632–637
and growth, 600–602
market allocations, 603
transition to, 611–624
and waste reduction, 609
Sweden
nuclear power plants, 175
refund system for abandoned automobiles, 207
Synergistic effects, 80, 515
Synthetic Fuel Corporation, 172
Synthetic natural gas, 159
Systems dynamics, 4

Tampering, automobile pollution control, 455
Tangible benefits, of environmental projects, 84
Taxation
energy tax, 171
export taxes and farming, 264